PRINCIPLES
OF
ORGANISATIONAL
BEHAVIOUR

SECOND EDITION

Michael Morley, Sarah Moore, Noreen Heraty, Margaret Linehan and Sarah MacCurtain

GILL & MACMILLAN

Gill & Macmillan
Hume Avenue
Park West
Dublin 12
with associated companies throughout the world
www.gillmacmillan.ie

0 7171 3670 1

Index compiled by Cover to Cover
Design and print origination in Ireland by O'K Graphic Design, Dublin

The paper used in this book is made from the wood pulp of managed forests. For every tree felled, at least one is planted, thereby renewing natural resources.

A catalogue record is available for this book from the British Library.

TABLE OF CONTENTS

PREFACE

Welcome to the second edition of *Principles of Organisational Behaviour*. Arising from lecturer and student feedback on the first edition, we have revised the text and added several new features.

The text is now presented in four key sections. Section 1 introduces organisational behaviour and places it within its historical context. Section 2 focuses on the nature of the individual. It explores personality, perception and cognition, individual learning, emotion, stress and psychological well-being and motivation. Section 3 examines key issues in an organisational context. Organisational communication, structure, culture, work systems, leadership, conflict, power, politics, ethics and organisational change are all analysed. Finally, Section 4 turns to contemporary debates in organisational behaviour and explores the topics of diversity management, women in organisations and working abroad.

In addition to the five new chapters contained in this edition, readers will also encounter several new features within each chapter. These include definitions of key concepts, a section on ongoing debates/advanced concepts and end of chapter multiple choice questions. Suggested key readings are also highlighted as prescient contributions from the broader literature on each topic. Our hope is that these new features, together with the updated content, offer an accessible map through the dynamic field that is organisational behaviour.

A number of colleagues have provided on-going support and assistance in the preparation of this second edition and we would like to take this opportunity to place on record our thanks to them. At the outset we wish to acknowledge the contribution of Professor Patrick Gunnigle. Paddy was a co-author with us on the first edition and although he is no longer involved, his original material and valuable insights remain an important feature of this second edition. We would also like to acknowledge the support of the Dean of the Kemmy Business School at the University of Limerick, Professor Donal A. Dineen, and the Head of the Department of Adult and Continuing Education at Cork Institute of Technology, Paul O'Mahony. Finally, our thanks to each and every one of our colleagues at the Department of Personnel and Employment Relations, University of Limerick and the Department of Adult and Continuing Education, Cork Institute of Technology, for their on-going collaboration.

SECTION ONE

INTRODUCING ORGANISATIONAL BEHAVIOUR

INTRODUCING 1
ORGANISATIONAL BEHAVIOUR

Learning Objectives

- To introduce key concepts in organisational behaviour.

- To trace the historical roots of the field in scientific management, Fordism, bureaucracy and the human relations movement.

- To outline contemporary perspectives in organisational behaviour – general, open and socio-technical systems theory.

- To introduce dominant methodologies employed in conducting research in organisational behaviour.

- To outline contemporary debates in the field, including social constructionism, postmodernism and the use of metaphors as a way of capturing the nature of organisational life.

INTRODUCTION

There are few laws or absolutes that govern 'proper' conduct for organisational stakeholders or predict their behaviour with any certainty. Through empirical investigation, we have arguably learned as much about those things that do not work as we have about those things that do. Most social scientists' experience demonstrates that there is a multiplicity of factors that shape and determine the behaviour of people at work, and consequently any investigation of behaviour in the workplace necessitates a rather broad treatment.

In this book we seek to describe and examine the complex work organisation from a behavioural perspective. Our particular concern is to provide some explanations of why people behave the way they do at work. In this respect, organisational behaviour as a subject can be seen to be interdisciplinary and concerned with integrating explanations, messages and lessons from the fields of psychology, social psychology, political science and sociology in so far as they relate to people at work and assist in explaining and predicting workplace interactions. Indeed, virtually all of the founding fathers of organisational behaviour, such as Kurt Lewin, Elton Mayo, Rensis Likert and Victor Vroom, were researchers from older social/psychological disciplines, many of whom found new homes in schools of management and business. While these multifaceted interdisciplinary roots have given rise to concerns about the utility of organisational behaviour in some quarters, we have come a long way in this fledgling discipline, with organisational behaviour now viewed as a serious and intellectually rigorous area of research and teaching.

Most scholars would agree that while its roots can be traced to a much earlier era, organisational behaviour began to emerge as a mature field of study in the late 1950s and early 1960s. Of particular significance in bringing about this development was the landmark study at the Western Electric Hawthorne plant, which eventually gave rise to the human relations movement. In this introductory chapter, we commence by defining key concepts in organisational behaviour. Following this, we trace the historical roots and introduce contemporary theories of organisational behaviour. We also present the debate on methodological approaches and rigour in organisational behaviour. The final section of the chapter presents ongoing debates and advanced concepts in the field.

HISTORICAL ROOTS

Historically, the precursor of the modern 'organisation' consisted of the medieval guild arrangement, a simple tripartite organisation between the apprentice, the journeyman and the master based upon a system of task-oriented status structures in which obedience to a wide range of technical rules was required (Offe 1976; Hardy and Clegg 1996). The emergence of an industrial society brought with it a new order dominated by complex institutional arrangements not easily understood by reference to the largely agrarian society from which they had sprung. We now live in an organisational/institutional world from which we can rarely escape (Huczynski and Buchanan 1991; Furnham 1997). Large-scale organisations have revolutionised the economic, technical, political, social and cultural fabric of our society, and whether as an internal/direct or external/indirect stakeholder, they play an important role in all our lives. Purposeful large-scale organisation has become one of the most important resources of the developed world and one which most developing regions eagerly embrace. This complexity has given rise to a body of knowledge on theories of industrial/business management and corporate governance and control that can be intellectually stimulating and practically relevant.

There are many ways one can conceptualise the elements of organisational design, and to understand this complexity and analyse organisations from different perspectives is an important area of knowledge (Kotter *et al.* 1979; Dawson 1996). Achieving it, on the other hand, is a difficult task because both the way in which the phenomenon of organising is characterised and the theoretical and methodological equipment thought most appropriate for its analysis have undergone significant changes in recent years (Reed 1992).

Management theories leading to today's contemporary ideas of organisational behaviour did not really emerge until the Industrial Revolution of the 1700s and the 1800s, with which came dramatic changes that demanded new ways of working and managing. Innovations in technology meant that traditional work practices were superseded by new forms of mass production requiring large numbers of workers and managers who knew how to co-ordinate these workers and their tasks in an effective and efficient manner.

These dramatic changes and the challenges associated with such changes brought an interest in developing general theories of management to the fore. This quest for a general theory of management has not abated, but rather has changed dramatically throughout the years and continues even now.

DEFINITIONS OF KEY CONCEPTS

Scientific management
A set of principles for organising work in order to increase efficiency and to give greater control over tasks to management.

Bureaucracy
A form of organisation that is characterised by high levels of formality, hierarchy, rules and procedures and specialisation of tasks.

Human relations school
A perspective of organisations that emphasises the importance of social processes in work, of which interpersonal relationships and group membership are an important part.

General systems theory
Views the organisation as a collection of interrelated parts working together towards a common goal and where the whole is greater than the sum of the parts.

Social constructionism
Focuses on interaction between the actor and the world and attributes importance to the actor's ability to interpret the social world. Views the organisation as a socially constructed reality.

Postmodernism
A way of thinking that rejects the modernist perspective and one universal truth. It is political in orientation and celebrates uncertainty and groups on the periphery of society.

Metaphor
Metaphors provide us with alternative ways of viewing things by comparing an unfamiliar concept with a more familiar one, with the purpose of emphasising certain associations between the two, e.g. he was a mountain of strength.

SCIENTIFIC MANAGEMENT

The first of these general theories took the form of management principles designed to increase productivity and efficiency. The founder of scientific management was Frederick Taylor, a man who has become synonymous with the 'rationalisation' of organisations.

Taylor called for heightened efficiency supported by a piece-rate incentive system in which workers were paid according to the amount of work they performed at a given time. In order to prevent a practice he called 'systematic soldiering' – the conscious and deliberate restriction of output by workers – the work was broken down into the smallest possible components and each part of the task was measured in order to find the 'one best way' of performing that task. This new system allowed management to define and control what tasks workers would perform and in what way they would approach it. The main principles of scientific management are outlined in Table 1.1.

Table 1.1 Frederick Taylor's Principles of Scientific Management

1. Assign all responsibility for the organisation of work to the managers rather than the workers.
2. Use scientific methods to determine the one best way of performing each task, thus increasing efficiency.
3. Select the person most suited to each job to perform that job.
4. Train the worker to perform the job correctly.
5. Increase the predictability of job performance through the standardisation of tasks.
6. Monitor work performance to ensure that specified work procedures are followed correctly and that appropriate results are achieved.
7. Provide further support by planning work assignments and eliminating interruptions.

Source: Adapted from Huczynski and Buchanan (2001)

The distinction between management being the brains and workers being the brawn of the organisation is an important one, for with it came the shift in control of work tasks from workers to management. While Taylor saw himself as being a man of the people, workers saw him in a very different light. Many associated Taylor with the erosion of craftsmanship and the demise of worker solidarity. His experience of systematic soldiering led him to distrust employees working in groups (Huczynski and Buchanan 2001). Thus, in order to combat this practice of restricting output within groups, Taylor offered differential pay for performance, a practice that deterred working in groups and encouraged individualistic behaviour.

Taylor is often accused of treating man as a machine, and indeed some of his writings would suggest he considered workers to be raw materials to be moulded by management. However, when studying scientific management it is necessary to consider the historical context of his work. Taylor is a product of a time where a social welfare system was absent and financial issues were of paramount importance to the workers (Huczynski and Buchanan 2001). He believed he was on the side of both workers and management and that scientific management would lead to mutual benefits and rewards – higher wages *and* higher productivity. What he did not expect was the negative and often fierce reactions from both employees and managers. Employees felt he was responsible for deskilling labourers, dividing workers and increasing redundancy. Managers either resisted his ideas, believing they reduced their control over their choice of work practices, or else implemented them selectively. Many workers complained that as their output increased, management required them to produce more for the same rewards (George and Jones 2002).

Scientific management is faulted for neglecting the social aspects of work and assuming that motivation is based solely on economics. It failed to appreciate the meanings workers would put on the new procedures and how they would react to being timed and closely supervised (Huczynski and Buchanan 2001). Scientific management has been criticised generally for ignoring the psychological needs and capabilities of workers and for 'dehumanising' work.

While many have mixed views about the merits of scientific management and feel Taylor's ideas may be 'intellectually unfashionable' (Kanigel 1997), there is no denying the mark he has left on Western society. Taylor bestowed upon us a preoccupation with time, efficiency, measurement and standardisation still very evident in today's world of work.

Fordism

A man who was greatly influenced by Taylor's thinking was Henry Ford. While Taylor is considered to have had a more profound and far-reaching impact (Kanigel 1997), Henry Ford has become synonymous with mass production and the assembly line. Taylor's influence may be evident in every aspect of society, but Ford's impact on manufacturing should not be underestimated. Ford was an avid proponent of Taylor's principles, which is evident in many of the novel practices Ford introduced to his company. When Ford established his company in 1903, the manufacture of cars was the domain of skilled craftsmen. However, this was about to change as Ford quickly set about changing the way the motor car was produced. Because Ford could not find enough craftsmen to produce the amount of cars he required, he applied Taylor's principles to the area of car production. In order to meet the growing demand for cars, Ford forever changed the way they were made. Instead of requiring highly trained craftsmen, Ford made it possible for the man on the street to manufacture quality cars. In order to do this, tasks were broken down to the smallest possible components and single-purpose machinery was installed to manufacture standardised parts (Huczynski and Buchanan 2001, 2004).

Yet perhaps Ford's biggest innovation was the creation of the assembly line. Until then, employees moved from car to car. Now, however, the car moved past the men. Thus, the moving assembly line was born, a development that plays a pivotal role in manufacture today, since with the assembly line came increased control over employees. The line imposed the working speed that Ford wanted upon the workers and increased production from twenty-seven cars per day in 1908 to 2,000 cars by 1923 (Huczynski and Buchanan 2001, 2004). Ford's dream of mass production was realised and the Model T for all was no longer a dream but a reality.

In order to achieve his goal, Ford had taken car production out of the hands of craftsmen and placed it in the hands of a standardised and semi-skilled workforce. What was once meaningful and skilful work was now a series of monotonous and repetitive tasks completed by a workforce as 'uniform and interchangeable as the parts they handled' (Huczynski and Buchanan 2001: 429). In order to manage this workforce, Ford created an environment that emphasised discipline and control. Workers were closely monitored both inside and outside the workplace. Such an authoritarian regime meant that labour turnover rocketed. Training costs were relatively low when measured on a per worker basis. However, given the large scale of production and the workforce, such a high volume of turnover threatened the high profits associated with mass production (Pietrykowski 1999). By 1913 the company had a turnover rate that was no longer sustainable, which was when Ford introduced the $5.00 a day wage and went from tyrant to god.

By doubling the minimum wage and cutting the working day from nine hours to eight, Ford found a solution, albeit a temporary one, to his absenteeism and turnover problem. Added to this achievement was the expectation that workers would spend the extra money on Ford's cars. In order to ensure that wages were spent on purchasing a Model T and not on other 'immoral' activities, Ford set up the Ford Sociology Department (FSD) in 1914. The establishment of the FSD reflected Henry Ford's interest in self-improvement and its central role was to ensure that Ford's employees were living in a manner he considered appropriate and moral. This interest in the personal domain of the worker and a desire to control every aspect of the worker's life can still be seen in certain modern-day organisations.

Like Taylor, Ford has many critics. He has been charged with deskilling, alienating and dehumanising workers, wiping out craftsmanship and establishing a regime of control and authoritarianism both inside and outside the workplace. However, others argue that his contribution to productivity should not be undermined and point out that Ford is also recognised as raising the standard of living. With mass production came mass consumption, so Ford's legacy meant that ordinary people could afford goods that were once beyond their reach. Now every man could own a Model T – but at what price?

BUREAUCRACY

While Ford and Taylor were preoccupied with the efficiency of production, Max Weber was interested in administrative efficiency. Weber's ideas on bureaucracy emerged in the beginning of the twentieth century, but like Taylor his thinking is still evident today. Weber described a rational and impersonal organisation where rules and procedures ensured predictability of behaviour. Some of the main characteristics of bureaucracy are:

- **Job specification:** Jobs are broken down into simple, routine tasks.
- **Rules and procedures:** Emphasis on rules and procedures that ensures consistency and reliability of behaviour.
- **Impersonality:** Procedures and rules are impersonal and apply to both management and non-management.
- **Hierarchy:** There is a hierarchy of authority. Those higher in the hierarchy have authority over those below them and ensure that they are working in the organisation's interests.
- **Selection and recruitment:** Emphasises the importance of expertise. Nepotism is eradicated.

- **Written records:** Records provide consistency and an 'organisational memory' (adapted from Mullins 2002).

As you may have noticed, many of the principles outlined above are similar to those outlined by Taylor. Both advocated that jobs should be broken down and routinised and both believed management had a legitimate authority, yet there are important differences between these two thinkers. Weber was cognisant of the negative ramifications that bureaucracy might have on those who worked within it and warned that humanity may become captive in the 'iron cage' of bureaucracy. Therefore, while there are similarities between the two perspectives, Weber was the more critical of the two in his understanding of organisational reality and the dehumanising nature of the 'rational' approaches.

Bureaucracy has been criticised for its overreliance on rules and regulations, resulting in rules becoming more important in their own right than as a means to an end (Mullins 2002), and is often associated with red tape and meaningless procedures. The dominance of rules and procedures stifles creativity and can lead to inflexible officious behaviour and what Merton (1940) referred to as a 'bureaucratic personality', someone who has a need for constraints and rules.

HUMAN RELATIONS SCHOOL

Although scientific management followers supported the scientific study of management, it was not until the 1920s that these ideas were formally evaluated (Wagner and Hollenbeck 1998). The Hawthorne studies, which began in 1924 at Western Electric's Hawthorne plant near Chicago, were among the first attempts to use scientific techniques to examine human behaviour at work. Initially the aim of the experiments was to explore the effects of workplace lighting on productivity levels. The experiment involved the segregation of two groups of workers engaged in the same task into two rooms. The lighting in one room only was reduced in ordered quantities in order to examine the effects on that group's productivity. However, there was no significant difference in productivity between the two work groups. Among other considerations, this 'interesting failure' led to further experiments, the most important being the relay assembly tests and the bank wiring room test (see pp 8–9).

The telephone relay assembly group consisted of five female operatives who were separated from the main assembly department by a ten-foot partition. For the first five weeks no changes were introduced to the group. After this period, the experimental change introduced was a variation in the method of payment. The women were no longer paid a group piece rate for the overall group, made up of 100 workers, but rather they were paid a group piece rate for their own work group, which consisted of five workers. This meant that each employee's wages would be more in proportion with her own individual effort, as the group had dropped from 100 to five, and also increased each individual's interest in the group's achievement (Mayo 1960). Other changes were initiated. Light refreshments, shorter working days and a variety of rest periods were introduced, with all except one showing an increase in productivity.[1]

---

1   In the sixth period the group was given six five-minute rests, which they found disruptive and output briefly decreased.

September 1928 was an important month in the Hawthorne studies. In September the group returned to the conditions of work that were in place before the experiments began, which meant that all rest periods, light refreshments and other concessions were brought to an end for a period of twelve weeks. The group's output rose to a point higher than any other period during the experiment. This was a seminal moment where it became clear that the changes introduced during the experiment could not be used to explain the group's continually increasing production. This surprising development led the researchers to conclude that social factors – workers' desire to satisfy needs, involvement at work, interpersonal relationships, support at work – may go a long way towards explaining the results of the Hawthorne experiments. Mayo (1960) argued that the experiment altered the work pattern of the group of the five women participating in the experiment. The group found themselves in what Mayo described as a new 'industrial milieu' in which their own self-determination and their social well-being were being prioritised. He argued that the changes introduced – rest pauses, food, etc. – at first operated mainly to convince them of the major change and to help them adapt. But once the new industrial milieu was established, the experimental changes were no longer important.

These results and the results of the bank wiring experiments (see below) raised serious questions about the efficiency-productivity focus of scientific management. Such questions sparked a growing interest in human issues in the workplace. From this the human relations school grew, directing attention away from scientific management and the control of workers to employee satisfaction and development in the workplace. The main conclusions from the Hawthorne studies are:

- People are motivated by more than just pay and working conditions.
- The importance of the work group needs to be recognised. Individuals are also members of groups and the effect of the group on the individual should not be ignored. Through their unofficial norms, groups can influence the work habits and attitudes of individual group members.
- Individuals have social and emotional needs. The need for recognition, support and a sense of belonging are more important factors in determining morale and performance than the physical conditions under which they work.
- Supervisors need to take workers' social needs and informal group dynamics into consideration in order to align these to the organisational objectives (adapted from Huczynski and Buchanan 2001).

THE BANK WIRING ROOM TEST

This experiment involved a group of fourteen men working in the bank wiring room. It emerged from observing these men that they formed informal cliques with their own group norms as to what constituted appropriate behaviour within the group. The group established their own means of working, and despite incentives where the more they produced the more they earned, they kept the level of output below the optimum level they were capable of producing. This behaviour emerged because the group felt that if they increased their output, the incentive rate would decrease and management's expectations regarding output would increase. Those who went over the group's agreed level of output were called *rate busters*. This experiment highlighted the importance of groups within the organisation in both controlling and motivating the group members (Mayo 1960).

Unlike scientific management and Fordism, the human relations school emphasises people over task, support over control and the importance of the group in shaping people's behaviour at work. Taylor was aware of the group's importance, but he distrusted groups and sought to dismantle them. In contrast, the human relations school uses the group as one of the core building blocks of the organisation and stresses the importance of employee participation, group norms and supportive relationships.

The human relations school has been criticised on several factors. They have been accused of oversimplifying organisational theory and of failing to take into account environmental factors. Other criticisms levelled at this perspective are that it overrelies on scientific methods and that its 'unitarist frame of reference' is too narrow in scope (Mullins 2002). However, the human relations school emphasised the importance of the social group in the workplace and gave rise to a more psychological approach to understanding organisations, something previous management theories had failed to do.

CONTEMPORARY THEORIES OF ORGANISATIONAL BEHAVIOUR

Both scientific management and the human relations school have useful insights to contribute to our understanding of organisational behaviour. Whereas scientific management emphasises the technical aspect of organisations and seeks 'one best way' of working, the human relations school stresses the human and social aspects of organisations. However, studying these theories in isolation can only take us so far. The systems approach merges these two perspectives by viewing organisations as a holistic entity that incorporates both structural and social elements that are inextricably linked.

GENERAL SYSTEMS THEORY

The general systems theory (GST) has its roots in the natural and physical sciences. One of the main thinkers behind this theory, Ludwig von Bertalanffy, was a biologist concerned with providing a hypothesis to explain all scientific phenomena. In doing so he recognised that all these phenomena were in some way linked, from entire societies right down to the atom, and referred to these phenomena as systems made up of different interrelated and interdependent parts (Hatch 1997). Each part affects all the other parts, and while each part can be examined and studied in isolation, to do so would fail to capture the essence of the whole. GST views the organisation as a system made up of many subsystems and the interrelationships of these subsystems create a dynamic and unique whole that is more than the sum of its parts.

Drawing on GST, Boulding, an American economist, provided a framework that identifies nine different levels of increasingly complex systems, ranging from low-level, simple, dynamic or cybernetic systems to complex, sophisticated social systems (Boulding 1956). While systems higher in the hierarchy are based on systems lower in the hierarchy, they cannot be reduced to these levels, as higher-level systems have unique characteristics that distinguish them from lower-level systems. This framework differentiates between closed systems (systems that are self-maintaining and do not require anything outside of themselves to operate) and open systems (systems that depend on their environment to support their existence). The open system theory provides us with a view of organisations that is essential to our understanding of contemporary perspectives of organisational behaviour.

OPEN SYSTEMS THEORY

In the open systems model, a system takes inputs from its environment and transforms these inputs into outputs, a cycle that sustains the life of the system. If we take the organisation as an example of a system, the inputs may include labour, technology, raw material and expertise, amongst others. These inputs will then be transformed through a variety of different production, administrative and social processes to become outputs, e.g. products or services (see Figure 1.1).

Figure 1.1 The Open Systems Theory of Organisations

Each system exists within a supersystem. For example, if the system under investigation is the organisation, the supersystem will be the environment within which the organisation exists. Each system will also have subsystems (those systems that are lower in the hierarchy and that exist within the system you are studying). In the organisation example, the subsystems would be the different departments within the organisation. The system you are analysing will determine the level of analysis. The higher the system is in Boulding's hierarchy, the higher the level of analysis (Hatch 1997). For example, taking the organisation as a whole as the system under analysis would involve a higher level of analysis than taking an organisational department as the system under analysis. The level of analysis will also determine what the supersystem and the subsystems are.

SOCIO-TECHNICAL SYSTEMS

The systems approach views the organisation as a whole and recognises that to examine the parts of the organisation separately would provide an incomplete picture of organisational life. The socio-technical systems approach focuses on the interrelationship between the organisation's technical and structural requirements and the social and behavioural elements. The idea of socio-technical systems originated from the Tavistock Institute, a group of social scientists in England interested in integrating the human relations perspective with the organisation's technical view. Its studies on changing technology in the coal mining industry and work redesign in Indian textile mills have been heralded as developing the concept of the socio-technical system, which has led to the more general open systems theory of organisations.

A major criticism of the open systems theory is the oversimplification of the human dimension of organisations. While it recognises the importance of the human aspect, the assumption that all components of the organisation work towards a common goal fails to reflect the complex and often contradictory nature of organisational life.

RESEARCHING BEHAVIOUR IN ORGANISATIONS

Having outlined the historical roots of the field, it is now appropriate to turn to how we build knowledge in organisational behaviour. We briefly introduce two perspectives on how to generate understanding in workplace behaviour, namely positivism and naturalism, and the associated research methods that may be employed. Like any of the behavioural sciences, organisational behaviour requires the utilisation of rigorous methodologies to better understand human behaviour in the workplace. There is no consensus about the best way to understand and describe social interaction at organisational level. The researcher must select from competing and conflicting views that in turn will likely give direction to all aspects of the enquiry. Gill and Johnson (1991) highlight that most researchers experience at least some tension between a view that highlights the supremacy of enquiry modelled on physical science on the one hand and the necessity to contextualise and individualise the investigation on the other. This selection of paradigmatic choice is therefore the starting point. Broadly speaking, the researcher can take a positivist or a naturalist route. In this way organisational behaviour researchers can be seen to be eclectic, with differing philosophical approaches giving rise to different research methods, depending upon the precise area of investigation.

Positivism assumes that there is an objective reality that is measurable and thus entails a marked preference for quantitative approaches to data collection to make these discoveries. This is because there is a widespread tendency to view quantitative survey and experimental research as suited to the confirmation or rejection of theoretical propositions and hypotheses (McNeill 1990). Positivism assumes that the world is knowable in objective terms – that there is an objective reality that can be discovered and explained by laws, theories, etc.

Positivist researchers believe that there is a single reality that can be segmented and broken down into quantifiable units or variables that can be independently studied and for which causal relationships can be identified. In this way it is believed that the various aspects of behaviour in the workplace can be described and linked to particular causes.

Once the causal relationship is known, it is believed that predictions can be made about the situations in which certain behaviours recur. In this way positivism assumes that for every action there is a corresponding cause. As a result, this approach takes its logic from the model of the physical sciences and applies this logic to the social world. Tiernan (1996: 135) summarises the central tenets of this approach.

> The positivist approach assumes that social research is similar in nature to that of the natural and physical sciences, namely, that knowledge can be viewed in an objective way and that such an objective reality can be developed and explained by causal theories and laws using quantitative analysis. As a consequence, in operational terms, positivism assumes that social phenomena like those of the natural and physical sciences can be broken down into quantifiable variables, studied independently and that theories and laws that predict future observations through causal analysis and hypothesis testing can be developed. The logic of the physical and natural sciences is, therefore, imposed on the social sciences. The tendency is to reduce human action to the status of automatic responses achieved by external stimuli, ignoring the subjective dimension of human action, namely, the internal logic and interpretative processes by which such action is created.

Among the most prominent positivist research methods are laboratory experiments, field experiments and, to a lesser extent, quantitative surveys. Laboratory experiments involve the researcher in testing the effects of one or more independent variables on one or more dependent variables through the utilisation of both control and experimental groups that are randomly selected. Here, the independent variable refers to that variable which has been identified as the possible cause of the phenomena under investigation, and the dependent variable is one that is thought to be causally linked to the independent variable and is therefore expected to change. Thus, in what is essentially an artificial environment that is dedicated to preserving controlled conditions, the researcher manipulates an independent variable and deduces that any changes in the dependent variable are as a result of that manipulation. In experiments of this nature, the researcher trades off realism/naturalism for precision and control. Associated advantages with this research method include the high level of control maintained by the researcher and the possibility of isolating only those variables under investigation and therefore eliminating 'experimental error'. Disadvantages include its artificial nature and thus its possible irrelevance to the real world (what naturalists describe as 'naïve realism'); the potential emergence of the 'Hawthorne effect', whereby participants alter their behaviour when they know they are under investigation; and issues associated with deception and ethics in social research.

Field experiments involve the researcher sampling and investigating behaviour in natural situations rather than attempting to replicate behaviour in a laboratory. Here, the researcher similarly utilises both control and experimental groups. While the natural setting is less controlled it clearly is more realistic than any laboratory-generated scenario, hence the field experiment typically provides the most generalisable findings.

Quantitative surveys are designed to collect data that allows the researcher to describe and/or analyse the world as it is and lie in the middle of the positivism/naturalism continuum. In this case the researcher typically defines an area of research and then designs a set of questions that will elicit the attitudes, beliefs and experiences of the respondents as they relate to the research under investigation. A sample of respondents is typically selected to represent a larger group. Respondents are then surveyed and the researcher makes inferences from their responses about the larger population. Among the key phases associated with quantitative survey design are choosing the topic to be studied, developing core research hypotheses, isolation of the population to be surveyed, preparation of the research questionnaire, conducting a pilot test, selecting a representative sample from the population, collecting the data and processing and analysing the results. Particular advantages associated with survey designs include their ability to be highly specific in terms of research objective; the high level of anonymity afforded to respondents; the possibility of targeting large numbers of people to be studied and the subsequent generalisability of results to the wider population under investigation; and the possibility of comparing results with other populations. Among the disadvantages are the limited scope for response, particularly where the questionnaire is highly structured, and the potential problem of a lack of validity, as the method uncovers what people say they are doing when they are filling out the questionnaire rather than what they are actually doing.

In recent times there has been considerable interest in alternative ways of understanding organisations. A growing number of researchers have become suspicious of the orthodox view that organisations can best be understood by using a positivistic perspective. The growing critique of positivism and the search for alternative epistemological and methodological foundations for the social sciences has led many researchers to veer towards the qualitative method of analysis. According to Gill and Johnson (1991), to this group, the positivist approach, with its search for an objective reality and universally applicable rules, has failed to capture and illuminate the substance, interrelatedness and totality of organisational life. The more subjective approach, described as naturalism, has parted company with the natural physical science methodology and borrows from a number of sources, such as anthropology, sociology and psychology, in an attempt to find more meaningful ways of investigating and understanding the reality of organisational life. This more qualitative approach to research is depicted as placing an emphasis on the discovery of the novel and the unfamiliar, which its more unstructured approach to data gathering is deemed to facilitate.

Naturalists argue that in contrast to physical objects and animals, human beings attach meaning to surrounding events and from these interpretations select courses of meaningful action that they can reflect upon and monitor (Gill and Johnson 1991). It is argued that such subjective processes are the sources of human behaviour explanations. Therefore, unlike physical objects, humans can become aware of predictions made about their behaviour and can alter it, thereby negating or moderating the prediction. The naturalist approach's aim is to understand how people make sense of their worlds, with human behaviour seen as purposive and meaningful rather than externally determined.

Thus, naturalistic researchers assume that objective knowledge is not available and stress the subjective experience of individuals. The naturalistic researcher believes that there are multiple realities subjectively constructed within each social setting, available only by considering the whole organisation. These socially constructed realities shift and change and thus cannot be predicted before an inquiry or completely controlled during research. To the naturalist the only way to understand an organisation is to become immersed in its world and inquire into whole systems, searching for changes, patterns and interrelationships.

According to Diesing (1972), the natural approach 'includes the belief that human systems tend to develop a characteristic wholeness. They are not simply a loose collection of variables; they have a unity that manifests itself in nearly every part.' Similarly, Tiernan (1996: 128) adds:

> In contrast to the deductive research methodology of the positivist approach, naturalism favours a more inductive approach. The essence of the inductive approach is that in order to understand social phenomena, such as an organisation, the researcher has to become immersed in its world and inquire into whole systems searching for patterns and explanations. Induction, therefore, begins with an observation of the empirical setting and then proceeds to construct theories about observed phenomena.

From this perspective it emerges that everything is interwoven and it is not necessary to distinguish between cause and effect. The overriding goal of the research is to provide a contextually bound picture of what is going on and to illuminate as much as possible how the organisation has constructed itself.

In order to understand whole systems and whole organisations, naturalistic inquirers favour qualitative research methods, such as participant observation, in-depth, open-ended/semi-structured interviewing and documentary evidence, which are the methods that allow the researcher to interact with the field site as collaboratively and intimately as possible. The purpose is to collect what Geertz (1970) has termed 'thick descriptions' of the way people create and sustain a social experience.

Originally associated with the early work of the Chicago school of sociology, participant observation involves the researcher playing a dual role, namely that of participant in everyday organisational activities and that of observer and recorder of the specific processes and interactions that are being investigated. Here, the researcher does not attempt to manipulate aspects of the research environment, but rather he/she records as much information as possible about the situation's characteristics and processes. While categories of behaviour may be selected for observation and recording methods devised, participant observation is typically unstructured, with the researcher being prepared to collect all data that might prove relevant to the inquiry. As a research tool it is primarily descriptive, often focusing on intragroup and intergroup interactions within organisations.

Advantages associated with this form of enquiry include its ability to reflect the reality of organisational life as it is occurring and its capacity to provide direct information through watching what people do and recording what they say, rather than asking about attitudes and feelings. Among the potential disadvantages are the possibility of the researcher being less than objective as a result of being acculturated into the environment, to the detriment of his/her research independence, and the potential for loss of control. It usually also requires considerable time commitments from the researcher.

The interview, normally described as a conversation with a purpose, is one of the most common methods of inquiry in organisational behaviour research. Interviews differ in terms of the extent to which they are structured. Semi-structured interviewing implies a questioning process that has been generically organised by the researcher before the interview takes place. Conversely, open-ended or unstructured interviewing implies that no predetermined structure has been prepared by the interviewer other than a reflection on what overarching areas the research is examining, and is therefore arguably closer to 'true conversation' than more structured interviews. Particular advantages include its flexibility and adaptability and its potential to deliver new or additional information through non-verbal cues. Disadvantages include the potential for interviewer bias, its time-consuming nature and the lack of anonymity for respondents.

Documentary evidence in organisational behaviour research refers primarily to written documents such as books, company magazines, papers, newsletters, memos, minutes of meetings and notice board displays. It may also refer to video material. Thus, it involves an analysis of materials that have been produced by individuals or organisations, not the researcher. This technique requires that the researcher do an in-depth content analysis of the documents in an attempt to make valid inferences from the data contained in the documents. In order that content analysis be executed effectively, the researcher must have a clear research question, make decisions about what sampling strategy to use when collecting documents, define the recording unit (typically the frequency with which a particular word occurs in the various documents being content analysed) and construct categories for analysis. Advantages associated with this research method include its unobtrusive nature and its potential for the provision of longitudinal data at relatively low cost. Common disadvantages include the possibility of bias or distortion, as documents used are typically written for purposes other than that of the research. The establishment of causal relationships is also problematic.

ONGOING DEBATES/ADVANCED CONCEPTS IN ORGANISATIONAL BEHAVIOUR

Thus far in this introductory chapter we have introduced organisational behaviour as a field. In tracing its historical roots, we looked at scientific management, Fordism, bureaucracy and the human relations school. We also set down more contemporary developments in the form of systems theory. Beyond these theoretical roots, we have also outlined key methods employed for researching behaviour in organisations.

In this section we now turn to ongoing theoretical and measurement debates in organisational behaviour, namely social constructionism, postmodernism and the use of metaphors as a means of providing insight into organisational life and behaviour.

SOCIAL CONSTRUCTIONISM

"If men define the situation as real, then they are real in their consequences." (Thomas and Thomas 1928)

Issues of social construction and sense making came to the fore in the 1960s, partly as a reaction against the dominance of the scientific approach to understanding organisations. Social constructionism rejects the scientific approach to understanding social phenomena and embraces the argument that representations are subjective, relative and arbitrary and focuses on the interaction between the actor and his environment. Closely related to social constructionism is Weick's theory of enactment (1969), which also focuses on subjective interpretations of organisational realities. Weick argues that in trying to interpret our world, we create meanings that we then assume to exist independently from the interpretations that created them. Our interpretation of reality will go on to affect how we behave and our behaviour will in turn shape that reality. Therefore, while the classical theories assume that individuals are shaped by the society in which they live, the social constructionist view sees the environment and the actor shaping each other through this process of sense making and action. Essentially, social constructionists argue that in attempting to conceptualise our world, we also construct it.

An important part of social constructionism is shared meaning. It recognises that the environment in which we live is social as well as material and that material structures are given meaning only by the social context through which they are interpreted. Social constructionists acknowledge that there is an important interplay between the social and the material world (Checkel 1998) and that it is through the interaction between ourselves and the material/physical world in which we live that reality is constructed. Therefore, it assumes that social order is based on the interpretations we assign and the meanings we convey in the process of social interaction.

Consider the university that you are now attending. Social constructionists argue that it is not the building itself that constitutes a university – after all, the building is just bricks and mortar – but rather, it is our shared understanding of that building as a place of advanced learning that makes it a university. Through rituals, symbols, language, structure and hierarchy, organisations create shared meanings about organisational phenomena and what it is to manage, to be managed, to be committed, etc. Social constructionism assumes that it is through these shared meanings that something exists 'objectively', for example, a chair is only a chair when we interpret it as a chair, otherwise it is just a collection of sticks. While the chair is a simplistic example, interpretation can become more difficult when we are considering more abstract entities. Blumer (1969) differentiates between three different types of entities/objects:

- Physical object, e.g. table, chair, car.
- Social object, e.g. mother, student, lecturer.
- Abstract object, e.g. idea, moral, principle.

As we travel down this list, it becomes more difficult to rely on shared meanings. Most people (at least in the Western world) will interpret a chair in the same way. However, this process of sense making becomes more complicated when the physical object also has a symbolic aspect. For example, while most people will interpret a car as a means of transport to get you from point A to point B, some will also interpret it as a status symbol or as a symbol of something out of their reach. Such difficulties increase when we consider social objects. For example, some might interpret a student as someone who is dedicated to learning, while others might interpret a student as someone who sleeps all day. When we consider abstract objects, such as principles and ideologies, shared meaning can be very difficult to achieve.

Some critics argue that the social constructionist theory fails to consider the importance of power. While social constructionism seeks to understand and describe organisational phenomena, critics maintain that it does not explore organisational life in a more political way. While the individual may shape his/her environment through his/her interpretations and actions, this influence is limited. Organisations are a reflection of the society in which we live and therefore recreate the values and meanings that are dominant in that society. We need to consider the importance of the dominant groups' influence in our society and how they may shape meaning and sense making. For example, the values and goals of organisations are expressed through seemingly legitimate rules, regulations and procedures, but who made those rules and regulations, and for whom are they made? Such rules reflect the balance of power and are derived from historical divisions of labour, class, gender and race. This is perpetuated through 'legitimate' organisational structures, rules, procedures, networks, coalitions, norms, dress codes, humour, stereotypes, etc. Once established, they become taken for granted and further 'legitimised'. For instance, the traditional belief that a woman's place was in the home is still evident in the work-home divide and the belief of some that family-friendly work policies are 'women's options'. This would suggest that in constructing reality, certain groups shape it more than others.

POSTMODERNISM

Postmodernism (PM) emerged as a reaction against classical/modernist preoccupation with control, hierarchy and rationalisation. The foundation belief of the postmodernist school is that reality is not objectively or subjectively determined, but rather socially determined. Originating in the arts and architecture, postmodernism sought to challenge the status quo and is therefore political in orientation. The term 'postmodernism' is difficult to define and some would even say that providing a definition of postmodernism would go against everything postmodernism stands for. However, there are dominant themes that underlie postmodernist thinking, outlined below.

Rejection of an Objective Truth and the Grand Narrative

PM challenges the modernist belief in an objective truth and argues that there is no one 'truth'. At the heart of postmodernist thinking is the belief that knowledge is fragmented, constructed and open to many different interpretations (Beardwell and Holden 1997). Postmodernism undermines what it refers to as the 'grand narrative' that has constructed twentieth-century thinking, which is a belief in a universal truth arrived at through scientific and rational means. It challenges the products of such thinking, such as notions of progress and the value of science. Postmodernism opposes the idea that science and technology will automatically enhance human progress, describing this assumption as the progress myth, and argues that progress is defined by those in power and provides justification for maintaining the status quo.

Deconstruction

Deconstruction is the exact opposite of construction. Instead of building up, it involves breaking down and dismantling what is already there. PM assumes that it is only through the destruction and negating of existing theories, assumptions and beliefs that we can become free from the constraints of current thinking. The act of deconstructing taken-for-granted 'truths' and unexamined assumptions like the progress myth above is an important facet of postmodernist thinking, providing distance between the individual and the socially and culturally defined ways of viewing the world (Hatch 1997), thus encouraging a plurality of interpretation rather than one right answer.

Fragmentation

The fragmentation of self and society is another important theme of postmodernism. PM partly draws from Freudian theory and argues against the modernist theory of the self as a unified and autonomous being. It argues that the breakdown of society, community and the family will lead to the fragmentation of the individual. This is further augmented by the lessening divide between work and home life and the multiple and often contradictory roles associated with current working practices, e.g. teleworking (Hatch 1997).

The Link between Language and Power

PM argues that language is more than just a reflection of society, rather, it creates society. Our experience of the world is structured through the language we use (Alveeson and Deetz 1999). Groups that have historically been marginalised and denied a 'voice' in the communicaton of public institutions, e.g. churches, government, etc., may find they do not speak the dominant 'language', which may further marginalise these groups. Bourdieu (1991) argues that language is not just about communicating; it is also a medium of power through which people get their story heard and pursue their own interests. The use of language can vary according to considerations such as race, class and gender.

The Link between Knowledge and Power

Postmodernists argue that the modernist preoccupation with control is still evident in today's organisation, but it has moved away from scientific management's control of labour to trying to control employees' perceptions and knowledge. PM challenges the ruling elite's authority and claims there are multiple and competing views of what is legitimate in organisations. It challenges the modernist view of management as the legitimate power so long as managers are guided by rational and objective principles of management (Hatch 1997). It calls for greater levels of participation by diverse and marginalised groups such as women, ethnic minorities and others traditionally denied a voice.

A complete and thorough discussion of postmodernism is beyond the scope of this chapter. However, despite widespread disagreement as to what actually constitutes postmodernism, there are certain commonalities and themes that have been presented above. Postmodernism involves multiple and competing interpretations, diverse realities and a constant questioning of taken-for-granted assumptions. It is therefore a challenging and difficult perspective to come to terms with. However, it is a perspective worth grappling with, as postmodernism provides unique and important ways of viewing the organisation.

While the ideas of postmodernism are proving attractive to many, some critics challenge this school of thought for failing to come to terms with some of its core themes (Mills and Simmons 1995). The concept of the self as fragmentary has been criticised for ignoring the fact that we 'live one life not several, our ability to choose which other "worlds" we wish to inhabit is very much dependent on our position in this world' (Marx Memorial Library bulletin, no. 117, 1992 as cited in Mills and Simons 1995).

A major criticism of PM is that while it attacks all other theories, it provides no alternative solution and has been unable to encourage radical change (Mills and Simons 1995). Postmodernism's acceptance of the chaotic and the fragmented is not accompanied by any attempt to counteract it.

OTHER WAYS OF VIEWING ORGANISATIONS – GARETH MORGAN'S METAPHORS

This chapter has discussed the many different perspectives of organisations that co-exist, and no single perspective can fully understand organisations in all their complexity. However, Morgan (1980) has provided an approach where different metaphors are used to incorporate the many different and often competing approaches to organisations and thereby increase our understanding of organisational life. Morgan emphasises the importance of metaphorical thinking and maintains that 'schools of thought in organisation theory are based upon the insights associated with different metaphors for the study of organisations, and the logic of metaphor has important implications for the process of theory construction' (1980: 611). Metaphors provide us with a new way of seeing and different metaphors can 'constitute and capture the nature of organisational life in different ways, each generating powerful, distinctive, but essentially partial kinds of insight' (1980: 611). The word 'partial' is important, as no one metaphor can fully capture the complexity of organisations, just as no one theory can. Metaphors concentrate on the similarities and therefore do not address the important differences that exist between two things, which can lead to important factors being ignored and limit our understanding of organisational life (Hatch 1997). Metaphors do, however, provide us with different lenses through which to view the organisation, each lens allowing us to gain more insights into the many 'realities' of organisational life. They can help us to ask different questions and recognise the importance of different information. While the modernist view of the organisation has been based predominantly on the machine and the organism metaphor, Morgan has produced new metaphors that add rich and creative dimensions to the study of organisations, some of which are briefly discussed below.

Organisations as Machines

This metaphor draws heavily from scientific management and views the organisation as something that can be controlled in a routine and predictable way. A machine is something that is rationally devised for a purpose; the machine metaphor therefore emphasises rationality and the achievement of goals. Organisational mechanisation is associated with routine, precision, time constraints, predetermined goals, repetition and control, concepts very much aligned to scientific management and Fordism.

While the machine metaphor is useful when the environment is stable and tasks are straightforward, like all metaphors, the machine is just one way of looking at the organisation and is quite a simplistic one at that. Some of the problems inherent in viewing the organisation as a machine include neglecting social/political and emotional aspects of organisational life and assuming that people act in predictable ways. This metaphor has also been criticised for creating organisational forms that have great difficulty in adapting to changing circumstances (Huczynski and Buchanan 2002).

Organisations as Organisms

This metaphor is based on the open systems theory of organisations, which views organisations as living entities that adapt to their environment in order to survive. Viewing organisations as organisms draws attention to the interrelatedness of all parts of the organisation and the importance of viewing the organisation in a holistic manner. Unlike the machine metaphor, it highlights the importance of adapting to the external environment in order to survive. Another strength is that in recognising the importance of all parts of the organisation, it takes into account the human aspect of organisational life. However, because it views all parts as working in unison together towards a common goal, it fails to consider the complexities of the human component (Rollinson and Broadfield 2002) and underestimates the power of the individual within the organisation.

Organisations as Cultures

This metaphor focuses on the symbolic aspects of organisational life and is rooted in the social constructionist perspective. It delves beneath the surface of organisational life in order to explore the effects of culture on human behaviour. It focuses on the less tangible aspects of organisational life, such as beliefs, values, customs and rituals, in order to understand why people behave the way they do. By viewing the organisation as culture, we see and understand particular events and behaviours in distinctive and penetrating ways. Morgan (1980) argued that the culture metaphor (as well as the theatre and political systems metaphors) introduce 'an explicitly social dimension to the study of organisations, and give particular attention to the ways in which human beings may attempt to shape organisational activities' (1980: 616). However, this metaphor is not without its problems, as Rollinson and Broadfield (2002) have observed. They recognise that while the machine and organism metaphors are easy to grasp and have their own logic, the culture metaphor has no 'overarching rationality' and even questions the usefulness of rationality in understanding organisations. This can make this metaphor difficult for us to understand, given the widespread acceptance of rationality and logic as tools for understanding.

Organisations as Political Systems

The political metaphor sees organisations as arenas of conflicts of interest and political wheeling and dealing. Unlike the machine and organism metaphors, it recognises that people may not have common goals and acknowledges the potential for conflict that differing goals and objectives may set in motion. It recognises that there are many different sources of power within the organisation and that people will compete and engage in political behaviour in order to pursue their own interests. Some of the main strengths of this metaphor are that it dispels the myth of organisations pursuing unitary goals, emphasises the political nature of organisations and recognises the complexities of the people who inhabit it. However, it has been argued that this metaphor overemphasises the competing and conflicting aspects of organisational life and fails to consider the potential for co-operation and collaboration that is also a fundamental part of organisational life (Rollinson and Broadfield 2002).

Organisations as Instruments of Domination

This metaphor views organisations as areas of domination and control. It emphasises the imbalance of power within organisations and views certain groups as imposing their will upon others. This metaphor has certain similarities with the postmodernist perspective in that it focuses on the social domination of many by a seemingly 'legitimate' few in power in order to maintain the status quo. Through this lens we view organisations as places where employees are exploited and controlled in order to pursue the goals of the few at the top. It draws our attention to the prevalence of bureaucracy, work hazards, stress and workaholism as modes of domination and echoes Weber's analysis of bureaucracy as an 'iron cage'. This metaphor also helps to understand how power within organisations reflects the power structures within the wider political environment and 'how societal divisions between classes, ethnic groups, men and women etc. are evident in the workplace' (1980: 618).

Table 1.2 Organisational Metaphors

Metaphor	Theoretical Perspective
Machine	Scientific management/Fordism
Organism	Open systems theory
Culture	Social constructionism
Political system	Postmodernism
Instrument of domination	Postmodernism

SUMMARY OF KEY PROPOSITIONS

- This chapter explored some of the different perspectives of organisational behaviour and how each perspective brings different insights to our understanding of organisations.
- It surveyed the modernist theories of organisational behaviour, focusing on scientific management, Fordism and bureaucracy, which all view the organisation in rational terms, highlighting efficiency, job performance and the role of managers in controlling the labour process. These theories fail to consider the importance of the emotional and social aspects of organisational life.
- It discussed the systems theory of organisations, where organisations are seen as life-sustaining entities that rely on the external environment for survival. This theory recognises the need for organisations to adapt to their surroundings, but oversimplifies the human aspect of organisations by assuming a unitary objective.
- Disillusionment with modernist thinking led to the emergence of social constructionism as an organisational theory, which focuses on the interaction between the individual and the social world in which they live and recognises that the organisation is subjected to symbolic interpretation.
- It looked at postmodernist thinking, focusing on some of the dominant themes from this perspective. Postmodernism rejects modernist thinking and celebrates paradox, uncertainty and deconstruction.
- Finally, this chapter discussed the importance of metaphors in aiding our understanding of organisations. It viewed organisations through the lens of the machine, organism, culture, political systems and instruments of domination metaphors.

DISCUSSION/SELF-ASSESSMENT QUESTIONS

1. In what ways do you think Taylorism is still alive and well today? Discuss the application of Taylorism in organisations today. What are the negative effects of Taylorism? What are the positive effects?
2. What are the different issues/problems that emerge when you view your university through the lens of the machine, culture and political systems metaphors? What other metaphors can you come up with that provide insightful ways of looking at your college? In what ways can the use of metaphors aid our understanding of organisations? In what ways can it inhibit our understanding?
3. How might social constructionism as a theory help us to understand the many political/ideological divides that exist today?
4. How do you think language is used to construct reality and identity? What functions might (a) the use of jargon and (b) managerial speak have in constructing certain realities?
5. What do you think Max Weber meant when he referred to the bureaucratic organisation as an 'iron cage'? In what way are some of today's organisations iron cages?

MULTIPLE CHOICE QUESTIONS

1. According to the human relations school:
   (a) Employees respond primarily to the social context of organisations, of which interpersonal relations are an important part.
   (b) The informal group can exercise strong controls over the work habits of employees.
   (c) The need for recognition and support at work can influence employees more than the physical working conditions.
   (d) All of the above.
   (e) None of the above.

2. Frederick Taylor:
   (a) Underestimated the importance of groups within organisations.
   (b) Believed that the relationship between management and employees was fundamentally adversarial in nature.
   (c) Is associated by some with the alienation and dehumanisation of workers.
   (d) All of the above.
   (e) None of the above.

3. Morgan's culture metaphor:
   (a) Focuses on the competing and conflicting aspects of organisational life.
   (b) Recognises that organisations are inherently political arenas where wheeling and dealing and game playing are rife.
   (c) Underestimates the potential for collaboration and co-operation within organisations.
   (d) All of the above.
   (e) None of the above.

4. Social constructionism:
   (a) Recognises the importance of both the individual and the environment in shaping behaviour.
   (b) Is political in orientation.
   (c) Advocates organisational change.
   (d) All of the above.

5. Systematic soldiering is:
   (a) A view among workers that increased production would lead to redundancies.
   (b) A group norm where workers produce below their optimum level.
   (c) The clear division of tasks between management and employees.
   (d) The breaking down of a job to its smallest components.

6. Which of the following themes are associated with postmodernist thinking?
   (a) The rejection of one universal truth and the acceptance of many, often contradicting, truths.
   (b) The belief in a 'grand narrative'.
   (c) Maintaining the status quo.
   (d) The celebration of certainty and 'one best way'.

(e) None of the above.

7. Bureaucracy is:
    (a) A form of organisation characterised by high levels of formality and rules and procedures.
    (b) For some, an 'iron cage'.
    (c) Characterised by the specialisation of tasks and hierarchy.
    (d) All of the above.
    (e) None of the above.

8. Viewing the organisation as a metaphor can:
    (a) Provide us with alternative lenses through which to view the organisation.
    (b) Provide us with a partial understanding of organisations.
    (c) Limit our understanding of organisations if used incorrectly.
    (d) All of the above.
    (e) None of the above.

FIVE SUGGESTED KEY READINGS

Alvesson, M. and Deetz, S., 'Critical theory and postmodernism: approaches to organizational studies', in S.R. Clegg and C. Hardy (eds), *Studying Organization: Theory and Method*, London: Sage 1999.

Hatch, M.J., *Organisation Theory: Modern, Symbolic and Postmodern Perspectives*, Oxford: Oxford University Press 1997.

Kanigel, R., *The One Best Way: Frederick Winslow Taylor and the Enigma of Efficiency*, London: Little, Brown 1997.

Morgan, G., 'Paradigms, metaphors and puzzle solving in organisational theory', *Administrative Science Quarterly* (1980), 605–20.

Morgan, G., *Images of Organization*, 2nd ed., London: Sage 1997.

REFERENCES

Alvesson, M. and Deetz, S., 'Critical theory and postmodernism: approaches to organizational studies', in S.R. Clegg and C. Hardy (eds), *Studying Organization: Theory and Method*, London: Sage 1999.

Beardwell, I. and Holden, L., *Human Resource Management: A Contemporary Perspective*, 2nd ed., London: Pitman Publishing 1997.

Blumer, H., *Symbolic Interactionism: Perspective of Method*, Englewood Cliffs, NJ: Prentice Hall 1969.

Boulding, K.E., 'General systems theory – the skeleton of science', *Management Science*, II/3 (1956), 197–208.

Bourdieu, P., *Language of Symbolic Power*, Cambridge, MA: Harvard University Press 1991.

Checkel, J.T., 'Social construction and integration', Arena working paper, www.arena.uio.no/publications/wp98 1998.

Dawson, S., *Analysing Organisations*, London: Macmillan 1996.

Diesing, P., *Patterns of Discovery in the Social Sciences*, London: RKP 1972.

Furnham, A., *The Psychology of Behaviour at Work*, London: Psychology Press 1997.

Geertz, C., 'The impact of the concept of culture on the concept of man', in E. Hammel and W. Simmons (eds), *Man Makes Sense*, Boston: Little, Brown 1970.

George, J.M. and Jones, G.R., *Organisational Behaviour*, 3rd ed., New York: Prentice Hall 2002.

Gill, J. and Johnson, P., *Research Methods for Managers*, London: PCP Ltd 1991.

Hardy, C. and Clegg, S., 'Some dare call it power', in S. Clegg, C. Hardy and W. Nord (eds), *Handbook of Organization Studies*, London: Sage 1996.

Hatch, M.J., *Organisation Theory: Modern, Symbolic and Postmodern Perspectives*, Oxford: Oxford University Press 1997.

Huczynski, A.J. and Buchanan, D., *Organisational Behaviour: An Introductory Text*, Hemel Hempstead: Prentice Hall 1991.

Huczynski, A.J. and Buchanan, D., *Organisational Behaviour: An Introductory Text*, 4th ed., Hemel Hempstead: Prentice Hall 2001.

Kanigel, R., *The One Best Way: Frederick Winslow Taylor and the Enigma of Efficiency*, London: Little, Brown 1997.

Kotter, J., Schlesinger, L. and Sathe, V., *Organization: Text, Cases and Readings on the Management of Organizational Design and Change*, Homewood, IL: Irwin 1979.

Mayo, E., *The Human Problems of an Industrial Civilization*, Boston: President and Fellows of Harvard College 1960.

Merton, R., 'Bureaucratic structures and personality', *Social Forces*, 18 (1940), 560–8.

McCourt, W., 'Discussion note: using metaphors to understand and to change organisations: a critique of Gareth Morgan's approach', *Organisational Studies*, XVIII/3 (1997), 511–22.

McNeill, P., *Research Methods*, London: Routledge 1990.

Mills, A.J. and Simmons, T., *Reading Organisational Theory: A Critical Approach*, Aurora, Ontario: Garamond Press 1995.

Morgan, G. 'Paradigms, metaphors and puzzle solving in organisational theory', *Administrative Science Quarterly* (1980), 605–20.

Mullins, L.J., *Management and Organisational Behaviour*, 6th ed., London: Pitman Publishing 2002.

Offe, C., *Industry and Inequality*, London: Edward Arnold 1976.

Pietrykowski, B., 'Beyond the Fordist/post-Fordist dichotomy: working through the second industrial divide', *Review of Social Economy*, LVII/2 (1999), 177–96.

Reed, M., *The Sociology of Organisations: Themes, Perspectives and Prospects*, Hemel Hempstead: Harvester Wheatsheaf 1992.

Rollinson, D. and Broadfield, A., *Organziational Behavior and Analysis: An Integrated Approach*, 2nd ed., Hemel Hempstead: Prentice Hall 2002.

Tiernan, S., 'Organisational transformation: the case of TEAM Aer Lingus', unpublished PhD dissertation, University of Limerick: Department of Management 1996.

Wagner III, J.A. and Hollenbeck, J.R., *Organizational Behaviour: Securing Competitive Advantage*, 3rd ed., New York: Prentice Hall 1998.

Weick, K.E., *The Social Psychology of Organizing*, Reading, MA: Addison-Wesley 1969.

SECTION TWO

THE NATURE OF THE INDIVIDUAL

PERSONALITY

Learning Objectives

- To explore how personality is defined in the organisational behaviour literature.

- To outline some of the major sources of personality difference.

- To set down the interdependence between inherited characteristics and those that are learned.

- To present key personality characteristics and orientations that have been linked to work behaviour and performance in organisations.

- To set out the advantages and disadvantages of adopting a trait approach to personality at work.

- To introduce a critical perspective on the five-factor (or 'big five') personality framework.

- To consider some of the ethical issues associated with determining or measuring personality in the workplace.

INTRODUCTION

People are different from one another. Perhaps it is this simple fact that creates frustrations within organisations, particularly when it comes to setting up controlled, predictable, manageable systems and working arrangements. Every individual is unique and complex, with his or her own orientations, predispositions and personality characteristics. Individuals often act in ways that are unexpected and surprising to others with whom they come in contact.

Personality is a common concept in everyday language that is often used in evaluative ways. Organisational practitioners regularly cite personality differences as one of the most problematic and stressful aspects of managing work in organisations. On the other hand, it is precisely the uniqueness and complexity of individuals that gives rise to some of the most positive sources of organisational achievement and performance.

Organisational behaviour literature has devoted significant attention to exploring and understanding the concept of personality, and over the years there has been some convergence in the research about the ways in which personality impacts on work behaviour and performance. This chapter will help you to develop a more focused understanding of the concept of personality and its impact within organisations. It will outline the importance of understanding dimensions of personality in organisational settings, will help you to consider some of the ethical constraints associated with identifying and measuring different types of personality at work and explore how research has been able to shed useful light on the concept of personality. It will also discuss how an understanding of the sources and impact of personality difference can have significant benefits, both for individuals themselves and for the organisations within which they work.

Organisational behaviour literature has witnessed a recent resurgence in interest in the impact that personality has on work behaviour and organisations (Robertson and Callinan 1998). Most people intuitively recognise that people's personalities have important implications for the organisations in which they work and empirical evidence supports intuitive hunches that personality is important. We are often judged on what people see as our traits or the stable psychological characteristics that give rise to our unique personality and patterns of behaviour. Many theorists and practitioners emphasise how influential an understanding of personality may be in helping organisations to function more effectively and in enhancing levels of self-awareness among individuals and groups at work. The recent popularity of the concept of emotional intelligence (Goleman 1996) emphasises the importance of 'knowing oneself' as a key ingredient. A focus on individuals' own personalities and how these might differ from those around them forms an essential part of enhancing this self-awareness.

DEFINITIONS OF KEY CONCEPTS

Personality
Generally defined using trait-related concepts as a stable set of psychological characteristics that are relatively unchanging over time that differentiate people from one another in a range of identifiable ways and that cannot be explained by the social or biological pressures of the moment.

Sources of personality difference
The main sources of personality difference explored in this chapter are genetic inheritance, gendering, family influences, culture and past experiences.

The nature/nurture debate
This debate addresses the classic question of to what extent our characteristics are inherited or learned. It engages us in attempting to understand how much of our personality is part of the genetic blueprint that we are born with and how much is a result of experiences that we encounter in our environment.

The 'big five' personality characteristics
Offering a framework of important personality factors that some research has found to be linked to behaviour and performance, the big five personality characteristics are

emotional stability, extroversion, openness to experience, agreeableness and conscientiousness.

Locus of control
Locus of control is a key personality characteristic that defines the extent to which one feels in control of one's environment (internal locus of control) or controlled by our environment (external locus of control).

Self-esteem
A key personality characteristic that defines an individual's own self-evaluation, which, although contextually determined, to some extent tends to be either broadly positive or negative.

Authoritarianism
This is a key personality characteristic that defines the extent to which individuals respect and legitimise formal authority in organisations.

Psychometric tests of personality
Structured, usually self-report questionnaires that attempt to measure various dimensions of personality.

Personality as reputation
This is a definition that focuses on external reputation as a way of assessing and categorising personality.

Construct validity of personality tests
The potential of a personality test to measure personality (and specified dimensions of personality) accurately and effectively.

Predictive validity of personality tests
The potential of a personality test to predict aspects of performance or behaviour.

DEFINING PERSONALITY

It is not easy to define personality. In doing so it is just as important to consider what personality is not as well as what it is. People in organisations often attribute behaviour to personality characteristics, when in fact the behaviour is being influenced by other factors within the system (Pomice 1995). Problems can all too easily be attributed to personality 'flaws', personality clashes or personality conflicts when actually there may be structural problems that need to be addressed or other organisational processes causing difficulties (Thomas 1976). Rose (1975) demonstrates that much of the early literature from the human relations school 'overattributes' events to people's personalities without recognising the influences of external factors like group dynamics, power and politics, authority structures and other constraints or behavioural ingredients in the workplace.

This is not to underestimate the powerful influence that personality can have on behavioural patterns and interactions at work. However, as with all key concepts in organisational behaviour, an examination of the influence of personality variables must be undertaken in conjunction with the consideration of a wide range of other factors. It is simplistic to suggest, for example, that someone has a 'personality flaw' even in situations where an individual appears to behave in ways that seem unacceptable or inexplicable. Anyone studying organisational behaviour should recognise that there are interdependent influences on behaviour and that personality is only one of a variety of different influences.

So what is personality? Traditional personality theorists say that personality is a stable set of psychological characteristics that can provide generalised predictions about a person's behaviour. They emphasise people's traits and explore personality as a unitary concept. More recently, however, cognitive/information-processing theorists have proposed that personality may not be as stable a set of characteristics as the traditional theorists suggest. Since the 1960s, cognitive models of behaviour have become more predominant, which view people as complex and sophisticated (though error-prone) information processors (Pervin 1990).

Table 2.1 Traditional and Cognitive Approaches to Personality

Traditional personality theory sees personality as:	Cognitive personality theory sees personality as:
• Stable and consistent. • Able to provide generalised predictions about individual behaviour. • Largely structured and stable. • Based on dispositions, needs and traits. • Based on the self as a single, unitary concept. • Flexible and at least somewhat choice based.	• Able to provide predictions about behaviour that are situation specific. • Largely a process characterised by development and fluidity. • Based on belief systems, inferential strategies and cognitive competencies. • Based on the self as composed of a diverse set of possibilities and potential.

Cognitive theories have now been incorporated into views on motivation, group dynamics, conflict and conflict management and other important organisational behaviour concepts, but the basis for this approach originated with the personality theorists. The cognitive approach sees personality as flexible and often context specific. Pervin (1990) provides a framework that outlines the differences between traditional and cognitive approaches to personality (see Table 2.1):

Essentially the traditional theorists imply that we may have little or no control over the kinds of people that we are and the sorts of personalities that we have. We are, according to traditional theorists, products of our genetic inheritance and our life experiences. Cognitive theorists do not ignore these influences either, but they suggest that people do have a choice about the types of personality characteristics they display. Cognitive theory considers that people have greater control over the ways in which they behave and that personality can be altered through those choices. Furthermore, these choices tend to focus on people's understanding of how certain behaviours will give rise to certain outcomes.

SOURCES OF PERSONALITY DIFFERENCE AND THE NATURE/NURTURE DEBATE

This section outlines some of the main sources of personality difference and explores the ways in which these sources might affect people's personality.

Why are people different? Most research points to a coherent list of sources of personality difference that are generally referred to as based on genetic inheritance, sex role socialisation, family and early childhood influence, cultural factors and experience-related impacts. More detail on each of these categories is outlined below.

GENETIC INHERITANCE

For centuries, philosophers and theorists have debated about whether individuals inherit their characteristics or whether they are acquired through learning, a question often referred to as the nature/nurture debate. Throughout history, theorists, philosophers and scientists have adopted various positions on the issue and there are some extreme arguments in the context of this debate. For example, some theorists have suggested that we are born without any psychological characteristics and that it is only our experiences in life that determine the kinds of characteristics we develop. Others highlight that our genetic blueprint can determine a vast number of personal characteristics, including such features as intelligence, levels of aggression, conservatism, creativity, rationality and so on. Most psychologists recognise that genetic inheritance plays at least some role in helping to determine personality characteristics.

Studies have shown, for example, that there is some evidence to suggest that there are certain personality dimensions that may be influenced at least in some way by the genetic patterns and codes that we inherit from our biological parents. Gottesman (1963) has addressed the nature/nurture debate by proposing the concept of the 'reaction range', which suggests that people inherit a range of potential characteristics and that experiences dictate which of these characteristics are activated by the environment or acquired experientially through the learning process.

SEX AND GENDER

One of the most important sets of features determined by people's genetic coding is their sexual characteristics. Sexual characteristics (which are inherited) have a strong effect on sexual identity or gender (which is learned as a result of the way that society interacts with individuals on the basis of their sex). Anthropologists have demonstrated that people in all societies and communities are socialised differently according to whether they are male or female and that this socialisation process (also known as gendering) can have at least some impact on the personality characteristics they develop. Sexual characteristics and sexual identity clearly demonstrate the interdependence of influence between what people inherit and what they learn.

FAMILY EXPERIENCES

An individual's family is usually the first social group to which he/she comes into contact. Parents act as powerful role models, giving their children normative examples of how adults behave. They selectively reward various behaviours and provide strong guidance to their children, which can affect various aspects of their personalities. Research and theory on dysfunctional families in which there is a serious and ongoing problem, such as alcoholism, abuse or illness, shows that early family experiences can 'create' certain types of personality characteristics among individuals (Wegscheider-Cruise 1987). Whatever the patterns of behaviour that individuals learn when they are young, it seems that their family can have a fundamental and intense impact on the characteristics that they bring with them into adult life. Families provide important early experiences for individuals that can help to shape personalities. The question then arises how it is that members of the same family can demonstrate such different personalities and psychological characteristics. Of course, there are other sources of personality difference, some influenced by such factors as family size, birth order, differential parental orientations towards children and so on. All of these influences can also have a significant impact on the way in which each individual personality emerges within any one family.

CULTURE

Different cultures have their own established and approved patterns of behaviour that are learned by members of that culture. Cultural norms can specify ranges of tolerable behaviour and impose serious restrictions on behaviour deemed by that culture to be unacceptable or intolerable.

LIFE EXPERIENCES

People who come from the same culture, the same family and even those who have identical genetic codes (as in the case of identical twins) are exposed to a different series of life experiences. Some researchers, such as Dunn and Plomin (1990), suggest that experiences outside the family can have an even stronger effect on personality development than those inside the family. It seems that the 'non-shared environment' of family members is an important factor in the attempt to understand the diversity of influences on personality development.

We have seen that personality develops as a result of a complex aggregation and interaction between an individual's genetic inheritance, their family membership, their cultural groups and their life experiences. The sources of personality difference are impossible to isolate and efforts to do so have led to excessive simplification of the causes of personality difference. In fact, it is important to emphasise the interdependence of influence of each of these factors upon the others. The combined influence of such sources of difference leads to a complex range of personality characteristics and combinations.

One way of disentangling the different characteristics to which these sources of diversity give rise is to focus on research that has linked specific aspects or factors of personality to behaviour and performance within work settings. There are five key factors (commonly known as the 'big five') that can help to identify meaningful differences in individual personalities in a way that some researchers have linked to observed differences in workplace behaviour. The next section provides an explanation of these factors.

THE 'BIG FIVE' PERSONALITY FACTORS

Given the wide-ranging research on personality and its impact in the workplace, it is perhaps surprising that there has been at least some significant convergence in evidence that links personality to work behaviour and performance (Nord and Fox 2002). This section explores five major personality factors that have consistently been found to impact on behaviour and performance at work. The fact that these findings have been established and confirmed in a wide variety of different types of personality-based research makes these five factors particularly worthy of attention, and because evidence of these five factors appears in many different cultural settings, some argue that they may be universally applicable despite other cultural differences that prevail in different national or social settings (McCrae and Costa 1997).

The big five personality factors are generally referred to using the following labels:
1. Emotional stability.
2. Extroversion.
3. Openness to experience.
4. Agreeableness.
5. Conscientiousness.

While research remains inconclusive and recent evidence continues to give rise to contradictory findings, these five factors have been frequently correlated with various aspects of work performance in a range of different cultural settings. In this section we suggest some of the most important reasons why such factors might be associated with work effectiveness and performance. However, keep in mind that later in the chapter a more critical note of caution will be introduced in order to discourage linear or automatic assumptions about the impact of these factors on specific work outcomes. To assume that there is an automatic or predictable relationship between any of these factors and work performance is to oversimplify the relationship between these dimensions of personality and individual performance within work settings. This will be explored in more detail at the end of this chapter.

EMOTIONAL STABILITY

Emotional stability is defined by an individual's ability to cope with stress, manage anxiety and respond in reasonable and consistent ways to the challenges that they may face in their lives. 'Neurotic anxiety' is a term originally coined by Sigmund Freud and refers to what he saw as every individual's struggle between their internal impulses to act and the pressures to behave in ways that are socially/contextually acceptable (Freud 1949). While an understanding of behaviour, psychology and personality has progressed considerably since Freud's work, the concept of emotional stability (and its opposite, neuroticism) still retains these connotations. The ways in which we reconcile our internal impulses with the social or organisational pressures of any situation is one way in which emotional stability or neuroticism tends to be assessed. It is intuitively appealing to assume that people who are emotionally stable are more likely to behave effectively in work situations than those who are less stable (or more 'neurotic', to use the original psychological term).

The burgeoning literature on emotional intelligence that will be explored in more detail in Chapter 5 reflects how emotional stability has become an attribute that has been increasingly ascribed to a wide range of social and organisational benefits, including enhancing such capacities as learning, leadership, technical performance, conflict management and concentration. It can be argued that the popular concept of emotional intelligence derives at least in part from research findings that suggest that there is a demonstrable link between emotional stability/neuroticism and work performance (Salgado and Rumbo 1997).

EXTROVERSION

In the 1960s, Hans Eysenck proposed that personality could be understood mainly by examining whether people were introverted or extroverted. This personality dimension refers to the extent to which different people are either reserved and internally oriented or outgoing and sociable. Steers and Mowday (1977: 67) define the introversion/extroversion dimension as follows: 'Introverts tend to focus their energies inwards and have a greater sensitivity to abstract feelings, whereas extroverts direct more of their attention towards other people, objects and events.'

Introverts generally tend to look inwards to their own thoughts, feelings and ideas and extroverts tend to look outwards to other people's actions and reactions. Theorists have suggested that introverts and extroverts demonstrate different kinds of behaviour patterns in the workplace, as outlined below:

Introverts

- Usually prefer to work in quieter places with less activity going on around them.
- Tend to be very clear about their own feelings and thoughts.
- Tend to be analytical (looking at different angles of a given problem).
- Tend to spend time thinking and reflecting about issues and ideas at work.

Thus, introverts are seen to be good at:

- Working on jobs that require reflection.
- Concentrating on difficult or time-consuming tasks.
- Being sensitive to their own positions and feelings towards work.

- One-to-one encounters, especially when sorting out a problem.
- Working independently on projects.

Introverts are seen as being less good at:

- Dealing with large groups of people.
- Speaking their thoughts and articulating their ideas.
- 'Networking' (developing important links with other people at work).
- Having to interact with a wide range of different people on an ongoing basis.

Extroverts

- Usually prefer to work with groups of people rather than on their own.
- Are vigilant about other people's actions and reactions at work.
- Prefer to operate close to the centre of the action at work.
- Appreciate attention and approval from others.
- Prefer to spend more time working with others than working alone.

Extroverts are seen to be good at:

- Dealing with large groups of people.
- Creating a friendly, open atmosphere at work.
- Putting other people at their ease.
- Talking to and interacting with a wide range of different people.

Extroverts are seen as being less good at:

- Working alone on deadlines.
- Reflecting on the key issues of the task at hand.
- Preparing carefully for meetings or key events.
- Thinking before acting.
- Concentrating on one task at a time.

OPENNESS TO EXPERIENCE

Through his clinical observations as a psychologist, Rogers (1961) proposed that people who are 'fully functioning' are those who are more likely to be open to feelings and experiences and to incorporate new experiences effectively into their understanding of themselves and the contexts within which they act. Openness to experience has been associated with more effective work performance, particularly in jobs requiring higher levels of interpersonal interaction, and when tested as a predictor of communication skills (Nikolaou and Robertson 2001). Openness to experience has variously been defined as a tolerance of ambiguity. People who are open to experience tend to be more predisposed to change and more willing to adapt in uncertain or changing circumstances.

AGREEABLENESS

Agreeableness simply refers to an individual's tendency to have satisfactory, easy and pleasant working relationships with those around them. The agreeable personality may be more likely to build effective networks and to develop strong, trusting working relationships with other people. It is intuitively appealing to assume that agreeableness is a characteristic that equals performance and success at work. Indeed, much of the literature on 'emotional intelligence' (Goleman 1996) implies that this is the case. A popular contemporary supposition is that the more agreeable people are, the more likely they are to create tolerable and comfortable interpersonal dynamics, which in turn will lead to more effective work outcomes. However, keep in mind that more recent research suggests that in certain settings there may be no significant relationship between agreeableness and work performance (Nelson *et al.* 1999). Such anomalies will be discussed in more detail later in this chapter.

CONSCIENTIOUSNESS

A series of research papers published in the 1990s seemed to suggest that one personality characteristic – conscientiousness – is frequently found to be most closely associated with effective job performance in a wide range of occupational settings (Barrick and Mount 1991; Salgado 1997). Conscientiousness has been linked to an individual's tendency to be competent, ordered, dutiful, achievement orientated, self-disciplined and deliberate (Costa and McCrae 1992).

Like the assumptions made about the agreeableness characteristic, the proposition that conscientiousness is linked to work performance is also naturally appealing. The research suggests that measuring someone's level of conscientiousness represents an effective route to predicting how well they will perform in their jobs across a range of different tasks. The research from the 1990s indicates that conscientiousness was the 'biggest of the big five' personality characteristics, and while there is no doubt that there are some links between work performance, behaviour and conscientiousness, you will be invited to challenge the assumptions that derive from these findings later in this chapter.

OTHER IMPORTANT PERSONALITY-RELATED CHARACTERISTICS

In addition to the big five personality factors, there are some commonly cited characteristics that have been linked to work behaviour in important ways. Three frequently considered variables – locus of control, self-esteem and authoritarianism – will be discussed in this section. Each of these concepts has the capacity to cast further light on an overarching understanding of personality and its associated dynamics.

LOCUS OF CONTROL

Rotter (1966, 1982) built on work by others in the area of learned helplessness in order to establish another personality dimension, that of 'locus of control'. This dimension (for which Rotter has developed a questionnaire-based measure) is based on social learning theory, which suggests that our experiences cause us to develop relatively stable personality traits that we bring to all situations in life.

Locus of control represents 'a generalised expectancy concerning the determinants of rewards and punishments in one's life' (Pervin 1990: 38). This is a personality dimension that refers to the extent to which people feel in control of what goes on around them. Rotter proposes that all individuals can be defined as having either an 'internal locus of control', i.e. people who believe that their own behaviour and actions will have a direct impact on what happens to them, or an 'external locus of control', i.e. people who believe that events in their lives are determined by more powerful people than themselves or by chance or fate.

Thus, locus of control is a concept that refers to how 'in control' people feel. 'Internals' feel that they are masters of their own destiny and are in control of what goes on around them, whereas 'externals' feel that they don't have much impact on what happens to them and that events in their lives will happen independently of their actions or influence.

Locus of Control and Behaviour

People with an internal locus of control tend to:

- make more decisions by themselves;
- be more politically and socially active because they believe this activity can help to change or shape different events;
- investigate their situations more actively; and
- be more likely to attempt to influence others and to take control of situations.

People with an external locus of control tend to:

- be less likely to demonstrate any of the above tendencies;
- prefer other people to direct their activities; and
- like other people to make decisions on their behalf.

Rotter's research originated from observations he made with his colleague Jerry Phares (1976) of a single individual. Their observations revealed that many of the problems encountered in one case were based on the individual's perceived control over his/her environment. Based on the hypothesis that locus of control was an important dimension that affects behaviour, these researchers carried out years of research before coming up with their first established measure of locus of control, which attempted to identify how individuals perceive the relationship between their own actions and the consequences of those actions. Rotter's main hypothesis centred around the principle that, through their life experiences, individuals learn whether to believe that rewards and punishments depend on their own actions or on variables external to themselves. Nowicki and Strickland (1981) later developed a test that builds on the locus of control concept. Table 2.2 shows a typical series of items contained in a locus of control questionnaire.

The personality dimension of locus of control has been supported as valid in several different studies. However, methods of establishing the locus of control of individuals (including the sample questionnaire outlined in Table 2.2) have been subjected to some criticism. Any questionnaire-based method of uncovering personality dimensions is vulnerable to problems of validity and reliability. These problems will be discussed in more detail later in this chapter.

Table 2.2 Typical Questions to Establish Locus of Control

- Do you believe that some people are born lucky?
- Do you believe that if someone studies hard they can pass any subject?
- Do you believe that many of the unhappy things that happen to people are due partly to bad luck?
- Do you believe that people's misfortunes result from the mistakes they make?
- Do you believe that the average citizen can have an influence on government decisions?
- Do you feel that you have a lot of choice in deciding who your friends are?
- Do you feel that people can get their own way if they just keep trying?

SELF-ESTEEM

This personality characteristic simply refers to the assessment that people make of themselves in their everyday lives. Coopersmith (1967) has shown how self-esteem is an extremely important psychological characteristic that can have a significant influence on behaviour, both in childhood and in adult life.

Individuals with high levels of self-esteem see themselves in a good light, have confidence in their abilities and don't spend too much time worrying about what other people think of them. People with low self-esteem have less confidence in their abilities, look for affirmation and approval from others and are more critical of themselves and their behaviour.

Trait theorists suggest that self-esteem is a relatively constant personality variable. However, any measures used to establish levels of self-esteem show that while there are general ranges within which individuals usually score, self-esteem can vary quite significantly over time, and even from day to day (Gleitman 1991).

Studies have shown that people with high self-esteem are generally more likely to:

- take more risks in choosing their jobs;
- be more assertive, more independent and more creative;
- develop effective interpersonal relationships;
- be less easily influenced by others' opinions; and
- set challenging goals for themselves at work.

People with low self-esteem are generally more likely to:

- be more dependent on and swayed by others' opinions;
- take fewer risks in all work-related activities; and
- set fewer and easier goals for themselves.

What Affects People's Self-esteem?

Like the other personality dimensions outlined in this section, early experience seems to play a central role in the development of high or low levels of self-esteem. Reflected appraisal (the assumptions that children make about themselves by studying the reactions of people close to them), degree of acceptance (the amount of affection, warmth and approval that children receive in the early years of their lives), clarity of boundaries (the extent to which parents establish and clarify guidelines of behaviour) and early experiences of democratic practices (the extent to which children are encouraged to take part in the identification and negotiation of boundaries and rules of behaviour) all appear to play a part in the development of levels of esteem. People who receive positive appraisals, high degrees of acceptance, clear rules of behaviour and who have experience of democratic practices may develop higher levels of self-esteem, which in turn can affect their behaviour in adult life (Coopersmith 1967). Self-esteem also has important implications for how people manage emotion and stress and has been linked to people's overall sense of psychological well-being. Further research and related ideas about self-esteem will be discussed in more detail in Chapter 5.

AUTHORITARIANISM

Important research carried out by Aronoff and Wilson (1985) identified a collection of behavioural tendencies which together can be referred to as the 'authoritarian' personality.

Aronoff and Wilson's research suggests that people with an authoritarian personality demonstrate the following tendencies:

- Sensitivity to status, formal authority and official rules. When operating in organisational settings, common authoritarian responses include submission (towards those perceived to be of a higher status) and aggression (towards those perceived to be of a lower status within the system).
- Sensitivity to any information that might reveal the nature of other people's status, given that this information will help to determine how to behave towards that person (aggressive/submissive).

The research also shows that authoritarian personalities are driven by a deep fear of failure, causing them to avoid tasks that are difficult, complex or ambiguous. They depend on the authority of their rank within their organisation when engaged in attempts to influence others, and as a result they much prefer to work in highly structured organisations where there are clear lines of authority and divisions of activity and responsibility.

Theorists have suggested that the authoritarian personality is linked to the concept of the 'bureaucratic personality' (Allinson 1990). The authoritarian has been found to be least comfortable and least able to cope at the early stages of a new task and particularly at times when change is being planned or is underway.

On the one hand it is important to avoid a simplistic attribution of organisational problems to personality defects, but on the other, it is impossible to deny that examples of dysfunctional behaviour relating to personality can be identified in organisational settings. Dixon (1976) has argued that the authoritarian personality can give rise to problematic patterns of behaviour within organisations. For example, it has been argued that because authoritarian personalities are more successful at climbing career ladders in traditional organisational settings (Hosking and Morley 1991), with time their patterns of behaviour can become reinforced and more intense.

PROBLEMS WITH TRAIT THEORIES OF PERSONALITY

The research that gave rise to the identification of the five-factor framework and such personality dimensions as locus of control, self-esteem and authoritarianism all largely assume that personalities are stable sets of characteristics that can determine people's behaviour and tendencies over the course of their lives. However, as Mischel (1968) points out, there is evidence to suggest that people behave much less consistently than many of the trait theories would suggest.

Individual personality traits, whether inherited or learned, may play a role in determining people's behaviours, but other situational influences are also important to consider. At work, group influence (Milgram 1963; Haney and Zimbardo 1977), organisational structures (Allinson 1990) and power relationships (French and Raven 1959) can all influence the ways in which people are likely to behave and suggest that personality may in fact be a flexible concept that adjusts in each individual according to the situations they encounter.

Most people can identify times when they have felt introverted and other times when they have been extroverted. Some situations may provide people with a sense of control over their lives, whereas others may cause them to feel out of control. Further, as mentioned earlier, people's levels of self-esteem may change from day to day. In assessing personality, it is important to keep in mind that while people may have certain tendencies or dimensions that affect their behaviour, situational variables are also powerful and may provide evidence that personality traits are not as constant or as apparent as traditional trait theorists might suggest.

MERITS OF TRAIT THEORIES OF PERSONALITY

Other studies have shown that people do sometimes demonstrate remarkable consistency of behaviour over time (Block 1977). Longitudinal studies show high levels of correlation between personality characteristics over ten- to twelve-year periods (Costa and McCrae 1980). Similarly, while there is strong evidence to suggest that people's personalities seem to change quite radically from one situation to another, there are other studies which show that cross-situational consistency in certain personality characteristics is also possible to establish (Epstein 1983).

Put more simply, the debate between trait and situational theories of personality shows how the concept of personality may be subject to a multiplicity of influences and how difficult it is to isolate causal variables. Indeed, the scientific basis for exploring personality dimensions and their causes is not robust and is often accused of being able to provide only the flimsiest evidence of reliability or validity. The next section outlines the pitfalls associated with attempting to measure personality.

ASSESSING PERSONALITY

Not only is the concept of personality hard to define, but even when a definition has been accepted and articulated there are fundamental difficulties associated with measuring or assessing individual personalities.

Attempts to develop structured personality tests have traditionally been attacked by conventional scientists for being inadequate in a number of ways. However, access to information about the sources of individual difference is already limited. One way of attempting to discover the way in which individuals differ and the reasons why they do is by asking people questions about their beliefs, values, feelings and likely behaviour. Established personality tests that address such questions to the individuals being tested can at least be evaluated for their consistency and their predictive validity. In the workplace, common personality tests like the 16PF and the Myers Briggs type indicator are used to help make decisions about recruitment, selection and promotion. However, the extent to which such tests provide valid information about individuals and their personalities is still subject to considerable dispute.

Predictive Validity

Personality tests are generally developed in order to predict how people will behave. However, the uniqueness and complexity of human nature has so far confounded all of psychologists' best attempts to provide any complete predictive framework for behaviour. Situations and people are so complex that even when certain personality dimensions or situational variables are isolated successfully, their ability to tell us anything about real-life situations is quite limited. It has regularly been suggested that common-sense methodologies for finding out about individuals' personalities are generally as effective (and sometimes more effective) than elaborate questionnaires that have been developed over long periods of time using large samples.

The Barnum Effect

The Barnum effect describes the tendency for people to be fooled by generic descriptions of their personality profiles. A little like horoscopes, some personality tests have been bestowed high levels of validity even when this is not the case. The following extract explaining the Barnum effect shows how this can sometimes happen.

There's One Born Every Minute!

'An early demonstration of the Barnum effect was performed by Bertrand Forer who asked the students of one of his classes to take a personality test (Forer 1949). This test made them list the hobbies, personal characteristics, secret hopes and ambitions of the person they would like to be. Forer promised that within a week he would give them a brief description of their personality based on the results of the test. True to his word, he gave each subject what appeared to be a personalised interpretation: a typed personality sketch with the student's own name written on the top. The subjects were assured that their privacy would be strictly respected.

'After reading the sketches, the students were asked to rate the effectiveness of the test in describing their personality using a scale from 0 ('poor') to 5 ('perfect'). They evidently thought that the test had done a good job, for their average rating was 4.3. There was only one thing wrong. Unbeknown to the subjects, Forer had given each of them the identical personality sketch.'

Source: Gleitman (1991)

THE 'SELF-REPORT' PROBLEM

Many classic personality tests require individuals to answer a series of questions about themselves. From this data, the assessors then infer through a variety of patterns, clues and evidence-based links what type of personality the individual possesses. This methodology is implicitly trait orientated, often failing to recognise that individuals may change and develop over time or even from moment to moment. Questionnaires and personality measures that do produce identical scores over time can be assumed to be more valid than those that don't and may support the case for the trait approach. Yet there are other problems with self-report questioning that cause difficulties for effective personality assessment.

- There is evidence to suggest that respondents to personality questionnaires often respond in a way that they think they are supposed to. This is especially the case if personality tests are being used as a mechanism for selecting people for jobs or promotion.
- Even if there are no positive or negative outcomes to be gained from various responses to a personality assessment, people often have built-in tendencies to answer in a particular way. We are often vulnerable to ego defence mechanisms that prevent us from recognising or identifying aspects of our personality that may have significant impacts on how we behave.
- People's own blind spots can cause them to give skewed responses to personality tests. Individuals are subjective about their own characteristics and about how they portray themselves to other people, so it is not always likely that they will be able to provide effective and accurate responses to questions about themselves.
- The construct validity of any measure refers to the extent to which the measure actually does test the variables that it sets out to test. It is difficult to establish the construct validity of personality tests. Instead of measuring personality as they set out to do, they may measure other variables, such as an individual's mood or current disposition, their aspirations, their illusions about themselves or their own assumptions of acceptability.

For these reasons, personality tests are prone to a variety of inaccuracies and pitfalls, particularly in relation to construct validity, predictive validity and generalisability.

ONGOING DEBATES/ADVANCED CONCEPTS IN PERSONALITY

A Critical Perspective on the 'Big Five' Personality Factors

Earlier in this chapter, five major personality factors were outlined that many theorists have argued are universally related to important aspects of work performance and behaviour. More recent research has subjected this assertion to further scrutiny and, while not dismissing these factors as unimportant, has ensured that excessively simplistic assumptions about the links between personality and work behaviour do not prevail. This section outlines a more critical perspective on the 'big five' personality factors and cites some interesting research that helps to avoid making simplistic assumptions.

For around the last twenty years, the five-factor model of personality has provided a measurable structure around which personality traits can be assessed and analysed (McCrae and Costa 1997). Many personality measures either implicitly or explicitly focus on these factors and attempt to identify some verifiable measures of emotional stability, extroversion, openness to experience, agreeableness and conscientiousness when it comes to understanding different personality types and orientations.

More recent research has found varying levels of support for the propositions accompanying the five-factor model. Nikolaou and Robertson (2001) provide a range of evidence that reminds us that the five personality factors that have gained so much credence should not automatically be seen as necessarily reliable or valid predictors of job performance and work behaviour. Conflicting, inconclusive, methodologically diverse and context- or job-specific findings uncovered by related studies demonstrate that the universal validity of some aspects of the five-factor model must continue to be subjected to critical scrutiny (Roberston *et al.* 2000). There are important considerations, such as type of occupation (Barrick and Mount 1991), cultural context (Nikolaou and Robertson 2001) and methodological approaches (Tett *et al.* 1991) that prohibit generalisations about the relationship between these features of personality and work behaviour or performance. For example, such studies have sometimes found only weak (and in some cases negative) correlations between job performance and conscientiousness, depending on the methodologies used, the types of samples being studied and the range of performance indicators being applied.

One of the most promising findings emerging from this recent research lies in the important correlations uncovered between personality factors, overall levels of job satisfaction and organisational citizen behaviours. The broadening of the research agenda to explore how personality may be linked in important ways to job satisfaction and work citizenship lays the path to further avenues of investigation that in the future may help to establish more clarity about how personality influences the many realms and dimensions of organisational experience.

Challenging Assumptions about Agreeableness and Conscientiousness at Work

Some of the more established research in the area of personality at work suggests that we need to surround ourselves with agreeable and conscientious people in order to ensure positive work outcomes. On the one hand, this assumption may seem like an obvious platitude, while on the other it has itself been subjected to some interesting challenges based on more recent findings. For example, Craik *et al.* (2002) have demonstrated that among managerial groups, disagreeableness (defined by such constructs as aggression, impatience and arrogance) is more closely linked to performance than agreeableness. In challenging the assumption that conscientiousness leads to higher levels of performance at work, Robertson *et al.* (2000) have also shown that 'managerial promotability' is negatively correlated with conscientiousness and is more likely to be linked with other constructs, such as eloquence, decisiveness, flexibility, innovativeness, motivation and persuasiveness. Interestingly, they also found that all of the correlations between those constructs and conscientiousness were negative. This throws some interesting light on the requirements of managerial career development in organisations and suggests either that promotability is not related to performance at work or (more likely) that there are dimensions of performance that have not been adequately isolated or explored in the literature.

PERSONALITY AND PROMOTABILITY

Promotable managers at work are:

- Self-motivated and enthusiastic (MOTIVATED).
- Clear and convincing when communicating with others (PERSUASIVE AND ARTICULATE).
- A source of new ideas (INNOVATIVE).
- Prepared to adapt to changing situations (FLEXIBLE).
- Prepared to take responsibility and initiate action (DECISIVE).

Source: Roberston *et al.* (2000)

CONTINUED LACK OF CLARITY OF THE PERSONALITY CONCEPT

While general definitions of personality have already been presented and compared at the beginning of this chapter, it is important to recognise that approaches to understanding personality have been somewhat distorted by another source of definitional ambiguity. As Nord and Fox (2002) explain, two qualitatively different ways of defining personality have emerged in the literature. One is 'personality as reputation', which defines personality as the traits that other people perceive an individual to possess (Hogan 1991). The other definition describes personality as the processes internal to an individual that can never be fully uncovered (or that may only be uncoverable through the kinds of self-report questionnaires that were critiqued earlier in this chapter). Attempts to recognise the difference between one's own and others' perceptions of personality have not yet been fully integrated in research or practice. However, the increasing popularity of such human resource development practices as 360-degree feedback, self-awareness training and higher levels of commitment to exploring interpersonal perception demonstrate that such differences are increasingly being recognised as important keys to organisational development.

ETHICAL AND MORAL ISSUES

There are ethical and moral constraints associated with attempts to measure or categorise personality. Labelling people according to different personality characteristics may be subject to misuse in organisational settings. Because there are no objectively perfect measures of personality, making selection, reward or promotion decisions based on an analysis of personality is fraught with ethical problems. Indeed, even if there were measures that could definitively identify employee personality types, their use would still have to be subjected to a critical ethical audit. We know that personality, while often defined as relatively stable, can also change or develop over time. The danger in assigning a personality label to an individual as a result of any structured or formal measurement technique is partially based on the risks that are linked to stereotyping or inappropriate labelling in organisational settings.

Of course, it can be argued that stereotyping and labelling occur regardless of the existence of formal measures of personality, but personality testing that risks being linked to individual rewards, sanctions or other outcomes may represent the institutionalising of a stereotyping process that would be particularly ethically unsafe. These concerns do not suggest that the exploration of personality preferences of individuals and groups within organisations cannot be conducted in ethically sound ways. Indeed, the process of developing a higher level of awareness of our own personalities and those of others can lead to a range of important benefits that can help to clarify career direction, preferred working environments, appropriate team roles and many other aspects of work dynamics. When personality is explored with a view to enhancing self-awareness and that of others in formative, confidential environments, it can enrich our understanding of how best to operate. Such explorations should, however, incorporate a consideration of questions that relate to the construct validity, reliability and utility of any personality-related tests.

STUDYING PERSONALITY AT WORK

All of the issues and concerns above suggest a number of important ideas about personality that are worthy of further consideration. First, on its own, personality cannot account for differences in work behaviour and success. Power, culture, perception and other organisational dynamics (many of which are explored in other chapters) all have an impact on organisational behaviour and must be considered in conjunction with characteristics that relate to individual personality. Second, a 'reductionist view' of personality, i.e. a view that sees personality as explainable by focusing on a small number of characteristics, such as 'the big five' outlined earlier, is inevitably going to lead to contradictory findings. Approaches to understanding personality must be multifaceted and context sensitive. A real understanding of how personality, work behaviour and work performance interact may only really be possible by examining fine-grained, context-specific, qualitative aspects of these factors, and the generalisability of such approaches is likely to be quite limited.

Nikolaou and Robertson (2001) conclude that there are some important theoretical and practical implications associated with current levels of personality-related knowledge.

Personality measures that are used in any context should be used in conjunction with a careful, context-sensitive analysis of job-relevant characteristics. For example, personality criteria relevant to occupations requiring significant interpersonal interaction may require a different subset of the five-factor model, i.e. agreeableness and openness to experience, than that which might be required for concentrated, solitary-type work. In addition, it is argued that 'a confirmatory approach should always be used when exploring the application of personality dispositions at work' (Nikolaou and Robertson 2001: 182), which means that it is important to generate evidence-based hypotheses about the kinds of personality characteristics that are likely to be relevant in any one work setting before moving to measure or assess individual personality types.

As with all organisational behaviour research, it is usually only reasonable to expect to establish 'probablistic' relationships between personality and various types of work performance and outcome.

SUMMARY OF KEY PROPOSITIONS

- This chapter explored the concept of personality and looked at some of the ways in which personality can affect individual behaviour at work.
- The distinctions between different personalities in the workplace can have a significant impact on the types of behaviours that manifest themselves. Understanding personality is a key requirement for understanding behaviour in organisations, and while there are many other factors which affect people's behaviour, personality generally has a consistent, stable effect that sometimes outweighs the influences that come from elsewhere.
- Definitions of personality vary considerably. For example, trait theorists define personality as a stable set of psychological characteristics associated with each individual. On the other hand, cognitive theorists see personality as characteristics which are flexible and adjustable according to the different cognitive assessments people make about the world around them.
- Personality can be seen to be shaped at least to some degree by a variety of identifiable sources. Common sources of personality difference include genetic inheritance, sex and gender, early family experience, cultural influences and life encounters. The importance and significance of each of these sources is still uncertain, but it is clear that there is a strong interdependence of influence between the variables outlined.
- The five-factor, or 'big five', model of personality suggests a limited number of identifiable characteristics that may be linked to behaviour at work. The possibilities and limitations associated with this model have been outlined.
- Personality has been found to influence behaviour in a variety of ways. Trait approaches identify different personality types that can be seen to exert significant influence on the ways in which people behave. Locus of control is a dimension that can affect the levels of control an individual perceives that he/she has over events in the workplace; self-esteem, or an individual's evaluation of himself/herself, can have an

impact on such patterns as job choices and goal setting; and authoritarianism is a personality dimension that determines the levels of status orientation that individuals demonstrate at work.

- The relationship between personality and other important work-related dynamics, such as job satisfaction and citizenship behaviour, were highlighted as representative of other exciting areas of investigation on which future research may be able to shed further light.

- This chapter also addressed the issue of personality assessment, showing how difficult it often is to develop effective measures of personality. With any personality test, problems of predictive and construct validity are likely to arise, making personality measurement and assessment a difficult task that is also accompanied by important ethical considerations.

DISCUSSION/SELF-ASSESSMENT QUESTIONS

1. Differentiate between trait theories and cognitive theories of personality. In your view, which is a more accurate perspective?

2. Have a nature/nurture debate in class – one side should propose that people inherit their personalities and the other that people learn or acquire their personalities through life experiences. Which side found it easier to assert their position? Why?

3. Develop a list of positive and negative behaviours that might occur in the workplace. See if you can identify personality traits that might have produced the behaviours you have identified. Are there other factors that might have given rise to these behaviours?

4. Why is it so difficult to measure or assess people's personalities? Discuss the principles of construct and predictive validity as they relate to personality assessments.

5. Imagine that you have been asked to come up with an accurate assessment of the personality characteristics of a fellow student or colleague. What steps would you take in preparing to carry out an assessment? What sources of evidence would you seek? What ethical considerations would you need to take into account?

MULTIPLE CHOICE QUESTIONS

1. All differences in the ways in which people behave at work can ultimately be explained by analysing individual personality. True or false?

2. Personality is:
   (a) Inherited and defined by our genetic make-up.
   (b) Learned by our interactions with our environment.
   (c) Influenced both by inherited and learned factors.

3. Locus of control refers to:
   (a) The extent of control we actually have over our environment.
   (b) The extent of control we typically feel that we have over our environment.
   (c) The extent of control that others exert on us.

(d) The location of power in any organisational setting.
4. Research shows that people with low self-esteem are likely to take more risks in choosing their jobs. True or false?
5. Research on authoritarianism has suggested that authoritarian personalities are:
   (a) More likely to try to exercise authority over people without regard to their status in the organisation.
   (b) Rarely concerned or perturbed by failure.
   (c) Highly sensitive to status, formal authority and official rules.
   (d) Not sensitive to social clues indicating status.
6. Traditional personality theory sees personality as:
   (a) Stable and consistent.
   (b) Unpredictable and ever changing.
   (c) Irrelevant to workplace settings.
   (d) Based on social and biological pressures of the moment.
7. Parents typically socialise their children differently depending on whether they are male or female. True or false?
8. In personality theory, emotional stability is a factor that typically refers to:
   (a) An individual's ability to conceal their emotions.
   (b) An individual's tendency to behave in emotionally open ways.
   (c) An individual's emotional state at any one point in time.
   (d) An individual's ability to respond in reasonable and consistent ways to the challenges that they may face in their lives.
9. Agreeableness is a trait that is always highly correlated with work performance. True or false?
10. Which of the following describes the Barnum effect?
    (a) An ability to evade responsibility.
    (b) A distortion of self-perception.
    (c) A tendency to be fooled by generic descriptions of personality profiles.
11. 'Personality as reputation' refers to:
    (a) The extent to which people work to display a certain set of traits to others.
    (b) The traits other people perceive an individual to have.
    (c) The public face deliberately presented by an individual.
12. Because there are no objectively perfect measures of personality, making selection, reward or promotion decisions based on measures of personality is fraught with ethical problems. True or false?

FIVE SUGGESTED KEY READINGS

Allinson, S., 'Personality and bureaucracy', in R. Wilson and S. Rosenfeld (eds), *Managing Organizations: Experiences, Texts and Cases*, New York: McGraw-Hill 1990.
Barrick, M. and Mount, M., 'The big five personality dimensions and job performance: a meta-analysis', *Personnel Psychology*, 44 (1991), 1–15.

McCrae, R.R. and Costa, P.T., 'Personality trait structure as a human universal', *American Psychologist*, 52 (1997), 509–16.

Nord, W.R. and Fox, S., 'The individual in organisational studies: the great disappearing act?', in S.R. Clegg, C. Hardy and W.R. Nord (eds), *Handbook of Organizational Studies*, London: Sage 2002.

Robertson, I. and Callinan, M., 'Personality and work behaviour', *European Journal of Work and Organisational Psychology* , VII/3 (1998), 321–40.

REFERENCES

Allinson, S., 'Personality and bureaucracy', in R. Wilson, and S. Rosenfeld (eds), *Managing Organizations: Experiences, Texts and Cases*, New York: McGraw-Hill 1990.

Aronoff, J. and Wilson, J.P., *Personality in the Social Process*, New York: Laurence Erlbaum 1985.

Barrick, M. and Mount, M., 'The big five personality dimensions and job performance: a meta-analysis', *Personnel Psychology*, 44 (1991), 1–15.

Block, J., 'Advancing the psychology of personality: paradigmatic shift or improving the quality of research?', in D. Magnusson and N. Endler (eds), *Personality at the Crossroads*, Hillsdale, NJ: Erlbaum 1977, 37–64.

Coopersmith, S., *The Antecedents of Self-Esteem*, San Francisco: Freeman 1967.

Costa, P.T. and McCrae, R.R., 'Influence of extraversion and neuroticism on subjective well-being', *Journal of Personality and Social Psychology*, 38 (1980), 36–51.

Costa, P.T. and McCrae, R.R., *Manual for the Revised NEO Personality Inventory*, Odessa, FL: Psychological Assessment Resources 1992.

Craik, K.H., Ware, A.P., Kamp, J., O'Reilly, C., Staw, B. and Zedeck, S., 'Explorations of construct validity in a combined managerial and personality assessment programme', *Journal of Occupational and Organizational Psychology*, 75 (2002), 171–93.

Dixon, N.F., *On the Psychology of Military Incompetence*, London: Jonathan Cape 1976.

Dunn, J. and Plomin, R., *Separate Lives: Why Siblings Are So Different*, New York: Basic Books 1990.

Epstein, S., 'The stability of behaviour: on predicting most of the people most of the time', *Journal of Personality and Social Psychology*, 37 (1983), 91–154.

Eysenck, H., *Dimensions of Personality*, London: RKP 1967.

French, J. and Raven, B., 'The bases of social power', in L. Cartwright and A. Zander (eds), *Group Dynamics: Research and Theory*, London: Tavistock 1959.

Forer, B.R., 'The fallacy of personal validation: a classroom demonstration of gullibility', *Journal of Abnormal and Social Psychology*, 44 (1949), 118–23.

Freud, S., *An Outline of Psychoanalysis*, New York: Norton 1949.

Gleitman, H., *Psychology*, 3rd ed., New York: Norton 1991.

Goleman, D., *Emotional Intelligence: Why It Can Matter More than IQ*, St Ives: Bloomsbury 1996.

Gottesman, I.I., 'Heritability of personality: a demonstration', *Psychological Monographs*, IX/77 (1963).

Haney, C. and Zimbardo, P.G., 'The socialisation into criminality: on becoming a prisoner and a guard', in J.L. Tapp and F.L. Levine (eds), *Law, Justice and the Individual in Society: Psychological and Legal Issues*, New York: Holt, Reinhart and Winston 1977, 198–223.

Hogan, R., 'Personality and personality measurement' in M.D. Dunnette and L.M. Hough (eds), *Handbook of Industrial and Organizational Psychology*, 2nd ed., ii, Palo Alto, CA: Consulting Psychologists Press 1991, 873–919.

Hosking, D.M. and Morley, I.E., *The Social Psychology of Organising: People, Processes and Contexts*, London: Harvester Wheatsheaf 1991.

McCrae, R.R. and Costa, P.T., 'Personality trait structure as a human universal', *American Psychologist*, 52 (1997), 509–16.

Milgram, S., 'A behavioural study of obedience', *Journal of Abnormal Psychology*, 67 (1963), 371–8.

Mischel, W., *Personality and Assessment*, New York: Wiley 1968.

Nelson, A., Robertson, I.T., Walley, L. and Smith, M., 'Personality and work performance: some evidence from small and medium sized firms', paper presented at the Occupational Psychology conference of the British Psychological Society, Blackpool, England 1999.

Nikolaou, I. and Roberston, I.T., 'The five factor model of personality and work behaviour in Greece', *European Journal of Work and Organisational Psychology*, X/2 (2001), 161–86.

Nord, W.R. and Fox, S., 'The individual in organisational studies: the great disappearing act?', in S.R. Clegg, C. Hardy and W.R. Nord (eds), *Handbook of Organizational Studies*, London: Sage 2002.

Nowicki, S. and Strickland, B., 'Locus of control', in R. Aero and E. Weiner, *The Mind Test*, New York: William Morrow 1981, 20–3.

Pervin, L.A., *Personality: Theory and Research*, 6th ed., New York: Wiley 1990.

Phares, E.J., *Locus of Control in Personality*, Morrison, NJ: General Learning Press 1976.

Pomice, E., 'Personality attributions and the work environment', *Working Woman*, VI (1995), 68–75.

Robertson, I. and Callinan, M., 'Personality and work behaviour', *European Journal of Work and Organisational Psychology*, VII/3 (1998), 321–40.

Robertson, I.T., Baron, H., Gibbons, P., MacIver, R. and Nyfield, G., 'Conscientiousness and managerial performance', *Journal of Occupational and Organisational Psychology*, 66 (2000), 225–44.

Rogers, C.R., *On Becoming a Person: A Therapist's View of Psychotherapy*, Boston: Houghton Mifflin 1961.

Rose, M., *Industrial Behaviour*, Harmondsworth: Penguin 1975.

Rotter, J.B., 'Generalised expectancies for internal versus external control of reinforcement', *Psychological Monographs*, LXXX/609 (1966).

Rotter, J.B., *The Development and Application of Social Learning Theory*, New York: Praeger 1982.

Salgado, J.F. and Rumbo, A., 'Personality and job performance in financial services managers', *International Journal of Selection and Assessment*, 5 (1997), 91–100.

Steers, R.M. and Mowday, R.T., 'The motivational properties of tasks', *Academy of Management Review* (October 1977), 645–58.

Tett, R., Jackson, D. and Rothstein, M., 'Personality measures as predictors of job performance: a meta-analytic review', *Personnel Psychology*, 44 (1991), 703–42.

Thomas, K., 'Conflict and conflict management', in M.D. Dunnette and B.M. Bass, *Handbook of Organizational Behaviour*, Chicago: Rand McNally 1976.

Wegscheider-Cruise, S., 'Choicemaking', *Health Communications*, II/4 (1987).

PERCEPTION AND COGNITION AT WORK

3

Learning Objectives

- To introduce the concepts of perception and cognition at work and their effects on organisational behaviour.

- To present the perceptual process and to explore the role that individual perception plays in the workplace.

- To highlight some of the major reasons why people are selective in the ways in which they perceive their environment.

- To explain how the context in which people receive information can have a significant influence on the ways in which they understand and deal with this information.

- To outline common distortions in perception that can prevent people from making an accurate assessment of their work environments.

- To review key cultural influences that can affect the ways in which people perceive their environments.

INTRODUCTION

How people perceive their environment is a fundamentally important consideration for understanding behaviour at work. People react to and interact with their work environments based on the perceptions that they develop. Understanding processes of perception and the ways in which they develop can help to explain how individuals make sense of and act upon the information they receive.

Research and experience show us that people rarely receive information passively, rather, we receive information in active and sometimes individually unique ways. Events, issues, changes, people, groups and activities are seldom interpreted in the same ways by different people. This chapter deals with the following issues relating to perception and reecognition at work: the process of perception, the development of common perceptual errors and biases, the ways in which information is organised and interpreted and the functions of attitudes. Such an exploration should help to clarify why perceptual processes and cognition are fundamental to our understanding of organisational behaviour.

DEFINITIONS OF KEY CONCEPTS

Perception
The psychological process through which people receive, organise and interpret information from their environment.

The process of perception
Involves sensing, selecting, organising, interpreting and responding to events, information or people in the environment.

Attribution
The term applied to the process through which people assign causes to events and actions.

Stereotype
A pre-established expectation about an individual or a group, often based on surface characteristics relating to physical appearance.

Projection
A perceptual process that occurs when we believe that other people see the world as we do.

The halo effect
A perceptual error that occurs when a single characteristic associated with an individual is used to generate a positive impression or assessment of that person.

The fundamental attribution error
A perceptual error that some theorists assume to be universal; defines the tendency for people to explain their own behaviour using external attributions and others' behaviour using internal attributions.

Attitudes
Can be defined as a person's relatively enduring disposition toward people, objects, events or activities.

Cognition
The process of thinking, knowing or mentally processing information.

Cognitive style
An individual's approach to organising and processing information.

PERCEPTION AND PERCEPTUAL INFLUENCERS

Perception can be defined as 'the psychological process through which people receive, organise and interpret information from their environment' (Atkinson *et al.* 1993). It is nearly impossible for people to avoid biases in perception and attitudes (Plous 1993). Everything we see and all the information we receive is actively processed by us, and our own perceptual and attitudinal systems have a fundamental effect on the events that occur around us. Our attitudes and perceptions can influence all aspects of the decisions that we make, both inside and outside the workplace. People behave in accordance with the way they perceive information (Stranks 1994). Definitions of perception focus on the idea that perception is a process, not a static or passive concept. People *receive* information from the outside world through the sensory channels of sight, hearing, touch, taste and smell, but they *perceive* information differently according to their attitudes, values, expectations, motives and contexts.

Sensing information from the environment is not an automatic given. Just because something is 'out there' doesn't mean that we will notice it or interpret it in an objective manner. Our perceptual processes influence not just how we see things, but also what we see and what we don't see. Once we have noticed something in our environment, individual perceptions will interpret that information in different ways.

Much research has been carried out by psychologists to determine how the perceptual process works (Rock 1983; Posner 1989; Osherson *et al.* 1990). This work focuses on how visual images are processed by the brain and the visual system, which has provided perceptual theorists with a good 'bottom up' grounding in key aspects of visual perception. For the purposes of understanding organisational behaviour, it is not necessary to investigate this type of visual research in too much detail. It is enough for us to know that our brains allow us to process information in such a way that we can normally differentiate objects from each other, i.e. figure ground perception, and we can perceive distance, depth, colour and patterns in the environment around us. But how do we use these perceptual skills to organise more complex perceptions about the environment?

STOP AND LOOK

Examine the photograph and briefly describe what you see. What kind of person are you looking at? What kinds of characteristics do you think this person possesses?

Now ask yourself how your perceptions might have been influenced by any prior knowledge you have about this person, what assumptions you made based on this person's physical appearance or facial expression and any contextual information that might have guided your perceptions.

To understand the perceptual process in any situation, it is important to focus on the three key factors that influence perceptions:
1. The individual perceiver.
2. The perceived.
3. The context or setting.

Figure 3.1 Factors that Influence Perception

Individual (the perceiver)	Contrast	Context (the setting in which perception takes place)
• Expectations • Motives • Object (what is perceived)	• Intensity • Motion • Repetition	• Physical factors • Social factors • Organisational factors

THE INDIVIDUAL

It is impossible to understand why someone perceives his/her environment in a particular way unless we have considered certain factors relating to that individual. Individual expectations, motivations, emotions, values and attitudes are characteristics which influence the perceptual process and which must be considered when attempting to understand perception.

INDIVIDUAL EXPECTATIONS

A person's expectations are important considerations when attempting to understand why that person perceives things in the ways that they do. Research as far back as the 1950s shows us that our expectations influence our perceptions in powerful ways (Bruner and Minturn 1955; see Figure 3.2).

Imagine this picture in colour, but the queen of hearts is black and not red, as is usually the case. Until you have really studied the picture, it can be difficult to see why it is a different or unusual image. Existing expectations can make people unobservant. Oftentimes, the stronger our expectations are, the less likely we are to notice any variations that emerge, which is an important perceptual tendency to consider when coming to grips with behaviour at work. Essentially, people often see only what they expect to see.

Figure 3.2 Expected and Unexpected Stimuli

INDIVIDUAL MOTIVES

Individual motives can have a significant effect on the way in which people interpret the environment around them. People don't just see what they expect to see. They often perceive things in the ways that they *want* to see them. At work, people often misinterpret negative messages, such as a poor performance appraisal or unfavourable signals in market trends, because they don't want to receive pessimistic or threatening information from their environment. Individuals have been found to be especially effective at screening out information that is unpalatable, difficult to face or in some way tells them things that they don't want to hear.

REACTIONS TO UNEXPECTED/UNWANTED STIMULI

Research has demonstrated that people can react in a variety of ways when they are exposed to information in their environment that is unexpected or in some way surprising to them (Bruner and Postman 1949). Using a black three of hearts as a stimulus, Bruner and Postman found that it took people more than four times longer to recognise that anything was strange or different about this image. Their research led them to identify four types of reactions to unexpected stimuli, which were termed dominance, compromise, disruption and recognition (see also Plous 1993).

Dominance Reaction

When we fail to recognise the nature of unexpected stimuli, our normal expectations are said to dominate the unexpected stimulus and prevent us from seeing anything different. Subjects who did not spot the black three of hearts and who claimed to have seen a red three of hearts or a black three of clubs reacted to the stimulus by having their normal expectations dominate their experience and their perceptions, thus preventing them from identifying the different nature of the image.

Compromise Reaction

When we recognise that a stimulus is unexpected but fail to identify the reasons why, it may be because our perceptual system is attempting to *compromise* for the unexpected stimulus. Some people who are exposed to a black three of hearts, for example, report that it appears greyish or purple in colour. This is a perceptual error that draws attention to the unexpected nature of the stimulus in some way, though failing to precisely or accurately pinpoint the manner in which the stimulus is different.

Disruption Reaction

Disruption in our perceptions occurs when we fail to detect even the recognisable aspects of an object. For example, on seeing a black three of hearts, some people fail to recognise even the familiar aspects of the image. While this type of reaction is relatively rare, it can happen to people when they are under pressure to react or if they are being bombarded with a series of different stimuli in rapid succession.

Recognition Reaction

Recognition occurs when individuals are accurate in their diagnosis of the nature of an unexpected stimulus.

Much of the perceptual research continues to confirm that individuals expect and want to see things in a certain way and that their perceptions are influenced by these expectations and motives. At work, for example, people quickly come to expect certain routine activities to be carried out in a particular sequence. Ego defence motivations also encourage people to believe that they are respected or that they are seen as good at what they do. It's worth remembering that our expectations and our motives can prevent us from being objective in our analysis of the real situation.

SOME GOOD ADVICE FOR DECISION-MAKERS

Before making an important judgment or decision, it often pays to pause and ask a few key questions:

- Am I motivated to see things a certain way?
- What expectations did I bring to the situation?
- Would I see things differently without these expectations and motives?
- Have I consulted with others who don't share my expectations and motives?

By asking such questions, decision-makers can expose many of the cognitive, emotional and motivational factors that lead to biases in perception.

Source: Plous (1993: 21)

THE PERCEIVED

It is not just our own motives and expectations that affect the way in which we perceive our environment or objects within it – the perceptual process centrally depends on the nature and characteristics associated with what we are perceiving. There are some basic principles of object perception that can affect people's ability to notice and perceive events or objects in their environment.

Principles of Object Perception

- **Contrast:** As shown earlier, perceptual theory demonstrates that people do not always spot the unexpected. On the other hand, it is also true that people are more likely to notice things that stand out from their environment, e.g. a bright red desk in a dingy room will attract our attention. People who look or act differently in contrast to others will often cause our attention and perceptions to be drawn towards them.

- **Intensity:** Intensity of an image or a sound will probably have a significant effect on the extent to which people become aware of that image or sound. For example, very loud noises tend to attract attention more effectively than those of a moderate intensity.

- **Motion:** Moving objects or people in motion tend to attract more perceptual attention than those that are still or motionless. We are more likely to notice someone moving through the workplace or an object flying through the air.

- **Repetition:** Information that is repeated over and over again can be more likely to be learned and recognised than information that only gets a single airing. However, our perceptions can screen out repeated information as if it is just background noise. A supervisor who continually reminds people to wear their hard hats or to keep their workplaces tidy may end up being ignored because of the repetitive nature of the message they are sending.

In asking why people see things in different ways it is important to consider not only what the expectations and needs of individual perceivers are, but also the nature of the objects, events or people that they perceive. This can help to explain why some events at work receive extreme reactions and others go almost completely unnoticed.

THE CONTEXT

A third factor that affects the ways in which we perceive our environment relates to the context or setting within which our perceptions occur. People do not perceive information in isolation; they interpret new information in light of the context within which they receive that material.

The physical, social and organisational setting in which we receive information can have an enormous effect on the ways in which we interpret and understand this information. When trying to understand meaning in someone's behaviour, we normally pay attention to certain contextual factors associated with it. If we see someone shouting, we look around to find out what they're shouting at. If we see someone crying, we search for further contextual information to help clarify the situational factors that may have given rise to this reaction. All behaviours that we see at work are usually interpreted within a complex contextual framework that we use to take important aspects of the environment into account when attempting to understand what's going on around us.

THE PROCESS OF PERCEPTION

Perception is a process involving a series of steps or stages. In reality it is difficult to see where one stage in the perceptual process begins and another one ends, but for the purposes of analysing perception it is useful to break the process down into its different stages in order to reach a more effective understanding of how perception works and how people come to make sense of what goes on around them.

Figure 3.3 outlines the key stages in and sequence of the perception process and shows how perceiving and reacting to events in our environment is not automatic – it depends on the unfolding of a sequence of stages, outlined below.

Figure 3.3 Stages in the Perception Process

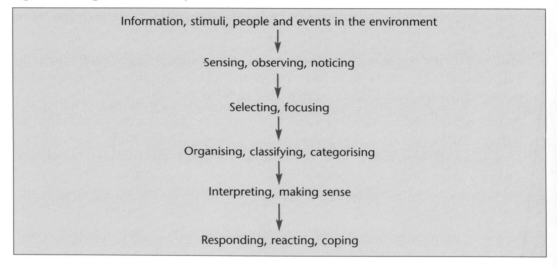

Information, stimuli, people and events in the environment

↓

Sensing, observing, noticing

↓

Selecting, focusing

↓

Organising, classifying, categorising

↓

Interpreting, making sense

↓

Responding, reacting, coping

INFORMATION, STIMULI, PEOPLE AND EVENTS IN THE ENVIRONMENT

An important principle of perception is that there are many more elements in our environment than we are ever likely to be aware of at any one point in time. People at work exist in environments that are complex and multidimensional. What they notice or become aware of depends on the individual factors, object features and contextual characteristics outlined in the last section. It is worth remembering that at work, it is not guaranteed that everyone will be aware of issues or information that may seem obvious to you.

SENSING, OBSERVING, NOTICING

People can't notice everything that goes on around them – if they did, they would be overwhelmed with information, overloaded with data from the outside world and, more than likely, unable to function effectively. From the time we are born, we learn to filter out information from the environment that is not relevant or important in our attempts to cope with and make sense of our world. This filtering mechanism is what determines the fact that people notice some aspects of their environment and do not sense other aspects. Our filtering system is sometimes overefficient in that it can filter out important information that might help us to operate better in various situations.

SELECTING, FOCUSING

One of the most important characteristics of an organisational leader is his/her ability to 'read the signs', that is, to be on the lookout for signals that say the market is changing or that various opportunities are becoming available. It is important not to filter out important information about the environment that might affect the organisation and its future (Kakabadse 1997). This closely relates to the process of selective perception at work.

Some people deliberately develop their perceptual abilities by constantly looking for signals or signs that need to be considered, such as when organisational survival or success is at stake. Indeed, research into the strategic management of organisations demonstrates that a 'careful assessment of the environment' is necessary if organisations are to successfully manage their strategic development (Pettigrew and Whipp 1991). People's ability in organisations to select and focus on the important aspects of the environment is crucial in determining subsequent action and behaviour and central to the concept of perception and the perceptual process.

ORGANISING, CLASSIFYING, CATEGORISING

Just as we cannot notice everything in the environment, we also cannot focus on everything. Our ability to organise, classify and categorise information can make it easier to focus on issues in a structured and coherent way.

In order to make sense of the environment, people develop coding systems to help them categorise the information that they receive. Typical coding systems used by individuals are known as schemas and scripts.

A *schema* is a mental framework that encompasses memories, ideas, concepts and programmes for action which are relevant to a particular object, event or person in the environment. People have schemas for various aspects of their environment (Weick 1983; Rumelhart 1984), such as self-schemas, which help us to organise and control information we receive relating to ourselves. Schemas can be complex or simple, but their function is generally to help people organise information about certain (usually important) aspects of their lives and environments.

Scripts are another way in which individuals organise, manage and classify the complex information they receive. Scripts are knowledge frameworks that describe the appropriate sequence of events in a given situation (Schermerhorn *et al.* 1994). Individuals at work tend to develop scripts for activities such as performance appraisals, interviews, meetings, lunch breaks, conversations with different people within the organisational setting and so on.

Generally, scripts and schemas make it easier for people to manage the diverse range of information they face every day and tend to define people's expectations about what they think they will see or hear at work. Keep in mind that expectations can in turn have an effect on the aspects of the environment that we pay attention to and those that we ignore. Thus, scripts and schemas provide a structure around which information is organised. If new information does not fit into our existing schemas, we may react in the ways outlined earlier in this chapter, i.e. dominance, compromise, disruption or recognition.

A Classic Example of Two Different Organisational Schemas

In the 1960s, Douglas McGregor suggested that there were two different and opposing views relating to people's behaviour at work, which have come to be known as Theory X and Theory Y and are classic examples of the kinds of schema that different people at work can have. These schema guide behaviour in sometimes very powerful ways (McGregor 1960).

The Theory X Schema
- People generally dislike work and therefore need to be coerced into working effectively.
- Most people dislike taking on responsibility.
- People generally prefer to carry out tasks that have been clearly defined by others.
- Most people lack creativity and are resistant to change.

The Theory Y Schema
- Work is as natural to individuals as play or rest.
- People who are committed to goals can achieve them through their own self-direction without the need for coercion or supervision.
- Most people actively seek out responsibility and like to be in control of their own actions.
- People are naturally creative and can solve problems without having to be told what to do.

You can see that if someone used Theory X as their guiding schema, their behaviour is likely to be quite different than if they were guided by Theory Y. Schemas guided by Theory X are more likely to result in supervisory behaviour that involves control and coercion of others, threats and punishment and generally discouraging people from making their own decisions or solving their own problems. Schemas guided by Theory Y are more likely to result in behaviour that involves encouraging people to direct, empower and motivate themselves and to take responsibility for their own actions.

Interpreting, Making Sense

In organisational settings, particularly those in which there are many people doing many different things, behaviour and events can often be bewildering to us. Psychologists tell us that when people do not understand or cannot make sense of what's going on, they experience 'psychological discomfort' (Festinger 1957) and are motivated to identify reasons and logic in others' behaviour. The concept of attribution is a way of attempting to define the rules that people use to explain their own and others' behaviour (Kelley 1973).

Attribution theory originates from the work of Heider (1958) and since then has come to be recognised as an important aspect of perceptual theory. Attributions are interpretations of the causes of behaviour. People make attributions about their own as well as others' behaviour. The types of attributions that people make have a proven influence on subsequent behaviours and interactions. Based on a series of investigations, Kelley (1967) showed that there are three basic information cues which people attend to when trying to establish the causes of people's behaviour:

1. **Consistency:** The extent to which a particular action is consistent with an individual's pattern of behaviour over time.
2. **Consensus:** The extent to which a particular individual action mirrors the actions of others in similar situtaions.
3. **Distinctiveness:** The extent to which a particular action is similar to or different from various other activities in which the individual is involved.

If you see someone you know behaving aggressively, you may try to attribute causes to that person's behaviour by implicitly addressing the following questions:

1. Has this person behaved aggressively in similar situations in the past?
   Yes = high consistency
   No = low consistency
2. Do other people behave aggressively in similar situations?
   Yes = high consensus
   No = low consensus
3. Does this person behave aggressively in different situations?
   Yes = low distinctiveness
   No = high distinctiveness

Our answers to these questions will affect the ways in which we explain the individual's behaviour. In situations where we perceive high consistency, low consensus and low distinctiveness, we tend to assume that the individual's behaviour is a result of their own personal characteristics. The way we then explain the behaviour is to say, 'He/she is just an aggressive person.' In situations where we perceive low consistency, high consensus and high distinctiveness, we tend to assume that the individual's aggressive behaviour occurred as a result of situational factors. We are more likely to assume that the person behaved aggressively because some environmental trigger gave rise to an aggressive response.

RESPONDING, REACTING, COPING

So far we have seen that how people identify, focus on, organise and make sense of information strongly affects the ways in which they are likely to behave. Perceptual processes play a central role in the ways in which people respond, react to and cope with their organisational environments. An enhanced understanding of the process of perception can help to shed important light on the complex network of behaviours that occur in organisations.

COMMON PERCEPTUAL DISTORTIONS

As with any psychological process, perception is vulnerable to a variety of errors. We have seen that people do not process information accurately or objectively, but rather, perception is a subjective process open to all sorts of inaccuracies, distortions and errors. Understanding perception requires a focus on the common distortions that people display in their attempts to make sense of the environment around them.

COMMON PERCEPTUAL DISTORTIONS

- Stereotyping.
- Projection.
- The halo effect.
- The fundamental attribution error.

Stereotyping

Because of the enormous amount of information that our brains have to process every day of our lives, people have a natural capacity to categorise, arrange and pigeonhole the information that they encounter as they interact with their world. This is a vital ability. We need to know how to recognise the differences between various aspects of our environment. It is important for us to be able to make a quick assessment of dangerous versus safe situations, helpful and unhelpful people at work or difficult or easy tasks. As we process information from the outside world, we tend to label it according to these kinds of concepts. We see some work situations as boring or interesting, worthwhile or useless, challenging or effortless and so on.

Similarly, we label people using categories like friendly/unfriendly, similar/different from us, attractive/unattractive, honest/dishonest and so on. But how do we decide on these labels? For example, what information do we use to decide whether we think someone is honest or dishonest, clever or dull? Research has shown that the kinds of information we use in assigning labels to others can simply be irrelevant and that people develop stereotypes about other people in often highly inaccurate ways.

A stereotype is a pre-established expectation about an individual or a group, often based on surface characteristics such as physical appearance, gender or race. Stereotypes allow those who hold them to reduce uncertainty about what people or groups are likely to want, believe or do (Rumelhart 1984).

Stereotypes are like social schemas that help people to make sense of other people and decide how they will develop their relationships and interactions with others. Yet while useful in helping people to manage diverse information, stereotypes can also be damaging and cause people to make mistakes in their assessment and evaluations of others.

Cultural stereotypes may be extremely inaccurate and yet can be widely held by various groups. Gender stereotypes can influence and differentiate people's behaviour depending on whether they are interacting with men or women, age stereotypes can cause people to discriminate against people who are young or old in work situations and socio-economic stereotypes can cause people to make inaccurate assumptions and attributions about people based on background information about where they live or observed differences such as those that relate to dialect, accent and appearance.

Projection

Projection is a perceptual process that occurs when we assume that other people think or are likely to act like us. Put simply, it occurs when we project our own thoughts and feelings onto someone else and assume that our thoughts and feelings belong to others. Egocentricity is another key psychological concept that is related to projection, that is, the less able someone is to see things from perspectives other than their own, the more likely they are to assume that other people are reacting, thinking or feeling in the same ways as they are. At work, it is easy to assume that people are motivated by the same things that motivate us, that they get annoyed by the same irritants, that they are driven by the same ambitions or that they are satisfied by the same rewards. Discovering that this is often not the case can be disorientating or at least surprising. It is possible to avoid excessive projection by endeavouring to see things from different perspectives and by exploring different viewpoints with others at work.

The Halo Effect

The halo effect occurs when a single characteristic associated with an individual is used to generate an overall impression or assessment of that person. In this way, someone who has one positive characteristic may be assumed to have a whole range of positive attributes, which may not necessarily be the case in reality. The halo effect is so called because one characteristic serves to create a saintly or inherently good overall impression of an individual.

The opposite of the halo effect (sometimes called the trident effect) occurs when one negative characteristic overshadows and dominates any positive attributes of an individual. Some studies suggest that the trident effect can be observed in selection interview situations, showing that negative information about a candidate tends to be weighted more heavily in the making of selection decisions than positive information (Binning et al. 1988). In organisational settings, unfair or inaccurate evaluations of people can have serious implications. It is important for organisational practitioners to equip themselves with an awareness of the common tendency to pay attention to one characteristic at the expense of another.

The Fundamental Attribution Error

We have already seen that attribution is a crucial stage in the perceptual process and evidence suggests that it is a stage in which people are particularly prone to error. 'The fundamental attribution error' finding proposed by Ross (1977) suggests that people are more likely to explain other people's behaviour by considering only internal/dispositional characteristics, such as the individual's personality, attitudes, motivations and so on, and to explain their own behaviour by considering external variables, such as circumstances, environmental influences, pressures from other people and other contextual factors. For example, on witnessing a car crash, the attribution error theory suggests that people are more likely to attribute the event to the internal characteristics of the driver, using explanations like 'He must be a very careless person', 'He wasn't looking where he was going' or 'He is not a good driver.' On the other hand, on being involved in a crash where they themselves were the drivers, explanations are more likely to involve external attributions, such as 'It was very dark', 'The other car was going too fast' or 'There was a dangerous bend in the road.'

Why do people make skewed or distorted attributions leading to notoriously subjective accounts of events and occurrences? It's partly because of the perceptual process and the fundamental attribution error. The fundamental attribution error can be made as a way of defending people's self-esteem, by allowing people to develop accounts in which it is possible for them to continue to think highly of themselves and to protect themselves from unpalatable truths about their own tendencies and behaviours. This relates to what was discussed in the first section of this chapter: people expect and want to see things in a certain way and will explain things to themselves in order to support these expectations and motivations.

However, recent investigations into the perceptual aspects of behaviour suggest that the fundamental attribution error may not be 'fundamental' in all cultures and that it is arguably a culturally influenced inaccuracy. Smith and Harris Bond (1993) point out that the fundamental attribution error is much less likely to be found in collectivist cultures than in individualist cultures (see the discussion on individualism in the next section). Hofstede (1983) found that Ireland ranks moderately to strongly individualistic as a culture, so it can be argued that people in the Irish cultural setting are less likely to make the fundamental attribution error than people from highly individualistic cultures, such as the US, Australia or Britain, but are more likely to make it than people from highly collectivist cultures, such as Asia, South America and China.

STOP AND DISCUSS

How can knowledge of common perceptual distortions help to prevent errors and problems in organisational settings?

Use the following typical work scenarios to explore this question.

* A selection interview.
* A performance appraisal.
* A team briefing/meeting.
* Training a new employee.

CULTURAL VALUES AND PERCEPTION

People see things in different ways depending on their cultural contexts. Chapter 9 explores the concept of organisational culture in more depth and demonstrates the different dimensions of culture that can affect organisational behaviour. Perception, or the way people select, organise and interpret information in the outside world, is often loaded with culturally defined influences that can sometimes make interaction between cultures difficult and bewildering.

Nations tend to share a broadly common history and heritage and are exposed to similar values, beliefs and social rules. While there is an increasing awareness that diversity exists and needs to be valued in any culture, a common set of value systems, beliefs and norms tends to permeate any one cultural setting. These value systems can provide a filter or lens through which members of that culture process and perceive information. Cultural differences in perception can help to explain many of the misunderstandings that can emerge between individuals and groups from different cultures.

Hofstede (1983, 1991) refers to culture as 'the collective programming of the mind which distinguishes the members of one group from another', explaining that the 'programmes' we have in our minds affect the way in which we process any new information we receive.

Using four main dimensions of culture, Hofstede has classified a wide variety of different countries according to their cultural values. The four values he identifies are power distance, uncertainty avoidance, individualism and masculinity/femininity.

POWER DISTANCE

Power distance refers to the extent to which people in a particular culture recognise and respect status differences between individuals. Power distance can be assessed by examining the extent to which, for example, employees are reluctant to or nervous about expressing disagreement with their managers.

UNCERTAINTY AVOIDANCE

While it is a general psychological principle that people tend to avoid or reduce uncertainty, it seems that some cultures are much more likely to tolerate high levels of uncertainty in the environment than others. The type of question asked to establish uncertainty avoidance in this study was: '[Do you agree that] company rules should not be broken, even if it's in the company's best interest?' and 'How long do you think you will continue working for this company?'. High uncertainty avoidance is assumed to exist if people tended to stick to established rules and avoid changes (like leaving one organisation for another).

INDIVIDUALISM

Individualism refers to the degree to which people in a particular culture pursue individual, autonomously selected goals in contrast to collectivist, group-oriented goals. Some cultures have been found to hold individualist values whereby competition, independent action and self-reliant activity is highly valued. Other cultures have more collectivist values that focus on the development and reward of group activity, e.g. family involvement, consensus building at work and so on.

MASCULINITY/FEMININITY

The masculinity/femininity dimension denotes the extent to which work values like high earnings, status, recognition and achievement are seen as important (this defines so-called 'masculine' cultural values) as opposed to values such as good working relationships, co-operative work atmospheres and interpersonal harmony (this defines so-called 'feminine' cultural values).

Since Hofstede defined these cultural value dimensions in the early 1980s there have been some criticisms of the validity and clarity of his definitions of culture and its characteristics. However, the large samples that he used in his research (117,000 individuals from a total of fifty-three different countries) and the statistical rigour of his analysis gives us one of the most comprehensive studies of the differences between cultures, their values and prevailing perceptual lenses through which different cultures look at the world. While there is some disagreement about aspects of the measures used in the study, differences and contrasts found in the research demonstrate that it is possible to show that there are prevailing or general tendencies for people from different countries to espouse and believe in very different kinds of work-based values.

What does this add to our knowledge of perception and the perceptual process? As mentioned at the beginning of this section, people see things in different ways according to their cultural values. Nationalities may strongly influence the perceptual process, and even though national barriers may be breaking down in Europe, evidence suggests that people still see themselves as having strong cultural identities. Being 'Irish', 'French', 'British', 'Italian', etc. is just as important to individuals now as it has ever been (Moore and Punnett 1994).

IRISH CULTURAL VALUES AS DEFINED BY THE HOFSTEDE FRAMEWORK

According to Hofstede's framework, Irish people score very low on the dimensions of power distance and uncertainty avoidance, very high on the dimension of individualism and particularly high on the 'masculinity' dimension. This may give us some important clues as to how Irish people are likely to interpret and process information, both within and outside their work settings. Priorities, values, beliefs and the rules of behaviour that we think are important may indeed give rise to some cultural stereotypes and may challenge others.

According to Hofstede's research (1983), Irish cultural values are more likely to be represented by:

- Relatively low amounts of respect and deference between those in 'superior' and 'subordinate' positions. For example, people surveyed were generally not afraid of or nervous about talking to their bosses.
- Relatively low emphasis on planning and stability as a way of dealing with life's uncertainty, revealing a 'take it as it comes' attitude to changes in life and work.
- Relatively high levels of importance attached to individual as opposed to collective achievement.

- Particularly high levels of importance attached to achievement, recognition and respect in working life.

While it can be convincingly argued that this profile provides an inevitably broad and sweeping generalisation of the values that Irish people hold and while changes in the economic, social and cultural environment may give rise to different overall patterns as time goes by, it is important to recognise that cultural factors do play an important part in influencing people's perceptions. In current organisational contexts, where global issues now affect a growing number of businesses, the influences of cultural diversity on differences in perception are more important than ever to pay attention to.

Although on the one hand people seem to be retaining a strong sense of their national cultural identities, on the other, circumstances dictate that more and more of us need to communicate effectively with people from a wide range of different cultural backgrounds. It is increasingly important for organisational members to understand some of the central reasons why people can perceive information differently as a result of the cultural influences to which they are exposed.

ATTITUDES AND PERCEPTION

People at work develop attitudes about a wide variety of issues, events and people in their environment and these attitudes are strongly connected with the perceptual process. In both theoretical and practical senses, the link between attitudes and perception is not always clear and the differences between these two concepts are not always easy to define, yet they are inextricably linked. For example, it might be argued that perceptual biases like stereotypes and halo effects contribute in powerful ways to the network of attitudes that individuals develop.

THE IMPORTANCE OF ATTITUDES IN THE WORKPLACE

Attitudes can be defined simply as a person's relatively enduring disposition toward people, objects, events or activities (Bird and Fisher 1986). These dispositions are evaluative in that they are usually positive or negative in orientation, they are acquired or developed over time and they are not immutable, although depending on the functions that they serve for the individual, some may be more fixed and difficult to change than others.

People develop attitudes at work that can affect and influence their behaviour. Students and researchers into organisational behaviour therefore need to consider how attitudes develop, what their functions are and how they affect behaviour. However, as with most concepts in organisational behaviour, such questions are not straightforward or easy to answer.

Also, if a purely managerialist perspective is adopted, then people's rights to develop their own attitudes, no matter how negative, are rarely considered. Indeed, the ethical or moral constraints associated with changing or manipulating people's attitudes have received little attention in management literature. However, regardless of the perspective taken, there are some theoretical foundations about attitudes that can be considered in objective ways and that can also help to enhance an understanding of the behaviour of people and groups within organisational settings.

In addressing the question of how attitudes influence behaviour, it is important to recognise that attitudes are neither necessary nor sufficient determinants of behaviour. In other words, just because you have, say, a negative attitude towards someone else at work does not necessarily mean that you will behave negatively towards them. Similarly, there may be times when even if you do have a positive attitude towards someone, circumstances and influences may cause you to behave negatively towards them.

Attitudes do not dictate or determine the kinds of behaviours that people engage in at work, but rather, they are facilitative or probabilistic causes of behaviour in the sense that they make it more likely, depending on a range of other variables, that someone will behave in a certain way towards others or in reaction to various events at work.

The Functions of Attitudes

Psychologists have developed a useful perspective on attitudes that helps to understand the function that they serve for the individual, rather than focusing (as much of the management literature does) on how attitudes affect the organisations within which they are developed. One of the first things that people often notice as newcomers to organisations is the variety of opinions and attitudes that people have about the same things. Psychologists have long argued that the reasons why attitudes are so prevalent and often so obvious at work are that they help people to make more sense of their world, develop a stronger sense of their own identities, protect their own egos from negative information about themselves or to gain more effective knowledge about what's going on around them (Katz 1960).

- **The knowledge function:** Attitudes can give meaning to our experience in the same ways that the perceptual processes help us to organise and categorise the world.
- **The utilitarian function:** Developing certain attitudes can help us to get the most out of our social situations.
- **The self-expressive function:** People are more likely to develop a coherent and somewhat consistent framework of attitudes which allow them and others to define the kinds of people that they are.
- **The ego defensive function:** We often develop attitudes simply to avoid potentially unpleasant information about ourselves and to project a positive self-image to ourselves. This might mean developing negative attitudes towards people who react badly towards us in the workplace as a way of explaining their behaviour in a way that does not threaten our own image of ourselves.

Being aware of attitudes, and more particularly knowing that people develop attitudes in order to fulfil some important psychological function, is important, especially if we are attempting to uncover the attitudes that people have or to change existing attitudes in an organisational setting.

COGNITION IN ORGANISATIONS

Cognition and perception are two inherently linked concepts, each influencing one another and both having important implications for how people behave in organisational settings. Cognition refers to the process of thinking, knowing or mentally processing information (Coon 1991). Many traditional topics in the field of organisational behaviour are now being influenced by what Markus and Zajonc (1985) described nearly twenty years ago as a cognitively orientated revolution in the psychological sciences. Since then, the role of cognition and cognitive processes has received more and more attention within the field of organisational behaviour. Indeed, how people think and how they process information in order to make sense is central to many of the other processes and dynamics explored in this book.

The Multidimensional Nature of Cognition

Cognition defines how people produce basic units of thought (images, concepts, language, symbols and even muscular responses) as well as how they solve problems and gain important insights about the world around them. Experimental research in psychology has given rise to a multidimensional understanding about how people think, demonstrating that our thinking processes are facilitated by our ability to generate concepts, produce images, store and retrieve information, make connections between unconnected stimuli in our environment and by generating solutions to problems through imagination. Almost everyone can produce visual images in order to try to comprehend situations more effectively (Kosslyn 1983) and it is this ability that allows us to think in both concrete and abstract ways about the world around us. Bruner (1966) has shown that our thinking processes are significantly aided by the use of our whole bodies (not just our brains) and that we 'store' information in our muscles and other kinaesthetic sensations as a way of helping us to think effectively and orientate ourselves towards our environment. Coon (1991) reminds us that most thinking is accompanied by muscular 'micromovements' throughout our bodies that help us to orientate ourselves towards ideas, concepts and memories in ways that can help us to think effectively and solve problems.

Multiple Intelligences and the Development of Cognitive Theory

In the early 1980s Howard Gardner proposed the theory of multiple intelligences, suggesting that there are many different ways in which people can understand and know the world around them. His work is still deemed to be one of the most important contributions to cognitive psychology. It proposes that different people may access ideas and knowledge and develop intelligence in different ways. Gardner suggests that there are many different forms of intelligence and proposes that they are common to all cultures. He cautions against our tendency in Western cultures to define intelligence in narrow terms or to measure intelligence using reductionistic scores and indicators that are restricted only to logical, linguistic and mathematical capacities. By extending definitions of intelligence and cognition, Gardner has demonstrated that cognition is a rich and diverse human function and that knowledge can be both accessed and created through our musical, spatial, bodily and personal/emotional capacities. How people and groups exercise and apply their cognitive capacities in organisations have critical implications for the study and understanding of behaviour at work.

ONGOING DEBATES/ADVANCED CONCEPTS IN PERCEPTION AND COGNITION AT WORK

COGNITIVE STYLE

Cognitive style is a concept that has recently received increasing attention in organisational settings. Metareviews, information networks and developing research into cognitive style have burgeoned, as evidenced in work by researchers such as Allinson and Hayes (1996, 1999), Kirton (1989), Kogan (1980) and Miller (1987). Many of these researchers have shown how cognitive style is another important characteristic with potential implications for individual and group performance at work.

Cognitive style can be defined as an 'individual's characteristic and consistent approach to organising and processing information' (Tennent 1988). There is a wide range of typologies that have attempted to explore this concept. Some evidence increasingly suggests that there is a single superordinate dimension associated with individual thinking styles, the poles of which are 'analytic' and 'intuitive', respectively.

* **Analytical cognitive styles:** People with broadly analytical cognitive styles are more likely to prefer structure when taking in and organising information and to approach data in a linear, sequential manner.
* **Intuitive cognitive styles:** People who express broadly intuitive information-processing preferences are more likely to be non-conformist, prefer open-ended tasks and approach information in holistic, non-sequential ways. They tend to seek overarching patterns in their interaction with different types of information.

ANALYTICAL AND INTUITIVE THINKERS IN ORGANISATIONAL SETTINGS

Much of the literature on cognitive style suggests that analytical and intuitive styles are complimentary in so far as the cognitive strengths of analytical thinkers tend to be the same dimensions in which intuitive thinkers are less competent and vice versa (Sadlier-Smith *et al.* 2000). In this way, it can be argued that significant synergies can be achieved by combining individuals with different ways of processing information to tackle specific problems, tasks or decisions. According to emerging evidence, intuitive thinkers are more likely to be comfortable with focusing on future possibilities and to derive insights from the serendipitous combination of different sources of information, which can significantly enhance the chances that they will identify creative solutions in their workplaces. On the other hand, intuitive thinkers are less focused on detail and less comfortable with working methodically through documents and the specifics associated with decision implementation. Analytical thinkers may be more likely to perceive and focus on important detail and to have more command over structuring and sequencing actions so that follow-through and closure can be achieved.

Like research on personality, however, the analytical and intuitive approaches to taking in and organising information may represent an excessively reductionistic approach to understanding cognitive processing styles, and at the very least needs to be integrated with broader concepts associated with cognition and cognitive processes.

BEHAVIOURAL DECISION THEORY

This is a field of organisational studies that explores how people use information and knowledge to make decisions. March and Simon (1958) identified a theory of 'bounded rationality' based on their research into decision-making behaviour in organisations. They were among the first theorists to recognise and explore the fact that people do not conform to the predictions that are based on traditional economic assumptions of total rationality, arguing instead that people make decisions whose rationality is bounded or constrained by cognitive limitations. They claimed through their observations that people are unable to evaluate decision options simultaneously and are less likely to choose optimal alternatives, but rather select ones that are 'good enough'. They also observed that people are inclined to reduce the amount of information processing they engage in by adopting rules of thumb and other cognitive shortcuts that make decision making more tolerable and comfortable. March and Simon showed how rational models are not the best predictors of human decision-making behaviour and were among the first theorists to demonstrate that such behaviour is influenced by psychological, cultural, social, perceptual and cognitive processes.

The use of heuristics has been identified as a human cognitive tendency and refers to strategies that limit the number of possibilities to be tried in solving problems or making decisions. Because cognitive capacities are limited, even in the most intelligent of humans, the use of heuristics represents an important route to decision making in organisations, particularly if time is short or problems are illuminated by limited amounts of formal or explicit information.

Table 3.1 shows some heuristic strategies that can aid creative thinking and cognition at work.

Table 3.1 Heuristic Strategies for Managing Cognitive Limitations and Making Decisions at Work

Comparisons Try to identify how the current state of affairs differs from the desired goal and then try to identify steps that would reduce the differences identified.
Reversal Try working backwards from the ideal state of affairs.
Bridging If you can't reach the goal directly, try to identify an intermediate goal or subproblem that at least gets you closer to the ultimate solution.

Representation
Represent the problem in other ways with graphs, diagrams or analogies.

Experimentation
Generate possible solutions and test it. Doing so may eliminate many alternatives or it may clarify what is needed for a solution.

Source: Adapted from Coon (1991)

TACIT OR IMPLICIT KNOWLEDGE

Human beings are not just processors of information, they are also creators of knowledge (Nonaka and Kenney 1991; Baumard 1999). Until recently, knowledge has largely been defined in terms of the tangible phenomena that demonstrate that knowledge, but it is important to recognise that most knowledge is not explicit. As Nonaka (1991) puts it, 'that which can be expressed in words and numbers, represents only the tip of the iceberg of the entire body of knowledge' (Nonaka, via Baumard 1999: 8). More attention is now being directed at the unspoken, implicit knowledge that is embedded within organisations. Intuitive knowledge, unconscious knowledge and creative processes that cannot be predicted or even sourced from conventional forms of organisational information have received more of a research focus in recent years. The idea that there are 'invisible forms of cognition' as well as more tangible or demonstrated types represents a relatively new and important avenue towards an enhanced understanding of how organisations and the people within them operate.

In order to understand the differences between tacit and explicit knowledge, have a look at Baumard's matrix (Table 3.2). He identifies that as well as a tacit/explicit dichotomy, knowledge in organisations can also be individual or collective. These dichotomies give rise to four inseparable but qualitatively different types of knowledge.

Table 3.2 Four Different Types of Knowledge

	Individual knowledge	**Collective knowledge**
Explicit knowledge	Techinical expertise	Rules, laws, regulations
Tacit knowledge	Intuitiveness	Wisdom of social practice

Source: Baumard (1999)

The fact that tacit knowledge may be unconscious, embedded in habit and social practice and based on the principles of intuition, which themselves are poorly understood, makes it a difficult subject to understand and study. However, what is clear is that tacit knowledge exists alongside explicit knowledge in organisational settings and may influence behaviour and organisational outcomes in a range of important ways.

SUMMARY OF KEY PROPOSITIONS

- This chapter has explored some of the central aspects of the processes and determinants of perception.
- Perception is a psychological process through which people receive, organise and interpret information from their environment.
- Three major factors influence the ways in which people perceive the world around them: the individuals themselves (and their expectations and motives for seeing things in a particular way), the characteristics of the object/person/event being perceived (including such features as contrast, motion, novelty, intensity and repetitiveness) and the context within which the perceptions are being formed (including physical, social and organisational aspects of the setting).
- People can react to unexpected or unwanted stimuli in a number of ways. Their expectations can completely dominate or distort the information they receive or they can cause people to fail to recognise important aspects of their environment.
- The perceptual process involves a series of stages, starting with sensing or observing stimuli in the environment and then selecting aspects of the stimuli, organising the information into manageable categories, making sense of the information and then responding in some way. The perceptual process is complex and involved and can give rise to distortions at any of the key stages identified.
- Common perceptual distortions include people's tendency to stereotype others, to assume that others see things in the same ways that they do (projection), to use a single characteristic to create an overall impression of another person (halo effect) and to attribute internal causes to other people's behaviour (the fundamental attribution error).
- Differences in cultural values can give rise to different ways of perceiving events, issues and people in the environment.

DISCUSSION/SELF-ASSESSMENT QUESTIONS

1. People often have to deal with unexpected or surprising events at work. Have you experienced situations in which the information you have received has been totally different from what you expected or what you wanted to hear? How did you react? Can you think of workplace examples of the different reactions to unexpected information that have been outlined in this chapter, i.e. dominance, compromise, disruption and recognition?

2. Imagine that you have an important message to send to all employees in a large organisational setting, for example, new regulations for safety procedures, the introduction of a product or the arrival of a new employee. What techniques would you use to make sure that everyone in the organisation was aware of the message that you wanted to get across? Discuss this in light of what you now know about perception and the factors that influence it.

3. Create your own simple self-schema by writing down six to eight key words that

define who you are as an individual. This list is an example of a self-schema – it represents a simple framework of information you probably use in some implicit way to organise new or complex information about yourself and allows you to classify your perceptions in a structured and predefined manner.

4.   Do you think that gender stereotypes exist at work or in other social settings? Are there strong gender stereotypes among organisations in Ireland? If so, how do you think they affect people's behaviour at work? Is it possible to identify different general categories of perception towards gender? (See the gender perception game in Appendix 3.1 for an engaging way of exploring this question in active discussion groups.)

5.   What do you think of Hofstede's cultural dimensions? Does the 'Irish profile' outlined in this chapter make sense to you? How can our understanding of culture and its influence on perception be enhanced by recognising the concept of subcultures, both within countries and within organisations? Think about how cultural dimensions outlined by Hofstede might affect people's perceptions of various situations in work.

6.   What is tacit knowledge? In what ways does it differ from explicit knowledge in organisations? (To find out more about tacit knowledge read Baumard, *Tacit Knowledge in Organizations*, London: Sage 1999.)

MULTIPLE CHOICE QUESTIONS

1.   The dominance reaction to unexpected stimuli occurs when:
   (a) Individuals perceive the world in a dominant, aggressive way.
   (b) Other people's attitudes dominate an individual's perception of events.
   (c) One source of information dominates an individual's overall perception of an external object.
   (d) An individual's own normal expectations dominate their experience and their perceptions.

2.   What is a stereotype?
   (a) A pre-established expectation about an individual or a group, often based on surface characteristics such as physical appearance, gender or race.
   (b) An accurate assessment of the characteristics of another person.
   (c) A negative assessment of another person or group.
   (d) A positive overall assessment of another person or group.

3.   What is the fundamental attribution error?
   (a) A common perceptual error where people are more likely to explain other people's behaviour by considering only internal/dispositional characteristics and to explain their own behaviour by considering external variables.
   (b) A common perceptual error that shows how accurate people's perceptions generally are.
   (c) A common perceptual tendency to explain one's own behaviour using internal attributions.

(d) A tendency to create complex explanations for unexpected events in the environment.

4. The halo effect is a perceptual error that describes:
   (a) A tendency to see everyone in a positive light.
   (b) A tendency to see oneself in a positive light.
   (c) A tendency to allow a single positive characteristic observed in someone else to dominate one's assumptions about that person.

5. Perception can be defined as:
   (a) The general functioning of our five senses.
   (b) The psychological processes through which people receive, organise and interpret information.
   (c) The way people view the world.
   (d) The development of logical processes through which decisions can be made.

6. What are the individual factors that influence perception?
   (a) Expectations and motives.
   (b) Ideas and insights.
   (c) Moods and dispositions.
   (d) Intelligence.

7. Moving objects tend to attract more perceptual attention than those that are not in motion. True or false?

8. From the time we are born we learn to filter out information that is not relevant or important to us. True or false?

9. Our filtering system never filters out important information. True or false?

10. In perception theory scripts are:
    (a) Written documents.
    (b) Specific, exact dialogues between two people.
    (c) Knowledge frameworks that describe the appropriate sequence of events in a given situation.
    (d) General attitudes towards other people.

11. In attribution theory, consistency refers to:
    (a) The stability of our reactions to events.
    (b) The stability of the ways in which we behave generally.
    (c) Our evaluation of the extent to which an action is consistent with someone's pattern of behaviour over time.

12. Attitudes serve several important psychological functions. True or false?

13. What is cognitive style?
    (a) The types of topics that people prefer to think about.
    (b) The emotional perspective brought to bear on someone's environment.
    (c) An individual's approach to organising and processing information.

14. People with broadly analytical cognitive styles are more likely to prefer open-ended tasks and approach information in holistic ways. True or false?

APPENDIX 3.1

THE GENDER PERCEPTION GAME©

(Moore 2002)

GUIDELINES FOR INSTRUCTORS, TUTORS OR DISCUSSION FACILITATORS

HOW THIS GAME CAN BE USED

This game is a tried-and-trusted classroom interaction experience developed and refined in real classroom settings (Moore 2002). It can be used to explore some of the common stereotypes, questions and attributions associated with gender in the workplace and works well as:

- a simple icebreaker or energiser;
- a structured way to get students of organisational behaviour to engage in lively discussion;
- a focused activity to help a group practise its skills in conducting useful dialogue between learners; and
- a qualitative diagnostic tool to help people identify different orientations towards gender perception.

BENEFITS OF THE GAME

This exercise leads to a lively and productive learning environment. It helps to 'unlock' groups that may be initially reluctant to engage in classroom-based learning discussions and it deals with the issue of gender perception in a sensitive but also intricate and effective way.

This game helps participants to engage in realistic, complex discussions without targeting or polarising participants. By providing a series of statements that are preconstructed, it allows for challenging and useful conversations about gender perception to take place within learning groups. It avoids the emergence of dysfunctional conflict that can arise if participants are expected to come up with their own statements about issues relating to gender perception at work.

To conduct this game in your learning setting, you will need:

- A pack of 'signs' or 'cards'. The signs can be roughly the size of an A5 page but can be as small as a playing card, depending on the size of the group. You will need forty-eight cards in total. Twenty-four should be pink and a single statement about women in the workplace (see lists of statements below) should be typed or clearly written on each. The other twenty-four should be blue and each should contain a single statement about men in the workplace. The statements range from positive to negative and should also be numbered from one to twenty-four (see list below) for later analysis.

- A large sheet that can be pinned to the wall and to which individual cards can be attached (using blu-tack).
- The sheet is illustrated below. Each quadrant should be big enough to accommodate about fourteen cards.

Perceptual naïveté	Perceptual integration
Perceptual 'blindness'	Perceptual hostility

LIST OF GENDER PERCEPTION STATEMENTS

Pink cards: Statements reflecting different types of perceptions about women (each statement is printed on a separate card/sign).

1. Women benefit from having other women as role models at work.
2. Women face challenges at work that are rarely encountered by men.
3. Women need more options for flexible work arrangements in order to manage the family/work balance.
4. We need special measures in place to help women with young children to participate in the workplace.
5. Women choose different careers than their male counterparts.
6. Women benefit from having mentors to help them navigate higher levels in the organisation.
7. Women nowadays generally have the same work opportunities as men.
8. There is no difference between men and women at work.
9. Generally women and men have access to the same social networks at work.
10. Gender should be ignored in organisational settings.
11. Whether you are male or female should never be taken into account at work.
12. In order to ensure equality at work, women must be prepared to do the same things at work that men are expected to do.
13. Women are fantastic workers.
14. Women have talents that men don't have.
15. Women are welcome in most organisational settings these days.
16. Women are better at dealing with people than their male counterparts.
17. Women are more intuitive than men.
18. Women are more sensitive to people's emotions than men are.
19. Women are generally not responsible for the primary or stable income of families and

so are less likely to have as much at stake as their male counterparts.

20. Women's place is in the home and they should be discouraged from activities that take them away from this primary domestic role.

21. Women are not as intelligent as men and their jobs should be designed accordingly.

22. Women are 'hormonal' at certain times of the month and managers should be on the lookout for mood swings among women workers.

23. Women with young children are more likely to be absent from work than men and so should be hired with more caution.

24. It is dangerous to put women in positions that have been traditionally held by men.

Blue cards: Statements reflecting different perceptions about men (each statement is printed onto a separate card/sign).

1. Men benefit from having other men as role models at work.

2. Men face challenges at work that are rarely encountered by women.

3. Men need more options for flexible work arrangements in order to manage the family/work balance.

4. We need special measures in place to help men with young children to participate in the workplace.

5. Men choose different careers than their female counterparts.

6. Men benefit from having mentors to help them navigate higher levels in the organisation.

7. Men nowadays generally have the same work opportunities as women.

8. There is no difference between men and women at work.

9. Generally women and men have access to the same social networks at work.

10. Gender should be ignored in organisational settings.

11. Whether you are male or female should never be taken into account at work.

12. In order to ensure equality at work, men must be prepared to do the same things at work that women are expected to do.

13. Men are fantastic workers.

14. Men have talents that women don't have.

15. Men are welcome in most organisational settings these days.

16. Men are more rational and objective than their female counterparts.

17. Men are more analytical than women.

18. Generally, men are more task orientated than women.

19. Men are generally not primarily responsible for arranging or providing child care for their families and so don't require special measures to help them cope with this added responsibility.

20. Men's place is at work and so they should be discouraged from engaging in activities that take them away from their primary economic role.

21. Men are not as intelligent as women and their jobs should be designed accordingly.

22. Testosterone makes men behave in more aggressive ways than women and managers should be on the lookout for this type of behaviour in men.

23. Men are more likely to suffer from illnesses that give rise to unexpected absences from work, e.g. heart disease or sports injuries, and so should be hired with more caution than their female counterparts.

24. It is dangerous to put men in positions that have been traditionally held by women.

Time to be allocated: Approximately one hour, including debriefing and plenary discussion.

Number of participants: This game can be played with any number of participants, but duplicate card/sign packs will be necessary for groups of a certain size. With one pack, the ideal group size is between ten and twenty.

Materials: Those described here, a spacious room and a clear wall for the poster session.

FORMATS FOR THE GAME

You can play the game using either of the formats listed below.

(a) Split the group into a male and female subgroup. Give a pack of pink cards to the female group and a pack of blue cards to the male group and ask them to sort the cards into three piles:

- Group 1: Statements that the group generally agrees with.
- Group 2: Statements that the group generally disagrees with.
- Group 3: Statements on which the group cannot reach agreement.

In order to control the time, assign a timekeeper and suggest that participants spend no more than one minute discussing each statement. Have a notetaker keep notes on the rationale for placing the different statements in different groups.

(b) Using the large sheet/poster described earlier, explain to the groups that the cards have been numbered according to which approach to gender perception each statement represents:

- Category 1: Statements 1–6 (perceptual integration).
- Category 2: Statements 7–12 (perceptual blindness).
- Category 3: Statements 13–18 (perceptual naïveté).
- Category 4: Statements 19–24 (perceptual hostility).

Have a representative from each group (preferably the notetaker) pick up only the group of statements that their group agreed with and ask him/her to pin them to the large sheet in the corresponding quadrant.

The final result for either format should be clusters of pink and blue cards distributed in various ways across the large sheet/poster. This sheet forms the basis of subsequent discussion/analysis/exploration/theory development. Participants should be encouraged to follow up this game with a search for statistics and data relating to gender that can clarify and demystify some of the issues that each group selected to agree on. The remaining card piles can be incorporated into the discussion. Of particular interest are the cards that group members couldn't agree on – this group of statements can help to demonstrate possible 'splits' in group approaches to gender perception and often reveals important aspects of a group's orientation to gender perception.

The information and ideas generated during the session can contribute to:

1. A better individual understanding of different approaches to gender perception and stereotyping in organisations.
2. A recognition that different perceptions towards gender can impact on individual and group experiences at work.
3. A satisfactory dialogue in which the principles of gender perception have been given an active airing.

FIVE SUGGESTED KEY READINGS

Festinger, L., *A Theory of Cognitive Dissonance*, Stanford, CT: Stanford University Press 1957.

Kelley, H.H., 'The processes of causal attribution', *American Psychologist*, 28 (1973), 107–28.

Plous, S., *The Psychology of Judgement and Decision Making*, New York: McGraw-Hill 1993.

Stranks, K., 'Perception and behavior: impact, influence and outcomes', *Management Review*, LXXXIV/3 (1994), 21–31.

Thompson, L.L., Levine, J.M. and Messick, D.M., *Shared Cognition in Organizations: The Management of Knowledge*, Cambridge: Sage 2000.

REFERENCES

Allinson, C.W. and Hayes, J., 'The cognitive style index: a measure of intuition-analysis for organizational research', *Journal of Management Studies*, XXXIII/1 (1996), 119–36.

Allinson, C.W. and Hayes, J., 'Cross-national differences in cognitive style: implications for management', *Journal of Human Resource Management*, V/2 (1999), 33–59.

Atkinson, R.L., Atkinson, R.C., Smith, E.E. and Bem, D.J., *Introduction to Psychology*, 11th ed., New York: Harcourt Brace 1993.

Baumard, P., *Tacit Knowledge in Organizations*, London: Sage 1999.

Binning, J.F., Goldstein, M.A., Garcia, M.F. and Scattaregia, J.H., 'Effects of pre-interview impressions on questioning strategies', *Journal of Applied Psychology*, LXXIII/1 (1988), 30–42.

Bird, C.P. and Fisher, T.D., 'Thirty years later: attitudes toward the employment of older workers', *Journal of Applied Psychology* (August 1986), 515–17.

Bruner, J.S., *Studies in Cognitive Growth*, New York: Wiley 1966.

Bruner, J.S. and Minturn, A.L., 'Perceptual identification and perceptual organisation', *Journal of General Psychology*, 53 (1955), 21–8.

Bruner, J.S. and Postman, L.J., 'On the perception of incongruity: a paradigm', *Journal of Personality*, 18 (1949), 206–23.

Coon, D., *Essentials of Psychology*, New York: West Publishing 1991.

Festinger, L., *A Theory of Cognitive Dissonance*, Stanford, CT: Stanford University Press 1957.

Gardner, H., *Frames of Mind: The Theory of Multiple Intelligences*, London: Fontana 1983.

Heider, F., *The Psychology of Interpersonal Relations*, New York: Wiley 1958.

Hofstede, G., 'Dimensions of national cultures in fifty countries and three regions', in J. Deregowski, S. Dzuirawiec and R. Annis (eds), *Explications in Cross Cultural Psychology*, Lisse: Swets and Zeitlinger 1983.

Hofstede, G., *Culture and Organizations: Software of the Mind*, London: McGraw-Hill 1991.

Kakabadse, A., 'The billion-dollar manager: global leadership for the next millennium', paper delivered at the Annual John Lovett Memorial Lecture, University of Limerick 1997.

Katz, D., 'The functional approach to the study of attitudes', *Public Opinion Quarterly*, 24 (1960), 163–204.

Kelley, H.H., 'Attribution theory in social psychology', in D. Levine (ed.), *Nebraska Symposium on Motivation*, Lincoln, NE: University of Nebraska Press 1967.

Kelley, H.H., 'The processes of causal attribution', *American Psychologist*, 28 (1973), 107–28.

Kirton, M.J., *Adaptors and Innovators: Styles of Creativity and Problem Solving*, London: Routledge 1989.

Kogan, N., 'Cognitive style and reading performance', bulletin of the Orton Society, 30 (1980), 63–78.

Kosslyn, S.M., *Ghosts in the Mind's Machine*, New York: Norton 1983.

Lindsay, G. and Aronson, E. (eds), *The Handbook of Social Psychology*, New York: Random House 1985.

March, J.G. and Simon, H.A., *Organizations*, New York: Wiley 1958.

Markus, H. and Zajonc, R.B., 'The cognitive perspective in social psychology', in D. McGregor (1960), *The Human Side of Enterprise*, New York: McGraw-Hill 1985.

McGregor, D., *The Human Side of Enterprise*, New York: McGraw-Hill 1960.

Miller, A., 'Cognitive style: an integrated model', *Educational Psychology*, VII (1987), 251–68.

Mohan, M., 'The influence of marital roles in consumer decision making', *Irish Marketing Review*, VIII (1995), 97–106.

Moore, S. and Punnett, B.J., 'Expatriate and spousal adjustment: a pilot study in the midwest region', *Irish Business and Administrative Research*, 15 (1994), 178–84.

Nonaka, I. and Kenney, M., 'Towards a new theory of innovation management: a case study comparing Canon Inc. and Apple Computer Inc.', *Journal of Engineering and Technology Management*, VIII (1991), 67–73.

Osherson, H., Kosslyn, P. and Hollerbach, J., *Invitation to Cognitive Science: Visual Cognition and Action*, ii, Cambridge, MA: Blackwell 1990.

Pettigrew, A. and Whipp, R., *Managing Change for Competitive Success*, Oxford: Blackwell 1991.

Plous, S., *The Psychology of Judgement and Decision Making*, New York: McGraw-Hill 1993.

Posner, E., *Foundations of Cognitive Science*, Hillsdale, NJ: Erlbaum 1989.

Rock, I., *The Logic of Perception*, Cambridge, MA: Bradfors Books/MIT Press 1983.

Ross, L., 'The intuitive psychologist and his shortcomings: distortions in the attribution process', in L. Berkowitz (ed.), *Advances in Experimental Social Psychology*, New York: Academic Press 1977.

Rumelhart, D.E., 'Schemata: the building blocks of cognition', in R.J. Spiro *et al.* (eds), *Theoretical Issues in Reading Comprehension*, Hillsdale, NJ: Erlbaum 1980.

Rumelhart, D.E., 'Schemata and the cognitive system', in R.S. Wyer and T.K. Scrull (eds), *Handbook of Social Cognition*, i, Hillsdale, NJ: Erlbaum 1984.

Sadlier Smith, E., Spicer, D.P. and Tsang, F., 'Validity of the cognitive style index: replication and extension', *British Journal of Management*, XI (2000), 175–81.

Schermerhorn, J.R., Hunt, J.G. and Osborn, R.N., *Managing Organizational Behavior*, 5th ed., New York: Wiley 1994.

Smith, P.B. and Harris Bond, M., *Social Psychology Across Cultures: Analysis and Perspectives*, Hertfordshire: Harvester Wheatsheaf 1993.

Stranks, K., 'Perception and behaviour: impact, influence and outcomes', *Management Review*, LXXXIV/3 (1994), 21–31.

Tennent, M., *Psychology and Adult Learning*, London: Routledge 1988.

Thomas, K., 'Conflict and conflict management' in M.D. Dunnette (ed.), *Handbook of Industrial and Organizational Psychology*, Chicago: Rand McNally 1976.

Thompson, L.L., Levine, J.M. and Messick, D.M., *Shared Cognition in Organizations: The Management of Knowledge*, Cambridge: Sage 2000.

Weick, K., 'Managerial thought in the context of action', in S. Srivastiva and associates (eds), *The Executive Mind*, San Francisco: Jossey-Bass 1983.

LEARNING AND THE INDIVIDUAL 4

Learning Objectives

- To define learning and explain its significance in understanding behaviour in organisations.

- To distinguish between single and double loop learning.

- To differentiate between various theories of learning and how these might be applied to individuals at work.

- To develop understandings of individual differences and how people learn.

- To understand the key principles underpinning adult learning in organisations.

INTRODUCTION

While behaviour in organisations is largely governed by individual, group and organisational processes, learning as a concept bridges all three strata since learning can occur at all levels and through a variety of formal and informal systems. Indeed, in recent times we have witnessed a consistent organisational focus on the importance of the individual's contribution to successful functioning, which has led to a situation whereby employees are increasingly being viewed as critical competitive resources which, if developed effectively, are seen to add significantly to the attainment of strategic business goals. Boud and Garrick (1999: 1) persuasively argue that modern organisations ignore learning at the cost of their present and future successes and that in the complex enterprises of the new millennium, learning has moved from the periphery – from something that prepared people for employment – to the lifeblood which sustains them. They go on to caution that there are few places left for employees at any level who do not continue to learn and improve their effectiveness throughout their working lives. Likewise, there is no place for managers who do not appreciate their own vital role in fostering learning (Boud and Garrick 1999: 1).

Therefore, it is pertinent that some attention is given to how and why individuals learn and how the organisation as a system can facilitate continuous learning. The reader should be aware that in this chapter we focus solely on learning and the individual in the workplace context. Debates on learning as an organisational phenomenon, including 'organisational learning', 'the learning organisation' and 'knowledge management', are treated in Chapter 10, where we examine learning as an organisational context dynamic.

In this chapter we explore the dimension of learning from the individual's perspective. In particular, we identify the range of critical learning theories that have informed our understanding of the individual's learning process. Furthermore, we focus on key learning criteria and the notion of learning transfer as it applies to learning in the organisation. Finally, we turn our attention to the complex issue of how individuals learn in organisations, and particularly the dynamics of adult learning.

Definitions of Key Concepts

Learning
A process through which individuals acquire and assimilate new knowledge and skills that results in relatively permanent behaviour changes. Learning may be conscious or unconscious, formal or informal and requires some element of practice and experience.

Single loop learning
Is said to occur where actions lead directly to consequences – if the consequences are not those desired, then the actions are changed and the process continues. Single loop learning is useful for routine, repetitive issues and is helpful for getting the job done.

Double loop learning
Occurs where mismatches are corrected by first examining, questioning and altering the underlying systems and then changing the actions. In an organisational context, double loop learning is required for complex, non-programmable issues where a number of variables can be said to influence the learning situation.

Behaviourist theories
View learning in terms of a stimulus and a response whereby behaviour can be determined by reinforcement (via rewards or punishment).

Cognitive theories
Suggest that learning is about how the environment is perceived by the individual and how individuals interact with that environment. Learning in this context is not predictable and varies considerably between individuals.

Social learning
Suggests that most learning centres around observing the behaviour of others and interpreting the outcomes of that behaviour. If the outcomes are perceived to be positive then that increases the likelihood that that behaviour will be copied (modelled).

Learning style
Refers to each individual's preferred way of receiving and interpreting information.

Learning transfer
A process whereby learning in one activity is transferred to another form of activity.

Pedagogy
Refers to the art and science of teaching children and can be classified as a content-based approach that forms the foundation for most school-based education.

Andragogy
A process-based approach to learning that is held to be more appropriate when dealing with adult populations.

DEFINING LEARNING

A fundamental question for students of organisational behaviour concerns how individuals acquire the various abilities and skills required for survival in a complex social environment. In this respect we can postulate that learning is an integral feature in helping us understand behaviour in the organisation. Therefore, any discussion on learning as a concept must necessarily be prefaced by an attempt to define the concept itself. By its very nature learning is difficult to define, since there is no complete agreement on the parameters of learning or where learning crosses over into other behavioural determinants. Finding a conclusive definition of learning is therefore difficult and perhaps counterproductive.

A narrow definition might suggest that learning is broadly consistent with education and so learning takes place at school or within formal learning environments. Viewed this way, learning is held to be a deliberate activity that occurs within identified parameters or set boundaries. Such a definition is overtly restrictive and largely unacceptable in the context of organisational behaviour, since it does not recognise the range of learning opportunities available to individuals in their employment in an organisational setting.

A more acceptable definition of learning might be that it is a process through which individuals assimilate new knowledge and skills that results in relatively permanent behaviour changes. Here behaviour should be taken to include both observable activity and internal processes such as thinking, attitudes, feelings and emotions. Burns (1995) cautions that there are many situations where what is learned may not manifest itself in observable behaviour until later (latent learning). For example, it is possible to learn how to do something simply by watching someone else do it. Here the learner's behaviour does not change at the time, but this does not mean that no learning has occurred. Presented with that same situation sometime in the future, it is entirely possible that the learner will reproduce the behaviour he/she observed earlier. Much of children's learning can be seen to occur through such observation. Thus, learning can be conscious or unconscious, formal or informal, though most would agree that it tends to require some element of practice and experience if it is to 'stick' or result in some permanent behaviour change. This notion of learning resulting in an observable change in behaviour is well captured by McGeehee (1958: 2), who described learning thus:

> You have seen people in the process of learning, you have seen people who behave in a particular way as a result of learning and some of you have 'learned' at some time in your life. In other words, we infer that learning has taken place if an individual behaves, reacts, responds as a result of experience in a manner different from the way he formerly behaved.

Table 4.1 Learning and Training Compared

Comparison Factor	Learning	Training
Focus of activity	On values, attitudes, innovation and outcome accomplishment.	On knowledge, skills, ability and job performance.
Clarity of objectives	May be vague and difficult to identify.	Can be specified clearly.
Timescale	Continuous.	Short term.
Values that underpin activity	Assumes continuous change. Emphasises breakthrough.	Assumes relative stability. Emphasises improvement.
Nature of learning process	Instructional or organic.	Structured or mechanistic.
Content of activity	Learning how to learn, values, attitudes relevant to work.	Knowledge, skills and attitudes relevant to specific job, basic competencies.
Methods used	Informal learning methods, learner-initiated methods.	Demonstration, practice, feedback.
Outcomes of process	Individuals learn how to learn and create their own solutions.	Skilled performance or tasks that make up a job.
Learning strategy used	Inductive strategies.	Didactic tutor centred.
Nature of process	Inside out, seeks to do for self.	Outside in, done by others.
Role of professional trainer	To facilitate and guide.	To instruct, demonstrate and guide.
Document trainer philosophy	Existentialism: self-managed process.	Instrumentalism: transferring knowledge using formal methods and measuring results.
Type of need emphasised	Individual and organisational needs.	Organisational needs.
Process of evaluation	Continuous evaluation.	Evaluation against specific job performance standards.
Link with organisational missions and stategies	Not necessarily linked to organisation's mission and goals.	Directly aligned with organisation's vision and requirements for success.
Payback to organisation	Immediate and ongoing.	Almost immediately in terms of skilled performance.

Source: Garavan *et al.* (1995)

It is important at the outset to differentiate learning from training. In its most basic sense, training refers to the acquisition of knowledge, skills and abilities required to perform effectively in a given role. In an organisational context, training tends to be associated with the range of abilities required for the specific job by the individual. Learning, on the other hand, is a much broader concept than training in that it is not limited to any organisational role that an individual may hold. However, learning is a necessary occurrence in any training intervention. In other words, training will not be effective unless some learning has occurred. Garavan *et al.* (1995) differentiate between learning and training along a number of key characteristics (see Table 4.1).

Learning is thus concerned with changes in an individual's behaviour that endure over time. In terms of organisational behaviour, learning refers to the assimilation of new knowledge that leads employees to behave in a new or different way. However, learning does not exist in a vacuum and so organisations must make some attempt to facilitate individual learning if employees' full potential is to be harnessed in pursuit of greater organisational efficiency.

This brings us to another concept that requires some attempt at definition, namely the learning organisation. The literature on the learning organisation as a distinct concept is relatively new, and again, while there is no agreement on what exactly constitutes a learning organisation, it is generally described as a participative learning system that places an emphasis on information exchange and being open to enquiry and self-criticism. We will be dealing with this as an organisational context issue in Chapter 10.

An important distinction should also be drawn between two types or categories of learning, developed by Argyris and Schön (1978), namely single loop learning and double loop learning. Single loop learning is said to occur where actions lead to consequences – if the consequences are not those desired, then the actions are changed and the process continues. Single loop learning is useful for routine, repetitive issues and for getting the job done. Argyris (1992) uses an electrical engineering analogy to demonstrate single loop learning – a thermostat is programmed to detect states of 'too hot' or 'too cold' and to correct the situation by turning the heat on or off. Thus, whenever an error is detected and corrected without questioning or altering the underlying values of the system, the learning is said to be single loop. Double loop learning, on the other hand, occurs where mismatches are corrected by first examining and altering the underlying systems and then changing the actions. Returning to the thermostat analogy, if the thermostat asked itself such questions as why it was set at 68 degrees or why it was programmed as it was, then it would be a double loop learner. In an organisational context, double loop learning is required for complex, non-programmable issues where a number of variables can be said to influence the learning situation. Argyris and Schön (1978) differentiate single and double loop learning as follows in Table 4.2.

Newman (2000) argues that learning in organisations occurs through routines that are repeated and modified and is organised by schemas (mental maps) that help to assimilate, process and interpret information. She argues that most learning involves incremental change in routines within the existing schema, which she terms first order learning, single

Table 4.2 Single and Double Loop Learning

Features of Single Loop Learning	Features of Double Loop Learning
Goals designed unilaterally based on local information and reinforcing behaviour.	Individuals, groups and departments are open with data.
Individual/organisational objectives to be winners.	Interests and understandings move beyond functional and hierarchical boundaries.
Information is a power resource and kept 'close to one's chest'; little sharing of information.	Decisions through partnership, not imposition.
Emphasis on rationality and objectiveness on the surface, even if it is clearly inappropriate.	Norms and values open to change. Communality in values and perceptions an objective.
Conflict not confronted, but smoothed over or postponed.	Shared ownership and commitment.
Attractive in that it is familiar, measurable and reflects functional activities.	Policies and strategies seen as open and complex.

Source: Adapted from Argyris and Schön (1978)

loop learning or learning through exploitation. As long as existing routines can be interpreted as achieving organisational goals, they will be repeated and first order learning will dominate, i.e. individuals becoming better at what they do. She further suggests that second order learning, double loop learning or learning through exploration involves the search for new routines and schemas and is most likely where goals or aspirations are not being met, when existing routines become ineffective or when new information cannot be understood within the currently accepted schema. Since the business world today is increasingly complex and uncertain, it is arguable that double loop learning is more necessary than ever before.

Having defined learning it now becomes pertinent to explore some of the key learning theories that have informed our understanding of the learning process. However, in advance of doing this let us rid ourselves of two omnipresent myths about learning, namely that learning is always positive and beneficial, and second, that learning is always an eagerly anticipated and fun process. In relation to the former, it may be overly optimistic to suggest that all learning results in improved performance. For example, March and Olsen (1976) suggest that learning that is based on misunderstandings or on misdirected responses to external or internal signals will give rise to a distorted type of learning, while March (1991) argues that in the long run, overly adaptive processes may be self-destructive. Furthermore, individuals and groups can learn new things that may be undesirable from an organisation's perspective and these may survive and be perpetuated, i.e. use of shortcuts, inappropriate behaviour, reinforcement of restrictive practices and so forth. In relation to the latter, Schein dismisses the popular notion that learning is fun (Coutu 2002). He believes that learning and the change that inevitably accompanies it is a complex process, often more a source of frustration than achievement for groups and individuals. He argues that once one has established attitudes about work and life, one does not particularly want to change them. It can be painful to replace something that is already there with some new learning. Billet (1999) similarly suggests that learning in a work setting can be challenging in multiple ways, citing a number of specific work examples where the opportunities or demands for learning can be inwardly approached with anxiety or even as threats to individuals' perceived ability to cope. Such examples include being asked to comprehend a new process, product or set of ideas; utilising a new way of dealing with these ideas (IT) or a new way of interacting with others and handling oneself; and interacting with individuals from other professional domains within organisational networks or with diverse team members in a multinational team setting.

However, while it is to be expected that there will be some level of learning anxiety, the learning process can be greatly facilitated if the individual fundamentally accepts the need to learn and by the provision of a safe learning environment characterised by good training, coaching, group support, feedback and positive incentives. This supportive learning environment idea will be taken up further in Chapter 10.

THEORIES OF LEARNING

The dimensions of individual learning have been the focus of considerable research and experimentation over time and a range of theories has been advanced to explain how individuals acquire and assimilate knowledge. The early roots of learning theory may be traced back to Plato and Aristotle and the notion of the 'trained mind', whereby training is seen to require extensive self-discipline and control. Luminaries such as these proposed that the exercise of mental faculties, e.g. reason, memory, willpower, etc., was crucial to the development of the individual and ultimately of the community at large. However, it is in the previous two centuries that some of the most important research into learning has occurred, which now informs our current understanding of the process of learning. Luthans (1992) indicates that a theory's purpose is to better explain the phenomenon under investigation, thus a true theory can be universally applied and allow one to predict outcomes with reliability and validity. In this way, a perfected theory of learning would be able to explain all aspects of learning (how, why and when), have universal application, i.e. to children, college students, managers and workers, and predict and control learning situations (Luthans 1992: 208).

To date, however, no such theory of learning exists, for while there is some broad agreement on many of the principles of learning, considerable divergence remains as to the theory underpinning such principles. Thus, a considerable number of theories on learning have been proposed, the more instructive of which are discussed here under the classification of behaviourist theories, cognitive theories and experiential theories. Centrally, what distinguishes these theoretical approaches to understanding learning is their conceptualisation of humans in the social world, namely whether the individual may be viewed as a passive learner reacting to external stimuli; whether the individual may be considered an active participant in the learning process by assimilating, interpreting and interacting; or whether the individual rather more deliberately seeks out opportunities for knowledge acquisition and self-development. Beyond their theoretical contributions, such theories also have a range of practical applications to the design and delivery of training and development programmes, work structuring and organisational social networks.

BEHAVIOURIST THEORIES

The behaviourist school is perhaps the most dominant in terms of early learning research and suggests that learning is a function of experience, i.e. that ideas that are experienced together tend to be associated with each other. At the theory's core lies the question of how to get individuals to habitually respond in a particular way to a particular situation, i.e. how to condition behaviour. It is suggested that behaviour can be conditioned in essentially two ways: as a response to an external stimulus, referred to as 'classical conditioning', or through reinforcement (positive or negative), referred to as 'operant conditioning'.

Classical Conditioning

Often referred to as learning by association, classical conditioning was derived from the scientific experiments of Ivan Pavlov (1849–1936) and probably represents the most famous study ever completed in the behavioural sciences. Pavlov attributed learning to the association between a stimulus and response (S-R) and sought to test this using dogs in a laboratory experiment. When Pavlov presented dogs with a piece of meat they automatically salivated – this salivating represented an unconditioned or reflexive response to the smell of the meat. Thus, the meat in this case was an unconditioned stimulus, i.e. nothing was done to it to make the dogs salivate. When Pavlov rang a bell, however, nothing happened. Then Pavlov started to ring a bell each time he gave the dogs a piece of meat until such time as the dogs began to salivate each time the bell was rung, regardless of whether there was meat present or not. This is known as classical conditioning – the dogs were conditioned to believe there was meat on the way as soon as they heard the bell, and so they started to salivate. In this experiment the saliva produced represents a conditioned response to a conditioned stimulus, i.e. the bell. Thus, making no assumptions about the thinking or feeling processes that might be implied in this experiment, Pavlov merely described or predicted overt behaviour and demonstrated the connection between stimuli and responses in learning. Thus, the learner is conditioned (learns) to emit a response (salivation) that was originally attached quite naturally to another stimulus (the meat) to a new stimulus (the bell). Classical conditioning is basically passive, where an event occurs and the individual reacts in a specific (conditioned) way. There must always be an existing S-R link available. Classical conditioning thus suggested that in order to change human behaviour, some form of further conditioning is required.

Operant Conditioning

Following in the behaviourist tradition and dedicated to providing an understanding of how we learn through the use of selective rewards and punishments, B.F. Skinner (1904–1990) mainly focused on the concept of reinforcement of behaviour and on how associations are formed between a stimulus and response. He suggested that classical conditioning was limited since it only explained reflexive or involuntary responses, and since human behaviour is so complex, learning must be a function of more conscious behaviour. Using rats in his experiments, Skinner designed a particular type of box that had a lever inside. When this lever was pressed it released food into the box. Over time, the rats learned that the more the lever was pressed, the more food they received. Since the rats were extremely hungry each time they were put into the box, it is not surprising that they spent a considerable amount of time pressing the lever. This experiment demonstrated the link between a stimulus and response whereby when the rats behaved in a certain way (pressing the lever) they were rewarded (received food), and this behaviour was reinforced through the continual rewarding with food whenever the lever was pressed. A central feature, therefore, of operant conditioning is what happens as a consequence of a particular behavioural response.

At the core of this behaviourist perspective lies the principle of behaviour modification, which essentially refers to attempts to control individual behaviour through the systematic reinforcement of behaviours that are deemed to be desirable. This reinforcement points to the process through which certain consequences serve to strengthen a particular behaviour. It basically centres on the 'law of effect', which states that behaviour will be repeated or avoided depending on whether the consequences are positive or negative. There are three types of reinforcement that are relevant in an organisational behaviour context: positive, negative and punishment.

- **Positive reinforcement:** Is used to increase the frequency of desirable behaviour, whereby positive consequences are applied in order that a particular type of behaviour is encouraged and so increases the frequency with which it may occur again. For example, an employee who performs above expectation in their job is praised, given a bonus, promoted to encourage them to continue to work well, etc. In other words, an employer accentuates the positive behaviour in order to eliminate the likelihood of any negative behaviour occurring.

- **Negative reinforcement:** Is also used to increase the frequency of desirable behaviour. In this situation, however, a particularly undesirable consequence is withdrawn in order to increase the frequency with which desired behaviour occurs. Luthans (1992) refers to this as a form of social blackmail. An organisational example of this type of reinforcement might be where a threat of punishment or disciplinary action is withdrawn as soon as an employee behaves in a manner that is desired by the organisation. Thus, an individual will behave in a particular manner to avoid being punished.

- **Punishment:** Is used to decrease the frequency of undesirable behaviour. Here, a useful example might be an organisation's disciplinary procedure, which seeks to eliminate undesirable behaviour (such as unauthorised absences) through the imposition of sanctions.

Luthans (1992) illustrates the differences between classical and operant conditioning as follows.

Table 4.3 Classical vs. Operant Conditioning

Classical Conditioning		
	Stimulus (S)	**Response (R)**
The individual …	is stuck by a pin	flinches
	is tapped below the kneecap	flexes lower leg
	is shocked by an electrical current	jumps/screams
	is surprised by a loud sound	jumps/screams
Operant Conditioning		
	Response (R)	**Stimulus (S)**
The individual …	works	is paid
	talks to others	meets more people
	enters a restaurant	obtains food
	enters a library	finds a book
	works hard	receives praise and a promotion

Source: Luthans (1992: 210)

In most organisations, the two key reinforcement mechanisms are feedback on performance (to encourage/discourage good/bad behaviour) and money (to reward desirable behaviour).

Overall, while behavioural theories have added considerably to our understanding of how people learn, their work did not prove acceptable to other researchers in the field of learning as related to human behaviour. Essentially, behaviourist approaches were viewed as mechanical and rigid, giving little emphasis to an individual's ability to interpret and evaluate stimuli and generate a response. It is argued that human behaviour is particularly complex and that learning and behaviour are not necessarily synonymous. For example, even though learning may have taken place, e.g. an individual knows that driving fast in foggy conditions can be extremely hazardous, this individual may choose not to apply this learning, e.g. may still be unwilling to drive slowly. Thus, while learning and behaviour are undoubtedly interrelated, they are not necessarily one and the same thing.

COGNITIVE THEORIES

In organisation behaviour, the cognitive approach is often used as a valued means of explaining motivation in the organisation (see Chapter 6 for a detailed treatise on motivation theories and processes). The cognitive approach to learning primarily sets out to describe the person as a knowing being. The emphasis in this approach is on the significance of the role of experience, the development of meaning and the use of problem solving and insight as the sources of learning central to the individual. Studies by German Gestalt psychologists early in the twentieth century demonstrated that individuals are constantly confronted by a mass of stimuli and that they actively impose some order on this so that that they can understand it. Burns (1995) suggests that in this way, cognitive theory accounts for the different ways in which individuals make sense of their environment because it acknowledges each individual's different past experiences, needs, expectations and aspirations. The early advocates of cognitivism, such as Wertheimer (1889–1943) and Kohler (1887–1967), were particularly interested in the subject of perception, i.e. in how human beings and animals 'see' their world, and from their experiments they demonstrated that learning is a matter of assembling one's world into meaningful patterns, rather than just making connections between separate elements. This view of perception was encapsulated in the statement that 'the whole is greater than the sum of its parts' (the Gestaltist perspective), thus the focus of cognitivists is on the structure and processes of human competence, i.e. the role that memory, intuition, perception and information processing have on learning. Thus, while the behaviourist theories view learning in terms of a stimulus and a response whereby behaviour can be determined by reinforcement (via rewards), the cognitive approach suggests that learning is about how the environment is perceived by the individual and how that learning can be stored away until it is required (latent learning); for example, a student attends lectures, tutorials, reads notes and materials and assimilates information that will be used later to (hopefully) pass an exam.

Insight is considered to play a significant role in the cognitive approach to learning in terms of how an individual perceives his/her environment. Specifically, three stages are involved:

1. The individual understands the situation and identifies a problem to be solved.
2. He/she thinks about the problem and the context within which it occurs.
3. He/she experiences a sudden flash of inspiration where a solution suddenly becomes evident.

Such insight is usefully demonstrated in the experiments conducted by Kohler (1925) during the 1920s. Working with chimpanzees, Kohler discovered that apes were able to work things out in their minds rather than having to go through the process of trial and error associated with operant conditioning. In summary, he illustrated this mental problem solving as follows. He had a chimp confined in a cage and outside of the cage, beyond his reach, was a piece of fruit. Within the cage was a short stick and close to the piece of fruit outside of the cage was another, longer stick. He observed as the chimp tried to grasp the fruit with his outstretched hand and failed; he then watched the chimp pick up the short stick in his cage and attempt to use this to reach the fruit and pull it in – the stick was too short so he gave up and threw it down. The chimp then attempted to escape from the cage, to no avail. After a short while he noticed the chimp stare at the long stick outside of the cage. Without pausing, the chimp used the short stick to drag the longer stick into the cage and then used the longer stick to pull in the fruit. Naturally, he then ate the piece of fruit.

As demonstrated in this experiment, insight represents the dawning of understanding, whereby a person grasps the essentials of a problem, formulates a solution and then applies the learning from this experience to a future occasion while acknowledging the learning situation. Its principal relevance in organisational behaviour is to situations of a complex, problem-solving nature.

In summary, the cognitive perspective assumes that one can never truly predict behaviour since behaviour is contingent on how each individual perceives, constructs and interprets their environment and subjectively correlates this with his/her past experience.

Social Learning Theory

Sometimes referred to as observational or imitation learning, social learning as a separate theory seeks to combine both the behaviourist and cognitive approaches to learning. Associated with the work of Miller and Dollard (1950), social learning suggests that individuals learn not just by doing but also by watching others and repeating their actions. More recently, Bandura (1986: 5) argues that learning must be more than conditioning and that while reinforcement has a considerable influence on an individual's behaviour, 'most of the behaviours that people display are learned either deliberately or inadvertently through the influence of example.' In practice, this suggests that individuals observe each other on a continuous basis, and where they perceive a positive consequence of certain behaviour, they will tend to emulate that behaviour and thereby achieve the positive outcomes associated with it. This is known as social modelling. In a work situation, for example, a new employee may adopt an approach to a difficult supervisor that seems to work for more established workers and thereby hope to achieve the same positive result. This observational approach to learning has a range of applications in the workplace and occurs both formally and informally. It constitutes a core element of on-the-job training and experiential learning and is largely responsible for the way in which new recruits are socialised into the organisation.

Learning that is acquired through experience is often referred to as implicit learning, which essentially suggests that individuals can acquire complex knowledge without ever being aware that they are learning (Green and Shanks 1993). Implicit learning is thought to be the foundation for tacit knowledge and can be used to solve problems as well as make reasonable decisions about novel circumstances. Knowledge acquired through implicit learning is not amenable to verbal reports, whereas explicit learning, which proceeds with the individual's awareness of what is being learned, is verbally reportable. Raelin (1997) suggests that implicit learning serves as the base for conscious operations and that reflection is thought to contribute to the learning experience to the extent that learners are active observers. Again, this brings us back to the work of Bandura (1986), who suggests that people often learn behaviours from observing others before performing the behaviour themselves and use this as a means of reflecting on the causes and consequences of particular modes of behaviour.

Clearly, the legacy of individual psychology has had a considerable influence on our understanding of individual learning in an organisational context. Learning theory based on behavioural theories represents a still-common view of conditioned learning. In an organisational context, this learning can be perceived as a trial-and-error procedure or as a search among alternative routines where routines are likely to be used when they have previously resulted in a positive outcome (positive reinforcement). The cognitive perspective acknowledges that each individual brings a unique set of experiences and expectations to the organisation that can shape the level of learning that takes place and the degree to which the learning becomes a significant aspect of subsequent behaviour.

LEARNING STYLES AND PREFERENCES

The various theories of learning present learning as a complex process of acquiring knowledge, understanding, skills and values in order to be able to adapt to the environment in which we live. Various psychologists have provided further insights into how individuals learn and interact with their environment. Piaget (1963), for example, proposes that all individuals develop schemas or particular ways of thinking that are used to interpret experiences. New knowledge is then assimilated into these schemas or ways of thinking. When an experience occurs that challenges these existing schemas, the individual goes through a process of reassessing them and adapting or accommodating new ways of thinking as a result as required. Thus, the individual is in constant interaction with the environment, responding to and re-evaluating existing ways of thinking and acting.

Kolb (1984) developed a highly influential model of experiential learning, which presents learning as an ongoing cyclical process whereby knowledge is created through the transformation of experience and a reflective process. In this model, the cycle begins

Figure 4.1 Kolb's Learning Cycle

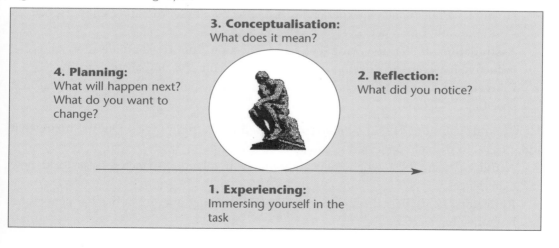

3. **Conceptualisation:**
What does it mean?

4. **Planning:**
What will happen next?
What do you want to change?

2. **Reflection:**
What did you notice?

1. **Experiencing:**
Immersing yourself in the task

with a concrete experience of some kind that provides a stimulus for observation and reflection. These observations evolve into a more generalised theory from which new actions and their implications can be deduced. These concepts are then tested in a new situation, which provides a fresh experience and thus the cycle begins again. Kolb's model suggests that individuals learn in four particular ways – through immediate concrete experiences, through observation and reflection, through abstract conceptualisation or through active experimentation.

Kolb's model highlights a number of important characteristics associated with experiential learning, as follows.

1. Learning is a continuous process associated with experience.
2. Rather than being passive recipients of knowledge, learners need to actively explore and engage with their environment in order to generate new experiences and new ways of viewing things.
3. Learners need to actively reflect on their experiences – to think about what they mean and how they might fit with existing knowledge and assumptions.
4. Learners need to experiment with new ways of doing things in order to adapt to the evolving circumstances of their environment.
5. Learning is social and the sorts of life experiences individuals have shape the way they learn.

This process view of learning suggests that learning from experience involves a number of discrete phases, which has led some researchers to believe that individuals have developed sets of preferences for receiving and processing information, i.e. that we are capable of being more 'efficient' learners when we are presented with information in a way that is closely aligned with these developed preferences. Kolb himself conducted extensive investigations into how individuals learn from their experiences and developed what he termed a Learning Styles Inventory or questionnaire. This inventory identifies a set of preferred 'learning styles' that are held by individuals.

- **Accommodators:** 'Hands-on' learners who have a strong preference for concrete experiences and active experimentation – learn primarily from doing.
- **Divergers:** Prefer concrete experiences, but reflect on these from different perspectives – observe rather than act.
- **Assimilators:** Prefer to swing between reflection and conceptualisation and use inductive reasoning to develop new theory – like concepts and abstract ideas.
- **Convergers:** Favour taking ideas and testing them out in practice – practical and specific.

Honey and Mumford (1992) similarly developed a Learning Styles Questionnaire that identifies four discrete preferred approaches to learning.

- **Activists:** Learn best when they are actively involved in concrete tasks and new experiences.
- **Reflectors:** Learn best through reviewing and thinking over what has happened and how they have acted.

- **Theorists:** Learn best by relating new information to concepts or theories.
- **Pragmatists:** Learn best when they can relate new information to real-life issues.

The authors are careful to note that individuals may have more than one preferred method of learning – depending on the circumstances – but argue that each of us can identify more fully with one style preference over the others.

Together, research on learning styles and preferences suggests that individuals learn in different ways and that this has considerable implications for how learning opportunities are presented and delivered in the organisational situation. For example, some individuals may learn more effectively in a structured training environment using concrete examples, whereas others might prefer a more informal conceptual framework. Mumford (1989) suggests that a failure to take account of different learning styles can have seriously negative implications for the training process, while Arment (1990) indicates that:

- by the time we reach adulthood, each of us has developed our own method of learning, reflected in a unique and well-established learning style;
- trainers also have well-established learning styles and preferences; and
- the more compatible the style of learning with the approach to training adopted, the more likely it is that a positive learning experience will occur.

LEARNING STYLES THEORY: WHAT THE EXPERTS SAY

Can we accurately and predictably measure a learner's preferred or dominant learning style though the use of instruments and inventories?

DAVE KOLB: Few, if any, individual-difference tests can measure an individual with complete accuracy. For this reason, the Learning Style Inventory (LSI) is not recommended as a tool for individual selection purposes. However, the LSI has considerable construct validity, that is, significant and replicated patterns of relationships predicted by experiential learning theory. For example, individuals who score high on Concrete Experience … tend to have greater interpersonal skills, have educational backgrounds in the liberal arts and are in people-oriented careers such as sales or human resources. Individuals who score high on Abstract Conceptualization, on the other hand, tend to have greater cognitive skills, be educated in the sciences and be in technical and scientific careers. But there are always exceptions to these trends. For this reason, we do not refer to the LSI as a test but rather an experience in understanding how you learn.

PETER HONEY: Preferences, i.e. likes and dislikes, are more subjective and therefore harder to measure accurately than observable, manifest behaviors. Behaviors are much easier to predict. The trouble with the notion of a style is that it is a mixture of internal preferences and external behaviors, and these are not always aligned. For example, someone might prefer to ponder a problem or sleep on it before deciding on a course of action, but because of constraints or a 'go-go, can-do' culture, makes a hasty decision. So, I'm confident that the behavioral tendencies typical of learning 'style' can be predictably measured, but less confident about measuring the underlying preference.

Is there unequivocal, empirical evidence to validate the practical relationship between learning style and learning effectiveness?

PETER HONEY: Yes, but there are two sorts of learning effectiveness. People can either play to their strengths and in so doing become better at selecting learning opportunities that suit their style, or they can set to work to become better all-round learners by investing extra effort in underdeveloped or underutilized styles. The former is easier; the latter is the ultimate challenge.

LYNN CURRY: The research that has been done in learning styles has been plagued with serious design flaws that tend to cast doubt on the purported results or at least limit the applications. Various reviews have been done in this area, however, and I think the thrust of the evidence is positive. There is a particularly strong relationship in those individuals without style flexibility, which is the ability to match their learning processes to the learning environment encountered. When the environment is consistent with their inflexible styles, they do at least OK. When the learning environment is not conducive to their inflexible styles, they do less well and have to work harder with predictable threats to motivation and engagement.

Should we teach exclusively to an individual's preferred style?

DAVE KOLB: Tracking of students in education by whatever criteria is generally a bad idea, as it tends to stigmatize and stereotype learners, preventing them from developing their full learning potential. It is more effective to design curriculum so that there is some way for learners of every learning style to engage with the topic, so that every type of learner has an initial way to connect with the material, and then begin to stretch his or learning capability in other learning modes.

PETER HONEY: Teaching exclusively to an individual's preferred style, if indeed it was possible, would undoubtedly be convenient and comfortable for the learner. But so much of what is involved in effective learning would be missing – having to struggle, taking a risk, picking yourself up after a setback and having another go, and learning from failure and mistakes.

Is an individual's learning style stable over time, task, problem and situation?

DAVE KOLB: Test-retest studies of the LSI suggest that learning style is relatively stable over time. However, cross-sectional studies suggest that learning style does change as a function of career path and life experience. For example, engineers who remain bench engineers throughout their career retain the converging (abstract and active) learning style typical of the engineering profession, but engineers who become managers become more concrete because of the interpersonal job demands of that role. Similarly, a study of the accounting profession showed that accounting students had diverse learning styles, entry-level accountants were converging, and intermediate-level accountants were even more so. Senior-level accountants had accommodating (concrete and active) learning styles.

PETER HONEY: It depends whether we are talking about the preference or the behavior part of the style. The underlying preference is more consistent and durable. The behaviors, however, are changeable depending on circumstances or will. The nature of my work, having to pay close attention to detail for example, would affect my behavior but I could, and I do, discipline myself to compensate for a 'weaker' style. My self-imposed discipline of keeping a written learning log, for example, forces me to invest more effort in reflecting and surfacing lessons learned than my activist/pragmatist preferences would allow.

Are learners adept at finding their own path through content?

LYNN CURRY: The evidence is that this is not true. The best references here are from the European line of research into learning instructional preferences. Scores are high when the individual's learning approach happens to match the performance expectations of the course or performance situation. When approach and performance expectation do not match, poor scores result. Those with flexibility about style can adapt easily within some range of learning environments. Learning environments that are inconsistent or oppose their native learning style will further challenge those without the style flexibility, or those at the borderline of their general competence to learn at all.

PETER HONEY: Most learners are unaware of their style and are bombarded by diverse learning materials. It is all very hit-and-miss and inefficient. Much more work remains to be done on how to tailor content. At the moment, people hide behind an ostensible multimedia/blended approach claiming that it provides something for all. This is, however, just a sop and another version of one-size-fits-all. My experience is that people who are aware of their learning style preferences, who understand the need to continuously improve their learning capabilities (learn to learn), and who have access to sound guidance are in a far better position than those who are left to their own devices.

How can we best make use of learning styles in the corporate environment?

DAVE KOLB: In addition to the obvious applications of experiential learning theory and the LSI to the design and conduct of corporate training programs, these ideas can also be used to promote learning throughout the organization. Managers' understanding of their learning style can help them understand and improve the way they make decisions. Understanding the learning styles that are characteristic of different organizational functions also can improve cross-functional communication. A study of the demise of a once highly profitable high-tech firm when its patent expired and competition entered the market showed a culture dominated by engineers with the converging style who would not accept high-level marketing personnel hired to create a more market-oriented culture.

PETER HONEY: Use information about the mix of learning style preferences to arrive at a learning strategy that would build learning into the system/processes so that it becomes a 'requirement.' Too often, organizations say that learning is a priority, but then they adopt an 'it's-up-to-you' approach, making it an optional activity. E-learning has, if anything, exacerbated this with the expectation that people will somehow find the space and time to do it. I see learning styles as just one piece of the jigsaw puzzle. Other pieces are about the motivation to learn, the skills to learn and the learning environment. The challenge to create learning-friendly work environments is as great as it ever was.

LYNN CURRY: The quickest and most cost-effective use of cognitive and learning styles in corporate environments is to provide comprehensive, detailed and interpreted information to employees about their own styles. This will allow individuals to use that personal information to better structure their coping strategies and achievement tactics.

Compilation of this individual information into a group composite would indicate to peers, team leaders and supervisors the necessity of offering alternative working structures to what is currently in place or personally preferred by the supervisor. Further supervisory development may be necessary in order to assist leaders to develop these alternative structures within time and resource constraints. Even if alternative structures cannot be provided, this knowledge of style differences should enable everyone to respond more effectively to the style outliers in the workplace.

What areas of learning style would most benefit from further research?

PETER HONEY: Everything! In particular, I'd say we need much more research on learning behaviors. What ways of behaving increase the amount and relevance of what is learned and people's willingness to share what they have learned for the good of the organization? We also need more research on the specific links between different styles and different types/methods of learning.

LYNN CURRY: A range of experimental design flaws plagues this literature including (but not limited to) over-generalization based on measurement of one isolated construct, often assessed on only one occasion and with only one instrument; only one or sometimes no independent measure of behavior change; and no attempt to control for interacting and confounding variables such as gender, IQ, ability or initial capability in target behavior, time-on-task and teacher expectation.

The result is that the research base is not a strong and consistent platform guiding the application of learning or cognitive style. These same criticisms can, however, be applied to the wider body of educational literature. Considerable service to the field could be made through relatively modest-scale studies that addressed any one, and preferably more, of the above limitations.

DAVE KOLB: Our latest research on experiential learning and the LSI is focused on developing more fine-grained descriptions of individuality in learning – the Adaptive Style Inventory – in order to respect individual uniqueness and avoid the stereotyping that can result from having only four learning styles. Also we are studying ways to promote adaptive flexibility in learning using this new inventory.

Source: DelahoUssaye 2002

THE TRANSFER OF LEARNING

The term 'learning transfer' refers to the extent to which skills and abilities acquired during a learning session are applied back to the job situation or to the learning of a new, but related, skill. Reid *et al.* (1992) distinguish between two types of positive learning transfer: vertical and lateral. Vertical transfer occurs where one subject area acts as a basis for another, i.e. a foundation course in general business forms the basis upon which students/learners can progress to greater specialism/diversification and where they can apply the general principles learned at foundation level. In training terms this involves the acquisition of additional knowledge/skills that builds upon existing skills and abilities.

Lateral transfer occurs where the same type of stimulus requires the same response. In this respect, training simulates a particular type of task and provides the learner with an opportunity to practise in a 'safe' environment. Reid *et al.* (1992) use the example of training simulations that are used to train aircraft pilots. Buckley and Caple (1990) indicate that positive transfer will have taken place if the learner is able to apply on the job what has been learned in training with relative ease (lateral), or is able to learn a new task more quickly as a result of earlier training on another task (vertical).

It is possible that in some circumstances negative transfer occurs, which may be as a result of past learning experiences that contradict present practice, i.e. a driver who learns to drive on one side of the road and might find it difficult to drive on the opposite side while abroad – this is particularly so in cases where the driver is distracted or stressed. The particular choice of training method, style of trainer or indeed the training situation might, individually or combined, serve to inhibit the learning process and thus result in negative learning transfer.

As discussed earlier, reinforcement plays a key role in encouraging/discouraging particular behaviour, with feedback and money identified as two particular organisational tools in behaviour modification. Latham and Crandall (1991) identify pay and promotion policies as key organisational variables that influence the level of learning transfer because they affect outcome expectations. Bandura (1986) suggests that learners may believe that they are capable of performing a specific behaviour but may choose not to do so because they consider it will have little or no effect on their status in the organisation.

ADVANCED CONCEPTS/ONGOING DEBATES IN INDIVIDUAL LEARNING

ADULT LEARNERS AT WORK

'Competitive functioning' has become the byword for a refocusing on various measures to improve employee motivation and morale as a means of increasing productivity and effectiveness. The shift in recent times has been towards creating an organisational environment that enables employees to learn and develop and thereby heighten productivity. In empowerment and total quality cultures, for example, individuals are expected to accept greater responsibility at their level of operations and to follow a path of continuous improvement. At the core of such cultures lies the recognition that employees have far more to offer than just performing work in a functional manner. This recognition is neatly articulated by both Barrow and Loughlin (1992) and Boud and Garrick (1999), who suggest that opportunities and problems within work are creating the need for new knowledge and understanding, such that modern organisations require that employees:

- have the ability to learn new skills and adapt to changing circumstances;
- can conceptualise the contribution of their role to organisational effectiveness;
- are capable of working in flatter structures and without supervision;
- have the ability to manage the interface between customers and the organisation;
- adapt flexibly to match the requirements of capital accumulation; and
- possess capabilities such as problem solving, creative thinking and innovativeness.

In short, this suggests that we are witnessing a strongly market-driven emphasis on learning in the organisational context where there is a major impetus to learn now built into work. Learning in an organisational context is not necessarily straightforward, however, and it requires a considered realisation that the kinds of activities that individuals engage in or are presented with will ultimately determine what they learn – and whether that learning will be of value to the organisation. The quality of that learning and the prospect of it being meaningfully transferred and used in the job situation are highly dependent on the levels of support and guidance provided to the learners. These issues need to be addressed if, as Boud and Garrick (1999) suggest, the workplace can represent a powerful and important site of learning.

Having established that learning inherently concerns some change in behaviour, it becomes pertinent to explore some of the principles underpinning effective learning as they can be applied in an organisational context. Our principle aim is to attempt to understand the dynamic, complex and diverse nature of adult learning. Here, what distinguishes the adult learner from the child and how adults approach learning are critical questions to ask in a context highlighting the importance of lifelong learning and continuous development. There is a vast range of abilities across organisations and, concomitantly, a wide variety of learning needs. Burns (1995) argues that while some of this learning may take place outside of the organisation, perhaps in a formal educational setting, much of this learning cannot be separated in time or place from work. Indeed, Brookfield (1986) notes that most adult learning is not acquired in formal courses, but is gained through experience or through participation in an aspect of social life such as work, community action or family activities.

Two broad approaches have been developed for the teaching of children and adults that are based on recognised differences in capabilities, experiences and knowledge. These approaches are termed pedagogy (a content-based approach that forms the foundation for most school-based education) and andragogy (a process-based approach that is held to be more appropriate when dealing with adult populations). The differences between the approaches are less concerned with the age of the learners (children versus adults), but rather are more associated with the broad educational philosophy underpinning them.

As traditionally conceived, pedagogy essentially refers to the art and science of teaching children. Pedagogy per se does not assume a single methodology, but rather refers to the general practice of teaching children, involving a range of appropriate methods. Here, the learning curriculum, in terms of what is to be learned, how it is to be learned and when it is to be learned, is primarily determined by the teacher or educational authority. The learner in this situation is usually a passive recipient[1] with limited life experience who is required to absorb and store information (or received wisdom) and to be able to reproduce it at a later stage for some predetermined purpose (usually examination). This approach to learning has as its core the objective of preparing the learner for some future event (life after formal education in most instances) and so it tends to be drawn from a wide canvas of foundation education. The learner has virtually no control of either the learning content or process. This approach suggests a rather mechanistic approach to learning that primarily ignores the particular needs and motivations of the individual learner.

Andragogy, a term devised by Knowles (1978, 1984), arose from a concerted debate about the appropriateness of traditional pedagogical learning approaches for adults. Specifically, it arose from the premise that adults are self-directing individuals with a wealth of life experiences that cognitively influence what and how they learn. Moreover, it recognises that there is considerably less homogeneity between a group of adults in an

---

1   It is recognised that not all school-based learning today is passive, which is evidence of concerted efforts being made to make learning more interactive and discursive.

organisational training session and a group of first class children in a classroom. Burns (1995) argues that an adult's ability to learn may depend as much on lifestyle, social roles and attitudes as it does with innate ability to learn. Furthermore, he notes that adults can judge the value of a learning activity and its relevance to their own lives, which has considerable implications for the way adult learning events are constructed and delivered.

PRINCIPLES OF EFFECTIVE ADULT LEARNING

Each individual brings a unique set of experiences and expectations to the learning event that can shape the level of learning that takes place and the degree to which the learning becomes a significant aspect of subsequent behaviour. The humanist psychologist Carl Rogers (1969) has had a considerable influence on our understanding of adult education and learning and argues that the focus of learning is best directed at the experiences of the learner rather than at the actions of the trainer. He distinguished between meaningless, oppressive and alienating learning and significant, meaningful, experiential learning, which is self-initiated and involves the whole person (Rogers 1969: 5), and focused the educational debate on how to facilitate rather than direct the learning of others. Garavan *et al.* (1995) summarise a number of principles underpinning Rogers's work and it is recognised that these principles hold true for all learning situations, irrespective of the age of the learner.

- Individuals have a natural tendency and potential for learning.
- Significant learning takes place when the subject matter is perceived as relevant by the learner.
- Learning that involves change in oneself is threatening and may be resisted.
- Much of what individuals learn is acquired by 'doing'.
- Learning is facilitated when the learner actively participates in the learning process.
- Self-initiated learning involving the whole person (emotionally and intellectually) is the most lasting and pervasive form of learning.
- Learning about the process of learning is essential to enable individuals to cope with change.
- The facilitator's task is to provide an environment in which individuals can set their own learning goals.

A key requirement is that learning events are presented in such a manner that they allow individuals to learn, retain and use this learning over time. Revans (1982), for example, identifies four cardinal conditions of successful learning that are widely referred to today:

1. That individuals are motivated to learn of their own volition and not solely at the will of others (goal directed).
2. That individuals can identify themselves with others who may not only share their needs, but who may also satisfy some of these needs (social dimension to learning).
3. That individuals can try out any new learning in actions of their own design (practice).
4. That within a reasonable lapse of time, individuals can attain first-hand knowledge of the results of their learning efforts (feedback).

Various sets of adult learning principles – derived in part from evidence of what constitutes effective and satisfying learning – have been developed over the years and are epitomised in the work of Brookfield (1986: 9). He proposed six principles of effective practice in facilitating learning that include voluntary participation, mutual respect, collaborative spirit, action and reflection, critical reflection and self-direction and demonstrating an awareness of the importance of the social context in adult learning. These learning principles place a number of implicit requirements on both the design and delivery of learning activities within organisations that can be summarised as follows.

- **Motivation to learn:** The employee as learner must want to learn and thus, in order to be committed to the process, must perceive that the learning event will result in the achievement of certain desired goals. This links back with the notion of adults being self-directed.

- **Involvement of the learner:** The learning or training activity should be seen as an active rather than a passive process. Pont (1991) suggests that adults learn more effectively when they are actively involved in the learning process.

- **Meaningfulness of the material:** The nature of the learning intervention must be seen to be relevant to the employee's work. Wexley and Latham (1991), for example, suggest that to increase meaningfulness, learners should be provided with an overview of the material to be learned; the material should be presented using examples, concepts and terms familiar to the learner; material is sequenced in a logical manner; and finally, complex intellectual skills are composed of simpler skills and the attainment of these subordinated skills is essential before the complex skills can be acquired.

- **Reinforcement and feedback:** Employees should be given an opportunity to practise what they have learned and be provided with continuous feedback on their performance. This facilitates continuous improvement and employees can engage in setting goals to heighten the learning process. In tandem with this, the learning event must allow employees sufficient time both to absorb the material and practise/test new knowledge and skills. This is perhaps one of the most difficult aspects of learning in an organisation since time to reflect is often very difficult to build into individual jobs, yet unless learners have time and space to think about and reflect on what has been learned and how it can be usefully applied, it is difficult to see how meaningful learning can occur.

A range of other factors can be seen to impact significantly on adults' learning experience, including the individual's age (which can affect attitudes to, motivations for and interests in learning), their level of intelligence and ability (affects preferences for structured versus unstructured learning events), their background and emotional disposition (can result in predetermined perceptions of the value of learning) and as discussed earlier, their learning style and preference.

Finally, let us revisit a key point made in the introduction to this chapter – that learning may not always be perceived in a positive light by the adult learner. For the most part, learning presents personal challenges as well as intellectual ones. Barnett (1999) cautions that learning can be very unsettling, particularly in a work situation where we have to disclose that we have much to learn. He suggests that admitting that we do not know all the answers can impact on our sense of self within the organisation and may well be something that individuals prefer to avoid if at all possible. This has appreciable implications for the learning environment that exists within the organisation and is a topic that is addressed in detail in Chapter 10.

SUMMARY OF KEY PROPOSITIONS

- Learning can be defined as the process through which individuals assimilate new knowledge and skills that results in relatively permanent changes in behaviour. This learning can be conscious or unconscious, formal or informal and requires some element of practice and experience.
- Learning differs from training in that training tends to be more immediate and job related, while learning focuses on behaviour changes that endure over time.
- Single loop learning is used for routine, repetitive issues (action – outcomes – actions), while double loop learning is more complex and requires that the individual question why such behaviour is occurring.
- Behaviourist theories of learning suggest that learning is a function of experience. Classical conditioning refers to reflexive or involuntary learning that is a function of the connection between a stimulus and a response. Operant conditioning focuses on the concept of reinforcement and the consequences of particular behavioural responses to a stimulus.
- Cognitive theories set out to describe an individual as a knowing being and suggest that memory, intuition and perception of the environment all play an important role in explaining how individuals learn.
- Social learning theory suggests that behaviour, and therefore learning, is a function of how individuals perceive each other and that people imitate behaviours that are deemed to result in positive consequences.
- Learning transfer refers to the extent to which skills and abilities acquired during a training session are applied to the actual work situation or to the learning of a new, but related, skill.
- Adult learning is a complex phenomenon that is largely based on experience and reflection. This suggests that effective learning in an organisational context is dependent on a range of variables that allow the learner to be an active participant in learning situations that are perceived as meaningful and valuable and which allow for reflection and practice of new learning.
- An individual's propensity to learn is determined by a range of variables such as age, education, motivation, learning style and learning delivery.

DISCUSSION/SELF-ASSESSMENT QUESTIONS

1. Define learning.
2. Contrast the behavioural and cognitive theories of learning. How have they helped our understanding of human learning?
3. What is learning transfer? How might learning transfer be maximised?
4. How does adult learning differ from more traditional classroom learning?
5. What core features of adult learning should be considered before undertaking some form of learning in an organisation?

MULTIPLE CHOICE QUESTIONS

1. Learning can be defined as:
   (a) A temporary change in behaviour resulting from experience.
   (b) A change in attitude but not behaviour.
   (c) A relatively permanent change in behaviour.
   (d) Best illustrated through physical conditioning.
2. Social learning:
   (a) Is associated with social outings.
   (b) Is based on learning through observation.
   (c) Has replaced the cognitive theories of learning.
   (d) Is only associated with childhood learning.
3. Reinforcement is:
   (a) Based mostly on contrived rewards.
   (b) Associated solely with punishment.
   (c) Mainly associated with cognitive theories.
   (d) Associated with social modelling.
4. Double loop learning:
   (a) Occurs where mismatches are corrected by first examining and altering the underlying systems and then changing the actions.
   (b) Is required for complex, non-programmable issues where a number of variables can be said to influence the learning situation.
   (c) Occurs where interests and understandings move beyond functional and hierarchical boundaries.
   (d) All of the above.
   (e) None of the above.
5. Cognitive theories suggest that learning is about how the environment is perceived by the individual and how individuals interact with that environment. True or false?
6. Operant conditioning is associated with the work of:
   (a) Skinner.
   (b) Kolb.
   (c) Boyatzis.
   (d) Bandura.
   (e) All of the above.

7. Cognitive theories:
   (a) Primarily set out to describe the person as a knowing being.
   (b) Emphasise the significance of the role of experience.
   (c) Focus on the development of meaning.
   (d) Use problem solving and insight as the sources of learning central to the individual.
   (e) All of the above.
   (f) None of the above.
8. Kolb's model of experiential learning (1984) :
   (a) Presents learning as an ongoing cyclical process whereby knowledge is created through the transformation of experience and a reflective process.
   (b) Begins with a highly abstract experience of some kind, which provides a stimulus for observation and reflection.
   (c) Suggests that individuals learn in one specific way, namely abstract conceptualisation.
   (d) All of the above.
   (e) None of the above.
9. From the Learning Styles Inventory, *accommodators* are:
   (a) Learners who have a preference for concrete experiences, but who reflect on these from different perspectives.
   (b) 'Hands-on' learners who have a strong preference for concrete experiences and active experimentation.
   (c) Learners who prefer to swing between reflection and conceptualisation and use inductive reasoning to develop new theory – like concepts and abstract ideas.
   (d) All of the above.
   (e) None of the above.
10. With respect to learning transfer, vertical transfer occurs where one subject area acts as a basis for another. True or false?

FIVE KEY READINGS

Bandura, A., *Social Learning Theory*, New Jersey: Prentice Hall 1977.

Berryman, S., 'Learning for the workplace', *Review of Research in Education*, XIX (1993), 343–404.

Green, R.E. and Shanks, D.R., 'On the existence of independent explicit and implicit learning systems: an examination of some evidence', *Memory and Cognition*, XXI (1993), 304–17.

Mainemelis, C., Boyatzis, R. and Kolb, D., 'Learning styles and adaptive flexibility: testing experiential learning theory', *Management Learning*, XXXIII/1 (2002), 5–33.

Raelin, J., 'A model of work-based learning', *Organisational Science*, VIII/6 (1997), 563–78.

REFERENCES

Argyris, C., *On Organizational Learning*, Cambridge, MA: Blackwell 1992.

Argyris, C. and Schön, D., *Organizational Learning: A Theory-in-Action Perspective*, Reading, MA: Addison-Wesley 1978.

Arment, L., 'Learning and training: a matter of style', *Industrial and Commercial Training*, XXII/3 (1990).

Bandura, A., *Social Foundations of Thought and Action*, Englewood Cliffs, NJ: Prentice Hall 1986.

Barnett, R., 'Learning to work and working to learn', in D. Boud and J. Garrick (eds), *Understanding Learning at Work*, London: Routledge 1999.

Barrow, M. and Loughlin, H., 'Towards a learning organisation: the rationale', *Industrial and Commercial Training*, 24 (1992), 3–7.

Billet, S., 'Guided learning at work', in D. Boyd and J. Garrick (eds), *Understanding Learning At Work*, London: Routledge 1999.

Berryman, S., 'Learning for the workplace', *Review of Research in Education*, XIX (1993), 343–404.

Boud, D. and Garrick, J., *Understanding Learning at Work*, London: Routledge 1999.

Boydell, T.H., *A Guide to the Identification of Training Needs*, 2nd ed., London: British Association for Commercial and Industrial Education 1976.

Brookfield, S., *Understanding and Facilitating Adult Education*, San Francisco: Jossey-Bass 1986.

Buchanan, D. and McCalman, J., *High Performance Work Systems: The Digital Experience*, London: Routledge 1989.

Buckley, R. and Caple, J., *The Theory and Practice of Training*, London: Kogan Page 1990.

Burgoyne, J., 'Management development for the individual and the organisation', *Personnel Management* (June 1988).

Burns, R., *The Adult Learner at Work*, Sydney: Business and Professional Publishing 1995.

Calvert, G., Mobley, S. and Marshall, L., 'Grasping the learning organisation', *Training and Development* (June 1994).

Coutu, D., 'The anxiety of learning', *Harvard Business Review*, LXXX/3 (2002), 100–7.

Daft, R., *Organization Theory and Design*, 5th ed., New York: West Publishing 1995.

DeGeus, A., *The Living Company: Growth, Learning and Longevity in Business*, London: Nicholas Brealey 1997.

DelahoUssaye, M., 'The perfect learner: an expert debate on learning styles', *Training*, XXXIX/5 (2002), 28–35.

Foley, G. (ed.), *Understanding Adult Education and Training*, NSW: Allen & Unwin 1995.

Garavan, T., Costine, P. and Heraty, N., *Training and Development in Ireland: Context, Policy and Practice*, Dublin: Oak Tree Press 1995.

Green, R.E. and Shanks, D.R., 'On the existence of independent explicit and implicit learning systems: an examination of some evidence', *Memory and Cognition*, XXI (1993), 304–17.

Gunnigle, P., Heraty, N. and Morley, M., *Personnel and Human Resource Management: Theory and Practice in Ireland*, Dublin: Gill & Macmillan 1997.

Gunnigle, P., Morley, M., Clifford, N. and Turner, T., *Human Resource Management in Irish Organisations: Practice in Perspective*, Dublin: Oak Tree Press 1997.

Hatch, M.J., *Organization Theory*, New York: Oxford University Press 1997.

Heraty, N. and Morley, M., 'A review of issues in conducting organisation level research with reference to the learning organisation', *The Learning Organisation*, II/4 (1995), 27–36.

Hodgetts, R., Luthans, F. and Lee, S., 'New paradigm organisations: from total quality to learning to world class', *Organisation Dynamics*, XXII/3 (Winter 1994).

Honey, P. and Mumford, A., *Manual of Learning Styles*, London: Peter Honey 1992.

Iles, P., 'Developing learning environments: challenges for theory, research and practice', *Journal of European Industrial Training*, XVIII/3 (1994).

Knowles, M., *The Adult Learner: A Neglected Species*, Houston, TX: Gulf Publishing 1978.

Knowles, M., *Andragogy in Action*, San Francisco: Jossey-Bass 1984.

Kohler, W., *The Mentality of Apes*, New York: Harcourt Brace 1925.

Kolb, D.A., *Experiential Learning – Experience as a Source of Learning and Development*, New Jersey: Prentice Hall 1984.

Latham, G.P. and Crandall, S.R., 'Organisational and social influences affecting training effectiveness', in J.E. Morrison (ed.), *Training for Performance*, Chichester: Wiley 1991.

Law, C., *Helping People Learn*, Cambridge: Industrial Research Unit 1986.

Leavitt, B. and March, J., 'Organisational learning', *Annual Review of Sociology*, XIV (1988), 319–40.

Luthans, F., *Organizational Behaviour*, 5th ed., New York: McGraw-Hill 1992.

March, J.G., 'Exploration and exploitation in organizational learning', *Organizational Science*, II (1991), 71–87.

March, J.G. and Olsen, J.P. (eds), *Ambiguity and Choice in Organizations*, Oslo: Universsttetsforlaget 1976.

Marsick, V. and Watkins, K., 'Envisioning new organisations for learning', in D. Boud and J. Garrick (eds), *Understanding Learning at Work*, London: Routledge 1999.

Matthews, J. and Candy, P., 'New dimensions in the dynamics of learning and knowledge', in D. Boud and J. Garrick (eds), *Understanding Learning at Work*, London: Routledge 1999.

McGeehee, W., 'Are we using what we know about training? – Learning theory and training', *Personnel Psychology* (Spring 1958), 2.

McGill, M., Slocum, J. and Lei, D., 'Management practices in learning organisations', *Organisation Dynamics* (Spring 1992).

Miller, N.E. and Dollard, J.C., *Personality and Psychotherapy*, New York: McGraw-Hill 1950.

Mumford, A., *Management Development Strategies for Action*, London: Kogan Page 1989.

Pedler, M., Boydell, T. and Burgoyne, J., 'Towards the learning company', *Management Education and Development*, XX/1 (1989).

Perry, B., *Enfield: A High Performance System*, Digital Equipment Corporation: Educational Services Development and Publishing 1984.

Piaget, J., *The Origins of Intellegence in Children*, New York: Norton 1963.

Pogson, P. and Tennant, M., 'Understanding adult learners', in G. Foley (ed.), *Understanding Adult Education and Training*, NSW: Allen & Unwin 1995.

Pont, T., *Developing Effective Training Skills*, Maidenhead: McGraw-Hill 1991.

Raelin, J., 'A model of work-based learning', *Organisational Science*, VIII/6 (1997), 563–78.

Reid, M., Barrington, H. and Kenney, T., *Training Interventions*, 2nd ed., London: IMP 1992.

Revans, R., 'Action learning: the skills of diagnosis', *Management Decision*, XXI/2 (1982), 46–52.

Rogers, C., *Freedom to Learn*, Westerville, OH: Merrill 1969.

Rowden, R., 'How attention to employee satisfaction through training and development helps small business maintain a competitive edge: a comparative case study', *Australian Vocational Education Review*, III/2 (1997), 33–41.

Senge, P., *The Fifth Discipline*, New York: Doubleday 1990.

Skinner, B.F., *The Behaviour of Organization*, New York: Appleton-Century-Crosts 1938.

Stata, R., 'Organisational learning – the key to management innovation', *Sloan Management Review*, XXX/3 (Spring 1989).

West, P., 'The learning organisation: losing the luggage in transit?', *Journal of European Industrial Training*, XVIII/11 (1994).

Wexley, K. and Latham, G., *Developing and Training Human Resources in Organizations*, New York: HarperCollins 1991.

EMOTION, STRESS AND WELL-BEING

Learning Objectives

- To establish the importance of emotion in the workplace and the concept of emotional intelligence in organisations.

- To distinguish between different types of emotion and their effects on behaviour at work.

- To introduce the concept of emotional labour.

- To introduce the concept of stress, its definitions, sources and influences at work.

- To highlight self-esteem as an antidote to stress and a protector of well-being.

- To examine the roles that trust, mistrust and paranoia play in organisational settings.

- To outline the experience of 'flow' in work activity and the kinds of characteristics associated with engaged, enjoyable and optimal experience at work.

INTRODUCTION

Life at work can be extremely satisfying and motivating on one hand, but on the other it can be emotionally difficult and stressful. Certainly, working in any type of organisation is not without its complications, uncertainties, frustrations and challenges. Being in paid employment requires interactions that involve dealing with conflict, sorting out problems and reacting to unexpected crises.

Many workplaces involve coping with negative interpersonal dynamics that can sometimes manifest themselves in, for example, extreme forms of bullying and harassment-related behaviour. While it is probably unreasonable to assume that working life will be completely stress free, organisations are increasingly being held to account for the psychological well-being of their employees. Structures, systems and organisational cultures that facilitate unacceptable levels of stress or that do not protect employees from excessively and persistently emotionally intolerable situations require serious critical examination.

In this chapter, we will examine some of the most important factors that can give rise to psychological well-being at work. While you have seen in Chapter 2 that self-esteem is an important personality-related characteristic, this chapter will explore the concept of self-esteem in more detail, highlighting the potential benefits that high self-esteem can bestow upon individuals and on their organisations.

DEFINITIONS OF KEY CONCEPTS

Emotion
A physical and psychological state of arousal that manifests itself in both positive and negative ways at work.

Emotional labour
Having to express emotions we do not feel or suppress emotions we do feel as part of our role responsibilities at work.

Emotional intelligence
The ability to perceive, assimilate, understand and manage our own and others' emotions.

Stress
Is variously defined as:
- a perceived imbalance between demand and response capability, under conditions where failure to meet demand has important consequences;
- a general feeling of tension, anxiety and pressure; and
- a 'fight or flight' response mechanism to a threatening situation.

Self-esteem
Self-esteem (also briefly defined in Chapter 2 as a dimension of personality) is a concept that can help us to understand a range of issues associated with emotional and psychological well-being. Defined as an individual's overall positive evaluation of themselves, researchers have proposed that it is made up of two distinct dimensions: competence (an individual's belief in his or her own ability or efficacy) and worth (an individual's belief in his or her own inherent value as a human being).

Trust
The acceptance of broad mutual expectations between people and the sense of assuredness that these expectations will continue to be met without the need for monitoring, control or other forms of surveillance.

Paranoia
An inflexible tendency to behave in suspicious or untrusting ways towards other people, irrespective of evidence, contexts or outcomes.

Flow
The absence of negative or conflicting emotions when engaged in a task. Flow is characterised by the focused, controlled, unself-conscious engagement in a challenging task that contains clear goals and leads to immediate performance feedback.

EMOTION IN THE WORKPLACE

For many years, the concept of motivation has been a prominent one in organisational behaviour (OB) literature. However, it is only relatively recently that the broader concept of emotion has received critical attention in organisational settings. While human emotional states have always played a central part in the reality of organisational life, until quite recently they tended to have been ignored or dealt with in relatively sketchy ways by researchers and theorists in the field (see Fineman 1993; Watson 2001). While some key texts and research did take place in this area before the 1990s (see Hochschild 1983; Rafaeli and Sutton 1987; Van Maanen and Kunda 1989), it was not until the mid- to late 1990s that specialists in organisational behaviour and management started to express and display a much more active interest in emotions at work.

Fineman (1993) criticises traditional management and OB researchers and theorists for ignoring this important dimension of behaviour in organisations and calls for a much more in-depth treatment of the richness and complexity of people's emotional life at work. He is critical about the fact that instead of addressing real, expressed emotions in workplace situations, theorists talk only in what he refers to as 'emotionally anorexic' terms. Instead of happiness, love, fear, hate and passion, all of which are 'true' emotions experienced by people in real-life organisational settings, Fineman proposes that theorists engage in an unnecessary and misleading sanitisation of these concepts. He argues that they refer instead to such emotionally sterile concepts as 'satisfaction', 'positive or negative affect', 'cognitive dissonance', 'self-actualisation' and 'motivation'. While these are all valid concepts in the field of organisational behaviour, he proposes that simpler, more direct definitions might help us to explore emotion in ways that could significantly enhance our understanding of why people behave in certain ways in organisational settings.

Since that criticism was articulated, work in the area of emotion has developed considerably. Goleman's popular focus on emotional intelligence in the workplace has been met with enthusiastic interest from both organisational practitioners and theorists, and more academic work by such researchers as Ashforth and Humphrey (1995) and Weiss and Cropanzano (1996) has started to set the scene for an increasingly comprehensive understanding of emotions at work. Indeed, it has been striking to witness the explosion of literature focusing explicitly and strongly on emotion along with its sources, effects and outcomes at work. Ashkanasy and Daus (2002: 77) suggest that 'the issue of emotions in the workplace is shaping up as one of the principal areas of development in management thought and practice in the 2000s.'

STOP AND DISCUSS

If emotions are such a central and important part of organisational life, can you suggest some of the main reasons why they were they ignored for so long by organisational theorists and researchers? Why were emotions not considered worthy of explicit attention?

> How do emotions integrate with the classic topics associated with organisational behaviour literature, e.g. personality, group dynamics, leadership, motivation and conflict?

The traditional reluctance to address emotions in organisations from a theoretical perspective probably lies (at least in part) in the vast and incalculable nature of human emotional life. As a result, in the past this realm was left to such professionals and practitioners as counselling psychologists in personal, confidential settings rather than to the more measured work of management theorists or organisational behaviour experts. Despite changes in management and organisational theory, there is still a long history of rationalism, control and focus on logic – a history that has not been easy to do away with or to transform. It is only recently that mechanistic, modernist models of organisational functioning have been augmented by postmodern, multilayer analyses of work situations.

Emotions are difficult to control and calculate, but they are also often difficult to encounter. If you have ever been in a situation where someone in a formal work setting expressed an intense emotion, e.g. anger, sadness, fear, you will already know that this can be a challenging and sometimes paralysing experience. It is the same reluctance that people often experience in the face of emotion at work that may have kept researchers and theorists away from this area for so many years.

In addition, there are ethical issues relating to the privacy of individuals and groups that may have been central to the avoidance of emotions at work in traditional literature. As Watson (2002: 139–40) puts it:

> When … working as researchers, or as thoughtful managers in specific organisational situations, we feel uncomfortable about invading the privacy of the people we come across. We might ask whether we have the right to enquire too deeply into the emotional states and the private feelings of the people we meet in work situations. This would be a proper ethical question to ask. Yet if we want to understand the full complexities of organising and managing work, we need to attend to matters of feeling and emotion in the workplace.

Despite the traditional reluctance of researchers and practitioners to explore emotions in direct and explicit ways, hints and clues about the centrality of emotion in organisations have actually existed for a long time in the literature. The concepts of inspirational or 'transformational' leadership (see Chapter 12) highlight the important skills required by leaders in harnessing the emotions of their followers. The quest to fulfil basic and higher-order needs in motivational theory recognises that, for example, the need for love plays a central part in people's lives (although interestingly, the original term 'love needs' in Maslow's hierarchy of needs model tended to be replaced by the more sterile term 'esteem needs', reflecting Fineman's (1993) criticism of the OB literature in general). Stress and stress management are areas that have received enormous attention in the literature, and the links between emotion and stress, while not always explicit, are intuitively clear.

Managing conflict, interacting in groups, communicating well – all these themes resonate with ideas about people's emotional lives. It is little wonder that emotion is now being treated as a central concept in organisational behaviour research, despite the tendency in the past to make only indirect or hazy reference to it.

While the exploration of emotion as a topic in management and OB has been a recent phenomenon, psychological theory and research have tackled different types of emotion for many years, and it is from this discipline that we derive many of the definitions and conceptualisations.

EXPLORING EMOTION

The word 'emotion' is derived from the verb 'to move'. Our bodies become aroused during emotional episodes and change from a steady baseline state to a much more stimulated condition. Emotions motivate us to act. Plutchik (1980) demonstrates that emotion is linked to our basic human adaptive behaviours that in different situations cause us either to attack others or defend ourselves, help others, seek out comfort and safety and survive. While human emotions can be disruptive and damaging in certain situations, it is worth remembering that their main function is as an aid to survival. If we did not experience fear in the face of danger, we would be less likely to react and cope with threats that might compromise our safety.

Much of the literature on emotion in organisations focuses on the idea that the 'emotional mind' is much faster at reacting to events or experiences than the 'rational mind'. The way our brains work determines that what we do and how we think is driven by the emotions that we experience, which influence our thinking both quickly and powerfully. As soon as we encounter significant events in our environment, our emotional minds snap into action much faster than the rational, analytical, reflective part of our brain (Ekman 1992). It is always worth remembering that people have emotional reactions before they have rational ones. Thus, the emotion literature argues that it is how we feel that influences what we think, not the other way around. Managers who are aware of and sensitive to people's emotionality will be able to interact with people more successfully than those who adopt a purely rational model.

Emotions in workplace settings can be used in pragmatic ways to yield higher levels of performance. Many effective leaders have actively worked to inspire emotion among their followers to develop such reactions as loyalty, devotion and trust. Passion, commitment, motivation and concentration all derive from emotional states and can result in outstanding organisational performance. Later in this chapter we will see how the psychology of optimal experience and performance mainly derives from the harnessing of our emotions in positive ways in order to produce exceptional results.

TYPES OF EMOTION

How many emotions are there? Is there a hierarchy of emotions? In 1980, Robert Plutchik attempted to answer these questions and his research yielded a proposition that there are eight basic or primary emotions, which when combined in various ways lead to a further eight more complex or 'mixed' emotions. Table 5.1 outlines his proposition that there is a group of both basic and complex emotions, with complex emotions being the result of a combination of pairs of basic emotions.

Table 5.1 Plutchik's Model of Primary and Mixed Emotions

Primary emotions	Anger
	Disgust
	Sadness
	Surprise
	Fear
	Acceptance
	Joy
	Anticipation
Complex (mixed) emotions	Contempt (anger and disgust)
	Remorse (disgust and sadness)
	Disappointment (sadness and surprise)
	Awe (surprise and fear)
	Submission (fear and acceptance)
	Love (joy and acceptance)
	Optimism (joy and anticipation)
	Aggression (anticipation and anger)

Source: Adapted from Coon (1991)

STOP AND DISCUSS

Critically consider the propositions contained in Table 5.1. Do you think it is possible to generate an accurate model of emotion that identifies such basic and complex emotions as those outlined above? What important emotions does Plutchik's model omit? (Jealousy? Enjoyment? Shame?) Generate your own list of emotions based on your work/life experiences and explore how such emotions may have shaped or influenced your behaviour in particular situations.

Can we feel more than one or two emotions at the same time?

Try to identify combinations other than those identified by Plutchik. What effects are different emotions likely to have in organisational settings?

Can you think of any real-life examples of either positive or negative emotional effects at work?

EMOTIONAL LABOUR

Not only does work give rise to a range of possible emotions, it also constrains the expression of those emotions in ways that can lead to negative outcomes for individuals and their organisations. Emotional labour refers to employment-related requirements that force individuals to express emotions they do not feel, e.g. happiness and cheerfulness in service settings, or to suppress emotions that they do feel, e.g. anger or dislike towards colleagues, customers or bosses. Of course, it is important in any social situation to be able to control our emotions, but it has been argued that the kinds of emotional control that are expected of people in some work situations can be extremely restrictive and can cause them to feel that their personal integrity has been somehow compromised.

The first studies that addressed emotion in the workplace tended to focus on this idea of emotional labour at work. Hochschild (1983) described the difficult dynamics associated with containing or expressing certain emotions at work on a continuous basis. Through detailed analyses of the behaviour of different workers, Hochschild examined the strategies that individuals use to cope with highly emotionally charged situations.

EMOTIONAL INTELLIGENCE

Emotional intelligence was first defined by Salovey and Mayer (1990) and can be seen as the capacity to notice and handle emotional signals and information in one's environment. Emotional intelligence is an important and established concept in organisational theory and practice today. Goleman (1996) shows how emotional intelligence includes self-awareness, impulse control, persistence, motivation, empathy and social skill. It has been claimed that even more than conventional notions of intelligence as measured by IQ (intelligence quotient) tests, emotional intelligence is what differentiates people both in the workplace and in life. According to Goleman, people who are emotionally intelligent are more likely to live happy, productive and successful lives in comparison with people who lack emotional intelligence.

A recent model of emotional intelligence (Salovey and Mayer 1990) incorporates four key factors: emotion perception, emotion assimilation, emotion understanding and emotion management.

Emotion Perception

Emotionally intelligent people are sensitive to emotional information in their environment and are able to pick up even subtle changes in someone's behaviour that indicate a change in emotional state. Vigilance about how people are feeling allows us to recognise emotional information more readily, which is a primary ingredient of emotional intelligence – we cannot be emotionally intelligent unless we are emotionally perceptive. The perception of emotion provides an important foundation upon which emotional intelligence is exercised.

Emotion Assimilation

Emotionally intelligent people are able to assimilate the emotional information that they perceive into coherent, ordered patterns. Being able to assimilate emotion requires the capacity to differentiate between different types of emotion, both in ourselves and in others. Assimilation allows us to look at the emotions that we perceive and to sort, prioritise and explain their existence in different contexts. Assimilation of emotion requires 'walking around' the emotional experience in order to analyse and gain insight into different perspectives on the emotional experience. Seeing emotion from the perspective of different people, focusing on the negative and positive aspects of an emotional state and identifying underlying causes of emotional signals are all part of the ability to assimilate effectively (Jordan *et al*. 2002).

Emotion Understanding

Being able to perceive and assimilate emotions are preconditions for emotion understanding (Salovey and Mayer 1990). Emotion understanding refers to the ability to gain insights into 'emotional dissonance', i.e. feeling two conflicting emotions at the same time, and to adopt a positive perspective on emotional transitions, such as those associated with grief and loss. Understanding that there may be a progression and transition of different emotions in response to an external event sets the scene for effective emotional management, which is an essential dimension of emotional intelligence.

Emotion Management

Managing our emotions does not mean repressing them in the ways suggested by the emotional labour literature outlined earlier. Rather, it requires that we regulate and moderate the expression of emotion in order to maximise our ability to achieve positive outcomes for ourselves and others in organisational settings. Research demonstrates that open expressions of emotions such as anger in organisations can create negative work outcomes and damage relationships in both the short and the long term (Fitness 2000). The ability to disconnect from emotions in certain contexts, without ignoring or failing to tackle the causes that led to them, is a central dimension of emotion management. Conversely, good emotion managers can also harness and express emotion at important times in order to achieve positive results. As Jordan *et al*. (2002: 366) state, 'connecting with one's feelings of anger … may be useful if this feeling provides motivation.'

PAYING ATTENTION TO EMOTION AT WORK

The research and reflection that have recently taken place in the field of organisational behaviour suggest that if we ignore emotions, we do so at our peril. In the words of Goleman (1996: 163):

> [The future of] all corporate life [will be one in which] the basic skills of emotional intelligence will be ever more important, in teamwork, in co-operation, in helping people learn together how to work more effectively. As knowledge based services and intellectual capital become more central to corporations, improving the way people work together will be a major way to leverage intellectual capital, making a critical competitive difference. To thrive if not survive, corporations would do well to boost their collective emotional intelligence.

STRESS AT WORK

Unlike the concept of emotion, stress at work has appeared in management and OB research for many years. Of course, the emotional dimension of stress may seem obvious, but some of the more conventional definitions emerging from the 1960s and 1970s often tended to adopt a cognitive (thinking-related) rather than an emotional (feeling-related) orientation towards the experience of stress.

Stress in the workplace may not always be damaging, but it does have the potential to inflict damage on the individual and create negative results for the organisation. The following are three definitions of stress.

- A perceived imbalance between demand and response capacity, under conditions where failure to meet demand has important consequences (McGrath 1976).
- A general feeling of pressure, anxiety and tension.
- A fight or flight capacity to any threatening situation.

These different definitions each tell us something important about stress and what it means. First, people who experience stress at work often report that it arises due to a feeling that they won't be able to meet their goals or carry out the tasks that are required of them. If people feel that their future work lives will be affected by their current inability to carry out a task, the experience of stress is likely to arise. There are many reasons why people may feel unable to carry out the tasks required of them at work. Being overloaded with work, being unsure about appropriate steps to take, not having enough information or feeling that skills and abilities are inadequate for the tasks at hand are all possible reasons why someone might feel that there is an imbalance between the demands being made upon them and their capacity to respond effectively to those demands.

Almost everyone is familiar with the 'general feeling of pressure, anxiety and tension' that accompanies stress. Excessive levels of stress give rise to unpleasant or uncomfortable experiences. When people experience stress they are generally motivated to decrease the levels that they feel or to eliminate the source of the stress.

Stress can also be defined as a fight or flight response capacity to a threatening situation. As identified earlier, emotions exist in order to help us to survive. As an emotionally laden experience, stress causes us to react to real or perceived threats in our environment. In the face of threat, our bodies become ready for fight or flight – heart rate increases, blood pumps around the body faster than usual, palms start to sweat and adrenalin is released into the system. This creates extra energy in individuals, which can help them to concentrate and focus on the problem they are facing or the threat that is challenging them. On the other hand, oftentimes the energy that is created cannot be released fully in normal work situations. This extra energy can create the feeling of tension referred to above.

SOURCES OF WORK STRESS

How do people become excessively stressed at work? Cooper *et al.* (1988) provide a useful framework for identifying various sources of pressure at work, showing that there is a variety of potential causes of stress to which individuals may be vulnerable at different times in their working lives (Table 5.2).

Table 5.2 Sources of Work Stress

- Workload.
- Job conditions.
- Role conflict and ambiguity.
- Career development.
- Interpersonal relationships in the organisation.
- Conflict between demands at work and demands outside work.

Source: Cooper *et al.* (1988)

The different sources of stress show how diverse the experience of stress may be, depending on situations and settings. While one person may be stressed because of the clashing demands between their home and work responsibilities, someone else may be stressed because of a bad relationship with their boss. Moderate levels of stress may actually help people to perform, but as stress levels increase (perhaps as a result of an increase in the number of different sources of work stress) people's well-being and performance become significantly more likely to suffer. As well as the potential problems associated with poor work performance, organisations have a moral and legal responsibility to ensure that individuals are not exposed to levels of stress that may have an adverse effect on their health.

RESPONDING TO STRESS

People can respond to stress in various ways. Eysenck (1996) shows how different types of responses can be categorised into different coping classifications (Table 5.3).

Table 5.3 Stress Coping Classifications

Task-focused coping
- Establish priorities.
- Come to terms with the nature and parameters of the problem.
- Spend time thinking about the stressful event and work out strategies for coping with similar future events.

Emotional coping
- Vent frustrations by expressing anger, irritation or anxiety.
- Blame oneself for being too emotional about the situation.
- Re-enact a stressful situation in an emotionally expressive way.

Avoidance coping
- Put the problem out of one's mind.
- Take time away from the source of the stress.
- Engage in behaviour that temporarily relieves the symptoms of stress, e.g. drinking, smoking or eating.

Source: Eysenck (1996)

Some coping mechanisms are effective in that they help people to overcome or deal with stresss in a positive way. Others are less effective in that they may not remove the source of stress or may cause the individual to create more harmful situations for themselves, e.g. excesssive drinking in order to avoid stressful situations.

In the quest for high levels of motivation at work, managers should be mindful that pressures to perform and achieve can create high stress levels, which may be damaging to both the individual and their organisation.

ONGOING DEBATES/ADVANCED CONCEPTS IN STRESS AND WELL-BEING

This section explores several key concepts that are linked to emotion, stress and psychological well-being at work, namely self-esteem, trust, mistrust, paranoia and flow in organisations. Recent research and evidence have identified that these factors add to our understanding of organisations' emotional life. This section also outlines the current ideas and organisational implications associated with these concepts.

SELF-ESTEEM: A RESERVOIR THAT NOURISHES PSYCHOLOGICAL WELL-BEING

Self-esteem has been defined and explored in Chapter 2 as an important dimension of personality. It is treated again here as a source of emotional health in organisations, where it can be conceptualised as a sort of psychological reservoir that feeds our sense of well-being (Cast and Burke 2002). The reservoir gets built up when individuals 'verify' their sense of themselves by interacting with other people. The reservoir gets depleted when there is a lack of self-verification in group settings.

Self-esteem is best understood as an important part of the basic human process of establishing our identity and of constructing a coherent self-image that allows us to function within our environments. Gecas (1982) proposed that self-esteem is made up of two separate dimensions: competence and worth. The competence-based dimension of self-esteem relates to an individual's perception that they are capable of having a meaningful and effective impact on their environment. Competence-based self-esteem (or 'efficacy-based' self-esteem) at work relates to the extent to which people believe that they are able to carry out the activities and deliver on the responsibilities associated with their jobs. The more we feel capable and competent at our jobs, the higher the levels of efficacy-based self-esteem we can be said to have. The worth-based dimension of self-esteem relates to the overall sense that people feel they are of intrinsic value, a sense that is independent of their beliefs about their own competence or efficacy. This is arguably a more important dimension of self-esteem. To believe that we are people of value and worth is fundamental to our psychological health. If we believe this, regardless of our perceptions of what we can or cannot do, then we are more likely to be buffered from psychological damage in the workplace, even at times when we are not sure about our abilities to engage in certain activities or to achieve certain outcomes.

Evidence shows that childhood experiences carry more weight in the building of our self-esteem than those we encounter later in our lives (Erikson 1963; Connolly et al. 1988).

Receiving love and endorsement from other people is usually the way in which we bolster our self-esteem, and since our sense of ourselves is 'constructed' during childhood, the messages that we get as children from other people about how valued and important we are have a more powerful impact on our sense of ourselves. Like many psychologists, Rogers (1961) proposes that self-esteem is most likely to have been built and generated during people's childhood, but unlike some of his predecessors he believes that self-esteem can also be enhanced all the way though our lives. In any case, people's levels of self-esteem have an important impact on behaviour at work. Generally speaking, if we don't feel positive about our efficacy and worth at work, we are likely to behave in ways that may be qualitatively different from those that do.

Self-esteem has been identified as an important moderator of a range of organisational experiences, including job insecurity (Jordan *et al.* 2002), the receipt of performance feedback (Moore and Kuol 2003), work commitment (Krecker 1994) and job-related tension (Arnold *et al.* 1991). Taking performance feedback as an example, levels of self-esteem can fundamentally affect the ways in which people react to positive and negative feedback at work. Giving feedback to individuals and groups with a view to enhancing performance is arguably one of the most interpersonally challenging tasks for managers, supervisors or consultants in organisational settings. Someone with high levels of self-esteem is likely to react quite differently to positive or negative performance feedback than someone with lower levels of self-esteem. If negative feedback is given to someone who already has no sense of competence or self-worth, particularly if that feedback is delivered in an unconstructive way, the results are more likely to have discouraging and even devastating effects. Someone with a strong sense of competence and self-worth, however, has a psychological buffer which protects them from being dismayed or overwhelmed by such negative feedback.

In general, strong and positive self-esteem represents a fundamental source of psychological well-being. Self-esteem is established in childhood, but can be positively or negatively affected all through our lives, depending on the types of experiences we encounter and the ways in which we receive verification from others, particularly those with whom we have significant personal or working relationships. It is clear from this analysis, then, that organisations should pay attention to important ways in which their employees' self-esteem can be boosted and protected.

TRUST AND PARANOIA IN ORGANISATIONS

The importance of trust is not only central to emotional well-being, it also plays an essential role in developing effective relationships between people at work – relationships that are likely to lead to a whole range of positive work outcomes (for example, see Fox 1974; Barber 1983; Zucker 1986). Like the concept of emotion, trust has received increasing attention in organisational research and we have witnessed the escalation of research papers and reflections in the literature that demonstrate the extent to which it is a concept that is currently seen as worthy of scrutiny (for example, see Mayer *et al.* 1995). It has been argued that in dynamic social systems such as those that prevail in organisations, trust may represent one of the most important preconditions for increasing a wide range of significant work-based benefits. Trust can be seen as a vital resource within organisations in so far as it represents one of the emotionally based dynamics that allows people to proceed with their working lives on the basis of reasonable assumptions about other people. This satisfies our need to reduce uncertainty and complexity within organisational environments (Albrow 1997). Watson (2002: 431), for example, defines high-trust relations as being represented by 'a situation in which each party to a relationship feels able to take it for granted that broad mutual expectations established between them will be met and continue to be met without the need closely to specify those expectations or to monitor their fulfillment.'

The literature suggests, then, that within any organisation, when levels of trust are high it is likely that desirable work outcomes will result. Instead of a lazy complacency, trust seems to engender 'self-fulfilling prophecies' or positive assumptions that by their very nature give rise to positive responses from others. When people are trusted to do their best, to act in good faith and to deliver on their responsibilities (in the same way as McGregor's Theory Y assumptions, outlined in Chapter 3, would predict), it seems more likely that people will respond in positive ways. Thus, it could be said that the existence and persistence of trust tends to endorse its causes in ways that can be self-sustaining. The evidence that high-trust groups create high-performance environments suggests that fostering and maintaining trust may represent an important source of competitive advantage for organisations that has a concrete effect on organisational outcomes.

Then why has the literature also found that trust can be so elusive, fragile and difficult to maintain (e.g. Gambetta 1988; Slovic 1993)? Kramer (2002) identifies that much mistrust emerges from states of uncertainty in organisations and that since organisational uncertainty is almost inevitable, especially as organisations become larger and more complex, then mistrust is an almost inevitable part of many organisational settings. Defined as an 'absence of confidence in the other, a concern that the other may act so as to harm one, that he does not care about one's welfare, intends to act harmfully or is hostile' (Govier 1993: 240), mistrust can be either rational or irrational. It should be pointed out that rational distrust is a functional response to untrustworthy situations and that engendering trust at all costs is not in the interest of individuals or groups at work. As Grove (1996) has suggested, mistrusting people in one's environment may be more likely to help one to survive and navigate the political terrain of organisational life.

Preconditions for Paranoia at Work

Paranoia has been defined as non-rational mistrust. Deutsch (1958: 171) has defined this as an 'inflexible, rigid, unaltering tendency to act in a ... suspicious manner, irrespective of the situation or the consequences of so acting.' Organisational paranoia may emerge when rational mistrust developed in one setting is applied to new settings, even when mistrust is neither warranted or productive. Kramer (2002) proposes that certain organisational preconditions foster paranoia. Broadly, these conditions are:

- organisations in which less information is transmitted to fewer people;

- organisations defined by hierarchical structures with high power distance;
- organisations where social distinctiveness exists, i.e. those in which certain people may feel socially distinctive by virtue of their gender, age, race, socio-economic background, etc.;
- organisations in which tenure status is typically low; and
- organisations which employ methodologies to subject employees to surveillance and monitoring.

While rational mistrust is an adaptive orientation towards untrustworthy situations, non-rational mistrust or paranoia, facilitated by the organisational conditions outlined above, are dysfunctional ways of making sense of work environments and are likely to have negative impacts not just on organisational productivity and performance, but also on people's basic psychological well-being. In the words of Kramer (2002: 24), 'paranoid social cognition can be viewed as a sensemaking process gone seriously awry.'

FLOW

If organisational paranoia is at one end of the spectrum of psychological well-being, the concept of flow is at the other. 'Flow' is a term originally coined by Csikszentmihalyi (1990) that relates to the psychology of optimal experience. It is seen as a psychological state that can significantly enhance quality of life, both within and beyond the workplace. Organisational theorists have become interested in the concept of flow because of the range of positive work outcomes with which it has been associated, including creativity, motivation, persistence, curiosity and productivity. It is argued that an organisation's psychological health can be defined by the extent to which the work involves opportunities to enter the state of flow.

What is flow and why has it recently been identified as one of the ways in which we can understand important aspects of psychologically healthy work? Essentially, flow refers to the absence of negative or conflicting emotions when engaged in a task. It represents the focused deployment of emotions in order to learn and perform. It is a state of self-forgetfulness where we find ourselves completely 'in the moment'. It has been referred to as 'pure motivation', where one's complete absorption in a task allows us to bring all of our skills, abilities and attention to its successful completion. Everyone has experienced flow at some stage in their lives. It may be the case that certain types of work and tasks may be intrinsically motivating because of the opportunities they provide us to enter a flow-like state. Csikszentmihalyi (1990) proposes that flow can be described as having several essential elements, which can help to explain why it is an intrinsically enjoyable and psychologically healthy experience.

The Characteristics of Flow

Flow exists in that sometimes elusive zone between boredom on the one hand and anxiety on the other. We cannot enter the focused state of flow if we are in a state of boredom. Because flow requires energy, focus and commitment, being bored or understimulated is not a precursor for engaging in flow-like activity. On the other hand, if we are overstimulated and anxious, confidence, which is an essential feature of flow, is also likely to diminish. In order to facilitate flow, activities must do the following.

- **Involve challenge and skill.** Flow can be described as a state in which an individual uses his or her skills and talents to the best of their abilities in order to achieve a particular task or outcome. A sense of challenge is often enhanced when competition is introduced or when there is some sense that one is testing their skills in a way that will provide them with an assessment of how such skills compare to those of others. Most trainers or teachers can vouch for the enhanced levels of enjoyment that often arise when they introduce 'safe' competition into learning activities.

- **Involve the fusion of action and awareness, or 'total focus'.** Flow can be described as a state of engagement that is so absorbing it prevents us from getting distracted by periphery anxieties, niggling doubts or off-putting thoughts. Work tends to be stressful when it causes people to be pulled in all directions, when people are engaging in one task but thinking about another or when they can't fully focus on the things that we are being asked to do. Flow is the opposite of that distracted state and arises when external worries disappear and our awareness merges completely with the task that we are focusing on.

- **Contain clear goals and feedback.** Flow can be described as associated with activities that allow us to see clearly what it is that we are aiming for and to have inbuilt indicators that tell us when we have reached our goal. The intrinsic satisfaction that comes with performance feedback builds not only our levels of motivation (see the theories of motivation outlined in Chapter 6), but also provides the type of verification that people require in order to nourish their sense of competence and self-esteem.

- **Include a perception of control.** Flow is also associated with an individual sense that they are in control of their environment. It has long been held that a sense of control over our environment (e.g. Rotter 1966) is likely to give rise to a range of positive states of mind. When someone is in a state of flow they do not experience the sense of helplessness or lack of control that is often associated with stressful work. In the words of Csikszentmihalyi (1990: 59), 'the flow experience is typically described as involving a sense of control – or, more precisely, as lacking the sense of worry about losing control that is typical in many situations of normal life.'

- **Eliminate self-consciousness and time consciousness.** Linked to the other characteristics outlined above, people in a state of flow are not conscious about how they appear to other people. It is not the loss of the self that occurs here, because consciousness and independent action are required, but rather a loss of any worry about how others perceive our activities. Similarly, the loss of any normal sense of time is characteristic of flow. Think back to the last experience you had that caused you to lose track of time. Perhaps this experience will give you some clue about what kind of work or activity might help you to enter the elusive state of flow.

Note that just as mistrust is not always a bad thing in organisational settings, flow is not always an entirely positive state. There are risks associated with becoming addicted to the experience of flow, which arguably manifest themselves in different forms of workaholism

(Burke 2000). Some forms of workaholism may represent an excessive or uncontrolled compulsion to engage in flow at the expense of other dimensions of one's life.

SUMMARY OF KEY PROPOSITIONS

- This chapter has focused on key aspects of emotion, stress and psychological well-being at work. It has shown how the concept of emotion, while traditionally ignored in organisational and management theory, is now receiving increasing attention.
- It has explored the concepts of emotional intelligence and emotional labour and their effects on both organisational performance and individual well-being.
- The chapter also highlighted the more established concept of stress as an important experience to understand in the workplace. There are many sources of stress and people can make attempts to cope with stress through task orientation, emotional expression or avoidance.
- Finally, in the advanced concepts section of this chapter, emerging ideas that are gaining a foothold both in theory and in practice were explored, including the recent reinforcement in the literature of the importance of the established concept of self-esteem as a protector of psychological well-being at work; the role of trust and mistrust along with the organisational conditions that foster paranoia among individuals and groups; and the concept of flow as an important (but not entirely risk free) source of high-quality work.
- Keep in mind that the principles of emotion, stress and psychological well-being incorporate important managerial responsibilities. By focusing on the evidence associated with key research relating to these concepts, it is possible for management theory and practice to become more focused on insightful, ethical and enlightened orientations towards people and their experiences at work.

DISCUSSION/SELF-ASSESSMENT QUESTIONS

Read the following article and explore the questions that follow.

Bricklayer who became a folk hero by blowing the whistle on sleaze

No one ever said James Gogarty was easy to get on with. He was a stern father, a tough boss, a cranky pensioner. He fought with picket lines, threw fits of rage, drove hard bargains. Having grown up the hard way, he demanded the same high standards as he imposed on himself. As an employer and company 'fixer' he brooked no opposition and was prepared to cut corners. As an old colleague from the building industry once said of him: 'Talk to Gogarty? You might as well talk to a jackass.' Gogarty was also, by his own admission, mired in corruption. He went to Ray Burke's house in June 1989, knowing that the politician was to receive a payoff designed to secure the rezoning of lands owned by Gogarty's company, JMSE. All of which makes the 85-year-old an unlikely hero this weekend after the publication of Mr Justice Flood's report. But hero he is. He blew the whistle, and the whole edifice of lies came tumbling down. Would there were more of his ilk. But it didn't come about easily or prettily. Gogarty's initial motivation was revenge. He was angry at JMSE and its millionaire owner, Joseph Murphy senior, for failing to reward his loyalty with a decent pension. When he started spilling the beans, he told everyone the long saga about the pension and threw in the encounter in Burke's house as an afterthought. At first, no one wanted to know. He brought his grievances to the attention of Nora Owen, Michael McDowell and other politicians, but nothing happened. Prominent journalists walked away from the story of the decade, because they couldn't see the story behind the story. It took a £10,000 reward offered by two anti-corruption campaigners to get things going – not that Gogarty was interested in the money. His allegations started appearing in Sunday newspapers and the process that culminated in this week's report got underway. Having decided to tell all, Gogarty stuck to his story through thick and thin. At times, it was one frail pensioner versus the rest – lawyers, spin doctors, the political establishment, JMSE and some of the media. His early relations with the Flood tribunal were turbulent, with Gogarty threatening to withdraw his co-operation. However, a personal meeting between the septuagenarian judge and the octogenarian whistleblower established a basis of trust and Gogarty became the tribunal's 'star' witness. Those first weeks of his evidence in 1999 were dramatic days. Gogarty caught the mood of the nation with his shocking tales of corruption, his David and Goliath struggles against the establishment and his railings against the legal profession.

Hundreds came to see him in action and cheer him on in his battles. Nightly re-enactments of the evidence on Vincent Browne's radio show made him a household name. By the time he completed his evidence, his departure was greeted with matinee idol-style adulation.

Since then he has disappeared into relative obscurity in North Dublin whence he came. This weekend, Gogarty is said to be 'quietly pleased' about Mr Justice Flood's verdict. He has had countless requests for interviews and photographs but doesn't wish to enter the limelight. The relief is even greater for his wife Anna, for whom the ordeal of the past decade can now finally be consigned to the past.

Gogarty was one of the old school – thrifty, hardworking and tough. Born in Kells in 1917, he left school after the inter cert to work as a bricklayer. He served in the reserve Gardaí while attending night school and emerged with a degree 17 years after starting.

It was in 1968 that Gogarty's career took its final, fateful turn. He went to work for Joseph Murphy senior, who ran his operations from off-shore tax havens. Gogarty managed his Irish interests, which included JMSE, a huge land bank of industrial land in north Dublin and the Gaiety Theatre.

He was the epitome of the loyal company executive; in one letter he even [referred to himself as] 'your loyal servant'. He took sandwiches to work rather than spend unnecessarily at the company's expense. In his late 60s, he spent several years working on Murphy's behalf in the UK, living in hotels and seeing Anna and his six children only at weekends.

He ran the Irish end of Murphy's empire with an iron hand. When a strike broke out at Moneypoint, in Co. Clare where JMSE had a €13 million contract to build an electricity generating station, there were allegations of intimidation. Gogarty also presided over the slow decay of Turvey House, a fine old north Dublin period house that lay on lands owned by Murphy, which were earmarked for building development.

Whatever Murphy wanted, Gogarty did his bidding. It was no different in 1989, Mr Justice Flood has now decided, when JMSE and the developer Michael Bailey decided to do a deal on the north Dublin lands and the money was paid to Ray Burke.

In the 1990s, it all went sour between Gogarty and his boss. Gogarty pressed for his pension and even corralled some money which was due to JMSE as a bargaining chip. He took legal action against the company and won. In 1994, Murphy's son rang him late one night, delivered a tirade of abuse threatening to 'break every bone in your fucking body'. Out of this bitter dispute came the nugget of information which culminated in this week's report. We still don't know the whole truth about who gave how much to Ray Burke and, most important of all, why. By now, we'll probably never know.

But as Gogarty himself memorably said: 'The answer is out there, it's flowing in the wind.'

Source: Paul Cullen, *The Irish Times*, 28 September 2002

1. Discuss the role that emotion played in the events outlined in the above case. Can you identify or list a range of different emotions appearing in this story? What important insights can be gained by engaging in an emotional analysis of relationships and dynamics at work?

2. Try to identify two different instances in your own work or life, one in which mistrusting someone led to positive results for you and one in which mistrusting someone gave rise to negative results. What were the differences between these events? How (if at all) were the negative outcomes addressed or resolved? How do the differences between these events help to differentiate between functional mistrust and paranoia?

3. Develop a written strategy for diagnosing and addressing levels of organisational trust, mistrust and paranoia within an organisation that you are familiar with.

4. Earlier in this chapter you read that 'organisations should pay attention to important ways in which the self-esteem of their employees can be boosted and protected.' Suggest what organisational interventions might enhance and maintain self-esteem among individuals and groups. Refer to literature on motivation, group dynamics and areas dealt with in other chapters of this textbook. Refer as well to Goleman's (1996) suggestions for the provision of emotionally intelligent performance feedback (see 'The Artful Critique' in *Emotional Intelligence*, London: Bloomsbury 1996, 153).

5. Workaholism was mentioned briefly at the end of this chapter as a way of moderating the evangelical pursuit of 'flow' in organisations. To find out more about the concept of workaholism, have a look at the following key reading: Burke, R.J., 'Workaholism in organisations: concepts, results and future research directions, *International Journal of Management Reviews*, II/1 (2000), 1–16. On reading this, critically analyse the concept of flow and consider the possibility that states of flow in organisational settings may lead to a range of negative work outcomes.

MULTIPLE CHOICE QUESTIONS

1. The concept of emotion in organisations did not receive much attention from traditional organisational behaviour theorists because:
    (a) Emotion was not an important concept to understand.
    (b) An exploration of emotions was banned before the 1990s.
    (c) Emotions may have been seen as vast, incalculable, unanalysable and ethically inappropriate domains of inquiry.
2. 'Emotion' derives from the word 'to move'. True or false?
3. The emotional part of our mind is much slower at reacting to events or experiences than the rational part of our mind. True or false?
4. Emotional labour can be defined as:
    (a) Working in situations that are generally difficult or challenging.
    (b) Engaging in work that requires us either to display emotions we do not experience or to suppress emotions that we do experience.
    (c) Working in situations where other people display high levels of emotion.
5. Indicate which of the following four statements is untrue.
    (a) Self-esteem can be conceptualised as an important source of emotional health.
    (b) Self-esteem has not been linked to any positive outcomes for individuals or their organisations.
    (c) Self-esteem has been found to be an important moderator of a range of organisational experiences, including perceptions of job insecurity and performance feedback.
    (d) Low self-esteem has been found to have negative effects on people's perceptions of themselves.
6. Which of the following statements is true?
    (a) Trust in organisations has no effect on organisational behaviour or performance.
    (b) Trust in organisations could damage group morale by giving rise to false assumptions.
    (c) Trust can be elusive, fragile and difficult to maintain in organisations.
7. Emotional intelligence refers to:
    (a) The number of emotions we are capable of feeling.
    (b) The range of emotions we display.
    (c) The capacity to notice and handle emotional signals in one's environment.
    (d) The ability to exploit the emotional states of others.

8. The competence-based dimension of self-esteem relates to:
   (a) Other people's views of our overall levels of intelligence.
   (b) Our own perceptions that we are capable of having a meaningful impact on our environment.
   (c) Others' perceptions of our ability to impact our environment.
   (d) None of the above.
9. When rational mistrust developed in one setting is applied to new settings, even when mistrust is neither warranted nor productive, organisational theorists refer to this as:
   (a) Attitude problems.
   (b) Personality issues.
   (c) Organisational paranoia.
10. 'Flow' is characterised by:
    (a) Stressful work conditions.
    (b) Difficult work conditions.
    (c) Work conditions in which there is an absence of negative emotion.
11. The experience of flow contains elements of boredom and anxiety. True or false?

FIVE SUGGESTED KEY READINGS

Ashkanasy, N.M. and Daus, C., 'Emotion in the workplace: the new challenge for managers', *Academy of Management Executive*, XV/1 (2002), 76–86.

Burke, R.J., 'Workaholism in organisations: concepts, results and future research directions', *International Journal of Management Reviews*, II/1 (2000), 1–16.

Fitness, J., 'Anger in the workplace: an emotion script approach to anger episodes between workers and their superiors, co-workers and subordinates', *Journal of Organisational Behaviour*, 21 (2000), 147–62.

Goleman, D., *Emotional Intelligence: Why It Can Matter More than IQ*, London: Bloomsbury 1996.

Van Maanen, J. and Kunda, G., 'Real feelings: emotional expression and organisational culture', *Research in Organisational Behaviour*, 11 (1989), 43–103.

REFERENCES

Albrow, M., *Do Organisations Have Feelings?*, London: Routledge 1997.

Arnold, J., Robertson, I.T. and Cooper, C.L., *Work Psychology*, London: Pitman 1991.

Ashforth, B.E. and Humphrey, R.H., 'Emotion in the workplace: a reappraisal', *Human Relations*, XLVIII (1995), 97–125.

Ashkanasy, N.M., 'Studies in cognition and emotion in organisations: attribution, affective events, emotional intelligence and perception of emotion', *Australian Journal of Management*, XXVII (2002), 11–20.

Ashkanasy, N.M. and Daus, C., 'Emotion in the workplace: the new challenge for managers', *Academy of Management Executives*, XV/1 (2002), 76–86.

Barber, B., *The Logic and Limits of Trust*, New Brunswick, NJ: Rutgers University Press 1983.

Baumeister, R.F., *Self-esteem: The Puzzle of Low Self-regard*, New York: Plenum 1993.

Burke, R.J., 'Workaholism in organisations: concepts, results and future research directions', *International Journal of Management Reviews*, II/1 (2000), 1–16.

Cast, A.D. and Burke, P.J., 'A theory of self-esteem', *Social Forces*, LXXX/3 (2002), 1041–68.

Connolly, J.A., Doyle, A.B. and Reznik, E., 'Social pretend play and social interaction in preschoolers', *Journal of Applied Developmental Psychology*, IX/3 (1988), 301–13.

Coon, D.C., *Essentials of Psychology*, 5th ed., St Paul, MN: West Publishing 1991.

Cooper, C., Sloan, S. and Williams, S., *The Occupational Stress Indicator*, Oxford: NFER-Nelson 1988.

Cullen, P., 'Bricklayer who became a folk hero by blowing the whistle on sleaze', *The Irish Times*, 28 September 2002.

De Vellis, R.F., De Vellis, B.M. and McCauley, C., 'Vicarious acquisition of learned helplessness', *Journal of Personality and Social Psychology*, XXXVI (1978), 894–9.

Ekman, P., 'Facial expressions of emotion: new findings, new questions', *Psychological Science*, III (1992), 34–8.

Erikson, E.H., *Childhood and Society*, 2nd ed., New York: Norton 1963.

Eysenck, M., *Simply Psychology*, Sussex: Psychology Press 1996.

Fineman, S. (ed.), *Emotion in Organisations*, London: Sage 1993.

Fitness, J., 'Anger in the workplace: an emotion script approach to anger episodes between workers and their superiors, co-workers and subordinates', *Journal of Organizational Behaviour*, XXI/2 (2000), 147–62.

Fox, A., *Beyond Contract: Work, Power and Trust Relations*, London: Faber 1974.

Gambetta, D., 'Can we trust trust?', in D. Gambetta (ed.), *Trust: Making and Breaking Cooperative Relationships*, Cambridge: Basil Blackwell 1988.

Gecas, V., 'The self concept', *Annual Review of Sociology*, VIII (1982), 1–33.

Goleman, D., *Emotional Intelligence: Why It Can Matter More than IQ*, London: Bloomsbury 1996.

Greenberg, J. and Baron, R.A., *Behaviour in Organizations*, 6th ed., New Jersey: Prentice Hall 1997.

Grove, A., *Only the Paranoid Survive: How to Survive the Crisis Points that Challenge Every Career*, New York: Doubleday 1996.

Hatfield, E., Cacioppo, J.T. and Rapson, R.L., *Emotional Contagion*, New York: Cambridge University Press 1994.

Hayes, N., *Foundations of Psychology*, London: Routledge 1994.

Hochschild, A.R., *The Managed Heart: Commercialisation of Human Feeling*, Berkeley, CA: University of California Press 1983.

Ilgen, D.R. and Davis, C.A., 'Bearing bad news: reactions to negative performance feedback', *Applied Psychology: An International Review*, XLIX/3 (2000), 550–65.

Jordan, P.J., Ashkanasy, N.M. and Hartel, C.E.J., 'Emotional intelligence as a moderator of emotional and behavioural reactions to job insecurity', *Academy of Management Review*, XXVII/3 (2002), 361–72.

Mayer, R.C., Davis, J.H. and Schoorman, F.D., 'An integrative model of organizational trust', *Academy of Management Review*, XX (1995), 109–34.

McGrath, J., 'Stress and behaviour in organizations', in M. Dunnette (ed.), *Handbook of Industrial and Organizational Psychology*, Chicago: Rand-McNally 1976, 1351–96.

Meelad, T., Seanai, A. and Seanai, E., 'Thoughts on learned helplessness', *Psychology Today*, VI (1953), 39–54.

Miles, E.W., Hatfield, J.D. and Huseman, R.C., 'Equity, sensitivity and outcome importance', *Journal of Organizational Behaviour*, XV/7 (1994), 585–96.

Moore, S. and Kuol, N., 'Reactions to performance feedback by academic faculty: challenging the classic assumptions', conference paper presented at the 7th Conference on International Human Resource Management, University of Limerick, June 2003.

Murray, H.A., *Explorations in Personality*, New York: Oxford University Press 1975.

Plutchik, R., *Emotion*, New York: Harper & Row 1980.

Rafaeli, A. and Sutton, R.I., 'Expression of emotion as part of the work role', *Academy of Management Review*, XII/1 (1987), 23–37.

Ribeaux, P. and Poppleton, S.E., *Psychology and Work: An Introduction*, London: Macmillan, Business Management and Administration Series 1978.

Rogers, C., *On Becoming a Person: A Therapist's View of Psychotherapy*, Boston: Houghton-Mifflin 1961.

Salovey, P. and Mayer, J., 'Emotional intelligence', *Imagination, Cognition and Personality*, IX (1990), 185–211.

Seligman, M.E.P., 'Fall into helplessness', *Psychology Today*, 7 (1973), 43–8.

Slovic, P., 'Perceived risk, trust, and democracy', *Risk Analysis*, XIII (1993), 675–82.

Van Maanen, J. and Kunda, G., 'Real feelings: emotional expression and organisational culture', *Research in Organisational Behaviour*, XI/6 (1989), 43–103.

Warr, P., *Work, Jobs and Unemployment*, London: Macmillan 1984.

Watson, T.J., *Organising and Managing Work*, Essex: Prentice Hall 2002.

Weiss, H. and Copranzano, R., 'Affective events theory: a theoretical discussion of the structure, causes and consequences of affective experiences at work', *Research in Organisational Behaviour*, XVIII (1996), 1–79.

Zucker, L.G., 'Production of trust: institutional sources of economic structure', in B.M. Staw and L.L. Cummings (eds), *Research in Organizational Behavior*, viii, Greenwich, CT: JAI Press 1986.

MOTIVATION

Learning Objectives

- To define motivation and identify the essential elements of the motivation process.

- To show how an understanding of the psychological effects of unemployment can help to explain the motivation to work.

- To apply broad concepts of individual behaviour to the motivation process at work.

- To critically evaluate central theories of motivation.

- To analyse issues of motivation using a variety of theoretical concepts.

- To identify trends in motivational research during the 1990s.

INTRODUCTION

This chapter provides a theoretical overview of the behavioural concepts of motivation, which is central to the treatment of organisational behaviour. Motivation – or what drives people to perform in their work settings – is a subject that has received enormous attention in the literature. Employee performance is frequently described as a joint function of ability and motivation, and one of the primary tasks facing a manager is motivating employees to perform to the best of their ability (Moorhead and Griffin 1998). In fact, motivation has been described as 'one of the most pivotal concerns of modern organisational research (Baron 1991: 1).

From the classic 'hierarchy of needs' theory proposed by Maslow (1943) to the network of expectancies and outcomes outlined by the expectancy theorists, there has been a variety of attempts to establish how efforts at work are initiated, sustained and directed. Interest in research in relation to employee motives and needs peaked in the 1970s and early 1980s, with the last fifteen years seeing little empirical or theoretical research (Ambrose and Kulik 1999). The majority of research on motives and needs in the 1990s falls into three areas: an examination of the job attributes that motivate individuals, research that examines the need for achievement and research on the Protestant work ethic.

Motivation is an important concept, both from a managerial and individual perspective. However, while motivation is important, the relationship between motivation and performance is not straightforward, as motivation and job performance are not synonymous (for example, see Greenberg and Baron 1997). Work motivation is viewed as an invisible, internal, hypothetical construct (Pinder 1998). We cannot actually see work motivation, nor can we measure it directly. Instead, we rely on established theories to guide us in measuring the observable manifestations of work motivation. In exploring motivation, this chapter highlights a definition of motivation and outlines the key theoretical perspectives that have been adopted in relation to this concept.

DEFINITIONS OF KEY CONCEPTS

Motivation
The set of forces that leads people to behave in particular ways.

Need
Something an individual must have in order to survive.

Want
Something an individual would like to have.

Primary needs
Things people require to sustain themselves.

Secondary needs
Are learned from the environment and culture.

Motive
A person's reason for choosing a behaviour.

Protestant work ethic
The degree to which people place work centrally in their lives.

Need theories
What drives behaviour and initiates motivation.

Process theories
How motivation occurs.

Reinforcement theory
Influences behaviour through rewards and punishment.

NEEDS AND MOTIVES IN ORGANISATIONS

A need is something that an individual must have in order to survive and is therefore physiological in nature, for example, water, food and shelter. In an organisational context, an employee will need money in order to satisfy these basic needs. There is a distinction between a need and a want. A want is something an individual would like to have rather than something which is needed for their survival.

Motivated behaviour usually begins when a person has one or more important needs, which can be grouped into two categories: primary and secondary needs. Primary needs are things that people require to sustain themselves. Needs of this type are instinctive and physiologically based. Secondary needs, on the other hand, are requirements based more in psychology and are learned from the environment and culture in which the person lives.

Secondary needs often arise in organisational settings, so it is important to consider them when examining motivated behaviour. For example, if employees are to be satisfied with their psychological contracts with their organisation, the inducements offered by the organisation must be consistent with their own unique needs. A nice office and job security may not be sufficient if the employee is primarily seeking income and promotion opportunities. People's needs also change with time. Thus, efforts designed to motivate employees to behave in a certain way may lose their effectiveness as employees satisfy one set of needs and begin to identify another set.

A motive is a person's reason for choosing one behaviour from among several choices. Motives are derived from needs in that most behaviours are undertaken to satisfy one or more needs. Needs, motives and behaviour are interrelated, as a need serves as a stimulus for action. Motives are the channels through which the individual thinks the need can best be satisfied, thus reflecting the person's behavioural choices. Finally, the manifestation of motives is actual behaviour.

APPROACHING THE THEORY OF MOTIVATION

Behaviourist and experimental psychology has traditionally had problems trying to come to grips with the broader questions about human nature. As a result of the dominance of these two traditions in European and American psychology for most of [the past] century, many aspects of human life remain very little researched – although with the increasing acceptance of qualitative methodologies, many of these areas have started to come into focus. This is a recent development, however, and their omission has left many gaps and distortions in accepted psychological knowledge.

Motivation is one of those areas which became distorted as a result of the emphasis on laboratory studies of overt behaviour. A typical psychology textbook of the 1960s or 1970s will have a chapter on motivation which will almost inevitably be devoted to research into psychological drives such as hunger and thirst; with some discussion of neural mechanisms underlying these drives. If the authors were being really radical, they might even include Maslow's hierarchical model at the very end of the chapter.

But what about the other reasons why people do things? In fact a great deal of psychology is concerned with human motivation. But those aspects of human motivation which are to do with social or personal motives tend not to come under the same heading – they are treated under social psychology or personality theory, or something quite different. If they are all brought together as aspects of motivation though, they produce a very interesting and much fuller picture of why people do things.

Source: Hayes (1994: 438)

DEFINING MOTIVATION

The word 'motive' comes from the Latin word for 'move' (*movere*). Maund (1999: 87) defines motivation as 'the process by which an individual wants and chooses to engage in certain specified behaviours.' The concept of motivation is used and referred to often in organisational contexts. From a personal perspective, most people are familiar with times when they find it difficult to be interested in or feel energetic about work that they have to do. At other times or in other contexts, however, people can feel focused, can be eager to start a task, maintain high levels of energy and interest while the job is underway and derive high levels of satisfaction once it has been completed. Low or high levels of motivation have an effect on the experience and perceptions of work and can (but not necessarily) be related to performance. Motivation is the set of processes that stimulate, guide and sustain human behaviour towards accomplishing some goal.

STIMULATING BEHAVIOUR

In an effort to understand what stimulates or initiates behaviour, theorists have proposed that in order for any behaviour to be initiated, that behaviour needs to be triggered by some driving force that influences an individual. For example, a feeling of hunger is the driving force that causes people to be motivated to search for ways of acquiring food; a need for achievement may be the driving force that motivates people to attempt to accomplish challenging work-related goals; or curiosity at work may be the driving force that motivates people to try out new ideas or experiment with new combinations of activities. A driving force is essentially anything that triggers a certain behaviour.

GUIDING BEHAVIOUR

Behaviour may be initiated by some driving force, but it is guided or directed by the decisions that the individual makes as to what the best alternatives to select are in order to achieve the goal that they are pursuing most effectively. Events in the environment may cause individuals to make a new decision or to change a course of action that they are pursuing. A change in perception about the appropriateness of a given goal or about the appropriateness of certain activity in the achievement of a goal are the types of events that can serve to direct people's behaviour during the process of motivation.

SUSTAINING BEHAVIOUR

Motivated behaviour varies in its overall levels of robustness. What is it that sustains behaviour towards the achievement of a certain goal? How long will someone persist in attempting to achieve a particular goal? The stronger or more robust the motivated behaviour, the more likely someone is to persist in the achievement of the relevant goals. Thus, key questions that relate to motivation are:
- What initiates behaviour?
- What directs behaviour?
- What sustains behaviour?

These are important preliminary questions to ask in attempting to understand the complex and multifaceted concept of motivation, and the theories of motivation outlined in this chapter each address at least one of these three questions.

Different individuals aim for different kinds of goals in their lives. The different goals that people set are often pursued at different levels of intensity and immediacy, depending on experienced needs at a particular point in time, so the theories of motivation do not always account for these individual differences. Theoretical frameworks of motivation have often been criticised as inadequate in some way in the face of the uniqueness and complexity of the human spirit.

Attempting to explain all human motivation processes under a single framework has proved to be a daunting theoretical task. Nevertheless, different theories make different contributions to a more complete understanding of motivation. There are two major categories of motivation theory: need or content theories and process theories, which will be discussed later in this chapter.

EFFECTANCE MOTIVATION

Psychologists have proposed that people are dispositionally motivated to deal and interact with their environments in effective and functional ways (White 1959). It has been demonstrated that children are driven to be effective and that learning to master the environment is an important motivator for individuals, so much so that it drives behaviour from an early age.

Motivation patterns at work may also be characterised by effectance motivation. However, because different people master their environments in very different ways in their work settings, it is difficult to identify a theoretical model that describes, explains or predicts individual motivation patterns in any comprehensive way. The basic proposition of effectance motivation is that people want to be capable members of society and so are anxious to grasp and master the aspects of society that are valued.

WHY DO PEOPLE WORK?

Some psychologists suggest that to humans (and indeed to other animals), work is as natural as rest or play. Anthropologists have also found that all societies engage in work-based, organised activity of some kind, even though the nature of these activities may vary dramatically from one culture to another. Warr's studies (1984) have outlined some of the psychological effects of unemployment, which may help to clarify some of the answers to the question of why people are motivated to work.

PSYCHOLOGICAL EFFECTS OF UNEMPLOYMENT

Financial anxiety
Financial pressures are an almost inevitable feature of unemployment, and studies have shown that worries about money are a strong predictor of overall anxiety levels in unemployment situations.

Loss of 'traction' or life structure

Employment seems to create a structure and direction that may not be as easy to attain in situations of unemployment. Traction is a concept which refers to the structure in people's lives that helps to direct their energies. It provides a focus and creates various landmarks in life that can help to provide people with a sense of progress and achievement. For example, people at work look forward to their weekends and their holidays. They may feel a sense of achievement on Fridays when the week is complete or at the end of any day. People who are unemployed often report a feeling that every day is the same and that there is nothing particular to look forward to. Although, of course, it is possible to create one's own structures and frameworks in life, it appears that this is harder for people who are not involved in some form of paid or unpaid work.

Less decision making

When people are unemployed they are not answerable to an employer and are not subjected to rules and regulations that they may find stressful or unacceptable. However, while in theory there may be more freedom, generally people find that there is less to be free about. Decisions tend to be seen as less important and less significant, which may have an effect on overall levels of self-esteem and confidence.

Less skill development

Organisations have the potential to provide people with an effective arena for developing their skills. Opportunities for training and development may be more available and employers may carry some or all of the costs of skill or competence enhancement. Without a job, people may find that their opportunities for skill development are not as easy to create without an organisation's backing.

Increase in psychologically threatening activities

Looking for another job, risking rejection, having to reorganise loan payments or other financial-related worries generally give rise to an increase in psychologically threatening activities.

Loss of status

The attitudes towards unemployment that exist in society can make people feel less important and less valuable as members of that society. Even the words that our society uses to describe unemployment are charged with negative connotations; for example, the word 'redundant' (literally meaning something which no longer has a use) is commonly used to describe people who have lost their jobs. In implicit and explicit ways, 'not having a job' is often seen and described in highly negative ways, leading to an overall sense of a lowering of status.

Source: Adapted from Warr (1984)

Warr's study of the psychological effects of unemployment has been generally supported by more recent studies exploring the same concept. For example, surveys have shown that aspects of work that are motivating include having control over activities, using knowledge and experience, having a variety of things to do, earning money, making friends and doing a job that people respect (Handy 1990). If people suffer psychological ill effects when out of work, then we can infer that they may be motivated to work in order to avoid these effects or to seek out the positive outcomes that work can provide.

Thus, it can be argued that people work in order to:

- protect themselves from financial anxiety;
- gain structure and momentum in their lives;
- develop their skills and knowledge;
- have an arena in which to exercise control and make decisions;
- protect themselves from psychologically threatening activities to which they may be more vulnerable outside employment; and
- enhance or maintain their perceived status in their lives and communities.

Defining work in the narrow terms of 'paid employment' can prevent an effective analysis of the issue of motivation. Many people work in non-paid situations and derive similar benefits from their work as those in paid employment. Indeed, there are arguments that suggest that no one should be labelled unemployed and that motivation does not derive from work or even from employment, but rather from activity. To illustrate this point, Handy (1990: 20) proposes ways in which we can start to think more broadly about the nature of 'employment' and 'unemployment' and how these concepts may relate to motivation:

> We should stop talking and thinking about employment and employees. They are words, after all, which only entered the English language some hundred years ago. If work were defined as activity, some of which is paid for, then everyone is a worker, for nearly all of their natural life. If everyone were treated as self-employed during their active years, then by law and logic they could not be unemployed.

Some people argue that many of the psychological effects of unemployment are attributable to the attitudes, perceptions, labels and evaluations that society places on people who do not work in conventional, paid employment, and that the label 'unemployment' can itself be demotivating. It is worthwhile thinking of motivation in a wider sense than in the conventional context of organisational settings, as people are motivated by a wide range of needs, activities and goals. Motivation manifests itself in a myriad of ways, from running companies to running marathons. A broader view of the phenomenon of motivation can help managers to understand the passion and commitment to which it sometimes gives rise – even if this is not always easy to apply or capture in all work settings.

PROTESTANT WORK ETHIC

The Protestant work ethic represents the degree to which individuals place work at or near the centre of their lives. The Protestant work ethic has become conceptualised as a key individual difference variable that may influence adults' work attitudes and behaviours. Research during the 1970s and 1980s demonstrated that individuals who score highly on the Protestant work ethic are more satisfied with their jobs, more involved with their jobs, more committed to their organisations and more likely to stay with their organisations (Furnham 1990). Research by Weaver (1997) reported that self-employed individuals more strongly endorsed Protestant work ethic beliefs than organisationally employed individuals. Research investigating whether there has been a decline in Protestant work ethic, achievement and affiliation between 1973 and 1993 concludes that there has been no decline in work ethic in the US or Britain (Tansey *et al*. 1997). Research on the Protestant work ethic has expanded in scope, examining a broad range of outcome variables, e.g. fitness centre use, intrinsic motivation and absence attributions. The following theories help in understanding motivational structures, processes and outcomes.

HISTORICAL PERSPECTIVES ON MOTIVATION

THE SCIENTIFIC MANAGEMENT APPROACH

The traditional approach to understanding employee motivation is best represented by scientific management and the work of Frederick Taylor. Scientific management was developed primarily in the US and focused chiefly on the efficiency of individual workers. Taylor assumed that employees are economically motivated and work to earn as much money as they can. While working as a foreman at Midvale Steel Company in Philadelphia from 1878 to 1890, Taylor became aware of a phenomenon he called soldiering – employees working at a pace much slower than their capabilities. Because most managers had never systematically studied jobs in the plant – and, in fact, had little idea how to gauge worker productivity – they were completely unaware of this practice.

To counteract the effects of soldiering, Taylor developed several innovative techniques. For example, he scientifically studied all the jobs in the Midvale plant and developed a standardised method for performing each one. He also installed a piece-rate system in which each worker was paid for the amount of work that individual completed during the workday rather than for the time spent on the job. Taylor believed that money was the only important motivational factor in the workplace. Other assumptions were that work is inherently unpleasant for most people and that the money they earn is more important to employees than the nature of the job they are performing. Hence, people could be expected to perform any kind of job if they were paid enough.

Scientific management paved the way towards improved productivity, but its failings quickly became apparent. It did not consider the social context of work and the workers' psychological needs for attachment to the work process itself. Researchers recognised that scientific management's assumptions about motivation could not always explain complex human behaviour. The next perspective on motivation to emerge was the human relations approach.

THE HUMAN RELATIONS APPROACH

The basic premises underlying the human relations approach were that people respond primarily to their social environment, that motivation depends more on social needs than on economic needs and that satisfied employees work harder than unsatisfied ones. Favourable employee attitudes, such as job satisfaction, were presumed to result in improved employee performance, a perspective that represented a fundamental shift away from the philosophy and values of scientific management. The human relations approach arose from the Hawthorne studies, which were conducted between 1927 and 1932 at Western Electric's Hawthorne plant near Chicago.

The Hawthorne studies were a series of early experiments that focused new attention on the role of human behaviour in the workplace. In the first major experiment, for example, researchers monitored how productivity changed as a result of the effects of different levels of lighting. The researchers systematically manipulated the lighting of the area in which a group of women worked. The group's productivity was measured and compared with that of another group (the control group), whose lighting was left unchanged. Not until the lighting had become almost as dim as moonlight did productivity start to decline, which led the researchers to conclude that lighting had no relationship to productivity. In turn, these findings served as a catalyst for other major research projects designed to learn more about the role of human behaviour at work.

Table 6.1 Theory X and Theory Y

Theory X Assumptions	Theory Y Assumptions
1. People do not like work and try to avoid it.	1. People do not naturally dislike work; work is a natural part of their lives.
2. People do not like work, so managers have to control, direct, coerce and threaten employees to get them to work toward organisational goals.	2. People are internally motivated to reach objectives to which they are committed.
3. People prefer to be directed, avoid responsibility and want security; they have little ambition.	3. People are committed to goals to the degree that they receive personal rewards when they reach their objectives.
	4. People will seek and accept responsibility under favourable conditions.
	5. People have the capacity to be innovative in solving organisational problems.
	6. People are bright, but under most organisational conditions their potentials are underutilised.

Source: McGregor (1960)

The works of Douglas McGregor and Abraham Maslow illustrate the values of the human relations approach to motivation. McGregor identifies two opposing perspectives that he believes typify managerial views of employees. Some managers, McGregor says, subscribe to what he labels Theory X, whose characteristics are summarised in Table 6.1. Theory X takes a pessimistic view of human nature and employee behaviour and in many ways it is consistent with the premises of scientific management. A much more optimistic and positive view of employees is found in Theory Y, also summarised in Table 6.1. Theory Y, which is generally representative of the human relations perspective, is the approach McGregor himself advocates.

The human relations approach left many questions regarding motivation unanswered. However, one of the primary theorists associated with this movement, Abraham Maslow, helped develop an important need theory of motivation.

NEED/CONTENT THEORIES OF MOTIVATION

Need theories of motivation focus on the question 'What initiates or stimulates behaviour?' By focusing on the different types of needs that people experience and by exploring which needs are most important at any one point in time, need theorists implicitly assume that needs are the most important determinant of individual levels of motivation. In attempting to answer the question 'What motivates people to work?', the need theorists would say that people are motivated by needs, particularly those that are strongest and most salient to them at a particular time.

MASLOW'S HIERARCHY OF NEEDS THEORY

Maslow's hierarchy of needs theory (1943, 1954, 1970) has been widely quoted in organisational behaviour texts all over the world. In fact, Maslow was a humanistic psychologist, never claiming to be an expert in organisational contexts and processes. However, organisational theorists (notably Hall and Nougaim 1968) have traditionally borrowed strongly from the ideas promoted by him, applying them to motivation in the workplace.

Figure 6.1 Maslow's Hierarchy of Needs

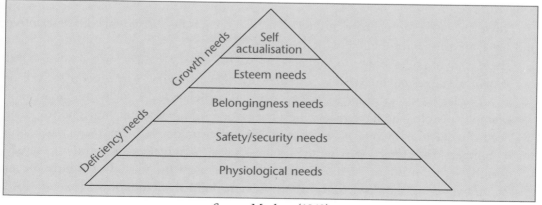

Source: Maslow (1943)

According to Maslow, needs at the lower level of the hierarchy dominate an individual's motivational drive as long as they continue to be unsatisfied. Once they are adequately satisfied, they move into a 'higher' need category, being motivated by a different set of needs. Maslow identifies a total of five different need types. He also identifies two broader categories: deficiency needs (physiological and safety needs) and growth needs (belongingness, esteem and self-actualisation needs). All of these are important needs to consider in the workplace as well as in wider contexts.

- Physiological needs include basic deficiency needs for water, oxygen, rest, sexual expression and physiological tension release.
- Safety needs include needs for security, comfort, tranquillity and freedom from fear.
- Belongingness/social needs include the need to belong, to love and to be loved.
- Esteem needs include needs for confidence, sense of worth and competence, self-esteem and respect from others.
- Self-actualisation refers to the need to realise one's full human potential, to achieve long-term goals in life and to become everything that one is capable of becoming.

The strongest implication emerging from the hierarchy is that unless people's basic deficiency needs are satisfied, they will not be motivated to pursue goals that relate to higher-order needs. Therefore, activities that demand organisationally popular dimensions of teamwork, 'empowerment', creativity, innovation or knowledge enhancement will not be relevant or important to people who do not earn enough money to survive or who are not sufficiently protected from danger in their workplace. According to Maslow's theory, people in low-paid work or who face hazardous or dangerous environments in the workplace will be less interested in developing social networks, achieving high status in their jobs or realising their potential in other ways.

A Brief Critique of Maslow

There is a certain intuitive appeal to Maslow's 'hierarchy of needs' theory. It recognises that needs motivate people in different ways and assumes that if someone experiences deficiency needs they will not be motivated to grow or develop until those needs have been satisfied. Furthermore, it identifies important categories of individual needs and encourages us to consider the variety of needs that at different times stimulate or initiate behaviour.

However, as a comprehensive model of motivation, it is insufficient in both descriptive and predictive terms for the following reasons.

1. There is plenty of evidence to suggest that needs are not organised in the hierarchical structure suggested in Maslow's framework. On a regular basis, people sacrifice lower-order needs in order to satisfy those at a higher level on the hierarchy. For example, people who have risked their lives to save other people, thus ignoring their needs for safety in favour of, say, attachment or esteem needs; people who have gone on hunger strike, thus depriving themselves of basic survival needs in order to satisfy a higher-order need; or even someone who has stayed up all night to study for an exam, bypassing the need for sleep in order to fulfil their individual potential. All

provide clear evidence that need order is not as straightforward or as linear as the hierarchy suggests.

2. An implicit assumption of Maslow's hierarchy is that need deprivation is what motivates people's behaviour. The theory is based on a 'fulfilment progression' dynamic which indicates that as soon as a need has been sufficiently satisfied it ceases to be a motivator. There is a connotation inherent in this assertion which suggests that in any attempts to motivate people, needs should be deprived in order to sustain motivated behaviour.

This second implication points to a flaw in the theory, both intuitively and empirically. Need deprivation may motivate for a certain length of time, after which its effects may yield quite the opposite reaction. If people are continually denied an opportunity to satisfy needs that they are experiencing, this eventually leads to demotivated, apathetic and disheartened behaviour (for example, see Seligman 1973).

ALDERFER'S ERG THEORY

Alderfer (1972) proposes that there are three broad need categories: existence (roughly corresponding to Maslow's physiological and safety needs), relatedness (corresponding to Maslow's belongingness needs) and growth (corresponding to Maslow's esteem and self-actualisation categories). Responding to the problematic 'fulfilment progression' dimension proposed by Maslow, Alderfer suggests that motivated behaviour can be activated either via 'need fulfilment, progression' or by another dynamic referred to as 'need frustration, regression'.

- **Fulfilment progression:** Once a need is satisfied in someone, he/she ceases to be motivated by that need category and moves on to another, higher-order category of needs.
- **Frustration regression:** If a need is consistently frustrated, an individual 'regresses' to being motivated by lower-order needs that are already being fulfilled to a sufficient degree.

MCCLELLAND'S ACHIEVEMENT MOTIVATION THEORY

Work by David McClelland (1961), which gained popularity around the same time as Maslow's theory, proposes that there are three key needs which motivate people's behaviour at work. Unlike Maslow, McClelland's work is grounded more firmly within organisational settings and may relate more directly to patterns of work and how people operate within organisational structures. According to this theory, needs that people experience can be directly related to people's work preferences. The three needs that he identifies are the need for achievement, the need for power and the need for affiliation.

These are need categories that are learned through life experiences, and any one person will tend to be more driven by one of the three needs that are identified. McClelland's research has shown that people who are mainly driven by a need for achievement will have distinctly different work preferences than those driven by a need for power or by a need for affiliation. Table 6.2 summarises the preferences that have been found to be associated with each of the three need categories in this theory.

Table 6.2 Preferences Associated with Needs

Individual Needs	Work Preferences
Need for achievement	**People driven by a need for achievement are motivated to:** • set challenging but achievable goals; • work on goals that they have set for themselves; and • receive timely and accurate feedback about their performance.
Need for power	**People driven by a need for power are motivated to:** • influence and affect the behaviour of others; • position themselves within organisational settings so that they can legitimately control situations; and • receive attention and recognition through having mobilised others' activity.
Need for affiliation	**People driven by a need for affiliation are motivated to:** • develop strong interpersonal ties at work; • work in situations where they are given the opportunity to interact with others; • receive approval from others; and • spend time in social settings.

Source: McClelland (1961)

The needs identified by McClelland can be useful in helping managers to recognise the diversity of behaviours that people display at work. Recognising individual differences is an important starting point in attempting to understand motivation, and McClelland's propositions make some progress towards this goal. People with a need for power will behave in very different ways than people with a need for achievement and affiliation.

McClelland's model provides the field of organisational behaviour with more food for thought in relation to needs and driving forces. The methodologies through which he gathered his data were also quite innovative at the time the theory was developed. He used thematic aperception tests (TATs) in order to ascertain the needs that were operating in any one individual, which were projective tests that displayed pictures to subjects, asking them to create their own story about what the picture was about. Qualitative analyses of the responses given provided information and perspectives which McClelland believed allowed him to infer whether someone was driven by achievement, affiliation or power.

Another technique involved asking people to tell stories or to finish stories that had been started by someone else. By exploring the content, language and imagery of the stories, McClelland attempted to determine the dimensions of achievement, affiliation or power motivation.

This methodology was inevitably criticised for being too subjective and not testable according to rigorous or valid measures. However, his methodologies marked an important contribution to an increasingly popular approach in organisational behaviour for exploring intangible concepts like motivation, culture and personality. Many qualitative researchers argue that the language, imagery and stories that people use contain important clues to the sorts of inner drives that direct and sustain their energies.

Furthermore, McClelland's work yielded some interesting intercultural observations, particularly with respect to the need for achievement. McClelland argues that the differences in achievement motivation observed in different cultures is reflected in each culture's use of literature and imagery and that language is an important source of evidence which can help to establish the intensity with which different needs are experienced in any one culture.

Table 6.3 Two Factor Theory

Satisfiers/Motivators	Dissatisfiers/Hygiene Factors
• Sense of achievement. • Recognition. • Responsibility. • Nature of the work. • Personal growth and advancement.	• Salary/pay. • Job security. • Working conditions. • Level and quality of supervision. • Company policy and administration. • Interpersonal relations.

HERZBERG'S TWO FACTOR THEORY

Frederick Herzberg (1950) provides a perspective on needs that adds another consideration to the area of needs and the motivation to which they give rise. His research suggests that there are two types of factors in the workplace. One set of factors (called satisfiers or motivators) is capable of motivating people to perform, and the other set of factors (called hygiene/maintenance factors or 'dissatisfiers') only has a negative or dissatisfying impact if they are absent, but are not capable of motivating behaviour when present. The two sets of factors his research identified are summarised in Table 6.3.

While the methods that Herzberg used to reach his conclusions were also criticised for their questionable rigour and validity, the principle that he highlights is still worth considering in work settings, though perhaps not in the rigid way that his theoretical assertions suggest. His theory has been criticised for its method boundedness, that is, similar findings have only been established using the same methods applied in the original study. The original work elicited information from respondents by requesting them to do the following.

1. 'Tell me about a time when you felt exceptionally good about your job.' Responses to this request were assumed to be the factors that people found motivating.

2. 'Tell me about a time when you felt exceptionally bad about your job.' Responses to this request were assumed to be the factors that people found demotivating or dissatisfying.

When other samples of respondents have been asked directly what motivates them at work, responses have yielded very different patterns of results. It may be that potential problems with the construct validity of Herzberg's work have led to an inaccurate or at least an overly rigid framework.

A key criticism often directed at Herzberg is his assertion that money is not a motivator. People often intuitively respond quite fiercely to any suggestion that money is not capable of motivating people's work. For example, studies have shown that people with high needs for achievement rank money very highly on their list of motivators in that it can be a tangible and measurable way of gauging their progress and performance. In addition, money itself is capable of fulfilling a wide range of needs outlined by many of the content theorists, thus it cannot be so easily dismissed as incapable of motivating behaviour.

However, there is some strong evidence in applied settings that money can play a dissatisfying role and be at least less able to give rise to motivated behaviour than other factors. For example, bonus schemes or yearly percentage increases can become institutionalised in organisational settings such that they are seen as a condition of the job and only serve to create dissatisfaction if they are not received and fail to motivate people in any directed or sustained way.

This example draws attention to a series of ideas that relate to process theories of motivation, that is, a comparison between what people expect and what they get in organisational settings is an important consideration when attempting to explain motivation at work. This comparison will be explored in more detail later in the section that deals with the process theories of motivation.

THE CONTRIBUTION OF NEED THEORIES TO THE STUDY OF MOTIVATION

Need theories provide useful direction for recognising and understanding that there are different types of needs that, when experienced, will give rise to different types of motivated behaviour. However, it is far from certain that there are only five broad categories of needs. Alderfer (1972) identifies only three major need categories, while Murray (1975) proposes a long list of different categories.

Indeed, it may not be as important to know exactly what needs people experience and how they can be categorised as it is to understand some of the individual processes associated with motivation. It seems that efforts to classify these experiences will almost inevitably lead to imprecise generalities or to cumbersome lists, neither of which are particularly useful in the development of sound theoretical principles.

Any need theory focuses on the identification of the nature of the needs that people experience that motivate them to behave in certain ways. As such, it can be argued that none of them go far enough in the quest to understand motivation. As the process theorists have shown, there is more to motivation than simple responses to experienced needs.

Table 6.4 Need/Content Theories of Motivation

Theory	Summary	Comment
Maslow's hierarchy of needs (1943)	Five levels of needs arranged in a hierarchy. People not conscious of needs, but normal people proceed to make predictable climb from bottom to top: psychological —> safety —> belogingness —> esteem —> self-actualisation.	Widely known and influential because simple and plausible. But note that Maslow made original proposal after studying mentally ill patients. There is little supporting evidence from studies of people at work.
Alderfer's ERG theory (1972)	Condensed Maslow's list into three levels – existence, relatedness and growth. Suggested a continuous rather than a strict step-by-step progress. Frustration at one level may lead to regression to the next one down.	An attempt to overcome some of Maslow's weaknesses. Experiments showed that existence needs were more important if they were less fulfilled, but did not support the notion of a rising hierarchy.
McClelland's achievement motivation theory (1961)	McClelland proposes that some important needs are not inherited but are learned. Most frequently studied are the needs for achievement, affiliation and power. People with strong needs in these categories are often found in the roles of entrepreneur, team co-ordinators and top managers of large hierarchies.	Compared with other need/content theories, McClelland's work looks more towards senior managers' development. Rather than focus on management skill, he argues that attention should be given to developing the drive for achievement.
Herzberg's two factor theory (1950)	Two different factors affect motivation at work. Hygiene factors prevent dissatisfaction but do not promote more satisfaction, even if provided in abundance. Motivators, or growth factors, push the individual to greater performance.	Herzberg's contribution was to recognise that the opposite of dissatisfaction is not satisfaction, but rather no dissatisfaction. Both hygiene factors and motivators are important, but in different ways. His theory is based on field studies and has direct implications for job design.

PROCESS THEORIES OF MOTIVATION

There is no doubt that the content/need theories of motivation make an important contribution to the understanding of motivation at work, particularly via the identification of factors and needs that drive behaviour. Need theorists are centrally focused on the question 'What drives behaviour and what initiates motivation?' and broadly maintain that people experience needs and respond in a way that will satisfy whatever need they feel most intensely. The process theorists' work proposes that people are more complex, more pragmatic and more contemplative than the need theorists suggest or at least imply.

Process theorists have collected evidence to show that before people exert energy in pursuit of any goal, they go through a decision-making process that:

- explores the validity of the goals that they are pursuing;
- examines the extent to which they are likely to achieve objectives by pursuing a particular course of action;
- compares their situation to others;
- investigates the difference between what they put into work and what they get out; or
- in some way considers the benefits associated with devoting energy to a particular activity or set of activities at work.

In analysing what motivates people at work, process theories focus not only on what people want from their work situations, but how they believe they can get it.

Table 6.5 Performance Expectations

	Example statements which which may reveal that the expectation does exist	**Example statements may reveal that the expectation does not exist**
Effort performance expectancy	'If I work hard, I know I'll achieve results.'	'No matter how hard I work, I never seem to be able to reach my targets.'
Performance outcome expectancy	'If I achieve results, I'll get a rise.' 'If I meet my targets this year, I'll be promoted.'	'Even if I achieve the results, I'm not at all sure that I'll get rewarded for it.' 'My boss isn't interested in promoting me no matter how good she thinks I am.'
Valence	'It's really important I get a rise this year.' 'I really hope that I'll be promoted by the end of this year.'	'I don't really care whether I get a rise or not – after tax it's not worth much to me anyway.' 'I wouldn't care if I never got promoted.'

EXPECTANCY THEORY

The original expectancy theory (Vroom 1964) identifies three important expectations that individuals bring to the workplace:

1. That effort will lead to performance (effort – performance expectancy).

2. That performance will lead to a further outcome(s) (performance – outcome – expectancy).
3. That each outcome is perceived to have a certain value (valence).

Vroom proposes that the strength of someone's motivation can be established by using the following formula.

Motivation = effort performance expectancy x performance outcome expectancy x valence

This means that each of the three expectations outlined are equally important in establishing or determining levels of motivation. Table 6.5 demonstrates the types of statements that can reveal the existence or strength of an individual's expectations with respect to performance, outcomes and value of outcomes.

Empirical work on expectancy theory declined substantially in the 1990s, which likely reflects the theory's maturity. Expectancy theory generated great interest following its introduction in the 1960s. Most of the basic questions about expectancy theory have been examined, but there have been few advances in this research in the 1990s (Ambrose and Kulik 1999).

PORTER AND LAWLER

As a way of extending the original expectancy theory, Porter and Lawler also consider the role that abilities and role perceptions play in producing various outcomes. In addition, they draw an explicit difference between intrinsic and extrinsic rewards, the former being rewards that are generated by the individuals themselves, e.g. a sense of achievement,

Figure 6.2 Porter and Lawler's Extension of the Model of Motivation

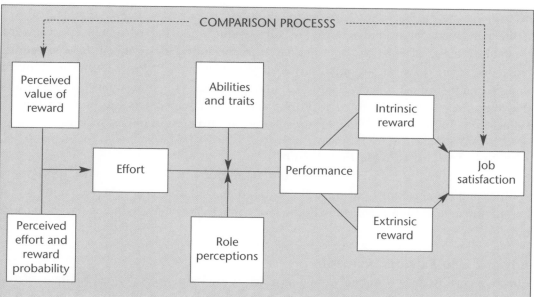

Source: Porter and Lawler (1968)

personal satisfaction, a feeling of pride in work, etc., and the latter being rewards that are provided from external sources, e.g. pay, promotion, praise, recognition, etc.

Like the original expectancy theory, Porter and Lawler also highlight that before people make a decision to exert effort they need to value the rewards that are available, and to feel that if they do exert effort that the rewards will be available to them.

Perceived Value of the Reward

Porter and Lawler's model highlights that before people give their effort and commitment to any activity, they ask themselves 'What's in it for me?' and that people are constantly engaged in a process of examining the value of the rewards or benefits that are associated with the effort involved.

Perceived Effort-Reward Probability

It's not enough that people value the potential rewards associated with an activity – they must also believe that they are capable of carrying out that activity successfully or that the rewards that they are being promised are actually going to materialise on completion of the task. When perceived effort-reward probability is high, then the individual has confidence in their ability to carry out the tasks and that the rewards will be available once the task has been completed. When perceived effort-reward probability is low, the individual does not have confidence in their ability to carry out the tasks or they are not confident for some reason that the rewards for carrying out the tasks will be available once the required tasks are complete. Perceived effort-reward probability is a function of the individual's faith and belief in their own capacities and/or their faith in the likelihood that rewards will be administered by the organisation.

Effort

If the perceived value of the reward is high enough and the perceived effort-reward probability exists at least to some degree, then the individual is likely to exert effort. However, effort does not automatically lead to performance. Most people can think of times when their most concerted efforts did not give rise to the performance or the results that they expected. Highlighted in Porter and Lawler's model is the identification of factors that intervene to facilitate or impede the path from effort to performance.

Abilities, Traits and Role Perception

In order for effort to translate into performance, individuals need to have appropriate abilities and traits to carry out the tasks required as well as a clear role perception and a good knowledge of the parameters of the tasks or activities they are being asked to carry out.

Intrinsic and Extrinsic Rewards

Effective performance is unlikely to be repeated if individuals do not receive the rewards that they expected. Porter and Lawler assert that motivation is not sustained just because a particular need is experienced or activated. Motivated activity must give rise to results and rewards. These rewards can be intrinsic, e.g. an inner sense of achievement, or extrinsic, e.g. a pay rise, a promotion or some other externally provided reward.

Overall Levels of Satisfaction

The combination of intrinsic and extrinsic rewards experienced or provided to individuals leads to overall levels of satisfaction. These overall levels are compared to the individual's original expectations and if they compare favourably, that is, if rewards are the same or better than expected, then motivated behaviour is likely to continue. If the rewards compare unfavourably to original expectations, that is, if rewards are worse than originally expected, then motivated behaviour will decrease and may eventually disappear altogether.

Unlike the need theorists, expectancy theories recognise the role of conscious thought processes and assert that people's personal calculations, expectations and evaluations are central to a comprehensive understanding of how the process of motivation works.

EQUITY THEORY

Adams's equity theory (1963) is based on the assumption that the most important motivator for individuals is the perception that they are being treated fairly in comparison to other people in the same context. According to this theory, people's motivation to be treated fairly is so overwhelming that they become involved in any number of 'strategies' to reduce situations of injustice or inequity.

Like the other process theories, Adams asserts that it is individuals' own conscious evaluations of their situation and their work outcomes that drive the motivation process and can explain the bases of motivation at work.

Adams's research indicates that people are constantly engaged in three main evaluative processes:

1. A comparison between their work inputs and their work outcomes.
2. A comparison between other people's work inputs and outcomes.
3. An analysis of these two comparisons.

It is the perception of equity and balance between an individual's rewards and those of others that maintains their levels of motivation. As soon as people feel (or even suspect) that they are being treated unfairly in comparison to others, their framework of motivation can change quite radically in a variety of different ways.

An individual will conclude that they are being treated unfairly if their ratio of inputs and outcomes does not match the input/outcome ratios of 'comparison others', i.e. people to whom the individual compares themselves (see Table 6.6). Adams states that when individuals compare their own work inputs and outcomes with those of others, they are motivated to maintain their levels of input just as long as they feel that they are being treated fairly. Someone who puts in an eight-hour day and gets paid, say, €48 would expect someone else who puts in four hours to get paid €24. This means that both people are getting treated equally according to their inputs. However, if their 'comparison other' gets more or less per hour than they do, a situation of perceived inequity is said to have arisen.

Table 6.6 Key Terms Associated with Adams's Equity Theory

Inputs	• 'Anything a person perceives as an investment in the job and worthy of some return' (Ribeaux and Poppleton 1978).
	• Individuals can consider a wide range of factors to be work inputs, valuable assets or contributions that they bring to their jobs.
	• Inputs can include time, effort, commitment, loyalty, qualifications, skills, attitudes or competencies.
Outcomes	• Any outcomes that a person receives from doing their job.
	• Outcomes can include money, respect, satisfaction, friendship, skill acquisition, status, fringe benefits, bonuses and so on.
'Comparison others'	• Other people with whom people compare themselves.
	• People tend to compare themselves with people doing the same or similar jobs. However, they may rule out comparing people who have different qualifications or different levels of experience.
Perceived equity	• Occurs when the individual perceives that he/she is being treated fairly when compared to their comparison others.
Perceived inequity	• Occurs when the individual perceives that he/she is being treated unfairly when compared to their comparison others.

Of course, time is not the only work input that may be considered and money not the only outcome. People may choose from a wide range of different inputs and outcomes when they are evaluating whether or not they are being treated fairly.

There are two types of perceived inequity that people can experience.
- **Negative inequity:** When people feel that the unfair treatment affects them in negative ways, such as less pay or fewer positive work outcomes than other people in the same or similar work situations.
- **Positive inequity:** When people feel that the unfair treatment affects them in positive ways, for example, they receive more positive work outcomes than their colleagues, including pay, fringe benefits, skill development, interpersonal contact, etc.

When people are happy that they are being treated fairly, they are motivated to maintain the status quo by maintaining their current levels of input. However, if they perceive that they are being treated unfairly, then according to this theory, they may respond in any one of the following ways.
1. Changing their level of input to the job.
2. Changing the outcomes they receive.
3. Changing other people's inputs or outcomes.
4. Changing their perception of their or others' inputs/outcomes.
5. Changing their comparison others.
6. Leaving the work situation in which they feel unfairly treated.

1. Changing work inputs

If inequitable treatment is perceived, the individual may lower their inputs by putting in less effort or time (if they feel they are being treated worse than others) or increase their inputs by working harder (if they feel they are being treated better than others).

2. Changing work outcomes

If people feel that their outcomes are less than other people in the same situation, they may try to increase their outcomes by appealing to their bosses, supervisors or trade unions. They may bring the inequity to public attention in some way in an effort to establish or to restore a level of equity.

There is less evidence to support the hypothesis that people will try to decrease their outcomes even in situations where they feel that they are receiving more for their inputs than others are. However, Adams's theory suggests that this is also a possible response when people feel that they are being treated better than other people to whom they compare themselves. More recent research by Miles *et al.* (1994) has demonstrated that different individuals vary in their levels of 'equity sensitivity'. Their research has identified evidence which suggests that some people are more 'benevolent' than others and as a result more likely to highlight situations of positive inequity, i.e. situations where they perceive that they are being treated or rewarded more favourably than others in their work situation.

3. Changing others' inputs/outcomes

Similar efforts may be made to redress the perceived inequity by attempting to change other people's inputs (encouraging them to increase or decrease their inputs) or other people's outcomes.

4. Changing perceptions of own or others' inputs/outcomes

Adams argues that people's perceptions are what influence their behaviour most strongly. In order to redress a situation of perceived inequity, changes in perception may be just as powerful as any real changes in the environment, and because people feel uncomfortable when they perceive inequity, they may voluntarily re-evaluate the situation and become satisfied that they are not being treated unfairly in comparison to others. Some people find the experience of inequity so intolerable that failure to change the situation may cause them to reconsider their original assessments. Thus, for example, someone who sees that they are being paid less than others doing the same work may introduce other variables into the equation for their considerations. They may look at the amount of experience others have or other people's level of skill or qualifications and then establish that they are not being treated unfairly once these considerations are accounted for. By changing perceptions, people can convince themselves or become convinced that they are being treated fairly.

5. Changing comparison with others

Sometimes perceptions cannot be changed. In situations where there is obvious favouritism in an organisation, individuals may restore feelings of equity by ceasing to consider certain individuals as comparable to them. Someone who is picked out for special treatment, e.g. the boss's son/daughter, may be getting a better deal than everyone else, and one way of overcoming a personal feeling of inequity is to recognise the special circumstances surrounding a certain individual and stop using this individual as a measure of equity. Of course, legislation and other policy-based rules should prevent any individual from receiving special treatment, but in situations where it does arise a sense of inequity may be overcome via perceptual changes as well as actual ones.

6. Leaving the situation

Adams argues that if someone continues to feel unfairly treated even after efforts to redress the balance (either actually or perceptually) have been made, they will quit their jobs. It has been recognised, especially in times where alternatives are unavailable, that many people tolerate high levels of perceived inequity without ever leaving their jobs. However, it is also possible to withdraw psychologically from work and working life. Adams says that people who experience negative inequity for any length of time are likely to withdraw in some way from their jobs, even if this means simply allowing their levels of motivation on the job to decrease or to disappear. Essentially, the equity theory highlights the importance that a feeling of fairness plays in people's motivational processes.

Research has shown that the equity theory appears to have more global applicability than other motivation theories that may be more culturally biased. Because many of the original theories of motivation derive from American researchers, a common allegation is that they may be limited in their applicability to the American cultural context. Equity theory has shown higher levels of applicability in a variety of cultural settings, including Europe and China (Shenkar and Von Glinow 1994). Soon after equity theory's appearance in the literature, Weick (1966) described it as one of the most useful organisational behaviour theories, and several reviews concluded that the evidence for equity theory was generally strong (Greenberg 1982; Mowday 1991).

Generally, research evidence is particularly supportive of the theory in situations of underpayment or other forms of negative inequity (Crosier and Dalton 1989). It seems that the concept of fairness is an important one in a wide variety of cultural and organisational settings. Anecdotal evidence abounds in the Irish context as much as anywhere. Examples of intense reactions to inequitable situations are everywhere. 'It's not fair' is a commonly used phrase in situations where people are demotivated or where they are attempting to make efforts to establish and maintain fair treatment for themselves and for others with whom they identify. Theory and evidence frequently suggest that organisational fairness pervades the psyche of organisational members and the groups that represent them.

Equity research during the 1990s explored a range of employee behavioural reactions to inequity, including illegal behaviours, performance appraisal and salary decisions. The bulk of research, however, continues to rely on attitudinal measures such as satisfaction, commitment or self-reported measures of intentions to change effort or to look for another job. According to Ambrose and Kulik (1999), there is a definite need to explore the effects of inequity on employees' behaviour over an extended time period.

GOAL SETTING AND MOTIVATION

People can be motivated by the needs that drive them, the cognitive processes that help them to calculate 'what's in it for them', but also by goals and targets which can help them to direct, measure and assess their performance in tangible and often effective ways.

Setting goals at work has been found in some settings to be an effective way of unlocking motivational processes in individuals and groups. To motivate people, Latham and Locke (1979), among others, have found that setting goals elicits higher performance levels than in the absence of goals. However, goal setting is not a simple management technique that necessarily increases effort and performance in any linear or automatic way. Combined with effective and equitable reward systems, developed in a participative context and accompanied by accurate and timely feedback on the levels of achievement, organisations can benefit by setting challenging but achievable goals and targets for their employees. Table 6.7 outlines how some goals can motivate performance in a positive way and how others can be demotivating.

Table 6.7 Goals and Performance

Goals can motivate people to perform when they are:	Goals can be demotivating when they are:
• Specific and clear. • Challenging but achievable.	• Non-specific and ambiguous. • Impossible or too easy to achieve (excessively difficult goals eventually become ignored or cause high levels of stress with low levels of performance; excessively easy goals set a ceiling on performance).
• Flexible when the task is novel or ambiguous to give people time to explore the parameters of the new activities involved.	• Inflexible in times of change, uncertainty, crisis or novelty.
• Agreed on by those required to achieve the goals.	• Imposed without consultation or communication.
• Monitored and reviewed so that people can be provided with effective feedback on their performance towards the attainment of the goals.	• Rarely reviewed or only mentioned when people are not achieving them.

Goal-setting theory is another helpful perspective on motivation that can be useful in enhancing our understanding of some of the triggers and directors of motivation and sustained behaviour at work. Multiple reviews of the goal-setting literature have concluded that there is substantial support for the basic principles of goal-setting theory.

One new trend of research on goal-setting theory during the 1990s was to study the effects of difficult goals. The research focused on personal (self-set) goals. Self-set goals are frequently more desirable than assigned goals because they automatically engender high commitment (Hinsz et al. 1997). In addition, individuals who reject assigned goals may set personal goals that exert an impact on performance. However, a difficulty in using self-set goals is encouraging people to set challenging goals. Ambrose and Kulik (1999) conclude that it is somewhat difficult to draw firm conclusions about theory advancements resulting from goal-setting research published in the 1990s, as the subset of variables examined and the predicted (and tested) relationships are rarely the same, making comparisons across studies extremely difficult.

REINFORCEMENT PERSPECTIVES ON MOTIVATION

A final element of the motivational process focuses on why some behaviours are maintained over time and why other behaviours change. Reinforcement theory is largely based on the work of B.F. Skinner (1938) and focuses on influencing behaviour through rewards and punishments, or reinforcement. Reinforcement is defined as any effect that causes behaviour to be repeated or inhibited, which can be positive or negative. The process of shaping behaviour through reinforcement is called behaviour modification, or operant conditioning. Reinforcement theory is based on the assumption that behaviour that results in rewarding consequences is likely to be repeated, whereas behaviour that results in punishing consequences is less likely to be repeated.

In organisations, there are four kinds of reinforcement that can result from behaviour. Two kinds of reinforcement strengthen or maintain behaviour, whereas the other two weaken or decrease behaviour. Positive reinforcement strengthens behaviour and describes a satisfying consequence from following a desired behaviour. Ranging from a simple 'well done' to changes in pay and prospects, such actions increase the chance of similar behaviour being repeated. The other method of strengthening desired behaviour is through avoidance, which strengthens behaviour by allowing escape from an undesirable consequence. For example, if an employee improves the standard of work, the supervisor may stop criticising or watching very closely.

Punishment means negative consequences for undesired behaviour. The assumption is that the unpleasant consequence will reduce the likelihood that the employee will choose that particular behaviour again. Extinction is used to weaken undesired behaviours by ignoring or not reinforcing that behaviour. Extinction involves the withdrawal of rewards in light of undesired behaviour. Responses such as withdrawal of praise or pay increases by managers may result in the undesired behaviour fading away.

Not only is the kind of reinforcement important, but when or how often it occurs is also crucial. There are various strategies for timing or scheduling reinforcement. A fixed-interval schedule provides reinforcement at fixed intervals of time, regardless of behaviour. An example of a fixed-interval schedule of reinforcement is the weekly or monthly paycheque. This method provides the least incentive for good work, because employees know they will be paid regularly regardless of their effort or lack of it. A variable-interval schedule provides reinforcement at varying intervals of time. Rewards are based on assessments at unpredictable intervals, for example, random visits or inspections of employees' work.

A fixed-ratio schedule provides reinforcement after a fixed number of behaviours, regardless of the time interval involved, such as payment by weight in fruit picking. A variable-ratio schedule provides reinforcement after varying numbers of behaviours are performed based on random work samples, for example, random checks on sales calls leading to sales bonuses.

Ambrose and Kulik (1999) observe that the primary accomplishment in research on reinforcement theory during the 1990s is the renewed interest in punishment as an influence on employee behaviour, with initial results suggesting that it is an area that warrants additional attention.

ONGOING DEBATES/ADVANCED CONCEPTS IN MOTIVATION

CROSS-CULTURAL PERSPECTIVES ON MOTIVATION

To a large extent, motivation is culturally conditioned and learned. Since most motivation theories have been developed in North America and the West, these concepts therefore reflect Western assumptions about human nature. Yet not all Western cultures view motivation the same way.

Maslow's need hierarchy, for example, has been criticised from a cross-cultural perspective. Hofstede, a leading international cultural expert, argues that in countries with cultures that value uncertainty avoidance (like Japan and Greece), job security and lifelong employment are stronger motivators than self-actualisation (Hofstede 1980). Also, in certain European countries, like Norway, Sweden and Denmark, that value and reward quality of life as much as – if not more than – productivity, social needs are stronger motivators than self-esteem or self-actualisation needs (which are higher-order needs in Maslow's hierarchy).

A further example is that in countries that value collectivist and community practices over individualistic achievements, belonging and security are higher-order needs (in contrast to Maslow's hierarchy). One study found that China's hierarchy of needs differs significantly from that of Maslow's. Cultural assumptions underlying Chinese management practices suggest that the nation has priority over everything, with loyalty to the country of utmost importance. Communal property is more important than private possessions, collectivism is seen as the best economic mechanism and emphasis is placed on group forces for motivational purposes (Nevis 1983). The conclusion, therefore, is that need hierarchies differ with culture. Maslow's needs may thus be universal, but the logic or the sequence of the hierarchy is likely to differ from culture to culture.

Herzberg's two factor theory also does not hold up across cultures. A study showed that interpersonal relationships and supervision in New Zealand act as motivators, not hygiene factors; that is, they reduce dissatisfaction (Hines 1973). Hofstede also notes that cultures influence factors that motivate and demotivate. For example, collectivist societies, such as Scandinavian countries, use organisational restructuring strategies (forming work groups to enhance interaction) to increase quality of work life, whereas more individualistic societies, like the US, focus on job enrichment to increase individuals' productivity.

Similarly, Vroom's expectancy theory (1964) is also subject to cross-cultural influences. Vroom's expectancy theory works best in individualistic cultures in which people are viewed as 'rational maximisers of personal utility' and where need fulfilment and expectancies of future achievement are determinants of performance and satisfaction. In collectivist societies, individuals have different types of commitments and links to their organisation, work and to what influences success and satisfaction. For example, in many collectivist societies in the Middle East and Asia, individuals are rewarded not primarily on the nature of the job or achievements, but rather more on relationships with supervisors, owners and co-owners. The accompanying rewards are less likely to be individual incentives like pay or promotion and are more likely to be job security. Expectancy theory is still applicable to different types of societies; the types of rewards, motivations and expectancies simply differ from those in many Western societies (Weiss 1996).

McClelland's motivation theory (1961) holds up better under the test of cross-cultural analysis. Even so, his methods can be questioned as to whether they actually identify and 'detect' achievement and power as defined by other peoples and other cultural business practices. There are societies, like Tahiti, that do not follow McClelland's logic (Miller and Kilpatrick 1987). It is important for human resource managers working with different cultures to realise that not everyone in a culture will share all of its basic societal values, but these values can certainly influence unspoken beliefs, attitudes and motivations.

PREFERENCES FOR JOB CHARACTERISTICS AND REWARDS IN DIFFERENT COUNTRIES

In recruiting new employees as well as managing present ones, it is important to know what their preferences are for the various rewards and inducements organisations can offer in exchange for becoming and remaining productive employees. Preferences vary around the world. Multinational companies and expatriate managers need to be aware of these preferences so that they can target their recruiting messages, reward systems and management styles accordingly.

Table 6.8 shows importance ranks for ten job characteristics by employees in four nations. Interesting work is ranked first in the US but seventh in China. Being in on things is third in the US and last in China. These differences suggest that job enrichment, empowerment and participative management may be better received by US than Chinese employees. Employees in China and Taiwan should be very attracted by good wages, whereas this seems to be much less important to Russian employees (at least it was at the time this data was collected). An additional item that was rated separately as most important by employees in China was employer-subsidised housing, yet this is something that few Western managers would think of as a reasonable benefit for employees.

Table 6.8 Ranked Preferences for Job Characteristics

Job Characteristic	US	People's Republic of China	Taiwan	Russia
Interesting work	1	7	5	3
Appreciation of work done	2	5	4	7
Being 'in on things', being well-informed and involved	3	10	8	2
High job security	4	6	1	6
Good wages	5	1	2	10
Promotion within the organisation	6	4	3	1
Good working conditions	7	2	7	9
Personal loyalty from superiors	8	3	9	4
Tactful discipline	9	9	10	5
Help with personal problems from superiors	10	8	6	8

Source: Fisher and Yuan (1998); Silverthorne (1992)

DO REWARDS MOTIVATE PERFORMANCE?

Kohn (1993) claims that systems for rewards and pay for performance are fundamentally flawed and incapable of motivating performance, stating that rewards elicit temporary compliance at best and do not motivate sustained changes in attitude or commitment. He calls rewards as manipulative and controlling as the threat of punishment, saying that 'do this and you'll get that' is not really very different from 'do this or here's what will happen to you'. He cites laboratory research showing that people become less interested in performing inherently interesting tasks after being paid contingently than when paid at an hourly rate or not paid at all.

Kohn believes that individual incentives breed unhealthy competition among co-workers, reduce teamwork, risk taking and creativity and lead to political behaviour, short-term fixes and cover-ups of errors. He claims that managers use incentives as a cheap and easy way to increase employee effort when they should be concentrating instead on deeper causes of performance problems, such as poor job design, lack of feedback and ineffective leadership.

These arguments seem to be of two kinds: first, that the concept of using rewards to motivate performance is simply wrong, and second, that some individual incentive plans are badly designed and reward the wrong thing. Let us consider the first type of argument – that rewards simply cannot work, no matter how well designed. It is true that most people resent being closely controlled by others and that some reward systems, especially piece-rate incentives or systems that rely on supervisors' subjective judgments, can be seen as very controlling. There is also research, however, showing that performance-contingent pay can actually increase employees' feelings of control by giving them the ability to determine how much they earn. Further, most pay-for-performance systems provide more than just the extrinsic reward of money. Earning more money under these systems also conveys feedback and recognition that a job was done well and is appreciated. Research shows that when the information/feedback value of a reward is seen as more salient than its controlling aspects, intrinsic motivation is enhanced.

Other research shows that when pay is a normal, expected part of a setting, it does not harm and may even increase intrinsic motivation. Certainly, people expect to be paid for their performance at work, so money need not reduce intrinsic motivation in that context. Thus, it seems that the concept of rewards for performance is not flawed. The execution of reward systems, however, can leave much to be desired and sometimes negative consequences do flow from poorly designed incentive systems. Too much focus on getting things done with incentives may distract management from exploring other causes of and solutions for performance problems. A balanced approach is needed, bearing in mind that it is possible to design incentive systems to reward teamwork and creativity and that profit-sharing or gain-sharing systems can increase commitment and interest in business performance among employees.

SUMMARY OF KEY PROPOSITIONS

- This chapter explored the concept of motivation, the study of which aims to address three key questions: What initiates behaviour? What directs behaviour? What sustains behaviour?
- An exploration of the psychological effects of unemployment may provide some important insights into why people are motivated to work. In general terms, people are motivated to be protected from excessive financial anxiety, to have structure in their lives, to develop skills and knowledge, to make decisions and to enhance or maintain their perceived status in their lives.
- The content theories of motivation focus on the needs that people experience and how these needs might drive or initiate behaviour. Maslow's hierarchy of needs, Alderfer's ERG theory, McClelland's achievement motivation theory and Herzberg's two factor theory all attempt to explain, from a variety of perspectives, the role that needs play in motivating people's behaviour. Need theories are useful, but do not provide a comprehensive base for understanding motivation at work.
- Process theories are based on the assumption that individuals and groups consciously think about the effort that they expend at work and its relative utility in reaching valued goals.
- Expectancy theories and equity theories focus on how people consider or weigh up various factors that contribute to their decisions to engage in effort at work.

- Goal setting is another method for understanding what motivates people in the workplace. Goals can be an important motivator, but only when they satisfy essential criteria. Goals should be clear, specific, agreed upon, flexible in certain situations and people should be given timely and accurate feedback about their levels of goal attainment.
- Another method of understanding motivation is reinforcement theory, which focuses on influencing behaviour through rewards and punishments, or reinforcement. Reinforcement can be positive or negative. The scheduling or timing of reinforcement is important, and this can be done through fixed-interval schedules, variable-interval schedules, fixed-ratio schedules and variable-ratio schedules.

DISCUSSION/SELF-ASSESSMENT QUESTIONS

1. Compare three different need theories of motivation. In what ways are they similar and how do they differ in their approaches to motivation at work?
2. Which of the motivation theories discussed in this chapter has the most practical value for managers? Which one has the least practical value?
3. Assess the arguments for and against performance-related pay in light of various motivation theories.
4. Discuss the advantages and disadvantages of expectancy theory to practising managers.
5. Some researchers have argued that understanding human behaviour at work is the single most important requirement for managerial success. Do you agree or disagree?

MULTIPLE CHOICE QUESTIONS

1. The starting point of the motivational process is (are):
   (a) Efforts to fulfil needs.
   (b) Needs.
   (c) Experience of satisfaction.
   (d) Performance.
2. Which of the following perspectives on motivation concerns 'what' motivates people as opposed to 'how' they are motivated?
   (a) Process.
   (b) Content.
   (c) Equity.
   (d) Expectancy.
3. Which of the following factors would not be included in Maslow's physiological needs category?
   (a) Air.
   (b) Food.
   (c) Shelter.

    (d) Positive self-image.

4. At the bottom of the needs hierarchy are:

    (a) Physiological needs.

    (b) Belongingess needs.

    (c) Esteem needs.

    (d) Security needs.

5. The need to have a safe physical and emotional environment is:

    (a) An esteem need.

    (b) A physiological need.

    (c) A security need.

    (d) A social need.

6. The need to continue to grow, develop and expand our capabilities is:

    (a) An esteem need.

    (b) A social need.

    (c) A self-actualisation need.

    (d) A security need.

7. Which of the following is a content/need theory of motivation?

    (a) Two factor.

    (b) Expectancy.

    (c) Equity.

    (d) Security.

8. Which of the following is one of the contentions of ERG theory?

    (a) More than one level of needs can operate simultaneously.

    (b) Employees are primarily motivated by money.

    (c) Satisfaction is contingent on hygiene factors.

    (d) Few people are motivated by a need for achievement.

9. Relatedness needs correspond most closely to Maslow's:

    (a) Physiological and safety needs.

    (b) Belongingness and safety needs.

    (c) Self-actualisation and the need for self-esteem.

    (d) Belongingness and the need for the esteem of others.

10. Which of the following is a motivator according to Herzberg's theory?

    (a) Pay.

    (b) Working conditions.

    (c) Hygiene factors.

    (d) An opportunity to show what you can do.

11. Which theories of motivation deal with 'how' people are motivated?

    (a) Content.

    (b) Need.

    (c) Learned need.

    (d) Process.

12. The theory that says motivation is a function of how much we want something and how likely we think we are of getting it is:
    (a) Expectancy theory.
    (b) Equity theory.
    (c) Two factor theory.
    (d) Hierarchy of needs theory.
13. Which of the following is a process theory of motivation?
    (a) Maslow's needs hierarchy.
    (b) Alderfer's ERG theory.
    (c) McClelland's achievement motivation theory.
    (d) Equity theory.
14. Which motivational theory is based on the idea that employees compare their inputs and outcomes to some other person to determine if they are being fairly treated?
    (a) Expectancy.
    (b) Equity.
    (c) Hierarchy of needs.
    (d) Two factor.
15. Giving prestigious job titles would be one way to satisfy people's need for:
    (a) Esteem.
    (b) Belongingness.
    (c) Self-actualisation.
    (d) Safety.
16. All of the following are parts of the expectancy model except:
    (a) Effort.
    (b) Performance.
    (c) Satisfaction.
    (d) Outcomes.
17. What is the meaning of the term 'valence' as it is used in expectancy theory?
    (a) The overall level of individual motivation.
    (b) A subjective probability estimate that effort will lead to performance.
    (c) The value an individual places on outcomes.
    (d) A subjective probability estimate that performance will lead to rewards.
18. According to the Porter-Lawler extension of equity theory:
    (a) Performance may lead to satisfaction.
    (b) Satisfaction causes performance.
    (c) The performance-to-reward expectancy influences valence.
    (d) Satisfaction, as modified perceived equity of rewards, leads to performance.
19. According to equity theory, all but which of the following are inputs to a job?
    (a) Pay.
    (b) Education.
    (c) Time.
    (d) Effort.

20. The need that people have to work with others, to interact and to have friends is the need for:
    (a) Achievement.
    (b) Esteem.
    (c) Security.
    (d) Affiliation.

FIVE SUGGESTED KEY READINGS

Ambrose, M. and Kulik, C., 'Old friends, new faces: motivation research in the 1990s', *Journal of Management*, XXV/3 (1999), 231–92.

Furnham, A., Bond, M., Heaven, P., Hilton, D., Lobel, T., Masters, J., Payne, M., Rajamanickam, R., Stacey, B. and Van Daalen, H., 'A comparison of Protestant work ethic beliefs in thirteen nations', *Journal of Social Psychology*, CXXXIII (1993), 185–97.

Herzberg, F., 'One more time: how do you motivate employees?', *Harvard Business Review* (January/February 1968).

Pinder, C., *Work Motivation in Organizational Behavior*, New Jersey: Prentice Hall 1998.

Steers, R.M. and Porter, L.W. (eds), *Motivation and Work Behaviour*, London: McGraw-Hill 1987.

REFERENCES

Adams, J.S., 'Towards an understanding of inequity', *Journal of Abnormal and Social Psychology* (November 1963), 422–36.

Alderfer, C.P., *Existence, Relatedness and Growth*, New York: Free Press 1972.

Ambrose, M. and Kulik, C., 'Old friends, new faces: motivation research in the 1990s', *Journal of Management*, XXV/3 (1999), 231–92.

Baron, R.A., 'Motivation in work settings: reflections on the core of organizational research', *Motivation and Emotion*, XV (1991), 1–8.

Crosier, R. and Dalton, K., 'Equity theory examined', in D. Smith (ed.), *Motivation and Control in Organizations*, New York: Baron Press 1989.

Fisher, C.D. and Yuan, A., 'What motivates employees? A comparison of U.S. and Chinese responses', *International Journal of Human Resource Management*, IX (1998), 516–28.

Furnham, A., *The Protestant Work Ethic*, London: Routledge 1990.

Greenberg, J., 'Approaching equity and avoiding inequity in groups and organizations', in J. Greenberg and R.L. Cohen (eds), *Equity and Justice in Social Behavior*, New York: Academic Press 1982, 337–51.

Greenberg, J. and Baron, R.A., *Behavior in Organization*, 6th ed., New Jersey: Prentice Hall 1997.

Hall, D.T. and Nougaim, K.E., 'An examination of Maslow's need hierarchy in an organisational setting', *Organisational Behaviour and Human Performance*, 3 (February 1968), 12–35.

Handy, C., *The Age of Unreason*, London: Arrow 1990.

Hayes, N., *Foundations of Psychology*, London: Routledge 1994.

Herzberg, F., 'One more time: how do you motivate employees?', *Harvard Business Review* (January/February 1968).

Hines, G., 'Cross-cultural differences in two-factor theory', *Journal of Applied Psychology*, LVIII/5 (1973), 375–7.

Hinsz, V.B., Kalnbach, L.R. and Lorentz, N.R., 'Using judgmental anchors to establish challenging self-set goals without jeopardizing commitment', *Organizational Behavior and Human Decision Processes*, LXXI (1997), 287–308.

Hofstede, G., 'Motivation, leadership and organization: do American theories apply abroad?', *Organizational Dynamics* (Summer 1980), 42–63.

Kohn, A., *Punished by Rewards: The Trouble with Gold Stars, Incentive Plans, A's, Praise and Other Bribes*, Boston: Houghton Mifflin 1993.

Lathan, G.P. and Locke, E.A., 'Goal setting – a motivational technique that works', *Organizational Dynamics* (Autumn 1979), 68–80.

McClelland, D.C., *The Achieving Society*, Princeton, NJ: Van Nostrand 1961.

McGregor, D., *The Human Side of Enterprise*, New York: McGraw-Hill 1960, 33–4, 47–8.

Maslow, A.H., 'A theory of human motivation', *Psychological Review*, 50 (July 1943), 370–96.

Maslow, A.H., *Motivation and Personality*, New York: Harper 1954.

Maslow, A.H., *Motivation and Personality*, revised ed., New York: Harper & Row 1970.

Maund, L., *Understanding People and Organisations: An Introduction to Organisational Behaviour*, Cheltenham: Stanley Thornes 1999.

Miles, E.W., Hatfield, J.D. and Huseman, R.C., 'Equity, sensitivity and outcome importance', *Journal of Organizational Behaviour*, XV/7 (1994), 585–96.

Miller, J. and Kilpatrick, J., *Issues for Managers: An International Perspective*, Homewood, IL: Irwin 1987.

Moorhead, G. and Griffin, R.W., *Organizational Behavior: Managing People and Organizations*, 5th ed., Boston: Houghton Mifflin 1998.

Mowday, R.T., 'Equity theory predictions of behavior in organizations', in R.M. Steers and L.W. Porter (eds), *Motivation and Work Behavior*, 5th ed., New York: McGraw-Hill 1991, 111–31.

Murray, H.A., *Explorations in Personality*, New York: Oxford University Press 1975.

Nevis, E., 'Using an American perspective in understanding another culture: towards a hierarchy of needs for the People's Republic of China', *The Journal of Applied Behavioral Science*, XIX/3 (1983), 249–64.

Pinder, C., *Work Motivation in Organizational Behavior*, New Jersey: Prentice Hall 1998.

Porter, L. and Lawler, E., *Managerial Attitudes and Performance*, Homewood, Il: Dorsey Press 1968.

Ribeaux, P. and Poppleton, S.E., *Psychology and Work: An Introduction*, London: Macmillan, Business Management and Administration Series 1978.

Seligman, M.E.P., 'Fall into helplessness', *Psychology Today*, 7 (1973), 43–8.

Shenkar, O. and Von Glinow, M.A., 'Paradoxes of organisational theory and research: using the case of China to illustrate national contingency', *Management Science*, XL (1994), 56–71.

Silverthorne, C.P., 'Work motivation in the United States, Russia, and the Republic of China (Taiwan): a comparison', *Journal of Applied Social Psychology* (1992), 1631–69.

Skinner, B.F., *The Behavior of Organization*, New York: Appleton-Century-Crofts 1938.

Steers, R.M. and Porter, L.W. (eds), *Motivation and Work Behaviour*, London: McGraw-Hill 1987.

Tansey, R., Hyman, M.R., Zinkhan, G.M. and Chowdhury, J., 'An advertising test of the work ethic in the U.K. and the U.S.', *Journal of International Consumer Marketing*, IX (1997), 57–77.

Vroom, V., *Work and Motivation*, New York: Wiley 1964.

Warr, P., *Work, Jobs and Unemployment*, London: Macmillan 1984.

Weaver, C.N., 'Has the work ethic in the USA declined? Evidence from nationwide surveys', *Psychological Reports*, LXXXI (1997), 491–5.

Weick, K.E., 'The concept of equity in the perception of pay', *Administrative Science Quarterly*, XI (1966), 414–39.

Weiss, J.W., *Organizational Behavior and Change: Managing Diversity, Cross-cultural Dynamics, and Ethics*, New York: West Publishing 1996.

White, R.W., 'Motivation reconsidered: the concept of competence', *Psychological Review*, 66 (1959), 297–333.

SECTION THREE

THE DYNAMICS OF ORGANISATIONAL CONTEXT

THE DYNAMICS OF COMMUNICATION

Learning Objectives

- To introduce and define the concept of communication.
- To outline the communication process.
- To assess listening skills.
- To present a model of how managers communicate and depict information flow in the organisation.
- To outline the barriers to communication and set out the characteristics of effective communication.
- To present information on the role of communication in leading-edge companies.
- To highlight key issues around the use of the organisational grapevine.
- To outline some communication issues that arise in international firms.

INTRODUCTION

Early discussions of management gave little emphasis to communication. Although it was implicit in the management function of command and the structural principle of hierarchy, Luthans (1992) argues that the early theorists never fully appreciated its significance or completely developed or integrated it into management theory. Traditionally, information has gone up the management hierarchy to where decisions were made and then back down to where they were implemented. However, since Mintzberg's (1975) work on the manager's job, there has been clear evidence that managers spend a good deal of their time in face-to-face exchange with employees as part of their organisational role.

Today, everyone knows that communication is vital to the organisation and communication is now accepted as one of the core management processes. Nearly every aspect of the way people are managed involves critical elements of communication. Indeed, Smythe (1995: 31) goes so far as to say that 'the "discipline" of organisational communication has arrived.' However, not everyone is able to create the type of information-rich environment that is necessary in today's competitive world. Communicative interactions in the form of meetings, e-mail, phone calls, memos, interviews, reports, advertisements, etc. make communication a pervasive feature of organisations. Any individual who is to be an effective member of an organisation must be a competent communicator, and for an organisation to be effective, its communication must be effective. Creating the right communications environment may require a large-scale change in attitudes and approaches of all organisational stakeholders and a climate of trust that encourages the free flow of ideas.

DEFINITIONS OF KEY CONCEPTS

Communication
The process of sending and receiving messages with attached meanings, with the ultimate meaning in any communication being created by the receiver or perceiver of the message.

Organisational communication
Viewed as an ongoing process that includes patterns of interaction between organisational members that both emerge from and shape the nature and actions of the organisation and the events within it.

Noise
A term used to describe any barriers to or disturbance within the communication process that disrupts it and distorts or interferes with the transfer of messages.

Non-verbal communication
Includes all of the elements associated with human communication that are not expressed orally or in writing.

Communication channels
The formal and/or informal mechanisms/routes by which the message is transmitted from the sender to the receiver.

Grapevine
The informal, person-to-person, unofficial communication network that permeates the organisation. Communication spread through this network is not officially sanctioned and does not necessarily flow along an established chain of command.

Interest in business communication has seldom been higher than it is today (McClave 1997), largely because pay-offs are found both in terms of employee satisfaction and organisational performance. According to the broader literature, effective communication has the potential to foster greater commitment (Kane 1996; Lippit 1997), is a significant predictor of job satisfaction (Miles et al. 1996), acts as a conduit for the promotion and development of collaboration between organisational stakeholders (Bolton and Dewatripont 1994; Mintzberg et al. 1996), facilitates the diffusion of teamwork (Lawson and Bourner 1997; Pettit 1997) and can prove significant in improving internal control and facilitating strategy development (Steinberg 1998). As Ludlow and Panton (1992: 3) summarily outline, communication is important in performance terms because it keeps people in the picture, gets people involved with the organisation, increases motivation to perform well, increases commitment to the organisation, makes for better relationships and understanding between boss and subordinate and helps people understand the need for change, how they should manage it and how to reduce resistance to it.]

Similarly, in an attempt to highlight the importance and economic values of information and communication systems, Woods (1993: 7) assesses the potential of a variety of different communication channels for addressing the broad human and institutional development functions on which growth and success depend.

Table 7.1 indicates the relative potential of a host of different communication channels for developing what are viewed as critical functions.

Table 7.1 Comparative Potential of Different Communications Media

Functions	Communication Media							
	Press	Books	Radio	TV	Phone	Phone+	Computers	Informatics
Topical information	XXX		XX	XXX	XX	XX	X	XX
Formal education	X	XX	X	X	X	XX	XX	XXX
Two-way communication			X		XXX	XXX	X	XXX
Interactive learning		X			X	XX	XX	XXX
Skill development		X		X	X	XX	XX	XXX
Motivation	X	X	X	XX	XX	XX	X	XX
Entertainment	X	X	X	XXX		X	X	XXX
Group decisions	X		X	XX	X	XX	X	XXX
Data supply	X	XX				XX	XX	XXX
Data processing						X	XXX	XXX
Planning		X			XX	XX	XX	XXX
Design		X				X	XX	XXX
Financing					X	X	XX	XXX
Monitoring					X	XX	XX	XXX
Financial control		X			X	XX	XX	XXX

Notes:

1. 'Phone' refers to traditional, voice-only telephone services. 'Phone+' (also called 'telematics') is what becomes possible with teleconferencing and with networks and databases where telephony links remote computers to mainframe computers. 'Informatics' goes beyond telematics reorder by decentralising substantial memory and processing power to local level and linking the uses of the whole family of digital technologies.

2. Printed and broadcast media have potential in most of the functions other than those for which they are given a rating in Table 7.1, but their relative potential in those functions is small.

3. One can argue over the relative potential of one communication medium over another. For example, is TV more entertaining than radio or books? What is their potential in supplying data? A medium able to communicate sound, pictures, graphics and script has a greater

potential in these fields than media able to communicate only with literate people. In the past, broadcast media had the disadvantage that the information and the entertainment they offered was sent at the broadcaster's convenience, not the viewer's or listener's. (Video recorders were used to overcome this difficulty in relation to TV.) However, more recent media, which have the real-time capacity to provide information interactively and learning and entertainment materials on demand, demonstrate far greater potential than those that cannot.

Source: Woods (1993: 8)

By way of tapping into this potential, there is now clear evidence that organisations across Europe are going beyond trite statements about their employees being their major asset to actually developing and increasing the amount of communication and consultation in which they involve those employees (Brewster *et al.* 1994). The considerable moves that have been made by many employers in Europe to expand the degree of information given to the workforce irrespective of legal requirements is clear, which reflects a central theme of standard concepts of modern people management – the requirement to generate significant workforce commitment (Mayrhofer *et al.* 1997). Kar (1972) estimates that between forty and sixty per cent of work time in a typical manufacturing plant can involve some phase of communication, while Beach (1970) estimates that top- and middle-level executives devote sixty to eighty per cent of their total working lives to communication. Thus, for management as well as organisational theorists, communication is the key element and theoretical construct, respectively, for describing and explaining organisational phenomena. Weick (1989: 97) states that 'interpersonal communication is the essence of organisation because it creates structures that affect what else gets said and done by whom.' Even more significant is communication in the conceptualisation of organisations made by sociological systems theory. Luhmann (1987) argues that communications are the basic elements of social systems, and the (latent) structures that form and guide communications are particularly relevant if one is interested in organisations' behaviour.

DEFINING COMMUNICATION

Communication has many definitions – at least 100 according to Goldhaber (1990). However, it may be studied from different perspectives. In this chapter we are concerned about how information is exchanged and shared in the organisational context.

Axley (1996) defines communication as a process of sending and receiving messages with attached meanings, with the ultimate meaning in any communication being created by the receiver or perceiver of the message. Alternatively, Fisher (1993) suggests that communication may be defined as consisting of two types of actions: those that create messages or displays and those that interpret messages or displays. A display consists of information not necessarily intended as a message but from which an observer can derive meaning. A principle of communication holds that 'a person cannot not communicate'.

Thus, one's clothing, posture or facial expression make a meaningful display, whether or not we intend them as messages.

Organisational communication is similar to other forms of communication in that it involves making and interpreting message displays, but it also differs since it is viewed as an ongoing process that includes patterns of interaction between organisational members that both emerge from and shape the nature and actions of the organisation and the events within it. McClave (1997: 20) simply refers to it as internal communication, which is the exchange of information that occurs among people within the organisation that can occur in a formal or informal way. Formal organisational communication generally follows the formal organisation structure and employs methodologies sanctioned by management. Informal organisational communication springs up by virtue of common interests between people in organisations, which may be caused by work, social or outside relationships. The most powerful channel is the 'grapevine', which McClave (1997: 24–5) argues has several positive features, including the fact that it is often the only source of vital information for employees, it acts as a social glue in holding the organisation together and, contrary to popular belief, grapevine information has been found to be mainly accurate. It has been estimated that managers receive over half the information they need for planning purposes through the grapevine.

Price (1997: 349) conceives of organisational communication simply as the degree to which information is transmitted among members of the organisation. While this transmission assumes many forms (formal discussions between superiors and subordinates, informal conferences among subordinates, publication of various types of newsletters, production of radio and television programmes, posting of announcements on bulletin boards, the use of public address systems and so forth), he notes that four broad dimensions are found in the extant literature. Concurring with many writers, the first and most pervasive distinction is between formal and informal communication. As we have highlighted, the basis of this distinction is whether the transmission is official or unofficial.

The second common distinction Price identified is between vertical and horizontal communication. Vertical communication refers to the transmission of information in superordinate-subordinate relationships, whether from superordinate to subordinate or from subordinate to superordinate. Horizontal communication refers to the transmission of information among peers.

A third distinction advanced also differentiates between personal and impersonal communication. The basis of this distinction is whether or not the information is transmitted in situations where mutual influence is possible. Personal conversations and telephone calls are examples of personal communication, whereas the mass media is an example of impersonal communication.

Fourth, Price distinguishes between instrumental and expressive communication. The transmission of information necessary to do a job is instrumental communication, whereas expressive communication refers to the residual category of non-job information.

Thus, to a large extent an organisation *is* communication, both formal and informal, vertical and horizontal, personal and impersonal and instrumental and expressive. Fisher

(1993: 3) notes that this is more true than ever now because the information age is upon us. Sophisticated communication technologies bring outside information into organisations faster and in greater volumes than ever before. In this vein, Wilson *et al.* (1986) take a more contingency view of organisational communication, suggesting that it is an evolutionary, culturally dependent process of sharing information and creating relationships in environments designed for manageable, goal-oriented behaviour. The primary purpose in organisational communication is thus to achieve 'co-ordinated action' (Baskin and Aronoff 1980). Just as the human nervous system responds to stimuli and co-ordinates responses by sending messages to various parts of the body, communication co-ordinates the various parts of the organisation.

THE PURPOSE OF COMMUNICATION

In the organisational context communication may serve several major functions, among which are motivating the workforce, controlling member behaviour, persuading and influencing, aiding decision making and assisting in employee retention.

Communication is important in the context of motivating a workforce. Maitland (2002) notes that effective internal communication is an essential weapon in the battle to motivate employees, yet research shows that all too often key workers essential to an organisation's competitiveness are unhappy about the quality and the quantity of the information that they receive. In this context, Maitland suggests that a systematic approach is required as the best way forward in improving the situation. First, a serious diagnosis is necessary in order to unearth exactly what employees really think. The information garnered from this exercise should then be used to establish the key drivers of employee satisfaction. Once the organisation then establishes which of these offers the greatest room for improvement, an action plan should be devised to effect the key drivers. According to Maitland, this plan should be accompanied by measurable targets by which the organisation's performance may be judged.

Communication can also serve to control organisational member behaviour. Robbins (2001) suggests that communication acts to control in several ways. Thus, he highlights that when employees are required to first communicate any job-related grievance to their immediate boss, to follow their job description or to comply with company policies, communication is performing a control function. Informal communication, he suggests, also controls behaviour. For example, he suggests that when work groups tease or harass a member who produces too much, they are actually informally communicating with and controlling that member's behaviour.

Communication is similarly important in the context of persuading and influencing employees. This is particularly true in the context of leadership communication, where it is argued that organisational leaders can improve their relationships with members by focusing on developing their interpersonal communication strategy (Campbell *et al.* 2003). Leaders are encouraged to develop higher-quality relations with their employees to increase communication satisfaction. Close attention should be paid to the interactional and communicative behaviours that build rapport. Campbell *et al.* (2003: 189) suggest that less effective leaders might improve their success in interactions with members by choosing a communication strategy based on the following heuristic.

- Am I striving to consolidate internal processes, maximise output, adapt or build human commitment by communicating this message?
- Do I intend to inform, direct, consult or build trust with the member?
- How urgent is my need to communicate with the member?
- What is the quality of my current relationship with the member?
- Will the member's wants or rights be threatened by my message?
- Should my primary message be on my message or my relationship?

[Communication is an important aid to decision making within the organisation.] Effective decision making requires appropriate, timely information transmitted to the appropriate people.]

Communication is important in employee retention as well. Thornton (2001) highlights that keeping good employees is probably one of the most important issues facing organisations today. She notes that while there are a variety of reasons why people leave organisations, all too often they leave because they feel that they are not valued and because management fail to communicate with them or listen to their opinions. She suggests that the reality of limited resources and pressing and heavy demands means that internal communication often does not get the attention it requires. Managers and supervisors need to create an environment where employees have the information they need to do their job, where they feel respected and valued and where communication is truly a priority. Consequently, according to Thornton, when people have the information they need to perform their jobs and communication is at optimal levels across the organisation, it stands to reason that employee morale, productivity, effectiveness and efficiency will also be at optimal levels. Under these circumstances, she notes that employees are more likely to stay in their jobs than look for greener pastures.

By way of building and promulgating a strategy to enhance employee retention, Thornton suggests that a complete programme of employee communication tools, programmes and training in addition to the support and commitment of the leadership of the organisation is necessary. It is suggested that an effective strategy aimed at ensuring employee retention might have the following multiple elements.

- Determining the employees' needs and preferences.
- Using multiple channels to communicate, including (but not limited to) brochures, manuals, phone, e-mail, intranet, CD-ROM, meetings, face-to-face encounters, posters, videos, conferences, staff gatherings, information sessions, work groups, newsletters, displays, notice boards, memos, reports and even the grapevine.
- Ensuring that employees get reliable, timely, up-to-date news about what is happening in the organisation and the information they need to do their job, to feel part of a team and to feel pride in being part of something bigger.
- Constantly measuring and evaluating the effectiveness of the tools and activities, i.e.

in addition to asking people if they like publications, videos or brochures, asking people to evaluate what they learn from them and what difference they make in their behaviour, satisfaction levels, knowledge or ability to do the job.
- Supporting and bolstering the informal communication in the organisation.

THE COMMUNICATION PROCESS

The key elements in the communication process are illustrated in Figure 7.1. Arguably one of the most influential linear models, its earlier iterations did not include a feedback loop. The key elements in the communication process include a source, who encodes the intended meaning into a message, and a receiver, who decodes the message. The receiver may or may not give feedback to the source. Noise is the term used to describe any barriers to or disturbance within the communication process that disrupts it and distorts or interferes with the transfer of messages.

Figure 7.1 The Communication Process

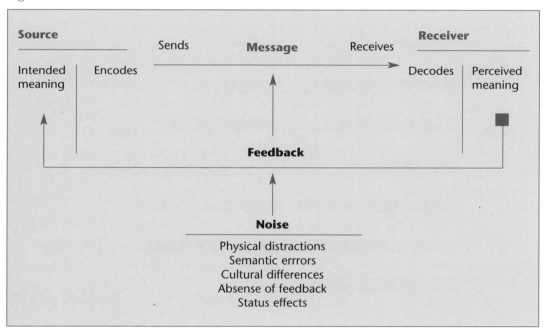

Source: Based on Shannon and Weaver (1949)

The information source is a person or group trying to communicate with someone else. Reasons for why the source is communicating could include changing the receiver's attitudes, knowledge or behaviour. In group or organisational communication, an individual may send a message on behalf of the organisation. The source is responsible for preparing the message, encoding it and entering it into a transmission medium.

The next step in the communication process is encoding, the process of translating an idea or thought into meaningful symbols that can be transmitted. The symbols may be words, numbers, pictures, sounds or physical gestures and movements. The source must encode the message in symbols that the receiver can decode properly, i.e. the source and the receiver must attach the same meaning to the symbols. When we use the symbols of a common language, we assume that those symbols have the same meaning to everyone who uses them. Yet the inherent ambiguity of symbol systems can lead to decoding errors. The resulting message may be written (letters, memos, reports, manuals, forms), oral (formal speeches, informal conversations, group discussions), non-verbal (including human elements such as facial expressions or body language) or perhaps some combination of these. This message is then translated through various possible channels, or delivery media, which are the path of transmission.

Figure 7.2 presents the results of a Europe-wide survey on the common methods organisations use to communicate with their employees. It presents the overall averages across Europe of organisations reporting an increase and/or decrease in the use of various methods. Overall one can see a definite increase in the use of various communication fora.

Figure 7.2 Common Methods Used by Organisations to Communicate with Employees

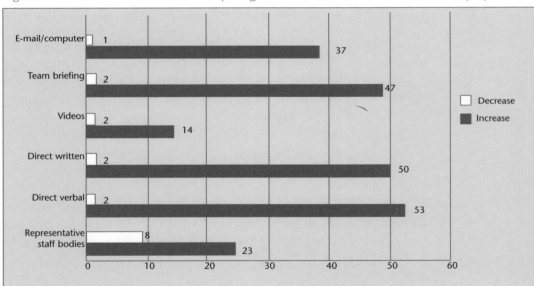

Source: Mayrhofer *et al.* (1997)

Critically, the choice made here relating to the channels can have an important impact on the communication process, as different media have different capacities for carrying information. Some messages are better handled by specific channels, while some individuals are not particularly comfortable with certain channels. Organisations typically produce a great deal of written communication of many kinds. A letter is a common formal means of communicating with an individual, often someone outside the organisation. Internally, probably the most frequent form of written communication is the memo, which tends to address single topics, and while more impersonal than other modes, they are less formal than letters. Reports are typically used to present the results or progress of specific projects and are often a central aid to decision making.

The most common form of organisational communication is oral, which is particularly powerful because it includes not only the speaker's words but also their changes in tone, pitch, volume and speed. People will typically draw upon all of these cues associated with oral communication for the purpose of understanding the message.

Non-verbal communication includes all of the elements associated with human communication that are not expressed orally or in writing (Moorhead and Griffin 1995). Human elements include facial expressions and physical movements that may be conscious or unconscious. Among the common facial expressions which have been identified and classified are interest/excitement, enjoyment/joy, surprise/startle, distress/anguish, fear/terror, shame/humiliation, contempt/disgust and anger/rage. Body language elements (referred to as the study of kinesics) that are often drawn upon during the communication process include eye contact, which expresses a willingness to communicate, sitting on the edge of the chair, which may indicate nervousness or anxiety, or folded arms, which might signal a certain defensiveness. Drooped shoulders, a furrowed brow, talking with your hands and the tilt of the head may all prove to be important.

Ekman and Friesen (1969) have identified five categories of body expressions that we commonly use as part of our communication repertoire.

- **Emblems** refer to common gestures that may substitute for the use of words. The conventional wave of the hand as a gesture of goodbye is a classic emblem.
- **Illustrators** serve to accompany and complement spoken language and are used for emphasis or directions. For example, when being asked what time it is, if one holds up three fingers while saying it is three o'clock, one is making use of an illustrator.
- **Regulators** control verbal interaction. For example, when you nod your head while someone is talking to you, this signals that they should continue.
- **Affect displays** reveal the emotional state of the communicator, e.g. a frown or a clenched fist indicating anger.
- **Adaptors** are non-verbal habits unique to the individual, for example, scratching one's nose or pulling at one's ear.

Thus, the possible elements involved in decoding can be complex. Decoding is the process by which the receiver of the message interprets its meaning. The receiver will typically draw upon their knowledge and experience to decode the message. The meaning the receiver attaches to the symbols must be the same as the meaning intended by the source for effective communication to have taken place. The receiver of the message may be an individual, a group or an organisation.

A critical skill necessary for the proper reception of the message is good active listening, which means the receiver has a definite responsibility, i.e. not passively absorbing the message, but rather actively trying to grasp its facts and the emotions.

LISTENING SKILLS ACTIVITY

Good listening skills are essential for effective communication and are often overlooked when communication is analysed. This self-assessment questionnaire examines your ability to listen effectively. Work through the following statements, marking 'Yes' or 'No' in the space next to each one. Mark each statement as truthfully as you can in light of your behaviour in the last few gatherings or meetings you have attended.

	Yes	No
1. I frequently attempt to listen to several conversations at the same time.		
2. I like people to give me the facts and then let me make my own interpretation.		
3. I sometimes pretend to pay attention to people.		
4. I consider myself a good judge of non-verbal communication.		
5. I usually know what another person is going to say before he or she says it.		
6. I usually end conversations that don't interest me by diverting my attention from the speaker.		
7. I frequently nod, frown or in some way let the speaker know how I feel about what he or she is saying.		
8. I usually respond immediately when someone has finished talking.		
9. I evaluate what is being said while it is being said.		
10. I usually formulate a response while the other person is still talking.		
11. The speaker's 'delivery' style frequently keeps me from listening to content.		
12. I usually ask people to clarify what they have said rather than guess at the meaning.		
13. I make a concerted effort to understand other people's point of view.		
14. I frequently hear what I expect to hear rather than what is said.		
15. Most people feel that I have understood their point of view when we disagree.		

Scoring: The correct answers according to communication theory are as follows:

No for statements 1, 2, 3, 5, 6, 7, 8, 9, 10, 11, 14.
Yes for statements 4, 12, 13, 15.

If you missed only one or two responses, you strongly approve of your own listening habits and you are on the right track to becoming an effective listener. If you missed three or four responses, you have uncovered some doubts about your listening effectiveness and your knowledge of how to listen has some gaps. If you missed five or more responses, you probably are not satisfied with the way you listen and your friends and co-workers may not feel you are a good listener, either. Work on improving your active listening skills.

Source: Glenn and Pond (1989)

There is a final aspect of our communication model/process which Shannon and Weaver (1949) originally neglected to consider, namely feedback. When we communicate face to face we get some instant feedback on how our message has been received and interpreted and our ability to exchange meaning effectively is greatly enhanced by this rich feedback loop (Buchanan and Huczynski 1997). Feedback allows us to constantly check the accuracy of the coding and decoding processes. With more formal and remote methods, at worst feedback can be non-existent or perhaps at best slow and unreliable, thus we need to take more care in coding the message.

HOW MANAGERS COMMUNICATE

Thornton (2001) summarises a variety of survey results by stating that 'a manager's number one problem can be summed up in one word: communication.' This is rather unsurprising, since for approximately eighty per cent of all managers, most time is spent on verbal communication. Luthans and Larsen (1986) combined the direct observation of managers in their natural setting with self-report measures to try to determine how they actually communicated. The model presented in Figure 7.3 depicts the results.

Figure 7.3 How Managers Communicate: The Managerial Communication Model

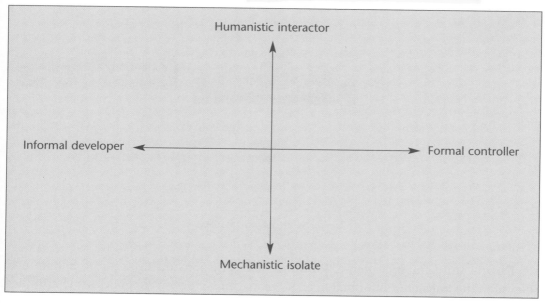

The first dimension of the managerial communication model represents a continuum ranging from the humanistic interactor (who frequently interacts both up and down the organisation hierarchy and exhibits human-oriented activities) to the mechanistic isolate (who communicates very little, except on a formal basis). The other dimension describes a continuum from the informal developer (who communicates spontaneously in all directions and exhibits activities related to developing his or her people) to formal controller (who uses formally scheduled communication interaction and exhibits monitoring/controlling activities). This empirically derived model describes two major dimensions of managerial communication. It provides a framework for how managers communicate on a day-to-day basis and, according to the authors, can be used as a point of departure for formally defining communication and the processes and systems of communication in today's organisations.

As highlighted earlier in this chapter, the flow of communication internally through formal channels in the organisation may be in different directions, namely downward, upward and/or lateral.

Figure 7.4 Direction for Information Flow in Organisations

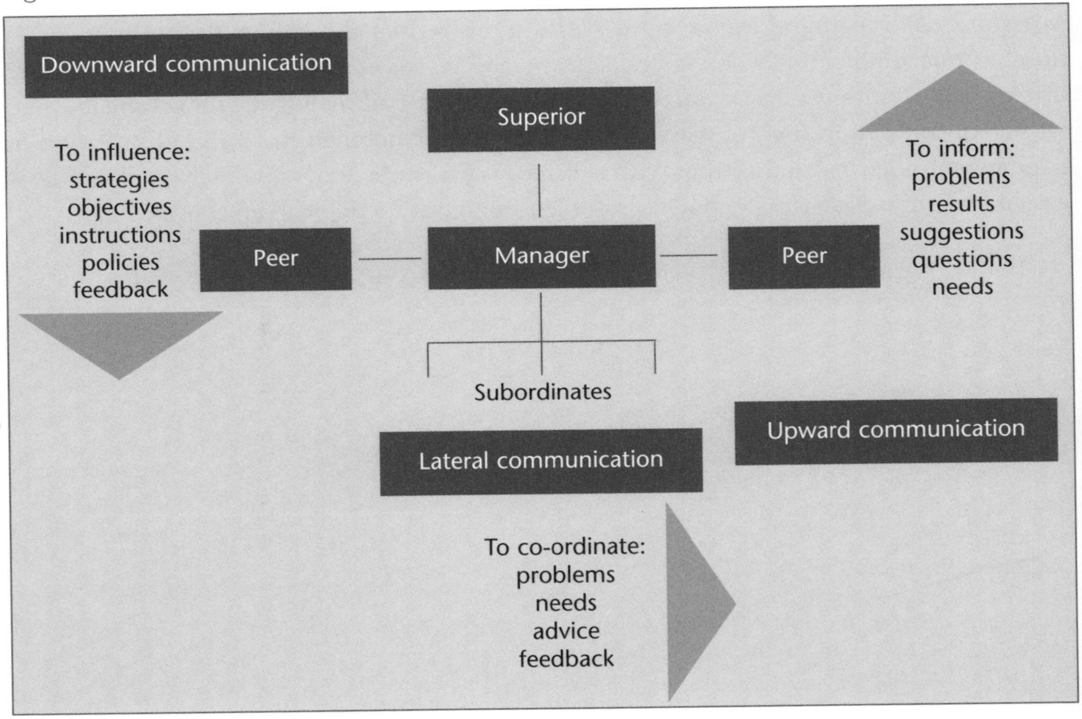

Source: Schermerhorn (1996)

Downward communication follows the chain of command from top to bottom and 'describes the transfer of information about management decisions, policies and attitudes to those lower in the hierarchy' (McClave 1997: 22). It is typically used for reiterating the nature of key strategic decisions and providing information on business performance results. The downward messages also consist of information that is necessary for any staff to carry out their work, such as policies and procedures, orders and requests that are passed down to the appropriate level in the hierarchy. Upward communication describes the flow of messages from lower to higher levels in the hierarchy. Upward messages are reports, requests, opinions and perhaps complaints. Sideways or lateral messages are between different departments, functions or people at the same level in the organisation and serve the important purposes of informing, supporting and co-ordinating activities across internal organisational boundaries.

INDIVIDUAL AND ORGANISATIONAL BARRIERS TO COMMUNICATION

Barriers to communication, often referred to as 'noise', are obstacles that distort or block the flow of needed information, thus interrupting the organisation's performance orientation and preventing people from exchanging ideas and emotions as effectively as they might wish. The barriers may be associated with the individual or the organisation.

- **Message uncertainty:** We may often be unclear about what exactly it is we want to communicate. It may be lack of understanding on our part, it may be that we are not certain about what message the receiver needs in order to achieve the desired effect or perhaps it may be that we are uncertain about how much information is necessary.

- **Perceptual selectivity and/or incompatible viewpoints:** People can take in and understand only a certain amount of information at one time. Perceptual distortions can be caused by having a poor self-concept or self-understanding or a poor understanding of others. People may fail to communicate because they see the world in very different ways, so shared understanding may be impossible for them.

- **Language differences:** The same words can mean different things to different people. Semantic problems occur when people use either the same word in different ways or different words in the same way. Problems of this nature also occur when people use jargon that they expect others to understand or language that is outside the other's vocabulary.

- **Implicit assumptions:** Beliefs that the communicator holds without being fully aware of them and without having thought them through. Communication will likely fail if the sender and the receiver have different assumptions about some aspect of the message and are unaware that they differ.

- **Status and authority effects:** Social factors within an organisation that lead to mistrust between its members or groups. Effects such as these are particularly common in hierarchical structures. Task differentiation and specialisation at different levels in the organisation result in differences in jargon, training and work focus that may impair organisation members' understanding of each other.

- **Lack of feedback:** Anything that keeps the sender from knowing that the other has received, acknowledged and understood the message. Although one-way communication is quicker, two-way is more accurate. While it may be difficult, in complex situations it helps both sender and receiver to measure their understanding and may improve their joint commitment to the issues at hand.

- **Lack of consultation/involvement and/or deception:** Tendency to avoid the input of people who will be affected by or who are capable of improving a decision. A person may sometimes decide that it is not in his or her best interests to tell other people all they might like to know, so the person refrains from communication. Or perhaps the communication is ambiguous, involving messages that it is known will be misinterpreted. Or people may simply tell lies, hoping that they will not be caught out or, if they are, that the receiver will be powerless to do anything about it.

CHARACTERISTICS OF EFFECTIVE COMMUNICATION

Effective communication is a critical organisational process as well as a key skill for managers. Dawson (1996: 193) identifies five characteristics of an ideal communication process.

1. **Accuracy:** The message clearly reflects intention and truth as seen by the sender and is received as such.
2. **Reliability:** Diverse observers would receive the message in the same way.
3. **Validity:** The message captures reality, is consistent, allows prediction and incorporates established knowledge.
4. **Adequacy:** The message is of sufficient quantity and appropriate timing.
5. **Effectiveness:** The message achieves the intended result from the sender's point of view.

McClave (1997: 14–15) outlines critical principles of effective communication from both the perspective of the communicator/sender and the receiver/perceiver.

Table 7.2 Principles of Effective Communication

As communicator:
Think carefully about your objectives before communicating: Ask yourself what you are trying to achieve. Do you want to inform, persuade, advise or consult the receiver? What kind of response do you need?
Put yourself in the receiver's shoes: Remember that the receiver's perception or frame of reference may not be the same as your own.
Choose the right medium or combination of media: Difficulties can arise if the wrong medium is used. For instance, when giving a talk, you may leave the audience bewildered if you try to describe a complicated process by means of speech alone. A combination of words and graphics may be necessary.
Organise your ideas and express them carefully: Take time to structure your ideas in a logical sequence. In choosing your words, take into consideration the understanding and linguistic ability of the receiver ... Use language suited to the context in which communication is taking place ...

Language that is appropriate to the shop floor may be very inappropriate in a committee meeting.

Consider the context: Breakdowns in communication often occur because the receiver is given information at the wrong time or in the wrong place. Even a very important message can be promptly forgotten if the receiver is busy or preoccupied in thought. In general, always put yourself in the receiver's position and try to anticipate any difficulties or concerns he may have.

Check for feedback: Make sure your message has been received and understood … Be prepared to repeat or re-explain if necessary.

As receiver:

Give the message your full attention: Many messages are misunderstood because the receiver is daydreaming or not concentrating. Focus on the message and try to ignore or remove distractions.

Interpret the message correctly: Interpreting the message requires effort. If you are unsure about what is being said, ask for clarification. Check the meaning of unfamiliar words or references. Be alert for non-verbal nuances that may subtly alter the meaning of the communication.

Keep an open mind: You should not allow dislike of the communicator or disagreement with his beliefs to influence your judgment. Try to acknowledge your own prejudices and make an objective assessment of the message, no matter what your relationship with the sender.

Record information you are likely to forget: Listeners in particular should take the time to jot down factual information they are likely to forget.

Respond appropriately: Respond positively to the communicator by providing feedback, following up enquiries or taking whatever other action is necessary.

Source: McClave (1997: 14–15)

THE ROLE OF THE COMMUNICATIONS FUNCTION IN LEADING-EDGE ORGANISATIONS

According to Morley *et al.* (2000), in the modern organisation the importance of effective communication is emphasised by three core factors: the increasing importance of information as an organisational function, the increasing recognition that it is only through exploiting employees' ideas and talents that organisations will be able to compete and survive and the need to convince employees that working for the organisation is something they should be committed to and to which they should devote their ideas, energy and creativity. In the high-performance organisation, information is viewed as a tool, not a privilege. The overarching philosophy is that everyone in the organisation must have access to the maximum amount of information that it is reasonable to be able to assimilate, understand and utilise. In a debate on the role and significance of communication in today's business environment, Smythe (1995), writing in *People*

Management, argues that the role of internal communications in an organisation is no longer limited to merely providing information to employees; rather, in the present business environment it has a role to play in defining and improving the relationship between employers and employees and in helping in the management of strategic, structural, technological and process changes within the organisation.

Of greater significance, Smythe's research identifies eight practical roles that the communication function will likely perform in leading-edge organisations, namely acting as the cultural conscience of the organisation, the communication planner, the communicator of decisions, the facilitator of revisioning, the provider of the big picture context, the facilitator of real-time listening, the facilitator of consultation, involvement and empowerment and the integrator of the internal culture and the external brand.

THE CULTURAL CONSCIENCE OF THE ORGANISATION

Smythe argues that the style of relationships between people in the organisation is one of the most tangible experiences that employees have of the organisation's culture and that relationships are the prime conduit or window through which employees experience, learn and contribute to the organisation's culture. In this respect he suggests that organisational communication can provide the instruments to measure relationship styles and facilitate debate among the leaders of the organisation on what kinds of relationship styles will be most useful.

> Becoming the organisation's conscience is important if, as seems likely, the styles of relationship are critical to retaining customers, employees and productive supplier and partner alliances … The communication role is to understand the expectations and ethics that the organisation must be aligned with. Consequently it must facilitate the articulation of values and behaviour that should characterise relationships between employees and between employees and key external groups (Smythe 1995: 27).

THE COMMUNICATION PLANNER

Traditionally, communication and information in the organisational context were rather more scarce than they are today. Smythe notes that the dramatic increase in the volume of communication brings with it the challenge of reconciling the needs and capacity of the audience. He suggests that this role should fall to a communication planner, who acts as a negotiator between the suppliers of information on the one hand and notes the capacity of employees to digest information on the other. The communication planner would thus act in the manner of an air traffic controller, permitting digestible quantities of information at any one time to be discharged to employees.

TRANSPARENCY OF DECISIONS

While institutional secrecy was the order of the day in earlier times, such constraints are becoming less and less common. Today, Smythe notes, instant communication is a role born of necessity. Decision makers require speed of implementation and recipients want clear, quick and honest reporting. The implication of this, he suggests, is the necessity to give communicators access to the decision-making fora of the organisation and to use modern, speedy technologies to distribute information.

FACILITATOR OF REVISIONING

The research demonstrates that organisations with vision sparkle with new ideas and take big leaps, often risky ones, to gain competitive advantage. Smythe argues that the quest to build a visioning ethos into organisations has fallen into the barren territory of producing mission statements that inspire no one, and, in a compelling fashion, he suggests that 'the real task is to hijack the often dull planning process to license a period of imagination.' The communication role here is to build inspiring revisioning into the planning process and to channel the results into the communication and transmission of the big picture.

BIG PICTURE CONTEXT

Here Smythe argues that issues need to be dealt with as part of an overall organisational plan and the communications role is to creatively use the channels and media of communication to tell stories about new procedures, processes and products and to put them in the context of the overall vision. He states that people react well to working in the context of a compelling vision.

REAL-TIME LISTENING

It is argued that the basis of a good relationship is good listening skills. (If you have not already done so, take some time to complete the Listening Skills Activity presented earlier in this chapter.) In a more macro way there is a need to reflect on how the organisation as a whole listens. Real-time listening is a continuous process and is deemed critical to the organisation's ongoing psychological health. One needs to be continuously versed in what concerns people have, what they want to know more about and what they have heard from the organisation and from each other. Thus, it is suggested that there must be processes in place to listen and to engage management in hearing what has been fed back so that there is a real connection between communication and listening.

PRODUCTIVE CONSULTATION, INVOLVEMENT AND EMPOWERMENT

This is a theme that we have already visited in this book. The central issue here, according to Smythe's reflections, is the attitude that management has about the role of employees in the decision-making process. Are employees there to implement the ideas of the few without questioning these ideas or influencing them? Or is it worth taking the time to seek and make use of employee input?

INTEGRATOR OF INTERNAL CULTURE AND EXTERNAL BRAND

Finally, Smythe highlights as an emerging communication role that which aims to reconcile the thinking and the programmes conceived by the inward- and outward-facing disciplines of the organisation so that the promises that the organisation makes and the experiences of its customers are aligned.

Promoting knowledge-sharing behaviour is also important in leading-edge companies. According to Seeley (2000), its importance should not be underestimated and a carefully tailored communication plan that lays the groundwork for disseminating essential messages may prove useful in the context of managing and mastering ongoing change in organisations. Seeley suggests that a communication plan helps in articulating messages and explaining the processes through which they will travel to their audiences. The components of a typical communication plan in this regard include:

- a defined change stage;
- a message;
- the target audience;
- the delivery method;
- responsibility for delivering the message;
- delivery timing; and
- the feedback mechanism for evaluating the process.

The feedback process considers the effectiveness of the message in terms of the medium used to deliver it and its ability to shape the audience's understanding of the knowledge-sharing behaviours that the organisation is interested in promoting. Seeley cites the example of Warner-Lambert, the pharmaceutical company, where in an effort to create an environment rich in information sharing, two key behaviours are encouraged. First, employees are encouraged to reach out to their colleagues to tap into their knowledge base in pursuit of the kind of information that typically resides in their heads and nowhere else. Second, the company is looking to its employees to develop a willingness to share their knowledge assets with a larger audience.

ONGOING DEBATES/ADVANCED CONCEPTS IN COMMUNICATIONS

In this section we touch upon two ongoing issues of significance in communications research and writing, namely the implications of internationalisation for communication and the role and value of the grapevine in organisational life.

GLOBALISATION AND CROSS-CULTURAL ISSUES

Communication plays a central role in the realm of international business.

> All international business activity involves communication. Within the international and global business environment, activities such as exchanging information and ideas, decision-making, negotiating, motivating and leading are all based on the ability of managers from one culture to communicate successfully with managers and employees from other cultures (Adler 1991: 64).

Literature on international human resource management and cross-cultural management stresses that cross-border communication happens constantly in multinational companies. This includes communications between expatriates and host country members as well as between employees of various offices in different countries (Dowling *et al.* 1994; Briscoe 1995). Exactly how does internationalisation and globalisation impact communication in an organisation? According to Wilson *et al.* (2001), communication is impacted in many ways and those charged with the responsibility of information dissemination should recognise, among other things, the differences between national cultures, the subtleties of language, the semiotic meaning of designs and the influence of politics and religion on work in certain countries. They consider what global communication has meant for several international organisations and unearth what tools and initiatives they have established to find success in a global era. They suggest that 'as business becomes even more global, communicators need to rise to the challenge. This will mean building partnerships across continents, increasing knowledge of the nuances of foreign cultures, and expanding horizons to take in the full view of what's to come.' Below is Wilson *et al.*'s account of Ericsson and how they have handled some of the communications challenges that arise from being a global player.

MANAGING COMMUNICATION IN A GLOBAL CONTEXT: THE CASE OF ERICSSON

As the world's leading supplier of telecommunications, Ericsson is a truly global organization. Based in Sweden, the company has been active worldwide since 1876 and today operates in more than 140 countries. Four out of every 10 mobile calls in the world are handled by Ericsson equipment.

Roland Klein, senior VP of *communication*, explains the challenge of structuring an effective *communication* department across the globe. 'It would be unrealistic to think you could manage *communication* on a local level in each country. The organization must establish a strong core *communication* team in media, investor and employee relations that puts messages out in a professional way – one company, one voice.'

Klein is responsible for worldwide *communication* and his key stakeholders are analysts, employees and the media. His rationale for this particular focus is that the links between investors and the media are much stronger now than in previous times. Today's media relations are driven by stock market news and company performance is often gauged by yesterday's news.

To create consistent messages across multiple locations, Klein suggests that a strong central content platform and action plan is needed to communicate to the local level. Global company statements should be based on a single source. His feeling is that it's much more effective if this is developed in a central *communication* department with input from the regional PR managers. It's equally important for the head of *communication* to work closely with the CEO and other top management because the proximity to senior leaders is critical for *communication* to be strategic.

Creating global communication guidelines

Balancing collaboration with central office leaders and maintaining close contact with the regions is a key skill for global communicators. At Ericsson, regional communicators support the two-way flow of information between their region and headquarters, as well as safeguard the local quality of statements, set up standards, and keep their region's employees up-to-date. To help them in their work, Klein's team has developed four instruments as guidelines for the *communication* team. These help to reduce information overload and ensure consistency in *communication*.

The first tool is the 'Ericsson Story,' a living document that changes to reflect the company's business strategies. The eight-page document illustrates Ericsson's business goals and competitor advantages. It focuses on main strategies and these points are supported by market statistics.

The second tool is a 'spokesperson brief.' This comes out after every quarterly earning report. It's a 30–40 page document that outlines what is public information and sets parameters for discussing the company in public. This ensures consistency and clear definitions for everyone who speaks on behalf of the company.

The third instrument is a perception-tracking system to monitor the reputation and issues of the largest of the 12 markets. It's produced every month. Based on published material, Ericsson assesses if the image in the region is aligned with the corporate strategy. This gives a clear understanding of the current state of affairs and flags up key issues. It's an early warning system that helps to hone global and local *communication*.

The fourth is an integrated *communication* plan that defines messages and actions for the next six months. It outlines the major factors of reputation, the PR objectives, and the metrics of what to achieve. Local communicators can develop their own programs based on these content and issue-driven action plans.

Communicating to global management

Ericsson restructured the internal *communication* team radically [during 1999 to 2001]. The new team now performs a strategic function as a support for management, preparing and advising on *communication* in each region. Their goal is to provide a comprehensive package across the organization, empowering managers to communicate most effectively to their staff.

The team also changed its tools to steer the department away from simply pushing out information in newsletters and on the Internet. Television webcasts are a more direct way of connecting with employees and also reaching different time zones when replayed. The team began frequent conference calls with Ericsson's top 400 managers. *Communication* drove the agenda for the managers' presentation materials and the schedules for discussing strategic changes to the employees. If customers were affected in the region then the *communication* team produced a customer Web site. This, too, helped to keep Ericsson's global message consistent.

Empowering employees

Employees don't rely on formal processes. The company is very project-oriented – talented staff are drawn together for customer-driven projects. 'At Ericsson you can't rely on your superiors. You have to find your way on your own. We have an entrepreneurial structure where people are allowed to do many things for the sake of investment,' says Klein. Employees take a lot of responsibility quickly and work quite independently at Ericsson. But at the same time there is a strong command centre that dictates behaviour and spending patterns. Doing this helps employees to react quickly to changing environments – [in 2000] there was a 40 percent increase in growth; [in 2001] it slowed to almost zero, which is not an unusual degree of change in the telecommunications market.

Ericsson aims to communicate its market-driven approach across all its global businesses so that as a group it can react quickly to the market. The softening economy has called for a large shift in business strategy, and unfortunately led to some layoffs. Klein believes it's important to be swift and decisive both in altering the course of the business and in communicating it to employees. 'When making tough decisions, it's important to come forward quickly and say, "this is what is needed even though it is hard." Employees shouldn't hear it first from unions. They need to hear it from us.' Focusing on internal *communication* was key to keeping employees on board. Building trust in changing times is never easy, but it's supported by Ericsson's communication structure which equips managers with the *communication* tools they need to provide employees with important news.

Source: Wilson *et al.* (2001)

THE GRAPEVINE AND THE E-GRAPEVINE

Often derided as the enemy of good management and something which must be eliminated and stamped out, the grapevine remains omnipresent in organisational life. It has been estimated that up to seventy-five per cent of employees hear about organisational matters and issues in the first instance through the organisational grapevine. It has also been suggested that a common perception among employees is that communication and information sourced via the grapevine is more reliable than formally sanctioned communication. Without question, the grapevine remains an important element of any organisation's communication armoury and it is one which is worth trying to understand. Among the grapevine's main characteristics are the fact that it is not controlled by management, it is perceived by most employees to be a source of credible information and it is largely used to serve the people within it (Robbins 2001).

Karathanos and Auriemmo (1999) note that over the past few years, research has shown that, properly managed, an active grapevine can assist in keeping company lines of communication open and may even assist in boosting the overall health of an organisation. Thus, while managers may have typically done their best to suppress this mechanism of communication, some are now beginning to reappraise its value. The authors suggest that attempts at phasing out the grapevine are unwarranted and unproductive, and while it does not always deliver information in an ideal manner, its advantages may in fact outweigh its disadvantages. They cite a number of core advantages, as follows.

- While the grapevine has a reputation for disseminating unreliable information, research shows that information via the grapevine is reliable and accurate, making this means of communication an asset to the organisation. Grapevine transmissions are within a range of accuracy of somewhere between seventy-five and eighty per cent (Davis 1969).

- The messages sent via the grapevine are generally characterised by a degree of timeliness. Generally, the speed of transmission through the grapevine is far faster than information received through formally sanctioned channels.

- The grapevine may often serve as an important communication channel for testing employees' reactions to news, events, planned changes, etc. (what Wells and Spinks (1994) refer to as 'trial balloons'). It allows employees to decide and plan a reaction when the formal communication is circulated. It may also give employees the opportunity to provide input/feedback to senior management before final decisions are made. This may prove particularly important when 'bad' news will subsequently be coming through the formal channels.

- Another advantage it offers is that it can transmit messages in a multidirectional manner, something which is unlike most formal channels that follow a rigid, linear path down the organisational hierarchy.

- The grapevine can serve as an outlet for stress release. It is argued that employees frequently need an opportunity to let off steam but may be unable to do so through formal communication lines, fearing embarrassment or repercussions. The grapevine provides them with a mechanism through which they can share their personal feelings and opinions.

- Finally, the grapevine may serve as an indicator of organisational health. It can spotlight issues and problems important to an organisation. Effects of policies and procedures often may be measured with informal communication. Also, organisations with strong formalised structures that inhibit communication outside these structures may benefit from a grapevine that supplements formal channels.

Among the core disadvantages cited by Karathanos and Auriemmo (1999) are the following.

- While research indicates that a good deal of information passed through the grapevine is accurate, a percentage is inaccurate. Furthermore, virtually all the information that passes through the grapevine is undocumented and thus is open to alteration and misinterpretation as it is transmitted. While the core message may be largely resistant to major alterations, some critical details may be eliminated in a process known as 'leveling', while more dramatic issues may be hyped up each time the information is being recycled.

- Another potential problem is the threat of legal action arising from inaccurate information. Several organisations internationally have found themselves defending lawsuits arising from false information circulating in this way.

Table 7.3 Views About the Grapevine

Favourable views

'I use the grapevine as an important medium – I listen to it (or at least get views on it from those in the know) and occasionally feed it, according to communication needs at the time. You'll never stamp it out, so work with it.' (Mark Godson, Global Marine Systems Ltd)

'The most positive use of the grapevine for me is using it as a way of tapping into people's concerns, priorities and interests. The straight-talking feedback you tend to get in canteens, photocopier rooms, etc. is great at almost every stage of the communication process.' (Bob Hammond, Post Office Ltd)

'The grapevine can be used to our advantage. Good, accurate information can be fed to it by whatever means as long as misinformation is killed. A good grapevine should be used as a barometer of every company. Let's be honest: it beats the hell out of some surveys.' (Philip Allen, Viridian Group)

Less favourable views

'We should be all about promoting best practices. Communicating strategic information by leaving a memo on the copying machine is about as diametrically opposed to a best practice as anything I can think of. Ditto for accepting the fact that your senior executives will chat with the rank and file in the smoking room only. If your company is utterly opposed to honest and candid communication with employees, you have two choices: be an accomplice to such worst practices or get out. I would get out fast. There are plenty of other organisations that will value sound internal communication practices.' (Thomas Lee, Arceil Leadership Ltd)

'Rumor mills are the product of an unhealthy culture where either people in the know can't be trusted or there's a vacuum of hard information on issues of concern to employees.' (Dean Williams, Williams Savvy & Associates)

Source: Thatcher (2003)

Thus, although the grapevine has always been with us, in today's business world managers are beginning to confront another new, interesting challenge in this sphere, namely the 'e-grapevine'. Burke and Wise (2003) note that e-mail allows workplace tales to spread faster than ever, but without the opportunity for non-verbal cues and interactivity, e-mail makes it even harder for employees to accurately interpret the message. Beyond e-mail, they also point out that managers have become increasingly concerned about disgruntled employees who anonymously post inaccurate or unfair electronic information on the Internet, in chat rooms or other virtual spaces beyond an intranet firewall.

SUMMARY OF KEY PROPOSITIONS

- Communication is involved in all of an organisation's activities and is the process by which two or more parties exchange information and share meaning. The purposes of communication in organisations are to achieve co-ordinated action, share information and express feelings and emotions.
- Organisations depend on complex flows of communication – upward, downward and laterally – to operate effectively.
- People communicate in organisations through written, oral and non-verbal means.
- The communication process involves a source encoding a message into symbols and transmitting it through a medium to a receiver who decodes the message and responds with feedback as a means of verifying the meaning of the original message.
- In the modern organisation, the importance of effective communication is emphasised by three core factors: the increasing importance of information as an organisational function, the increasing recognition that it is only through exploiting employees' ideas and talents that organisations will be able to compete and survive and the need to convince employees that working for the organisation is something they should be committed to and to which they should devote their ideas, energy and creativity.
- Those charged with the responsibility of information dissemination in an organisation operating internationally should be especially aware of, among other things, the differences between national cultures, the subtleties of language, the semiotic meaning of designs and the influence of politics and religion on work in certain countries.
- While many may have typically done their best to suppress the grapevine as a mechanism of communication, some are now beginning to reappraise its value. Research has shown that, properly managed, an active grapevine can assist in keeping company lines of communication open and may even assist in boosting an organisation's overall health.

DISCUSSION/SELF-ASSESSMENT QUESTIONS

1. How is communication in organisations an individual as well as an organisational process?
2. What place do informal communication channels have in organisations today?
3. Describe the main barriers to communication you are familiar with and give an example of each.
4. Think of a situation in which you felt there was a communication problem. Outline the things you would do to improve communication in that situation.

MUTLIPLE CHOICE QUESTIONS

1. Early discussions of management gave little emphasis to communication. True or false?
2. Effective communication has the potential to:

(a) Foster greater commitment.

(b) Be a significant predictor of job satisfaction.

(c) Facilitate the diffusion of teamwork.

(d) Prove significant in improving internal control.

(e) All of the above.

(f) None of the above.

3.   Which of the following is not a characteristic of an ideal communication process?

(a) Accuracy.

(b) Reliability.

(c) Validity.

(d) Insufficiency.

(e) Effectiveness.

4.   Estimates suggest that that top- and middle-level executives devote what percentage of their total working lives to communication?

(a) Sixty to eighty per cent.

(b) Eighty to one hundred per cent.

(c) Forty to sixty per cent.

(d) Twenty to forty per cent.

5.   In the organisational context, among the major functions which communication may serve are:

(a) Motivating the workforce.

(b) Controlling member behaviour.

(c) Persuading and influencing.

(d) Assisting in employee retention.

(e) All of the above.

(f) None of the above.

6.   Vertical communication refers to:

(a) The transmission of information in superordinate-subordinate relationships, whether from superordinate to subordinate or from subordinate to superordinate.

(b) The transmission of information among peers.

(c) Social factors within an organisation, particularly common in hierarchical structures, that lead to mistrust between its members.

(d) Perceptual selectivity and/or incompatible viewpoints.

(e) All of the above.

(f) None of the above.

7.   An important rule of active listening is to avoid reflecting back or paraphrasing what the other person has said. True or false?

8.   While new communication technologies present us with the possibility of dealing with large amounts of information simultaneously, such technologies may also result in organisational communication becoming:

(a) More personal.

(b) Less personal.

(c) Less participative.
(d) Less accessible.
(e) All of the above.
(f) None of the above.
9. The grapevine can have a positive impact on communication in organisations. True or false?
10. Kinesics refers to:
   (a) The feedback mechanisms deployed for evaluating the process of communication.
   (b) Body language elements that are often drawn upon during the communication process.
   (c) Communication planners who act in the manner of an air traffic controller, permitting digestible quantities of information at any one time to be discharged to employees.
   (d) Managers responsible for ensuring that the maximum amount of information that it is reasonable to be able to assimilate, understand and utilise is passed on to people at the appropriate time.

FIVE SUGGESTED KEY READINGS

Clampitt, P.G. and Downs, J.D., 'Employee perceptions of the relationship between communication and productivity: a field study', Journal of Business Communication, XXX (1993), 5–28.
Kurland, N. and Hope-Pelled, L., 'Passing the word: toward a model of gossip and power in the workplace', Academy of Management Review, XXV/2 (2000), 428–38.
Luthans, F. and Larsen, J., 'How managers really communicate', Human Relations, XXXIX/2 (1986), 161–78.
Pearce, W.B., Communication and the Human Condition, Carbondale, IL: Southern Illinois University Press 1989.
Weick, K.E., 'Theorizing about organizational communication', in F. Jablin, L. Putnam and K. Roberts, Handbook of Organizational Communication: An Interdisciplinary Perspective, Newbury Park: Sage 1989, 97–122.

REFERENCES

Adler, N., International Dimensions of Organizational Behavior, 2nd ed., Boston: Kent 1991.
Axley, S., Communication at Work: Management and the Communication-Intensive Organization, Westport: Quorum Books 1996.
Baskin, O. and Aronoff, C., Interpersonal Communication in Organizations, Santa Monica, CA: Goodyear 1980.
Beach, D., Personnel: The Management of People at Work, New York: Macmillan 1970.
Bolton, P. and Dewatripont, M., 'The firm as a communication network', Quarterly Journal of Economics, CIX/4 (1994), 809–40.

Brewster, C., Hegewisch, A., Mayne, L. and Tregaskis, O., 'Employee communication and participation', in C. Brewster and A. Hegewisch (eds), *Policy and Practice in European Human Resource Management*, London: Routledge 1994.

Briscoe, D.R., *International Human Resource Management*, Englewood Cliffs, NJ: Prentice Hall 1995.

Buchanan, D. and Huczynski, A., *Organizational Behaviour: An Introductory Text*, Hemel Hempstead: Prentice Hall 1997.

Burke, L. and Wise, J., 'The effective care, handling and pruning of the office grapevine', *Business Horizons*, XLVI/3 (2003), 71–6.

Campbell, K., White, C. and Johnson, D., 'Leader member relations as a function of rapport management', *The Journal of Business Communication*, XL/3 (2003), 170–94.

Clampitt, P.G. and Downs, J.D., 'Employee perceptions of the relationship between communication and productivity: a field study', *Journal of Business Communication*, XXX (1993), 5–28.

Davis, K., 'Grapevine communication among lower and middle managers', *Personnel Journal* (April 1969).

Dawson, S., *Analysing Organisations*, London: Macmillan 1996.

Dowling, P.J., Schuler, R.S. and Welch, D.E., *International Dimensions of Human Resource Management*, Belmont: Wadsworth 1994.

Ekman, P. and Friesen, W., 'The repertoire of non-verbal behaviour: categories, origins, usage and coding', *Semiotics*, I (1969), 63–92.

Fisher, D., *Communication in Organizations*, St Paul, MN: West Publishing 1993.

Glenn, E. and Pond, E., 'Listening self-inventory', *Supervisory Management* (January 1989), 12–15.

Goldhaber, G., *Organizational Communication*, Dubuque, IA: W.C. Brown Press 1990.

Kane, P., 'Two-way communication fosters greater commitment', *HR Magazine*, XLI/10 (1996), 50–4.

Kar, L., *Business Communication: Theory and Practice*, Homewood, IL: Irwin 1972.

Karathanos, P. and Auriemmo, A., 'Care and feeding of the organizational grapevine', *Industrial Management*, XLI/2 (1999), 26–31.

Kurland, N. and Hope-Pelled, L., 'Passing the word: toward a model of gossip and power in the workplace', *Academy of Management Review*, XXV/2 (2000), 428–38.

Lawson, J. and Bourner, T., 'Developing communication within new workgroups', *Journal of Applied Management Studies*, VI/2 (1997), 149–68.

Lippit, M., 'Say what you mean, mean what you say', *Journal of Business Strategy*, XVIII/4 (1997), 17–21.

Ludlow, R. and Panton, F., *The Essence of Effective Communication*, Hemel Hempstead: Prentice Hall 1992.

Luhmann, N., *Soziale Systeme*, Frankfurt: Suhrkamp 1987.

Luthans, F., *Organizational Behaviour*, New York: McGraw-Hill 1992.

Luthans, F. and Larsen, J., 'How managers really communicate', *Human Relations*, XXXIX/2 (1986), 161–78.

McClave, H., *Communication for Business*, Dublin: Gill & Macmillan 1997.

Maitland, R., 'Words are not enough', *People Management*, VIII/12 (2002), 62.

Mayrhofer, W., Brewster, C. and Morley, M., 'Communication and consultation in European organisations', paper presented to the workshop on the Impact of Strategy, Job Design and Organisational Structure on HRM, Cádiz, Spain, 25–28 May 1997.

Miles, E., Patrick, S. and King, W., 'Job level as a systematic variable in predicting the relationship between supervisory communication and job satisfaction', *Journal of Occupational and Organizational Psychology*, LXIX/3 (1996), 277–93.

Mintzberg, H., 'The managers' job: folklore and fact', *Harvard Business Review* (July/August 1975), 49–61.

Mintzberg, H., Jorgensen, J., Dougherty, D. and Westley, F., 'Some surprising things about collaboration: knowing how people connect makes it work better', *Organizational Dynamics*, XXV/1 (1996), 60–72.

Moorhead, G. and Griffin, R., *Organizational Behaviour: Managing People and Organizations*, Boston: Houghton Mifflin 1995.

Morley, M., Mayrhofer, W. and Brewster, C., 'Communication in organizations: dialogue and impact', in C. Brewster and H. Holt Larsen (eds), *Human Resource Management in Northern Europe: Trends, Dilemmas and Strategy*, Oxford: Blackwell 2000, 147–70.

Pearce, W.B., *Communication and the Human Condition*, Carbondale, IL: Southern Illinois University Press 1989.

Pettit, J., 'Team communication: it's in the cards', *Training and Development*, LI/1 (1997), 12–16.

Price, J., 'Handbook of Organisational Measurement', *International Journal of Manpower*, XVIII/4, 5, 6 (1997).

Robbins, S., *Organizational Behaviour*, New York: Prentice Hall 2001.

Schermerhorn, J., *Management*, New York: John Wiley & Sons 1996.

Seeley, C., 'Communication plans to stimulate', *Total Communication Measurement*, II/6 (2000), 5.

Shannon, C. and Weaver, W., *The Mathematical Theory of Communication*, Urbana, IL: University of Illinois Press 1949.

Smythe, J., 'Harvesting the office grapevine', *People Management*, I/18 (1995), 24–31.

Steinberg, R., 'No, it couldn't happen here', *Management Review*, LXXXVII/8 (1998), 68–73.

Thatcher, M., 'The grapevine: communication tool or thorn in your side?', *Strategic Communication Management*, VII/5 (2003).

Thornton, S., 'How communication can aid retention', *Strategic Communication Management*, V/6 (2001), 24–8.

Weick, K.E., 'Theorizing about organizational communication', in F. Jablin, L. Putnam and K. Roberts, *Handbook of Organizational Communication: An Interdisciplinary Perspective*, Newsbury Park: Sage 1989, 97–122.

Wells, B. and Spinks, N., 'Managing your grapevine: a key to quality productivity', *Executive Development*, VII/2 (1994), 24–7.

Wilson, G., Goodhall, H. and Waagan, C., *Organizational Communication*, New York: Harper & Row 1986.

Wilson, R., Thomas-Derrick, A. and Wright, P., 'What globalisation means from communication', *Strategic Communication Management*, V/6 (2001), 14–19.

Woods, B., *Communication, Technology and the Development of People*, London: Routledge 1993.

THE DYNAMICS OF GROUPS AND TEAMS AT WORK

8

Learning Objectives

- To outline the benefits of groups and be aware of the main reasons why people are organised (or organise themselves) into groups at work.

- To present the different stages that groups go through, from the time they form to the time they disband.

- To introduce the concept of group cohesiveness, how it develops and what its benefits are.

- To highlight the effects of excessive cohesiveness in groups.

- To explain how group decision making can be improved by helping people to be more objective and sometimes more critical of group decisions.

- To describe the concept of teamwork and why it is important in the context of organisations.

- To outline the common problems that arise when teams are being developed and how to avoid them.

- To present the different roles that people can play within their team.

- To highlight important features associated with good teams and ways in which these features can be introduced into teamwork situations.

INTRODUCTION

This chapter specifically addresses the concept of groups and teams at work. From an organisational behaviour perspective, it is important to have a good understanding of how people behave in groups and how teams are developed successfully. Group influence, group formation, the development of norms in groups and various outcomes of group interaction are central concepts in building an understanding of the ways in which people operate at work. This chapter explores some of the central theoretical foundations of organisational group dynamics and explains key concepts associated with group behaviour.

The concept of a 'team' is also central to organisational life and is semantically different from definitions of groups. The language of teams is used regularly in organisational settings, and many strategists and human resource specialists believe in and champion the benefits and advantages of team-based activity at work. Even a brief examination of the literature on organisational behaviour shows the enormous popularity that the concepts of teams and team building have gained.

There is a wide range of evidence that advocates team concepts, both from an individual and an organisational perspective. It has been claimed that people who are members of cohesive teams are likely to report higher levels of motivation, satisfaction and self-esteem at work, and organisations that have successfully implemented team initiatives have been found to report higher levels of productivity and effectiveness overall. However, some perspectives on teams suggest that there is much inaccurate or manipulative hype surrounding the concept. Argyris (1990), for example, proposes that teams, in the real sense of the word, do not always exist in the ways that organisations would like to think that they do (for example, claiming that 'the management team is a myth'). Others say that the team concept is simply a manipulative and exploitative tool used by managers to get more out of their employees.

These ideas will be developed in this chapter and you will be invited to engage in critical reflection in order to explore some of the key questions and findings that relate to the functioning of groups and teams in working environments.

DEFINITIONS OF KEY CONCEPTS

Psychological definition of a group
Any number of individuals who interact with each other, are psychologically aware of each other and perceive themselves to be a group (Schein 1988).

The Hawthorne effect
Based on early research that has come to be associated with the human relations school of organisational behaviour, the Hawthorne effect refers to the fact that when people are aware they are being observed, their behaviour is likely to be different than when they are not aware of being observed.

Group norms
Unwritten rules of behaviour to which all or most members of a group are expected to conform.

Group context
The physical, psychological, cultural and organisational situation within which a group operates.

Group structure
The internal context of a group, defined by the ways in which tasks and responsibilities are distributed and the different roles and status occupied by each member of the group.

> The stages of group formation
> A theoretical identification of different key phases of a group's development. The four stages are forming, storming, norming and performing.
>
> Group cohesiveness
> The extent to which group members share close and positive working relationships.
>
> The groupthink phenomenon
> Defined by seven key characteristics of highly cohesive groups, the groupthink phenomenon emerges in groups that have typically experienced success and agreement in the past. This can lead to poor decisions, as courses of action are less likely to be subjected to the scrutiny they require.

THE NATURE OF GROUPS

The exploration of motivation in Chapter 6 provided evidence that the need for 'belongingness' is an important motivator as well as a strong human need (Maslow 1943; Alderfer 1972). Most people gain much from belonging to groups, either inside or outside their organisations. Of course, it's not just individuals who benefit from groups. Organisations purposely arrange people into work groups in order to deal with large, difficult or complex activities.

BENEFITS OF GROUPS TO INDIVIDUALS

Of course, group membership is not just an organisational phenomenon, but rather is something that people are exposed to from the moment they are born by joining a family or social unit. Group membership continues to be part of their experience right through the various stages of their development (Hellriegel *et al.* 1989). By the time an individual joins an organisation as an employee, he or she will probably have had a wide variety of experiences in group settings and learned to play certain roles and satisfy a range of social needs. People have a tendency to join groups, not least because of the benefits that they derive from group membership. Personal benefits from group membership include the following.

- Groups provide people with friendship, social support and a sense of belonging.
- Groups help people to be more aware of their own identity, i.e. who they are and what they represent in relation to others around them.
- Groups (particularly at work) can help to lighten someone's workload or make the work process easier by providing extra input to complete a difficult or demanding task.
- Groups help people to become involved in a common activity, which may further their own development or career. For example, group involvement can help people to become more creative, more aware of a diversity of issues or even more skilled than they would have been outside the group.

BENEFITS OF GROUPS TO ORGANISATIONS

Not only do individuals like to be part of a group at work (for the reasons outlined above), but bringing people together is also good for the organisation, especially if what has to be done is difficult, complicated, strenuous or time consuming. Groups are good for organisations because of the following reasons.

- When people get together in groups, the subsequent combination and integration of skills, ideas and perspectives may provide a more cohesive set of competencies that aid in the completion of difficult tasks.
- When people get together in groups, certain problems and decisions may be easier to solve or make.
- Group work can often yield higher levels of commitment and participation than might be possible when people work apart. By satisfying individual affiliation and social needs, group membership can encourage continued commitment in work situations. Organisations recognise the need for their employees to be committed to their organisations, and creating good working groups is one way of achieving this objective.
- When people get together in groups they can often help to resolve conflicts that might never have been dealt with if people were kept apart. Organisations bring people together in order to help them to discuss such problems and issues so that unnecessary or dysfunctional conflict does not arise.

However, despite the potential benefits outlined above, groups and group formation do not always create these benefits for their organisations. Groups can also cause difficulties for organisations, in ways which will be discussed later in this chapter.

DEFINITION OF A GROUP

The concept of a group can be interpreted in a number of ways. It might be argued that a nation of people can be regarded as a group (in the sense that everyone shares a common national identity) or that an organisation is a group (in that all people within its walls are members of one specific establishment). However, from a behavioural perspective, there are several factors required before a collection of individuals can be defined as a group. A common and often quoted definition of groups comes from Schein (1988): 'a group is any number of people who interact with each other, are psychologically aware of one another and perceive themselves to be a group.' Participants in groups are generally defined by an identifiable membership, 'group consciousness', a sense of shared purpose, interdependence, interaction and an ability to act in a united manner (Mullins 1996).

Perhaps the most effective definitions of groups are those that are multidimensional, recognising their structural, dynamic and contextual aspects. From a contextual point of view, prerequisites such as interdependence of tasks and goals (Lewin 1947), the existence of a common fate (Lewin 1948; Campbell 1958) and the psychological perception that the group exists (Schein 1988) may all provide a rationale for differentiating between groups and non-groups in any social setting. Also, structural issues such as the roles, relationships and status of each member (Sherif and Sherif 1979) play an important part in differentiating between one type of social group and another and can be seen as important contextual determinants of group interaction.

In terms of process, such dynamics as interaction (Schein 1988) and face-to-face contact (Bales 1950; Homans 1950) also help to refine our understanding of what a social group represents. Group dynamics depend on the formal and informal tasks and objectives for which the group exists. The discussions and activities in which group members engage as well as the outcomes achieved can all be seen to relate to group task or content.

From a subjectivist perspective, the existence of a group and group membership may depend entirely on the 'self-categorisation' referred to by Turner (1982). From an objectivist perspective, a group is more likely to be defined according to some externally identified assignment, title or arrangement. Brown (1988: 2–3) augments existing definitions like the one provided by Schein above and proposes that 'a group exists when two or more people define themselves as members of it and when its existence is recognised by at least one [non-member].'

It is reasonable to argue that unless individuals in the group perceive themselves to be members and define themselves as such, then the existence of that membership is questionable and the sustainability of the group in terms of its processes and outcomes is unlikely to be maintained. Therefore, unless group members see themselves to be somehow part of the group, the ability to define a collection of individuals as a group becomes precarious.

THE IMPORTANCE OF GROUPS

Organisational theory once spent relatively little time concerned with questions about how people behaved and how they interacted with one another at work. In the midst of the Industrial Revolution, Frederick Taylor wrote *The Principles of Scientific Management* and his work was symptomatic of the mechanistic, hyper-rational thinking that had become dominant in much of management thought, both in the US and Europe. Tayloristic thinking did not account for or consider the social dimension of the human experience. People were seen as commodities and resources that could be applied to organisational problems in much the same ways as machines. Of course, it can be convincingly argued that this kind of thinking still prevails in at least some current organisational contexts today. From a theoretical perspective, research and hypotheses that support the mechanistic application of 'human resources' to the workplace can be seen to have originated from the beginning of the Industrial Revolution.

With the arrival of the Industrial Revolution, new machinery, new technology and new organisational structures became more sophisticated and more complicated than the simpler social and work-orientated structures that had gone before, but formal knowledge about how people were likely to behave in large organisational settings did not progress as fast as the new forms of organisations themselves. It was not until the 1920s that researchers began to consider the importance of social and intergroup dynamics at work.

The now famous Hawthorne studies (explored below) provided some of the first evidence that social and group dynamics were starting to be seen as important considerations for understanding behaviour at work. The Hawthorne studies gave rise to a new school of thought in the area of organisational theory that came to be known as the human relations school.

It can be argued that while the human relations school led to more enlightened understanding of important behavioural issues at work, the iron fist of industrialism did not disappear, rather, it just became hidden by a velvet glove (Mills and Simmons 1995). Others argue that the naked exploitation that had characterised employers' approaches to the workforce in the early part of the century was at least somewhat tempered by the arrival of the human relations school (Huczynski and Buchanan 1996), which started to alert theorists and practitioners to the importance of recognising the individual's social needs and of allowing groups to participate at least in some way in decisions that affected their working lives.

THE HAWTHORNE STUDIES

Between 1924 and 1927 a series of studies was carried out at the Hawthorne plant of the Western Electric Company in the state of Illinois in the US. The initial impetus of this research was driven by a focus on scientific principles of the workplace. The types of research questions that the investigators were originally interested in addressing related to how the physical surroundings of the organisation could enhance productivity and efficiency. Elton Mayo and his colleagues were interested in answering the following key research question: Would improvements in the physical surroundings, such as better lighting, have any effect on worker productivity?

Results of the Hawthorne Studies

After testing different levels of light intensity and other aspects of physical working conditions, measuring changes in productivity and then analysing the results, the researchers were initially disappointed. Even after elaborate adjustments in the physical conditions under which employees were working, they were unable to establish any relationship between characteristics of the work surroundings and the workers' productivity. In some groups output fluctuated randomly, while in others it appeared to increase. For one group in particular, it seemed that regardless of the alterations made in the environment, productivity increased. Baffled by these results, the researchers began to consider psychological factors that might be responsible for the increased productivity.

Eventually, after a series of different tests with two main groups within the Western Electric Company, the researchers concluded that far more important than any physical characteristics of work surroundings were the human factors associated with the activities that people are asked to engage in. Conditions of the experiment were such that people who had previously never been consulted about or involved in decisions relating to their work were suddenly being selected for special treatment, and high levels of interest in every aspect of their behaviour were being demonstrated. Most importantly, according to the reports of the studies, the subjects were given an opportunity to work together in a social group setting and had more of an opportunity to get to know each other than would otherwise have been the case (Mayo 1933; Roethlisberger and Dickson 1939). The most powerful proposal coming from the Hawthorne studies was that people prefer to work in groups and that people are likely to be more productive when they work together in participative group settings.

Despite many criticisms of the methodologies and findings associated with the Hawthorne studies, they represent one of the important original studies that helped to shape a more robust understanding of organisational behaviour. Schermerhorn *et al.* (1996: 710) summarise their contribution as follows:

> It is what the Hawthorne studies led to in terms of future research that counts most, rather than what they actually achieved as research. The studies represent an important historical turning point that allowed the field of management a new way of thinking about people at work. They extended the thinking of researchers beyond the concern for physical and economic considerations alone and clearly established the managerial significance of the psychological and sociological aspects of people as human beings. As a result the Hawthorne studies have had a major impact on what we study as part of organisational behaviour. This legacy includes an interest in the group as an important force in the work setting and the importance of social relationships as a determinant of behaviour at work.

More detail about the common criticisms of the Hawthorne studies will be explored in the advanced concepts section later in this chapter.

THE HAWTHORNE EFFECT

The Hawthorne studies gave rise to the expression 'the Hawthorne effect', which refers to the simple principle that when groups of people are aware that they are being observed, their behaviour is likely to be somehow different from when they are not being observed. This is a useful principle, not least because it draws attention to one of the methodological problems of studying human behaviour. It is not always easy to discover people's natural tendencies in groups. In order to study groups we often need to observe their behaviour, yet by observing group behaviour, it is possible that we will get a distorted picture of that group's natural behaviour and tendencies.

GROUP NORMS

A group norm is an unwritten rule of behaviour shared by all members of the same group. There are certain codes of behaviour in groups to which almost every member of the group is expected to conform. A norm is a rule that people must generally stick to if they are to continue to be accepted by the rest of the group. Norms are rules of behaviour which are set down by the group itself through the set of behaviours that is displayed within it. Group members informally develop and implicitly define acceptable ranges of tolerable behaviour that occur within that group. It is not necessarily managers or supervisors who decide what norms exist within the group, and sometimes formal structures, systems and rules stand in direct contrast to the range of norms that emerge.

Norms are not always under the control of people higher up in the organisation and they may not always encourage behaviour that is good for the organisation. In addition, small groups inside the organisation can band together and set goals for themselves that can be either compatible or incompatible with those of the organisation. Group norms are difficult to change because they are usually developed for behaviour that is important for the survival or benefit of the group members, regardless of whether they are good for the overall organisation, for productivity or for effectiveness.

Being part of a group may be accompanied by moderate or serious disadvantages for the individual. Membership may require sacrificing aspects of one's individuality and suppressing personal values or views; it may expose individuals to uncomfortable social arenas; it may force co-operation in situations where there is an urge to compete or withdraw; it may require considerable extra commitment, effort and dedication to particular activities; and it may alienate group members from non-members who may be socially or politically important in other contexts. These are just some of the examples of the drawbacks that may develop as a result of joining and maintaining membership of social and organisational groups.

On the other hand, group membership may bring special privileges, such as recognition, protection or prestige, which may be considered valuable or important enough to outweigh the associated disadvantages. In many social settings, groups can provide benefits ranging from psychological satisfaction to physical survival. The perception of the relative advantages and disadvantages of group membership often depends on whether original joining conditions were voluntary or involuntary, pleasant or unpleasant (Festinger 1957; Aronson and Mills 1959) and whether group pressure to conform is either moderate or severe (Kiesler and Kiesler 1969). However, establishing the level of choice and constraint to which individuals are exposed when joining certain groups is not a straightforward process. Some membership may appear entirely voluntary when in fact subtle pressures are being brought to bear on joining decisions. On the other hand, individuals may claim not to have had a choice in joining a particular group, even though the decision was mostly attributable to their own preferences with no external pressure. For political, psychological or self-justification reasons, personal freedom of choice is not always revealed. In summary then there are advantages, disadvantages, motives and pressures associated with the decision to join a group in any setting.

GROUP CONTEXT

The context within which a group operates can be analysed from several perspectives. Bateman and Zeithaml (1989) refer to the 'psychological context' of groups in strategic settings. This concept defines the cognitive, emotional and behavioural frameworks that provide a context for group action and interaction.

Initiation and precedent setting is largely connected with the context within which the group emerges and initiation ceremonies or rituals can often give important clues as to the basic contextual features of the group, as they often characterise group activation and may reflect and illuminate the group contexts upon which activities, interactions and outcomes are built (Moreland and Levine 1982). Evidence has repeatedly shown that initiation of a group not only changes the way in which individuals define themselves, but also gives rise to an effort to define and explore the identity, purpose and value of the group itself (Brown 1988). Important precedents may be set that can have a fundamental effect on the ongoing dynamics that characterise the group.

One of the ways of facilitating an identification of the important aspects of group context is to analyse the dynamics associated with group initiation. This early phase in the group's development is generally charged with high levels of uncertainty and ambiguity (Wilson 1994). Under such circumstances, members may attempt to reduce uncertainty through the development of a shared language and through the use of symbolism (Poole *et al.* 1990; Prasad 1993). Initiation activities such as introductions, receptions, organisation-wide communications regarding the new group, etc. represent 'transition rites' (Van Maanen 1976) that acknowledge that there has been a significant change from one state of affairs to another. This may reflect important contextual information about the culture, values, pressures, influences and expectations at play, even before the group begins to address the purposes for which it has been formed. This information may in turn come to define the group more clearly as events unfold.

Group initiation is also a time where the group's context and dynamics may be somewhat blurred. Members can originate from different personal contexts and bring with them a variety of assumptions, perspectives, needs and goals. Depending on how the early stages are managed, this context may be reshaped or manipulated in sometimes quite subtle ways in order to facilitate the achievement of the group's goals/activities/functions as defined at a particular point in time.

INTERDEPENDENCIES OF TASK AND FATE AS KEY CONTEXTUAL GROUP FACTORS

Past events are likely to have some impact on the shape of any current group context. For example, norms or 'ranges of acceptable behaviour' (Sherif and Sherif 1979) arise through members' experience of events and then become contextual fixtures within a group, allowing for the development of clearer ideas about what is socially appropriate and inherently acceptable for the group (Brown 1988). Group norms may take time to develop, but when they do, they often guide group behaviour in identifiable and powerful ways.

Two contextual fixtures that Brown (1988) identifies as important influencers of dynamics, such as cohesiveness and group identity, are based on the concept of interdependence. First, 'interdependence of fate' has been found to influence feelings of cohesiveness, group membership and motivation to band together (Jacobsen 1973; McCarthy 1979), which can affect the ways in which members perform together to produce effective outcomes.

Second, 'interdependence of task' refers to a more specific type of interdependence.

When individuals share a common objective and when each member must play a role in the achievement of this objective, task interdependence can be said to be high (Brown 1988; Saavedra *et al.* 1993). This plays a part in the group's definition and identity. Task interdependence may give rise to the emergence of coalitions within organisations (Narayanan and Fahy 1982), which may further clarify the relationship between one group and another.

Contextual factors relevant to groups include such concepts as interdependence, psychological frameworks and past events that lead to group norms. The existence of such factors can be identified and clarified through an examination of various sources of evidence, such as the differences in group roles as evidenced in group interaction and activity, and observations of the ways in which tasks are defined, objectives are set and outcomes are reached. An analysis of the context of a group draws on evidence that demonstrates the dynamics of group initiation and development as well as data that provides background information on events and structures that were a social reality prior to the group's existence.

GROUP STRUCTURE

Group structure can be viewed as part of the group's internal context (Collins 1981). Role differentiation and the extent to which this exists within a group is one of the central dimensions of group structure. The functions of this differentiation include such practical issues as division and distribution of activities, coherence and predictability of group operations and the psychological functions of self-definition within the group (Brown 1988). Status differentiation is a second important structural variable, and the extent to which this exists may serve to provide explanations of how and why group members behave in the ways that they do.

In any group setting, evidence of role and status differentiation should be sought in order to build a meaningful picture of the process, content and outcomes of a particular stream of group behaviour. The chain of command that exists within and between groups gives rise to an important set of relationships and may serve to clarify the routines or patterns by which groups become characterised (Collins 1981).

Bales (1953) was among the first social researchers to point out the potential diversity of major group processes and to trace different types of behaviours that operate simultaneously and that may give rise to competing demands being made on the group. Group theorists often point out that dynamics within groups are characterised by complexity, ambiguity and often apparent chaos (Janis 1982). Much of this complexity may be attributable to the emotional and social needs that reach the surface of group activity and may conflict with or delay the completion of formal group tasks.

Activity that demonstrates individual emotion or shows concern for the feelings of others can be referred to as 'socio-emotional activity' (Bales 1953). Socio-emotional behaviour has also been referred to as 'maintenance behaviour' (Marcic 1992), and rather than conflicting with the requirements of the task, may indirectly support or facilitate the achievement of group goals. Maintenance activities, while fulfilling social and/or emotional needs, may be necessary for group effectiveness rather than superfluous to or conflicting with it (Schein 1988; Marcic 1992). Such behaviours are seen to maintain the working order of the group, create an appropriate climate within which to accomplish tasks and allow for the development of relationships that lead to collaboration and good use of various member resources.

THE STAGES OF GROUP DEVELOPMENT

Evidence suggests that groups of individuals brought together for a particular purpose experience different dynamics and behaviours according to their stage of development. It is increasingly being recognised, for example, that 'groups are systems, often changing in social and work processes throughout the time of their existence' (Miller 2002). Recognising that groups do not stay the same and that they experience significant relationship and task-related changes over time continues to be an essential key to understanding and managing group dynamics at work (Marks *et al.* 2001).

It generally takes time before a group is up and running and achieving the goals for which it came together. As far back as the 1960s, theorists and research began to identify the dynamic nature of groups. Tuckman (1965) famously observed and reported the classic stages of group development, outlined below.

THE FORMING STAGE

The forming stage of group development is characterised by the first phase of development, in which group membership and group goals are clarified. Basic issues are established, which help to give the group its identity and set it apart from the rest of the organisation. At the forming stage of group development, group members may clarify the following issues: Who will be the leader or organiser of the group? Will people from outside work be allowed to participate? How many times will the group meet? For how long will the group stay together? Essentially, the forming stage can be defined as the stage at which the ice is broken between group members and initial ground rules are set.

THE STORMING STAGE

Once the basics have been clarified, a group moves on to the second stage of development, known as the storming stage. The kinds of behaviours that are evident at this stage usually include some conflict. At this stage, a deeper level of understanding emerges as people get to know each other better. There may be conflict over who occupies the leadership role (for example, an individual who was originally accepted as the leader may show that they are not completely committed to the goals of the group and a more suitable candidate for leadership may emerge or be chosen by other members).

This stage is characterised by a re-evaluation of the original assumptions that people have made about the reasons for the group's existence and an elucidation of the part that each person plays within the group.

THE NORMING STAGE

This stage is where the group starts to focus on its activities and establishes set norms and ways of doing things. It is often when the talking ends and the 'doing' starts. At this stage, people have usually identified each group member's particular strengths and are learning to use these strengths to their best advantage. Similarly, certain weaknesses may have been identified, which are also recognised when the group is together.

This stage is defined by the establishment of group norms. Acceptable behaviour is clarified and members become aware of what they are expected to do and how they are expected to behave.

THE PERFORMING STAGE

The performing stage is ideally the final phase of development that the group will reach. While in any group there may always be room for improvement, the performing stage is when people tend to have 'got it right'. They have resolved any of the confusion and conflict that may have existed at earlier stages, they are happy with the part that each member is playing in the group setting and they are achieving their goals as effectively as possible. At this stage the group can be seen as having reached maturity, where communication does not break down and where everyone knows what they have to do, achieves personal fulfilment from their membership and contributes in an important way to the group's success.

These four stages may not always be an accurate description of what really goes on in groups. It is useful to examine what can and does happen when groups get together and develop, but these stages are only pointers to the potential that groups have to develop successfully. The stages of forming, storming, norming and performing really describe the ideal and successful ways in which groups should develop.

However, what should happen is not always what does happen. It is often the case that groups get 'stuck' at one of the first three levels and never actually reach the stage where they are performing effectively together. In addition, more recent research has given rise to observations that are often quite different from those outlined in the original model of group formation or development (for example, see Miller 2002). An alternative to Tuckman's stage theory is Gersick's 'punctuated equilibrium model' (1988, 1989), which also suggests that we need to pay attention to temporal changes in the group's existence. It argues that rather than a sequential, developmental set of stages, groups experience stable phases of equilibrium, punctuated or interrupted by compressed, brief periods of major change. Gersick's theoretical model implies that in order to achieve significant change in group settings, we need to be aware of these windows of opportunity for change, as the prospects of achieving radical developments are quite limited in the context of the generally stable equilibrium. Whatever the experiences of any specific group may be, it remains important that we understand how group history and development impact on factors such as cohesiveness and the ability to perform effectively.

DEVELOPING COHESIVE GROUPS

The concept of group cohesiveness is an important notion in the theoretical and practical understanding of group behaviour (Hosking and Morley 1991). Cohesiveness has been described as the cement 'binding together group members and maintaining their relationships with one another' (Schacter 1951: 229). The concept of cohesiveness is not always defined with such certainty, but while it has traditionally been referred to as a complex and ambiguous term (Allport 1962), the intuitive meaning is generally described as a condition in which group members feel bonded together in ways that reinforce the existence, maintenance and purpose of the group (Budge 1981). The following are the common characteristics of cohesive groups.

- **High levels of communication:** Studies have shown that the more that people talk or communicate with others in the group, the more likely it is that they will become cohesive (Cook 1978; Hogg 1992).
- **Group size:** The number of people in a group also affects cohesiveness. If a group is too large, it is harder for every member to feel that they really belong. Psychologists have suggested that anything above twelve members can significantly reduce the group's ability to become cohesive (Schein 1988).
- **Co-operation and competition:** Experimental studies have shown that co-operative group behaviour is more likely to lead to group cohesiveness (Hogg 1992). Research has concluded that if group members spend more time co-operating with each other, they are more likely to feel that they belong to the group and to continue to be committed to the group, whereas competition inside the group can cause the group to pull apart rather than feel cohesive. However, Myers (1962) found that given certain aspects of the group contexts, cultures and values, team members expressed greater esteem for one another where there were high levels of competition.
- **A feeling of acceptance:** If each group member feels accepted by his or her group, cohesiveness is also more likely to be high (Hogg 1992).
- **Outside threat:** If a group experiences a threat from outside of the group, they will be more likely to band more closely together than might have been the case previously. If conflict arises between one work group and another, these groups may become more internally cohesive, developing a unity of purpose in an effort to strengthen themselves against what they perceive to be an outside threat (Thomas 1976).
- **Success and performance:** The more successful a group feels and the more it achieves rewards for what it does, the more likely it is that the group members will enjoy belonging to the group. Group cohesiveness can be created or strengthened by the successful achievement of the goals that the group has set (Janis 1972).

These factors, along with successful development as outlined in the last section, all contribute to the feeling of belongingness and commitment generally referred to as cohesiveness (Budge 1981). Evidence does show that cohesive group members usually enjoy group membership and experience higher levels of self-esteem by remaining part of the group. In organisational settings, the existence of group cohesiveness can contribute to the morale, commitment and performance of each group member.

However, too much group cohesiveness can sometimes make group members unrealistic in their aims and objectives, as well as in their assessment of their strengths. There are some reasons why group cohesiveness sometimes causes groups to make bad decisions, outlined below.

THE GROUPTHINK PHENOMENON

'Groupthink' (Janis 1972) is a concept that has become associated with the workings of groups in organisations. In this section we investigate what it means and why it can be another important label in helping to understand group behaviour.

While we have seen that group cohesiveness is associated with significant benefits, sometimes groups can become so cohesive that they are unaware of what is going on around them and as a result may ignore or be less responsive to cues in the rest of the organisation (Kim 2001).

Groupthink is what happens when people in a group become so close (or cohesive) that any disagreement between people becomes less and less likely to occur. As a result, the group members develop a way of thinking that prevent them from being critical about what they are doing or the ways in which they are doing it. The people in the group are then less likely to question the reasons for their actions. If this happens, the group can become blind to its weaknesses or potential weaknesses, because agreeing with each other becomes more important than doing the right things or being effective in achieving their goals. Too much agreement can lead to a false sense of security, where everyone feels high levels of comfort in the group and no one is prepared to rock the boat by pointing out weaknesses or mistakes that are being made.

The following are some of the factors that Janis (1972) has identified, which together give rise to what he calls the 'groupthink phenomenon'.

- **A feeling of invulnerability:** When groups achieve a record for excellent or highly successful performance, they can develop the feeling that they are invincible. The group's success can lead to a false sense of security that prevents members from being realistic in their evaluation of the risks associated with various subsequent courses of action.
- **False logic:** Groups that are very cohesive will often develop a false logic about what they are capable of doing. They try to rationalise their actions even if there is evidence from outside the group that this logic is flawed.
- **A feeling that the group is morally right:** Groups can start to feel justified in their decisions even if it means that individuals may suffer, that they will incur costs which could have been avoided or that in some way they are in breach of moral or ethical codes of behaviour. There can be a tendency for highly cohesive groups to ignore the moral implications of their activities.
- **Shared stereotypes:** Groups that experience 'groupthink' can be quick to stereotype anyone who criticises or disagrees with what the group is doing.

- **Pressure:** Individual members who do express reservations or doubts about the group's collective decisions can experience direct pressure from other members not to emphasise their doubts, to agree with the majority or, in some instances, to withdraw or resign from the group.
- **Self-censorship:** Group members in a highly cohesive group may be reluctant to communicate anything negative about the group to other people in the organisation. This results in an inadequate exploration and analysis of what the group is doing.
- **An illusion of agreement or unanimity:** Groups often become convinced that everyone agrees with the group's decisions. This can prevent members from exploring or even expressing their doubts about particular courses of action.

These are all factors that can cause a very cohesive group to make the wrong decisions, and taken together they explain the 'groupthink phenomenon'. In the next section you'll see that managing groups effectively involves helping to prevent this from happening.

How to Deal with 'Groupthink'

- Ask each group member to be a critical evaluator of all ideas and suggestions generated by the group.
- Encourage people to voice and explore their doubts.
- Create subgroups with different leaders to work on the same problem.
- Invite outside experts to observe and react to group discussions.
- Have a different member act as 'devil's advocate' at each group meeting.
- Hold 'second-chance' meetings once an initial decision is made.

Source: Adapted from Janis (1982)

TEAMS IN ORGANISATIONS

There are many potential definitions of teams in organisations. Teams can be structured in a variety of ways and fulfil a variety of purposes. Despite the potential diversity of the team concept, an organisational team can be broadly defined as 'a small group of people with complementary skills who work together to achieve a common purpose for which they hold themselves collectively accountable' (Schermerhorn *et al.* 1996). A team can also be defined as a group of people that has fine-tuned its performance, built on its skills and is constantly improving itself as well as contributing to the improvement and success of its organisation (Katzenbach and Smith 1993).

Types of Organisational Teams

Top Management Teams

The 'top management team' is the leading group in an organisation – the group of people who operate at the strategic apex of the organisation. Issues they are responsible for addressing relate to the organisation's long-term direction. However, many people who are at the top of their organisations will tell you that the group of people they are accompanied by do not behave like a team at all. A top management team can only be considered to be a team if it fulfils the broad definition outlined above.

Project Teams

Project-based teams can be created in organisations in order to investigate and address certain issues or problems for which a solution is sought. Project teams can be multistatus and multidisciplinary and, as a beneficial by-product, yield increased levels of cross-functional interaction, allowing individuals from one part of the organisation to gain insights into the problems or concerns of people in other divisions or at other levels. A multidisciplinary project team is a group of people who have been drawn together from various departments and divisions, often in order to exchange different perspectives on common organisational issues in order to identify and sometimes implement solutions.

Functional Teams

Functional teams are made up of groups of people who carry out functionally specific tasks within the organisation. Organisations that refer to their 'sales teams', their 'marketing teams', their 'research teams' and so on are referring to functional groups that may have in some way developed team-like characteristics.

While there are various team labels in organisations, there are both theorists and practitioners who readily admit that so-called teams do not necessarily fit the description in the real sense of the word (see the definitions of teams above). What organisations refer to as teams can often simply be a label for a group of people who may or may not be working well together as a team (for example, see Argyris 1990). A group of people and a team of people have the same potential for performance. Organisations often devote enormous effort to try to convert groups of people into 'teams' in an attempt to realise this potential.

Furthermore, the emergence of new types of team arrangements, facilitated by emerging organisational technologies, has led to a new set of potential dynamics and ways of working together that present novel opportunities and challenges not previously encountered in more conventional settings. The increasing existence of virtual teams, for example, presents team structures and work methodologies that may be radically different from those patterns and dynamics that have existed in traditional team settings (Matthews and Gladstone 2000).

It is often difficult to be exactly sure what combination of factors leads to organisational effectiveness. For one thing, the concept of effectiveness is difficult to define. People within the organisation may have different views about what effectiveness means. Marketing people may believe that organisations are effective to the extent that they promote their brands and attract customers to buy their products or services; personnel people may believe that effectiveness depends on the organisation's ability to attract, select, motivate, train and retain good-quality people; the finance department may see organisational effectiveness as the ability to keep costs low and revenues high; and research and development may consider organisational effectiveness to be characterised by the organisation's ability to develop new products and advance innovative ways of doing things.

Organisational effectiveness is not an objective standard to which all organisations can aspire in any straightforward way. It means different things to different people, and depending on the roles that people play in their organisations, the pursuit of organisational effectiveness can be characterised by a variety of very different perspectives, by conflict and by efforts to pursue goals that are at least sometimes mutually exclusive. The personnel department may be eager to develop new training initiatives that may be seen by the finance department as too costly. Marketing people may put the R&D department under pressure to speed up the product development cycles so that they can get the product to market as fast as possible, while the R&D people claim that they need more time if they are to make any real or substantial breakthroughs in a particular area.

Organisational effectiveness can be attributed to a variety of different activities, variables and events both inside and outside the organisation. It may be difficult to establish in any truly objective way why some organisations succeed and others fail. Organisations that introduce new initiatives like team activities and team-based structures may also have a variety of qualities and characteristics that make them successful or that contribute to their organisational effectiveness. Sometimes it is difficult to be sure that an organisation is effective because of its team orientation or that a team orientation exists because an organisation is effective.

Techniques for better management of organisations sit side by side with a myriad of other variables – economic conditions, the history of the organisation, random (or at least unpredictable) changes in market demands, earthquakes, hurricanes, assassinations, oil crises, droughts, wars, terrorist actions and other global events can all impact on organisations and their ability to survive in ways that may override or eliminate the benefits of any of the microprocesses introduced by managers within the company. Ireland exists within a small, open economy, which often makes the country all the more vulnerable to the peaks and troughs of bigger economies and worldwide events.

Nevertheless, initiatives that involve team creation and team-based activity can and do make a difference in individual companies. It is simplistic to say that team-based organisations will automatically be successful. A more accurate perspective incorporates the idea that organisational productivity can be facilitated by a team orientation in conjunction with a wide variety of other factors, both internal and external to the organisation.

WHEN TEAMWORK IS APPROPRIATE

Not all work situations demand teamwork. However, in today's complex business environments, more and more organisations are adopting team-based activities and philosophies. When a task requires teamwork, it usually means that the following factors exist.

• Working together will produce better results than working apart.

- The task requires a wide mixture of different talents and skills.
- The job needs constant adjustment in what people do and in how work is co-ordinated.
- Competition between individuals is likely to be damaging.
- The pressure of the job creates more stress than one single person could comfortably handle.

CHARACTERISTICS OF EFFECTIVE TEAMS

An effective team should have all or most of the following characteristics (adapted from Woodcock 1979).

- Clear objectives that have been agreed upon by all team members.
- A relaxed and informal atmosphere where people are allowed to express their opinions and ideas.
- Support and trust between all members.
- Honest, direct and constructive processes for criticising and analysing ideas and activities.
- Fair distribution of tasks.
- An accurate awareness of performance levels and capabilities.
- An ability to deal with disagreements.
- Appropriate leadership.

ONGOING DEBATES/ADVANCED CONCEPTS IN GROUPS AND TEAMS

A CRITIQUE OF THE HAWTHORNE STUDIES

As outlined earlier, the Hawthorne studies are still recognised as an important turning point in the development of theory about organisational behaviour and groups operating within organisations. However, there are several legitimate criticisms about the perspectives adopted, the methodologies used and the results reported.

First, while the researchers on the Hawthorne project heralded a fundamental change in the ways in which organisations were to be understood and studied, many people argue that they actually served to reinforce rather than to undermine the original Taylorist assumptions guiding most management thinking of the time. As Mills and Simmons (1995: 11) point out:

> Scientific management … is a strand of [organisational theory] which arose out of the needs of employers to increase their employees' efficiency. Similarly, the human relations strand of organisational behaviour developed out of the specific concerns of the Western Electric Company to improve productivity. This led to the development of organisational principles that were managerialist in nature, that is, that take the defined needs of those in charge of organisations as the starting point for the developments of research foci and projects … [As a result] managerialist approaches

to organisations have developed into a strong and dominant orthodoxy and alternative ways of viewing organisations have been treated as deviant and non-legitimate theories of organisation.

While a managerialist perspective is obviously an important standpoint from the point of view of understanding organisational behaviour, it is not the only one. An excessive emphasis on purely managerial concerns can prevent the consideration of alternative viewpoints and thus restrict the sound development of knowledge in the area.

More recently, however, attempts have been made to redress this paradigmatic imbalance in the organisational behaviour literature. For example, Morgan (1986) and Mills and Murgatroyd (1991) encourage us to use perspectives other than purely managerialist ones to help explain the nature of organisations and organisational group dynamics.

Second, the Hawthorne studies have been criticised for failing to recognise the 'sex power differential' (Stead 1978). Of the two main groups studied, one ('the relay assembly group') was all female and the other ('the bank wiring group') was all male. As Acker and Van Houten (1974: 156) argue:

> The [male and female groups] were studied in different ways. [The male group was] free to continue their usual work practices, including the autonomy to develop and maintain their own work norms. The [female group] on the other hand [was] carefully recruited, closely supervised and in numerous ways told that they should improve their productivity.

There were strong differences in the findings between the male and female groups studied. Most striking was the fact that the all-female group increased its productivity and the all-male group restricted its outputs. These important results and contingencies were underemphasised in the reporting of the research, thus disregarding possibly one of the most interesting and important aspects of the study.

Third, the cultural specificities of the study make the results difficult to validate across cultures and over time. There were no studies to which this research could be compared for cultural differences. In Ireland or in other European countries, similar studies at the time might have suggested different patterns of behaviour according to various cultural dimensions (Hofstede 1991). However, such information is not available.

PITFALLS IN THE PROCESS OF GROUP DEVELOPMENT

Earlier in this chapter we explored the commonly cited stages of group formation. This section explores some of the pitfalls that may be associated with each of these stages.

Why Groups May Get Stuck at the Forming Stage

People sometimes find that when a group forms there is an inability for group members to break the ice and to start communicating about the reason they have formed. If this happens and if such a problem continues, the reason for forming will become very hard to clarify and the group may break up or fizzle out.

If there is a constant inflow of newcomers at the forming stage, it becomes difficult to set objectives or to agree on who should occupy the leadership role, and so effective group formation may be difficult or impossible.

If for other reasons (such as people being coerced into group membership) there is little or no commitment to the purpose of the group, then formation will be half-hearted and the group is unlikely to successfully progress on to the next stages of development.

Why Groups May Get Stuck at the Storming Stage

People often find it difficult to cope with the storming stage because it is usually the first time when conflict or disagreement occurs. The group is still fragile and can easily come apart if this conflict is not resolved successfully.

Again, if group members do not learn to interact, cope effectively with conflicts that arise and operate beyond formal, surface introductions and clarifications, it will be much more difficult for effective development to progress.

Why Groups May Get Stuck at the Norming Stage

If people don't recognise their own strengths and weaknesses or what is expected of them by other members of the group, it can be difficult for effective norms to be established. Also, if people don't feel comfortable enough to voice their opinions about what they think is good or bad about the group, they won't have a chance to make the most of the skills that do exist and work on developing the skills that don't.

One of the most important things about achieving a good atmosphere for groups to develop successfully is to be able to recognise the above pitfalls and to avoid them or cope with them if they arise.

Team Tasks and Processes

In order for a team to perform effectively there are two different aspects of its functioning that people need to concentrate on, which are what the team is doing and how it is doing it. In other words, the team must attempt to perfect the task it has to complete and the process by which it goes about achieving the task.

The Team Process

How the team operates is just as important as what it does. When people talk about team processes, they refer to the following types of behaviours.
- Activities and discussions that help the team to remain in good working order.
- Maintaining a good work atmosphere.
- Developing and keeping good working relationships.
- Dealing with tension and conflict within the team.
- Keeping communication open between all team members.
- Meeting regularly.
- Sharing information.

- Offering praise and encouragement to one another.
- Accepting one another's points of view.

All of these kinds of behaviours help the team to maintain the qualities that make it a team. The second pillar of good team behaviour is task-oriented activity.

The Team Task

Teams are brought together to achieve certain goals, thus they need to be focused on these goals and monitor how close they are to achieving them. Task behaviours refer to the following types of activities.

- Proposing, agreeing and reviewing tasks or goals.
- Solving problems relating to these tasks or goals.
- Collecting relevant information and facts about the tasks.
- Exploring alternative courses of action and generating ideas.
- Reaching decisions about what needs to be done.
- Sticking to deadlines.
- Concentrating on the quality of the work.

PROBLEMS WITH DEVELOPING TEAMS

The language and rhetoric of teams, team building and team success has sometimes led to an image of teamwork that at one extreme is unrealistic and at the other is charged with cynicism and mistrust (Carson 1992). In order to develop a balanced picture of the potential benefits of teams, the following issues should be considered.

Inadequate Attention to Team Characteristics

It is easy to give lip service to team development in organisations by simply using the label 'team' when referring to groups of people that are in reality loosely connected within a structure. Various team characteristics can have a strong effect on the performance of the team.

Research carried out on top management teams in the Irish setting demonstrates that top team characteristics are an important consideration where various aspects of the team's performance are concerned, particularly pioneering behaviour (for example, see Moore *et al*. 1996).

TOP TEAMS AND PIONEERING

Our findings suggested that there are several links between top management team characteristics and pioneering behaviour.

1. Boundary spanning

Firstly, a strong relationship was found between pioneering and 'boundary spanning'. Boundary spanning refers to the extent to which a top management team communicates and interacts across various organisational boundaries. Boundaries between departments and other groups may serve to undermine communication and innovation, unless such boundaries are spanned effectively. Indeed, our study found that the more a team was involved in boundary spanning activity, the more likely it was to be a pioneer. This also reflects previous evidence which suggests that boundary spanning is an effective way of facilitating the recognition of new opportunities. For example, Quinn (1985) argues that not only must organisations have a strong market orientation at the very top of the company, but also that mechanisms must exist which facilitate boundary spanning between technical, marketing and top management functions. Boundary spanning is itself an indicator of an organisation's ability to recognise new opportunities. Evidence from our study supports this assertion.

2. Stock options, company shares and risk-taking activity

As mentioned earlier, really creative teams need to operate in environments where risk is tolerated and where experimentation with new ideas includes at least some allowance for failure.

Our study found a statistically significant relationship between the risk dimension of pioneering behaviour and specific aspects of top management team compensation arrangements. For example, the more stock options offered to top management team members, the more likely the team was to demonstrate pioneering behaviour. It appears that the option to buy stock at some point in the organisation's future encourages risk-taking which leads to innovation and pioneering.

On the other hand, it was also found that top managers of pioneering companies hold relatively less company shares. Our findings suggest that stock options have a positive relationship and share ownership has a negative relationship with risk-taking behaviour. It also appears then, that when top managers actually own considerable shares in the organisation, their tendency to take risks may be significantly reduced.

3. Age profile of the top management team

Several studies have in the past suggested that older decision-makers have more cognitive limitations and are less adept at handling information than their younger counterparts (see Kirchner 1958; Weir 1964). It has also been proposed that the age profile of the top management team has a significant bearing on the firm's risk orientation (Hambrick and Mason 1984). Older managers, it is argued, are less likely to take risks when deciding on future strategies and may rely on incremental change processes rather than quantum leaps in product portfolios, strategic options and so on (Johnson 1990). The stereotype of the older manager is that he/she possesses less physical and mental stamina, has greater psychological commitment to the organisational status quo and sees financial and career security as his/her primary goal.

Contrary to these assertions, our research reveals that pioneering organisations are more likely to have older rather than younger top managers at the helm. How do we explain these surprising findings? Perhaps the benefits of experience bestow knowledge and confidence in older managers which facilitate a more risk-tolerant style, and that the stereotypes of older managers have been exaggerated in the past. Another explanation might be found in the relative youth of the sample we chose. The average age in our sample is 44 years. Other studies such as those carried out by Wiersema and Bantel (1992) and O'Reilly and Flatt (1989) used samples with considerably higher average ages (56 and 53 years respectively).

Future investigation may reveal an 'inverted U-shaped' relationship between age and risk-taking behaviour. In other words, there may be an optimal age profile associated with risk-taking. If the age profile of a top management team is above this optimal level, risk-taking and innovation may be reduced due to the implementation of more conservative strategies. However, if it is below a certain age, risk-taking may not occur due to a lack of experience, confidence, knowledge structures and so on.

4. Educational profile of the top management team

We found that pioneering firms have relatively less educated top managers. While further research may be necessary to clarify the relationship between educational level and pioneering, this is nevertheless an interesting finding.

While education continues to be one of the primary criteria for selection or promotion within the managerial ranks of organisations, it appears that there is a limit to which education is associated with innovative or risk-taking behaviour. Perhaps this is because more educated managers tend to be more exhaustive in their search for information than their less educated counterparts (Hambrick and Mason 1984). The search for more information is obviously time-consuming and by its very nature is intrinsically less risk-orientated than the decision which is made more quickly, but with less information. An extensive, comprehensive search for information is more likely to be associated with linear, logical top management team dynamics. This type of orientation may be more likely to appear in teams with extensive educational experience and qualifications. Norburn (1989) says that while educational level does differentiate top managers from other organisational members, their success or failure may be more likely to be associated with factors such as breadth and multiplicity of experience. If pioneering is a contributor to organisational success, our findings suggest that higher levels of education may not be as necessary as previously assumed. In some contexts, educational levels may even hinder the risk tolerance associated with creativity, innovation and pioneering.

5. Team homogeneity and speed of strategic response

Fast strategic adjustment is an important stage in the pioneering process. Part of our study attempted to isolate certain variables that might be associated with a top team's ability to adjust speedily to new strategies, product innovations and so on. We hypothesised that if top team members were all similar in certain aspects (age, length of time in the organisation and education level), they would be faster to adjust strategically than those teams which were more diverse in terms of age, tenure and education. Our hypothesis was derived again from work by O'Reilly and Flatt (1989) and Wiersema and Bantel (1992) who suggested that homogeneity or similarity of top management teams can lead to less conflict at times when implementation is taking place, and faster, more effective communication. It has been suggested on the one hand that the more alike the top management team feels, the stronger the team norms and the better the communication patterns, the faster decision consensus is reached. On the other hand, team member homogeneity may lead to high levels of group cohesiveness which has been shown to be linked with some dysfunctional characteristics. Excessive group conformity is an example of such dysfunctionality, leading to poor decision quality and sometimes excessive risk-taking (e.g. Janis 1971).

In the light of previous evidence we expected to find some relationships between homogeneity and pioneering. However, our study yielded no evidence of any relationship between top management team homogeneity and pioneering behaviour. Based on our evidence, homogeneity of age, tenure and education are not factors when considering whether a team is likely to be pioneering in its strategic orientation.

Of course we cannot assume that other dimensions of homogeneity such as personality, gender, background and so on might not demonstrate a relationship with pioneering. Undoubtedly, there is scope for further investigation here.

To summarise, we found that pioneering in organisations was positively related to such factors as TMT boundary spanning behaviour, the existence of stock options and a higher average TMT age profile. We found that it was negatively related to share ownership among TMT members and higher levels of TMT educational qualifications. We found no significant relationship between TMT homogeneity of age, organisational tenure or education.

Our research has identified certain TMT factors that appear to be related to an organisation's ability to pioneer. These findings should be supplemented by further research and investigation, and may provide implications for the selection, compensation and development of top management team members in the future.

Source: Moore *et al.* (1996)

OTHER POTENTIAL PROBLEMS WITH TEAMS AT WORK

Autonomy vs. Accountability

As more and more organisations use the methodologies of self-managed teams, autonomous work groups and cross-functional teams, the problem of accountability often becomes an issue (Carson 1992). Individual accountability is often easier to establish than team accountability, especially because responsibility over tasks and outcomes can become ambiguous. While there is a wide variety of evidence that demonstrates the benefits of teams, the potential of team working can be lost when accountability is not considered. Some researchers and practitioners argue that while teams need to be put in place, the team's energy needs to be harnessed by maintaining the principle of individual accountability.

Too Much or Too Little Conflict

Effective teams are made up of individuals who occupy a variety of complementary roles. One of the problems associated with developing teams relates to the difficulty of the negotiation and agreement of the various roles that each individual should take on. There may be struggles over who should become the team leader, who should facilitate activity and where the real expertise lies. Because teams often demand a wide variety of different types of skills and perspectives, it is common to encounter clashes when priorities are being established (Brown 1988).

However, teams should also be characterised by healthy levels of conflict. Confrontation of divergent views is an important principle of effective teams (Thomas 1976) and unless conflict can be expressed, important and creative ideas in the team may be lost (Harrison 1972).

Too Much or Too Little Control

Ideally, when groups of people become teams they should start to create results far beyond what would have been possible before. Given the right conditions, teams have the capacity to be highly creative and innovative (for example, see Prince 1970). In cross-functional teams in particular and because of the ways in which individuals combine to form a team, plenty of new ideas become available and are discussed. This is one of the benefits of teamwork. Teamwork can help people to become more innovative, which is one of the central reasons why efforts to create teams emerge. However, such creativity becomes less likely if too much control is exerted over people. If a team is not given the freedom to explore new ideas and come up with its own solutions to specific problems, many of the benefits of teamwork can be lost. Because teams inevitably exist within a given organisational structure and because power is distributed in certain ways within that structure, teams are generally subject to a certain level of control and co-ordination.

Some control and co-ordination is of course necessary, otherwise activities become disjointed and confused. Someone (perhaps a team leader) needs to be given a certain amount of controlling power in order to ensure that the team gets its job done in the best way possible. Control is particularly important when there are pressing deadlines that have to be met.

Creating effective teams is accompanied by the difficulty which many organisations experience in striking a balance between too much and too little control (Carson 1992). Too much control smothers potential creativity, whereas too little results in time wasting and confusion.

Not Enough Training

If people are not trained for teamwork and for the specific tasks that they are required to complete, then they will not be able to operate successfully in a team situation. Training is particularly important during those times when an organisation is undergoing a lot of change and where new practices are being introduced. Unless organisations are prepared to invest in training people for the ways in which their jobs are changing and in training them to be a team member, the benefits of teamwork will undoubtedly suffer.

Unsuitable or Defensive Management Philosophy

If top management does not agree with the idea of teamwork, it is much less likely that the reality of teams will ever get off the ground. Teams need the support of top management and management must support teams through their actions as well as through what they say. Top management is often the rock upon which good teamwork perishes. For teams to work properly, they must operate in an atmosphere of openness and trust. Communication must be as honest and upfront as possible. This is a philosophy that many top managers can find threatening. Creating teams means giving teams the power and authority to make many of their own decisions, which means taking power away from where it traditionally lies. As a result, such managers may work against the principle of teamwork rather than for it, and consequently people remain divided and the benefits of teamwork may again be lost.

Unfair Rewards

Effective teams can help to yield positive results for their individual members and their organisations. If used at appropriate times and if managed well, their benefits can far outweigh the costs of developing them. Effective teams are usually very aware of their successes as well as their failures, and unless the organisation is prepared to reward the achievements that they produce, dissatisfaction among team members is likely. If a team is not rewarded, its members will begin to feel undervalued within the organisation. As a result, morale and motivation may be lost. This is another way in which teamwork can be damaged.

Teamwork involves people working together to produce work of high quality by pooling their resources and maximising the potential of each individual. It also requires integrating activity in a co-ordinated and organised way. The best way to do this is to generate and agree on specific aims. As soon as people have been given goals, it becomes much easier for them to know where they're going and to organise themselves to achieve these goals.

Resistance to Change

If people are not accustomed to being part of a team, then there are many reasons why the prospect of team participation may be intimidating. Teamwork places numerous demands on people, can carry negative associations and the introduction of teamworking can result in resistance to the concept. Negotiation and agreement of the terms of teamwork initiatives need to be carried out from the outset.

People need to feel responsible for their own development within the team, need to be given the authority to make their own unique contribution to the team and everyone in the team should be consulted about everything to do with the team.

It must be recognised that everyone has an important contribution to make. One way of showing this is to make sure that people communicate their ideas, are asked about any proposals that are being made and that their contributions are taken seriously. If people get the chance to participate, they will be more likely to be committed to the team's aims and believe in what the team is all about.

Laying the groundwork for good team development involves keeping all of the above points in mind and ensuring that people are clear about the kinds of things that good teamwork can uncover in an organisation. The potential pitfalls associated with creating teams can be avoided if the team members and their leaders are observant and prepared.

TEAM CREATIVITY

More and more, teams are being brought together in organisations not just to enhance the conditions for collaboration, but to increase overall levels of organisational creativity. An understanding of the creative process and how it unfolds in team settings is becoming an important dimension in team development.

Creativity has been defined and gauged in a wide variety of ways. Generally, though, creativity can be said to require a multiplicity of attributes, including such properties as curiosity, self-confidence, optimism, flexibility, humour, imagination, openness to experience, tolerance of ambiguity, independence, originality, responsiveness, motivation and freedom from the fear of failure. These attributes are not just a function of individual differences and personality, but also of the types of organisations within which individuals and groups operate and the climate that is fostered within group settings. Creative thinking is facilitated and constrained by many contextual and organisational variables, and the ability for teams to be creative may depend on a combination of any of the following factors.

Team Composition

The various mix of individual personalities, levels of self-esteem, cognitive styles and abilities, task-relevant knowledge and skill, past reinforcement history, etc. may have a fundamental effect on a group's ability to be creative, develop vision and manage the creative process. Traditional managers are often evaluated for competencies such as logic, analytical skills and organising ability, which are typically 'left brain' capabilities. Developing creative energy involves facilitating 'right brain' skills such as imagination, conceptualisation and intuition and ensuring that there is a good mix of both types of ability. Generally, group diversity tends to have a positive effect on creativity and diversity of individual behaviour and style can have a positive bearing on overall group effectiveness, including the capacity to create a meaningful and worthwhile vision of the future.

Leadership Style and Team Atmosphere

Evidence has repeatedly shown that democratic, collaborative leadership styles are positively correlated with creativity in organisations and that autocratic leadership styles are negatively correlated with effective idea generation and innovative outcomes. The prevalence of status consciousness, rule-bound behaviour and unequal power distribution may inhibit the free exchange of ideas, which (at least to some extent) is why it is difficult for traditionally bureaucratic organisations to achieve high levels of creativity.

There are a number of ways in which some of the negative effects of bureaucratic behaviour can be overcome. Leaders need to encourage and reward 'devil's advocacy' within organisational groups; be impartial, at least at the early stages of a group process, such as vision development and problem solving; gather as much relevant information from as many sources as possible; check agreement from all group members on an ongoing basis; detect any residual doubts, second thoughts or reservations; and uncover progressive ideas from those who might be inhibited about or unaccustomed to voicing their views. It is possible to create open and confrontational group atmospheres where members feel free to experiment with ideas, propose alternatives and disagree with the majority view in the interests of effective task accomplishment. Leaders can set important precedents by encouraging and rewarding dissenters from the outset and ensuring that all participation is recognised and integrated into either the content or the process of group activity.

Knowledge Banks and Creative Use of Existing Information

Research on organisational innovation and, more recently, on creativity has supported the notion that an elaborate variety of available resources is positively associated with high rates of innovative thinking. Evidence strongly suggests, for example, that the existence and development of a 'bank' of knowledge to which groups have open access is a worthwhile resource that can aid the initiation and progress of beneficial creative processes. While existing knowledge often confers the ability to recognise the relative importance of new information, it is also important for groups not to become constrained by current frames of reference. For real benefit to be derived, the acquisition and assimilation of information is not enough. Unless this information is exploited in focused, appropriate and original ways, its benefits may be lost. An organisation's capacity to exploit information effectively does not just depend on its ability to obtain information from external sources. It is also important that information transfer within and between key internal groups occurs frequently and effectively.

INITIATING AND DEVELOPING THE CREATIVE PROCESS WITHIN GROUPS AND TEAMS

Teams that have been charged with the responsibility for complex and non-routine tasks need to spend time agreeing and developing effective processes that will ensure that maximum benefit is gained from their activities. This is especially important in a context where time is precious and resources are scarce. While the creative process is not easy to analyse, it has been suggested by behavioural theorists that it is characterised by four major stages.

1. **Preparation:** This is an active process whereby information is gathered from both traditional and non-traditional sources. 'Creative decision-makers study the issues surrounding a decision and participate extensively in group meetings where new ideas and alternative points of view abound' (Griffin and Moorhead 1995: 255). It is desirable at this stage that participants in the creative process are encouraged to be relatively unbridled by practical issues associated with implementation. Of course, practical considerations must become part of the emerging plan for action, but if this happens too early on, good ideas and important perspectives may never come to light

and the value of group energy may become caught up in operational rather than strategic issues.

2. **Incubation:** The incubation stage is characterised by such cognitive processes as reflection and consideration. This is more likely to occur outside formal meetings, during informal discussions where developing ideas are 'thrown around'. It is useful to spend time trying to find different ways of viewing various issues and involving non-members, i.e. those outside the formally created committees/groups, in in-depth discussions about emerging patterns of thought.

3. **Illumination:** The illumination stage involves the development of effective insights whereby a set of conceptual breakthroughs paves the way towards the implementation of good ideas. Insight often involves lateral thinking and a sudden mental reorganisation of the elements of a problem that make the solution obvious, or at least clearer than originally was the case. Participants in the creative process need to work on the skills associated with the development of effective insights, which include selecting information relevant to a problem and ignoring distractions, bringing together apparently unrelated but useful pieces of information and comparing new problems with the existing base of knowledge and information.

4. **Verification:** Creative insights and visions must finally be verified and validated. This happens when the gaps between the ideal and the real begin to close. People may start to suggest ways in which visions of the future can be realised given current strengths and weaknesses in the system and recognising opportunities to be exploited and existing restrictions to be overcome. Practical operational issues must be considered at this stage and first steps towards the realisation of the vision need to be initiated.

SUMMARY OF KEY PROPOSITIONS

- This chapter introduced some of the original theoretical foundations of groups and group development in organisational settings. Most of the research about groups and group dynamics is managerialist in its perspective on organisational analysis. Nevertheless, groups can be very useful, not just for organisations but also to fulfil the needs of individual group members.

- A review of the original Hawthorne studies shows that the experiments were flawed in some serious ways, but that they led to the central propositions that people often prefer to operate in groups and that creating organisational groups can enhance organisational effectiveness.

- Group norms were discussed and described as unwritten rules of behaviour to which each member is expected to conform. It was pointed out that some group norms create effective and productive ways of doing things, but that others can be damaging for the organisation to which the group belongs.

- Group development has been described as comprising four key stages (forming, storming, norming and performing). In ideal situations, different issues relating to the group are resolved at different stages, but these stages of group development don't always reflect reality.

- Group cohesiveness is a sense of belongingness and commitment to a group that keeps group members together. It arises as a result of several factors in the course of a group's existence, which include good levels of communication and co-operation, acceptance of all group members, commitment to the survival of the group and a general atmosphere of success. Group cohesiveness, while desirable in a group, can sometimes be damaging due to what has come to be known as the 'groupthink phenomenon'.
- The concept of groupthink was explained and explored. It was described as behaviour that emerges when people become so close that any disagreement is less and less likely to occur. The group is prevented from being realistic or critical about what they are doing and the ways in which they are doing it. The causes of groupthink were outlined.
- Teamwork was described as people working together to produce work of high quality by pooling their resources and maximising each individual's potential. Good teamwork requires the integration and co-ordination of activities and is particularly appropriate under certain conditions. There are two different sets of behaviours that are useful for teams: task behaviours, i.e. getting the job done, and process behaviours, i.e. keeping the team together.
- There are some common organisational problems that can combine to prevent a group from becoming a team, which were explored in the advanced concepts section of this chapter.
- We examined some of the useful roles that should be played in teams along with some of the behaviours that can be damaging to team performance, and we looked at several of the main characteristics of effective teams.

DISCUSSION/SELF-ASSESSMENT QUESTIONS

1. Think of a group to which you belong. See if you can give any examples of group norms from the definition provided in this chapter.
2. Discuss the kinds of activities that effective teamwork involves.
3. Outline your views on some of the ways in which creativity in teams can be enhanced.
4. Do you think that the stages of group formation outlined in this chapter paint an unrealistic picture of what really happens in group situations?
5. Is group cohesiveness always a positive factor that enhances successful group performance?
6. Is your group a team? Think of a group of people with whom you work or have worked and ask yourself: Do I achieve results that far exceed what I could do alone? Does the activity I am engaged in involve pooling resources, i.e. skill, effort, commitment and creativity? Does the work in this group go beyond satisfactory, standard performance and reach levels of truly high quality? Am I maximising my potential as a member of the team?

    Possible problems are that maybe the group is made up of the wrong people or perhaps the group does not have the right mix of skills and attitudes to become a team.

Is this a problem in the group in which you work? What skills are missing? How could they be developed? Perhaps there are too many unnecessary controls on group members so that they are afraid of or prevented from coming up with their own ideas as to how the work should be done. Ask yourself if you have ever had ideas about improving teamwork or other work processes which you did not voice. Are there too many rules that prevent you from being creative? If so, what are these rules and why do you think they exist?

On the other hand, teamwork may not exist because of too little control. Is the work that you do in groups disorganised or disjointed? Are people unsure as to where everyone fits in and what they are expected to do? Do people have enough training to organise themselves into an effective working team?

MULTIPLE CHOICE QUESTIONS

1. Reorder the following stages of group formation according to Tuckman's classic theory sequence, outlined in this chapter.
   (a) Performing.
   (b) Forming.
   (c) Norming.
   (d) Storming.
2. The groupthink phenomenon emerges in groups when:
   (a) There is an inappropriate emphasis on group cohesiveness and agreement at the expense of decision quality.
   (b) There is an inappropriate emphasis on decision quality at the expense of group cohesiveness.
   (c) There is too much conflict in the group.
   (d) Groups are not skilled enough to solve problems.
3. Which of the following represents a beneficial aspect of belonging to a group?
   (a) A guaranteed mix of talents.
   (b) The chance that synergies will exist between members.
   (c) Certainty that work will be completed.
4. To be defined psychologically as a group, members must perceive themselves to be a group. True or false?
5. The Hawthorne studies concluded that physical surroundings were more important for group effectiveness and performance than behavioural factors. True or false?
6. A group norm is:
   (a) A formal written rule to which all members must comply.
   (b) A prevailing group attitude.
   (c) An unwritten rule of behaviour shared by all or most members of the group.
   (d) A legal group requirement.
7. Which of the following is a common characteristic of cohesive groups?
   (a) Plenty of conflict.

(b) Fear and mistrust.

(c) Likelihood that agreement will be reached quickly.

(d) Unconventional leadership style.

8. People find it difficult to cope with the storming stage of group development because it is usually the first time when conflict or disagreement between group members occurs. True or false?

9. The incubation stage of group creativity is characterised by:

(a) The development of effective insights.

(b) Reflection and consideration.

(c) The gathering of information.

(d) Verification and validation.

FIVE SUGGESTED KEY READINGS

Gersick, C.J.G., 'Time and transition in work teams: toward a new model of group development', *Academy of Management Journal*, XXXI (1988), 9–41.

Kim, Y., 'A comparative study of the abeline paradox and groupthink', *Public Administration Quarterly*, XX/3 (2001), 168–89.

Matthews, J.J. and Gladston, B., 'Extending the group: a strategy for virtual team formation', *Industrial and Commercial Training*, XXXII/1 (2000), 24–30.

Miller, D., 'The stages of group development: a retrospective study of dynamic team processes', *Canadian Journal of Administrative Sciences*, XX/2 (2003), 121–34.

Tuckman, B.W., 'Development sequence in small groups', *Psychological Bulletin*, LXIII (1965), 419–27.

REFERENCES

Acker, L. and van Houten, D.R., 'Differential recruitment and control: the structuring of organisations', *Administrative Science Quarterly*, IX/2 (1974), 152–63.

Adair, J., *Teams and Team Development*, London: Ashridge Press 1986.

Alderfer, C.P., *Existence, Relatedness and Growth*, New York: Collier Macmillan 1972.

Allport, F.H., 'A structuronomic conception of behaviour: individual and collective', *Journal of Abnormal and Social Psychology*, 64 (1962), 3–30.

Argyris, C., *Overcoming Organizational Defences*, Needham Heights, MA: Allyn and Bacon 1990.

Aronson, E. and Mills, J., 'The effect of severity of initiation on liking for a group', *Journal of Abnormal and Social Psychology*, 67 (1959), 31–6.

Bales, R.F., *Interaction Process Analysis: A Method for the Study of Small Groups*, Reading, MA: Addison-Wesley 1950.

Bales, R.F., *Task Roles and Social Roles in Problem-Solving Groups*, New York: Holt, Reinhart and Winston 1953.

Bateman, T.S. and Zeithaml, C.P., 'The psychological context of strategic decisions: a model and convergent experimental findings', *Strategic Management Journal*, X/1 (1989), 59–74.

Belbin, R.M., *Management Teams: Why They Succeed or Fail*, London: Heineman 1981.

Belbin, R.M., *Team Roles at Work*, Oxford: Butterworth-Heinemann 1993.

Brown, R., *Group Process*, London: Blackwell 1988.

Budge, S., 'Group cohesiveness re-examined', *Group*, 5 (1981), 10–18.

Campbell, D.T., 'Common fate, similarity and other indices of the status of aggregates of persons as social entities', *Behavioural Science*, 3 (1958), 14–25.

Carson, N., 'The trouble with teams', *Training*, XXIX/8 (1992), 38–40.

Collins, R., 'On the microfoundations of macrosociology', *American Journal of Sociology*, 15 (1981), 984–1013.

Cook, S.W., 'Interpersonal and attitudinal outcomes in co-operating interracial groups', *Journal of Research and Development in Education*, XII (1978), 97–113.

Festinger, L., *A Theory of Cognitive Dissonance*, Stanford, CT: Stanford University Press 1957.

Gersick, C.J.G., 'Time and transition in work teams: toward a new model of group development', *Academy of Management Journal*, XXXI (1988), 9–41.

Gersick, C.J.G., 'Marking time: predictable transitions in task groups', *Academy of Management Journal*, XXXII (1989), 274–309.

Griffin, R. and Moorhead, G., *Organizational Behaviour: Managing People and Organizations*, Boston: Houghton Mifflin 1995.

Hambrick, D. and Mason, P., 'Upper echelons: the organization as a reflection of its top manager', *Academy of Management Review*, 9 (1984), 193–206.

Handy, C., *Understanding Organisations*, London: Penguin 1988.

Harrison, R., 'When power conflicts trigger team spirit', *European Business* (Spring 1972), 57–65.

Hellriegel, D., Slocum, J.W. and Woodman, R.W., *Organizational Behaviour*, 5th ed., St Paul, MN: West Publishing 1989.

Hofstede, G., *Cultures and Organizations: Software of the Mind*, London: McGraw-Hill 1991.

Hogg, M.A., *The Social Psychology of Group Cohesiveness: From Attraction to Social Identity*, Reading, MA: Addison-Wesley 1992.

Holden, L.P., 'The team manager as visionary and servant', *Managers Magazine*, LXIII/11 (1988), 6–9.

Homans, G.C., *The Human Group*, New York: Harcourt Brace Jovanovich 1950.

Hosking, D.M. and Morley, I.E., *A Social Psychology of Organising*, Hemel Hempstead: Harvester Wheatsheaf 1991.

Huczynski, A. and Buchanan, D., *Organizational Behaviour: An Introductory Text*, 2nd ed., Hemel Hempstead: Prentice Hall 1996.

Jacobsen, S.R., 'Individual and group responses to confinement in a skyjacked plane' *American Journal of Orthopsychiatry*, XLIII (1973), 459–69.

Janis, I.L., 'Groupthink', *Psychology Today*, XLIII (1971).

Janis, I.L., *Victims of Groupthink*, New York: Houghton Mifflin 1972.

Janis, I.L., *Groupthink*, 2nd ed., New York: Houghton Mifflin 1982.

Johnson, M., 'Age differences in decision making: a process methodology for examining strategic information processes', *Journal of Gerontology*, Psychological Sciences, 45 (March 1990), 75–8.

Katzenbach, J.R. and Smith, D.K., *The Wisdom of Teams: Creating the High Performance Organization*, Boston, MA: Harvard Business School Press 1993.

Kiesler, C.A. and Kiesler, S.B., *Conformity*, Reading, MA: Addison-Wesley 1969.

Kim, Y., 'A comparative study of the abeline paradox and groupthink', *Public Administration Quarterly*, XX/3 (2001), 168–89.

Kirchner, W., 'Age differences in short term retention of rapidly changing information', *Journal of Experimental Psychology*, 55 (1958), 352–8.

Lewin, K., 'Group decision and social change', in T.N. Newcomb and E.L. Hartley (eds), *Readings in Social Psychology*, New York: Holt, Reinhart and Winston 1947.

Lewin, K., *Resolving Social Conflicts*, New York: Harper 1948.

Marcic, D., *Organizational Behaviour: Experiences and Cases*, New York: West Publishing 1992.

Marks, M.A., Mathieu, J.E. and Zaccaro, S.J., 'A temporally based framework and taxonomy of team process', *The Academy of Management Review*, XXVI/3 (2001), 356–76.

Maslow, A.H., 'A theory of human motivation', *Psychological Review* (July 1943).

Matthews, J.J. and Gladston, B., 'Extending the group: a strategy for virtual team formation', *Industrial and Commercial Training*, XXXII/1 (2000), 24–30.

Mayo, E., *The Human Problems of an Industrial Civilisation*, New York: Macmillan 1933.

McCarthy, M., *Missionaries and Cannibals*, New York: Hodder & Stoughton 1979.

Miller, D., 'The stages of group development: a retrospective study of dynamic team processes', *Canadian Journal of Administrative Sciences*, XX/2 (2002), 121–35.

Mills, A. and Murgatroyd, J., *Organizational Rules: A Framework for Understanding Organizational Action*, Milton Keynes: Open University Press 1991.

Mills, A.J. and Simmons, T., *Reading Organizational Theory: A Critical Approach*, New York: Garamond 1995.

Moore, S., Morley, M., Fong, C., Flood, P., O'Regan, P. and Smith, K., 'Taking the lead: an investigation into the process of top management team pioneering', in B. Leavy and J. Walsh (eds), *Strategy and General Management: An Irish Reader*, Dublin: Oak Tree Press 1996.

Moorhead, G. and Griffin, R.W., *Organizational Behavior: Managing People and Organizations*, 4th ed., Boston: Houghton Mifflin 1995.

Moreland, R.L. and Levine, J.M., 'Socialistion in small groups: temporal changes in individual-group relations', *Advances in Experimental Social Psychology*, 15 (1982), 137–92.

Morgan, G., *Images of Organisation*, London: Sage 1986.

Mullins, L., *Management and Organisational Behaviour*, 4th ed., London: Pitman Publishing 1996.

Myers, A., 'Team competition, success and the adjustment of group members', *Journal of Abnormal and Social Psychology*, 65 (1962), 325–32.

Narayanan, V.K. and Fahy, L., 'The micro-politics of strategy formulation', *Academy of Management Review*, XVII/1 (1982), 25–34.

Norburn, D., 'The chief executive: a breed apart', *Strategic Management Journal* (January/February 1989), 1–15.

O'Reilly, C. and Flatt, S., 'Executive team demography, organizational innovation and firm performance', working paper, Berkeley, CA: University of California 1989.

Poole, P.P., Gioia, D.A. and Gray, B., 'Influence modes, schema change and organisational transformation', *Journal of Applied Behavioural Science*, 4 (1990), 23–40.

Prasad, P., 'Symbolic processes in the implementation of technological change: a symbolic interactionist study of work computerisation', *Academy of Management Journal*, XXXVI/6 (1993), 1400–29.

Prince, G., *The Practice of Creativity*, New York: Harper & Row 1970.

Quinn, J., 'Managing innovation: controlled chaos', *Harvard Business Review* (May/June 1985), 73–84.

Roethlisberger, F.J. and Dickson, W.J., *Management and the Worker*, Cambridge, MA: Harvard University Press 1939.

Saavedra, R., Earley, P. and Van Dyne, L., 'Complex interdependence in task performing groups', *Journal of Applied Psychology*, LXXVIII/1 (1993), 61–72.

Schacter, S., 'Deviation, rejection and communication', *Journal of Abnormal and Social Psychology*, XLVI (1951), 190–207.

Schein, E.H., *Organizational Psychology*, 3rd ed., New York: Prentice Hall 1988.

Schermerhorn, J.R., Osborn, R.N. and Hunt, J.G., *Managing Organizational Behaviour*, New York: Wiley 1996.

Sherif, M. and Sherif, C.W., 'Research on intergroup relations', in W.G. Austin and S. Worchel (eds), *The Social Psychology of Intergroup Relations*, Monterey, CA: Brooks/Cole 1979, 7–18.

Stead, B.A., *Women in Management*, New York: Prentice Hall 1978.

Taylor, F.W., *The Principles of Scientific Management*, New York: Harper & Row 1947.

Thomas, K., 'Conflict and conflict management', in M.D. Dunnette (ed.), *Handbook of Industrial and Organizational Psychology*, Chicago: Rand McNally 1976, 889–935.

Tuckman, B.W., 'Development sequence in small groups', *Psychological Bulletin*, LXIII (1965), 384–99, 419–27.

Turner, J.C., 'Towards a cognitive redefinition of the social group', in H. Tajfel (ed.), *Social Identity and Intergroup Relations*, Cambridge: Cambridge University Press 1982, 15–40.

Van Gennep, A., *The Rites of Passage*, Chicago: University of Chicago Press 1960.

Van Maanen, J., 'Breaking in: socialisation to work' in J. Dubin (ed.), *Handbook of Work, Organization and Society*, Chicago: Rand McNally 1976.

Weick, K., 'Organisations as loosely coupled systems', *Administrative Science Quarterly*, IV/2 (1977), 132–51.

Weir, M., 'Developmental changes in problem solving strategies', *Psychological Review*, 71 (1964), 473–90.

Wiersema, M. and Bantel, K., 'Top management team demography and corporate strategic change', *Academy of Management Journal*, 35 (1992), 91–121.

Wilson, I., 'Strategic planning isn't dead – it changed', *Long Range Planning*, XXVII/4 (1994), 12–24.

Woodcock, M., *Team Development Manual*, Aldershot: Gower 1979.

THE DYNAMICS OF ORGANISATIONAL STRUCTURES AND CULTURE

9

Learning Objectives

- To define organisational structure.

- To provide an outline of the components of organisational structure.

- To examine various approaches to organisational structure.

- To define organisational culture and examine its characteristics.

- To examine core contributions to culture.

- To highlight ongoing debates in organisational structure and culture.

INTRODUCTION

What sort of structure do organisations need to operate effectively in today's complex environment? This is a key question and one that is difficult to answer. Developing a structure that supports the strategic and operational goals of the organisation is, without doubt, a challenging task. The way in which the structure manifests itself will determine how efficiently and effectively its activities are carried out. Knowledge of that structure is a critical first step to understanding the processes which occur within the organisation and detailing its structure is the most accessible way of describing it, yet a solely structural analysis is incomplete.

Structure seems to provide the basic framework, but an understanding of cultural processes is also necessary in order to get a more meaningful picture of what happens in modern organisations. Culture is a necessary condition for a co-ordinated organisational structure and, according to Hoe (2003: 110), should be viewed as a positive force. Often referred to as 'the way we do things around here' or the unwritten rules that govern behaviour in the organisation, it is an ideology that holds an organisation together and is the product of social interaction, influenced by all organisational participants (Shearer *et al.* 2001). This chapter concentrates on both of these aspects of organisational life, based on the premise that both structure and culture serve as functional buttresses designed to control, co-ordinate and direct organisational members in their work.

ORGANISATION STRUCTURE

Organisation structures provide the task and authority relationships that give meaning for people in their work. Structure refers to the relationships among the parts of an organised whole: it is a social creation. In this way structure is seen to consist of hard and soft components (Wang and Ahmed 2003). Mintzberg (1983), in his acclaimed work *Structure in Fives*, simply defines it as 'the sum total of the ways in which labour is divided into distinct tasks and then its co-ordination is achieved among these tasks.' Thus, organisations create structure to facilitate the co-ordination of activities and to control the actions of their members. The structure defines tasks and responsibilities, work roles and relationships and channels of communication. It creates a framework through which the activities of the organisation can be directed and controlled.

The design of an appropriate structure is a critical activity and involves the development of a framework which is compatible with the needs of the particular business or institution. While classic thinking suggested that rationality in structuring was attained through a single best way of doing things, more recent work suggests that there is no one best approach (for example, see Drucker 1999).

THE COMPONENTS OF STRUCTURE

Organisational structure has multiple dimensions. Tiernan *et al.* (1996) highlight that, arising from the mainstream literature, the main components of organisational structure can be classified into two critical areas: structural configuration and structural operation.

Structural configuration refers to the size and shape of the structure and can be assessed from the organisation chart. Structural operation focuses on the processes and operations of the organisational structure.

Table 9.1 Components of Organisational Structure

Structural Configuration	Structural Operation
Division of labour.	Formalisation.
Spans of control.	Decision making.
Hierarchical levels.	Responsibility.
Departmentalisation.	Authority.

Source: Tiernan *et al.* (1996)

STRUCTURAL CONFIGURATION

Division of Labour

The division of labour defines the distribution of responsibilities and refers to the extent to which the work of the organisation is broken down into different tasks to be completed by different people. As far back as 1776 Adam Smith, in *Wealth of Nations*, illustrated the concept of the division of labour in a pin manufacturing firm:

> One man draws out the wire, another strengthens it, a third cuts it, a fourth points it, a fifth grinds it at the top for receiving the head; to make the head requires two or three distinct operations; to put it on is a peculiar business, to whiten the pins is another; it is even a trade by itself to put them into the paper; and the important business of making a pin is, in this manner, divided into about eighteen distinct operations.

The classical theorists were strong advocates of the division of labour, viewing it as a means of significantly increasing the organisation's economic efficiencies.

Span of Control

Span of control refers to the number of subordinates who report to a single supervisor or manager and for whose work that person is responsible. This concept is related to the notion of hierarchy. Generally, the broader the span of control, the fewer the number of levels in the hierarchy. With wider spans of control, employees tend to have more freedom and discretion. In contrast, narrow spans of control usually lead to high levels of supervision. With effective spans of control employees can be given a degree of freedom, while at the same time having some form of guidance from a supervisor should assistance be necessary.

Several theorists have attempted to identify what the optimal span of control might be. Mintzberg (1979) concludes that the size of the span depends on a number of factors, not least the degree of specialisation, the similarity of tasks, the type of information available, the need for autonomy, direct access to supervisors and the abilities and experience of both supervisors and employees.

Hierarchical Levels

The number of levels and the extent of hierarchy outline the reporting relationships within the organisation from top to bottom.

Departmentalisation

The classical theorists argued that activities in an organisation should be specialised and grouped into departments. This element of structural configuration is essentially concerned with the co-ordination of the organisation's various activities. There are four main forms of departmentalisation an organisation might adopt, namely functional, divisional, geographic and matrix.

Functional departmentalisation is one of the most frequently occurring modes of co-ordinating and is one where the activities are grouped together by common function. This form is typically found in small or medium-sized companies or in those companies where only a few products are produced. It is seen to be most effective in a stable environment where the technology used by the organisation is of a routine nature, where there is low interdependence between departments and the organisation is controlled through the vertical hierarchy, i.e. formal authority in the organisation lies with senior managers in the functional department.

Under a divisional approach, the organisation uses the products or services, project groups or projects as the basis for differentiating the company. The distinctive feature is that the divisions of the organisation are grouped according to their organisational outputs. Thus, an organisation that manufactures four distinct products may create a subdivision for each product. A product-based structure is an example of divisional departmentalisation.

With geographical departmentalisation, the organisation is structured around activities in various geographical locations. This approach is common among organisations that provide goods or services over a wide area. Each region or country may have distinct tastes or needs and organisations may find it more appropriate to respond to these particular needs by locating in that region.

Functional, product or geographic departmentalisation may be combined to form what is termed a matrix approach, whereby functional departmentalisation and product lines are typically overlaid to form a grid. It may be required by an organisation whose structure is multifocused, needing to emphasise both product and function at the same time.

STRUCTURAL OPERATION

Formalisation

Formalisation refers to the degree to which rules and procedures shape the jobs and tasks completed by employees, and consequently the degree to which the jobs within the organisation are standardised. Organisations are said to be highly formalised if their work activities are governed by many rules and procedures. The degree of formalisation can vary widely between and within organisations. The critical purpose of formalisation, according to Mintzberg (1979), is to predict and control how employees behave on the job.

Decision Making

Decision making may be centralised or decentralised. Centralisation refers to the degree to which decision making is concentrated at a single point in the organisation. An organisation characterised by centralisation is inherently different from one that is described as decentralised. In a decentralised scenario, action can be taken more quickly to solve problems, more individuals typically provide input into the decision and individuals are less likely to feel alienated or divorced from critical aspects of their working lives.

Responsibility

Responsibility is essentially an obligation to perform. When one is given rights, one also assumes a corresponding obligation to perform. In the organisational setting managers and supervisors are responsible for achieving certain goals and for the conduct of their subordinates.

Authority

Authority refers to rights inherent in a managerial position to give orders and expect those orders to be obeyed. It is power that has been legitimised within a certain social context. In the case of organisational authority, the social context is the organisation and the authority is associated with the position in the hierarchy.

Mintzberg (1983: 4–20) offers a slightly different analysis, arguing that five co-ordinating elements seem to explain the fundamental ways in which organisations co-ordinate their efforts: mutual adjustment, direct supervision, standardisation of work processes, standardisation of work outputs and standardisation of worker skills. These, he suggests, should be considered the most basic elements of structure, the glue that holds organisations together.

Mutual adjustment achieves the co-ordination of work by the simple process of informal communication. The success of the undertaking depends primarily on the specialists' ability to adapt to each other. Direct supervision achieves co-ordination by having one person take responsibility for the work of others, issuing instructions to them and monitoring their action. In effect, one brain co-ordinates several hands. Mintzberg argues that work may also be co-ordinated without either mutual adjustment or direct supervision per se, but rather through standardisation. Co-ordination, he suggests, is achieved on the drawing board before the work is undertaken.

There are three basic ways to achieve such standardisation. Work processes are standardised when the contents of the work are specified or programmed. Outputs are standardised when the results of the work are specified or programmed. If neither the work nor the outputs are standardised, the worker who comes to work may be. Skills and knowledge are standardised when the kind of training required to perform the work is specified. These five co-ordinating mechanisms typically occur in a sequence so that as organisational work becomes more complicated, the desired means of co-ordination seem to shift from mutual adjustment to direct supervision to standardisation (often of work processes, but may be outputs or knowledge and skills). However, typically organisations will not rely on any single co-ordinating mechanism, but will mix them. Thus, a certain amount of mutual adjustment and supervision will always be evidenced, regardless of the extent of standardisation. This is variously reflected in the major schools of thought that have dominated the extant literature.

For Child (1984: 7), designing an appropriate structure for an organisation centres around five major issues.

1. Should jobs be broken down into narrow areas of work and responsibility so as to secure the benefits of specialisation? Or should the degree of specialisation be kept to a minimum in order to simplify communication and offer members of the organisation greater scope and responsibility in their work? Another choice arising in the design of jobs concerns the extent to which the responsibilities and methods attached to them should be precisely defined.

2. Should the overall structure of an organisation be 'tall' rather than 'flat' in terms of its layers of management and its spans of control? What are the implications for communication, motivation and overhead costs of moving towards one of these alternatives rather than the other?

3. Should jobs and departments be grouped together in a 'functional' way according to the specialist expertise and interests that they share? Or should they be grouped according to the different products and services which are being offered or the different geographical areas being served?

4. Is it appropriate to aim for an intensive form of integration between different segments of an organisation or not? What kind of integrative mechanisms are there to choose from?

5. What approaches should management take towards maintaining adequate control over work done? Should it centralise or delegate decisions? Should a policy of formalisation be adopted? Should work be subject to close supervision?

SCHOOLS OF THOUGHT ON ORGANISATION STRUCTURE

While different schools of thought provide rather different answers to these critical questions on how to approach the issue of structuring the primary reporting relationships, the majority of approaches promulgate a systems approach to understanding organisation structure and its interplay with strategy and structure. Writers from a variety of disciplinary backgrounds, including economics, management, psychology, political science and sociology, have contributed towards the development of theories describing the structure of organisations. Here we review three prominent strands of this literature: classical, contingency and more recent innovations and adaptations.

THE CLASSICAL SCHOOL OF THOUGHT

The classical school of thought advocated a universalist approach to organisational structure, arguing that there was one best way to structure the organisation's activities and offering prescriptions on designing for best fit in all situations. One of the most significant contributions was made by Henri Fayol (1841–1925).

Table 9.2 Fayol's Fourteen Management Principles

1. **Division of labour:** Divide work into specialised tasks and assign responsibility to individuals.
2. **Authority:** Equal delegation of responsibility and authority.
3. **Discipline:** Establish clear expectations and penalties.
4. **Unity of command:** Each employee should report to one supervisor.
5. **Unity of direction:** Employee efforts should be guided to achieve organisational goals.
6. **Subordination of individual interests to general:** Group interests should not precede the general interests of the organisation.
7. **Remuneration:** Equitable rewards for work.
8. **Centralisation:** Decide the importance of superior and subordinate roles.
9. **Scalar chain:** Lines of authority and communications from the highest to the lowest level.
10. **Order:** Order tasks and materials to support organisational direction.
11. **Equity:** Treat employees fairly.
12. **Stability of tenure:** Minimise turnover to ensure loyalty of personnel.
13. **Initiative:** Employees should have freedom and discretion.
14. **Esprit de corps:** Unity of interest between management and workers.

Fayol emphasised that his principles of management should be applied in a flexible way. Tiernan *et al*. (1996) argue that his principles remain important not only because of the influence they have had on succeeding generations of managers, but also because of the continuing validity of the work.

Equally influential in the classical school was the sociologist Max Weber (1864–1920), who concentrated in a more specific way than Fayol on how to structure the organisation for success. When he analysed organisations, he found the concept of bureaucracy to be an 'ideal' form of organisation structure. He advanced the critical elements of 'ideal bureaucracy' as a means of promoting efficiency in organising and a structure based on knowledge and ability rather than on favouritism, which he found prevalent at the time. It had six critical elements.

1. **Division of labour:** Tasks were divided and delegated to specialists so that responsibility and authority were clearly defined.
2. **Hierarchy:** Positions were organised in a hierarchy of authority from the top of the organisation to the bottom, with authority centralised at the top.
3. **Selection:** Employees were recruited on the basis of technical qualifications rather than favouritism.
4. **Career orientation:** Managers were viewed as professionals pursuing careers rather than having ownership in the organisation.
5. **Formalisation:** The organisation was subject to formal rules and procedures in relation to performance.
6. **Impersonality:** Rules and procedures were applied uniformly to all employees.

The strength of bureaucracy was in its standardisation. Employee behaviour was controlled and made predictable through adherence to rules and procedures. For Weber, bureaucracy represented the most efficient form of social organisation, largely because it was rational, logical and focused on goal attainment. It emphasised a narrow division of labour, narrow spans of control, many levels of hierarchy, limited responsibility and authority, centralised decision making and high formalisation. Tiernan *et al.* (1996) note:

> The bureaucratic structure was particularly popular in large organisations as it allowed such organisations to perform the various routine activities needed for effective operation. This structure became the dominant form of structure used by the majority of organisations, as it appeared to offer an efficient form of structure and was technically superior to any other form.

Jackall (1988) argues that large bureaucratic corporations operate on the basis of such values as control, order, elitism, pragmatism and competition for status. In fact, the bureaucratic context typically brings together men and women who initially have little in common with each other except the impersonal frameworks of their organisation. Indeed, the enduring genius of the organisation form is that it allows individuals to retain diverse private motives and meaning for action as long as they publicly adhere to agreed-upon rules.

THE CONTINGENCY SCHOOL OF THOUGHT

Contingency approaches to organisational structure became popular in the 1950s and 1960s and were developed to overcome many of the inadequacies associated with the classical school. Essentially, contingency approaches argue that there is no one best way of structuring an organisation.

> The most appropriate structure depends on a number of contingencies or structural imperatives. The three most popular contingencies are size, technology and the environment ... Each of these imperatives has been widely researched by different theorists and no single theorist or researcher can be attributed with the formulation of contingency theory (Tiernan *et al.* 1996).

The size imperative argues that the most appropriate structure for an organisation is determined by its size. Kimberly (1976) has argued that the measurement of size is important and can include employees, profit, turnover and sales. Larger organisations are generally more complex and bureaucratic (Blau and Schoenherr 1971). Increased size, therefore, leads to more complexity, which in turn leads to more bureaucratic structures to facilitate control (Robey 1991). Size is an important contingency that also determines the most appropriate type of structure. As the organisation increases in size, the original structure is simply unable to handle the complexity. Similarly, a small organisation does not need so many bureaucratic structures and controls to operate effectively.

The most influential work within the technology imperative was completed by Woodward (1965), who sought to examine whether spans of control and hierarchical levels have universal application. She studied the performance and structure of 100 UK manufacturing organisations and concluded that different technologies create different kinds of demands on organisations, which are met by different types of structure. In other words, the most appropriate structure was dependent upon the technology used.

Woodward identified three different types of technology.

1. **Unit production** occurs where one or a small number of finished goods are produced according to a customer specification, for example, tailor-made clothes or specially printed cards or invitations.

2. **Mass production** occurs where large batches of standardised goods are produced on an assembly line by assembling parts in a particular way, such as car manufacturers.

3. **Continuous process production** occurs where raw materials are transformed into finished goods using a production system whereby the composition of the raw material changes, for example, the manufacture of pharmaceuticals.

Woodward concluded that successful organisations displayed an appropriate fit between the technology used and the structure.

More recent work on an extension of contingency theory has been advanced by Mintzberg (1981), who identifies a range of structures and situations in which they are most commonly found. Mintzberg's framework provides guidelines for the choice of an appropriate structure depending on the organisation's age, its external environment and the nature of its employees. Mintzberg argues that a vitally important consideration in structuring an organisation is to achieve a match or fit between the various parts. In this sense, there must be a fit between the structure, the structural imperatives (size, technology and environment), the organisation's strategy and the various components of the structure (co-ordination, division of labour, formalisation and decision making). If these various elements do not fit together, then the structure will be ineffective (Mintzberg 1981).

Mintzberg identifies five types of structure, namely simple, machine bureaucracy, professional bureaucracy, divisionalised and adhocracy.

Mintzberg's Structure Types

The simple structure is found in small, relatively new organisations that operate in a simple and dynamic environment. Direct supervision is the main co-ordinating mechanism, which means that a supervisor or manager co-ordinates employees' activities. The structure is quite organic with little specialisation and little formalisation. The CEO holds most of the power and decision-making authority. Due to its simple yet dynamic environment, it must react quickly to changing events.

A machine bureaucracy corresponds to a typical bureaucracy and can be found in large, mature organisations operating in a stable and simple environment. Standardisation of work processes is the main co-ordinating mechanism, which means that the methods employees use to transform inputs into outputs are standardised. There is a strong division of labour, high formalisation and centralised decision making. Due to its stable and simple environment the machine bureaucracy does not have to change or adapt quickly.

Professional bureaucracies are usually professional organisations located in complex and stable environments. The primary co-ordinating mechanism is the standardisation of employee skills, which means that the skills or inputs into the various processes are standardised. The division of labour is based on professional expertise and little formalisation exists. Decision making is decentralised and occurs where the expertise is based. An example of a professional bureaucracy is a hospital or university.

The divisionalised structure is found in old and large organisations operating in simple and stable environments with many distinct markets. In fact, it could be a machine bureaucracy divided into the different markets that it serves. Decision making is split between headquarters and the divisions and standardisation of outputs is the main co-ordinating mechanism used. Due to the fact that control is required by headquarters, a machine bureaucracy tends to develop in each of the divisions.

An adhocracy is found in young organisations operating in complex and dynamic environments, normally in a technical area. Co-ordination is achieved by mutual adjustment, which means that employees use informal communication to co-ordinate with each other. Decision making is spread throughout the organisation and there is little formalisation. Specialists are placed in project teams to achieve the organisation's work. This form of structure is designed to encourage innovation, which is very difficult to do with the other structures.

Recent Thinking on Organisation Structure

Tiernan (1996) and Tiernan et al. (2002) argue that there have been two major evolutions in organisational structure to date. The first occurred in the early 1900s and involved a recognition of the independent roles and function of management and ownership. The second evolution took place some twenty years later and introduced the command/control organisation (more commonly termed bureaucracy), with which we are so familiar today. Now organisations are coming to terms with the third evolutionary period. The shift this time is from bureaucratic hierarchical forms to more flexible and adaptable forms.

Figure 9.1 Mintzberg's Structual Types

Structure	Characteristics	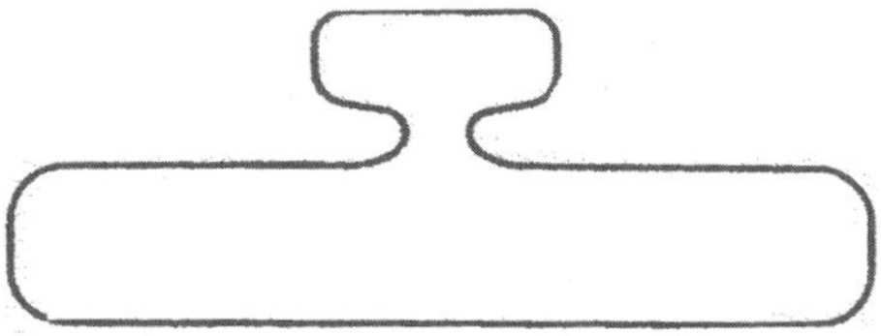
The Simple Structure	**Prime Co-ordinating Mechanism:**	Direct supervision
	Key Part of Organisation:	Startegic apex
	Main Design Parameters:	Centralisation, organic structure
	Situational Factors:	Young, small; non-sophisticated technical system; simple, dynamic environment; possible extreme hostility or strong power needs of top managers; not fashionable
The Machine Bureucracy	**Prime Co-ordinating Mechanism:**	Standardisation of work processs
	Key Part of Organisation:	Technostructure
	Main Design Parameters:	Behaviour formalisation, vertical and horizontal job specialisation, usually funtional groupings, large operating-unit size, vertical centralisation and limited horizontal decentarlisation action planning
	Situational Factors:	Old, large; regulaing, non-automated technical system; simple, stable environement; external control; not fashionable
The Professsional Bureucracy	**Prime Co-ordinating Mechanism:**	Standardisation of skills
	Key part of Organisation:	Operating coree
	Main Design Parameters:	Training, horizontal job specification, vertical and horizontal decentralisation
	Situational factors:	Complex, stable environment; non-regulating, non-sophisticated technical systems; fashionable

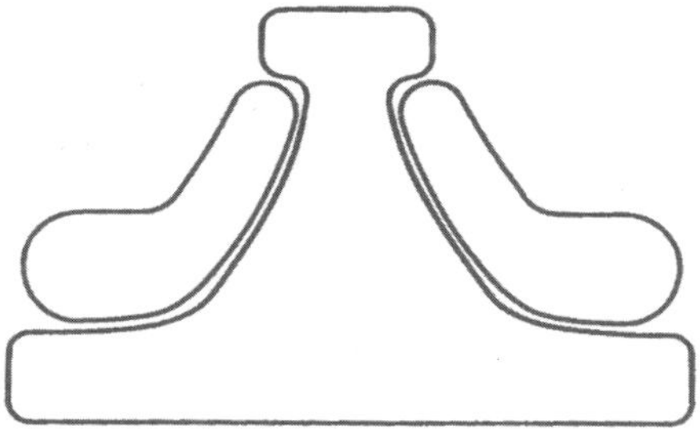

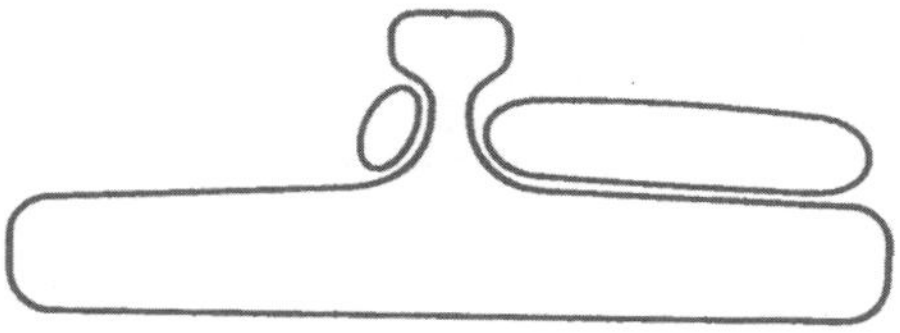

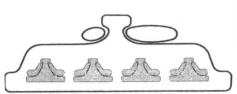

The Divisionalised Form

Prime Co-ordinating Mechanism:	Standardisation of outputs
Key Part of Organisation:	Middle line
Main Design Parameters:	Marketing grouping, performance control systems, limited vertical decentralisation
Situational Factors:	Diversified markets (particularly products or services); old, large; power needs of middle managers; fashionable

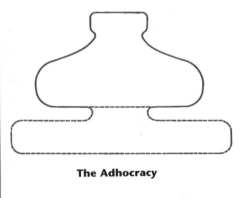

The Adhocracy

Prime Co-ordinating Mechanism:	Manual adjustment
Key Part of Organisation:	Support staff (in the administrative adhocracy; together with the operating core in the operating adhocracy)
Main Design Parameters:	Liaison devices, organic structure, selective decentralisation, horizontal job specification, training, functional and market grouping concurrently
Situational Factors:	Complex, dynamic (sometimes disparate) environment; young (especially operating adhocracy); sophisticated and often automated technical systems (in the administrative adhocracy); fashionable

Source: Mintzberg (1983)

Bureaucracy has been the dominant form of organisation structure used by organisations. The main reason for its dominance is that it is a rational and efficient form of structure when the environment is simple and stable. However, when the external environment becomes complex and dynamic, the rigidity of the bureaucratic structure hampers its ability to be flexible and adaptive. Recent trends in organisational structure have centred on the need to achieve competitive advantage in an increasingly complex, dynamic and competitive environment (Tiernan *et al.* 1996).

Many of the developments have built on Mintzberg's conceptualisations of the influence of the business environment on the organisation's structure. Drucker (1992) has argued that due to the nature of the current business environment, organisations are now undertaking fundamental changes to their structures. To achieve competitive advantage, organisations must be flexible and adaptive and must respond to and anticipate change in the business environment. Many organisations have looked to organisational structure as a means of providing such flexibility and adaptability. As a result of the nature of the business environment and the ineffectiveness of traditional bureaucratic structure, organisations have experimented with four main structural trends (for a detailed discussion see Tiernan 1993, 1996).

The first trend has been towards flatter, less hierarchical structures. Reducing the layers in the hierarchy is designed to reduce costs, free up information flows, speed up communications and allow more innovative ideas to flourish. Organisations, therefore, are reducing hierarchy to more manageable levels. According to Tiernan, organisations have also widened the traditional division of labour. Previously, individuals were boxed into segmented and isolated work tasks with little knowledge or training in other areas. Due to the need to be more flexible, many organisations have now widened job categories and trained employees to be multiskilled. Changing attitudes among the workforce have led to the creation of new structures that allow individuals to have more responsibility and authority over their work and a larger role in decision making. The final trend has been to move away from segmented and isolated work to team-based operations. Organisations are experimenting with task forces for short-term problem-solving exercises and with cross-functional and cross-hierarchical teams to achieve longer-term objectives. Organisations are also introducing team mechanisms for completing tasks. Such team mechanisms have been called self-managed teams and autonomous work groups and they complete the organisation's work with a supervisor's guidance.

Network Structure

As a result of these trends, new organisational forms have emerged, prominent among them the so-called 'network structure'. Baker (1992) views the network organisation as a market mechanism that allocates people and resources to problems and projects in a decentralised manner. The network organisation seeks to manage complex relationships between people and departments within the organisation, and sometimes external groups such as suppliers and customers (Tiernan *et al.* 1996). Rather than allocating responsibility and authority in line with the traditional hierarchy, the network organisation shares responsibility, authority and control among people and units that facilitate the co-operation necessary to achieve organisational goals. In this approach, the organisational units retain considerable autonomy, but collaborate extensively through networking between units. Goold and Campbell (2003) note:

> The organisation is largely self-managing, but has sufficient structure, process and hierarchy to achieve co-ordination and implement the corporate strategy. The objective is to obtain the benefits of interdependence that are designed into a typical matrix, but without sacrificing clear responsibilities, managerial initiative and accountability, speed of decision making and lean hierarchy. To design a structured network it is necessary to achieve clarity about each unit's role without hemming managers in with too much detail ... Organisations designed in this way will have enough but not too much structure.

They offer the following example of the soccer team as an illustration of the network.

Soccer Teams as Structured Networks

A good illustration of the structured network concept is a soccer team. The coach will decide the overall formation – for example, 4-4-2 – in which the team will play. Within this formation each player should understand his or her basic role (e.g. striker, wingback, central defender, and so on). Players' roles determine their basic responsibilities, including their individualised specialised tasks and how they should combine together with other members of the team. The coach will also work with the team to develop both its tactics and some pre-rehearsed moves. For example, the tactics may include close man-to-man marking of certain dangerous players on the other side, how to operate the offside trap, and when to use wingbacks in attacking moves down the flanks. For free kicks around the penalty area and corners, there is likely to be a repertoire of planned moves, carefully worked through on the training ground, in which each player knows exactly what to do. As the game unfolds, the coach may modify either the overall formation or the tactics, and the captain on the pitch will also exert an influence on how members of the team play their roles.

So successful football teams operate with quite a high level of designed-in structure (e.g. players' roles within a 4-4-2 formation), process (e.g. agreed tactics and rehearsed moves) and hierarchy (e.g. authority of coach and captain). But everyone recognises that all the players must be free to make their own judgements about how to handle specific situations as they emerge. A tactical manual that tried to prescribe each player's every move would not only be impossible to produce and hopelessly inflexible, but would also stifle the creativity and flair of the talented individuals that make up the team. Most of the play needs to depend on spontaneous decisions by each player, within the context of their agreed roles, not on pre-determined tactics and moves. Too much structure is just as dangerous as too little.

Ideally therefore the team just has enough structure for all the players to combine well together, but not so much that initiative, flexibility and speed are sacrificed. Most of the play will be guided by voluntary networking between individual players who are all free to make their own decisions and choices. But the formation and tactics laid down by the coach give enough coherence and co-ordination for the whole team to play well together. This is the essence of a structured network. It is the difference between the Brazilian side that almost failed to qualify for the 2002 World Cup (a collection of supremely talented individuals who failed to collaborate and combine together) and the Brazilian side that won the trophy (the same individuals, but playing effectively together as a team).

Source: Goold and Campbell (2003)

Cluster Structure

The cluster organisation has emerged as a radical and innovative form of organisational structure in which groups of employees are arranged like grapes growing on a common vine. A cluster is a group of employees from different disciplines who work together and are undifferentiated by rank or job title. No direct reporting relationships exist within the clusters and support areas only have a residual hierarchy.

The cluster is accountable for its business results and has a customer focus. It develops its own expertise, shares information broadly and pushes decisions towards the point of action. The central element of the cluster organisation is the business unit which is a profit centre. The cluster organisation contains other forms of clusters including project teams, alliance teams, change teams and staff units. In the cluster organisation staff units run their own businesses selling to internal and external customers where possible (Tiernan *et al.* 1996).

The cluster organisation has become popular in professional organisations, but it is unlikely that the cluster approach would suit all organisations. High-volume, low-variance activities are poorly suited to clusters, since the work cannot be made more challenging and interesting. In such a situation there is little scope for increasing responsibility and discretion. It is also difficult to see how traditional assembly line organisations could adopt such a structure, as it would involve eliminating all hierarchy and job titles. The cluster organisation, therefore, may be the most appropriate structure for professional organisations, rather than mass production organisations.

ORGANISATION CULTURE

While an organisation's effectiveness and success is determined in large measure by a well thought-out structure, it would be unwise to ignore the considerable impact of an organisation's culture on its performance. As Dawson (1996: 142) notes:

There has been a growing realisation on the part of organisational theorists as well as practitioners that structure … can only go so far in either providing the social mechanisms for co-ordination and control from a managerial perspective or in explaining human behaviour as work from a theoretical perspective. Structure … seems to provide the basic framework, but cannot either determine organisational life, or fully account for the effects of the organisation on people's behaviour.

Throughout human history, cultures have provided much of the additional guidance needed for human beings to collectively survive, adapt and achieve (Geertz 1971). Similarly, cultural processes underlie much of what happens in modern organisations, prescribing some behaviours and forbidding others. They also influence the emotional responses that people have, filtering the way people view and interpret their worlds. Consequently, as Trice and Beyer (1993) point out, the relative neglect of cultural processes in the study of organisations is unfortunate, given the central role that they play in channelling human behaviour. In an organisational setting, culture gives meaning to each person's membership in the social stage that is the workplace (McLarney and Chung 2000).

Organisational cultural research underwent a major revival in the 1980s with the emergence of the excellence literature (Peters and Waterman 1982), the high-performance literature (Vail 1982) and the Japanisation thesis (Ouichi 1981), all of which have been interpreted to mean that attention to culture pays off and can be critical for organisational adaptability, performance and productivity. In a similar vein, and approximately at the zenith of this cultural revival, Deal and Kennedy (1982) persuasively argue that the culture of an organisation can similarly be managed towards achieving greater effectiveness. There was a growing realisation that structural, rational approaches to understanding organisations missed crucial aspects of how organisations function (Pondy and Mitroff 1979) and a call was made for the establishment of corporate culture as a school of thought within organisational behaviour (Schein 1985). Overall there has been a substantial amount of work done in recent years on organisation culture, and while scholars have reached a consensus regarding the existence of a culture in every organisation, the term carries with it a degree of ambiguity and it is difficult to find a measure of agreement about its precise meaning and scope (Hoe 2003).

DEFINING AND MEASURING ORGANISATIONAL CULTURE

The issue of defining organisational or corporate culture remains contentious. There are probably as many definitions of culture as there are writers who discuss it. Arguably some are unnecessarily complex and academic. Hatch (1997) provides a set of selected definitions that reveals the diversity of views that permeate the literature (Table 9.3).

Table 9.3 Selected Definitions of Organisational Culture

Elliott Jaques (1952: 251): 'The culture of the factory is its customary and traditional way of thinking and of doing things, which is shared to a greater or lesser degree by all its members, and which new members must learn, and at least partially accept, in order to be accepted into service in the firm.'

Andrew Pettigrew (1979: 574): 'Culture is a system of publicly and collectively accepted meanings operating for a given group at a given time. This system of terms, forms, categories, and images interprets a people's own situation to themselves.'

Meryl Reis Louis (1983: 39): 'Organisations [are] culture-bearing milieus, that is, [they are] distinctive social units possessed of a set of common understandings for organising action (e.g., what we're doing together in this particular group, appropriate ways of doing in and among members of the group) and languages and other symbolic vehicles for expressing common understandings.'

Caren Siehl and Joanne Martin (1984: 227): ' ... organisational culture can be thought of as the glue that holds an organisation together through a sharing of patterns of meaning. The culture focuses on the values, beliefs and expectations that members come to share.'

Edgar Schein (1985: 6): 'The pattern of basic assumptions that a given group has invented, discovered, or developed in learning to cope with its problems of external adaptation and internal integration, and that have worked well enough to be considered valid, and, therefore, to be taught to new members as the correct way to perceive, think, and feel in relation to these problems.'

John van Maanen (1988: 3): 'Culture refers to the knowledge members of a given group are thought to more or less share; knowledge of the sort that is said to inform, embed, shape, and account for the routine and not-so-routine activities of the members of the culture ... A culture is expressed (or constituted) only through the actions and words of its members and must be interpreted by, not given to, a fieldworker ... Culture is not itself visible, but is made visible only through its representation.'

Harrison Trice and Janice Beyer (1993: 2): 'Cultures are collective phenomena that embody people's responses to the uncertainties and chaos that are inevitable in human experience. These responses fall into two major categories. The first is the substance of a culture – shared, emotionally charged belief systems that we call ideologies. The second is cultural forms – observable entities, including actions, through which members of a culture express, affirm, and communicate the substance of their culture to one another.'

Source: Hatch (1997)

A straightforward definition is advanced by Hellreigel *et al.* (1992). They define organisation culture as the philosophies, ideologies, values, beliefs, assumptions, expectations, attitudes and norms shared by the members of the organisation and includes the following dimensions:

- observed behaviour and the language commonly used when people interact;
- the norms shared by working groups throughout the organisation;
- the dominant values held by an organisation, such as product quality or price leadership;
- the philosophy that guides an organisation's policy towards employees and customers;
- the rules that a newcomer must learn in order to become an accepted member; and
- the feeling or climate conveyed in an organisation by the physical layout and the way in which its members interact with customers or other outsiders.

Schein (1985: 169) suggests that organisational culture refers to a system of shared meaning held by the members that distinguishes the organisation from other organisations. This system of shared meaning essentially represents a critical set of characteristics that the organisation values.

Hofstede (1991) describes how, from his perspective, people acquire mental programs, or the 'software of the mind', which create patterns of thinking, feeling and action. He suggests that culture is about the collective programming of the mind which distinguishes the members of one group or category of people from another.

Through a review of the extant literature, Robbins (1991: 573) identifies ten characteristics that 'when mixed and matched, tap the essence of an organisation's culture.'

1. **Individual initiative:** The degree of responsibility, freedom and independence that individuals have.
2. **Risk tolerance:** The degree to which employees are encouraged to be aggressive, innovative and risk seeking.
3. **Direction:** The degree to which the organisation creates clear objectives and performance expectations.
4. **Integration:** The degree to which units within the organisation are encouraged to operate in a co-ordinated manner.
5. **Management support:** The degree to which management provide clear communication, assistance and support to their subordinates.
6. **Control:** The number of rules and regulations and the amount of direct supervision that is used to oversee and control employee behaviour.
7. **Identity:** The degree to which members identify with the organisation as a whole rather than with their particular work group or field of professional expertise.
8. **Reward system:** The degree to which the reward allocations, that is, salary increases, promotions, etc., are based on employee performance criteria in contrast to seniority, favouritism, etc.
9. **Conflict tolerance:** The degree to which employees are encouraged to air conflicts and criticisms openly.

10. Communication patterns: The degree to which organisational communications are restricted to the formal hierarchy of authority.

Each of these characteristics is seen to exist on a continuum from low to high, and by examining and appraising the organisation on these characteristics, an overall composite picture of the organisation's culture can be gleaned. This picture, however it looks, creates a degree of order, particularly for the members of the organisation in what is a very uncertain, disorderly business environment. It can thus prove to be an important coping mechanism.

Culture does not exist in a vacuum but is linked to larger cultural processes within the organisation's environment. Every organisation expresses aspects of the national, regional, industrial, occupational and professional cultures in and through which it operates (Phillips *et al.* 1992). Hatch (1997: 200) argues that:

> Each organisation is formed, in part, through cultural processes established by a variety of environmental actors. However, the most immediate source of outside influence on the organisational culture is found within the organisation – its employees. Before joining an organisation, employees have already been influenced by multiple cultural institutions such as family, community, nation, state, church, educational system and other work organisations, and these associations shape their attitudes, behaviour and identity … Because of this it is difficult to separate an organisational culture from the larger cultural processes.

From a research, conceptualisation and measurement perspective, organisational culture can be viewed either as a 'variable' (for example, see Deal and Kennedy 1982) or as a 'metaphor' (for example, see Morgan 1986). The meaning one attaches to culture will fundamentally influence the likely methodologies employed in researching the phenomenon. Those who argue that culture is a variable believe that culture is an objective reality that can be isolated and measured and is something that management can alter for the purpose of achieving organisational objectives. This is what Daft (1989) calls 'culture at the surface level' that is bound up with the slogans, symbols and ceremonies that signify underlying values.

> This dominant perspective holds that corporate culture is 'out there' existing independently of employees and alongside company objectives, technology and structure. It consists of a single set of shared and consistent values and beliefs embedded in stories and symbols, and which are transmitted by company rites and rituals. These act to eliminate ambiguity for members as to how they should think and act. Most importantly corporate culture is capable of being consciously created and managed (Buchanan and Huczynski 1997: 514).

Those who suggest that it is a metaphor believe that culture is a mental state not easily pinned down or altered to suit particular ends. Also referred to as the 'subsurface level of culture', the unwritten norms and values are critical for guiding and influencing employee behaviour (Daft 1989). Culture here exists in and through the social action of the actors, and therefore supports the notion that competing subcultures, for example, affiliated to particular departments in the organisation, could exist. As Buchanan and Huczynski (1997: 515) point out, culture is deeper than its simple symbolic manifestations:

> Stories, rituals, material symbols and language within organisations are a means of transmitting culture, but are not culture itself ... This perspective ... offers management fewer levers with which to shape it or use it as a tool of control. Although managers might be able to change the outward manifestations of culture to some degree, the basic assumptions of company employees will remain the same.

CULTURAL MANIFESTATIONS AND CHARACTERISTICS

Cultural expression in an organisation has several manifestations that can be observed for the purpose of understanding the dominant values of the culture (Table 9.4).

Williams *et al.* (1989) have identified six elements that characterise organisational culture. Culture is:

- learned;
- both input and output;
- partly unconscious;
- historically based;
- held rather than shared; and
- heterogeneous.

Table 9.4 Manifestations of Corporate Culture

• **Rite:** Relatively elaborate, dramatic, planned set of activities that consolidate various forms of cultural expressions into one event, which is carried out through social interactions, usually for the benefit of an audience.
• **Ceremonial:** A system of several rites connected with a single occasion or event.
• **Legend:** A handed-down narrative of some wonderful event that is based in history but has been embellished with fictional details.
• **Story:** A narrative based on true events – often a combination of truth and fiction.
• **Symbol:** An object, act, event, quality or relation that serves as a vehicle for conveying meaning, usually by representing another thing.
• **Language:** A particular form or manner in which members of a group use vocal sounds and written signs to convey meanings to each other.
• **Physical setting:** Things that surround people physically and provide them with immediate sensory stimuli as they carry out culturally expressive activities.
• **Artefact:** Material objects manufactured by people to facilitate culturally expressive activities.

Source: Trice and Beyer (1984)

Culture is learned because individual beliefs, attitudes and values are gained from the individual's environment, and therefore culture can be seen to be gained from the environment which is common to all its members, both internal and external.

In terms of culture being both an input and an output, the argument is that the culture that people learn (input) affects the way they act in the future (output). The strategies, structures, procedures and behaviours adopted by management affect the work environment of the future. However, the managers, if they are members of the organisation for some time, are themselves a product of the culture and the strategies which they have implemented. Thus, people create a culture by their actions, the way they behave, etc. and this culture in turn affects how they behave in the future. Arguably, therefore, culture is often highly resistant to change.

Culture is seen to be partly unconscious because individuals' commonly held beliefs in organisations may exist at an unconscious level. This may occur simply because conscious beliefs and underlying attitudes become so commonplace that they are taken for granted and so become the norm over time, or because members unconsciously process information that influences the way they think. Williams *et al.* (1989) suggest that individuals process information at various levels of consciousness and that information processed below the threshold of awareness can critically influence behaviour in organisations.

Culture is seen to be historically based, largely as organisations are developed from the original assumptions, strategies and structures made by their founders. Once the organisation has made a strategic decision, this limits the degree of freedom for succeeding generations. The die has been cast and these assumptions may be present many generations after their foundation. The original culture influences successive generations because decisions affecting the future of the organisation are made within the context of existing culture, e.g. Guinness, Marks & Spencer and Bewleys.

A key feature of culture in organisations and in society is that mostly it is commonly shared. Generally, individuals discuss and reach consensus on how to think and behave in a given situation, i.e. they agree to hold common values. Individuals within a given organisation will come to adopt similar ways of thinking and behaving even though they may be widely separated geographically or functionally, which seems to give culture its slightly mystic quality. In reality, though, this common thought and behaviour results from common learning, common history and a common environment.

In practice, culture is also likely to be heterogeneous or not completely integrationist. Most organisations are characterised by subcultures that form around different roles, functions and levels. Probably very few beliefs, attitudes or values are completely common to all members. Subcultures tend to develop in large organisations to reflect common problems, situations or experiences that members face. Also labelled a 'differentiation perspective on culture', generally subcultures comprise the dominant core values of the accepted organisation's culture plus a set of additional values and/or meanings that are specific to the function or group. Most organisations generally comprise an executive culture focusing upon managing and resourcing and a blue-collar culture focusing upon production. Subcultures of a greater or lesser significance exist in any culture, which can often be beneficial if they instil a sense of common purpose and identity within a given department. Equally they can be highly detrimental if they limit co-ordination or cause unhealthy conflict across the organisation.

Trice and Beyer (1993), in their influential treatise on the cultures of work organisations, argue that cultures are characterised by being collective, emotionally charged, historically based, dynamic, inherently symbolic and, at the same time, inherently fuzzy. Cultures are not produced by individuals acting on their own. They emerge and are given meaning as individuals interact with one another. 'Cultures are the repositories of what their members agree about and persons who do not endorse and practise prevailing beliefs, values, and norms become marginal and may be punished or expelled. Belonging to a culture involves believing what others believe and doing as they do – at least part of the time!' (Trice and Beyer 1993: 5).

Cultures are emotionally charged because their substance and forms are infused with emotion as well as meaning, and cultures may assist in directing emotion into socially accepted channels. Cultures develop over time and cannot be completely divorced from their histories, as they will be derived from the context in which people have found themselves. Despite this link with the past, cultures are dynamic phenomena continuously sprouting variants, depending on what the preferences of a given generation are. They are inherently symbolic because symbolism itself is important for expressing and communicating the essence of the culture. However, they are also fuzzy because many symbols can be difficult to interpret and can have multiple meanings.

Swe and Kleiner (1998) note that a culture's strength broadly depends on three factors:
1. The pervasiveness of the norms and behaviours in the explicit culture and the pervasiveness of the values and beliefs in the implicit culture.
2. The pervasiveness of the beliefs and behaviours themselves.
3. The consonance between the explicit and the implicit cultures.

Strong cultures ultimately work at the implicit level of basic assumptions and beliefs, and they suggest that an organisation that creates a strong culture has employees who believe in its products, its customers and its processes because the culture is part of the employees' own identity.

BENEFITS OF A POSITIVE CULTURE

An organization that is able to maintain a positive culture is likely to enjoy many benefits. When organization members identify with the culture, the work environment tends to be more enjoyable, which boosts morale. When considering corporate culture, it is helpful to consider actual companies that have demonstrated the positive effects that a corporate culture can have.

Wal-Mart
Wal-Mart's founder, Sam Walton, showed concern and respect for his employees from

the company's inception (*Discount Store News* 1999). This created an environment of trust that persists to this day. Walton also modeled the behavior that he desired from his employees, especially customer service (both to internal and external customers), by visiting his stores, meeting customers, and greeting employees by their first names. Walton also embraced and encouraged change in order to remain competitive, and developed employees by having them work in a variety of positions (*Discount Store News* 1999). Wal-Mart considers its culture the key to its success, and to this day employees continue to think about 'how Sam would have done it' when making decisions.

Southwest Airlines

Another good example of a positive corporate culture is Southwest Airlines. The company's relaxed culture can be traced directly to its CEO and co-founder Herb Kelleher. Kelleher encourages employees to be very informal and have fun at their jobs. This is evident to anyone who has flown on Southwest and heard the jokes that the stewardesses tell. Kelleher fosters this type of culture by engaging in unusual acts, such as arriving at shareholder meetings on a motorcycle wearing jeans and a t-shirt, or holding a 2 a.m. barbeque for the company's mechanics who work the night shift (Donlon 1999). He even challenged another company's CEO to an arm-wrestle to settle a dispute over the use of a slogan. Kelleher also strives to value Southwest's employees, acknowledging births, deaths, marriages, and other events in their lives by sending a note or card. Employees are encouraged to pitch in where needed, a fact that is evident in airports where pilots are often seen checking passengers, for example. This has allowed Southwest to have a turnaround time at airport terminals that is less than half the industry average. In order to maintain the culture, prospective employees are carefully screened to make certain that they will fit in.

Hewlett Packard

Hewlett Packard is an example of a company that has been successful in improving its culture. A few years ago, employees at the company's Great Lakes division had begun to feel the stress and pressure of their jobs. Attrition rose to 20 per cent and over 50 per cent of employees surveyed reported feeling 'excessive pressure' on the job. This led the company to make some unusual changes in order to improve the culture. Employees are now required to formulate three business and three personal goals each year. Employees are encouraged to cheer on fellow employees who achieve personal goals, such as spending time with their children or getting away for a round of golf. Only two years into the program, the company reports no loss in productivity despite the reduced hours employees now work and has seen an increase in its retention rate. This success is attributed to the fact that managers strongly supported the program and modeled it in their own personal lives (Cole 1999).

Changing corporate culture

The preceding examples show that a positive culture can make a significant contribution to organizational success while a negative one can lead to failure. While it is easiest to establish a desirable corporate culture during a company's infancy, it has been shown in practice that culture can be changed for the better. In order to go about changing corporate culture, top management must first understand the culture, as it exists today. This can be accomplished by surveying employees on important topics such as their perceptions of and identification with the corporate values and mission, interactions with other employees both inside and outside of their departments, beliefs about whether they are treated fairly, and so on. This will help management to determine the type of culture that exists and to identify areas for change.

Source: Sadri and Lees (2001)

On occasion, organisations may exhibit different culture types, representing a misalignment between the 'espoused' and the 'actual' culture. As Buch and Wetzel (2001: 40) note:

> Almost everyone has been in an organization that says one thing but does another. Think about statements centered on quality, teamwork, customer service, or safety. For example, consider the organization with safety banners posted prominently in the production area alongside an unguarded, pinch-point-laden machine. This illustrates the two types of cultures present – simultaneously – in many organizations. The safety banners are examples of 'espoused culture' and the unguarded machine is an example of 'true culture'. Where there is a gap between the two types of culture, as in this example, a misalignment exists that can be very harmful to the organization and its members.

In their work, Buch and Wetzel advance a process that can be used to identify such cultural misalignments. They offer 'An Action-Oriented Culture Analysis' (see below) for diagnosing a cultural misalignment, arguing that if a misalignment is identified, organisational leaders can choose from a range of strategic and tactical initiatives designed to realign the cultural elements.

AN ACTION-ORIENTED CULTURE ANALYSIS

Step 1: Learn (a mental model of culture)

The first step is to introduce organizational members to the knowledge and skills necessary to conduct a cultural analysis. This can be facilitated by an internal or external change agent. Theories of both organizations and culture should be presented and discussed. An understanding of open systems theory is helpful because culture is a reflection of many subsystems (i.e. managerial, political, strategic, social, technical, structure) at work (Daft 1998), and a change in one may have unexpected effects on another. The goal of this stage is to help the leadership team develop a mental model that brings culture to a conscious level for analysis. This can be accomplished through operational definitions of artifacts, espoused values, and BUAs, reinforced with examples and self-analysis exercises.

Step 2: Observe ('walkies' and 'talkies')

This stage in the process involves the active collection of artifacts (walkies) and espoused values (talkies). Walkies and talkies are ideally gathered during a 'field trip' of the organization, department, or office; fortunately, there are a great many places to collect both. It may be the most enlightening to begin outside, in the parking lot, on the grounds, and by the entrances ... those places first observed by outsiders. What messages are the artifacts sending? Are these messages congruent with the organization's values and assumptions? As artifacts are noted, we recommend recording them on an action register, project management table, or data collection sheet.

Then bring the field trip indoors, focusing first on documentation. Collect and record as many relevant documents as possible, everything from values statements and strategic plans to operating procedures, human resource manuals, and employee evaluations. Another favorite place to unearth culture is in status symbols embedded in hallways, offices, meeting rooms, and workspaces. Cultural clues can be found in architecture, dress codes, furniture, company stories, acronyms, greetings, news letters, banners, casual conversations, and formal speeches. You may even want to record quotes from conversations, speeches, meetings, video presentations, and the grapevine, which is the ultimate source or reflection of an organization's true culture.

This 'observe' stage may be extended to include more formal interviews with new, established, and departing employees. New employees are a great source of anecdotal information about what they have had to change to adjust to the company. New employees must decipher the correct way to dress, act, interact, and behave. On the flip side, the evaluation and dismissal processes in an organization yield powerful information about culture. Exit interviews would highlight how an individual did not fit. 'In a sense, deviants represent and define a culture's boundaries' (Sathe 1985). Performance evaluation data may also yield clues by revealing who fits and who does not; often these are more a result of culture than performance.

Step 3: Infer (basic underlying assumptions from artifacts and espoused values)

The purpose of this phase is to infer deeper meaning from the artifacts and espoused values discovered in Step 2. What hidden basic underlying assumptions do they reveal? Again, we recommend that basic underlying assumptions be recorded in the table next to their corresponding artifacts and espoused values. The table will immediately reveal any discrepancies between the two, which represent 'cultural misalignment' as described above. It is also helpful to record the organizational subsystem involved (i.e. structure, compensation, management, social, and technical).

Finally, it must be decided whether to change or reinforce any misalignments or even alignments that are not congruent with future direction. A 'yes' decision may lead to one of three types of change initiatives:

1. tune-ups;
2. rebuilds; and
3. replacements.

Tune-ups are actions taken during the analysis or recently thereafter. We highly recommend taking trash bags, hammers, pliers, and bolt cutters on the field trip so that misaligned artifacts can be removed immediately. However, do not be surprised when employees react with shock or anxiety: 'My boss said this was okay?' 'Are you sure we are allowed to do this?'

Tune-ups can be tremendous confidence builders or they can kill the entire process if the participants are reluctant to act (even when approvals have been garnered). One supervisor actually quaked in anxiety over removing a nonfunctional mirror (so deformed it resembled a circus mirror) even though his plant manager, screwdriver in hand, was a member of our cultural exploration into the factory. However liberating, tune-ups involve relatively shallow change, mostly limited to the level of artifacts.

Rebuilds are intermediate actions that take one to six months to complete. They often require process or system redesign, associated approvals, and the collaboration of other organizational members. Rebuilds can begin the longer process of culture change because, at this level, they often require structure-based changes. The key to identifying rebuilds is the need to change a process, system, or structure. Rebuilds represent deeper change than tune-ups, often affecting espoused values and behaviors.

Replacements are longer-term interventions that take over six months to complete. They often require significant resources and adjustments to core values. They will most certainly reside in a business plan or strategic plan and represent full-blown cultural change. This type of work is definitely not trivial, instead 'requiring carabiners, grappling hooks, and long, long ropes' (Robbins and Finley 1996). This is change at the deepest level of culture.

Source: Buch and Wetzel (2001)

PERSPECTIVES ON CULTURE

The literature abounds with theories and models seeking to clarify the concept of culture, 'many of which are inconsistent with each other and fail to provide clear guidelines for measurement' (Buchanan and Huczynski 1997: 512). Here we review five critical contributions to the literature:

- Charles Handy's work on culture and structure compatibility.
- Building on Handy's work, Trompenaars and Hampden-Turner's organisational culture typology.

- The excellence school and its attempts to link culture and performance.
- Schein's contribution on what to look for when trying to discover the essence of the culture.
- Hofstede's work on larger national cultural systems, embracing the notion that the organisation and its culture is largely a manifestation of this larger system.

HANDY ON ORGANISATION CULTURE

In his work *Understanding Organisations* (1976), Charles Handy, drawing upon earlier research by Harrison (1972), developed a four-way typology of common cultural types, namely power, role, task and people orientations.

Power Orientation

In an organisation that demonstrates a power orientation, the organisation will attempt to dominate its environment and those who are powerful within the organisation strive to maintain absolute control over subordinates. Work is typically divided by function or product and the organisation structure tends towards a traditional framework, presented as a web structure.

Figure 9.2 Power Culture

Culture	Diagrammatic representation	Structure
Power or club		Web

Source: Handy (1976)

The functions or departments are represented by lines radiating out from the centre, but the essential feature is that there are also concentric lines representing communications and power. The further away from the centre one is, the weaker the degree of power and influence that one possesses. The organisation is dominated from the centre. Decisions can be reached quickly, but the quality of the decision depends to a large extent upon the ability of managers in the inner circle, who in turn are dependent upon their affinity and trust, both within the organisation and with suppliers, customers and other key stakeholders and influencers. Employees are rewarded for effort, success and compliance with essential core values. Change is very much determined by the central power source.

While this type of culture places a lot of faith in the individual, the organisation operates with apparent disregard for human values and general welfare and is highly competitive. It is often seen as tough and/or abusive and may suffer from low morale and high turnover in the middle layers as individuals fail or opt out of the competitive atmosphere.

Role Orientation

An organisation that is role oriented aspires to be as rational and orderly as possible. In contrast with the wilful autocracy of the power culture, there is a preoccupation with legitimacy, loyalty and responsibility, as the culture is built around defined jobs. Rules and procedures dominate, creating many bureaucratic characteristics. People fit into jobs and are recruited for this purpose, hence rationality and logic are at the heart of the culture, which is designed to be stable and predictable. The culture is represented by the greater temple design since the strengths of the organisation are designated to be in the pillars, which are co-ordinated.

Figure 9.3 Role Culture

Culture	Diagrammatic representation	Structure
Role	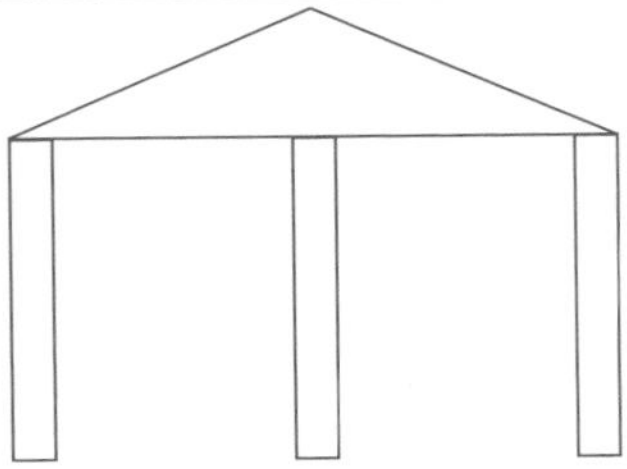	Greek temple

Source: Handy (1976)

However, although the organisation's strength is in the pillars, power lies at the top. There remains a strong emphasis upon hierarchy and status, with rights and privileges clearly defined and adhered to. Conflict is regulated by rules and procedures, predictability is high and stability and respectability are valued almost as much as competence. While high efficiency is possible in stable environments, Handy argues that role culture is less suitable for dynamic environments or situations. Communication goes up and down the organisation, but is less likely across the organisation between departments or sections. Decisions continue to be the reserve of those at the top, which may mean that leader satisfaction is high, but people lower down the organisation may feel frustrated and lacking in status.

Task Orientation

In such organisations, functions and activities are all evaluated in terms of their contribution to organisational goals. In the task culture management is concerned with continuous and successful problem solving and performance is judged by the success of task outcomes. The culture is depicted as a net because for particular problem situations, people and other resources can be drawn from various parts of the organisation on a temporary basis. Once the problem is dealt with, individuals will move on to different tasks, and consequently discontinuity is a key element.

The attainment of goals is the pervasive ideology in task-oriented organisations. Nothing is allowed to get in the way of task achievement. If individuals do not have the necessary technical skills or knowledge, they are retrained or replaced. Emphasis is placed on the development of meaningful flexibility, hence project groups and collaboration between groups is commonplace. Expertise is the major source of individual power and authority. This culture is adaptable and individuals retain a high degree of control over their work; it is common in volatile environments.

Figure 9.4 Task Culture

Culture	Diagrammatic representation	Structure
Task	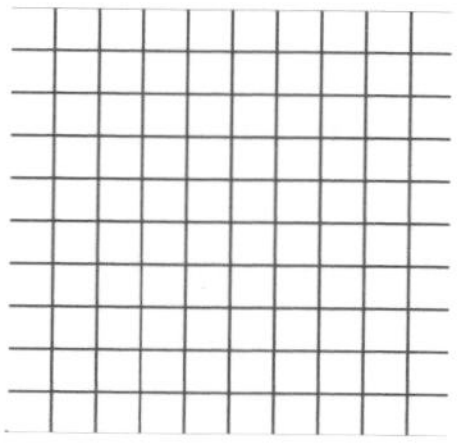	Net

Source: Handy (1976)

People Orientation

This type of culture differs from the other three, since in this instance the organisation exists primarily to serve the needs of its members, providing a service for individual specialists that they could not provide for themselves. Authority in the environment sense is redundant, although where necessary it may be assigned on the basis of task competency. In place of formalised authority, individuals are expected to influence each other through example and helpfulness. Consensus methods of decision making are preferred, as the figure illustrates, and roles are assigned on the basis of personal preferences and the need for learning and growth.

Figure 9.5 People Culture

Culture	Diagrammatic representation	Structure
Person or existential	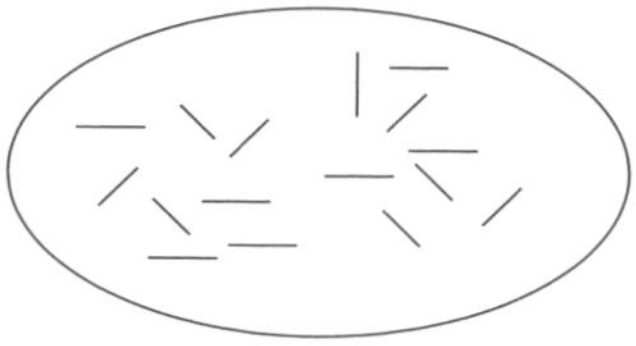	Cluster

Source: Handy (1976)

In a people-oriented culture people are not easy to manage as there is little influence that can be brought to bear on them, and being professionals, alternative employment is often easy to obtain. The psychological contract thus stipulates that the organisation is subordinate to the individuals and depends on the individual for its existence. Clearly, many organisations cannot exist with this kind of culture since organisations tend to have objectives above and beyond the collective objectives of those who comprise them. The culture is most often found in clubs, societies and professional bodies.

TROMPENAARS AND HAMPDEN-TURNER'S ORGANISATIONAL CULTURAL TYPOLOGY

Building on the work of Charles Handy and based on data gathered from several hundred respondents across several countries, Trompenaars and Hampden-Turner (1999) categorise organisational culture into four main types derived from two core dimensions, namely equity-hierarchy and person-task orientation.

Four organisational culture types are advanced, namely the Family, the Eiffel Tower, the Guided Missile and the Incubator.

- **The Family (a power-oriented culture):** This culture is characterised by strong emphasis on the hierarchy and an orientation towards the person. Individuals within this organisational form are expected to perform their tasks as directed by the leader, who may be viewed as the caring parent. Subordinates not only respect the dominant leader or father figure, but they also seek his/her guidance and approval.
- **The Eiffel Tower (a role-oriented culture):** A strong emphasis on the hierarchy and an orientation towards the task characterises this culture. The 'Eiffel Tower' image is intended to symbolise the typical bureaucracy – a tall organisation, narrow at the top and wide at the base, where roles and tasks are clearly defined and co-ordinated from the top. Authority is derived from a person's position or role within the organisation, not the person himself or herself.
- **The Guided Missile (a task-oriented culture):** Trompenaars and Hampden-Turner's third type of organisational culture is characterised by a strong emphasis on equality and an orientation toward the task. The motto for this cultural type is 'getting things done'. Organisation structures, processes and resources are all geared toward achieving the specified task/project goals. Power is derived from expertise rather than the formal hierarchy.
- **The Incubator (a fulfilment-oriented culture):** This culture is characterised by a strong emphasis on equality as well as an orientation toward the person. The purpose of the organisation in such a culture is to serve as an incubator for the self-expression and self-fulfillment of its members.

EXCELLENCE IN ORGANISATION CULTURE

It has been suggested that a strong organisation culture can help an organisation to successfully implement new business strategies and can also help the organisation achieve levels of excellence. For example, studies of Japanese methods of management suggest that the high levels of excellence achieved and the success of their organisations are partly explained by a strong organisation culture that encourages employee participation, job security and open communication. Cultural strength denotes the agreement among organisation members about the importance of specific values. If widespread consensus exists about the importance of those values, the culture is said to be cohesive and strong. If little agreement exists, the culture is described as weak (Arogyaswamy and Byles 1987).

Among the most popularised findings on the relationship between culture and excellence are those reported by Peters and Waterman in their book, *In Search of Excellence* (1982). They argue that excellent organisations do not insist on sticking to the rules but get on with the job. They identify what their customers want and ensure that they get it. People within the organisation are encouraged to use their own initiative and to take risks. They view employees as a key resource and encourage harmonious relations. Managers in these organisations are in touch with the workforce and the organisation sticks to what it knows best. From their research in forty-three 'high-performing' American companies, the authors identify six main attributes that characterise the cultures of 'successful' organisations.

- **A bias for action, for getting on with it:** These organisations do not feel that they have to constantly stick to the rule book, rather they 'do it, try it, fix it'.
- **Close to the customer:** Customers are seen as all-important and the organisation can learn from them. Customers are provided with quality, service and reliability.
- **Autonomy and entrepreneurship:** Risk taking and innovation are encouraged in the organisation. People are allowed the freedom to be creative.
- **Productivity through people:** The excellent organisations treat their employees as a key resource. They encourage good management/labour relations and accept that their employees *are* the organisation.
- **Hands-on, value driven:** These organisations feel that their philosophy and values are tied in to success. Managers at all levels spend a considerable time walking around, assessing what is going on and being seen to do so.
- **Stick to the knitting:** Excellent organisations concentrate their energies and resources on running what they know how to run. They do not waste time with other kinds of business where they do not have the same competency.

An emphasis on these values found favour and resonance with top managers, as witnessed by the number of organisations that attempted to transform their culture. The teachings of the 'excellence school' seemed to promise flexibility and innovation, together with employee commitment and loyalty while avoiding the rigidities of bureaucracy. However, as history was to demonstrate, 'excellent companies could fall from grace' (Dawson 1996: 159). A short two years after the publication of *In Search of Excellence*, many commentaries began appearing about the less-than-excellent fortune of many of the organisations investigated by Peters and Waterman. The erstwhile champions of excellence have now moved on from prescribing universal recipes for success, having declared that the era of sustainable excellence has ended and that managers need to learn to thrive on chaos. 'Having found one way to excellence they must learn that sticking to that managerial knitting will not necessarily stand them in good stead even in the medium term' (Dawson 1996: 160).

SCHEIN ON ORGANISATION CULTURE

Schein (1984, 1985) developed what has arguably become one of the most influential theories of organisational culture from a methodological/measurement perspective. He argues that culture exists at three different levels: at the surface level there exists a series of artefacts, underneath these artefacts there are a series of held values and at the deepest level there is a set of core assumptions. Artefacts are the visible, tangible and audible remains of behaviour that are grounded in cultural norms, values and assumptions. Hatch (1997: 216) suggests that artefacts might include physical manifestations such as buildings, dress/appearance and/or logos; behavioural manifestations such as rewards/ punishments, communication patterns and/or ceremonies; and verbal manifestations such as jokes, jargon, nicknames and/or anecdotes and stories. Values are guarded principles that give definition to the culture. They may not be as visible as artefacts, but they are typically more conscious than assumptions. Assumptions are taken for granted and likely exist outside ordinary awareness.

Figure 9.6 Three Levels of Organisational Culture

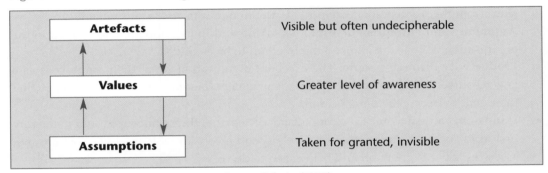

Source: Schein (1985)

According to Schein, culture and its maintenance is driven from the centre out, from the central assumptions, values and norms to the surface artefacts that we can observe. However, once the artefacts appear on the surface, they in turn begin to be interpreted in ways that can again eventually influence the values and assumptions that gave life and meaning to them in the first instance.

CULTURE AND THE WIDER SOCIETY: THE WORK OF HOFSTEDE

We mentioned earlier that culture does not exist in a vacuum and that it is difficult to separate an organisational culture from the larger cultural processes. While the nature of the industry acts as a determinant of the organisation's culture (specific industries have certain cultural characteristics that become manifest in the organisation's culture), there is little disputing the fact that the organisation's culture is more broadly developed by the prevailing national culture within which it operates (see also the discussion on cultural values and perception in Chapter 3). Geert Hofstede carried out a cross-cultural study to identify the similarities and differences among 116,000 employees of the same multinational organisation located in forty countries. His overall aim was to identify broad parameters of differences between national cultures and establish the impact of culture differences on management. From his research he identified four such value dimensions, which he claims discriminate between national cultures: power distance, uncertainty avoidance, individualism/collectivism and masculinity/femininity.

1. **Power distance:** The extent to which individuals accept that power is distributed unequally. Thus, high power distance implies a high acceptance of power inequalities in that society.

2. **Uncertainty avoidance:** The extent to which individuals feel uncomfortable with uncertainty and ambiguity and as a consequence seek to develop ways of working that limit their exposure to uncertainty and ambiguity.

3. **Individualism/collectivism:** The extent to which there is a preference for membership of tightly knit collectives with strong bonds of loyalty and mutual care or a preference for a more loosely knit society in which individuals and their families are rather more independent.

4. **Masculinity/femininity:** A preference for achievement and assertiveness rather than a preference for modesty and caring.

Figures 9.7 and 9.8 present the results of Hofstede's cluster analysis in the form of what he himself refers to as a series of cultural maps. While some concern has been voiced that the country differences found in Hofstede's research are not representative due to the single company sample, further research by him and others supports many of these dimensions

Figure 9.7 Position of Forty Countries on Power Distance and Individualism

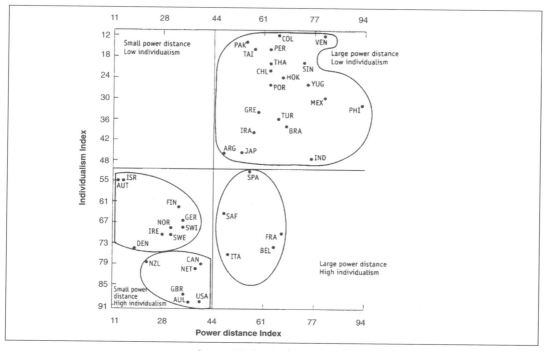

Source: Hofstede (1980, 1991)

Figure 9.8 Position of Forty Countries on Uncertainty Avoidance and Masculinity Dimensions

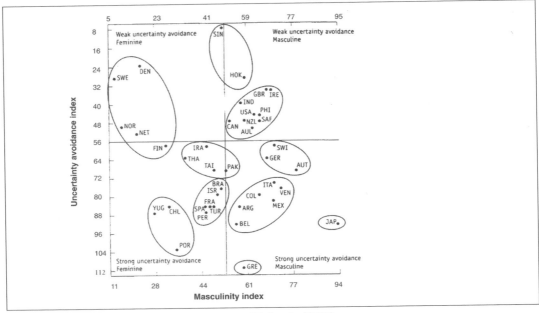

Source: Hofstede (1980)

Power Index Key

ARG	Argentina	FRA	France	JAP	Japan	SIN	Singapore
AUL	Australia	GBR	Great Britain	MEX	Mexico	SPA	Spain
AYT	Austria	GER	Germany	NET	Netherlands	SWE	Sweden
BEL	Belgium	GRE	Greece	NOR	Norway	SWI	Switzerland
BRA	Brazil	HOK	Hong Kong	NZL	New Zealand	TAI	Taiwan
CAN	Canada	IND	India	PAK	Pakistan	THA	Thailand
CHL	Chile	IRA	Iran	PER	Peru	TUR	Turkey
COL	Columbia	IRE	Ireland	PHI	Philippines	USA	United States
DEN	Denmark	ISR	Israel	POR	Portugal	VEN	Venezuela
FIN	Finland	ITA	Italy	SAF	South Africa	YUG	Yugoslavia

Hofstede argues that the first two dimensions (power distance and uncertainty avoidance) have the strongest influence on organisations and that the different combinations and permutations of power distance and uncertainty avoidance are suggestive of different perspectives on the process of organising. Organisations in countries with high power distance tended to have more levels of hierarchy (vertical differentiation), a higher proportion of supervisory personnel (narrow spans of control) and more centralised decision making. Those countries with high uncertainty avoidance tended to have organisations that are more highly formalised, as evidenced by the greater emphasis on proceduralisation and rule making, and management tended to be more risk averse. Countries that demonstrated high collectivism had a preference for group/collective decision making and for seeking out co-operation and consensus. The countries that ranked high on masculinity demonstrated a management style less focused on the employee or the development of strong social relationships and more on the execution and completion of the task. More feminine-orientated countries tended to view the managerial role as one which needed to demonstrate a concern for employee well-being.

According to Hofstede's cluster analysis, Ireland ranks with Finland, Norway, Sweden, Denmark and Germany as a country in which one witnesses small power distance and reasonably high levels of individualism. However, Ireland ranks with Britain, Canada, New Zealand and South Africa in terms of being a largely masculine culture with low uncertainty avoidance. Small power distance combined with low uncertainty avoidance values incline to a view of an adhocracy, or village market.

Drawing upon Hofstede's work and upon a broader extant literature, Dineen and Garavan (1994) provide a more socially embedded set of prominent Irish cultural characteristics (with stronger explanatory power) that are important in the context of better understanding Irish business (Table 9.5).

Table 9.5 Prominent Cultural Characteristics Found in Ireland

Cultural Characteristic	How it Manifests Itself in Ireland
Individualism vs. collectivism.	Relatively moderate degree of individualism.
Pride in the country.	Moderate to high.
Attitude to time.	Plenty of time, not viewed as tangible commodity.
Attitude to work and achievement.	Reasonable work ethic, but ambivalent towards achievement.
Uncertainty avoidance.	High degree of uncertainty avoidance.
Relationships to nature.	High attachment to nature.
Youth orientation of society.	Considerable extolling of youth values.
Attachment to hierarchy.	Very high attachment.
Attitude to competition.	Competition not overemphasised.
Talent for motivating a workforce.	Moderate ability.
Formality/informality.	Relatively informal in one-to-one relationships.
Reputation for marketing push.	Very poor.
Masculine/feminine values.	Predominantly masculine values.
Creativity and willingness to exploit innovation.	Moderate willingness.
Acceptance of business by the public.	High level of acceptance.
Co-operation/conflict.	High degree of co-operation encouraged.
Attitude towards foreign influences.	Healthy attitude.
Willingness to delegate authority.	Poor.

Source: Dineen and Garavan (1994)

ONGOING DEBATES/ADVANCED CONCEPTS IN ORGANISATIONAL STRUCTURES AND CULTURE

CULTURE AS AN INSTRUMENT OF DOMINATION

One important debate in the area of organisation culture refers to the extent to which culture and culture management reflect little more than an attempt by the dominant coalition in the organisation to control organisational members.

Ogbor (2001) presents the debate and summarises the literature in a dialectical way, cogently arguing that it is possible that corporate culture may be viewed as an organisational practice that fosters consciousness, identity-securing practices, employee empowerment and the promotion of diversity in the workplace. In this way it can be positively seen as the conflict-reducing glue that provides harmony and liberation to members of the organisation. Conversely, corporate culture can also be a source of alienation and serve as an instrument of domination dedicated to the hegemonic perpetuation of managerial ends. In this respect it is squarely viewed as a tool for repression. In the former perspective, therefore, culture is both positive and functional while in the latter it is manipulative and disruptive.

So-called 'critical theorists' have led the charge in advancing the latter. Critical theorists take the view that if the concept of culture in the organisational context is not subjected to a critical perspective, it remains a legitimate and dominant ideology that is socially constructed to reflect and legitimise the power relations of managerial elites within the organisation (Alvesson 1991; Alvesson and Berg 1992; Willmott 1993). Following Morgan's (1980) metaphors of organisation, the view is that attention should be drawn to that fact that the organisation is best understood as an instrument of domination because of the imbalance of power between different groups within the organisation and the desire by certain 'managerial elite' groups to impose their will on others.

SUMMARY OF KEY PROPOSITIONS

- The structure defines tasks and responsibilities, work roles and relationships and channels of communication. It creates a framework through which the organisation's activities can be directed and controlled.
- The main components of organisational structure can be classified into two critical areas: structural configuration and structural operation.
- The classical school of thought advocated a universalist approach to organisational structure, arguing that there was one best way to structure the organisation's activities. It offered prescriptions on designing for best fit in all situations.
- Contingency theory argues that the most appropriate structure for an organisation depends on its size, technology and environment.
- Mintzberg's framework provides guidelines for the choice of an appropriate structure depending on the organisation's age, its external environment and the nature of its employees.

- Under more recent innovations, cluster-based structures have emerged. A cluster is a group of employees from different disciplines who work together and are undifferentiated by rank or job title. No direct reporting relationships exist within the clusters and support areas only have a residual hierarchy.
- Organisation culture can be defined as the philosophies, ideologies, values, beliefs, assumptions, expectations, attitudes and norms shared by the organisation's members.
- Organisation culture does not exist in a vacuum, but rather is linked to larger cultural processes within the organisation's environment. Every organisation expresses aspects of the national, regional, industrial, occupational and professional cultures in and through which it operates.
- The manifestations of culture include rites, ceremonials, legends, stories, symbols, language, physical setting and artefacts.
- Handy, drawing upon earlier research, developed a four-way typology of common cultural types, namely power, role, task and people orientations.
- The 'excellence' school argued that a strong organisation culture can help an organisation successfully implement new business strategies, and can also help the organisation achieve levels of excellence.
- Schein argues that culture exists at three different levels: at the surface level there exists a series of artefacts, underneath these artefacts there are a series of held values and at the deepest level there is a set of core assumptions.
- Hofstede identifies four value dimensions, which he claims discriminate between national cultures: power distance, uncertainty avoidance, individualism/collectivism and masculinity/femininity.

DISCUSSION/SELF-ASSESSMENT QUESTIONS

1. Distinguish between the 'formal' and the 'informal' organisation. Does the informal organisation reinforce or contradict the formal organisation structure?
2. Examine the different types of departmentalisation an organisation can use. What factors influence the choices that organisations make here?
3. Do different organisational structures make different behavioural demands on employees and management?
4. What are the functions of an organisation's culture?
5. How would you go about measuring an organisation's culture?
6. From your reading of this chapter, what is the evidence to suggest that the formation and development of an organisation's culture are subject to external influences and processes?

MULTIPLE CHOICE QUESTIONS

1. Organisation structure is:
   (a) The sum total of the ways in which labour is divided into distinct tasks and co-ordination is achieved among these tasks.

    (b) The framework of task and authority relationships that provides meaning for people in their work.

    (c) That which defines tasks and responsibilities, work roles and relationships and channels of communication.

    (d) All of the above.

    (e) None of the above.

2.   Organisation culture is:

    (a) The customary and traditional way of thinking of and doing things, which is shared to a greater or lesser degree by all its members.

    (b) The glue that holds an organisation together through shared patterns of meaning.

    (c) Collectively accepted meanings operating for a given group at a given time.

    (d) All of the above.

    (e) None of the above.

3.   Span of control refers to:

    (a) The ability of the line manager to manage and control annual budgets.

    (b) The procedures operated for discipline handling.

    (c) The number of subordinates who report to a single supervisor or manager and for whose work that person is responsible.

    (d) All of the above.

    (e) None of the above.

4.   The classical school of thought, advocating a universalist approach to organisational structure, is associated with the work of:

    (a) Michael Dursey.

    (b) Peter Farmer.

    (c) Henri Fayol.

    (d) Chris Brewster.

    (e) All of the above.

    (f) None of the above.

5.   Among the elements of Weber's 'ideal bureaucracy' was:

    (a) Division of labour.

    (b) Selection based on qualifications.

    (c) A managerial career orientation.

    (d) All of the above.

    (e) None of the above.

6.   Based on Mintzberg's formulation, an adhocracy is:

    (a) Found in mature organisations operating in relatively stable environments.

    (b) Characterised by highly centralised decision making.

    (c) Designed to encourage innovation.

    (d) All of the above.

    (e) None of the above.

7.   The characteristics of the cluster organisation include:

    (a) Groups of employees from different disciplines who work together.

(b) Groups that are largely undifferentiated by rank or job title.

(c) The absence of direct reporting relationships within the clusters.

(d) All of the above.

(e) None of the above.

8. Cultures are emotionally charged because their substance and forms are infused with emotion as well as meaning. True or false?

9. According to Handy, in an organisation that demonstrates a power orientation:

(a) The organisation will tend to be dominated by its environment.

(b) Work is typically divided by function or product.

(c) Powerful organisational members typically relinquish control to subordinates.

(d) The organisation structure tends towards an innovative network framework.

(e) All of the above.

(f) None of the above.

10. The excellence school is associated with the work of:

(a) Hofstede.

(b) Schein.

(c) Drucker.

(d) Peters and Waterman.

(e) Trice and Beyer.

FIVE SUGGESTED KEY READINGS

Drucker, P., 'The coming of the new organization', *Harvard Business Review*, 66 (1992), 33–5.

Hofstede, G., *Cultures and Organizations: Software of the Mind*, London: McGraw-Hill 1991.

Mintzberg, H., 'Organizational design: fashion or fit', *Harvard Business Review*, 59 (1981), 103–16.

Pettigrew, A., 'On studying organisational culture', *Administrative Science Quarterly*, 24 (1979), 570–81.

Trice, H. and Beyer, J., 'Studying organizational cultures through rites and ceremonials', *Academy of Management Review*, 9 (1984), 653–59.

REFERENCES

Alvesson, M., 'Organisational symbolism and ideology', *Journal of Management Studies*, XXVIII/3 (1991), 207–25.

Alvesson, M. and Berg, O., *Corporate Culture and Organizational Symbolism*, Berlin: Walter de Gruyter 1992.

Arogyaswamy, B. and Byles, C., 'Organizational culture: internal and external fits', *Journal of Management*, 13 (1987), 647–59.

Blau, P. and Schoenherr, R., *The Structure of Organizations*, New York: Basic Books 1971.

Buch, K. and Wetzel, D., 'Analyzing and realigning organizational culture', *Leadership and Organization Development Journal*, XXII/1 (2001), 40–4.

Buchanan, D. and Huczynski, A., *Organizational Behaviour: An Introductory Text*, 3rd ed., Hemel Hempstead: Prentice Hall 1997.

Child, J., *Organization: A Guide to Problems and Practice*, London: Harper & Row 1984.

Daft, R., *Organization Theory and Design*, 3rd ed., St Paul, MN: West Publishing 1989.

Dawson, S., *Analysing Organisations*, London: Macmillan 1996.

Deal, T. and Kennedy, A., *Corporate Cultures: The Rites and Rituals of Corporate Life*, Reading, MA: Addison-Wesley 1982.

Dineen, D. and Garavan, T., 'Ireland, the emerald isle: management research in a changing European context', *International Studies of Management and Organisation*, XXIV/1, 2 (1994).

Drucker, P., 'The coming of the new organization', *Harvard Business Review*, 66 (1992), 33–5.

Drucker, P., *Management Challenges for the 21st Century*, New York: HarperCollins 1999.

Fayol, H., *General and Industrial Management*, London: Pitman 1949.

Geertz, C., 'The impact of the concept of culture on the concept of man', in E. Hammel and W. Simmons (eds), *Man Makes Sense*, Boston: Little, Brown 1971.

Goold, M. and Campbell, A., 'Structured networks: towards the well-designed matrix', *Long Range Planning*, XXXVI/5 (2003), 427–39.

Handy, C., *Understanding Organisations*, London: Penguin 1976.

Harrison, R., 'How to describe your organization', *Harvard Business Review* (September/October 1972).

Hatch, M., *Organization Theory: Modern, Symbolic and Postmodern Perspectives*, Oxford: Oxford University Press 1997.

Hellreigel, D., Slocum, J. and Woodman, R., *Organizational Behavior*, New York: West Publishing 1992.

Hoe, S., 'Book review: understanding organizational culture', *Leadership and Organization Development*, XXIV/2 (2003), 110.

Hofstede, G., *Culture's Consequences: International Differences in Work Related Values*, Beverley Hills, CA: Sage 1980.

Hofstede, G., *Cultures and Organizations: Software of the Mind*, London: McGraw-Hill 1991.

Jackall, R., *Moral Mazes*, New York: Oxford University Press 1988.

Jaques, E., *The Changing Culture of a Factory*, New York: Dryden Press 1952.

Kimberly, R., 'Organisational size and the structuralism perspective: a review, critique and proposal', *Administrative Science Quarterly*, XXI/2 (1976), 571–97.

Louis, M., 'Organisations as culture bearing milieu', in L. Pondy, P. Frost, G. Morgan and T. Dandridge (eds), *Organizational Culture*, Greenwich, CT: JAI Press 1983.

McLarney, C. and Chung, E., 'What happened is prologue: creative divergence and corporate culture fabrication', *Management Decision*, XXXVIII/6 (2000), 410–19.

Mintzberg, H., *The Structuring of Organizations: A Synthesis of Research*, New York: Prentice Hall 1979.

Mintzberg, H., 'Organizational design: fashion or fit', *Harvard Business Review*, 59 (1981), 103–16.

Mintzberg, H., *Structure in Fives: Designing Effective Organizations*, Englewood Cliffs, NJ: Prentice Hall 1983.

Morgan, G., *Images of Organisations*, London: Sage 1986.

Ouichi, W., *Theory Z: How American Business Can Meet the Japanese Challenge*, Reading, MA: Addison-Wesley 1981.

Peters, T. and Waterman, R., *In Search of Excellence: Lessons from America's Best Run Companies*, New York: Harper & Row 1982.

Pettigrew, A., 'On studying organisational culture', *Administrative Science Quarterly*, 24 (1979), 570–81.

Phillips, M., Goodman, R. and Sackmann, S., 'Exploring the complex cultural milieu of project teams', *PM Network*, VII/00 (1992), 820–6.

Pondy, L. and Mitroff, I., 'Beyond open system models of organization', *Research in Organizational Behaviour*, I/1 (1979), 3–39.

Robbins, S., *Organizational Behaviour: Concepts, Controversies, and Applications*, New York: Prentice Hall 1991.

Robey, D., *Designing Organizations*, Homewood, IL: Irwin 1991.

Sadri, G. and Lees, B., 'Developing corporate culture as a competitive advantage', *The Journal of Management Development*, XX/10 (2001), 853–9.

Schein, E., 'Coming to a new awareness of organisational culture', *Sloan Management Review*, XXV (1984), 3–16.

Schein, E., *Organizational Culture and Leadership*, San Francisco: Jossey-Bass 1985.

Shearer, C., Hames, D. and Runge, J., 'How CEOs influence organizational culture following acquisitions', *Leadership and Organizational Development Journal*, XXII/3 (2001), 105–13.

Siehl, C. and Martin, J., 'The role of symbolic management: how can managers effectively transmit organisational culture?', in J. Hunt, D. Hosking, C. Schriesheim and R. Steward (eds), *Leaders and Managers: International Perspectives on Managerial Behavior and Leadership*, New York: Pergamon 1984.

Swe, V. and Kleiner, B., 'Managing and changing mistrustful cultures', *Industrial and Commercial Cultures*, XXX/2 (1998), 66–70.

Tiernan, S., 'Innovations in organisational structure', *IBAR*, XIV/2 (1993), 57–69.

Tiernan, S., 'The management of change in team Aer Lingus', in *Proceedings of the First Irish Academy of Management Conference, Management Research in Ireland: The Way Forward*, Cork: University College September 1996.

Tiernan, S., Morley, M. and Foley, E., *Modern Management*, Dublin: Gill & Macmillan 1996.

Tiernan, S., Flood, P. and Murphy, E., 'Employee reactions to flattening organizational structures', *European Journal of Work and Organizational Psychology*, XI/1 (2002), 47–67.

Trice, H. and Beyer, J., 'Studying organizational cultures through rites and ceremonials', *Academy of Management Review*, 9 (1984), 653–9.

Trice, H. and Beyer, J., *The Cultures of Work Organizations*, Englewood Cliffs, NJ: Prentice Hall 1993.

Trompenaars, F. and Hampden-Turner, C., *Riding the Waves of Culture*, 2nd ed., Nicholas Brealey 1999.

Vail, P., 'The purposing of high performing systems', *Organizational Dynamics* (Autumn 1982).

Van Maanen, J., *Tales of the Field: On Writing Ethnography*, Chicago: University of Chicago Press 1988.

Wang, C. and Ahmed, P., 'Structure and structural dimensions for knowledge based organisations', *Measuring Business Excellence*, VII/1 (2003), 51–62.

Weber, M., *The Theory of Social and Economic Organization*, New York: Free Press 1964.

Williams, A., Dobson, P. and Walters, M., *Changing Culture*, London: Institute of Personnel Management 1989.

Willmott, H., 'Strength is ignorance, slavery is freedom: managing culture in modern organisations', *Journal of Management Studies*, XXX/4 (1993), 515–52.

Woodward, J., *Industrial Organisations: Theory and Practice*, London: Oxford University Press 1965.

THE DYNAMICS OF ORGANISATIONAL LEARNING

Learning Objectives

- To introduce the topic of organisational learning and outline its key constituent elements.

- To distinguish between individual and organisational perspectives on learning.

- To describe the 'learning organisation' paradigm.

- To delineate organisational learning processes and classify different learning process types.

- To outline why organisations sometimes fail to learn.

INTRODUCTION

The topic of organisational learning, as it is linked with work-based learning, training and development, has become one of the fastest-growing research and teaching interests within the management canon. There is no precise or measurable conception of organisational learning that adequately accounts for the range of influences upon it. Indeed, organisational learning does not sit comfortably within the domain of a singular theoretical discipline, nor is it a discipline in itself. As a result, issues relating to the continuous development of human resources within an organisational context are often dealt with in a fragmented manner and reflect the particular interests of the stakeholder involved.

Interest in the terminology of organisational learning has blossomed over the past thirty years. While widely acclaimed for their seminal work on organisational learning, Argyris and Schön (1996: xvii) themselves note:

> Twenty or twenty-five years ago organizational learning was a rare species among ideas ... With few exceptions ... organizational learning was largely absent from the scholarly literature of organizational theory ... Respected scholars ... found the idea confusing and, in some ways, repugnant ... Now, in the mid 1990s, it is conventional wisdom that business firms, governments ... even whole nations ... are all subject to a 'learning imperative', and in the academic as well as the practitioner world, organizational learning has become an idea in good currency.

Evidence of the fashionableness of the concept is readily available in both the academic and policy literature. In 1997 a policy paper (white paper) on human resource development was published by the Irish government, which concluded that in order to survive into the twenty-first century, every Irish organisation must strive to become a learning organisation. Emergence of the terms 'organisational learning' and 'learning organisation' in common parlance is also to be found in the US, where a study by the American Society for Training and Development (Weick and Westley 1997) reports that ninety-four per cent of respondents said it was important to build a learning organisation. More recently at the European Union summit meeting in Lisbon in 2000, the issues of lifelong education and learning were highlighted as critical components in ensuring a successful transition to a knowledge-based economy and society.

Clearly there is considerable evidence to suggest that the issue of organisational learning is a pressing one for organisations today – in rhetoric if not in practice. But what exactly do we mean when we talk about organisational learning? What is required for organisations to become effective facilitators of learning at work? These are some of the issues we will deal with in this chapter.

To start with, key contributions to the debate on the nature of organisational learning are reviewed. The origins of organisational learning (encompassing individualist and organisational roots) and the learning organisation paradigm are presented and discussed. Issues surrounding the process of organisational learning are evaluated and a synthesis of emergent themes is presented.

DEFINITIONS OF KEY CONCEPTS

Organisational learning
The intentional use of learning processes at the individual, group and system level to continuously transform the organisation in a direction that is increasingly satisfying to its stakeholders.

The learning organisation
An organisation where learning becomes a cultural practice that is affirmed through the development of a mission and value statements, workers' identification with corporate aims and the conceptualisation of an organisation as a site of ongoing learning.

Collective learning
The diffusion of knowledge, skills and know-how from individuals to the wider organisational community, where it is readily accessible to all.

Organisational learning mechanisms
Institutionalised structural and procedural arrangements that allow organisations to collect, analyse, store and use information.

> **Knowledge management system**
>
> Comprises mechanisms that generate information, transfer it and utilise it to create new connections and subprocesses.

DEFINING ORGANISATIONAL LEARNING

Without question, defining organisational learning in any meaningful way is problematic. Although interest in organisational learning has intensified over the last few years, it is still characterised as a murky field with little cumulative systematic research (Snyder and Cummings 1998). There is limited agreement on basic concepts and there are few attempts to provide integrative frameworks or to specify how organisational learning affects organisational performance. Popper and Lipshitz (2000) argue that the downside of the outpouring of publications on organisational learning is a confusing proliferation of definitions and conceptualisations that fail to converge into a coherent whole.

To illustrate this definitional milieu, Table 10.1 provides a range of definitions of organisational learning that have been proposed by organisational learning theorists over the last thirty years or more. The table further provides an indication of the prime unit or level of analysis of each of these contributions.

Table 10.1 Definitions and Perspectives of Organisational Learning

Author(s)	Date	Definition of Organisational Learning	Unit of Analysis
Bierly, Kessler and Christensen	2000	'The process of organisational learning and knowledge transfer provides a fundamental mechanism for the development of organisational wisdom ... enabled through an effective organisational communication system that encourages learning.'	Organisational
Solomon	1999	'Learning perceived as a concept of "repertoire" rather than as a developmental concept.'	Organisational
Nonaka	1996	'A company is not a machine but a living organism. Much like an individual, it can have a collective sense of identity and fundamental purpose. This is the organisational equivalent of self-knowledge.'	Organisational
Dodgson	1993	'The way firms build and supplement their knowledge bases about technologies, products and processes and develop and improve organisational efficiency and the broad skills of their workforce.'	Organisational
McGill *et al.*	1992	'An organisation's ability to gain insight and understanding from experience.'	Individual/ managerial

Simon	1991	'An organisation learns by learning from its members and ingesting new members.'	Individual
Huber	1991	'An entity learns if, through processing information, the range of its potential behaviours is changed.'	Organisational
Senge	1990	'Generative learning as learning that enhances capacity to create.'	Individual and organisational
Shrivastava	1983	'Conversion of individual knowledge and insights into a systematic organisational knowledge base which informs decision makers.'	Organisational
Argyris and Schön	1978	'Single loop and double loop learning.'	Individual and organisational
Cyert and March	1961	'Organisations learn ... we assume that organisations change their goals, shift their attention, and revise their procedures for search as a function of their experience.'	Organisational

The table illustrates the range of definitional viewpoints taken by various authors within the field of learning. Although there is considerable variation in the manner with which they define organisational learning, one can clearly discern two dichotomous approaches to the study of organisational learning: an individualist approach that focuses primarily on the individual learner to explain organisational learning and an organisational approach that views organisational learning as something more than the sum of individuals' learning. The former depicts individual members as agents of influence on organisational beliefs, while the latter suggests that organisations themselves can exhibit learning characteristics.

With respect to the individual level, the legacy of individual psychology has had a considerable influence on studies in organisational learning. Learning theory based on behavioural psychology grew from the early work of Pavlov and Skinner and represents a still-common view of conditioned learning. Here learning is represented in a stimulus-response relationship whereby behaviour can be determined by reinforcement (via rewards), resulting in changed behaviour. In an organisational context, learning tends to be perceived as a trial-and-error procedure or search among alternative routines, where routines are likely to be used when they have previously led to a positive outcome. Researchers who adopt this individualist perspective to organisational learning predominantly tend to view organisational learning as individual learning that occurs within an organisational context so that it represents an aggregate of individual learning processes (for a detailed discussion on individual learning, see Chapter 4).

More recently, however, the tendency has been towards describing organisational learning in terms of organisational processes and structures such that learning is embedded in routines, policies and cultures. Here the focus has been on building an environment that supports learning at work. Dixon (1994) describes such organisational learning as the intentional use of learning processes at the individual, group and system level to continuously transform the organisation in a direction that is increasingly satisfying to its stakeholders. In exploring a range of definitions of organisational learning, she isolates a number of key themes that can be seen to exist within this literature, namely:

- the expectation that increased knowledge will improve action;
- acknowledgement of the pivotal relationship between the organisation and its environment;
- the idea of solidarity, as in collective or shared thinking; and
- a proactive stance in terms of the organisation changing itself.

Her findings suggest that, however defined, organisational learning can be seen to be mediated by the learning of individual organisational members, but not explained by it. Coghlan (1997) postulates that organisational learning is concerned with the capacity or process within an organisation to maintain or improve performance based on experience – a systematic phenomenon that goes beyond the learning of individuals. Lundberg (1995) similarly proposes that individual learning is a necessary, though not sufficient, condition for organisational learning which is institutionally embedded. He argues that individual learning must first be shared through communication and that institutional processes play a critical role in ensuring that organisational learning takes place.

Findlay *et al.* (2000) note that while psychology has traditionally focused on the individual when considering learning, the bridge from individual to collective learning is generally held to be that organisational learning involves the sharing of knowledge, values or assumptions.

Kim (1993: 39) argues that there is an enduring and immeasurable relationship between individual and organisational learning and that one should not try to view them as separate processes:

> The importance of individual learning for organisational learning is at once obvious and subtle – obvious because all organisations are composed of individuals; subtle because organisations can learn independent of any specific individual but not independent of all individuals.

Both Argyris and Schön (1978, 1996) and Kim (1993) have attempted to bridge the gap between individual and organisational learning by proposing theories or frameworks that provide for some element of information sharing. Argyris and Schön, for example, developed shared theories of action, while Kim constructed shared mental models. In this way, both arguments propose that organisational learning occurs when inventions and evaluations of individual members are embedded in the organisation's theory in use of shared mental models.

Popper and Lipshitz (2000: 184) refer to organisational learning mechanisms (OLMs), which are seen as institutionalised structural and procedural arrangements that allow organisations to learn non-vicariously, i.e. to collect, analyse, store, disseminate and systematically use information that is relevant to their and their members' performance.

They allow for the interplay between individual- and organisational-level learning, since they represent organisational-level entities and processes on the one hand, but are operated by individuals and can be dedicated to facilitating learning or to disseminating what individuals and groups learn throughout the organisation.

Popper and Lipshitz argue that this approach permits one to view the organisation as capable of learning and of being able to be facilitated in building such capability, without using what they term metaphorical discourses (learning organisation) or positing hypothetical constructs (theories in use or shared mental maps). They conclude that individual- and organisational-level learning are similar in that they involve the same phases of information processing – collection, analysis, abstraction and retention. Yet they are dissimilar in that information processing is carried out at different systemic levels by different structures and because organisational learning involves the additional phase of transmission of information and knowledge among different people and organisational units.

Overall, there does appear to be some degree of consensus pertaining to the value of learning at the organisational level. Agarwal *et al.* (1997: 58) are instructive here:

> If the operational view of the organisation is seen in terms of a collection of procedures, routines, management initiatives, norms and cultures that will allow individuals to learn, then the objective leading to higher performance is a commitment to learning.

Put differently, the consensus view suggests that if learning is be harnessed for organisational purposes, then clearly there exists a need for a supportive environment to facilitate this learning. This requires that organisations develop a learning framework that will facilitate continuous development and improvement – specifically, institutional processes need to be developed that can support the transfer of what is learned by individuals to the organisation, and also be capable of storing and accessing what is learned. Tompkins (1995) describes this as collective learning, i.e. the diffusion of knowledge and/or skills from individuals to members of the collective, which increases the organisation's capacity to take effective action. Interpreted in this way, organisational learning can be viewed as a means of managing the environmental context to ensure both willingness and an ability to learn – the architecture of organisation-led learning. One suggested means of achieving this may be to develop what the literature terms 'a learning organisation'.

THE LEARNING ORGANISATION PARADIGM

Although the terms 'organisational learning' and the 'learning organisation' have often been used interchangeably, the broad body of evidence suggests that they are, in fact, quite distinct. This distinction is worth clarifying. Arguments in favour of organisational learning tend to be either analytical or normatively based. The analytic argument suggests that organisations must have the capacity to learn if they are to compete in their dynamic environments (Stata 1989; Daft 1994; Iles 1994; Edmondson and Moingeon 1998). The normative argument, on the other hand, proposes an 'ideal type' to which organisations should aspire in order to compete effectively, and organisational learning is seen as a critical means of achieving this ideal state (Senge 1990; Pedler *et al.* 1991). This normative argument suggests that organisational learning is likely to be productive if it is embedded in an appropriate learning mechanism within a facilitative environment or culture, i.e. a normative system of shared values and beliefs that shape how organisational members think, feel and behave. In condensed form, this is the 'learning organisation' as depicted in the literature.

The learning organisation literature is highly prescriptive, wherein, as Price and Shaw (1996) indicate, learning can so easily become a catch-all phrase that means whatever one wants it to mean, or as Hawkins (1994: 73) quips, 'the thing that everyone is searching for, and that no-one seems to have found.' Numerous definitions of the learning organisation have been proposed and some of these are included here to illustrate what Peters (1992: 385) laments as the 'maddeningly abstract or vague talk of learning organisations that perpetually falls short on the specifics.'

Some of the earliest proponents of the learning organisation concept were Pedler *et al.* (1991) and Senge (1990). Pedler *et al.* use the term 'the learning company' to describe an organisation that 'facilitates the learning of all its members and continuously transforms itself', while Senge (1990: 1) argues for the development of organisations 'where people continually expand their capacity to create results they truly desire, where new and expansive patterns of thinking are nurtured, where collective aspiration is set free, and where people are continually learning how to learn together.' This theme of developing an organisation's capacity is followed by Redding (1997: 62), who proposes that 'a company is a learning organisation to the degree that it has purposefully built its capacity to learn as a whole system and woven that capacity into all of its aspects: vision and strategy, leadership and management, culture, structure, systems and processes.'

Meanwhile, drawing from the knowledge management literature, Leonard-Barton (1992: 23) conceives of a 'learning laboratory' as:

> an organisation dedicated to knowledge creation, collection and control. Contribution to knowledge is a key criterion for all activities. In a learning laboratory tremendous amounts of knowledge and skill are embedded in physical equipment and processes and embodied in people.

Each of these definitions points to an ideal type to which organisations should aspire, although they are remarkably unforthcoming on how this ideal state is to be achieved.

The learning organisation concept is further confounded by descriptions of it as 'a work-in-progress, both conceptually and practically' (Calvert *et al.* 1994: 40) or as a 'journey rather than a destination' (West 1994).

Not all of the learning organisation literature is quite so heavy on rhetoric, however. Goh and Richards (1997: 575) describe learning organisations as those that 'identify and measure the essential organisational characteristics and management practices that promote organisational learning … that would enable managers to design interventions to overcome specific barriers in building a learning organisation.'

Similarly, Solomon (1999: 122) adopts a less idealised and prescriptive approach to the concept and proposes a more applied description of a learning organisation:

> While learning has always been a feature of working, learning at work has a new status in contemporary workforce discourse as learning is considered a part of everyday work. Learning becomes a cultural practice that is affirmed through the development of a mission and value statements, an identification of workers with corporate aims and the conceptualisation of an organisation as a site of ongoing learning.

Garavan (1997) suggests that the learning organisation might appropriately be viewed as a correction to the many efficiency and quality-driven initiatives that became popular during the 1980s. Meanwhile, Moss Jones (1992) proposes that while the terminology of the learning organisation is relatively new, it is based on a complex mix of ideas that have existed for quite some time. Indeed, Leitch *et al.* (1996) argue that, among others, the work of Revans (1982) has provided many of the foundations for current iterations of the learning organisation. Lawler and Ledford (1992) further argue that the learning organisation can be rooted in organisation theory, the quality movement and organisational development more generally.

In reviewing the learning organisation literature, Calvert *et al.* (1994: 40) draw three particular conclusions, as follows.

*   All organisations learn, hence learning is continuous.
*   All organisations learn at different levels of proficiency and at different paces.
*   To become a learning organisation, an organisation must find ways to make learning more intentional and more systematic; deliberate learning is more effective than learning that is left to chance.

The latter point perhaps best represents the central theme running through the often-amorphous learning organisation literature. Learning is intentional and the organisation, through its structure, culture and systems, is designed to learn. Moreover, the emphasis moves from improving efficiency and towards fostering creativity and innovation. Hawkins (1994) suggests that this change in emphasis challenges a commonly held assumption that learning is problem centred or concerned with the adaptation of existing routines and systems. Indeed, Senge (1990) notes that adaptability is not sufficient, as it is only the first stage in moving towards a learning organisation, while Slater and Narver (1995) argue strongly for a move away from responsive learning and towards generative learning that, of itself, is 'frame breaking'.

Kofman and Senge (1993: 19) extend the debate by arguing that the learning required in becoming a learning organisation is transformational learning, which is less about tools and techniques and more about who we are and how we can help each other. Kapinsky (1995: 18) supports this collectivist perspective and suggests that a learning organisation makes work as a collective human product possible through the development of empowered work teams that collaboratively manage their everyday work practices. Dovey (1997: 333) further takes up this 'community of practice' idea and suggests that as learning organisations evolve, the competitive individualism that has characterised modern capitalist cultures gives way to a form of communal learning whereby the interdependence of all members of the organisation, and their collective responsibility for meaningful survival, is acknowledged and cherished.

CRITICISMS OF THE LEARNING ORGANISATION

The learning organisation literature is not uncontested. On assessing the learning organisation literature, Smith and Tosey (1999: 70) suggest that if the capability and disposition for an organisation to measure its progress is absent, headway in substantive, wide-scale learning organisation development is seriously jeopardised. Instead, they propose that it is best to conceive of reaching the learning organisation ideal as a social process rather than as a scientific one. Goh and Richards (1997) argue that learning organisation implementation has been hindered by the lack of a measurable approach, while Allen (1997) and Gardiner and Whiting (1997) all note the significant absence of even the measurement of learning activity in much of the extant literature on learning organisations.

Henderson (1997) argues that organisational learning is difficult and the achievement of the learning organisation almost impossible, since learning is often perceived as a nice outcome of managerial action rather than the original intention. He further quotes Leonard-Barton (1992), who points out that organisations structured along the lines of a learning laboratory remain isolated exceptions.

As noted earlier, the notion of shared experience is endemic in the learning organisation literature, posited in an often vague attempt to create an ideal type of organisation. One critical problem with this type of approach is the implicit assumption that learning is the goal/end, rather than, in fact, the means to an end. It suggests that shared experience supersedes shared interests – this is not altogether plausible in all circumstances, since shared experiences are determined by the context within which they occur rather than as a result of learning, and so a myriad of factors can intervene in the relationship.

There is thus limited evidence to support the view that the learning organisation rhetoric can be transferred into practice. Raper et al. (1997) suggest that it represents nothing more than aspirations and prescriptions, while Loh (1997: 18) suggests that there is no agreement on what constitutes a learning organisation except that it requires adeptness at translating new knowledge into new ways of behaving.

Leitch et al. (1996: 33) deduce that 'we are a long way from creating a pure or perfect learning organisation since it is not possible, from existing accounts, to describe exactly how one is created', a conclusion that was also reached by Goh and Richards (1997: 575), who note that 'there is still no systematic, measurable approach available for the practical application of this concept in organisations.'

ACTIONING ORGANISATIONAL LEARNING: THE ORGANISATIONAL LEARNING PROCESS

Schendel (1996: 3) suggests that the *process* of learning, rather than *what* is learned, may well be what is more important and that the ability to develop organisational capability may be more important in creating competitive advantage than the specific knowledge gained. In articulating this learning process, Argyris and Schön (1978) developed their widely cited typology that distinguishes between two types of learning: single loop learning and double loop learning. Single loop learning is commonly used in routine work where actions are largely repetitive with little change. Double loop learning is associated with situations where change is a regular feature and where learners are required to think through actions and question whether a change in behaviour is required (constantly assessing and questioning how they perform their work).

Huber (1991) was perhaps one of the earliest theorists to singularly adopt a knowledge creation perspective to the organisational learning discussion. Interestingly, the knowledge management literature, built upon similar premises, began to emerge soon afterwards (towards the mid-1990s). In seeking to describe how organisational learning occurs, building on earlier work by Daft and Weick (1984), Huber (1991) identifies a number of processes associated with organisational learning – knowledge acquisition, information dissemination, information interpretation and organisational memory. Acquisition refers to knowledge gained from monitoring the external environment and using information systems to manage, store and retrieve information at will, carrying out research and development and carrying out training and development. Not only does the organisation acquire external knowledge, but it also rearranges existing knowledge and existing knowledge structures. Information dissemination refers to the process by which an organisation shares information among its members and units, thereby promoting learning and producing new knowledge or understanding. There must be opportunities to use the knowledge, particularly in a group setting – such as through group-oriented tasks – in order to promote collective learning. Interpretation refers to the manner in which information is given meaning and a common understanding, which is then stored in the organisation memory to be extracted for future use.

While Bhatt (2000) argues that defining knowledge accurately is difficult, Nonaka and Takeuchi (1995: 90) describe it as a justified belief system. In a complex and dynamic environment belief systems do not remain static, but rather are in continuous flux and readjusted through the process of social interaction and information exchange. This can occur between organisational members, organisational members and external environments and organisational members and the various internal environments. Knowledge is a changing reality that is observed and realised through multiple interactions and information exchange. To update and refine knowledge, organisations are required to interact with their environments and readjust their belief systems. Nonaka (1996: 19) contends that this process centres on:

... the recognition that creating new knowledge is not simply a matter of 'processing' objective information. Rather, it depends on tapping the tacit and often highly objective insights, intuitions and hunches of individual employees and making those insights available for testing and use by the company as a whole.

There is clearly a close connection between developing learning capability and knowledge creation in organisations and this is keenly reflected in the extant literature, which has witnessed the common adoption of the knowledge management terminology into the HRM literature more generally. Qureshi (2000) views the diffusion of information as the organisation's critical knowledge base and argues that this diffusion is affected by the learning processes that encompass the individual's effort and the group and organisation's collective experience. As such, mechanisms that generate information, transfer it and utilise it form a vital component of the survival and ongoing development of any organisation. He suggests that it is a matter of knowing how to learn and to understand how knowledge is organised and shared. Argyris and Schön (1978) add that the experiences of others, the stories that they tell and the understandings that they share all comprise the know-how that contributes to an organisation's ability to perform and react to its environment. A track record in accumulating prior knowledge improves an organisation's ability to accrue more knowledge and learn more easily. Weick and Roberts (1993) suggest that the extent to which organisational members are creative and willing to learn co-operatively can simplify the process of knowledge creation in the organisation, while Adler *et al.* (1999) posit that management's main task can be said to create an environment of interaction between individuals and the organisation for strengthening each other's knowledge base.

Snyder (1996) proposes that organisational knowledge consists of three essential elements: skills, cognitions and systems. Organisation skills include the technical, professional and social expertise of organisation members, i.e. the know-how of the organisation. Cognitions refer to the information, ideas, attitudes, norms and values shared by organisation members, i.e. including the know-why of the organisation. Organisation systems include the structures, procedures and policies related to performing tasks, co-ordinating resources and managing external relationships. Combined, these three elements represent organisational learning in action.

Candy and Matthews (1998) suggest that the workplace can perform a number of particular learning functions for employees, such as:

- representing a site for formally accredited learning;
- representing a site for complex technical interaction and problem solving;
- representing a site for sharing and creating knowledge;
- representing a part of the knowledge society; and
- representing an organic entity, capable of learning and adapting in its own right.

Learning is an individual activity in the first two instances above, where knowledge exists largely outside of the learner and is there to be assimilated. However, much workplace learning is collective and socially shared. As indicated earlier in the discussion, communities of practice build up in each workplace where much of the process of generating, distributing and applying knowledge occurs in team settings. Here the group creates knowledge for its members, for itself as a system and for others, using processes of framing, reframing, experimenting, crossing boundaries and integrating perspectives. Nonaka and Takeuchi (1995) describe how the processes move from the personal to the social, building on tacit as well as explicit knowledge in what they term a 'knowledge-creating spiral' (Figure 10.1).

Figure 10.1 Nonaka and Takeuchi's Spiral of Knowledge

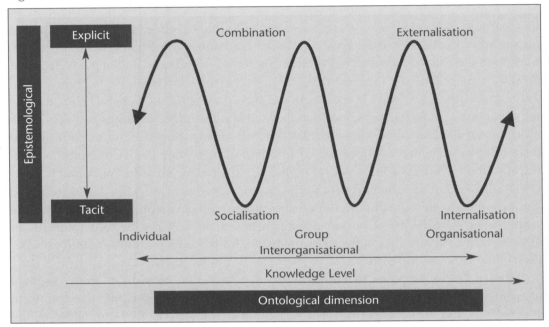

Source: Nonaka and Takeuchi (1994)

This spiral of knowledge suggests that new knowledge begins with the individual, and when this knowledge is translated into some new process or activity, then that individual's personal knowledge is transformed into organisational knowledge that is valuable to the company as a whole. Making personal and tacit knowledge available to others is a central mission within the knowledge-creating company.

When we speak of knowledge we need to clearly distinguish what is meant by knowledge. Firms can be seen to possess two types of knowledge – explicit and tacit. Explicit knowledge is that which can be written down, encoded, explained or understood by anyone with a basic understanding of the generic technology (inside or outside the organisation), since this knowledge is universal and transparent. Tacit knowledge and skills consist of that unwritten know-how and know-why quality which is understood only by the person, unit or firm that has long worked with it on a deeply personal or embedded level. Tacit knowledge essentially becomes part of the mental thought processes of the person creating and applying it. Within organisations, tacit knowledge and skills are often the result of sustained learning by individuals and teams where the skills become deeply embedded and ingrained. This knowledge becomes so specific and intrinsic that it is difficult for those outside the firm to decipher and imitate it. This tacit knowledge can frequently remain locked within the experience of individual employees or managers who may have no desire or see no necessity to explain it to other organisational members, and in so doing perpetuate the problem. This knowledge can easily be lost where such individuals choose to leave the organisation and thereby take the knowledge with them.

Green and Shanks (1993) argue that learning acquired through experience is often referred to as implicit learning, i.e. the acquisition of complex knowledge that takes place without the learner's awareness that he/she is learning. Implicit learning is thought to be the foundation for tacit knowledge and can be used to solve problems as well as make reasonable decisions about novel circumstances. Knowledge acquired through implicit learning is not amenable to verbal reports, whereas explicit learning, which proceeds with the subject's awareness of what is being learned, is verbally reportable. Reflection is thought to contribute to learning through experience to the extent that learners are active observers. Indeed, Bandura's social learning theory (1977) suggests that people often learn behaviours from observing others before performing the behaviour themselves and use this as a means of reflecting on the causes and consequences of particular modes of behaviour. Saul (1997) adds that organisations are part of the mechanism through which society advances and reproduces itself. Individuals both shape and are shaped by their social contexts and so they bring to the workplace a variety of knowledge, experiences and insights that can be capitalised upon. As learning takes place in communities of practice, so must the organisation be structured and managed in order to allow for information to be exchanged and applied.

In seeking to explain how organisations develop knowledge and learning capability, Miller's work on organisational learning (1996) is particularly instructive. He explores a number of dimensions that determine the ways in which organisations can learn and builds these into a typology of organisational learning. In order to understand how organisations can learn, he suggests that one must first appreciate two important dimensions of theories of organisation. The first dimension is the extent to which human or organisational action is constrained by cognitive, political or resource factors. He illustrates this by comparing voluntaristic theories of business strategy that envision few such constraints with more deterministic, bureaucratic or ecological theories that anticipate many such limitations. Here he compares economic theories that emphasise methodical and intentional behaviour with institutional theories that envision emergent and spontaneous behaviour far less driven by technical or economic norms. He goes on to identify the voluntarism-determinism axis as gauging the extent to which people and their institutions are deemed intelligent and autonomous rather than entities severely restricted in cognition and action (Berger and Luckmann 1966; Burrell and Morgan 1979). The debate centres on theorists of strategic choice, which are highly voluntaristic (Ansoff 1979; Porter 1985), versus bureaucratic theorists that view behaviour as being constrained (Cyert and March 1961).

Table 10.2 Types of Organisational Learning Processes

Level of Voluntarism	Mode of Thought and Action	
	Methodical	**Emergent**
Few constraints	**Analytic:** Concerned with evaluating achievements against predetermined objectives. Learning occurs through intensive and systematic information gathering from inside and outside of the organisation. A wide variety of alternatives are considered before a rational choice is made. *Example*: Developing a grand plan for the organisation. *Problem*: Can result in tunnel vision and limit radical change.	**Synthetic:** Learning is intuitive and holistic, such as the ability to generate global insights about issues. It may be internal to the individual and even unintentional. It involves being creative in how one looks at the world and in seeking connections between various elements that may not appear connected. *Example*: Developing synergies between various organisational units or pulling things together in a new way.
Action constrained	**Experimental:** Refers to incremental, bounded, problem-driven research aimed at finding an adequate solution or a satisfactory answer. One explores complex environments in a gradual, piecemeal way in an effort to see how it affects local operations. *Example*: Occurs during attempts at adaptation or renewal or changes to product lines or methods.	**Interactive:** Social and political activity result in contrasting ideas and conflicting objectives that force/limit choices of action. It involves learning by doing, by bargaining and trading with various organisational stakeholders and by 'reading people'. *Example*: An individual or department trying to achieve local objectives.
Action and thought constrained	**Structural:** Driven by routines that standardise information processing and behaviour. This form of learning is as a result of analytic learning since it tends to specify how to carry out roles and tasks efficiently. Structural learning is a form of programmed learning. *Example*: Using quality control routines to refine existing practices rather than to create new ones.	**Institutional:** Learning is a product of indoctrination, either subtle or direct, that results from laws, social norms or personal values that shape thinking. This form of learning tends to be led from the top of the organisation and reinforced through role models, status rituals, special procedures, language and the like. *Example*: Using organisational myths and legends to reinforce organisational values.

Source: Miller (1996)

His second dimension that contrasts theories of organisation measures whether decisions are based on methodical analyses and concrete standards versus emergent intuitions and subtle values. Transaction cost theories, industrial organisation economics and proponents of corporate planning tend to view managers as intentionally rational actors who make decisions by systematically analysing hard information about competitive options and costs. In contrast, institutional theories and theories of entrepreneurship emphasise how organisational actions are more spontaneous and emergent, driven by subtle normative considerations, fads and rituals or even personal motives. Methodical inquiry is analytical, systematic and deductive. Examples of methodical learning include systematic analyses of competitive markets and business strategy, experimentation with products or technologies that aim to reduce costs or increase profits or the use of statistical quality control procedures to determine process design. Emergent rationality is more spontaneous and intuitive and centres on instincts and impressions. Examples of emergent learning include conceptual insights that can provide a new vision for the organisation or it can come from the social and political interchanges managers have with individuals inside and outside of the organisation.

These paradigmatic distinctions suggest an important difference in the way organisations can learn. Miller (1996: 488) constructs six common types of organisational learning (three methodical and three emergent) that can vary in their approaches, outcomes and contexts depending on the level of voluntarism or constraint on thought and action.

Miller suggests that as we move down the table there is a tendency for learning to take place at lower levels of the organisation hierarchy – analytic and synthetic learning opportunities tend to be afforded to senior managers, experimental and interactive learning are frequently engaged in by middle managers, while structural and institutional learning take place below this level. Although one or two learning modes may dominate in many organisations, several modes may easily co-exist. There is an inherent danger in limiting particular learning modes to particular groups since decisions that are made may not be informed by those that have the most to contribute to them. The context within which all learning occurs has significant implications for the nature of that learning, i.e. levels of uncertainty, scarcity of resources, goal conflict or lack of clarity. Learning always involves a continual interaction between knowledge and behaviour. Miller (1996: 501) concludes by suggesting that as organisations progress through the life cycle they will tend to increase their use of the learning modes in approximately the following sequence: synthetic and analytic, institutional, experimental, structural and interactive.

Nevis *et al.* (1995) similarly worked on classifying types of learning processes in organisations. In their work on knowledge and learning, they conceptualise three stages in the organisational learning process: knowledge acquisition, knowledge sharing and knowledge utilisation. This framework forms the basis for their later identification of seven orientations to organisational learning (DiBella *et al.* 1996):

- **Knowledge source:** The degree to which organisations utilise information from internal or external sources. The use of external information is thought to classify organisations that are adaptive, while internal information refers to innovative organisations. Although innovation is generally perceived to be the more valued of the two, they argue that both approaches have merit.

- **Product-process focus:** The degree to which organisations concentrate on understanding their products and services or focus on the processes that underpin and support these products and services. Some organisations will give equal weight to both, while others concentrate on one at the expense of the other.

- **Documentation mode:** The extent to which knowledge is considered to reside within the individual and cannot be codified versus the implementation of mechanisms to translate personal knowledge into an organisational resource through the use of objective recording methods, hence knowledge becomes a collective commodity rather than an individual one.

- **Dissemination mode:** The extent to which the environment is designed to allow learning to evolve rather than one where learning is encouraged through more structured mechanisms. Informal learning modes include the promotion of dialogue through team working or the sharing of knowledge through 'communities of practice' (Seely Brown and Duguid 1991), where those working in the same field discuss information and problems.

- **Learning focus:** The degree to which the organisation focuses on improving the ways of understanding what is already known (single loop learning) versus using tools and methods to question the validity of what is already known (double loop learning). It is argued that poor organisational performance may be due to efficiency problems or to the inappropriateness of the assumptions underlying actions. Thus, for example, incremental and adaptive developments of products could be conceived as single loop learning. In contrast, innovation through the introduction of a completely new product could be viewed as an example of double loop learning.

- **Value-chain focus:** This refers to the particular part of the value chain that the organisation identifies as its core skills and where it consequently invests to develop and enhance those skills further. For example, some organisations are more design and make-end focused while others are more market and delivery-end focused.

- **Skill development:** The degree to which an organisation focuses on individual skill development versus team or group learning. Much of the learning organisation literature emphasises the significance of team learning over individual learning.

These learning orientations offer a useful way of describing what and how learning takes place. DiBella *et al.* (1996) argue that evidence of these different approaches to learning existing in the same organisation would give credence to the need for a pluralist model of organisational learning as opposed to the normative models currently emphasised. In practice, the authors note that an organisation can adopt more than one of these learning modes depending on how it is structured.

ONGOING DEBATES/ADVANCED CONCEPTS IN ORGANISATIONAL LEARNING

WHY DO ORGANISATIONS FAIL TO LEARN?

Much of the literature almost exclusively conceives of learning as a positive activity with attendant benefits for both the organisation and the individuals who populate it. It may be overly optimistic, however, to suggest that all learning results in improved performance for the organisation. For example, March and Olsen (1976) suggest that learning that is based on misunderstandings or on misdirected responses to external or internal signals will give rise to a distorted type of learning, while March (1991) argues that, in the long run, overly adaptive processes may be self-destructive. Indeed, Brunsson (1998) proposes that unlearning, like learning, might be useful to the organisation since it too can be perceived as a means of promoting change in an organisation. Hedberg (1981: 18) describes unlearning as a process through which learners discard knowledge, thus unlearning makes way for new responses and mental maps. Conceived thus, the question becomes less how well organisations learn and more how capable organisations are of unlearning old behaviours and perceptions and relearning when they face new situations. Brunsson (1998) argues that unlearning can support learning because as knowledge becomes stored in the organisation's memory, some means of unlearning become necessary to make room for more adequate interpretive frameworks and responses.

If we adopt the view that learning and unlearning are useful and necessary activities, then it follows that non-learning, or the inability to effectively learn, is dysfunctional for organisations. Non-learning will neither promote nor allow organisations to grow, nor to believe that they are changing or should change. Non-learning will effectively inhibit organisational improvement and growth since it will promulgate a culture where problems are passed on to someone else or moved into the future; old procedures are used to tackle new issues without any evaluation of their use and so attitudes and opinions remain unchallenged and unchanged and contradictions are accepted as par for the course (Brunsson 1998).

Why do organisations fail to learn effectively? It is likely that sometimes they become blind to new opportunities due to any number of reasons – lack of aspirations, lack of information, complacency, overconfidence or lack of awareness of how they can influence or indeed control their environment. Kim (1993) describes three types of learning 'disconnections' that can reduce the value of organisational learning: situation-specific learning where the individual does not absorb the learning and take that on to the next task; fragmented learning whereby the learning stays with the individual but is not transferred to the wider organisation, either through excessive individual isolation or demarcation and decentralisation; and opportunistic learning whereby individuals bypass standard procedures that are seen as intrusive or cumbersome. In a similar vein, March and Olsen (1976) pinpoint four conditions that can inhibit effective organisational learning.

- **Role-constrained learning:** The individual who acquires new insights is unable to influence behaviour in the organisation because he/she is 'low down' in the hierarchy.

- **Audience learning:** Influential individuals can influence others solely as a result of their important position, often in a spurious manner.
- **Superstitious learning:** The nature of environmental pressure is misunderstood such that organisational members imagine that certain actions produce certain responses, which is not the case.
- **Ambiguous learning:** Individuals simply fail to make connections between what the environment demands and what behaviour is required. As a result, decisions are avoided, more information is sought, plans are changed and the cycle continues.

The learning organisation literature postulates that everyone is a learner and that we can all learn from each other. We can, but can we? Barnett (1999) argues that this step is rarely taken and that while organisations can recognise that learning opportunities need to be opened up for individuals, the collective learning ideology is more difficult to take on board, since not every individual is willing or capable of dealing with the existential challenge that is inherent in being a 'learner'. He argues that at best the recognition that we are lifelong learners merely leads to the acknowledgment that learning opportunities need to be opened up to individuals. He also cautions that:

> Just as work can be demotivating, burdensome or threatening so too can learning, particularly if it is imposed on individuals and if they are poorly supported – in personal as well as well as resource terms – while they are struggling to learn. Learning can benefit from a supporting framework which is designed to address the existential anxiety of learning as much as it is designed to address the more material aspects of effective learning (time, space, money) (Barnett 1999: 37–8).

Work practices in many workplaces still reflect the hierarchical, fixed horizontal and vertical relationships where many workers have narrowly defined job duties and responsibilities characteristic of Fordism. Nevertheless, in terms of contemporary management philosophy there is a movement towards teamwork and flatter hierarchies where workers at various levels participate in decision making and where the different backgrounds, experiences and perspectives are understood to enhance teams' productive potential. As employees engage in diverse social activities and new language practices, workplace culture and a valuing of difference are seen as the basis for learning, for improved employee motivation, public image and organisational effectiveness.

Salaman (1995: 109) argues that it is difficult to achieve the premise of a learning organisation because the culture in most organisations is probably anti-learning due to the existence of rules, values and norms (probably all implicit and undiscussable) that encourage 'winning' over analysis and understanding, as well as protection and defensiveness. Learning must create mutual gains for all members of the organisation. Any increase in learning requirement must have some payback for employees in terms of increased employability, career development or ancillary benefits.

SUMMARY OF KEY PROPOSITIONS

- A consistent feature of the organisational learning literature is the difficulty in arriving at an acceptable definition of the very term 'organisational learning'. There appears to be no consensus as to the best means of understanding the nature of organisational learning.

- Organisational knowledge is more than facts and figures: it encapsulates relationships, biases, culture, motivating factors, reward systems and the like.

- Products and services are the resulting outputs of an organisation's work processes, and most work processes involve interdepartmental teamwork and co-operation between internal customers and suppliers. This suggests that the dominant paradigm should shift from a focus on task to a focus on work processes that need to be effectively integrated to achieve optimum performance. Therein lies the requirement for organisational learning.

- The capability to incorporate change into daily life is an enduring one, especially within the context of the prevailing business environment, and this ability to change can best be achieved if learning is integrated into the normal process of daily work.

- Two opposing perspectives were reviewed. One approach suggests that organisational learning is inherently concerned with the process of achieving consensus or a shared understanding, where learning is seen to occur as individuals converge upon a set of shared understandings or norms of how that organisation exists. An alternative view of organisational learning argues in favour of a fundamental review of these underlying assumptions and a persistent questioning of how things are done. This approach advocates a divergence of understandings and implies that organisations must develop incrementally towards higher-level learning.

- Researchers who adopt an individualist perspective to organisational learning predominantly tend to view organisational learning as individual learning that occurs within an organisational context so that it represents an aggregate of individual learning processes.

- More recently, there appears to be a growing tendency to describe organisational learning in terms of organisational processes and structures such that learning is embedded in routines, policies and cultures. These allow for an interplay between individual- and organisational-level learning since they represent organisational-level entities and processes on the one hand, but are operated by individuals and can be dedicated to facilitating learning or disseminating what individuals and groups learn throughout the organisation.

- With respect to the learning organisation concept, a central theme of this often-amorphous idea is that learning is intentional and that the organisation, through its structure, culture and systems, is designed to learn. Moreover, the emphasis is less on immediate efficiency improvements and more towards fostering creativity and innovation.

- An awareness of how one's actions impact upon and are influenced by the actions of others is critical in building up a community of practice that can reinforce learning and development.

- There is a close connection between developing learning capability and knowledge creation in organisations. Specifically, three stages in the organisational learning process – knowledge acquisition, knowledge sharing and knowledge utilisation – are seen to closely mirror the tenets of knowledge management.

DISUCSSION/SELF-ASSESSMENT QUESTIONS

1. Outline the main processes through which organisations can be said to learn.
2. Discuss the view that the learning organisation concept is overtly prescriptive and of little practical value for organisations.
3. Differentiate between explicit and tacit knowledge. How can tacit knowledge be developed and shared in organisations?
4. How does the knowledge management literature aid our understanding of learning in organisations?

MULTIPLE CHOICE QUESTIONS

1. The individualist approach to organisational learning depicts individual members as agents of influence on organisational beliefs. True or false?
2. In exploring a range of definitions of organisational learning, Dixon (1994) isolated a number of key themes that can be seen to exist within the organisational literature, including:
   (a) The expectation that increased knowledge will improve action.
   (b) Acknowledgement of the pivotal relationship between the organisation and its environment.
   (c) The idea of solidarity, as in collective or shared thinking.
   (d) All of the above.
   (e) None of the above.
3. Accepting that individuals do learn in organisations, this individual learning will always contribute to organisational learning. True or false?
4. Organisational learning mechanisms (OLMs) are associated with the work of:
   (a) Porter and Lorenz (1999).
   (b) Popper and Lipshitz (2000).
   (c) Princton and Lavelle (2001).
   (d) Purdue and Lally (2003).
5. In reviewing the learning organisation literature, Calvert et al. (1994: 40) conclude that:
   (a) Not all organisations learn.
   (b) Learning is static rather than continuous.
   (c) All organisations learn at different levels of proficiency and at different paces.
   (d) All of the above.

(e) None of the above.

6. Single loop learning is said to occur where actions lead to consequences and can be seen to be useful for routine, repetitive issues and for getting the job done. True or false?

7. Snyder (1996) proposes that organisational knowledge consists of three essential elements, namely:

(a) Wisdom, action and outcome.

(b) Skills, cognitions and systems.

(c) Reflexivity, deliberation and debate.

(d) Information, action and strategies.

8. Nevis *et al.* (1995) have classified three stages in the organisational learning process, namely:

(a) Knowledge acquisition, knowledge sharing and knowledge utilisation.

(b) Knowledge frameworks, knowledge development and knowledge supports.

(c) Knowledge fields, knowledge scale and knowledge institutionalisation.

9. According to March and Olsen (1976), among the conditions that can inhibit effective organisational learning are:

(a) Role-constrained learning, whereby the individual who acquires new insights is unable to influence behaviour in the organisation because he/she is 'low down' in the hierarchy.

(b) Audience learning, whereby influential individuals can influence others solely as a result of their important position, often in a spurious manner.

(c) Ambiguous learning, whereby individuals simply fail to make connections between what the environment demands and what behaviour is required.

(d) All of the above.

(e) None of the above.

10. The terms 'organisational learning' and 'the learning organisation' can safely be used interchangeably. True or false?

FIVE SUGGESTED KEY READINGS

Baldwin, T., Danielsen, C. and Wiggenhorn, W., 'The evolution of learning strategies in organizations: from employee development to business redefinition', *Academy of Management Executive*, XI/4 (1997), 47–58.

Dovey, K., 'The learning organization and the organization of learning', *Management Learning*, XXVIII/3 (1997), 331–49.

Easterby-Smith, M., 'Disciplines of the learning organization: contributions and critiques', *Human Relations*, L (1997), 1085–113.

Huber, G.P., 'Organizational learning: the contributing processes and the literatures', *Organizational Science*, II (1991), 88–115.

Popper, M. and Lipshitz, R., 'Organizational learning mechanisms: a cultural and structural approach to organizational learning', *Journal of Applied Behavioral Science*, XXXIV (1998), 161–78.

REFERENCES

Adler, P., Goldofters, B. and Levine, D., 'Flexibility vs. efficiency? A case study of model changeovers in the Toyota production system', *Organization Science*, X/1 (1999), 43–68.

Agarwal, R., Krudys, G. and Tanniru, M., 'Infusing learning into the information systems organization', *European Journal of Information Systems*, 6 (1997), 25–40.

Ansoff, H.I., *Implementing Strategic Management*, Englewood Cliffs, NJ: Prentice Hall 1979.

Argyris, C., *On Organizational Learning*, Oxford: Blackwell 1994.

Argyris, C. and Schön, D.A., *Organizational Learning: A Theory of Action Perspective*, Reading, MA: Addison-Wesley 1978.

Argyris, C. and Schön, D.A., *Organizational Learning 11: Theory, Methods and Practice*, Reading, MA: Addison-Wesley 1996.

Bandura, A., 'Self-efficacy: towards a unifying theory of behavioural change', *Psychological Review*, 81 (1977), 191–215.

Barnett, R., 'Learning to work and working to learn', in D. Boud and J. Garrick (eds), *Understanding Learning at Work*, London: Routledge 1999.

Berger, P. and Luckmann, T., *The Social Construction of Reality*, New York: Doubleday 1967.

Bierly, P., Kessler, E. and Christensen, E., 'Organisational learning, knowledge and wisdom', *Journal of Organisational Change Management*, XIII/6 (2000).

Billet, S., 'Guided learning at work', in D. Boud and J. Garrick (eds), *Understanding Learning at Work*, London: Routledge 1999.

Boud, D. and Garrick, J. (eds), *Understanding Learning At Work*, London: Routledge 1999.

Brunnson, K., 'Non learning organizations', *Scandinavian Journal of Management*, XIV/4 (1998), 421–32.

Bryans, P. and Smith, R., 'Beyond training: reconceptualising learning at work', *Journal of Workplace Learning*, XII/6 (2000), 228–35.

Burgoyne, J., 'Learning from experience: from individual discovery to meta dialogue via the evolution to transitional myths', *Personnel Review*, XXIV/6 (1995), 61–73.

Burgoyne, J., Pedler, M. and Boydell, T., *Towards the Learning Company*, London: McGraw-Hill 1994.

Burrell, G. and Morgan, G., *Sociological Paradigms and Organizational Analysis: Elements of the Sociology of Corporate Life*, London: Heinemann 1979.

Calvert, G., Mobley, S. and Marshall, L., 'Grasping the learning organisation', *Training and Development* (June 1994).

Candy, P.C. and Matthews, J.H., 'Fusing learning and work: changing conceptions of learning in the workplace', in D. Boud (ed.), *Current Issues and New Agendas in Workplace Learning*, Adelaide: National Centre for Vocational Educational Research 1998.

Coghlan, D., 'Organizational learning as a dynamic inter-level process', *Current Topics in Management*, XXII (1997), 27–44.

Cyert, R.M. and March, J.G., *A Behavioural Theory of the Firm:* Englewood Cliffs, NJ: Prentice Hall 1961.

DeGeus, A., 'Planning as learning', *Harvard Business Review*, LXVI (1988), 70–4.

DeGeus, A., *The Living Company: Growth, Learning and Longevity in Business*, London: Nicholas Brealey 1997.

DiBella, A.J., Nevis, E.C. and Gould, J.M., 'Understanding organizational learning capacity', *Journal of Management Studies*, XXXIII/3 (1996), 361–79.

Dixon, N.M., *The Organizational Learning Cycle: How Can We Learn Collectively?*, London: McGraw-Hill 1994.

Dodgson, M., 'Learning, trust and technical collaboration', *Human Relations*, 46 (1993), 77–95.

Dovey, K., 'The learning organization and the organization of learning', *Management Learning*, XXVIII/3 (1997), 331–49.

Edmondson, A. and Moingeon, B., 'From organizational learning to the learning organization', *Management Learning*, XXIX (1998), 5–20.

Findlay, P., McKinlay, A., Marks, A. and Thompson, P., 'Labouring to learn: organisational learning and mutual gains', *Employee Relations*, XXII/5 (2000), 485–502.

Garavan, T.N., 'Training, development, education and learning: different or the same?', *Journal of European Industrial Training*, XXI/2 (1997), 39–50.

Gardiner, P. and Whiting, P., 'Success factors in learning organizations: an empirical study', *Industrial and Commercial Training*, XXIX/2 (1997).

Garrick, J., *Informal Learning in the Workplace*, London: Routledge 1998.

Garrick, J., 'The dominant discourses of learning at work', in D. Boud and J. Garrick (eds), *Understanding Learning at Work*, London: Routledge 1999.

Garvin, J., 'Building learning organizations', *Harvard Business Review* (July/August 1993), 78–91.

Goh, S. and Richards, G., 'Benchmarking the learning capability of organizations', *European Management Journal*, 15 (1997), 575–83.

Green, R.E. and Shanks, D.R., 'On the existence of independent explicit and implicit learning systems: an examination of some evidence', *Memory and Cognition*, XXI (1993), 304–17.

Hamel, G., 'Competition for competence and interpartner learning within international strategic alliances', *Strategic Management Journal*, 12 (1991), 83–103.

Hawkins, P., 'Organizational learning', *Management Learning*, XXV/1 (1994), 71–82.

Henderson, S., 'Black swans don't fly double loops: the limits of the learning organization', *The Learning Organization*, IV/3 (1997), 99–105.

Huber, G.P., 'Organizational learning: the contributing processes and the literatures', *Organizational Science*, II (1991), 88–115.

Iles, P., 'Developing learning environments: challenges for theory, research and practice', *Journal of European Industrial Training*, XVIII/3 (1994).

Kapinski, R., 'The new competition and human resources: how disadvantaged are low income LDCS?', paper presented to the Oxford Conference: Globalisation and Learning, Oxford University 1995.

Kim, D., 'The link between individual and organisational learning', *Sloan Management Review*, XXXV/1 (1993), 37–50.

Kofman, F. and Senge, P., 'Communities of commitment: the heart of learning organizations', *Organizational Dynamics*, XXII/2 (1993), 5–23.

Lawler, E. and Ledford, G., *Doing Research That Is Useful for Theory and Practice*, San Francisco: Jossey Bass 1992.

Lei, D., Slocum, Jr., J.W., Pitts, R.A., 'Building cooperative advantage: managing strategic alliances to promote organizational learning', *Journal of World Business*, XXXII/3 (1997), 203–23.

Leitch, C., Harrison, R., Burgoyne, J. and Blantern, C., 'Learning organizations: the measurement of company performance', *Journal of European Industrial Training*, XX/1 (1996), 31–44.

Leonard-Barton, D., 'The factory as a learning laboratory', *Sloan Management Review* (Fall 1992), 23–8.

Lundberg, C.C., 'Learning in and by organizations: three conceptual issues', *International Journal of Organizational Analysis*, III/1 (1995), 10–23.

March, J.G., 'Exploration and exploitation in organizational learning', *Organizational Science*, II (1991), 71–87.

March, J.G. and Olsen, J.P. (eds), *Ambiguity and Choice in Organizations*, Oslo: Universtetsforlaget 1976, 54–69.

Matthews, J. and Candy, P., 'New dimensions in the dynamics of learning and knowledge', in D. Boud and J. Garrick (eds), *Understanding Learning at Work*, London: Routledge 1999.

McGill, M., Slocum, J. and Lei, D., 'Management practices in learning organisations', *Organisation Dynamics* (Spring 1992), 14.

Miller, D., 'A preliminary typology of organizational learning: synthesizing the literature', *Journal of Management*, XXII/3 (1996), 485–505.

Moss-Jones, J., *The Learning Organization*, The Open University: Unpublished thesis 1992.

Nevis, E., DiBella, A. and Gould, J., 'Understanding organisations as learning systems', *Sloan Management Review*, XXXVI/2 (1995), 73–85.

Nonaka, I., 'The knowledge creating company', *Harvard Business Review*, LXIX (1991), 96–104.

Nonaka, I. and Takeuchi, H., *The Knowledge Creating Company: How Japanese Companies Create the Dynamic of Innovation*, New York: Oxford University Press 1995.

Nonaka, I., 'The knowledge creating company', in K. Starkey (ed.), *How Organizations Learn*, London: Thompson 1996.

Pedler, M., Boydell, T. and Burgoyne, J., 'Towards the learning company', *Management Education and Development*, XX/1 (1989), 1–8.

Pedler, M., Boydell, T. and Burgoyne, J., *The Learning Company*, London: McGraw-Hill 1991.

Peters, T., *Liberation Management*, London: Macmillan 1992.

Popper, M. and Lipshitz, R., 'Organizational learning: mechanisms, culture and feasibility', *Management Learning*, XXXI/2 (2000), 181–96.

Porter, M., *Competitive Advantage*, New York: Free Press 1985.

Probst, G. and Buchel, B., *Organisational Learning: The Competitive Advantage of the Future*,

London: Prentice Hall 1997.

Qureshi, S., 'Organizational change through collaborative learning in network firms', *Group Decision and Negotiation*, 9 (2000), 129–47.

Quinn, J.B. and Paquette, P.C., 'Technology in services: creating organizational revolutions', *McKinsey Quarterly*, 3, (1990), 91-112.

Raelin, J.A., 'A model of work-based learning', *Organizational Science*, VIII/6 (1997), 563–78.

Raper, P.A., Ashton, D., Felstead, A. and Storey, J., 'Towards the learning organisation? Explaining current trends in training practices in the UK', *International Journal of Training and Development*, I/1 (1997), 9–21.

Redding, J., 'Hardwiring the learning organisation', *Theory and Development*, XV/8 (1997), 61–7.

Revans, R.W., *The Origins and Growth of Action Learning*, Sweden: Chartwell-Bratt 1982.

Rorty, R., *Consequences of Pragmatism*, Minneapolis, MN: University of Minneapolis 1982.

Salamon, C., 'Learning to manage the country nationals', *Personnel Journal*, LXXIV/3 (1995), 60–6.

Saul, R.J., *The Unconscious Civilisation*, Melbourne: Penguin 1997.

Schein, E.H., 'How can organizations learn faster?', *Sloan Management Review* (Winter 1985), 85–92.

Schendel, D., 'Editor's introduction to the 1996 winter special issue: knowledge and the firm', *Strategic Management Journal*, XVII (Special 1996), 1–4.

Senge, P., *The Fifth Discipline*, New York: Doubleday 1990.

Simon, H.A., 'Bounded rationality and organizational learning', *Organizational Science*, II/1 (1991), 125–33

Slater, S.F. and Narver, J.C., 'Market orientation and the learning organization', *Journal of Marketing*, 59 (1995), 63–74.

Smith, P.A. and Tosey, P., 'Assessing the learning organization: part 1 – theoretical foundations', *Learning Organization*, VI/2 (1999), 70–5.

Snyder, W., *Organization Learning and Performance*, Arbour: MI 1996.

Snyder, W. and Cummings, T., 'Organization learning disorders: conceptual model and intervention hypotheses', *Human Relations*, LI/7 (1998), 873–96.

Solomon, N., 'Culture and difference in workplace learning', in D. Boud and J. Garrick (eds), *Understanding Learning at Work*, London: Routledge 1999.

Starkey, K. (ed.), *How Organisations Learn*, London: International Thompson Business Press 1996.

Stata, R., 'Organisational learning – the key to management innovation', *Sloan Management Review*, XXX/3 (Spring 1989).

Tompkins, T.C., 'Role and diffusion in collective learning', *International Journal of Organizational Analysis*, III (1995), 69–85.

Vygotsky, L.S., *Mind in Society: The Development of Higher Psychological Processes*, Cambridge, MA: Harvard University Press 1978.

Watkins, K.E. and Marsick, V.J. (eds), *In Action: Creating the Learning Organization*, Alexandria, VA: American Society for Training and Development 1996.

Weick, K.E. and Roberts, K., 'Collective minds in organizations: heedful interrelating on flight decks', *Administrative Science Quarterly*, 38(1993), 357–81.

Weick, K.E. and Westley, F., 'Organizational learning: affirming an oxymoron', in S. Clegg, C. Hardy and W.R. Nord (eds), *Handbook of Organization Studies*, London: Sage 1996.

West, P., 'The learning organization: losing the luggage in transit?', *Journal of European Industrial Training*, XVIII/11 (1994).

THE DYNAMICS OF WORK SYSTEMS AND TECHNOLOGY

11

Learning Objectives

- To introduce the concepts of job design, work systems and technology.

- To review schools of thought on work systems and present historical and contemporary developments.

- To present some recent evidence on job design initiatives.

INTRODUCTION

A critical factor impacting on organisations and organisation behaviour is the work environment within which employees carry out their various tasks and responsibilities. The job represents the fundamental building block of the way in which work is organised and is the individual's primary point of contact with the organisation (Burr 2001). Parker *et al.* (2001) argue that in recent years, several factors have converged to render the topic of work design one of ongoing, continued importance, including the continuing and omnipresent concern about job simplification, increased emphasis on employee empowerment and a 'war for talent' in many industries, resulting in greater attention being placed on the creation of work that is attractive to the right candidate. This chapter considers the nature of work systems in organisations and evaluates the impact of technology on the design of both work systems and individual jobs in organisations.

DEFINITIONS OF KEY CONCEPTS

Work systems

The particular combination of job task, technology, skills, management style and personnel policies and practices present in an organisation.

Job design

Focusing on the tasks and activities that an employee completes in the organisation on a daily basis, job design is dedicated to changing the structure of jobs. Critical concerns relate to the degree of specialisation and direction afforded the individual in the completion of their tasks.

Scientific management
An approach to management and work organisation that emphasises the one best way to perform a task by applying scientific methods of enquiry.

Job enlargement
An individualistic approach to job design that focuses on the horizontal extension of the job as a means of broadening job scope and creating a more satisfying job.

Job enrichment
An individualistic approach to job design that focuses on the vertical extension of the job as a means of broadening job scope and establishing a more challenging, satisfying job.

Job characteristics model
Advanced by Hackman and Oldham, it seeks to identify job characteristics that satisfy higher-order needs and provide opportunities for achieving this satisfaction. It assumes that tasks are determined in terms of five core dimensions that are related to three critical psychological states and certain personal and work outcomes.

The 'quality of working life' (QWL)
An approach dedicated to addressing the overall quality of employee experiences in the workplace. While embracing job design as a critical influence on the quality of working life, this approach also looks at broader issues, such as employee empowerment, autonomy, participation, justice, working conditions and job security.

The high-performance work organisation
Typically having a distinctive structure that is designed to provide employees with skills, incentives, information and decision-making responsibilities that will lead to improved organisational performance and facilitate innovation, the main aim is to generate high levels of commitment and involvement of employees and managers.

Mass production
A production system in which large batches of standard products are manufactured in assembly line fashion by combining parts in a specified manner.

Just-in-time
An approach to system waste determination, problem solving at source and continuous process improvement.

Statistical process control
The use of statistical analysis to improve quality by reducing unwanted variation in industrial and management processes.

Our choice of the term 'work systems' is designed to embrace the different components that impact on how work is designed and carried out in organisations. In particular, it incorporates both the human and technical aspects of work organisation and job design. All too often one sees these two elements analysed exclusively: the technocratic approach ignoring critical human resource (HR) considerations and the HR approach failing to grasp the impact of technical complexities and realities. The description of work systems provided by Beer and his colleagues (Beer *et al.* 1985: 570) avoids this pitfall:

> The term work systems ... refers to a particular combination of job task, technology, skills, management style, and personnel policies and practices. These are seen as determining how work is organized and managed, how employees will experience work, and how they will perform.

The work system therefore incorporates the way in which the various tasks in the organisation are structured and impacts on issues such as organisation structure and job design. It reflects the interaction of management style, the technical system, human resources and the organisation's products or services (Figure 11.1). The nature of the goods and services being produced or delivered by an organisation plays a key role in determining the characteristics of work systems and job design. For example, organisations whose products require continuous process technology, such as cement production, must operate around-the-clock shift systems and ensure effective, ongoing maintenance to prevent a shutdown of the operating technology.

Figure 11.1 Work System and Job Design

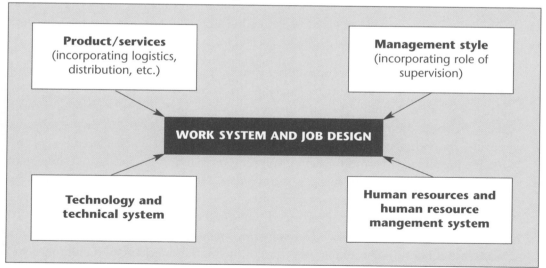

From an employee perspective, a key aspect of work systems is the design of individual jobs, which influences job content, autonomy and the role and extent of supervision. As such, the nature of work systems, particularly job design, significantly impacts on the extent to which work is intrinsically satisfying for employees. While technical considerations play an important role, decisions on the nature of work systems allow considerable scope for management discretion. Consequently, the particular approaches chosen also provide valuable insights into management beliefs about how employees should be managed, jobs structured and the role of supervision. While many boundaries are collapsing in the world of work (Engestrom 2000), many still remain and have their roots in earlier times. In this respect it is useful to review different work systems and their implications for organisations and workers.

A LOOK BACK: TASK SPECIALISATION AND THE DIVISION OF LABOUR

While work systems clearly existed in feudal times, it was the effect of technological advancements brought about by the Industrial Revolution which heralded the growth of large-scale organisations concerned with organising labour, capital and technology into effective production systems. In particular, the impact of technology allowed the creation of large-scale production systems (the new factories), which dramatically changed the nature of work. The key changes were that people worked together in much larger numbers and operated technology on a much larger scale than ever before; for example, individual cottage looms were replaced by much larger machines housed in new factory mills. This new technology required a large number of workers to operate effectively.

However, change was not confined to issues of scale: the nature of work carried out by these employees also underwent fundamental change. The factory system encouraged a high level of task specialisation: complicated job tasks were broken down into much smaller subtasks and technology was used to carry out, or at least aid, many of these sub-tasks. This process is normally referred to as the division of labour and is at the very core of the emergence of contemporary capitalist society.

> In precapitalist days, most people either directly produced their own subsistence or made some article that could be exchanged for subsistence: peasants grew crops; artisans produced cloth, shoes, implements. But as work became more and more finely divided, the products of work became ever smaller pieces in the total jigsaw puzzle. Individuals did not spin thread or weave cloth but manipulated levers and fed the machinery that did the actual spinning or weaving. A worker in a shoe plant made uppers or lowers or heels, but not shoes. None of these jobs, performed by itself, would have sustained its performer for a single day; and no one of these products could have been exchanged for another product except through the complicated market network. Technology freed men and women from much material want, but it bound them to the workings of the market mechanism (Heilbroner and Thurow 1984: 22).

The chief exponent of work systems based on the division of labour was Frederick Taylor, the 'father' of scientific management (Taylor 1947). Taylor's work focused on improving productive efficiency through greater standardisation of work systems and methods. In particular, Taylor encouraged more systematic approaches to the design of jobs and work systems, with specific emphasis on studying the 'best way' of doing particular jobs/tasks and then training workers in the requisite skills, and designing work systems to ensure workers followed this 'one best way'.

TAYLOR'S KEY PRINCIPLES OF SCIENTIFIC MANAGEMENT

* Develop a 'science' for every job, based on standardised work rules, motions and equipment/tools.
* Establish a clear division of tasks and responsibilities between management and workers.
* Careful, systematic selection and training of workers.
* Enlist co-operation of workers to operate in line with scientific management principles and provide appropriate economic incentives.

Taylor (1947: 109) explained his approach as follows:

> First, find, say, ten to fifteen different men who are especially skilled in doing the particular work to be organised; second, study the exact series of elementary operations or motions which each of these men uses in doing the work which is being investigated, as well as the implements each man uses; third, study with a stopwatch the time required to make each of these elementary movements and then select the quickest way of doing each element of the work; fourth, eliminate all false movements, slow movements and useless movements; fifth, after doing away with all unnecessary movements, collect into one series the quickest and best movements, as well as the best implements.

The key characteristics of such 'traditional' approaches to work systems and job design are summarised in Table 11.1. In evaluating the impact of scientific management, one of its important legacies is the notion that work 'planning' (seen as a management task) should be separated from work 'doing' (seen as a worker task). This separation delineated the primary role of management as that of establishing work standards, procedures and methods. Such approaches to work organisation were dominated by the desire to

Table 11.1 Key Characteristics of Traditional Approaches to Job Design

Characteristics	Outcomes
Bureaucratic organisation structure.	Tightly defined jobs.
Top-down management ethos.	Close supervisory control.
Work planning separated from execution.	Minimal employee autonomy or participation.
Task fragmentation.	Job specialisation.
Financial incentives based on performance.	Individual payment-by-results payment system.
Focus on 'one best way' of doing jobs.	Rigid training schedule.

maximise productive efficiency, which, based on Taylorist principles, has been a characteristic of employer approaches to job design since the early years of the twentieth century. Jobs were broken down into simple, repetitive, measurable tasks requiring skills that could be easily acquired through systematic job training. Taylorism helped improve efficiency and promoted a systematic approach to selection, training, work measurement and payment.

While scientific management approaches are often characterised as exclusively a pre-World War II phenomenon, their widespread application continues today. Huczynski and Buchanan (1991: 288) quote the role of Satosi Kamata, an assembly line worker in Toyota, Japan, in the 1980s:

> There is only one method of producing goods in the fastest way possible: standardized work. If we don't make the precise motions we're 'taught', it's absolutely impossible to do the required work in the required time. Under such a system, all movements must become mechanical and habitual.

An even more recent illustration is provided in the following comment from a recruit in one of the largest chicken processing companies in the US:

> The scene would have been downright medieval had the technology not been such a marvel. Each bird was hooked by its drumsticks to a shackle line, then carried through a series of precisely engineered turns ... Each of us was just given one task – a simple, rote, numbingly mechanical motion – and told to do it all day long (Jesse Katz, quoted in the *Los Angeles Times*, 11 November 1996).

Despite the immense productive efficiencies achieved as a result of the application of scientific management, it is also seen as the source of many of the problems associated with industrial work, such as high levels of labour turnover and absenteeism and low employee morale and motivation. Steers and Porter (1987: 459) offer this analysis:

> Early managerial approaches to job design ... focused primarily on attempts to simplify an employee's required tasks insofar as possible in order to increase production efficiency. It was felt that, since workers were largely economically motivated, the best way to maximize output was to reduce tasks to their simplest forms and then reward workers with money on the basis of units of output – a piecework incentive plan ... his [Taylor's] approach to simplified job design reached its zenith from a technological standpoint in assembly-line production techniques such as those used by automotive manufacturers ... On auto assembly lines, in many cases, the average length of 'work cycle' (i.e. the time allowed for an entire 'piece' of work) ranges from 30 seconds to one and a half minutes. This means that workers repeat the same task an average of at least 500 times per day. Such a technique, efficient as it may be, is not without its problems, however. As workers have become better educated and more organized, they are demanding more from their jobs. Not only is this demand shown in recurrent requests for shorter hours and higher wages,

but it is also shown in several undesirable behavior patterns, such as increased turnover, absenteeism, dissatisfaction and sabotage.

Indeed, one need only reflect on this analysis and the comments of the Toyota and chicken factory workers quoted above to gauge the negative effects of Taylorism. These traditional approaches to work systems and job design reflect a managerial desire to maintain control over the work process and maximise the productive efficiency of the organisation's technical resources. Choices on the organisation of work and the design of jobs were seen as primarily determined by the technical system. Management's role was to ensure that other organisational resources, including employees, were organised in such a way as to facilitate the optimal utilisation of the technical system. This approach often resulted in bureaucratic organisation structures, elaborate procedures and systems and top-down supervisory control. It also encouraged the fragmentation of jobs into simple, repetitive, measurable tasks that gave post-holders little autonomy. As noted earlier, such approaches to work organisation also reflected managerial assumptions about employees and how they should be managed. Close supervision, detailed work measurement and other types of job control often reflect a managerial belief that employees are inherently lazy and thus need to be coerced to work effectively. Such managerial thinking accords to McGregor's Theory X assumptions on employee motivation (see Chapter 6 and Table 6.1).

As a result of the negative consequences of scientific management approaches, particularly high employee turnover, absenteeism and monotony, the period since the 1930s has seen extensive experimentation in the area of work systems and job design. Much of this focused on restructuring organisations and jobs to incorporate greater scope for intrinsic motivation and to facilitate greater employee autonomy and involvement. Such approaches reflected more Theory Y assumptions in relation to employee motivation: workers are seen as willing and able to undertake challenging tasks and can do so in a self-directed manner (McGregor 1960). We now consider these approaches.

THE 'NEW' MODEL: MAKING JOBS MORE INTERESTING

While traditional approaches to work organisation and job design focused on breaking jobs down to improve efficiencies, many of the job redesign initiatives have sought to reconstitute job tasks to larger, 'whole' jobs. This alternative approach was based on the belief that employees gain most satisfaction from the work itself. Two particular themes characterise much of the work on job redesign, namely employee participation and job enrichment.

Let us first consider employee participation. We have already seen that scientific management approaches emphasised the separation of work planning from doing. Planning was seen as a managerial task, while doing was the job of the ordinary worker, whose role was tightly circumscribed to allow little or no scope for employee discretion. Thus, employee participation was not an issue once the 'one best way' of doing jobs was identified. Their role was to follow, not lead. In contrast, several proponents of job redesign identify increased employee participation as a key component of their approach (for example, see McGregor 1960; Beer *et al.* 1984, 1985). Their rationale is based on the premise that employees can be motivated by job content and desire involvement in decisions on their jobs and work systems: ' ... employees who are involved in decisions about their immediate work will take responsibility for reducing costs and improving quality in the same way managers are presumed to be able and want to do' (Beer *et al.* 1985: 575).

Increasing employee participation in job-related decisions is a key dimension of many job redesign initiatives, particularly those based on job enrichment (discussed below). This type of employee participation differs in extent and orientation from employee participation in higher-level, e.g. corporate, decision making. This latter form of employee participation is often the subject of industrial relations interactions and may be institutionalised through legislation or collective bargaining arrangements.

'Job enrichment' is a term that pervades the organisation behaviour literature. It is concerned with designing jobs in such a way as to provide 'job doers' with the opportunity to gain intrinsic satisfaction from their work. 'Job enrichment is the practice of building motivating factors into job content. This job design strategy ... seeks to expand job content by adding some of the planning and evaluating duties normally performed by the manager' (Schermerhorn *et al.* 1985: 209).

Job enrichment is seen as more comprehensive than other job redesign initiatives, such as job enlargement or job rotation. Job enlargement entails increasing job variety by combining more than one job task so that workers undertake more and different tasks than previously (Schermerhorn *et al.* 1985). Job rotation adopts a similar approach: workers move periodically between different jobs and thus experience a broader range of job tasks. A criticism of both job enlargement and job rotation approaches is that they only address task variety rather than level. Workers are exposed to a greater range of tasks, but the tasks themselves are of a similar level and require similar skills. Such initiatives are therefore seen as limited in their capacity to provide greater intrinsic satisfaction, as workers may simply find themselves undertaking more boring tasks than previously. Job enrichment is seen as avoiding this pitfall by increasing job level and challenge to provide greater opportunity for psychological growth (Gunnigle *et al.* 1997).

REDESIGNING JOBS THROUGH JOB ENRICHMENT

The work of Herzberg (1968) provides the basis for job redesign initiatives based on job enrichment, considered earlier in Chapter 6. Herzberg's dual factor theory identifies two key sets of factors which impact on employee motivation: 'hygiene' (or maintenance) factors are those associated with job context, such as pay, benefits and working conditions; 'motivator' factors, which are more concerned with job content, include issues such as responsibility, achievement and personal growth.

The essence of Herzberg's argument is that hygiene factors in and of themselves are not an adequate source of employee motivation, although they are highly important as a means of reducing dissatisfaction. When this is done, it is the motivator factors that stimulate employee motivation. The job enrichment approach is therefore based on the premise that employees gain most satisfaction from the work itself and that it is the intrinsic outcomes arising from doing meaningful and challenging work that motivates workers to perform well in their jobs. Given this premise, the challenge for organisations is to develop jobs which increase the capacity for intrinsic satisfaction, challenge and employee involvement. To this end Herzberg established the concept of 'vertical loading', the characteristics of which are outlined in Table 11.2.

Table 11.2 Increasing Job Challenge through 'Vertical Loading'

Principle	Motivators Involved
A. Removing some controls while retaining accountability.	Responsibility and personal achievement.
B. Increasing the accountability of people for their own work.	Responsibility and recognition.
C. Giving a person a complete natural unit of work (module, division, area, etc.).	Responsibility, achievement and recognition.
D. Granting additional authority to an employee in their activity: job freedom.	Responsibility, achievement and recognition.
E. Making periodic reports directly available to the worker rather than to the supervisor.	Internal recognition.
F. Introducing new and more difficult tasks than previously handled.	Growth and learning.
G. Assigning people specific or specialised tasks, enabling them to become experts.	Responsibility, growth and advancement.

Source: Herzberg (1968)

Probably the most comprehensive model of work redesign based on increasing job satisfaction and employee motivation is what has been termed the 'diagnostic approach to job enrichment'. This theory was initially developed by Hackman and Lawler in the early 1970s (Hackman and Lawler 1971) and was tested on a sample of telephone company workers. These tests provided favourable results and this work was refined by Hackman and his colleagues throughout the 1970s (see Hackman and Oldham 1980). This model is summarised in Table 11.3 and comprises four main components:

1. **Critical psychological states:** The key job conditions necessary to promote higher levels of employee satisfaction and motivation.
2. **Core job characteristics:** The key characteristics which need to be built into jobs to allow workers to achieve these critical psychological states.
3. **Implementation strategies:** The steps needed to ensure jobs are designed to incorporate the core job characteristics required to adequately enrich jobs.
4. **Personal and work outcomes:** The benefits of such work redesign initiatives for both individual workers and for the organisation.

Figure 11.2 Work Redesign: The Job Characteristics Model and Employee Motivation

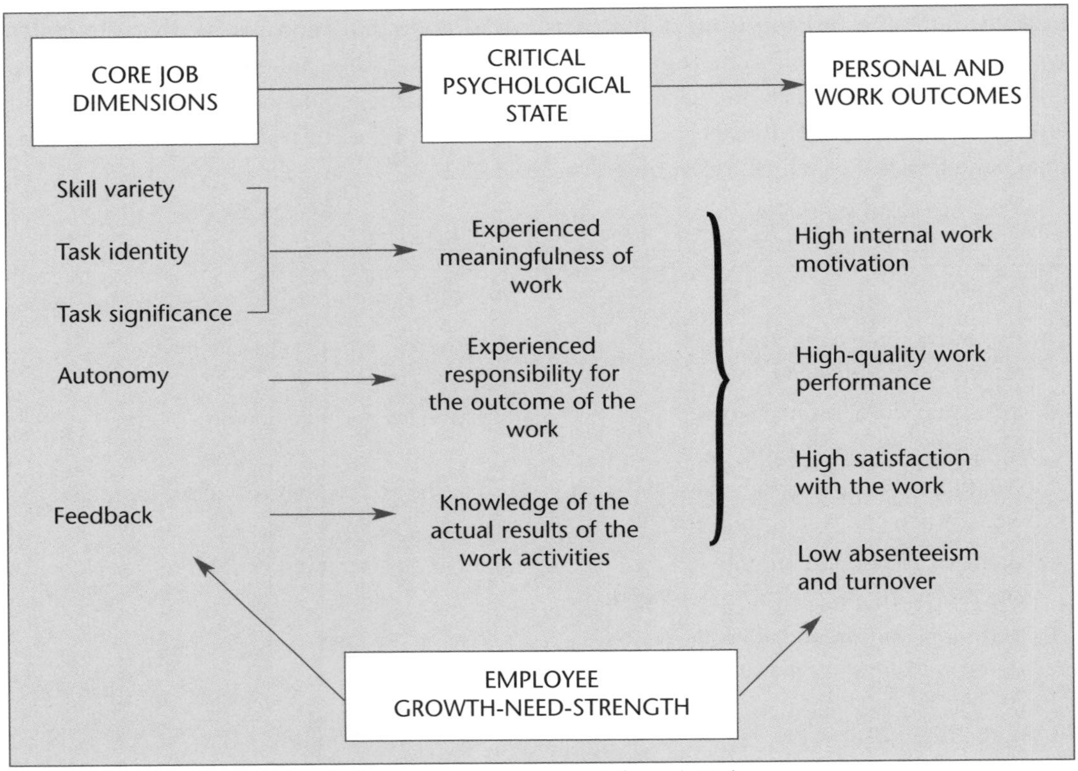

Source: Hackman and Oldham (1980)

At the core of Hackman and Oldham's approach (1980) is the need to design jobs to provide high levels of intrinsic rewards and satisfaction for workers. To this end, three basic conditions (the critical psychological states) were identified as necessary:
1. Work should be meaningful for the 'doer'.
2. 'Doers' should have responsibility for the results.
3. 'Doers' should get feedback on the results.

This approach suggests that it is the design of work and not the characteristics of the employee which have the greatest impact on employee motivation. Hackman and Oldham identify five 'core job characteristics' which need to be incorporated into job design to increase meaningfulness, responsibility and feedback.
1. **Skill variety:** Extent to which jobs draw on a range of different skills and abilities.
2. **Task identity:** Extent to which a job requires completion of a whole, identifiable piece of work.
3. **Task significance:** Extent to which a job substantially impacts on the work or lives of others, either within or outside the organisation.
4. **Autonomy:** Freedom, independence and discretion afforded to the job holder.

5. **Feedback:** Degree to which the job holder receives information on their level of performance, effectiveness, etc.

Having identified the factors necessary to promote satisfaction and intrinsic motivation, the next stage is to incorporate these characteristics into jobs through various job redesign strategies. Hackman and Oldham identify five implementation strategies to increase task variety, significance, identity and to create opportunities for greater autonomy and feedback.

1. **Form natural work groups:** Arrange tasks together to form an identifiable, meaningful cycle of work for employees, e.g. responsibility for a single product rather than small components.
2. **Combine tasks:** Group tasks together to form complete jobs.
3. **Establish client relationships:** Establish personal contact between employees and the end user/client.
4. **Vertically load jobs:** Many traditional approaches to job design separate planning and controlling (management functions) from executing (employees' function). Vertically loading jobs means integrating the planning, controlling and executing functions and giving greater responsibility to employees, e.g. responsibility for materials, quality, deadlines and budgetary control.
5. **Open feedback/communication channels:** Ensure maximum communication of job results, e.g. service standards, faults, wastage, market performance, costs.

The espoused advantages of redesigning jobs along the lines of Hackman and Oldham's job enrichment model are summarised thus:

> By redesigning jobs to increase variety, identity, significance, autonomy and feedback, the psychological experience of working is changed ... individuals experience the work as more meaningful, they feel more responsible for the results, and they know more about the results of their efforts. These psychological changes lead to many improved work outcomes which have been observed following the redesign of work ... (Beer *et al.* 1985: 576–7).

Hackman and Oldham thus argue that these changes have positive long-term benefits for both the organisation and the individual employee, such as increased motivation and improved performance. However, their theory also posits that not all workers are expected to respond favourably to job enrichment initiatives (Hackman *et al.* 1975). Employee 'growth-need-strength' is considered the most important source of variation in this respect: only those workers with a strong desire for achievement, responsibility and autonomy will be motivated by increased intrinsic satisfaction and hence motivated to perform better. For other workers, these changes may be a source of anxiety and lead to resentment and opposition to job redesign and other changes in the work system.

This 'diagnostic approach' to job enrichment has been tested in a variety of work contexts, such as banking, medicine and telecommunications. Schermerhorn *et al.* (1985:

213) suggest that while the results have been promising, further research is necessary to refine and support the concept:

> At the moment, researchers generally feel that job enrichment is not a universal panacea for job performance and satisfaction problems. They also recognize that job enrichment can fail when job requirements are increased beyond the level of individual capabilities and/or interests.

Figure 11.3 Growth Needs and Worker Responses to Job Enrichment

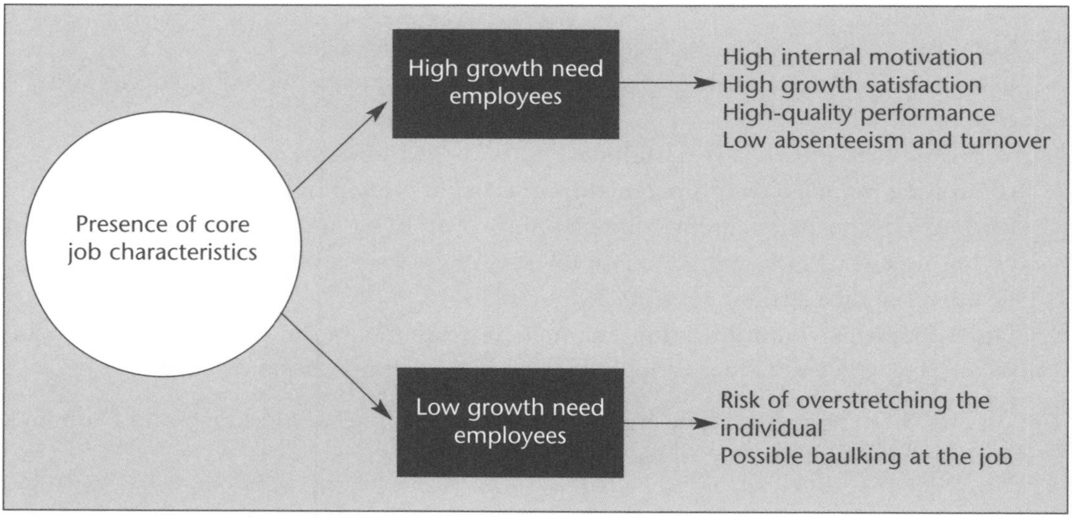

Source: Hackman (1975: 60)

IMPROVING THE QUALITY OF WORKING LIFE

While job enrichment clearly has the potential to positively impact on how employees experience work, its essential focus on job content has limitations. Numerous factors beyond the particular job and tasks undertaken impact on how employees experience work and working life, including issues such as working conditions, employee involvement and autonomy, work intensity and the nature of supervision. The 'quality of working life' (QWL) approach has its origins in developments in the US during the 1960s and 1970s (for example, see Walton 1973; Skrovan 1983). The QWL concept addresses the overall quality of employee experiences in the workplace. While embracing job design as a critical influence on the quality of working life, this approach also addresses broader issues, such as employee empowerment, autonomy, participation, justice, working conditions and job security. A particular stimulus for the QWL approach was a desire to improve the quality of work life for employees and avoid what were seen as characteristics of a low quality of working life. Table 11.3 summarises some of the main characteristics of low- and high-quality work life as identified in the extant literature (for example, see Schermerhorn *et al.* 1985; Steers and Porter 1987; Schuler and Jackson 1996).

Table 11.3 Indicative Characteristics of High- and Low-Quality Working Life

Low Quality of Working Life	High Quality of Working Life
• Jobs characterised by low levels of task significance, variety, identity and feedback.	• Adequate and fair reward systems.
• No or little employee involvement.	• Safe and healthy working conditions.
• Top-down communication.	• Opportunity to use personal capabilities.
• Inequitable reward systems.	• Opportunity for personal growth and development.
• Inadequate job definition.	• Integration into the organisation's social system.
• Poor employment conditions/hire-and-fire approach.	• High labour standards/employee rights.
• Discriminatory HR policies.	• Pride in relevance and value of work.
• Low job security.	• Balance between work and non-work roles.

A particular concern of QWL approaches was the desire to increase employee influence and involvement in work organisation and job design. Again, this challenges some traditional management assumptions about employees. It involves recognising that employees can and want to make a positive input into organisational decision making. It assumes that such involvement is valued by employees and results in increased commitment, responsibility and performance. Increased employee influence in work system design also addresses the issue of employee supervision as an aspect of the management role. If employees are to be involved in making decisions about the organisation of work and responsible for the subsequent execution of such decisions, much of the 'control' aspect is removed from the supervisory role. It therefore necessitates a change in attitude to workforce management – supervisors become less concerned with monitoring and controlling employee performance and more involved in advising and facilitating employees in carrying out their jobs.

This approach requires high levels of commitment and trust from both management and employees. Management must feel confident that employees have the required competence and will use their greater levels of influence positively and to the organisation's benefit. Employees must be happy that their increased commitment and sense of responsibility will not be abused or exploited by employers.

There are various mechanisms available to encourage increased levels of employee participation in the design and operation of work systems. Possibly the best-known approach is quality circles, which are small groups of employees and managers who meet together regularly to consider means of improving quality, productivity or other aspects of work organisation. They are seen as having played an important role in the success of Japanese organisations and have been successfully applied in Western economies, including Ireland.

There are numerous other participative and consultative mechanisms that may be established and can work effectively in an appropriate organisational environment, the creation of which has become an important concern for organisations. Past experiences in applying various techniques to improve employee motivation and involvement have demonstrated that these operate best where there is a change in the overall corporate approach. The issue for senior management is how to create a corporate culture whose values, beliefs and practices establish an organisational environment within which employees are highly committed to and work towards the achievement of business goals.

THE TREND TOWARDS HIGH-PERFORMANCE WORK SYSTEMS

The period since the late 1970s has witnessed dramatic advances in the area of technology, particularly information technology. Many of these advances, in both hardware and software, dramatically impact on work systems and employees' work experience. Many aspects of these developments also impact directly on our daily work routines: word processing, electronic mail, computerised procurement and stock control and online data access are just some of these developments.

More recent analyses of work organisation under such new technologies question the viability of pre-existing theories, such as those associated with task specialisation, job enrichment and improving the quality of working life. For example, Buchanan and McCalman (1989) point to the limited impact of job redesign theories and argue that this needs to be remedied:

> [Job design] has tended to be regarded as an isolated management technique aimed at local organisational problems and at individual jobs rather than realising that it must form part of the whole company philosophy, through all levels, if it is to be really successful.

More specifically, Maccoby (1988) criticises the partial nature of job redesign theories and suggests that they provide little insight into how workers can become more involved in 'the management of the business and work independently' (Maccoby 1988: 29; see also Huczynski and Buchanan 1991). Maccoby points to the significant impact of recent technological developments in altering requisite job skills – increasingly, many jobs demand skills such as data processing and retrieval and increased diagnostic/analytical/problem-solving abilities. In turn, these changing job demands impact on the training and education requirements in the workforce, often demanding increased levels of education. Maccoby also points to the impact of technology in changing the 'traditional' relationship between management and workers, embracing the potential to increase employee autonomy and team working, and also providing opportunities for greater worker interaction with suppliers and customers.

Others point to the impact of heightened competitive pressures in encouraging organisations to continuously improve performance on criteria such as responsiveness, quality and cost (Kochan *et al.* 1986; Buchanan 1994; Roche and Gunnigle 1995). Currently, a significant source of debate in relation to the nature of work systems and jobs is the increasingly competitive aspect of product and service markets. One can point to a number of reasons for this increase in competitive pressures, such as greater trade liberalisation, deregulation in capital, product and service markets, improved communications and transport infrastructures and greater market penetration by organisations from Asia (see Roche and Gunnigle 1995).

An important aspect of increased competitiveness is the pressure on organisations to increase speed to market, improve quality and cut costs. Indeed, the period since the 1980s seems to have witnessed some regression in the quality of work life, as workers are expected to undertake increased workloads and experience an intensification in the pace of work (for example, see Delbridge and Turnbull 1992; Sewell and Wilkinson 1992). These developments have particularly significant implications for Ireland as a result of its status as a small, open economy that is highly export oriented and reliant on mobile foreign investment. As a consequence, developments in the world economy have particularly significant implications for Irish organisations, requiring greater responsiveness to competitive pressures in an effort to maintain market share, while at the macro level efforts are focused on ensuring the business climate remains attractive to foreign investors.

Improved human resource utilisation through work systems design is often viewed as an important source of enhanced organisation performance. Of particular significance is the concept of 'high-performance work systems', which are viewed as notably different from preceding innovations in work organisation.

The concept of high-performance work systems is very much associated with the new 'high-tech' companies of the 1980s, especially those which located at greenfield sites in attempts to establish a fundamentally different type of organisation and organisation culture (see Lawler 1978, 1982; Buchanan and McCalman 1989). The essence of high-performance systems appears to lie in the adoption of a culture of continuous improvement and innovation at all levels in the organisation and the implementation of a range of work organisation and human resource systems to sustain and develop this culture, particularly team working, quality consciousness, employee autonomy and flexibility. They are also felt to reflect an increased management emphasis on developing broadly defined, challenging jobs within more organic, flexible organisation structures:

> The high performance work organisation has a distinctive structure which is designed to provide employees with skills, incentives, information and decision-making responsibilities that will lead to improved organisational performance and facilitate innovation … The main aim is to generate high levels of commitment and involvement of employees and managers … (Tiernan *et al.* 1996: 113).

High-performance work systems are thus seen as embracing much more than a change in the nature of jobs. Rather, they appear to welcome fundamentally different assumptions about organisational structure and orientation, so that all aspects of organisational management are altered to include a 'new' culture designed to improve performance and responsiveness through developing a more committed, flexible and skilled workforce. This interpretation is reflected in Buchanan's (1994: 101) conception of high-performance work systems:

> The term 'high performance' is used ... to refer to systemic, integrated developments in the application of autonomous group working, with multiple and related implications beyond the confines of the original technique, invading the domain of supervisory and management structures, and affecting also training and payment systems as well as other aspects of organizational design and working conditions.

As noted earlier, the primary motive behind the emergence of high-performance systems appears to lie in the pressures on organisations to improve their overall competitive position. This may explain its prevalence in high-tech sectors, especially electronics and software, which tend to be characterised by high levels of market volatility and product innovation. In relating the experience of Digital Equipment Corporation (possibly the most prominent early exemplar of high-performance work systems), Perry (1984: 191) notes how the company's Connecticut (Enfield) plant sought to respond to increased competition and product change:

> The goal at Enfield was flexibility: the capacity to respond quickly and effectively to an uncertain environment. Traditional ways to handle uncertainty had included the introduction of new procedures, changing the structure, employing more people, and tightening management controls. These strategies simply increased overheads, increased the complexity of the organization and generated more uncertainty. To deal with these issues, management decided to introduce a more participative style of decision-making, multi-skilled operating teams, an innovative rewards system, and systematic career planning and development. The plant manager's review of these changes revealed a 40 per cent reduction in product manufacturing time, a sharp increase in inventory turnover, a reduction of levels of management hierarchy to three, a 38 per cent reduction in standard costs, a 40 per cent reduction in overheads, and equivalent output with half the people and half the space (Buchanan 1994: 102; summary of more detailed review by Perry 1984).

High-performance work systems are also intimately linked to external standards – the idea that organisational performance should be disaggregated and compared to valid external standards such as cycle time, rework, labour costs and productivity (Vaill 1982). The external comparators may be other similar companies or simply other plants within the organisation's portfolio. The growth of total quality management, particularly quality accreditation schemes, has been an important catalyst in this regard. For example, companies that trade internationally often seek to achieve ISO 9000, which is a worldwide standard, while in Ireland the Quality Mark Scheme, introduced in 1982, is an increasingly important goal. In Ireland the diffusion of a quality orientation is reflected in the fact that by the end of 1993 over 1,000 organisations had been approved to ISO 9000 standard, and this number is increasing annually.

The use of external standards is seen as an important factor in differentiating high-performance work systems from quality of work life (QWL) and job enrichment approaches. The source of difference lies in the suggestion that QWL and job enrichment approaches stemmed from internal stimuli, primarily related to costs of negative employee behaviours such as absenteeism, turnover and boredom (see Buchanan 1994). As noted above, the stimulus for high-performance work systems related to external pressures to improve competitiveness on dimensions such as lower costs, better quality and greater flexibility. As such, Buchanan (1994) argues that the development of such systems is more strategic than operational, reflecting in particular managerial desires to improve competitiveness and customer service. Consequently, it is felt that the stimulus for the development of high-performance work systems is more enduring than those underpinning previous work redesign initiatives, and thus more likely to achieve greater practical diffusion and implementation.

KEY HUMAN RESOURCE DIMENSIONS OF HIGH-PERFORMANCE WORK SYSTEMS

It is clear from our preceding discussion on high-performance work systems that a critical focus of these systems entails the development of new or different approaches to the management of employees as well as in the structure of jobs and systems. In this way human resource policy governs work design in a corporate setting (Brewer 2000). These themes pervade both what is termed the 'high-performance' literature (Vaill 1982; Perry 1984; Lawler 1986; Buchanan and McCalman 1989) and, indeed, the 'excellence' literature (Peters and Waterman 1982; Moss Kanter 1983; Quinn Mills 1991). Almost all contributors highlight the need to empower employees in an attempt to make the organisation more effective. While commentators may differ on detail, there is overwhelming support for the use of group- or team-based work systems as a means of developing a highly skilled, flexible and motivated workforce within a leaner, flatter, more responsive organisation structure. This section seeks to identify some of the principal human resource dimensions that appear to characterise high-performance work systems.

Some of the most important early work on high-performance work systems was undertaken by Lawler in the US (Lawler 1978, 1982, 1986). He paid particular attention to newly designed plants that opened on greenfield sites and which were viewed as a new departure in terms of work systems and management style. Lawler sets out a list of organisational design features that he suggests significantly increase employee involvement in the workplace and help to improve organisational performance. While Lawler (1982) feels that this list is an ideal and not characteristic of any particular organisation, he argues that it most closely approximates to the configuration of employment practices adopted by companies which located at (or sometimes relocated to) greenfield sites in the US during the late 1970s and early 1980s. Lawler argues that such new plants were particularly likely to embody high-employee-involvement work systems and employment practices comprising mutually reinforcing arrangements and practices such as autonomous work groups, quality circles and gain-sharing plans (Lawler 1978, 1982, 1986). He describes the all-prevailing nature of changes in work systems and human resource practices in these new plants as follows: ' ... almost no aspect of the organisation has been left untouched. The reward systems, the structure, the physical layout, the personnel management system and the nature of jobs have all been changed and in significant ways' (Lawler 1978: 6–7).

Table 11.4 Organisational Characteristics of High-Performance, High-Involvement Work Systems

Organisational structure	Flat and lean. Enterprise oriented. Team based. Participative structure: councils, fora.
Job design	Job enrichment. Autonomous teams/work groups.
Information system	Open flow. Work/job focus. Decentralised and team/group based. Participatively established goals/standards.
Career system	Career tracks/ladders/counselling. Open job posting.
Selection	'Realistic' job preview. Team/group based. Potential- and process-skill oriented.
Training	Strong commitment and investment. Peer training. 'Economic' education. Interpersonal skills.
Reward system	Open. Skill based. Gain sharing/share ownership. Flexible benefits. All salary/egalitarian.
Personnel policies	Employment tenure commitments. Participatively established through representative group(s).
Physical layout	Based on organisational structure. Egalitarian. Safe and pleasant.

Source: Adapted from Lawler (1982)

Lawler thus argues that increased employee involvement levels and enhanced organisational performance outcomes are most likely to occur in these new plants because of their capacity to establish a totally 'congruent system' at the outset and to reinforce this desired approach through the selection of people who are 'compatible' with the new system. In the British context, a study of work practices (Income Data Services 1984) in four greenfield establishments also found evidence of innovation in work practices and identified six common features of greenfield sites:

1. Reduced number of management tiers.
2. Abolition of the roles of traditional supervisors and enhanced status of first-line managers.
3. Minimisation of status differentials between employee grades.
4. Greater devolution of responsibility for execution of work/tasks to employee groups.
5. Greater dissemination of information on work-related matters.
6. Greater emphasis on direct communication with employees through group meetings rather than trade unions.

Beaumont and Townley (1985) suggest that the key managerial concern in establishing at a greenfield site is related to the objective of introducing new methods of work organisation or new work practices, and argue that the essential attribute or component of the term 'greenfield site' is innovative work practices and arrangements. They suggest that such characteristics of greenfield sites reflect a management emphasis that is predominantly concerned with the achievement and maintenance of maximum flexibility in operations.

In evaluating the impact of high-performance work systems, it is useful to reflect on the extent to which this development represents a fundamentally new approach to the design of jobs and work systems. Huczynski and Buchanan (1991: 86) address this issue and identify the following distinctions between the high-performance work systems (HPWS) approach of the 1990s and the quality of work life (QWL) approach of the 1960s and 1970s.

- **More strategic focus:** It is argued that the HPWS approach seeks to improve organisational competitiveness through increased flexibility and quality, while the QWL approach primarily concentrates on achieving reductions in absenteeism and turnover.

- **Focus on performance rather than job experience:** The HPWS approach has a strong focus on performance criteria – increased employee autonomy is seen as leading to increased employee competence/skills, better decision making, greater flexibility/adaptability and better use of technology. In contrast, the major rationale of the QWL approach is based on improving employees' job experience – increased autonomy is seen as leading to increased worker satisfaction and a better job experience.

- **Major change in management style:** The HPWS approach is seen as requiring a fundamental overhaul of management style, necessitating major cultural change and redefinition of management's role, from top management down. The QWL approach appears to adopt a more limited approach, involving only a reorientation in the role of first-line supervisors.

- **Long-term comprehensive strategy:** The HPWS approach is seen as a major change initiative affecting the whole organisation and involving a long-term commitment by all parties. The QWL approach tends to be more of a quick fix applied to isolated and problematic work groups.
- **Representative of strategic human resource management:** Consistent with the argument that the 1980s and 1990s witnessed a move from reactive/operational personnel management to strategic human resource management (HRM), it is argued that HPWS is a key element of strategic HRM, while QWL is more of a personnel administration technique.

In essence it appears that while the high-performance concept has its roots in the individualistic and group approaches to job restructuring of previous decades, there is a shift in orientation away from job enlargement, job enrichment and quality circles towards a more all-inclusive approach, linking individual contributions, group performance and competitive advantage, which, according to Buchanan and McCalman (1989), affords a new acceptability to these traditional strategies. It also appears that high-performance work systems reflect a strategic shift in approaches to workforce management and may serve to encourage a wider understanding of the applications of traditional job restructuring techniques, variations of which have enjoyed a renaissance in recent times.

In Ireland, the first prominent examples of organisations that sought to develop high-performance work systems along the lines described above came from the ranks of firms which had experimented with such systems elsewhere. These were mostly US 'high-tech' companies such as Digital, Apple and Amdahl. More recently we have seen greater diversity in the range of companies undertaking such initiatives. One of the mostly widely quoted examples is that of Bord na Móna (see Magee 1991; O'Connor 1995). Here we find a semi-state company which by the 1980s faced severe competitive problems, particularly in relation to high costs, poor productivity and a pressing need to improve quality, performance and employee relations (Magee 1991). In an attempt to deal with these issues, the company undertook a number of radical initiatives. First, a new multidisciplinary and team-based management structure was established. The initial challenge was to reduce costs, which was addressed by a major redundancy programme that saw 2,500 workers (out of approximately 5,000) leave the company. After this, management initiated a more fundamental overhaul:

> It was recognised by everyone concerned … that cost-cutting through redundancy would not be enough. We had to change our work practices at the same time. We knew that a fundamental restructuring of how we did our business had to be undertaken to create flexibility in adapting to changing markets, to improve productivity and to improve our competitive position. After extensive negotiation, the 'enterprise scheme' was introduced with the full agreement and co-operation of all parties. The Bord na Móna enterprise scheme allows our staff to form their own autonomous enterprise units, which are team based and where the unit's earnings are directly related to performance and productivity. Our workers have become their own bosses (O'Connor 1995: 116).

The introduction of autonomous work groups (AWGs) meant that instead of working in isolation, the workers became team members. Leaders were selected for these AWGs, which then assumed responsibility and authority for the completion of tasks (Tiernan *et al.* 1996). In addition to the establishment of AWGs, Bord na Móna also reduced the number of levels in the management hierarchy. It seems that the results of these various changes have been extremely positive. Edward O'Connor, then managing director of the company, summed up the experience as follows:

> The spirit of enterprise this has brought into Bord na Móna has increased productivity per worker in a way that is truly amazing. Our productivity has increased by 75 per cent. Our people now make their own decisions and take their own risks. The series of work groups or enterprise units that have been set up have different structures, but essentially Bord na Móna supplies them with services and they produce quality peat, at a price which is agreed in advance. These are people who, formerly, did what they were told to do, got paid whether or not peat was produced, whether the sun shone all summer or whether it rained all the time … The new work practices and systems we have introduced amount to nothing less than a fundamental restructuring of the organisation (O'Connor 1995: 117).

HIGH-PERFORMANCE WORK SYSTEMS AND WORKING LIFE

While much of the organisation behaviour literature on high-performance work systems inevitably emphasises its human resource dimensions, it is important to note that these approaches also incorporate technical changes in the work process. In this respect two critical techniques that are commonly used are 'just-in-time' and statistical process control. Just-in-time (JIT) approaches focus on reducing waste, with particular emphasis on eliminating inventories (of materials, work in progress and finished goods). Statistical process control (SPC) approaches seek to apply rigorous statistical analysis of quality and performance levels to improve performance.

In evaluating the impact of high-performance work systems that incorporate JIT and SPC, an issue of particular significance is their impact on employees' work experience. This involves the coupling of initiatives to improve worker participation and autonomy, with particular management techniques designed to improve quality and productivity, especially just-in-time manufacturing systems and statistical process control. The combination of JIT and SPC approaches with initiatives to increased employee involvement and autonomy are often seen as the essence of moves towards total quality management or world-class manufacturing (see Gunnigle *et al.* 1995). The introduction of these initiatives is generally based on the premise that increase employee involvement/autonomy is consistent with the use of JIT, SPC or related techniques. Indeed, the argument that employee involvement/autonomy mutually complements the use of SPC and JIT is often a key selling point in encouraging employees to co-operate in the introduction of such approaches.

However, it should be pointed out that this is not necessarily the case (see the discussion below on the automobile industry). In her incisive review of the implications of techniques such as JIT and SPC for employees and their work experience, Klein (1989: 60) argues that such changes in production systems do not necessarily make for a more empowered workforce:

> In Japan ... where JIT and SPC have been used most comprehensively, employees are routinely organized into teams, but their involvement in workplace reform is typically restricted to suggestions for process improvement through structured quality control circles or *kaizen* groups. Individual Japanese workers have unprecedented responsibility. Yet it is hard to think of them exercising genuine autonomy, that is, in the sense of independent self-management.
>
> To be sure, managers can – and must – involve workers in workplace decisions. But the attack on waste, it must be understood, inevitably means more and more strictures on a worker's time and action. Our conventional Western notions of worker self-management on the factory floor are often sadly incompatible with the schedules, nature of supervision and reward systems. A particular and increasingly important influence is the role of technology. Indeed it is almost clichéd to speak of the accelerating rate of technological change and its impact in changing the way work is carried out.

Using examples from both the US and Japan, Klein (1989) argues that increased pressures and constraints on workers are common by-products of such manufacturing reforms. While allowing for greater employee involvement and autonomy than traditional assembly line systems, they are not conducive to the high levels of employee empowerment often thought to accompany such manufacturing reform and the move to high-performance work systems:

> True, under JIT and SPC, employees become more self-managing than in a command-and-control factory. They investigate process improvements and monitor quality themselves; they consequently enjoy immediate, impartial feedback regarding their own performance ... They also gain a better understanding of all elements of the manufacturing process.
>
> On the other hand, the reform process that ushers in JIT and SPC is meant to eliminate all variations within production and therefore requires strict adherence to rigid methods and procedures. Within JIT, workers must meet set cycle times; with SPC, they must follow prescribed problem-solving methods. In their pure forms, then, JIT and SPC can turn workers into extensions of a system no less demanding than a busy assembly line. They can push workers to the wall (Klein 1989: 61).

This analysis thus questions many aspects of the thesis that high-performance work systems necessarily contribute to an improved work experience. In particular, Klein (1989) points to important aspects of the work experience which may be lost as a result of recent manufacturing reforms using SPC and JIT, namely:

1. **Individual autonomy:** May be reduced due to the elimination of inventories under JIT, resulting in less slack or idle time, which in turn lessens the opportunity for workers to discuss issues, evaluate changes and make suggestions.
2. **Team autonomy:** May be reduced because of the greater interdependency between groups, due to the absence of buffer inventories with resulting work pressures reducing the time available to consider broader changes in the work process or system.
3. **Ability to influence work methods:** May be reduced because SPC sets strict guidelines for working methods and procedures.

However, this analysis does not necessarily mean that the adoption of high-performance work systems that adopt techniques such as JIT and SPC do not positively impact on the job experience of workers. Rather, it points to the fact that these techniques and systems may be applied in differing ways. Thus, the issue of management choice is important. Klein (1989) argues that the key to improving employee involvement and autonomy while instigating high-performance work systems is to provide for greater collaboration between teams and to allow greater opportunity for teams and individuals to propose and evaluate suggestions for changes in the work process and in the conduct of different jobs. Klein offers other suggestions to mitigate some of the more unfavourable effects of JIT and SPC:

- **Rethink zero inventory:** It is argued that the maintenance of some inventory is more sensible for a number of reasons, such as reduced employee stress, increased individual and team involvement, better quality of work life and as an insurance against system breakdown.
- **Emphasise work flow rather than pace:** Here Klein suggests that while JIT reduces worker ability to control work pace, the adoption of a *kanban* system will help improve individual initiative and individual and team communications by allowing workers to answer to each other rather than to the output of the system or to supervisors.
- **Focus on task design, not execution:** Based on the argument that task design allows greater opportunity for team involvement (once designed, there may be little capacity for changes to the mode of operation).
- **Give workers the right to move and choose (within limits):** Allow greater autonomy to workers to move between tasks and to teams in making decisions on issues such as interchangeability and working time (including breaks).
- **Allow for workplace management of quality and resources:** Give teams greater discretion (within budget) in making decisions on resource procurement and allocation, personnel selection and training, use of support services, rejection of defective materials and capacity to stop output of poor-quality goods.

A final and critical issue for organisations considering the adoption of high-performance work systems is the issue of employee expectations. It is important to avoid the common pitfall of promising more than can be delivered in terms of employee involvement and autonomy, which can quickly lead to widespread disillusionment among employees. One approach Klein (1989) suggests is to introduce SPC or JIT approaches before worker participation programmes. It's felt that this may remove confusion and reduce the likelihood of unrealised worker expectations:

If, for example, worker participation programs are implemented after JIT, there will be less confusion: workers will then not be invited to imagine greater freedom just when the new process takes freedom away. Even if some workers participate in the design of the system, this doesn't necessarily mean the plant will be operated by worker teams from the start. Besides, it is the task of managers, as always, to prepare the ground. They ought not to promise workers autonomy when they mean them to deliver an unprecedented degree of co-operation (Klein 1989: 66).

ONGOING DEBATES/ADVANCED CONCEPTS IN WORK SYSTEMS AND TECHNOLOGY

So far in this chapter we have considered different approaches to the design of jobs and work systems, notably those associated with scientific management, job enrichment, quality of work life and high-performance work systems. In so doing we have noted the impact of technological changes in critically impacting on work systems and job content. However, our perspective has primarily focused on microlevel developments at the level of the enterprise. It is therefore useful to conclude our analysis with a broader macrolevel analysis that considers developments in the technological environment and their impact on work systems. In so doing, particular emphasis is placed on contemporary developments, particularly the growth of 'lean production' techniques and quality improvement.

FORDISM: THE ZENITH OF MASS PRODUCTION

We have seen earlier in this chapter how developments in technology heralded what is often termed the Industrial Revolution, beginning in late eighteenth century Britain. Heilbroner and Thurow (1984) point out that this phase actually entailed a series of 'technological revolutions' whereby the means of production of different items underwent fundamental change. The industries affected were, firstly, spinning and weaving (late 1700s to early 1800s), then rail, shipping, steel, agricultural machinery and chemicals (mid-1800s) and finally, automobiles, electricity and consumer durables (early 1900s).

The move towards mass production represented a fundamental change from earlier craft-based methods of production. No industry typified the growth of mass production better than automobiles, and the chief exponent of this approach was Henry Ford and the Ford motor company. It is suggested that the automobile industry was the mass production industry (Sweeney 1997). It was based predominantly on scientific management principles, producing a limited range of models in very large volumes, in massive assembly plants, using rigid production methods whereby workers performed a series of highly specialised repetitive tasks at high speed. In a study by Womack et al. (1990), the main characteristics of Fordism are set out as follows.

- The complete and consistent interchangeability of parts and the simplicity of attaching them to each other.
- The fragmentation of production with 'interchangeable' workers performing work cycles of one to two minutes.

- The extreme horizontal division of labour, both in production work and indirect functions such as preparation, quality control, maintenance and repair.
- The use of dedicated machinery that can only do one task at a time and which embodies skills formerly carried out by craft workers.
- The vertical integration of production, with parts and components being manufactured in-house, and the manufacture of standardised products with minimum variation.

This same study suggests that mass production in the US had reached its heyday by the mid-1950s – three corporations (Ford, General Motors and Chrysler) and six models accounted for the overwhelming majority of all car sales. The demise of Fordism appears to stem from two sources. First, the growth of greater diversity in consumer demand (and also in supply by European manufacturers) lessened the demand for 'standard' products. However, another reason for the demise of mass-produced automobiles was related to human resource considerations. Workers were becoming increasingly disillusioned with the jobs they were asked to carry out, which was often manifested in industrial conflict. These labour pressures led to increased pay levels and reduced working hours. However, discontent associated with auto assembly often continued (Womack *et al.* 1990; European Industrial Relations Review 1992). A good example was the UK, where motor company strikes were an important characteristic of industrial relations during the 1960s and 1970s.

LEAN PRODUCTION AND THE IMPACT OF TOYOTISM

In 1990 researchers at the Massachusetts Institute of Technology (MIT) published the results of one of the largest studies undertaken in the automobile or any other industry (Womack *et al.* 1990). The study looked at ninety assembly plants in seventeen countries and concluded that the industrial world is experiencing the most revolutionary change since the growth of mass production, as Japanese-inspired 'lean production techniques begin to replace conventional means of mass production' (European Industrial Relations Review 1992: 13).

The focus on Japanese 'advantage' in the auto sector began in the 1960s and was largely attributed to lower labour costs, which gave a low-cost advantage to Japanese cars. However, the significant impact of Japanese competitors in the auto industry has been their ability to develop and sustain cost and quality advantages over time, particularly in foreign plants in countries such as the US and UK. The fact that these Japanese plants are located in the same regions as European and US auto manufacturers has served to focus attention on Japanese production methods and work systems, such as just-in-time and *kaizen* (continuous improvement).

In their attempt to discern the source of Japanese advantage, the MIT study concluded that their success was primarily due to what they termed 'lean production'. This term was used to indicate that it involved using less of almost everything when compared to mass production: half the human effort, half the manufacturing space, half the investment in tools and half the engineering effort (Womack *et al.* 1990). Additional advantages noted in the study included the need to carry lower inventory (less than half of that associated with conventional mass production), a lower level of defects and greater product variety.

The development of lean production is attributed to Eiji Toyota. It is reported that after a visit to a Ford assembly plant in Detroit, Eiji concluded that the methods used were excessively wasteful and that none of the indirect workers added value to the product. Together with his chief engineer, Taiichi Ohno, they set about developing the system which became known as lean production. The MIT study identified the main characteristics of lean production, or Toyotism, as follows.

- Workers are organised into teams with a leader who, unlike the mass production foreman, undertakes assembly work and fills in for absent workers. Teams are given responsibility for the functions previously carried out by indirect workers, such as simple machine maintenance, quality control, materials ordering and clearing up the work area.
- There is a 'zero defect' approach to production involving an effective system for immediately detecting defects and problems and tracing them to their root cause to make sure they do not recur. As the process is perfected almost no 'rework' is necessary.
- 'Lean' product development techniques, involving strong design team leadership, personnel continuity of development teams and an emphasis on communications and 'simultaneous development', drastically reduce the time and effort involved in manufacturing.
- Production occurs in small batches in order to eliminate the costs of high inventories of finished parts required by mass production systems. Cars are built to specific order with the assistance of flexible machinery and parts are delivered on a just-in-time basis.
- There is an absence of vertical integration. Instead, production of parts and components is rationalised through a hierarchy of suppliers. Thus, 'first tier' suppliers are responsible for working as an integral part of the development team, while 'second tier' suppliers are responsible for making the components required for the first tier supplier.

LEAN PRODUCTION: A POSITIVE WORK EXPERIENCE?

In evaluating the job experience of workers under lean production, we find some divided opinions. The MIT study suggests that while lean production requires very high effort levels from workers, it represents a more positive work experience than conventional mass production. The essence of the MIT argument is that lean production contrasts the mind-numbing stress of mass production by providing workers with the skills to exercise greater control over their work environment. This, they argue, leads to 'creative tension' at work, which requires high effort levels but also gives workers numerous ways to deal with work problems and challenges (Womack *et al.* 1990; European Industrial Relations Review 1992). The MIT study also compares lean production to what they term the 'neocraftmanship' model associated with some Swedish assembly plants. Again, they find that lean production systems provide a more rewarding and challenging work experience than that found in plants such as Volvo's Uddevalla facility, which the MIT study categorises as a very limited form of job rotation. In the Irish context, Mooney (1988) argues that work systems modelled around lean production principles represent a jettisoning of traditional approaches towards a more positive perspective on employees as 'human assets'.

Not everyone agrees with this benign analysis of the work experience under lean production. Earlier in this chapter we quoted an assembly line worker in Toyota (Japan) who emphasised the high pace and repetitive nature of the work undertaken (Kamata 1984). Similarly, Delbridge and Turnbull (1992: 58), in investigating one of the cornerstones of lean production, namely just-in-time (JIT) manufacturing systems, suggest that such systems can negatively impact on employees' job experience:

> Evidence from both Britain and America suggests that the experience of work under a JIT system involves work intensification, very little autonomy for the individual, a more complete system of management control and a concomitant decline in trade union (and worker) bargaining power. Team working, job rotation and flexibility are not the means of releasing the untapped reserves of human resourcefulness by increasing employee commitment, participation and involvement ... Rather they are the tools of work intensification and heightened management control. The emphasis is almost exclusively on the management, or more precisely the maximization, of human resources, involving an instrumental approach which is coherently integrated into corporate business strategy ... this is not so much a question of choice as necessity, since the JIT system increases the dependency of management on the workforce by removing all elements of slack or waste in the system.

In a review based on the experiences of the Swedish automobile industry, Berggren (1990) questions the MIT argument that lean production is fundamentally different from mass production. This study compares Japanese lean production systems with Swedish 'whole car' manufacturing systems. Berggren argues that lean production essentially represents another stage in the evolution of mass production, since it entails many of the core characteristics of that system: predefined work processes, short job cycles, repetitive tasks and intense supervision. He also points to the strong demands that lean production places on workers in areas such as working time, flexibility, effort levels and attendance. Berggren concludes that the further one moves away from assembly line work systems, the greater the improvements in terms of workers' job experience (on dimensions such as job satisfaction, challenge, stress and employee involvement). Clearly, such 'whole job' systems are quite different from assembly line systems in their rejection of task fragmentation and job specialisation.

This latter argument in relation to whole job systems versus assembly systems brings us to a traditional dilemma in the area of job and work system design, namely that concerning cost and profits. We have earlier noted that the 1990s were characterised by increased competitive pressures on organisations, such as the need to concurrently reduce costs and improve quality and service, the need to reduce cycle times and speed to market and the need to be more responsive to market trends. All these pressures combine to encourage management to seek improvements in their internal operating systems on dimensions such as costs, speed, quality and flexibility. While these pressures may occasionally serve to improve workers' job experience in areas such as job content and employee involvement, it is probably more likely to lead to greater job pressures on workers. This is particularly the case in highly competitive sectors where labour costs represent a high proportion of total production costs. In Berggren's study of the automobile industry, he concedes that the long-term viability of the Swedish 'whole car' manufacturing system is dependent not on the quality of the job experience, but rather on the extent to which it can be reconciled with profitability. If lean production systems can provide cars at lower cost and equal or better quality, then 'whole car' systems cannot compete with assembly line systems.

SUMMARY OF KEY PROPOSITIONS

- An organisation's work system incorporates the way in which various tasks are organised and carried out. It encompasses both human and technical aspects and critically impacts on the nature of the work environment, job content and management style.
- From a worker perspective, a key dimension of the work system is the design of individual jobs, which determines issues such as job content, skill level, extent of autonomy and involvement and the role of supervision.
- The Industrial Revolution witnessed a change from craft-based production systems to larger-scale mass production systems through what became termed the factory system. This system was based on a division of labour based on task specialisation – jobs were broken down into small subtasks that were comparatively easy to learn.
- Taylor developed the concept of scientific management, which embraced a high division of labour. Scientific management emphasised the achievement of high levels of productive efficiency through the standardisation of work methods. It also emphasised the identification of the best way of doing jobs and then the careful selection, training and reward of workers who followed this 'one best way'.
- A critical characteristic of scientific management was the separation of work planning (a management task) from work doing (an employee task).
- While scientific management led to significant improvements in performance, it was also identified as a source of workforce problems, particularly high levels of labour turnover and absenteeism and low employee morale and motivation. These problems were felt to stem from the repetitive and monotonous nature of highly specialised jobs under scientific management.
- The negative effects associated with scientific management led researchers and practitioners to search for ways to make jobs more satisfying and challenging for workers. Such approaches were generally termed 'job redesign' and invariably embraced attempts to reconstitute different jobs tasks into larger 'whole' jobs.
- The most notable job redesign initiative was termed the 'diagnostic approach to job enrichment'. This model, developed by Hackman and Lawler (1971) and based on

Herzberg's work on employee motivation, was grounded on the premise that workers gain the most satisfaction from work itself. It was therefore the intrinsic outcomes that arise from undertaking meaningful and challenging jobs that were seen as motivating workers to perform well.

- Using this premise, the researchers Hackman and Oldham (1980) developed their widely influential 'job characteristics model', which had four main components: critical psychological states, i.e. the key job conditions necessary to promote higher levels of employee satisfaction and motivation; core job characteristics, which must be built into jobs to allow workers to achieve the 'critical psychological states'; implementation strategies necessary to ensure that jobs are designed to incorporate the 'core job characteristics'; and the personal and work outcomes felt to accrue to individual workers and to organisations as a result of undertaking such job redesign initiatives.

- Three fundamental principles underpin the job characteristics model, namely that work should be meaningful for employees, they should have responsibility for the results of their work and also get feedback on these results.

- A criticism of the job characteristics model was its predominant focus on job content. Many commentators argued that broader organisational considerations should be taken into account in determining the 'total work experience'. This was the basis for what became known as the quality of work life (QWL) movement, which sought to improve the quality of work life for employees on dimensions such as autonomy and participation, working conditions, job security and social justice.

- More recently the predominant research focus has switched to the development of what is termed 'high-performance work systems' (HPWS). The HPWS approach is seen as more all-embracing than either job enrichment or QWL approaches. Its development appears to stem from two key sources: the increased competitive pressures faced by organisations and the impact of technological developments, particularly information technology, in changing the nature of organisations and jobs.

- The essence of HPWS appears to lie in the adoption of a culture of continuous improvement and innovation at all levels in the organisation and the implementation of a range of work organisation and human resource systems to sustain and develop this culture, particularly team working, quality enhancement, employee autonomy and flexibility. This approach was initially associated with the new 'high-tech' companies of the 1980s, particularly those that located at greenfield sites in attempts to establish a fundamentally different type of organisation and organisation culture.

- HPWS are therefore seen as embracing much more than a change in the nature of jobs. Rather, they are seen as incorporating fundamentally different assumptions about organisational structure and orientation so that all aspects of organisational management are altered to embrace a new culture designed to improve performance and responsiveness through developing a more committed, flexible and skilled workforce.

- HPWS approaches commonly involve the application of specific management techniques designed to improve performance, quality and cost effectiveness. The two most commonly used techniques are just-in-time (JIT), designed to eliminate inventories, and statistical process control (SPC), designed to improve quality and performance.

- A common criticism of the HPWS literature is the assumption that the adoption of techniques such as JIT and SPC are invariably conducive to increased employee involvement and autonomy. There is considerable research evidence which indicates that this is not necessarily the case, as in some ways JIT and SPC can act to limit or reduce employee involvement and discretion. If such techniques are to facilitate an improved work experience for employees, management must carefully consider how these systems are implemented and encourage greater individual and team collaboration in the work process.

- In evaluating alternative work systems, a useful example is the automobile industry. Often termed the first mass production industry, in recent decades it has undergone immense transformation. Companies in this sector appear to be moving away from conventional mass production assembly for both market and human resource reasons. However, different trends are discernible in this change. Of particular note is the emergence of Japanese lean production systems, which a recent study has labelled 'the most revolutionary change since Henry Ford's assembly line.' An alternative development in the industry has been a move away from assembly line approaches to 'whole car' systems using autonomous or partially autonomous work teams, an approach pioneered largely by Volvo in Sweden.

- The research evidence on the implications of these new developments for employees is mixed. Some commentators argue that while these approaches are more demanding in terms of worker effort, they also provide greater opportunity and challenge for workers in influencing the work system. Others are not so sure and point to the negative implications of new work systems, such as those based on just-in-time manufacturing and statistical process control. In particular they point to the increased pace and intensity of work, the greater stress on individual workers and the greater surveillance of work performance.

- These different perspectives highlight a traditional dilemma in the choice of work systems, namely the often contrasting pressures for low costs and high output on the one hand and the desire to create a positive work system and working environment on the other hand. In an era of increasing competitiveness and global competition, it is difficult to see a fruitful reconciliation of these conflicting pressures, particularly in industrial sectors that are exposed to high levels of market competition and volatility.

DISCUSSION/SELF-ASSESSMENT QUESTIONS

1. 'Management choices concerning work systems design will have a strong effect on worker satisfaction and performance.' Discuss.

2. Critically evaluate the impact of the Industrial Revolution on the development of work systems.

3. What do we mean by scientific management? How has scientific management affected the design of work systems in organisations?
4. Compare and contrast high-performance work systems and job enrichment.
5. Indicate what you see as the main characteristics of so-called high-performance work systems (HPWS). What do you feel have been the main factors which stimulated the development of HPWS?

MULTIPLE CHOICE QUESTIONS

1. The term 'work systems' refers to a particular combination of job task, technology, skills, management style and personnel policies and practices. True or false?
2. Among the core principles of scientific management are:
    (a) Flexibly designed jobs with a high degree of worker discretion.
    (b) The establishment of a clear division of tasks and responsibilities between management and workers.
    (c) Selection based on intuition.
    (d) The de-emphasising of economic incentives.
    (e) All of the above.
    (f) None of the above.
3. Under McGregor's Theory X, workers are seen as willing and able to undertake challenging tasks and can do so in a self-directed manner. True or false?
4. Job enrichment is:
    (a) Concerned with designing jobs in such a way as to provide 'job doers' with the opportunity to gain intrinsic satisfaction from their work.
    (b) The practice of building motivating factors into job content.
    (c) A job design strategy.
    (d) Concerned with expanding job content by adding some of the planning and evaluating duties normally performed by the manager.
    (e) The vertical extension of a job.
    (f) All of the above.
    (g) None of the above.
5. The job characteristics model was advanced by:
    (a) Huczynski and Buchanan.
    (b) Brewster and Mayrhofer.
    (c) Hackman and Oldham.
    (d) Newman and Hunter.
    (e) All of the above.
    (f) None of the above.
6. The quality of working life (QWL) concept addresses:
    (a) The overall quality of employee experiences in the workplace.
    (b) Employee empowerment, autonomy and participation at work.
    (c) Issues related to justice in the workplace.

(d) Working conditions and job security.

(e) All of the above.

(f) None of the above.

7. High-performance work systems are viewed as significantly different from preceding innovations in work organisation. True or false?

8. The essence of high-performance systems appears to lie in:

(a) The adoption of a culture of continuous improvement and innovation at all levels in the organisation.

(b) The implementation of a range of work organisation and human resource systems to sustain and develop a strong culture.

(c) The institutionalisation of team working, quality consciousness, employee autonomy and flexibility.

(d) All of the above.

(e) None of the above.

9. The 'greenfield site' is typically associated with innovative work practices and arrangements reflecting a management emphasis predominantly concerned with the achievement and maintenance of maximum flexibility in operations. True or false?

10. According to Womack *et al.* (1990), among the characteristics of Fordism were:

(a) Parts and components that were specific and not highly interchangeable.

(b) The extreme horizontal division of labour, both in production work and indirect functions, such as preparation, quality control, maintenance and repair.

(c) The use of general machinery that can perform multiple tasks.

(d) All of the above.

(e) None of the above.

FIVE SUGGESTED KEY READINGS

Buchanan, D. and McCalman, J., *High Performance Work Systems: The Digital Experience*, London: Routledge 1989.

Conti, R. and Warner, M., 'Taylorism, teams and technology in "reengineering" work organization', *New Technology, Work and Employment*, IX/2 (1994), 93–102.

Emery, F., 'Characteristics of sociotechnical systems', in L. Davis and J. Taylor (eds), *Design of Jobs*, London: Penguin 1972.

Hackman, J.R. and Lawler, E.E., 'Employee reactions to job characteristics', *Journal of Applied Psychology Monograph*, LV (1971), 259–86.

Womack, J.P., Jones, D.T. and Roos, D., *The Machine that Changed the World*, New York: Rawson Associates 1990.

REFERENCES

Beaumont, P.B. and Townley, B., 'Greenfield sites, new plants and work practices', in V. Hammond (ed.), *Current Research in Management*, London: Frances Pinter 1985.

Beer, M., Spector, B., Lawrence, P.R., Quinn Mills, D. and Walton, R.E., *Managing Human Assets: The Groundbreaking Harvard Business School Program*, New York: The Free Press 1984.

Beer, M., Spector, B., Lawrence, P., Quinn Mills, D. and Walton, R., *Human Resource Management: A General Manager's Perspective*, New York: The Free Press 1985.

Berggren, C., 'Det nya bilarbetet' ['The new automobile employment'], PhD dissertation, University of Lund, Sweden 1990.

Brewer, A., 'Work design for flexible work scheduling: barriers and gender implications', *Gender, Work and Organization*, VII/1 (2000), 33–44.

Buchanan, D., 'Principles and practice of job design', in K. Sisson (ed.), *Personnel Management: A Comprehensive Guide to Theory and Practice in Britain*, Oxford: Blackwell 1994.

Buchanan, D. and McCalman, J., *High Performance Work Systems: The Digital Experience*, London: Routledge 1989.

Burr, R., 'Self-management efficacy as a mediator of the relation between job design and employee motivation', *Human Performance*, XIV/1 (2001), 27–44.

Conti, R. and Warner, M., 'Taylorism, teams and technology in "reengineering" work organization', *New Technology, Work and Employment*, IX/2 (1994), 93–102.

Delbridge, R. and Turnbull, P., 'Human resource maximization: the management of labour under just-in-time manufacturing systems', in P. Blyton and P. Turnbull (eds), *Reassessing Human Resource Management*, London: Sage 1992.

Emery, F., 'Characteristics of sociotechnical systems', in L. Davis and J. Taylor (eds), *Design of Jobs*, London: Penguin 1972.

Engestrom, Y., 'Activity theory as a framework for analyzing and redesigning work', *Ergonomics*, XLVII/7 (2000), 960–74.

European Industrial Relations Review, 'Lean production – more of the same or revolution?', *European Industrial Relations Review*, 223 (August 1992).

Gunnigle, P., McMahon, G. and Fitzgerald, G., *Industrial Relations in Ireland: Theory and Practice*, Dublin: Gill & Macmillan 1995.

Gunnigle, P., Heraty, N. and Morley, M., *Personnel and Human Resource Management: Theory and Practice in Ireland*, Dublin: Gill & Macmillan 1997.

Hackman, J.R. and Lawler, E.E., 'Employee reactions to job characteristics', *Journal of Applied Psychology Monograph*, LV (1971), 259–86.

Hackman, J.R. and Oldham, G., *Work Redesign*, New York: Addison-Wesley 1980.

Hackman, J.R., Oldham, G., Janson, R. and Purdy, K., 'A new strategy for job enrichment', *California Management Review*, XVII (1975), 51–71.

Heilbroner, R.L. and Thurow, L.C., *The Economic Problem*, Englewood Cliffs, NJ: Prentice Hall 1984.

Herzberg, F., 'One more time: how do you motivate employees?', *Harvard Business Review* (January/February 1968), 115–25.

Huczynski, A. and Buchanan, D., *Organizational Behaviour: An Introductory Text*, Hemel Hempstead: Prentice Hall 1991.

Income Data Services, *Group Working and Greenfield Sites*, London: Incomes Data Services 1984.

Kamata, S., *Japan in the Passing Lane*, London: Allen & Unwin 1984.

Katz, J., 'The chicken trail: how Latino workers put food on America's tables', series in *Los Angeles Times*, x, xi, xii (November 1996).

Klein, J.A., 'The human costs of manufacturing reform', *Harvard Business Review* (March/April 1989), 60–6.

Kochan, T., Katz, H. and McKersie, R., *The Transformation of American Industrial Relations*, New York: Basic Books 1986.

Lawler, E.E., 'The new plant revolution', *Organizational Dynamics* (Winter 1978), 3–12.

Lawler, E.E., 'Increasing worker involvement to enhance organisational effectiveness', in P.S. Goodman (ed.), *Change in Organizations*, San Francisco: Jossey-Bass 1982.

Lawler, E.E., *High Involvement Management: Participative Strategies for Improving Organizational Performance*, San Francisco: Jossey-Bass 1986.

Maccoby, M., *Why Work?: Motivating and Leading in the New Generation*, New York: Simon & Schuster 1988.

Magee, C., 'Atypical work forms and organisational flexibility', paper presented to the Institute of Public Administration Personnel Management Conference, Dublin, 6 March 1991.

McGregor, D., *The Human Side of Enterprise*, New York: McGraw-Hill 1960.

Mooney, P., 'From industrial relations to employee relations in Ireland', unpublished PhD thesis, Trinity College, Dublin 1988.

Moss Kanter, R., *The Change Masters*, London: Unwin Hyman 1983.

O'Connor, E., 'World class manufacturing in a semi-state environment: the case of Bord na Móna', in P. Gunnigle and W.K. Roche (eds), *New Challenges to Irish Industrial Relations*, Dublin: Oak Tree Press 1995.

Parker, S., Wall, T. and Cordery, J., 'Future work design research and practice: towards an elaborated model of work design', *Journal of Occupational and Organizational Psychology*, LXXIV/4 (2001), 413–41.

Perry, B., *Enfield: A High Performance System*, Bedford, MA: Digital Equipment Corporation, Educational Services Development and Publishing 1984.

Peters, T. and Waterman, R., *In Search of Excellence: Lessons from America's Best Run Companies*, New York: Harper & Row 1982.

Quinn Mills, D., *Rebirth of the Corporation*, New York: John Wiley & Sons 1991.

Roche, W.K. and Gunnigle, P., 'Competition and the new industrial relations agenda', in P. Gunnigle and W.K. Roche (eds), *New Challenges to Irish Industrial Relations*, Dublin: Oak Tree Press 1995.

Schermerhorn, J.R., Hunt, J.G. and Osborn, R.N., *Managing Organizational Behavior*, New York: Wiley 1985.

Schuler, R.S. and Jackson, S.E., *Human Resource Management: Positioning for the 21st Century*, St Paul, MN: West Publishing 1996.

Sewell, G. and Wilkinson, B., 'Empowerment or emasculation? Shop floor surveillance in a total quality organisation', in P. Blyton and P. Turnbull (eds), *Reassessing Human Resource Management*, London: Sage 1992.

Skrovan, D.J., *Quality of Work Life*, Reading, MA: Addison-Wesley 1983.

Steers, R.M. and Porter, L.W., *Motivation and Work Behavior*, New York: McGraw-Hill 1987.

Sweeney, P., 'Structure, strategy and new product development in the automotive supply industry', unpublished MBS thesis, University of Limerick, Limerick 1997.

Taylor, F.W., *Scientific Management*, New York: Harper & Bros 1947.

Tiernan, S.D., Morley, M.J. and Foley, E., *Modern Management: Theory and Practice for Irish Students*, Dublin: Gill & Macmillan 1996.

Vaill, P.B., 'The purposing of high-performing systems', *Organizational Dynamics* (Autumn 1982), 23–39.

Walton, R.E., 'Quality of working life: what is it?', *Sloan Management Review*, XV (Fall 1973), 11–21.

Womack, J.P., Jones, D.T. and Roos, D., *The Machine that Changed the World*, New York: Rawson Associates 1990.

THE DYNAMICS OF ORGANISATIONAL LEADERSHIP

12

Learning Objectives

- To describe the nature of leadership.
- To differentiate between leadership and management.
- To summarise the functions of a leader.
- To review trait leadership theory.
- To examine behavioural leadership theory.
- To describe some contingency theories.
- To examine charismatic theories of leadership.

INTRODUCTION

While leadership means different things to different people, it is generally regarded as a critical factor in the success of any kind of social activity (Statt 1994). The burning cry in all organisations, according to Perrow (1973), is for good leadership, but we have learned that beyond a threshold level of adequacy, it is extremely difficult to know what good leadership is. Unlike some other aspects of organisational behaviour, there are many studies and a considerable body of knowledge on leadership, but the impetus for this development arguably springs from a dissatisfaction with many theories. Many studies of the concept point to the conclusion that it is a variable, contingent activity influenced by a whole series of external factors. However, despite the fact that there remain many unanswered questions, according to House and Aditya (1997) the various contributions have been cumulative and a great deal is known about the leadership phenomenon. Leadership may be interpreted in simple terms, such as 'getting others to follow', or interpreted more specifically, for example, as 'the use of authority in decision making'. It may be exercised as an attribute of position or because of personal knowledge or wisdom (Mullins 1991).

Leadership is a widely talked-about subject, yet at the same time it is somehow puzzling. The ability to provide effective leadership is one of the most important skills that a manager can possess. Manz and Sims (1991: 18) argue that:

> When most of us think of leadership, we think of one person doing something to another person. This is 'influence', and a leader is someone who has the capacity to

influence another. Words like 'charismatic' and 'heroic' are sometimes used to describe a leader. The word 'leader' itself conjures up visions of a striking figure on a rearing white horse who is crying 'Follow me!' The leader is the one who has either the power or the authority to command others.

Thus, there is little doubt that leadership is a skill that is respected and admired, but it appears rather elusive to many people. Pettinger (1994: 31) maintains that:

> Leadership is that part of the management sphere concerned with getting results through people, and all that entails and implies – the organisation of the staff into productive teams, groups, departments; the creation of human structures; their motivation and direction; the resolution of conflicts at the workplace; creating vision and direction for the whole undertaking; and providing resources in support of this.

A slightly narrower interpretation is advanced by Tannenbaum *et al.* (1961) when they suggest that leadership is an interpersonal influence that is exercised in a situation and directed through the communication process towards the attainment of a specified goal.

DEFINITIONS OF KEY CONCEPTS

Leadership
Where intentional influence is exerted by one person over others towards a shared goal.

Trait theories of leadership
The view that effective leaders possess certain exceptional characteristics.

Behavioural theories of leadership
Theory of leadership focusing on the behaviours that specific leaders exhibit based on a two-factor conception of leader behaviour.

Contingency theories of leadership
Takes into account the importance of situational factors when exploring what makes leaders effective.

Charismatic leadership theory
Belief that the leader has some special unique virtue, often heroic.

Transactional leadership
Involves an exchange or 'tit for tat' relationship between leader and follower.

Transformational leadership
Leads by inspiring and motivating followers, believes in commitment rather than compliance.

LEADERSHIP AND MANAGEMENT

In drawing attention to the distinction between leadership and management, Bennis (1989: 7) argues that in order to survive in the twenty-first century:

> We are going to need a new generation of leaders – leaders, not managers. The distinction is an important one. Leaders conquer the context – the volatile, turbulent, ambiguous surroundings that sometimes seem to conspire against us and will surely suffocate us if we let them – while managers surrender to it.

According to Bennis and Nanus (1985), 'managers do things right', while 'leaders do the right things'. While both leadership and management can be conceived of as being essentially about influence and the use of power, there is a strong argument to be made that leadership is a different concept than management per se. Hersey and Blanchard (1993) conceive of management as a special kind of leadership in which the achievement of organisational goals is paramount. The key difference between the concepts, they argue, therefore lies in the word 'organisation'. Leadership occurs any time one attempts to influence the behaviour of an individual or group, regardless of the reason. It may be for one's own goals or for those of others, and they may or may not be congruent with organisational goals. Critically, it is not axiomatic that every leader is a manager, though conversely, Mintzberg (1973) argues that leadership behaviour can be an integral part of a manager's job and in his research he identifies ten main roles grouped into three areas (Table 12.1).

Table 12.1 Managerial Roles Identified by Mintzberg

Interpersonal	Figurehead Leader Liaison
Informational	Monitor Disseminator Spokesperson
Decisional	Entrepreneur Disturbance handler Resource allocator Negotiator

According to Statt (1994), chief executives will spend much more of their time on the interpersonal roles than would more junior managers. However, this does not mean that they will be any more effective as leaders. He argues that the job titles, job descriptions and the amount of time the job demands for activity defined as leadership simply tell us *what* is done. It does not tell us *how* it is done, which is where leadership ability and effectiveness would come in. 'But in any organisation we tend to automatically look at the apex for evidence of leadership. Indeed, the greatest fallacy of leadership is that it always comes from the top down. It most certainly does not' (Statt 1994: 337). Many believe management and leadership to be more delineated as organisational and/or societal roles.

Management is more usually viewed as getting things done through other people in order to achieve stated organisational objectives. The manager may react to specific situations and be more concerned with solving short-term problems. Management is regarded as relating to people working within a structured organisation and with prescribed roles. To people outside of the organisation the manager might not be seen in a leadership role. The emphasis of leadership is on interpersonal behaviour in a broader context. It is often associated with the willing and enthusiastic behaviour of followers. Leadership does not necessarily take place within the hierarchical structure of the organisation. Many people operate as leaders without their role ever being clearly established or defined. A leader often has sufficient influence to bring about long-term changes in people's attitudes. Leadership can be seen primarily as an 'inspirational process' (Mullins 1991: 421).

Table 12.2 Distinguishing between a Manager and a Leader

Manager	Leader
Motivates people and administers resources to achieve stated organisational goals.	Motivates people to develop new objectives.
Short-range view.	Long-range perspective.
A copy.	An original.
Maintains.	Develops.
Focuses on systems and structure.	Focuses on people.
Implements.	Shapes.
Relies on control.	Inspires trust.
Eye on the bottom line.	Eye on the horizon.
Narrows down horizons.	Opens up horizons.
Rational.	Emotional.
Classic good soldier.	Own person.
Accepts the status quo.	Challenges the status quo.
Does things right.	Does the right thing.

Source: Adapted from Bennis (1989)

Zaleznik, of the Harvard Business School (1977), argues forcefully that there is a difference between leadership and management, and highlights a number of differences associated with their motivation, personal history and how they actually think.

- Managers tend to adopt impersonal or passive attitudes towards goals, whereas leaders adopt a more personal and active attitude towards goals.

- In order to get people to accept solutions, the manager needs to continually co-ordinate and balance in order to compromise conflicting values. The leader creates excitement in work and develops choices that give substance to images that excite people.
- In their relationships with other people, managers maintain a low level of emotional involvement. Leaders have empathy with other people and give attention to what events and actions mean.
- Managers see themselves more as conservators and regulators of the existing order of affairs with which they identify and from which they gain rewards. Leaders work in, but do not belong to, the organisation. Their sense of identity does not depend upon membership or work roles and they search out opportunities for change.

A common differentiation between leaders and management is that leaders are change oriented and focused on long-term strategy while managers are stability oriented and focused on the short term. Yukl argues against the perception of leading and managing being two mutually exclusive activities and maintains that people can use both types of behaviours. He goes on to argue that an effective leader will diagnose the situation and will 'lead' or 'manage' accordingly. Change-oriented 'leading' behaviour is more appropriate in times of environmental turmoil and when facing major threats or opportunities, and 'managerial' behaviour is more appropriate when the external environment is relatively stable and when the focus is on the maintenance of efficient operations (Yukl 1999). Considering leaders and managers as polar opposites may be oversimplifying what is involved in both of these activities. However, it is equally important to note that an individual can be a leader without being a manager, and a manager without being a leader.

LEADERSHIP FUNCTIONS

As far back as 1962, Krech et al. identified fourteen leadership functions that demonstrate the complexity of leadership. They saw the leader as:
- **Executive:** Top co-ordinator of the group activities and overseer of the execution of policies.
- **Planner:** Deciding the ways and means by which the group achieves its ends through both short-term and long-term planning.
- **Policy-maker:** The establishment of group goals and policies.
- **Expert:** A source of readily available information and skills.
- **External group representative:** The official spokesperson for the group, the representative of the group and the clearing house for outgoing and incoming information.
- **Controller of internal relations:** Determines specific aspects of the group's structure.
- **Purveyor of rewards and punishment:** Control over group members by the power to provide rewards and apply punishments.
- **Arbitrator and mediator:** Controls interpersonal conflict within the group.

- **Exemplar:** A model of behaviour for members of the group, setting an example of what is expected.
- **Symbol of the group:** Enhancing the group unit by providing some kind of cognitive focus and establishing the group as a distinct entity.
- **Substitute for individual responsibility:** Relieves the individual member of the group from the necessity of and responsibility for personal decision.
- **Ideologist:** Serving as the source of beliefs, values and standards of behaviour for individual members of the group.
- **Father figure:** Serving as focus for the positive emotional feelings of individual members and the object for identification and transference.
- **Scapegoat:** Serving as a target for aggression and hostility of the group, accepting blame in the case of failure.

More recently, Dawson (1996: 218) assembles what she describes as a 'long and incomplete list' of leadership functions. From a review of the extant literature, she argues that the list can be classified into five key areas: task functions, cultural functions, symbolic functions, political functions and relational functions. Task functions are largely concerned with task completion, while cultural functions are associated with creating and sustaining a performance culture and climate in the organisation. Symbolic functions are seen to be crucial, arguably because leaders are important for what they stand for as much as for what they actually do. Political functions are associated with the leader's role in relation to outsiders, while relational functions deal with the nature of the relationship between the leader and the followers.

Table 12.3 Leadership Functions

1. **Task functions**	
Strategist	Enunciating policy, objectives, goals.
Executive	Ensuring action to secure objectives.
Co-ordinator	Ensuring all parts and contributions fit together.
Procurer	Procuring important resources, including information.
Monitor/evaluator	Checking and evaluating performance.
Rectifier	Putting right or improving performance.
Problem definer	Identifying and conceptualising problems.
Problem solver	Identifying and implementing solutions in an imaginative way.
Expert	Supplying wisdom, skills and knowledge.
2. **Cultural functions**	
Missionary	Building a spirit of inquiry and commitment to continuous learning and improvement.
Role model	Setting an example of expected behaviour.
Ideologist	Originating and purveying values and sets of assumptions.
Consciousness raiser	Liberating followers' unconscious thoughts and aspirations.

3. Symbolic functions

Visionary	Formulating and communicating a view of the future.
Interpreter	Creating and managing meaning.
Father or mother figure	Providing a focus for identifications, reference and occasional rebellion.
Scapegoat	Acting as a target for blame and hostility.
Moral authority	Legitimating activities.

4. Political functions

Representative	Representing the group externally.
Politician	Securing external support.

5. Relational functions

Rewarder/sanctioner	Dispensing rewards and punishments
Coach	Encouraging and supporting others.
Arbiter and mediator	Working between different interest groups.
Teacher	Imparting knowledge and skills.
Welfare worker	Attending to group members' well-being.
Peacemaker	Securing consensus.
Referee	Ensuring fair competition.
Communicator	Ensuring open communications.
Honest broker	Securing trust between parties.

Source: Dawson (1996)

TRAIT THEORIES OF LEADERSHIP

It is almost a truism to suggest that good leadership is essential for business performance, but what makes a good leader? Among the earliest theories of leadership were those which focused on traits (Gibb 1947; Stogdill 1948). The earliest trait theories, which can be traced back to the ancient Greeks, concluded that leaders are born, not made. Up to approximately 1950 most studies sought to identify leadership traits, principally because prominent leaders seemed to possess certain 'exceptional characteristics'. Also known as the 'great man theory', the assumption was that it is possible to identify a unifying set of characteristics that make all great leaders great, and so psychologists set about looking for the personality characteristics or traits that distinguished leaders from other people. If the concept of traits was to be proved valid, there would have to be specific characteristics in existence that all leaders possessed. The trait theories argued that leadership is innate, the product of our parents given at birth. The chosen individuals are born with traits (particularly personality traits, though physical traits possibly had a role to play) which caused them to be self-selected as leaders. The findings emanating from this early work tend to disagree on what sets of traits distinguish leaders from followers. Among the characteristics identified are:

- intelligence;
- initiative;
- dependability;
- lateral thinker;
- self-assurance;
- maturity;
- visionary;
- social well-being;
- need for achievement;
- need for power; and
- goal-directedness.

The vast amount of research effort expended by psychologists on this topic up to the 1950s was reviewed in what Statt (1994: 326) refers to as 'a very important article' written by Stogdill (1948). Stogdill found that such people did tend to be higher in certain characteristics than other people, for example, intelligence, level of activity and social participation, but that this relationship was inconsistent, and even where it was found it was much less influential than had generally been assumed. He therefore concluded that while any useful theory of leadership had to say something about personal characteristics, by themselves they explained very little about leadership behaviour in organisations.

> Leadership was much more a matter of context and situation, Stogdill suggested. People who exhibited behaviour in one situation might not do so in another ... the reason for this was that whatever leadership may be it is always a relationship between people (Statt 1994: 326).

Overall, the research effort dedicated to the search for universal traits possessed by leaders resulted in little truly convincing evidence. Robbins (1991) goes so far as to say it resulted in 'dead ends'. Certainly, much of the research work has identified lists of traits which tend to be overlapping or contradictory and with few significant correlations between factors. As Luthans (1992) points out, only intelligence seemed to hold up with any degree of consistency, and when these findings were combined with those of studies on physical traits, the overall conclusion was that leaders were more likely to be bigger and brighter than those being led, but not too much so. Despite this, Stogdill argued that it was not entirely appropriate to abandon the study of traits and that the best way forward was to introduce an interactional element into the equation whereby traits and their significance/universality would be considered in the context of the situational difficulties or demands facing the leader.

However, this view that leaders are born and not made is much less widely held today. There has been an incremental shift away from this thinking for a number of reasons. First, the enormous range of traits potentially affecting leadership ability is problematic and there is a difficulty associated with measuring their existence. This is a critical weakness according to House and Aditya (1997), largely because there was little empirically substantiated personality theory to guide the search for leadership traits. The lists of traits tend to be exceptionally long and there is not always agreement on how they should be prioritised in terms of their importance. This resulted in an inability to produce many replicative investigations. Second, if we were to rely on birth alone to produce leaders, then potentially we would not have enough leaders to go around. Third, there is a growing body of evidence on the influence of nurturing and life experiences in this area. Fourth, our leadership needs are diverse and are commonly dispersed throughout society with the result that if the specific situational demands of the leader are taken into account, the replication problem once again raises its head.

Overall, many psychologists remain unconvinced that there is any link between any specific characteristics and any form of leadership, although there has been a resurgence of interest in this area in recent years, focusing on the emotional intelligence of the leader. (The area of emotional intelligence is discussed in more detail in Chapter 5.) Finally, from a methodological perspective it is likely that there will be some subjective judgment in determining who is regarded as an effective, 'good' leader (see Yetton 1984).

BEHAVIOURAL THEORIES OF LEADERSHIP

As convincing evidence failed to accumulate through trait-based research, researchers increasingly began to seek out behaviours that specific leaders exhibited. The central hypothesis in this school of thought was that critical specific behaviours differentiate leaders from non-leaders. Extensive research studies on behavioural classifications of leadership were conducted at Ohio State University (Stogdill and Coons 1957) and the University of Michigan (Likert 1961).

OHIO STATE UNIVERSITY LEADERSHIP STUDIES

These studies, which began in the 1940s, sought to identify and classify independent dimensions of leader behaviour. Questionnaires were designed containing a list of items detailing specific aspects of leadership behaviour. From a list of more than 1,000 dimensions, they eventually consistently identified two categories that accounted for most of the leadership behaviour, labelled initiating structure style and considerate style. Initiating structure style reflects the extent to which the leader defines and structures his/her role and the roles of the followers in achieving established organisational goals. The considerate style reflects the extent to which the leader focuses on establishing trust, mutual respect and rapport between himself/herself and the group of followers.

Both styles were found to be uncorrelated, thus potentially giving rise to four possible types of leadership behaviour:
1. Low on initiating structure style and low on considerate style.
2. High on initiating structure style and low on considerate style.
3. High on initiating structure style and high on considerate style.
4. Low on initiating structure style and high on considerate style.

Though criticised on methodological grounds, particularly for their reliance on questionnaires, the research demonstrated that leaders high in initiating structure style and high in considerate style were generally more likely to achieve superior performance among their followers. Followers were also more likely to describe feelings of satisfaction when compared with their counterparts operating under the leadership of those who were low on either style or both.

Figure 12.1 Four Leadership Styles

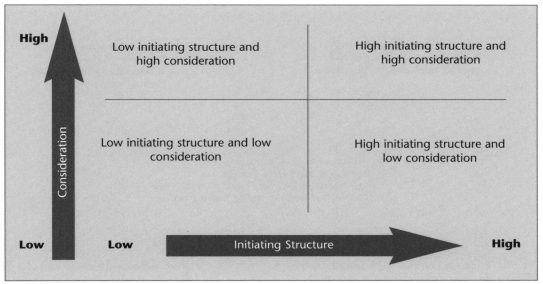

UNIVERSITY OF MICHIGAN STUDIES

Similar to the work being done at Ohio, the Michigan studies, under the direction of Rensis Likert, sought to examine the nature of the relationship between leaders' behavioural characteristics and performance effectiveness. The research resulted in a two-way classification of leadership, namely employee-oriented and production-oriented styles. The employee-oriented leader was one who emphasised interpersonal relations in the workplace, while the production-oriented leader concentrated on the technical aspects of the work. The results demonstrated that employee-oriented leaders consistently achieved higher productivity and higher job satisfaction among their work groups. Conversely, production-oriented leaders were more likely to be associated with lower group productivity and lower job satisfaction. However, it also emerged that employee-oriented and production-oriented approaches need to be balanced. Employee-oriented leaders who consistently achieved superior results recognised that production was one of the major responsibilities of their work.

THE MANAGERIAL GRID

The managerial grid advanced by Blake and Mouton (1962) has been particularly influential as a two-dimensional model of leadership. The grid, which has two axes (concern for people and concern for production), can be taken to represent the initiating structure style and the considerate style of the Ohio research, or the employee-oriented and production-oriented dimensions of the Michigan work. Their writings begin with the assumption that a manager's job is to foster attitudes about behaviour which promote performance, creativity and entrepreneurship. Such managerial competence can be taught and learned. Their managerial grid provides a framework for understanding and applying effective leadership.

Figure 12.2 The Blake and Mouton Grid

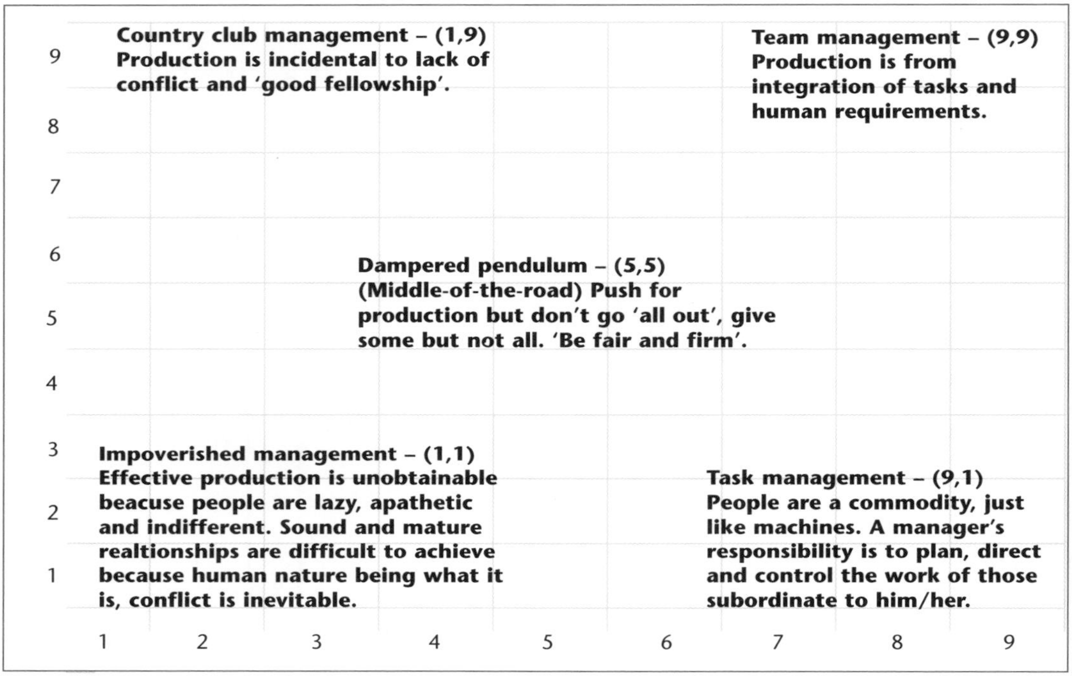

Source: Blake and Mouton (1962)

The grid results from combining two fundamental ingredients of managerial behaviour, namely a concern for production and a concern for people. Any manager's approach to their job will show more or less of each of these two fundamental constituents. They may show a high degree of concern for one or the other of these, or there is the possibility that they might lie in the middle with an equal concern for both. Different positions on the grid represent different typical patterns of behaviour. The grid indicates that all degrees of concern for production and concern for people are possible. Only five key styles are isolated for illustration.

- The 9,1 manager focuses almost exclusively on production issues. Thus, this type is one who expects schedules to be met and has a desire for the smooth running of production operations in a methodical way. Interruptions in this schedule are viewed as someone's mistakes. Disagreement is viewed as being dysfunctional and is seen as insubordination.
- The 1,9 management style, or country club style, almost exclusively emphasises people

concerns. People are encouraged and supported in their endeavours as long as they are doing their best. Conflict and disagreement are to be avoided and even constructive criticism is not seen as helpful as it interrupts the harmonious relationship.

- The 1,1 style, also known as impoverished management, signals little concern for either production or people. 1,1 managers avoid responsibility and task commitment. Leaders of this kind avoid contact where possible and display little commitment to problem solving.
- The 5,5 manager displays the middle-of-the-road style where they push enough to get acceptable levels of production, but in the techniques and skills that they use they also demonstrate a concern for people. They show a firm but fair attitude and have confidence in their subordinates.
- The 9,9 manager demonstrates a high concern for production and a high concern for people issues. This is a team manager whose goal is one of integration. They aim for the highest possible standard and insist on the best possible result for everyone. There is usually maximum involvement and participation, and the achievement of difficult goals is viewed as a fulfilling challenge. It is accepted that conflict will occur. When it happens it is handled in an open and frank manner and is not treated as a personal attack. This style, Blake and Mouton argue, is always the best style to adopt since it builds on long-term development and trust. This style of leadership, in order to be truly effective, requires an appropriate cultural fit. The value set of the whole organisation must seek to support this style of leadership.

CONTINGENCY LEADERSHIP THEORY

Contingency theories are based on the premise that the prediction of leadership success and effectiveness is more complex than the simple isolation of traits or behaviours. Situational variables, or the context in which leadership is occurring, are also viewed as having strong explanatory power. Both Fiedler's and House's theories are examined here.

FIEDLER'S THEORY

In the 1970s Fiedler conducted a series of studies dedicated to the leadership of work groups. Beginning with the assumption that anyone appointed to a responsible leadership position of this kind will possess the requisite technical expertise, his research question was what it is about leadership behaviour that leads to effective group working, 'effective' meaning how well the group performs the primary task for which it exists. Fiedler's research identifies two main leadership styles, namely 'relationship-motivated leaders' and 'task-motivated leaders'. The former get their satisfaction from having good relationships with others. They usually encourage participation and involvement and are always concerned about what the other team members think of them. Conversely, task-motivated leaders are strongly focused on the task. The emphasis is on proceduralisation and task completion.

Fiedler subsequently developed an instrument to classify these two styles (see LPC Activity below). The instrument asks leaders to review all people with whom they have ever worked and think of the one with whom they could work least well. They are then asked to rate this 'least preferred co-worker' (LPC) along a number of dimensions. Fiedler has found that relationship-motivated leaders will score relationship issues high in spite of their problems with the LPC. Conversely, task-motivated leaders were found to rate the LPC low on all dimensions. Fiedler emphasises that both these leadership styles can be useful and effective in appropriate situations. He thus argues that it is necessary to have a contingency perspective on leadership, because effective leadership will be contingent on the nature of the tasks to be completed and the context in which this is to be done.

LPC ACTIVITY

Think of the person with whom you work least well. He/she may be someone you work with presently, or may be someone you knew in the past. He/she does not have to be the person you like least well, but should be the person with whom you now have or have had the most difficulty in getting a job done. Describe this person as he/she appears to you by placing an X at the point at which you believe best describes that person. Do this for each pair of adjectives.

	8	7	6	5	4	3	2	1	
Pleasant	—	—	—	—	—	—	—	—	Unpleasant
Friendly	—	—	—	—	—	—	—	—	Unfriendly
Rejecting	—	—	—	—	—	—	—	—	Accepting
Helpful	—	—	—	—	—	—	—	—	Frustrating
Unenthusiastic	—	—	—	—	—	—	—	—	Enthusiastic
Tense	—	—	—	—	—	—	—	—	Relaxed
Distant	—	—	—	—	—	—	—	—	Close
Cold	—	—	—	—	—	—	—	—	Warm
Co-operative	—	—	—	—	—	—	—	—	Unco-operative
Supportive	—	—	—	—	—	—	—	—	Hostile
Boring	—	—	—	—	—	—	—	—	Interesting

Quarrelsome	_	_	_	_	_	_	_	_	Harmonious
	8	7	6	5	4	3	2	1	
Self-assured	_	_	_	_	_	_	_	_	Hesitant
	8	7	6	5	4	3	2	1	
Efficient	_	_	_	_	_	_	_	_	Inefficient
	8	7	6	5	4	3	2	1	
Gloomy	_	_	_	_	_	_	_	_	Cheerful
	8	7	6	5	4	3	2	1	
Open	_	_	_	_	_	_	_	_	Guarded
	8	7	6	5	4	3	2	1	

Scoring:

Your score on the LPC scale is a measure of your leadership style and it indicates your primary motivation in a work setting. To determine your score, add up the points (1 through 8) for each of the sixteen items. If your score is 64 or above, you are a high LPC person, or relationship oriented. If your score is 57 or below, you are a low LPC person, or task oriented. If your score falls between 58 and 63, you will need to determine for yourself in which category you belong.

Source: Fiedler and Chemers (1974)

HOUSE'S PATH-GOAL THEORY

Advanced by Robert House (1971) as a contingency theory of leadership, path-goal theory extracts critical elements from expectancy theory of work motivation and the Ohio State University research on behavioural aspects of leadership. House argues that leaders are effective if they can help subordinates identify a goal and then enable them to achieve it. The terminology 'path-goal' is used as a result of the belief that effective leadership is about clarifying the path to help others get from where they are to the achievement of their work goals and to smooth the journey along that path by reducing and/or eliminating roadblocks and pitfalls. House identifies four leadership styles – directive, supportive, participative and achievement oriented – and two classes of situational variables that influence the leadership behaviour-outcome relationship – the personal characteristics of the subordinates and the environment of the subordinates. These situational variables are seen to influence subordinates' perceptions and motivations and consequently the leader is advised to adopt the style which, in the given circumstances, is most likely to result in the identification and achievement of appropriate goals. Robbins (1991: 370) outlines a number of useful hypotheses that have emerged from path-goal theory research.

- Directive leadership leads to greater satisfaction when tasks are ambiguous or stressful than when they are highly structured and well laid out.
- Supportive leadership results in high employee performance and satisfaction when subordinates are performing structured tasks.

- Directive leadership is likely to be perceived as redundant among subordinates with high perceived ability or with considerable experience.
- The more clear and bureaucratic the formal authority relationships, the more leaders should exhibit supportive behaviour and de-emphasise directive behaviour.
- Directive leadership will lead to higher employee satisfaction when there is substantive conflict within a group.
- Subordinates with an internal locus of control (those who believe they control their own destiny) will be more satisfied with a participative style.
- Subordinates with an external locus of control will be more satisfied with a directive style.
- Achievement-oriented leadership will increase subordinates' expectancies that effort will lead to high performance when tasks are ambiguously structured.

ONGOING DEBATES/ADVANCED CONCEPTS IN LEADERSHIP

In the remainder of this chapter we visit four ongoing debates in leadership theory, namely a revised path-goal theory, the concept of transformational leadership, strategic leadership and top management teams and finally, some cross-cultural leadership issues.

REVISED PATH-GOAL THEORY

While House's path-goal theory has been extremely influential, it has been criticised for a number of reasons. House himself acknowledges that the original theory was very much a product of its time and relied heavily on the expectancy theory of motivation, a theory considered by many to over-rationalise individuals' behaviour. The theory also draws heavily from the behaviour theories of leadership, which focus on the person, and the task orientation theory of leadership. Both these theories fail to consider the effects of unconscious motives, affect, symbolic and emotional leader behaviours (House 1996). They also focus on leadership as a dyadic process (the effect of the leader on a subordinate) and fail to consider how leaders affect groups of people. House reformulated his theory in 1996, taking these concerns into consideration. In doing so he specified behaviours that enhance subordinate empowerment and satisfaction, and work unit and subordinate effectiveness. The revised theory addresses how leaders affect followers' motivation and abilities and work unit performance. It provides propositions to guide leader behaviour, some of which are outlined below (for a detailed discussed on House's reformulated path-goal theory, see House 1996).

1. Leader behaviour will enhance subordinate performance to the extent that their behaviour enhances task-relevant abilities of the work unit through role modelling and employee development.
2. Leader behaviour will enhance subordinate performance to the extent that their behaviour links the satisfaction of subordinates' needs with effective performance and complements subordinates' environment by providing psychological structure, support and rewards necessary for effective performance.

3. Leader behaviour will enhance work unity effectiveness to the extent that their behaviour encourages and facilitates collaborative relationships between employees and maintains positive relationships between the work units and the larger organisation.

The reformulated theory added several leader behaviours to the original theory. While the original theory identified four important leadership behaviours – directive, supportive, participative and achievement oriented – House's reformulated theory adds the following leader behaviours.

*   **Work facilitation:** Planning, scheduling, mentoring, coaching.
*   **Interaction facilitation:** Facilitating communication, teamwork, emphasising collaboration, encouraging positive relationships between employees.
*   **Group-oriented decision processes (how decisions that affect the group are made):** Posing problems, not solutions, to the group, encouraging balanced participation, searching for alternatives, encouragement of evaluation of alternatives.
*   **Representation and networking:** Communicating the importance of the group's work to those outside the organisation, networking.
*   **Value-based leader behaviour:** Articulation of a vision, display of passion for a vision, demonstration of self-confidence, use of symbolic behaviour.
*   **Shared leadership:** Manager and peer work facilitation, manager and peer interaction facilitation, manager and peer support.

While ten classes of leader behaviour may seem excessive, House argues that it is in fact strikingly parsimonious and argues that 'the essence of the theory is the meta proposition that leaders, to be effective, engage in behaviours that complement subordinates' environments and abilities in a manner that compensates for deficiencies and is instrumental to subordinate satisfaction and individual and work unit performance' (House 1996).

FROM TRANSACTIONAL TO TRANSFORMATIONAL LEADERSHIP

From the 1970s more research attention was paid to the hypothesis that more successful organisations (using objective performance indicators) have better top management leadership than less successful organisations. Dedicated to identifying 'charismatic' characteristics of leaders, it was viewed as important in the context of organisations attempting to transform traditional systems, methodologies and approaches in an attempt to meet the emerging strategic imperative. Bryman (1993) refers to the work in this area as the 'new leadership theories'. Research work emanating from both the US and the UK lent support to the hypothesis (see Goldsmith and Clutterbuck 1984; Peters and Austin 1985). The single factor that made the crucial difference was what Burns (1978) coined as 'transformational leadership'. Burns identifies two types of political leadership – transactional and transformational.

Table 12.4 Approaches of Transactional vs. Transformational Leaders

Transactional leaders
1. **Contingent reward:** Contracts exchange of rewards for effort, promises rewards for good performance, recognises accomplishments.
2. **Management by exception (active):** Watches and searches for deviations from rules and standards, takes corrective action.
3. **Management by exception (passive):** Intervenes only if standards are not met.
4. **Laissez-faire:** Abdicates responsibility, avoids making decisions.

Transformational leaders
1. **Charisma:** Provides vision and sense of mission, instils pride, gains respect and trust.
2. **Inspiration:** Communicates high expectations, uses symbols to focus efforts, expresses important purposes in simple ways.
3. **Intellectual stimulation:** Promotes intelligence, rationality and careful problem solving.
4. **Individual consideration:** Gives personal attention, treats each employee individually, coaches, advises.

Source: Bass (1990)

The more traditional transactional leadership involves an exchange relationship between leaders and followers, but transformational leadership is more about leaders adjusting their followers' values, beliefs and needs. Bass suggests that transactional leadership is largely a prescription for mediocrity, while transformational leadership consistently leads to exceptional performance in organisations that really need it. He argues that the development and utilisation of transformational leadership through a sustained focus on the human resource policy areas of recruitment, selection, promotion, training and development will yield dividends in the health, well-being and effective performance of the modern organisation. In response to the criticism levelled at transformational leadership on moral grounds, Bass and Steidlmeier (1999: 181) argue that their definition of true transformational leadership is rooted in moral grounds and is based on:

> the moral character of the leaders and their concerns for self and others, the ethical values embedded in the leader's vision, articulation, and program, which followers can embrace or reject and the morality of the processes of social ethical choices and action in which the leaders and followers engage and collectively pursue.

Transformational leadership theory has also been criticised for other reasons. Statt (1994: 339) describes it as the 'Loch Ness monster' of leadership theory. He accepts that while a number of perfectly sober observers claim to have seen it, he has never witnessed it. Furthermore, he suggests that upon close observation, transformational leadership represents a reversion to the much-maligned notion of the great man theory. Robbins (1991: 354) agrees that it does represent a return to traits, but from a different perspective:

Researchers are now attempting to identify the set of traits that people implicitly refer to when they characterise someone as a leader. This line of thinking proposes that leadership is as much style – projecting the appearance of being a leader – as it is substance.

While Yukl (1999) recognises that no one theory on leadership should be expected to include all aspects of leadership behaviour, he suggests that Bass's transformational leadership theory has some key omissions, including some task behaviours (team building, networking) and change-oriented behaviours (scanning and analysis of external environment).

A more serious criticism questions the methodological foundations of the theory. Most of the research to date has relied on Bass's original questionnaire, which has been criticised, or on qualitative research that largely describes leaders through interviews. In relation to the latter, Luthans (1992) cites Tichy and Devanna's research (1986) which, through a series of interviews with top managers in major companies, revealed that transformational leaders share the following characteristics.

- They identify themselves as change agents.
- They believe in people.
- They are courageous.
- They are visionaries.
- They have an ability to tolerate ambiguity, complexity and uncertainty.
- They are value driven.

FROM STRONG MAN TO SUPERLEADERSHIP

More recently it has been argued that leadership style may be better interpreted as being arranged along a continuum, with leadership approaches ranging from a completely 'strong man' approach dedicated to issuing strict instructions and tight supervision to one that is based on the principle of 'superleadership', the objective of which is to lead others to lead themselves. Table 12.5 presents a perspective on different approaches to leadership.

The authors argue that viewpoints on what constitutes successful leadership in organisations have changed over time. The strong man view of leadership is the earliest dominant form. Based on the principle of autocracy, the emphasis is on the leader's strength. The expertise for knowing what should be done rests entirely with the leader, and his/her power stems wholly from his/her position in the organisation. The second view of leadership is based on that of the transactor. The emphasis here is on the rational exchange process (exchange of rewards for work performed) in order to get employees to do their work. The focus here, according to the authors, is on goals and rewards, and the leader's power stems from his/her ability to provide followers with rewards. The third type of leader they identify is that of the visionary hero. The emphasis in this case is on the leader's ability to create highly motivating and absorbing visions. The focus in the relationship is on the leader's vision, and the leader's power is based on the followers' desire to relate to the vision. The final view of the leader is that of the superleader. Rather than using the title to create a larger-than-life type of figure, the authors argue that, ironically, the emphasis in this relationship is largely on the followers. The leader's objective is to help the followers to become self-leaders. Power is more evenly shared between the leader and the followers, the goal being to ensure that all followers experience commitment and ownership of their work.

Table 12.5 Four Types of Leaders

	Strong man	Transactor	Visionary hero	Superleader
Focus	Commands.	Rewards.	Visions.	Self-leadereship.
Type of power	Position/ authority.	Rewards.	Relational/ inspirational.	Shared.
Source of leader's wisdom and direction	Leader.	Leader.	Leader.	Mostly followers (self-leaders) and then leaders.
Followers' response	Fear-based compliance.	Calculative compliance.	Emotional commitment based on leader's vision.	Commitment based on ownership.
Typical leader behaviours	Direction command.	Interactive goal setting.	Communication of leader's vision.	Becoming an effective self-leader.
	Assigned goals.	Contingent personal rewards.	Emphasis on leader's value.	Modelling self-leadership.
	Intimidation.	Contingent material rewards.	Exhortation.	Creating positive thought patterns.
	Reprimand.	Contingent reprimand.	Inspirational persuasion.	Developing self-leadership through reward and constructive reprimand. Promoting self-leading teams. Facilitating a self-leadership culture.

Source: Manz and Sims (1989)

STRATEGIC LEADERSHIP AND THE IMPACT OF THE TOP MANAGEMENT TEAM

So-called strategic leadership (House and Aditya 1997) is concerned with those executives who have overall responsibility for the organisation. Until relatively recently this aspect of leadership was largely unresearched, but in a concerted effort to move beyond a simple examination of singular leaders at the top of organisations, recent research (Hambrick and Mason 1984; Bantel and Jackson 1989) has cast its net wider to focus on the cluster of executives who comprise the 'dominant coalition' in organisations. Thus, according to Hambrick (1994), the expression 'top management team' entered the leadership literature in about 1980 and has been pervasive ever since. Recently popularised organisational forms continually emphasise the concept of the team as a pivotal lever for sustained competitive advantage. The relative neglect of strategic leadership, according to House and Aidya (1997), is ironic since the study of effective organisational policies and strategies has been one of the most important foci of business school education ever since the founding of the earliest such schools. This collective group at the top of the organisational hierarchy will almost invariably have more influence on the course of the firm than any other people in the organisation. Thus, Hambrick (1994: 174) predicts that 'for those interested in explaining organisational outcomes, analytic attention to the group of executives at the top will not be misplaced.'

A comprehensive summary of the literature on strategic leadership in the form of the top management team is presented by Finkelstein and Hambrick (1996) when they debate whether or not the top management team actually matters. Based on studies of the characteristics of top executives that have been found to be associated with organisational effectiveness, they conclude that top managers do indeed matter, but they are often constrained by factors in their environments, organisational inertia and by their own limitations. Some of the most significant findings concern relationships between the composition and behaviour of the top management teams and important organisational outcomes, such as competitiveness and performance. Other prominent research has linked characteristics of top management teams to organisational diversification, innovation, strategic change and decline.

Research from the University of Limerick on top management teams provides some Irish evidence on strategic leadership (Flood and Smith 1994; Morley et al. 1996; Flood et al. 1997). Borrowing from trait and behavioural theories of leadership, the central question addressed was the extent to which the top management team demography and process variables impact (directly and indirectly) on the sales growth performance of thirty international divisions of US multinationals operating in Ireland. The demographic variables of this leadership group used in the research were as follows.

- **Job tenure:** The stability of employment of the members of the team.
- **Heterogeneity of experience:** The variety of previous industry experience in existence in the top management team.
- **Heterogeneity of education:** The dissimilarity of the educational backgrounds of the members of the top management team.
- **Functional heterogeneity:** The extent of functional diversity that exists within the top management team.

Team size refers to the number of participants/members in the team. The number of members is a critical element of group structure and composition. The process/behavioural variables used were as follows.

- **Social integration:** The extent to which the members of the top management team experience a sense of belonging and a sense of satisfaction with other members of the group.
- **Frequency of communication:** The amount of interaction between the team members (both formal and informal).
- **Communication informality:** The extent to which there is a preference among the members of the top management team for informal methods of communication, such as spontaneous conversations and chance meetings.

Table 12.6 Means and Standard Deviations

Variable	Mean	Standard Deviation
Job tenure	55.83	39.07
Social integration	3.51	0.428
Frequency of communication	0.026	0.472
Heterogeneity of experience (industry)	0.448	0.212
Communication informality	2.20	0.319
Heterogeneity of education	0.502	0.264
Team size	4.37	1.07
Functional heterogeneity	0.555	0.182
Number of permanent employees (1991)	171.26	179.75

Source: Morley *et al.* (1996)

Table 12.7 Multiple Regression

Variable	Beta	SE B
Job tenure	−0.030	0.001
Social integration	0.029	0.145
Frequency of communication	0.301*	0.128
Heterogeneity of experience (industry)	−0.763**	0.317
Communication informality	0.417*	0.179
Heterogeneity of education	−0.099*	0.233
Team size	−1.070**	0.083
Functional heterogeneity	0.677*	0.526
Number of permanent employees (1991)	0.249	0.108

Source: Morley *et al.* (1996)

A total of four top management team demography variables and two top management team process variables achieved significance in the analysis, suggesting that both demography and process variables are critical in explaining variation in company performance. Table 12.6 reports the means and the standard deviations of the variables in the study, while Table 12.7 reports the results of the multiple regression, with sales growth as the dependent variable.

Job tenure and levels of social integration pertaining in the top management team have no impact on sales growth in the organisations studied. In relation to the remaining variables, demographic and process characteristics are seen to have both a direct and indirect effect on sales growth. Team size and heterogeneity of industrial experience have a direct negative impact on sales growth. Conversely, functional heterogeneity has a direct positive impact. Variation in educational backgrounds has an indirect negative effect on sales growth. Finally, two process variables, namely communication informality and frequency of communication, are seen to be significant. Figure 12.3 graphically presents a path model of the results of the analysis.

Figure 12.3 Impact of Top Management Team Demography and Process on Firm Sales Growth

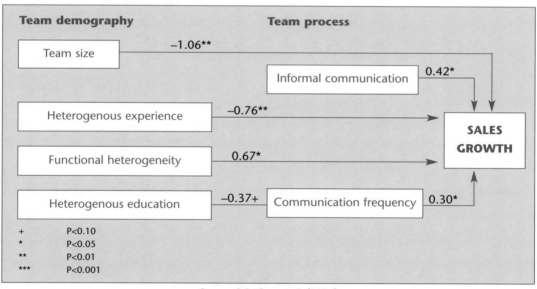

Source: Morley et al. (1996)

With respect to strategic leadership, this research does not support any pure demographic model. In relation to demography variables, team size has a direct negative relationship on sales growth, but the hypothesis that this occurs through negatively impacting on process is not supported. One would have anticipated that larger teams of leaders are arguably less socially integrated and encounter greater difficulties in communicating, which results in poorer performance. Job tenure has no impact on sales growth or indeed on leadership team processes. One would expect that this demographic variable would be positively related to performance through its impact on team process. The stability and familiarity that tenure should bring would be expected to positively influence social integration and communication and enhance organisational performance. This research suggests that heterogeneity of experience has a direct negative impact on sales growth. An explanation may be that teams with diverse experiential backgrounds encounter difficulties in decision making that hinders performance. Functional heterogeneity has a direct positive impact on sales growth. Variation in educational backgrounds has a negative impact on frequency of communication, suggesting that the amount of interaction between the members of the top management team is reduced where members of the team have diverse educational backgrounds. Social integration has no impact on sales growth in the Irish context, and the hypothesis that social integration is positively related to organisational performance finds no support. Communication informality and communication frequency have a positive impact on sales growth. As expected, informal communication would appear to facilitate the flow of communication and the number of interactions would appear to be related to performance.

CROSS-CULTURAL ISSUES AND LEADERSHIP

In exploring what makes a leader effective, it is necessary to take into consideration what leadership behaviour works and what doesn't work in different cultural settings. The majority of the leadership theories and research come from the US and Western Europe and are:

> individualistic rather than collectivistic; emphasising assumptions of rationality rather than ascetics, religion or superstition; stated in terms of individual rather than group incentives, stressing follower responsibilities rather than rights; assuming hedonistic rather than altruistic motivation and assuming centrality of work and democratic value orientation (House 1995: 443).

But not all cultures share these assumptions. One of the most significant cross-cultural leadership studies is GLOBE (Global Leadership and Organisational Behaviour Effectiveness), a programme exploring leadership and culture in sixty-one nations. GLOBE was conceived by Robert House, a leadership theorist we are already familiar with due to the prominence of his path-goal theory of leadership, and some of the questions posed by this project are outlined below (House *et al.* 2002).

- Are there leadership behaviours and attributes that are universally accepted?
- Are there leadership behaviours and attributes that are only accepted in certain cultures?
- What is the impact of societal culture on leader behaviour?
- What is the effect of violating cultural norms relevant to leadership behaviours?

In attempting to answer these questions, measures of societal and organisational culture were developed and the nine cultural dimensions studied in GLOBE are outlined below

(House *et al.* 2002). (Note: The first six culture items have their origins in Hofstede's (1980) dimensions of culture.)

1. **Uncertainty avoidance:** How comfortable the society/organisation is with uncertainty. Is there reliance on bureaucratic practices, social norms, etc. to alleviate uncertainty?
2. **Power distance:** The degree to which members are comfortable with imbalance in power.
3. **Collectivism I:** Societal collectivism – the degree to which the society/organisation rewards the collective distribution of resources.
4. **Collectivism II:** Group collectivism – the degree to which individuals are part of groups within their community and the loyalty they feel to their families, communities and organisations.
5. **Gender egalitarianism:** The degree to which society/organisation minimises gender role differences.
6. **Assertiveness:** The degree to which people will stand up for themselves and confront situations.
7. **Future orientation:** The degree to which people engage in long-term behaviour and look to the future.
8. **Performance orientation:** The extent to which performance is valued and rewarded.
9. **Humane orientation:** The degree to which societies/organisations encourage equality, fairness and altruistic behaviour.

The project also identified certain leadership behaviours, some of which are outlined below.

*   Charismatic/value based.
*   Team oriented.
*   Self-protective.
*   Participative.
*   Humane.
*   Autonomous.

While different cultures may vary regarding their conceptions of what makes a leader effective, the GLOBE findings suggest that certain aspects of charismatic/transformational leadership are universally endorsed as effective or outstanding, including trustworthiness, foresight, motivational ability and communication skills. However, other attributes of charismatic leadership were found to be culture specific, including risk taking, ambition and self-effacing behaviour. The acceptance of these behaviours may vary depending on the culture; for example, ambition may be less accepted in countries with low power distance.

SUMMARY OF KEY PROPOSITIONS

*   Leadership may be interpreted in simple terms, such as 'getting others to follow', or more specifically, for example, as 'the use of authority in decision making'. It may be exercised as an attribute of position or because of personal knowledge or wisdom.

- Leadership behaviour can be an integral part of a manager's job.
- Leadership activities can be classified into five key areas: task functions, cultural functions, symbolic functions, political functions and relational functions.
- Leadership trait theory argues that leaders are born and not made. Also known as the 'great man theory', the assumption was that it is possible to identify a unifying set of characteristics that make all great leaders great.
- Behavioural theories argue that specific behaviours differentiate leaders from non-leaders. Critical studies include the Ohio and Michigan studies and Blake and Mouton's managerial grid.
- Contingency theories are based on the premise that predicting leadership success and effectiveness is more complex than the simple isolation of traits or behaviours. Situational variables, or the context in which leadership is occurring, are also viewed as having strong explanatory power.
- Charismatic leadership has been directed at identifying behaviours that differentiate charismatic leaders from their non-charismatic counterparts. Transformational leadership has been influential here.
- Strategic leadership is concerned with those executives who have overall responsibility for the organisation – the top management team – and the impact of their characteristics and behaviours on organisational performance.
- We examined the cross cultural-leadership research, focusing on the GLOBE project.

DISCUSSION/SELF-ASSESSMENT QUESTIONS

1. 'Leaders are born, not made.' Discuss.
2. What are the main problems with trait theory of leadership?
3. What is the managerial grid?
4. What do you understand by contingency theory of leadership?
5. How might an organisation go about adopting the principle of superleadership?
6. What is strategic leadership?
7. Is charismatic leadership always an effective way of leading? Why or why not?
8. What are the differences between transactional and transformational leadership? In your opinion, are these leadership styles mutually exclusive? Why or why not?

MULTIPLE CHOICE QUESTIONS

1. According to the contingency theories of leadership:
   (a) Leaders are born, not bred.
   (b) Anyone can be a leader, if trained adequately.
   (c) It is vital to take into consideration the importance of situation when exploring leadership.
   (d) All of the above.
   (e) None of the above.

2. The great man theory of leadership defines a leader as:
    (a) Born with innate qualities.
    (b) Someone who has learned to adopt the appropriate leadership behaviours.
    (c) Someone who can take advantage of a situation.
    (d) Someone who will get their way no matter what the cost.
    (e) None of the above.

3. According to House's path-goal theory, directive leadership leads to greater satisfaction when:
    (a) Subordinates have an internal locus of control.
    (b) Tasks are ambiguous and stressful.
    (c) Tasks are highly structured and well laid out.
    (d) Subordinates are experts in their field.
    (e) All of the above.

4. Charismatic leadership involves:
    (a) The manipulation and coercion of followers.
    (b) The use of symbolic behaviour to gain commitment.
    (c) A 'tit for tat' relationship with followers.
    (d) A managerial approach to leading.
    (e) All of the above.
    (f) None of the above.

5. Transformational leadership involves:
    (a) Contingent reward.
    (b) Management by exception.
    (c) Laissez-faire leadership.
    (d) All of the above.
    (e) None of the above.

6. A definition of superleadership, according to the authors, would be:
    (a) An exceptional leader, but one who retains all the power.
    (b) A larger-than-life figure who is exceptional in every way.
    (c) A leader who empowers his/her followers and shares the leadership.
    (d) None of the above.

7. House's 1971 path-goal theory draws heavily from:
    (a) Expectancy theory of motivation.
    (b) Great man theory of leadership.
    (c) Equity theory of motivation.
    (d) All of the above.
    (e) None of the above.

8. Management, as opposed to leadership, is often associated with which of the following activities:
    (a) Solving short-term problems.
    (b) Keeping an eye on the bottom line.
    (c) Regulating the status quo.

(d) All of the above.

(e) None of the above.

9. The Blake and Mouton management grid identifies the following styles of management:

(a) Laissez-faire vs. participative.

(b) Country club, team, middle of the road, impoverished, task.

(c) Democratic vs. authoritarian.

(d) Transformational vs. transactional.

(e) None of the above.

FIVE SUGGESTED KEY READINGS

Den Hartog, D.N., House, R.J., Hanges, P.J., Ruiz-Quintanilla, S.A. and Dorfman, P.W., 'Culture specific and cross culturally generalisable implicit leadership theories: are attributes of charismatic/transformational leadership universally endorsed?', *Leadership Quarterly*, X/2 (1999), 219–57.

House, R.J., 'Path goal theory of leadership: lessons, legacy, and a reformulated theory', *Leadership Quarterly*, VII/3, (1996), 323–53.

House, R. and Aditya, R., 'The social scientific study of leadership: quo vadis?', *Journal of Management*, XXIII/3 (1997), 409–73.

Yukl, G., *Leadership in Organizations*, 5th ed., New York: Prentice Hall 2002.

Yukl, G., 'An evaluative essay on current conceptions of effective leadership', *European Journal of Work and Organisational Psychology*, VIII/1 (1999), 33–48.

REFERENCES

Bantel, K. and Jackson, S., 'Top management and innovations in banking: does the composition of the top team make a difference?', *Strategic Management Journal*, 10 (1989), 107–24.

Bass, B., 'From transactional to transformational leadership: learning to share the vision', *Organizational Dynamics* (Winter 1990), 22.

Bass, B.M. and Steidlmeier, P., 'Ethics, character, and authentic transformational leadership behaviour', *Leadership Quarterly*, X/2 (1999), 181–211.

Bennis, W., 'Managing the dream: leadership in the 21st century', *Journal of Organisational Change Management*, II/1 (1989), 7.

Bennis, W. and Nanus, B., *Leaders: The Strategies for Taking Charge*, New York: Harper & Row 1985.

Blake, R. and Mouton, J., 'The managerial grid', *Advanced Management Office Executive*, I/9 (1962).

Bryman, A., 'Charismatic leadership in business organisations: some neglected issues', *Leadership Quarterly*, IV (1993), 289–304.

Burns, J., *Leadership*, New York: Harper & Row 1978.

Conger, J., *The Charismatic Leader: Behind the Mystique of Exceptional Leadership*, San Francisco: Jossey-Bass 1989.

Conger, J. and Kanungo, R., *Charismatic Leadership*, San Fransisco: Jossey-Bass 1988.

Dawson, S., *Analysing Organisations*, London: Macmillan 1996.

Den Hartog, D.N., House, R.J., Hanges, P.J., Ruiz-Quintanilla, S.A. and Dorfman, P.W., 'Culture specific and cross culturally generalisable implicit leadership theories: are attributes of charismatic/transformational leadership universally endorsed?', *Leadership Quarterly*, X/2 (1999), 219–57.

Fiedler, F., *A Theory of Leadership Effectiveness*, New York: McGraw-Hill 1967.

Fiedler, F. and Chemers, M., *Leadership and Effective Management*, Glenview, IL: Scott, Foresman & Co. 1974.

Finkelstein, S. and Hambrick, D., *Strategic Leadership: Top Executives and Their Effects on Organizations*, St Paul, MN: West Publishing 1996.

Flood, P. and Smith, K., 'Top management team cohesiveness: impact on company performance', paper presented to College of Business Conference, Building an Effective and Cohesive Top Management Team, University of Limerick, May 1994.

Flood, P., Min Fong, C., Smith, K., O'Regan, P., Moore, S. and Morley, M., 'Top management teams and pioneering: a resource-based view', *International Journal of Human Resource Management*, VIII/3 (1997).

Gibb, C., 'The principles and traits of leadership', *Journal of Abnormal and Social Psychology*, XLII (1947), 267–84.

Goldsmith, W. and Clutterbuck, D., *The Winning Streak*, London: Weidenfeld & Nicolson 1984.

Hambrick, D., 'Top management groups: a conceptual integration and reconsideration of the "team" label', *Research in Organizational Behaviour*, XVI (1994), 171–213.

Hambrick, D. and Mason, P., 'Upper echelons: the organization as a reflection of its top managers', *Academy of Management Review*, IX (1984), 193–206.

Hersey, P. and Blanchard, K., *Management of Organizational Behavior: Utilizing Human Resources*, New York: Prentice Hall 1993.

Hofstede, G., *Culture's Consequences: International Differences in Work Related Values*, London: Sage 1980.

House, R., 'A path-goal theory of leader effectiveness', *Administrative Science Quarterly*, XVI (September 1971), 321–38.

House, R., 'A 1976 theory of charismatic leadership', in J. Hunt and L. Larson (eds), *Leadership: The Cutting Edge*, Carbondale, IL: Southern Illinois University Press 1977.

House, R.J., 'Path goal theory of leadership: lessons, legacy, and a reformulated theory', *Leadership Quarterly*, VII/3 (1996), 323–53.

House, R. and Aditya, R., 'The social scientific study of leadership: quo vadis?', *Journal of Management*, XXIII/3 (1997), 409–73.

House, R.J. and Shamir, B., 'Toward the integration of transformational, charismatic and visionary theories' in M.M. Chemers and R. Ayman (eds), *Leadership Theory and Research: Perspectives and Directions*, New York: Academic Press 1993.

House, R.J., Javidan, M., Hanges, P. and Dorfman, P., 'Understanding cultures and implicit leadership theories across the globe: an introduction to Project GLOBE', *Journal of World Business*, 37 (2002), 3–10.

Keating, M., Martin, G. and Donnelly-Cox, G., 'The GLOBE project: a case for interdisciplinary and intercultural research', in Proceedings of the 1st Irish Academy of Management Conference, Management Research in Ireland: The Way Forward, University College Cork, 12–13 September 1996.

Krech, D., Crutchfield, R. and Ballachey, E., *Individual in Society*, New York: McGraw-Hill 1962.

Likert, R., *New Patterns of Management*, New York: McGraw-Hill 1961.

Luthans, F., *Organizational Behavior*, New York: McGraw-Hill 1992.

Manz, C. and Sims, H., *SuperLeadership: Leading Others to Lead Themselves*, New York: Prentice Hall 1989.

Manz, C. and Sims, H., 'SuperLeadership: beyond the myth of heroic leadership', *Organizational Dynamics* (Summer 1991), 56–78.

Mintzberg, H., *The Nature of Managerial Work*, New York: Harper & Row 1973.

Moore, S., Morley, M., Fong, C., O'Regan, P. and Smith, K., 'Taking the lead: an investigation into the process of top management pioneering', in B. Leavy and J. Walsh (eds), *Strategy and General Management: An Irish Reader*, Dublin: Oak Tree Press 1996.

Morley, M., Moore, S. and O'Regan, P., 'The impact of the top management team on the sales growth performance of international divisions of US multinational enterprises operating in the Republic of Ireland', *Journal of Irish Business and Administrative Research*, XVII/1 (1996).

Mullins, L., *Management and Organisational Behaviour*, London: Pitman 1991.

Perrow, C., 'The short and glorious history of organizational theory', *Organizational Dynamics* (Summer 1973), 2–15.

Peters, T. and Austin, N., *A Passion for Excellence: The Leadership Difference*, New York: Random House 1985.

Pettinger, R., *Introduction to Management*, London: Macmillan 1994.

Robbins, S., *Organizational Behavior: Concepts, Controversies, and Applications*, Englewood Cliffs, NJ: Prentice Hall 1991.

Statt, D., *Psychology and the World of Work*, London: Macmillan 1994.

Stogdill, R., 'Personal factors associated with leadership: a survey of the literature', *Journal of Psychology*, XXV (1948), 35–71.

Stogdill, R. and Coons, A., *Leader Behavior: Its Description and Measurement*, Columbus, OH: Ohio State University Press of Bureau for Business Research 1957.

Tannenbaum, R., Weschler, I. and Masserik, F., *Leadership and Organization*, New York: McGraw-Hill 1961.

Tichy, N. and Devanna, M., 'The transformational leader', *Training and Development Journal*, (July 1986), 30–2.

Yetton, P., 'Leadership and supervision', in M. Gruneberg and T. Wall (eds), *Social Psychology and Organisational Behaviour*, Chichester: Wiley 1984.

Yukl, G., 'An evaluative essay on current conceptions of effective leadership', *European Journal of Work and Organisational Psychology*, VIII/1 (1999), 33–48.

Yukl, G., *Leadership in Organizations*, 5th ed., New York: Prentice Hall 2002.

Zaleznik, A., 'Managers and leaders: are they different?', *Harvard Business Review* (May/June 1977), 67–78.

THE DYNAMICS OF CONFLICT

13

Learning Objectives

- To consider the types of conflict that take place in organisational settings.
- To identify some of the key sources of conflict in organisations.
- To explain four key perspectives on organisational conflict.
- To consider some of the ways in which conflict at work can be managed and resolved.

INTRODUCTION

Whether conflict is viewed as desirable or otherwise, there is no escaping the fact that conflict exists and is endemic in all aspects of social interaction. For this reason, conflict can represent one of the most emotive aspects of organisational behaviour. It can arise for a variety of reasons, such as individual differences in goals, expectations, values, approaches to handling situations or perhaps due to personality clashes. Disagreements may thus arise over substantive issues relating to the manner in which work is carried out or be more emotionally or personally derived. In either case, conflict clearly constitutes a social process involving more than one person. When individual or group interests clash, as they inevitably will given the range and diversity of individual and group interests in organisations, it is likely that conflict will occur on occasion. The most visible organisational manifestation is probably industrial relations conflict, such as a strike or 'go-slow'. However, conflict can take numerous other forms, including conflicts between departments or work groups or individual, interpersonal conflict. How conflict is viewed and subsequently managed is perhaps the most telling aspect of the impact that conflict can have in an organisation. Properly managed, it can foster an understanding and valuing of differences that opens up new and different possibilities for action. Poorly handled or ignored, conflict can escalate (openly or covertly), resulting in an organisational environment that has detrimental implications for both individuals and organisation alike.

In this chapter we explore a number of dimensions of conflict in organisations. Here we look at definitional aspects of conflict and the various perspectives or schools of thought that influence how conflict is viewed in organisations. Next, the sources of conflict are examined and the process through which conflict manifests itself is discussed. Key strategies used for handling conflict are presented and the chapter concludes with a section detailing the complexities associated with group conflict in the organisation.

DEFINITIONS OF KEY CONCEPTS

Conflict
A process that begins when one party perceives that another party has negatively affected, or is about to negatively affect, something that the first party cares about (Thomas 1976).

Unitarist view of conflict
Conflict is seen as a negative factor that is harmful and therefore to be avoided.

Human relations or pluralist view of conflict
Conflict is a natural and inevitable feature of organisational life that cannot be eradicated.

Interactionist view of conflict
Conflict is not only a positive force but is necessary for effective group performance.

Radical view of conflict
Conflict in organisations is simply a manifestation of broader class conflict in relation to the distribution of power in society.

Functional conflict
Conflict that leads to positive benefits for the organisation.

Dysfunctional conflict
Conflict that leads to negative or damaging consequences for the organisation.

Conflict handling
An interactive process whereby the actions of one party impact on the behaviour of others involved. Parties to the conflict determine how they will approach the conflict situation, but they may alter their approach depending on how the other party approaches the conflict situation.

DEFINING CONFLICT

Conflict can be perceived in a variety of ways, depending on the perceptions of the individuals involved or on the particular circumstances or context within which it occurs. Conflict can be evaluated positively or negatively, be seen as rational or irrational, a worthwhile or fruitless activity. While numerous definitions of conflict exist, perhaps the most widely accepted definition is that proposed by Thomas (1976), who describes conflict as a process which begins when one party perceives that another party has frustrated (or is about to frustrate) some concern that it values. Essentially there are three core features underpinning the notion of conflict. In the first instance, conflict must be perceived by the parties to it, i.e. if no one is aware of a conflict, then conflict cannot be said to exist. Second, there must be some kind of opposition or incompatibility, i.e. different perspectives that are valued by the parties. Finally, there must be some form of interaction between the parties for it to be felt (except in the case of intrapersonal conflict, as described below).

Our most common image of conflict in organisations is probably that of collective conflict, involving some form of dispute between workers and management such as a strike or 'go-slow'. However, such employee relations conflict is only one form of conflict in organisations. Broadly speaking, conflict can be seen to occur at a number of specific levels, and the level at which conflict occurs will clearly have implications for how it is handled, if at all.

Intrapersonal conflict occurs within the individual. There are certain inner conflicts that an individual can experience which do not involve other individuals or groups. These conflicts may occur because of actual or perceived pressures from incompatible goals or expectations, i.e. being offered a promotion that involves considerably more money (positive and welcome aspect), but also requires relocation (not so welcome in terms of impact on personal life). While inner conflicts can give rise to other types of conflict, in themselves they are not interactive. Inner conflict can result in stress, uncertainty or anxiety, or alternatively it can be associated with positive decisions and effective individual development.

Interpersonal conflict occurs between two or more individuals who are in opposition to one another. This opposition may occur over substantive issues associated with work, such as goals or targets to be achieved, resource allocation or policies or procedures to be adopted. Interpersonal conflict can also be emotionally based (Walton 1969) and arise over feelings of anger, mistrust, dislike, fear, resentment and so forth. Almost everyone who has worked in an organisation will have experienced some degree of interpersonal conflict, which can occur between an employee and his/her manager or between two or more employees or managers.

Intergroup conflict occurs between groups in an organisation. Essentially, it refers to interpersonal conflict (either of a substantive or emotional nature) that extends beyond the individual level to incorporate groups. Organisations have tremendous potential for intergroup conflict. The fact that organisations are often designed so that people work in comparatively discrete units means that intergroup discord and rivalries inevitably arise. Common sources of intergroup conflict are those relating to resource allocation, interdependence and differentiation or where there is some structural or contingent factor affecting group functioning.

Interorganisational conflict is typically associated with competitive functioning within product or service markets where organisations compete for market share, resources or profits. It can also occur between organisations representing different interest groups, i.e. union and employer organisations in conflict over national pay deals, etc.

Conflict in organisations can thus be seen to occur for a variety of reasons. For example, conflict may occur where one individual feels that another is deliberately putting obstacles in the way of them achieving objectives; where managers pursue different goals than the employees for whom they are responsible; when two departments get involved in a competition over scarce resources; when various agreements are violated; or when basic rights within organisational systems are not taken into account. In this chapter, our main focus is on interpersonal conflict that involves two or more individuals or groups within an organisational setting.

PERSPECTIVES ON CONFLICT IN ORGANISATIONS

Our definition of conflict would suggest an acceptability of conflict as a feature of organisational life, in which case it becomes a managerial task to ensure that conflict does not have an unduly disruptive effect on the organisation. This brings us to a critical debate on how best to view conflict in organisations, i.e. what exactly the normality, desirability and legitimacy of conflict in organisations is (see Dunford 1992). There are a number of broad perspectives and frameworks that we can use to help understand traditional and more recent thinking on the role and utility of conflict in an organisational setting, and these are presented here for discussion (see Fox 1966, 1973; Edwards 1986; Huczynski and Buchanan 1991; De Dreu and Van de Vliert 1997).

THE TRADITIONAL OR UNITARIST VIEW OF CONFLICT

Early approaches to conflict assumed that all conflict was inherently bad. Conflict was seen as a negative factor that was harmful and therefore to be avoided and as stemming from some malfunction in the system, such as poor communication or lack of openness. The focus for management, then, was to find the source of this malfunction and 'fix it' in order that further conflict could be avoided.

Essentially, this unitarist perspective views conflict as an aberration which occurs because 'something has gone wrong'. Harmony and unity are seen as the natural state, with conflict an abnormal phenomenon which occurs as a result of some failure in the normal functioning of the organisation, such as poor communications, poor management or the work of 'troublemakers'. While viewing conflict as abnormal, the unitarist perspective also sees conflict as essentially negative and damaging to the organisation's normal harmonious, productive state. Thus, conflict is viewed as something which can and should be avoided. Where it does occur, management should take appropriate steps to eradicate it, most likely by addressing the source, i.e. improve communications or organisation design, train managers or get rid of troublemakers.

It is still commonplace for conflict to be viewed as an 'abnormal' or 'unnatural' phenomenon. Reasons for this are both numerous and complex. For example, Rollinson (1993) points to the effects of social institutions, such as the Church and some of the more traditional conceptions of the family, as significant factors in shaping attitudes to conflict, particularly in promoting the view that unity and harmony are the 'natural state' for organisations. 'Many of the important institutions in our society – the home, the Church, and so on – are founded on the premise that harmony is a natural state of affairs, and this has a powerful effect on the way conflict is regarded' (Rollinson 1993: 251).

Rollinson also points out that the influence of the classical management theorists, such as Taylor (1911) and Fayol (1949), succeeded in establishing the perception that conflict was abnormal in organisations. The contribution of the classical management theorists further led to a vision of the 'ideal' organisation as a smoothly run entity where management designed plans in a systematic fashion and all the constituent parts gelled to execute these plans. Unity and harmony were the bywords, whereas the existence of conflict was generally regarded as an unnatural state that wasted scarce resources by consuming management time and channelling employee energies in inappropriate directions. This perspective assumed goal congruity between all the parties in the organisation.

Clearly, such assumptions run contrary to evidence on the actual practice of organisational management. There is much evidence to suggest that different groups in any organisational setting are likely to have different goals and motives for behaving in the ways that they do. Organisational strategies, for example, may on the surface tell a story of cohesion and consensus, but in actual fact, any plan for the organisation's future usually requires addressing and accepting that there is often a wide diversity of different explicit and implicit goals within any one organisation. Usually the functioning of that organisation will depend on recognising and managing the conflicting interests, which are bound to lead to at least some levels of conflict.

THE HUMAN RELATIONS OR PLURALIST VIEW OF CONFLICT

The human relations view of conflict dominated conflict theory from about the start of the 1950s through to the mid-1970s. In essence, this approach took the view that conflict is natural and inevitable in all groups and organisations, and therefore, rather than seeking to avoid it (which is impossible), organisations and managers should accept it. This more realistic view proposes that conflict cannot be eradicated, but rather is to be expected and is indeed a normal phenomenon in organisations. Conflict is seen as a rational response, perhaps to oppressive or unjust management systems, or at least an inevitable feature of organisational life.

This essentially pluralist perspective views conflict as a naturally occurring phenomenon in organisations, arising from the differing perspectives and interests of all the groups and individuals who make up the organisation. Since conflict is seen as inevitable, management should therefore expect it to occur and should plan for this eventuality so that it can be handled successfully and not endanger the achievement of the organisation's primary objectives. Since conflict is not necessarily negative but can have beneficial effects, efforts should be concentrated on channelling functional conflict to realise such organisational benefits. The emphasis is therefore on the management of conflict as opposed to its elimination.

THE INTERACTIONIST VIEW OF CONFLICT

While the human relations or pluralist view accepts the inevitability of conflict, the interactionist perspective goes further by actually stimulating conflict and also instigating means for its resolution. This approach suggests that not only is conflict natural and inevitable, but it should be encouraged to avoid situations where harmonious and co-operative groups become static, apathetic and non-responsive to needs for change and innovation (De Dreu and Van de Vliert 1997). It is therefore appropriate to maintain a certain level of conflict to stimulate creativity and innovation. Thus, an 'acceptable' level of conflict is seen as both positive and necessary, particularly in creating a work environment which stimulates change and 'new' thinking.

THE RADICAL VIEW OF CONFLICT

The radical perspective is essentially grounded in Marxist theory of capitalist society and social change. Conflict in capitalist societies is seen as a symptom of the structural enmity which exists between capital and labour, employer and employee. Such enmity arises from the organisation of work in capitalist societies and the unequal distribution of power between the dominant establishment group that owns the means of production (employers, shareholders) and those whose labour is required to produce goods and services (workers). Therefore, conflict in organisations is simply a manifestation of broader class conflict in relation to the distribution of power in society, and organisations are just a microcosm of a broader class conflict between the 'bourgeoisie' (who control economic resources and political power) and the 'proletariat', with managers representing the interests of capital. In the radical perspective, conflict is seen as a means of instigating revolutionary change designed to dismantle the capitalist system, redistribute power in favour of workers and the working class and ultimately achieve a classless society.

In arguing that conflict can be a positive force in an organisation, it becomes necessary to further differentiate the conflict construct into two broad classifications – functional conflict and dysfunctional conflict. Automatically assuming that conflict is an entirely negative force in an organisation closes people off to the possibilities and opportunities that conflict episodes can unlock. On the other hand, assuming that conflict is always an opportunity for achieving positive outcomes is naïve and unrealistic. The extent to which conflict is functional or dysfunctional often depends on how the various parties involved manage the part that they play in conflict situations. In addition, and more recently, descriptions of functional and dysfunctional conflict are normally based on their differing effects on the organisation (Gibson et al. 1994). Functional conflict, then, can be described as that which leads to benefits for the organisation, while dysfunctional conflict encompasses that which damages the organisation, for example, through impeding the achievement of production targets or any action which threatens the survival or in some way damages the competitiveness of the organisation.

It is equally important to acknowledge that conflict can take differing forms, which can have either positive or negative effects. From a management perspective it is therefore necessary that conflict be managed as effectively, constructively and productively as possible. It was noted earlier that there are positive dimensions of organisational conflict. Thomas (1976) argues that unless organisational members recognise the potentially positive effects of conflict, the opportunity to learn and gain from situations of conflict can be lost. Conflict can motivate by energising the environment and the people who operate within it and can allow people to become clearer about their own positions, helping them to analyse and confront divergent views within the system. Furthermore, as noted by Thomas, the confrontation of divergent views can often lead to ideas of superior quality that may not have been considered at all if conflict had not arisen in the first place. Conflict can also act as a catalyst for change and innovation in organisations as well as serving as a 'pressure release' mechanism, allowing parties to vent opinions and positions which are a source of frustration and anxiety.

These differing perspectives on conflict are more than analytical categories. Rather, they play a critically significant role in influencing the reactions and behaviour of individuals and groups who are involved in conflict situations. For example, where conflict is viewed as unnatural and essentially disruptive, there will be little tolerance or accommodation of those that articulate or engage in actions that are in conflict with the expressed status quo. Alternatively, where conflict is viewed as natural or even beneficial, there will be concerted efforts to engage in activities that challenge established practice in favour of change or innovative approaches to viewing organisational situations.

SOURCES OF CONFLICT IN ORGANISATIONS

In studying the nature of conflict in organisations, it is important that we attempt to identify possible sources of conflict. It is also important to acknowledge that conflict is 'normal' in organisations, although, of course, excessive levels of conflict are undesirable. Huczynski and Buchanan (1991) identify five major sources of conflict in organisations:
- the employment relationship;
- competition over scarce resources;
- ambiguity over responsibility or authority;
- interdependence; and
- differentiation.

Commentators such as Allen (1971) argue that the structure of the employment relationship, which emphasises employer needs for productivity, cost effectiveness and change, is often at odds with employee needs for security, adequate rewards and opportunity for personal growth. It is therefore to be expected that in this 'labour for pay' exchange, interests will clash and result in conflict on occasion, e.g. pay disputes. However, the potential conflict is not simply confined to the 'financial exchange' dimension. The employment relationship also requires the ongoing exercise of employer/managerial authority over employees in the workplace on issues such as working time, work flow and task allocation (Reed 1989). Again, some degree of conflict here is inevitable, as differing interests clash and seek to establish their positions, e.g. disputes over demarcation or work loads.

Another obvious and significant source of conflict in organisations is that which may occur in relation to resource allocation decisions, examples of which include those relating to product development, financial investment and deployment of human resources. It is clear that some element of both interindividual, intergroup and intragroup conflict is inevitable in relation to decisions on the allocation of financial, technical and human resources.

Role ambiguity occurs when a person in a role is uncertain about their role and/or the role expectations of other members of their role set (for example, see Schermerhorn *et al.* 1985). Individual workers may often be unclear as to their particular job responsibilities or of the precise roles of other workers and managers. For example, there may be ambiguity in relation to lines of authority in areas such as reporting relationships and financial expenditure, which can lead to conflicts between individuals and groups in relation to divisions of responsibility and the exercise of authority.

The existence of some level of interdependence between individuals and work groups may also be a source of conflict in organisations. This is particularly pertinent where, for example, work flow or quality among one group of workers is contingent on the performance of other groups or individuals. If a group is unhappy about another group's performance, some level of conflict is likely to emerge.

A final source of conflict is differentiation, which Huczynski and Buchanan (1991: 550) define as 'the degree to which tasks and work of individuals or groups is divided.' It is suggested that such differentiation in organisations leads to the establishment of distinct work groups or cliques that establish their own 'norms, values and practices'. As a result those outside such groups may view such cliques with suspicion. In turn these distinct groups may themselves view 'outsiders' as 'lesser mortals'. Such perceptions will inevitably lead to some conflicts between individuals and groups. A common example where such conflicts can occur in the industrial relations sphere is in conflicts between skilled and unskilled work groups.

THE CONFLICT PROCESS

Most conflicts tend to develop in stages, which can be broadly termed potential opposition or incompatibility, realisation and personalisation, intentions and behaviour and outcomes, as follows.

STAGE 1: POTENTIAL OPPOSITION OR INCOMPATIBILITY

In the first instance there are conditions or circumstances that create the potential for conflict to arise, though conflict is not inevitable. These can typically result from communication problems (use of jargon, misinterpretation, insufficient information), structural problems (relating to formal work arrangements such as specialisation, resource allocation, leadership style and so forth) or personal variables (clash of personalities).

STAGE 2: REALISATION AND PERSONALISATION

Here, one of the factors outlined above affects something that one party cares about and that party then perceives the conflict situation. Not only does that party perceive the conflict but feels it, i.e. becomes emotionally involved and experiences anxiety, tension or hostility. This engagement or personalisation constitutes the essence of the conflict situation.

STAGE 3: INTENTIONS AND BEHAVIOUR

This is the stage where the 'aggrieved' party first takes a decision to act in a particular way (intention), but this is inherently based on how that party perceives that the other party is going to behave. The party then acts on that intention, manifesting in overt behaviour. At this stage the conflict becomes overt and can range from subtle or indirect actions/reactions to more direct, even aggressive or violent behaviours (depending on the nature of the conflict and how strongly it is felt). It is at this stage that the range of conflict-handling behaviours are initiated (these are discussed in the next section).

STAGE 4: OUTCOMES

The conflict-handling behaviour utilised will result in specific consequences and thus the outcomes of conflict can be either functional (resulting in some positive consequences) or dysfunctional (a negative outcome that adversely affects the relationship or activity). Functional conflict can be seen to have a number of positive outcomes for organisations, including improved quality of decision making, stimulating creativity and innovation, relieving boredom and improving communication and participation between groups. Dysfunctional conflict, on the other hand, can lead to damaging outcomes, such as emotional and physical damage to individuals, dissolution of trust, decreased productivity, reduced group cohesiveness and ultimately diminished organisational performance. We shall return to the outcomes of conflict towards the end of the chapter.

CONFLICT HANDLING AND RESOLUTION

A key theme in the preceding discussion is that some degree of conflict is inevitable in organisations. As such, a particular onus falls on management to develop effective strategies to deal with such conflict. Within the organisation, all levels of management have specific and important roles to play in conflict handling and resolution. Line managers and team leaders have a key role in dealing with individual conflicts and grievances. Senior management has overall responsibility for the development of effective strategies and policies to both limit the extent of conflict (particularly dysfunctional conflict) and to handle any more serious conflicts which arise. As discussed earlier, conflict in organisations should not necessarily be viewed in negative terms, and properly handled, conflict can have many positive effects, allowing individuals or groups to highlight and pursue issues of concern. While conflict often involves difficult and fraught interactions between individuals and groups, it may ultimately facilitate constructive change and development in organisations.

In evaluating alternative approaches to handling conflict, Schermerhorn *et al.* (1985) suggest that managers can react in the following ways.

- **Non-attention:** No deliberate attempt is made to deal with the conflict.
- **Suppression:** An attempt is made to quell the conflict, for example, by disciplining the individual(s) involved. However, suppression does not address the source of the conflict or seek viable long-term solutions.

- **Resolution:** Involves the search for long-term solutions to the source of conflict.

Using terminology traditionally used in relation to negotiations between two or more parties, Schermerhorn *et al.* also argue that attempts to manage conflict can result in lose-lose, win-lose and win-win outcomes. Lose-lose outcomes involve those where all parties to the conflict are unhappy with the outcome. Win-lose outcomes involve one party achieving its desired aims to the detriment of the other party, outcomes which often result from conflict suppression. Win-win outcomes involve all parties to the conflict gaining a satisfactory outcome. Such win-win outcomes ideally involve the elimination of the source of conflict and thus prevent it from arising again at some future stage.

CONFLICT-HANDLING STRATEGIES

While the three possible outcomes described above (win-win, win-lose, lose-lose) provide a convenient categorisation of conflict outcomes, a more pressing concern for managers confronted with conflict situations is what strategies might optimally be adopted to help resolve such conflicts. One of the most widely quoted models of conflict-handling strategies is that developed by Ken Thomas (Thomas 1976), summarised in Figure 13.1, and is based on two conflict-handling dimensions.

1. The assertiveness dimension, which measures how assertive or unassertive each party is in pursuing its own concerns or needs.
2. The co-operativeness dimension, which measures how co-operative or unco-operative each party is in satisfying the concerns or needs of the other party.

The interplay of these two dimensions produces five different conflict-handling orientations or behaviours that can be used in a variety of conflict situations.

1. Competition (assertive and unco-operative).
2. Collaboration (assertive and co-operative).
3. Compromise (moderate on both dimensions).
4. Avoidance (unassertive and unco-operative).
5. Accommodation (unassertive and co-operative).

Each behavioural style can be used in overt conflict situations and reflects the preferred approach to conflict handling given the relative extent of assertiveness and co-operativeness.

In a particular conflict situation, the selection of a specific conflict-handling orientation will be influenced by the extent to which there is a perceived conflict of interest between the parties and also by an assessment of the power and level of commitment of each party (see Dunford 1992). Such factors facilitate the identification of appropriate contexts for the adoption of particular conflict-handling orientations. Using empirical data, Thomas (1977) positioned each conflict-handling orientation within an 'appropriate' situation or context. The following section briefly describes each of Thomas's conflict-handling orientations and his conclusions in relation to their appropriate operational context (see Thomas 1976, 1977).

Figure 13.1 Conflict-Handling Orientations

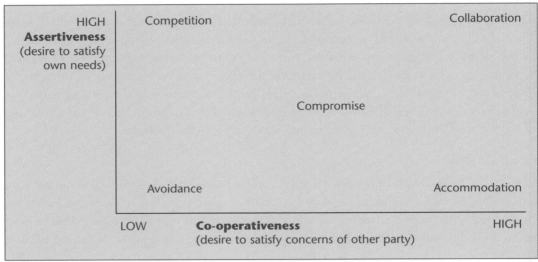

Source: Adapted from Thomas (1976: 900)

The competition orientation is characterised by a desire to win (dominate) at the other party's expense. It entails a highly assertive win-lose approach, involving the use of one particular power base and competitive strength to achieve their objectives regardless of the implications for the other party. This orientation is considered most appropriate in the following situations.

- When quick, decisive action is required, such as crisis situations.
- On critical issues where unpopular action is required, such as cost cutting, restructuring, enforcing unpopular rules or taking disciplinary action.
- In dealing with people or parties who are persistently competitive in the face of other non-competitive types of behaviour.

The collaborative orientation is characterised by a desire to achieve a mutually acceptable outcome that satisfies the interests of both parties. It requires a problem-solving orientation by both parties, i.e. a willingness to work through issues of conflict, confronting and dealing with problems so that each party benefits from the results. This orientation is considered most appropriate in the following situations.

- Where each party's concerns are too important to be compromised and thus some integrative solution is required.
- Where learning is the objective.
- When it is desirable to merge insights from parties holding different perspectives.
- When it is desirable to build consensus by taking account of the concerns of all parties in order to achieve the commitment of the parties involved.
- To effectively address the feelings of each party, which may have interfered with relationships.

It is also argued that groups that are likely to have to work together after a conflict episode are well advised to search for collaborative solutions to the conflict issues that they face.

The compromise orientation is characterised by a desire to seek solutions that partially satisfy the needs of each party. Certain trade-offs are used as keys to conflict resolution, with each party gaining something but also making concessions in relation to their own position so that satisfactory rather than ideal solutions are achieved. This orientation is considered most appropriate in the following situations.

- Where each party's goals are important, but not to the extent that would merit the effort or potential disruption associated with more assertive approaches.
- Where parties committed to mutually exclusive goals operate from a similar power base.
- To achieve temporary settlements in relation to complex issues.
- Where time constraints require that expedient solutions are achieved.
- As a back-up orientation when competition or collaboration approaches are unsuccessful.

The avoidance orientation is characterised by withdrawal from the particular conflict situation. It may involve ignoring the conflict, often in the hope that it will go away, and is commonly used as a result of one or both parties' inability to face up to the conflict and address it adequately. An avoidance orientation, entailing as it does a desire to dodge any manifestation of conflict, may lead to an effective withdrawal of a party from the conflict. Alternatively, a party may attempt to suppress the conflict by disguising or withholding any manifestation of that conflict. This approach may be particularly common where close personal relations exist between the parties and either party may choose to avoid confrontation. The avoidance orientation is considered most appropriate in the following situations.

- Where the issue is of minor importance or more important issues are pressing.
- When a party feels there is no chance of satisfying its concerns.
- Where the issues at hand have a potential for disruption that exceeds the potential benefits of resolution.
- To allow a 'cooling off' period.
- Where the collection of adequate information is of greater priority than reaching an immediate decision.
- Where others can resolve the conflict more effectively.
- When the issue at hand seems 'tangential or symptomatic of other issues' (Thomas 1977: 487).

The accommodation orientation is characterised by a desire to satisfy the concerns of the other party at the expense of one's own interests. It involves allowing the other party's wishes to rule and is often motivated by a stronger wish to maintain the working relationship between parties than to pursue one's other interests. This orientation is considered most appropriate in the following situations.

- Where a party finds it is wrong.
- When the issue at hand is more important to the other party than yourself – to satisfy others and to maintain co-operation/working relationships.
- To build 'credits' for dealing with subsequent issues.
- To minimise loss when faced with a losing situation.
- Where the maintenance of harmony and stability take priority.
- To allow subordinates to develop and learn as a result of their mistakes.

In evaluating approaches to conflict handling, it is important to note that conflict situations are dynamic in nature. Thus, the parties may start out with a particular conflict-handling orientation, but as the situation evolves the parties may alter their position as they gain insights into the other party's position or as power is exercised. Conflict handling is therefore an interactive process (Huczynski and Buchanan 1991) whereby the actions of one party impact on the behaviour of others involved. Such reactions and modifications are inherent to the conflict-handling process. It is often argued that collaboration, which scores high on both co-operativeness and assertiveness, is the 'ideal' strategy in conflict handling because it represents an explicit attempt to address the conflict head-on and treat the sources of such conflict.

However, it is important to acknowledge the reality that more often than not, many conflicts in organisations are resolved through some form of compromise. In no area is this more pertinent than in employee relations conflict. Indeed, perhaps the most widespread response to industrial conflict in the workplace has been the development of joint mechanisms to discuss and resolve issues of difference through negotiation (Gunnigle *et al.* 1995). Such institutionalisation of conflict is primarily characterised by the development of agreed procedures to facilitate conflict resolution. This reflects an implicit acceptance that issues of conflict will arise and is characteristic of the pluralist approach to employee relations discussed earlier. In creating institutions (such as negotiating structures) and procedures for handling employee relations and industrial conflict, the parties involved seek to create a framework through which the parties can interact, argue, disagree and agree while allowing for the ongoing operation of the business. Grievances, disputes and disciplinary procedures are a characteristic feature of Irish organisations and represent an important means of dealing with employee relations conflict at the level of the enterprise.

CONFLICT OUTCOMES

At the end of a conflict episode, some result will emerge: the conflict may be resolved, it may be suppressed or simply deferred to emerge again at some future stage. Such an outcome will have various implications for the participants. Where some solution is found, the parties may have particular responsibilities to execute to ensure that whatever agreement reached is put into practice. The outcome will also affect the perceptions, feelings and future conflict-handling orientations of the parties involved. For example, the parties may feel disappointed or happy with the outcome. This may in turn affect their future relationships and also cause them to adopt differing strategies in their future interactions.

Some of the most visible manifestations of conflict in organisations are evident in the employee relations arena, where conflict seems an inherent feature of organisational life and where some degree of industrial conflict is inevitable. It is possible to identify two broad forms of employee relations conflict here: unorganised, individual conflict and organised, collective conflict (Salaman 1992). Unorganised, individual conflict tends to represent spontaneous, reactive and random responses that do not form part of a conscious strategy on behalf of the proponents. Common outcomes of unorganised conflict include absenteeism, turnover, theft and many forms of industrial sabotage. Organised, collective conflict, on the other hand, encompasses more systematic, collective efforts in pursuing a conscious strategy through co-ordinated action designed to achieve specified objectives. The most common examples of organised employee relations conflict are strikes, go-slows, overtime bans and the withdrawal of co-operation. Examples of both types of conflict outcomes are presented below.

OUTCOMES OF CONFLICT IN ORGANISATIONS

Strike
Strikes are collective in nature and involve the temporary withdrawal of labour. Strike action can take different forms. Official strikes are defined as those which have been fully sanctioned by the union executive and normally occur after negotiations have failed to resolve the issue and when all due procedures have been exhausted. Unofficial strikes are those which have not been sanctioned by the trade union and tend to be quite reactive in nature, often sparked off by a particular event or incident at workplace level, such as the dismissal or suspension of a worker.

Withdrawal of co-operation
Collective in nature, this entails involving the withdrawal of representatives from joint institutions, strict interpretation of and rigorous adherence to procedure and absence of flexibility.

Work to rule
Collective in nature, this involves working only in accordance with the strict interpretation of written terms and conditions of employment, job description or other rules, such as those concerning safety or hygiene.

Overtime ban
Collective in nature, an overtime ban is a refusal to work outside normal contractual hours of work.

Go-slow
Collective in nature, in a go-slow employees work at a lower than average level of performance.

Sabotage

Individual in nature, sabotage is a conscious action to damage goods, equipment or other aspects of the work environment.

Pilfering and theft

Individual in nature, this involves stealing items owned by the organisation.

Absenteeism

Absenteeism has been generically defined as 'all absences from work other than paid holidays'. As such it is reckoned that only a small proportion of absenteeism may represent a form of conflict. Where it does, it tends to represent an individual response to perceived problems in the workplace.

Labour turnover

Labour turnover refers to the rate at which people leave the organisation. As with absenteeism, only a proportion of labour turnover in organisations is representative of conflict in organisations.

Lock-out

In the employee relations sphere in particular, it is important to acknowledge that employers may instigate a lock-out, which involves preventing the workforce from attending at work and is the equivalent of strike action by employees.

Source: Salaman (1992) Gunnigle *et al.* (1995)

Of course, this distinction is often more clouded in practice, particularly so in relation to the randomness and spontaneity of unorganised conflict. Blyton and Turnbull (1994) illustrate the difficulty in differentiating between organised and unorganised conflict by citing the 'blue flu' phenomenon in the New York Police Department, whereby all police officers report in sick on the same day. Such co-ordinated forms of traditionally 'unorganised' conflict are likely to become increasingly common as increased competitiveness and job insecurity render more organised methods, especially strikes, less attractive to workers due to loss of income and the possibility of dismissal. It is also clear that certain forms of apparently organised conflict can be quite reactive and spontaneous in nature. For example, so-called 'wildcat' strikes can occur when workers walk off the job in reaction to a particular incident but do not possess any overall strategy.

An important theme in our earlier discussion on conflict perspectives is that conflict in organisations can be functional, that is, it can have positive outcomes for the organisation and participants. For example, Dunford (1992: 229) identifies the following functional outcomes of organisational conflict.

- In conflict situations, differing viewpoints on an issue tend to be proffered: this can lead to the exploration of an array of different solutions and to the identification of 'superior' solutions.

- Conflict situations may lead the parties involved to reflect on their perspectives and commitment to particular issues, leading to potentially positive changes in their beliefs and approaches.
- It is likely that the tensions and interaction involved in conflict situations may lead to greater creativity in terms of approaches, solutions and future working arrangements.
- Conflict can serve to identify fundamental problems in the organisations which need to be addressed. The absence of any manifestation of such conflict may lead to such problems being suppressed and thus continue to impair the functioning of the organisations.

This latter point illustrates the dangers of passivity for organisations. The absence of conflict may lead to both excessive complacency about the extent of harmony in the organisation and to an organisational climate that is excessively rigid and overly committed to the status quo. This phenomenon led Robbins (1978) to suggest that organisations can suffer from a 'lack of conflict', and he identified a number of pointers to this 'condition', as illustrated below.

INDICATORS OF INSUFFICIENT CONFLICT IN ORGANISATIONS

- Managers who are surrounded by subordinates who always agree with their ideas.
- Subordinates who are afraid to admit to lack of knowledge or uncertainty.
- Excessive emphasis on reaching decisions through compromise so that decision makers lose sight of values, long-term objectives and organisational well-being.
- A managerial value system based on ensuring an impression of harmony and co-operation in their domains.
- Decision makers who are excessively concerned with others' feelings.
- A managerial value system that views popularity as more important than competence or performance in gaining organisational rewards.
- Excessive managerial concern with achieving decisions through consensus.
- Employees who demonstrate an unusually high resistance to change.
- Lack of new ideas being generated.
- Unusually low level of employee turnover.

It is important to note that these are merely indicators that an organisation may be suffering from a lack of conflict. Clearly, many of the phenomena detailed above may occur for extraneous reasons, for example, low labour turnover may be due to economic recession and high unemployment. Nevertheless, conflict stimulation may be used in organisations to achieve some of the positive outcomes mentioned earlier.

A pervasive theme in our consideration of conflict in organisations has centred around the issue of legitimacy, i.e. the extent to which conflict is seen as a natural phenomenon, or alternatively the extent to which conflict is seen as abnormal. Where conflict is seen as a natural state, it is likely that managers will focus on addressing the sources rather than the symptoms of conflict. It is also likely that various mechanisms will be established to facilitate conflict handling. Where conflict is seen as abnormal, management will often focus on eliminating conflict altogether. Open communications and high trust are often seen as the answer in this respect. Our conclusion is that some degree of conflict will inevitably occur in all organisations. Such conflict is inevitable because of the range and diversity of individual and group interests in organisations. However, such conflict is not necessarily negative, and indeed can have many positive benefits for organisations, particularly in facilitating grievance handling and changes in work practices, in stimulating creativity and in improving decision making. Because of the inevitability of some level of conflict arising, the area of conflict handling remains of critical concern for organisations if the attendant outcomes are going to result in appreciable benefits for the organisation and its members.

ADVANCED CONCEPTS/ONGOING DEBATES IN CONFLICT

CULTURE AND CONFLICT

As discussed in Chapter 9, culture is perceived to have a significant impact on the effectiveness and competitiveness of organisations (for example, see Peters and Waterman 1982; Kilmann 1989; Brown 1992). Lewis *et al.* (1997) argue that the effects of culture on the performance of an organisation depend not on the strength of the overall culture or on the individual components of that culture, but rather on the mix and weightings of the components of that culture. They cite the example of conflict, which they argue might be a healthy incentive for action and competition when present in some forms and degrees, but can be damaging when it becomes the culture's dominant feature. In a culture dominated by conflict, this excessive conflict can be seen to paralyse an organisation's ability to function since it is unable to set goals, organise staff, conduct productive meetings or solve problems in a meaningful way.

Given that many conflicts in organisations become institutionalised through common attitudes, values and rituals, conflict can become an undesirable part of an organisation's culture without members being consciously aware of its presence.

A problem for many organisations centres around striking a balance between a 'healthy degree of conflict' that is used to stimulate creativity and innovation and the development of a culture of conflict that is dysfunctional. In other words, how can an organisation control the type of conflict it encourages and not, in fact, encourage the 'wrong' type of conflict? Amason *et al.* (1995) identify two types of conflict: cognitive or issue-related conflict, which is seen to be beneficial to decision making, and affective conflict, which is described as a personalised type of conflict (an intolerance of others' opinions and motives) that erodes decision quality. Amason (1996: 126) further highlights the multidimensional nature of conflict and argues that that while one aspect of conflict enhances decision quality, another dimension attenuates consensus and affective acceptance. Managing conflict is inherently difficult in situations where conflict is not acknowledged or is hidden. Unresolved conflict in teams or groups or a refusal to discuss issues is highly dysfunctional and results in open hostility, while covert hostility can be seen as 'toxic' because it breeds a climate of distrust and secrecy.

GROUPS AND CONFLICT

With the internationalisation of business, diverse task groups, in terms of ethnic, geographic, cultural and functional diversity, are becoming more common and this diversity inevitably results in at least the potential for conflict to emerge. In the traditional model of group formation (see Chapter 8 for a detailed description), intragroup conflict is an inevitable feature of the 'storming' phase, as individuals express their individuality and seek to establish control within the group. Moreover, an inability to recognise individual differences and the positive benefits these differences can bring to a group can result in overt or covert conflict.

Smith and Berg (1987) suggest that conflict is a concomitant, attendant process of collective life that may be an inevitable and recurring feature of all group interactions. They also propose that conflict may be a result both of the inevitable differences of those individuals who comprise the group as well as the 'unconscious ambivalence' stirred by individuals becoming part of a collective. By way of illustration, they posit a set of seven group paradoxes that are seen as sources of potential conflict in groups.

GROUP PARADOXES WITH THE POTENTIAL FOR CONFLICT

The paradox of identity
The dilemma of the individual within a group who seeks to preserve an identity that remains differentiated from the group while the group seeks to maintain a coherent identity in the face of inevitable turnover in membership.

The paradox of disclosure
The dilemma of the individual who is willing to disclose themselves when they know the strengths and weaknesses of the group while the group is willing to reveal its weakness only when the individual discloses themselves.

The paradox of trust
The dilemma of who starts the trust-building process – the individual or the group?

The paradox of individuality
The dilemma arises from the group's dependency on it members' individuality and the individual's dependence on the group's commonality.

The paradox of authority
Members must subordinate their autonomy to the group for it to become strong enough to represent members' collective interests. Yet in authorising the group, members may diminish themselves and lessen the group's capacity to derive its potency from the strengths of its members.

The paradox of regression

Occurs when individuals permit part of themselves to let go in order to let the group integrate its parts into a whole. At the same time, the group has to develop in a collective way, which is established upon the individuality of each member.

The paradox of creativity

The creative process, the making of the new, involves destruction of the old, the very antithesis of what creativity symbolises. However, the refusal to destroy blunts creativity's possibilities for the group.

Source: Smith and Berg (1987: 633–58)

It is suggested, then, that conflict is an inherent aspect of all group functioning that can emerge at any stage, depending on the situation that the group finds itself in. Indeed, the very act of bringing people from different backgrounds or perspectives together may well be the reason that many groups fail to achieve their objectives (Appelbaum *et al.* 1998). Therefore, how conflict is managed is a critical determinant of group performance. This suggests that conflict resolution techniques or strategies for managing conflict behaviour are important not just in the early stages of group development, but throughout the duration of the existence of any group or team.

SUMMARY OF KEY PROPOSITIONS

- This chapter introduced the area of conflict in organisations. Conflict was defined as a process which begins when one party perceives that another party has frustrated (or is about to frustrate) some central concern of theirs.
- Conflict occurs whenever disagreement exists in a social situation over issues of substance or emotional discord. Our focus is on 'structurally derived conflict', which arises as a result of organisations' operation and structure.
- While traditional views of conflict held that any organisational conflict was negative and to be avoided, emerging views recognise that conflict is 'normal' and can have both negative and positive dimensions. The positive effects of conflict include its potential to energise and motivate people, to identify real problems that need to be changed and to allow people to express their feelings about issues that are causing stress and anxiety. The negative effects of conflict include its potential to entrench people into positions that cause damage to themselves and others.
- This chapter also explored four key perspectives on organisational conflict: the traditional or unitarist view, the human relations or pluralist view, the interactionist view and the radical view. Each of these perspectives represents different views about the functionality and legitimacy of conflict in organisations.
- There are five main sources of conflict in organisations: the employment relationship, competition over scarce resources, ambiguity over responsibility or authority, interdependence and differentiation.

- Employee relations conflict is a particular form of intergroup conflict stemming from differences between management (employers) and labour (normally organised in trade unions or similar bodies) in relation to the terms and regulation of the employment relationship.
- Senior management in organisations has responsibility for the development of effective strategies and policies to deal with organisational conflict.
- There are a number of different approaches to conflict handling which vary in their approach and effectiveness, namely non-attention, suppression and resolution. These differing approaches can result in either lose-lose (non-attention), win-lose (suppression) or win-win (resolution) outcomes for the participants.
- A key issue for organisations and particularly managers is the identification of effective strategies to deal with organisational conflict. Thomas (1976) provides us with a model based on the dominant orientations of the parties involved in a particular conflict situation. This model identifies five such orientations (competition, collaboration, compromise, avoidance and accommodation) based on the relative extent of assertiveness and co-operativeness of each party.
- Some organisations may suffer from a lack of conflict, which may lead to complacency about the extent of harmony in the organisation and to an organisational climate that is excessively rigid and resistant to change and development.
- Organisations must also be aware of the inherent problems with trying to stimulate conflict and the danger of developing a culture of conflict that is dysfunctional for all concerned.
- As business becomes increasingly global it is important that organisations address the issue of cultural diversity so as to both manage 'culturally derived' conflict effectively and to ensure that conflict-handling approaches are appropriate to the national cultures in which they are implemented.

DISCUSSION/SELF-ASSESSMENT QUESTIONS

1. Define conflict and give examples of different types of organisational conflict with which you are familiar.
2. Having explored four key perspectives on organisational conflict (unitarist, pluralist, interactionist and radical), which perspective appeals most to you? Identify a conflict situation with which you are familiar and identify the different accounts that might be given of this situation depending on what perspective on conflict is adopted.
3. Explain and explore the difference between functional and dysfunctional conflict at work.
4. As a class, split into small groups and assign one of five different behavioural approaches to conflict to each of your discussion groups, i.e. avoiding, accommodating, compromising, competing or collaborating. Identify examples of the behavioural approach that you have been assigned and generate two lists with the following headings: 'When [avoiding] should be used as an approach to conflict' and

'When [avoiding] should not be used as an approach to conflict'. After your subgroup discussions, regroup and exchange the results of your discussion with the groups that tackled different approaches.

MULTIPLE CHOICE QUESTIONS

1. 'Structurally derived conflict' refers to conflict that arises as a result of the organisation's operation and structure. True or false?
2. Conflict may have strong positive dimensions. True or false?
3. The unitarist view of conflict is that:
   (a) Conflict is not only a positive force but is necessary for effective group performance.
   (b) Conflict is seen as a negative factor that is harmful and therefore to be avoided.
   (c) Conflict in organisations is simply a manifestation of broader class conflict in relation to the distribution of power in society.
   (d) Conflict is a natural and inevitable feature of organisational life that cannot be eradicated.
4. Intergroup conflict refers to interpersonal conflict (either of a substantive or emotional nature) that extends beyond the individual level to incorporate groups. True or false?
5. The human relations view of conflict that dominated conflict theory from about the start of the 1950s through to the mid-1970s suggests that:
   (a) Conflict is natural and inevitable in all groups and organisations.
   (b) The avoidance of conflict is impossible and therefore, rather than seeking to avoid it, organisations and managers should accept it.
   (c) Conflict is not necessarily negative, but can have beneficial effects.
   (d) All of the above.
   (e) None of the above.
6. The main stages in the conflict process are:
   (a) Spotting negativity, intensity, engagement, interaction, outcomes.
   (b) Potential opposition/incompatibility, realisation, personalisation, intentions/behaviour and outcomes.
   (c) Strategising, deliberation, decision making, engagement, outcomes.
   (d) Planning, organising, resourcing, behaviourly engaging, outcomes.
7. The outcomes of conflict can be either functional (resulting in some positive consequences) or dysfunctional (a negative outcome that adversely affects the relationship or activity). True or false?
8. According to Thomas (1976), compromise as a conflict-handling orientation is appropriate where:
   (a) Each party's goals are important, but not to the extent that would merit the effort or potential disruption associated with more assertive approaches.
   (b) Parties committed to mutually exclusive goals operate from a similar power base.
   (c) Seeking temporary settlements in relation to complex issues is important.
   (d) Time constraints require that expedient solutions are achieved.

(e) All of the above.

(f) None of the above.

9.   Collaboration as a conflict-handling orientation is high in co-operativeness (desire to satisfy concerns of the other party) and low in assertiveness (desire to satisfy own needs). True or false?

10. A work to rule may be defined as:

(a) Collective in nature and involving the temporary withdrawal of labour.

(b) Collective in nature and involving the refusal to work outside normal contractual hours of work.

(c) Collective in nature and involving working only in accordance with the strict interpretation of written terms and conditions of employment, job description or other rules such as those concerning safety or hygiene.

(d) Collective in nature and involving the withdrawal of representatives from joint institutions.

(e) All of the above.

(f) None of the above.

FIVE KEY READINGS

Cosier, R.A. and Dalton, D.R., 'Positive effects of conflict: a field assessment', *International Journal of Conflict Management*, I (1990), 81–92.

De Dreu, C. and Van de Vliert, E., (eds), *Using Conflict in Organisations*, London: Sage 1997.

Jehn, K., 'A qualitative analysis of conflict types and dimensions in organizational groups', *Administrative Science Quarterly*, XLII/3 (1997), 530–58.

Lewis, D., French, E. and Steane, P., 'A culture of conflict', *Leadership and Organizational Development Journal*, XVIII/6 (1997), 275–82.

Robbins, S., '"Conflict management" and "conflict resolution" are not synonymous terms', *California Management Review*, XXI (1978), 67–75.

REFERENCES

Adler, N.J., 'Cross-cultural management research: the ostrich and the trend', *Academy of Management Review*, VI (1983), 65–83.

Allen, V., *The Sociology of Industrial Relations*, London: Longman 1971.

Amason, A., 'Distinguishing the effects of functional and dysfunctional conflict on strategic decision making: resolving a paradox for top management teams', *Academy of Management Journal*, XXXIX/5 (1996), 123–48.

Amason, A., Hochwarter, W., Thompson, K.R. and Harrison, A., 'Conflict: an important dimension in management teams', *Organizational Dynamics*, XXIV/1 (1995), 20–35.

Appelbaum, S., Shapiro, B. and Elbaz, D., 'The management of multicultural group conflict', *Team Performance Management*, IV/5 (1998), 211–34.

Bendix, R., *Work and Authority in Industry*, New York: Wiley 1956.

Blyton, P. and Turnbull, P., *The Dynamics of Employee Relations*, London: Macmillan 1994.

Brown, A., 'Organizational culture: the key to effective leadership and organizational development', *Leadership and Organizational Development Journal*, XIII/2 (1992), 3–6.

Cosier, R.A. and Dalton, D.R., 'Positive effects of conflict: a field assessment', *International Journal of Conflict Management*, I (1990), 81–92.

De Dreu, C. and Van de Vliert, E. (eds), *Using Conflict in Organisations*, London: Sage 1997.

Dunford, R.W., *Organisational Behaviour*, Wokingham: Addison-Wesley 1992.

Edwards, P.K., *Conflict at Work*, Oxford: Blackwell 1986.

Fayol, H., *General and Industrial Management*, London: Pitman 1949.

Fox, A., 'Industrial sociology and industrial relations', Research Paper No. 3 to the Royal Commission on Trade Unions and Employers' Associations, London: HMSO 1966.

Fox, A., 'Industrial relations: a critique of pluralist ideology', in J. Child (ed.), *Man and Organization*, New York: Halstead Press 1973.

Gibson, J.L., Ivancevich, J.M. and Donnelly, J.H., *Organizations: Behavior, Structure, Process*, Burr Ridge, IL: Irwin 1994.

Gunnigle, P., 'Collectivism and the management of industrial relations in greenfield sites', *Human Resource Management Journal*, V/3 (1995), 24–40.

Gunnigle, P. and Brady, T., 'The management of industrial relations in the small firm', *Employee Relations*, VI/5 (1984).

Gunnigle, P., McMahon, G.V. and Fitzgerald, G., *Industrial Relations in Ireland: Theory and Practice*, Dublin: Gill & Macmillan 1995.

Hofstede, G., *Culture's Consequences: International Differences in Work Related Values*, Beverly Hills, CA: Sage 1980.

Hofstede, G., *Cultures and Organizations: Software of the Mind*, London: McGraw-Hill 1991.

Huczynski, A.A. and Buchanan, D.A., *Organizational Behaviour: An Introductory Text*, London: Prentice Hall 1991.

Humphrey, P., *How To Be Your Own Personnel Manager*, London: Institute of Personnel Management 1979.

Jehn, K., 'A qualitative analysis of conflict types and dimensions in organizational groups', *Administrative Science Quarterly*, XLII/3 (1997), 530–58.

Kilmann, R.H., 'A completely integrated program for creating and maintaining success', *Organizational Dynamics*, XVIII/1 (1989), 5–19.

King, A.Y.C. and Bond, M.H., 'The Confucian paradigm of man: a sociological view', in W. Tseng and D. Wu (eds), *Chinese Culture and Mental Health: An Overview*, New York: Academic Press 1985.

Kochan, T.A., Katz, H.C. and McKersie, R.B., *The Transformation of American Industrial Relations*, New York: Basic Books 1986.

Lewis, D., French, E. and Steane, P., 'A culture of conflict', *Leadership and Organizational Development Journal*, XVIII/6 (1997), 275–82.

Marchington, M., *Managing Industrial Relations*, London: McGraw-Hill 1982.

McGovern, P., 'Union recognition and union avoidance in the 1980s', in *Industrial Relations in Ireland: Contemporary Issues and Developments*, Dublin: University College Dublin 1989.

McMahon, J., 'Employee relations in small firms in Ireland: an exploratory study of small manufacturing firms', *Employee Relations*, XVIII/5 (1996), 66–80.

Mintzberg, H., 'Patterns in strategy formulation', *Management Science*, XXIV (May 1978), 934–48.

Mintzberg, H., 'Opening up the definition of strategy', in J. Quinn, H. Mintzberg and R. Rames (eds), *The Strategy Process: Concepts, Contexts, and Cases*, Englewood Cliffs, NJ: Prentice Hall 1988.

Open University, 'International perspectives', Unit 16, Block 5, *Managing in Organizations*, Milton Keynes: Open University Press 1985.

Peters, T.J. and Waterman, R.H., *In Search of Excellence*, Sydney: Harper & Row 1982.

Poole, M., 'Managerial strategies and styles in industrial relations: a comparative analysis', *Journal of General Management*, XII/1 (1986), 40–53.

Reed, M., *The Sociology of Management*, Hemel Hempstead: Harvester Wheatsheaf 1989.

Robbins, S.P., *Managing Organizational Conflict*, Englewood Cliffs, NJ: Prentice Hall 1974.

Robbins, S.P., '"Conflict management" and "conflict resolution" are not synonymous terms', *California Management Review*, XXI (1978), 67–75.

Robbins, S.P., *Organizational Behavior, Concepts, Controversies, and Applications*, Englewood Cliffs, NJ: Prentice Hall 1986.

Rollinson, D., *Understanding Employee Relations*, Wokingham: Addison-Wesley 1993.

Rothenberg, H.I. and Silverman, S.B., *Labor Unions: How To Avert Them, Beat Them, Out-Negotiate Them, Live With Them, Unload Them*, Elkins Park, PA: Management Relations Inc. 1973.

Salaman, M., *Industrial Relations: Theory and Practice*, London: Prentice Hall 1992.

Schermerhorn, J.R., Hunt, J.G. and Osborn, R.N., *Managing Organizational Behavior*, New York: Wiley 1985.

Smith, K. and Berg, D., cited in Appelbaum, S., Shapiro, B. and Elbaz, D., 'The management of multicultural group conflict', *Team Performance Management*, IV/5 (1987), 211–34.

Sparrow, P. and Hiltrop, J.M., *European Human Resource Management in Transition*, Hemel Hempstead: Prentice Hall 1994.

Tang, S.F.Y. and Kirkbridge, P.S., 'Developing conflict management in Hong Kong: an analysis of some cross cultural implications', *Management Education and Development*, XVII/Part 3 (1986), 287–301.

Taylor, F., *The Principles of Scientific Management*, New York: Harper 1911.

Thomas, K., 'Conflict and conflict management', in M.D. Dunnette (ed.), *Handbook of Industrial and Organizational Psychology*, Chicago: Rand McNally 1976.

Thomas, K., 'Towards multi-dimensional values in teaching: the example of conflict behaviors', *Academy of Management Review*, II (July 1977), 484–90.

Walton, R., *Interpersonal Peacemaking: Confrontations and Third Party Consultation*, Reading, MA: Addison-Wesley 1969.

Walton, R.E. and Dutton, J.M., 'The management of interdepartmental conflict: a model and review', *Administrative Science Quarterly*, XIV (1969), 73–84.

THE DYNAMICS OF POWER, POLITICS AND ETHICS

Learning Objectives

- To introduce the concepts of power, politics and ethics.
- To outline the key sources of power available.
- To examine the uses of power.
- To highlight critical political tactics useful for influencing targets.
- To examine the sources of personal ethics.
- To review critical issues in social responsibility.

INTRODUCTION

Though traditionally neglected in the extant literature, power, politics and ethics are important concepts for explaining behaviour in organisations and, definitional quagmires aside, the concepts of 'political behaviour' and 'ethical conduct' are now well established in the management and organisational behaviour literature (Drory and Romm 1988; Turnipseed 2002). Analyses of power, politics and ethics cast light on the nature of the relationship between organisational stakeholders and are dimensions of every organisation. According to Finchman and Rhodes (1988), the study of power and political activity in organisations has some positive things to recommend it. First, they argue that the stress on 'real' organisational activity is fruitful when compared with the overly prescriptive approach of many managerial theorists. Second, they highlight the fact that this side of the management role has been played down until quite recently encourages a far greater interest in power and that any new approach which has the potential to take our understanding forward is wholeheartedly welcome. Thus, Pfeffer (1981: ix) notes that recent years have brought with them an increasing interest in a political perspective on organisational behaviour: 'this growing concern encompasses … topics as diverse as bargaining and influence strategies and the political aspects of organisation development and is at once welcome and long overdue.'

Power may be defined as the ability to engage in action, i.e. the extent to which individuals or stakeholders are able to pursue or convince others to take a certain course of action. The essence of power is control over others' behaviour. Politics, on the other hand, can be viewed as power in action and consist of strategies and tactics drawn upon for the purpose of influencing individuals and groups. Indeed, as early as 1936 Lasswell defined politics as the study of who gets what, when and how. Ethics can be conceived of as an individual's personal beliefs regarding right and wrong behaviour. Management ethics are the standards of behaviour that guide individual managers in their work. Thus, what constitutes ethical behaviour can vary from one person to another, and while ethics is relative and not absolute, when people talk about ethical behaviour they do usually mean behaviour that conforms to generally accepted social norms. From an organisational behaviour perspective, though, ethics is crucially defined in the context of the individual, which means that people have ethics and organisations per se do not. This chapter focuses on each of these three important dimensions of organisational life.

Definitions of Key Concepts

Power
The ability to engage in action, i.e. the extent to which individuals or stakeholders are able to pursue or convince others to take a certain course of action.

Reward power
Derives from the individual's control over resources and is dependent upon the ability of the power wielder to confer valued material rewards.

Coercive power
Refers to the power to punish or withhold reward and the power to threaten and use one's position to force others to take action.

Legitimate power
Is that which is exercised in accordance with organisational rules and with the authority of the organisation.

Referent power
Is contingent upon the charisma, interpersonal skill and/or personal attraction of the individual.

Expert power
Derives from know-how or expertise that sets the individual apart from others.

Politics
Power in action.

Organisational politics
Activities individuals and groups engage in to maintain their power and to obtain preferred outcomes.

Ethics
The philosophical study of moral values and rules.

Business ethics

An organisation's attitude and conduct toward its employees, customers, community and stockholders.

Whistleblowing

An organisational member's disclosure of confidential information which relates to some hazard, scam or other illegal or unethical conduct connected with the place of work.

DEFINING POWER

According to Statt (1994), one of the most striking aspects of our everyday experience of organisations is that some people seem to have more influence over what happens than others. The exercise of this influence is often referred to as having power. Power is an element in almost all social relationships. The concept of power is 'as ancient and ubiquitous as any that social theory can boast' (Dahl 1957: 201). Power and politics are major factors that cannot be ignored by anyone interested in understanding how organisations work and end up doing what they do effectively (French and Bell 1995). Tyson and Jackson (1992) argue that the concept of power is central to understanding organisational life because people devote much of their energies at work to trying to accomplish tasks either for themselves or on behalf of other people, while Walumbwa (1999) calls for the integration of the use of power and politics into training programmes in areas such as leadership, strategic planning, management development, re-engineering, team development and organisational transformation since they squarely form part of everyday organisational life. Power does not operate in a vacuum, but rather is context or relationship specific.

ILLUSTRATING POWER

Dawson (1996: 167–8) presents a series of mini case studies as a means of describing power relationships in which the desires, requests and interests of individuals or groups are frustrated either by the decisions or actions of other people or by characteristics of the technical and administrative system that has been created and developed.

In the *post office* a mother tries to obtain her child benefit aid and is told by the clerk, 'It's not my fault that you can't get your child benefit this week, it's just that your book has run out and your new book hasn't arrived yet. Probably that's because of the train drivers' strike delaying the post, but whatever the reason, I can't do anything about it; I've no authority to pay your benefit without a book.'

> The manager of a *purchasing department* of an electrical assembly factory complains to the sales representative of one of their suppliers about late deliveries. 'I'll see what I can do,' says the rep. 'The problem is that we are retooling one of our production lines and production are in difficulties. I'll do what I can about your order, but I can't promise anything in the immediate future. You see, production never consult us when they make changes and we have no power to insist. They should produce a lot of stock before shutting down, but they don't want to increase their stock levels.'
>
> In the post office scenario the claimant is less powerful than the officer, who is less powerful than the administrative system when it comes to determining whether or not a mother gets her child benefit.
>
> In the purchasing department scenario, the sales rep of the components factory is less powerful than the production manager over issues of inventory and production schedules. The purchasing manager of the assembly plant may have to bow to the suppliers in the short term, but in the long term he may well discover other suppliers and hence shift his power relationship with the components firm in a fairly dramatic way.

Source: Dawson (1996)

As noted above, power may be defined as the ability to engage in action, i.e. the extent to which individuals or stakeholders are able to pursue or convince others to take a certain course of action. Dahl (1957) defines power as a relation among social actors in which one social actor, A, can get another social actor, B, to do something that B would not otherwise have done. Thus, Pfeffer (1981) notes that power is about a force sufficient to change the probability of B's behaviour from what it would have been in the absence of the application of that force. Concomitantly, it is about resistance, i.e. the amount of resistance that B can advance because his/her wishes are being overridden. It is also about the likely conflict that will ensue. For Dahl and many other contributors, the acid test of a power relationship is the existence of this conflict of interests between people or groups.

Generally, definitions of power are synonymous with the concepts of authority and influence. Indeed, one of the earliest writers, Bernard (1938), defined power in terms of 'informal authority'. However, Luthans (1992: 427) draws important distinctions between the interconnected, though separate, concepts of power and authority and influence. Like many other contributors to the extant literature, he identifies power as the ability to get an individual or group to do something – to get the person or the group to change in some way. Authority, he argues, legitimises and is a source of power and is the right to manipulate or change others. Power need not be legitimate. Influence, he suggests, is usually conceived of as being broader in scope than power. It involves the ability to alter others in general ways, such as by changing their satisfaction and performance. While both influence and power are involved in the leadership process, influence is more closely associated with leadership. Thus, he suggests that authority is different from power because of its legitimacy and acceptance, and influence is broader than power.

Broadly speaking, the impetus for the study of power in organisations came from two rather different directions (see Hardy and Clegg 1996). One stream of research can be traced back to the early work of Max Weber, which has focused on the existence of conflicting, competing interests and has examined power from the perspective of domination. The pioneering sociologist Weber defined power as 'the probability that one actor within a social relationship will be in a position to carry out his own will despite resistance' (Weber 1947: 152). In this respect, Hardy and Clegg note that it has largely focused on how power becomes embedded in organisational structures and systems in a way that serves certain, but not all, interest groups in the organisation. Weber acknowledges that power is derived from having ownership of and controlling the means of production. However, it could not all be explained on the basis of ownership and non-ownership. Weber argues that power is also derived from knowledge of operations as much as from ownership. Most studies of power in organisations have focused on this type of power, what Pfeffer (1981) refers to as 'vertical or hierarchical power', or the power of supervisors over subordinates or bosses over employees.

The second major research root associated with power, according to Hardy and Clegg (1996), examined how groups acquire and wield power not granted to them under official arrangements. This line of research was more closely associated with management theorists who defined power as those actions that fell outside the legitimated structures and which threatened organisational goals.

> One consequence of the widespread, if implicit, acceptance of the hierarchical nature of power has been that social scientists have rarely felt it necessary to explain why it is that power should be hierarchical. In other words, in this stream of research the power embedded in the hierarchy has been viewed as normal and inevitable following from the formal design of the organisation. As such, it has been largely excluded from analyses that instead have focused on 'illegitimate' power, i.e. power exercised outside formal hierarchical structures and the channels that they sanction (Hardy and Clegg 1996: 624).

Finchman and Rhodes (1988) suggest that by considering the amount of resistance offered by those under power as well as the strength of the sanctions brought to bear by those in power, the different types of power can be seen to fall within a continuum. This, they suggest, represents the extent of conflict between the interests of the 'in power' group and the 'under power' group.

It is evident from this interpretation that power covers a very broad range of behaviours, from almost pure agreement to the resort to violence. In addition, the concept of authority overlaps with that of power, but they do differ. Garavan et al. (1993) suggest that power differs from authority in four key ways.

1. While authority usually operates in vertical directions down the organisational hierarchy, power typically operates in any direction.
2. While authority is often accepted by subordinates, power may not be accepted by those it is exercised upon.

3. In the organisational context, authority is vested in specific roles or positions in the organisation, whereas power may arise from different sources.
4. While authority can be identified from the organisation chart, power is less observable in this concrete way and consequently it is more difficult to identify and label.

Figure 14.1 Types of Power

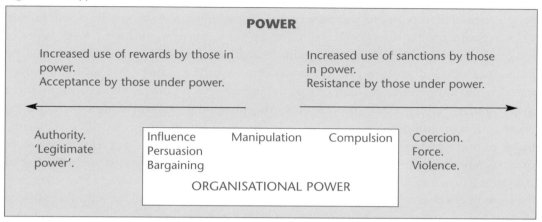

EXPLAINING THE SOURCES OF POWER

French and Raven (1959) advance several bases of power which reflect the different bases or resources that power holders might rely upon. The sources they identify are reward, coercive, legitimate, referent and expert power. Most discussions of power refer to these categories and they are considered a necessary foundation for understanding the multidimensional nature of the concept.

Reward power derives from the individual's control over resources and is dependent upon the ability of the power wielder to confer valued material rewards, such as pay increases or promotions. In addition, the target of this power must value these rewards. Luthans (1992) argues that to understand this source of power more completely, it must be remembered that the recipient holds the key. If managers offer subordinates what they perceive to be a reward but subordinates do not value it, then managers do not really have reward power. By the same token, there are instances where managers might not think that they are giving a reward to subordinates, but if subordinates perceive this to be rewarding, the managers nevertheless have reward power. Furthermore, there are instances where managers do not really have the rewards to distribute, but as long as their targets think they do, then in the targets' eyes they continue to have reward power.

Coercive power refers to the power to punish or withhold reward, the power to threaten and to use one's position to force others to take action. In both cases it is the desire for valued rewards or the fear of having them withheld that ensures the obedience of those under power (Finchman and Rhodes 1988). A coercive power source often relies on fear. This form of power has contributed substantially to the negative connotations that power has for many people. Managers generally have coercive power in that they can punish employees or they can threaten punishment. Some psychologists maintain that much organisational behaviour can be more accurately explained in terms of coercive power rather than on the basis of reward power.

Legitimate power is that which is exercised in accordance with organisational rules and with the organisation's authority. Finchman and Rhodes go so far as to say that it is identical with authority and depends upon the individual's belief in the right of senior people to hold their positions and their consequent willingness to accept the power holder. Thus, according to Luthans (1992), legitimate power stems from the internalised values of the other people, which gives the legitimate right to the agent to influence them. The individual with legitimacy is also in a position to reward or punish. As a source of power, it is dependent upon the position or role the person holds. Luthans (1992) outlines three major sources of legitimate power. First, the prevailing cultural values of a society, organisation or group determine what is legitimate. Certain groups, such as managers, males as opposed to females or the Church, may possess high levels of legitimate power in a society. Second, people may obtain legitimate power from the accepted social structure. Thus, arguably, when manual employees accept employment from a company, they are in effect accepting an established hierarchical structure and granting legitimate power to their supervisors. A third accepted source of legitimate power comes from being designated as the agent or representative of a powerful person, group or establishment. TDs, priests, members of the board of directors of a company or shop stewards would be examples here.

Referent power is contingent upon the charisma, interpersonal skill and/or personal attraction of the individual. Typically here the person under power desires to identify with these personal qualities and gains some satisfaction from being an accepted follower. It thus comes from the desire on the part of other people to identify with the individual wielding the power. They may wish to identify with the powerful person, regardless of the outcomes. In an organisational setting, referent power is arguably different from other types of power. Managers with referent power must be attractive to subordinates such that subordinates will want to identify with them, regardless of whether managers have the ability to reward or punish or whether they have legitimacy. Managers who depend on referent power must be personally attractive characters. Advertisers take advantage of this type of power when they use celebrities, such as sports stars, to do personal recommendation testimonial advertising.

Expert power, as the name suggests, derives from know-how or expertise that sets the individual apart from others. This source of power is determined by the extent to which others attribute knowledge and expertise to the power seeker. While all the major sources of power depend on the target's perceptions of the power holder, this is especially the case with expert power. The power holder must be seen to be convincing, trustworthy, honest and relevant before expert power is granted.

Finchman and Rhodes (1988) have identified a number of defects in French and Raven's classification. They argue that the reward and coercive forms of power identified are not in fact power sources in themselves, but rather merely describe the actions of people who have other power resources. In addition, they note that their legitimate and referent forms of power are taken from Weber's typology of authority, although without the addition of his third type, namely traditional authority. However, they do acknowledge that French and Raven's typology does serve to emphasise the fact that within organisations people can draw upon a broad range of different bases of power.

In a similar vein, Garavan *et al.* (1993) identify a range of power sources available to both internal and external organisational stakeholders.

- **Exchange power:** An internal stakeholder will have a lot of exchange power if he/she has control of a specific resource, a technical skill, specific information or a body of knowledge that is essential to the organisation's functioning. In order for a stakeholder to have exchange power, the particular resource must be concentrated and non-substitutable, which means that it is not available in other places.

- **Position in the hierarchy:** An individual's position in the hierarchy provides them with formal power over others in the hierarchy. This can be conceived of as authority.

- **Personal qualities/influence:** Some individuals may have specific personality characteristics which allow them to exercise influence. Influence might also arise because there is a high level of consensus within a particular department. An example here might include the existence of a persuasive personality, charisma or high energy levels.

- **The power of being there:** Individuals who have access to decision-making machinery and decision makers are said to have power. Stakeholders who may not have strong exchange power may have considerable influence because they are participating in the decision-making process. Access to those who have power is also a source of power in itself.

- **Ability to give rewards or to punish:** Individuals or stakeholders who can distribute rewards to those who carry out their wishes or who can distribute sanctions will have power. In the case of the former, people obey because they believe they will be rewarded in some financial or psychological way, and in the latter case, compliance is secured through fear of punishment or removal of rewards.

- **Perceived power:** A power situation can arise because the decision maker perceives the stakeholder to possess power. Managers who build up their power base can maintain their image long after their skills are no longer relevant to particular problems or environmental conditions. Managers can make others believe that they possess power.

- **Boundary management functions:** Individuals and stakeholder groups who help the organisation manage its external environment tend to have power, which arises because of their ability to reduce, control or absorb environmental uncertainty.

- **Control of strategic resources:** Stakeholders who control fundamental resources such as money, product design or human resources tend to have significant power.

The main sources of power for external stakeholders identified by Garavan *et al.* (1993) are as follows.

- **Creating dependency relationships:** External stakeholders, such as financial institutions or key suppliers, have considerable capacity to create dependency relationships. Porter (1985) argues that the capacity of a supplier to create a dependency relationship is contingent upon five major factors: the concentration of the suppliers vis-à-vis the industry they sell to, the degree of substitutability between the products of different suppliers and the amount of product differentiation, the amount of and the potential for vertical integration, the importance of the supplier to the buyer and the existence of switching costs if buyers want to switch suppliers.
- **Specialist knowledge and skills:** External stakeholders who possess specialist knowledge and skills critical to company success tend to have power. The extent of this power is contingent on the type of knowledge and expertise involved, how it impacts on the value chain, the supply of it in the external environment and the extent to which the organisation can create the knowledge or skill itself.
- **Links with internal stakeholders:** External stakeholders who have access to key internal stakeholders can generate significant power. This arises from the realisation that they develop relationships and are also influenced by the power of the internal stakeholder involved.
- **Concentration of external stakeholders:** The power of suppliers, buyers or distribution companies can be significantly influenced by their concentration. The greater the degree of concentration, the greater their potential to set their own terms and to negotiate favourable agreements and contracts.
- **Involvement in the strategy implementation process:** External stakeholders who support key links in the value chain can generate power. The knowledge this involvement generates can be used to the advantage of the external stakeholder and can allow them to dictate terms to the organisation.

INFLUENCING THE TARGETS OF POWER

Luthans (1992: 433) notes that while most discussions of power imply a unilateral process of influence from the agent to the target, the power relationship can be better understood by examining some of the target's characteristics. Drawing upon the work of Reitz (1987) he outlines a set of characteristics that have been identified as being especially important to the ability of targets to be influenced.

- **Dependency:** The greater the target's dependency on their relationship to agents (for example, when a target cannot escape a relationship, perceives no alternatives or values the agent's rewards as unique), the more targets are influenced.
- **Uncertainty:** Experiments have shown that the more uncertain people are about the appropriateness of a behaviour, the more likely they are to be influenced to change that behaviour.
- **Personality:** There have been a number of research studies showing the relationship between personality characteristics and 'influenceability'. Some of these findings are obvious (for example, people who cannot tolerate ambiguity or who are highly anxious are more susceptible to influence, and those with high needs for affiliation are

more susceptible to group influence), but some are not (for example, both positive and negative relationships have been found between self-esteem and influenceability).

- **Intelligence:** There is no simple relationship between intelligence and influenceability. For example, highly intelligent people may be more willing to listen, but because they also tend to be held in high esteem, they also may be more resistant to influence.
- **Sex:** Although it was traditionally acknowledged that women were more likely to conform to influence attempts than men because of the way they were raised, there is now evidence that this has changed. As women's and society's views of women's roles are changing, there is less of a distinction by sex of influenceability.
- **Age:** Social psychologists have generally concluded that susceptibility to influence increases in young children up to about age eight or nine and then decreases with age until adolescence, when it levels off.
- **Culture:** Obviously, the cultural values of a society have a tremendous impact on the influenceability of its people. For example, Western cultures emphasise individuality, dissent and diversity and tend to decrease influenceability, while others, such as many in the Far East, emphasise cohesiveness, agreement and uniformity, which tend to promote influenceability.

USE OF POWER

Power can be a fundamental part of the management process. Many commentators argue that introducing and effectively implementing strategic change requires the use of power and influence. Dawson (1996: 175) identifies three main sources of constraint that limit attempts to exercise power in pursuit of interest.

1. **Technological:** The parameters set by the plant, machinery and equipment.
2. **Administrative:** The parameters set by rules, procedures and formal structure.
3. **Ideological:** The views of those who are already in strong positions of power concerning what is feasible and desirable.

Table 14.1 Personal Power and Political Tactics

Expertise	Particularly significant where the skill is in scarce supply. It is possible to use mobility and the threat of leaving to gain support for certain changes of strategy, again dependent upon the manager's personal importance to the firm.
Assured stature	A reputation for being a 'winner' or a manager who can obtain results. Recent successes are most relevant.
Credibility	Particularly credibility with external power sources, such as suppliers or customers.
Control over information	Internal and external sources. Information can be used openly and honestly or withheld and used selectively – consequently, it is crucial to know the reliability of the source.

Group support	In managing and implementing change it is essential to have the support of colleagues and fellow managers.
Political tactics to obtain results	
Develop liaison	As mentioned above, it is important to develop and maintain both formal and informal contact with other managers, functions and divisions. Again, it is important to include those managers who are most powerful.
Present conservative image	It can be disadvantageous to be seen as too radical an agent of change.
Diffuse opposition	Conflicts need to be brought out into the open and differences of opinion aired rather than kept hidden. Divide and rule can be a useful strategy.
Trade-off and compromise	In any proposal or suggestion for change it is important to consider the needs of other people whose support is required.
'Strike while the iron is hot'	Successful managers should quickly build on successes and reputation.
Research	Information is always vital to justify and support proposals.
Use a neutral cover	Radical changes, or those which other people might perceive as a threat to them, can sometimes be usefully disguised and initiated as minor changes. (This is linked to the next point.)
Limit communication	A useful tactic can be to unravel change gradually in order to contain possible opposition.
Withdraw strategically	If things are going wrong, especially if the changes are not crucial, it can be a wise tactic on occasion to withdraw, at least temporarily.

- Politically successful managers understand organisational processes and are sensitive to others' needs
- Effective political action brings about desirable and successful changes in organisations – it is functional.
- Negative political action is dysfunctional and can enable manipulative managers to pursue their personal objectives against the organisation's better interests.
- The strategic leader needs to be an effective politician.

Source: Alen *et al.* (1979); Dixon (1982); Garavan *et al.* (1993)

MacMillan (1978) suggests that there are two basic options open to the strategist who wishes to bring about change: he/she can either structure the situation so that others comply with his wishes or he/she can communicate with people and seek to change their perceptions so that they see things differently and decide to do as he/she suggests. Arguably, in the former situation the strategist is using power bases as enabling resources, while in the latter situation he/she is seeking to use influence.

Table 14.2 Some Common Strategies for Developing and Using Power within an Organisation

Develop power by:
Creating dependence in others.
- Work in areas of high uncertainty.
- Cultivate centrality by working in critical areas.
- Develop non-substituable skills.

Coping with uncertainty on behalf of others.
- Prevention.
- Forecasting.
- Absorption.

Developing personal networks.
Developing and constantly augmenting your expertise.

Use power to:
Control information flows to others.
Control agendas.
- Issue definition.
- Order of issues.
- Issue exclusion.

Control decision-making criteria.
- Long-term vs. short-term considerations.
- Return vs. risk.
- Choose criteria that favour your abilities and contributions.

Co-optation and coalition building.
- External alliances, e.g. supplier or customer relationships, interlocking boards of directors.
- Internal alliances.
- Promote loyal subordinates.
- Appoint committees.
- Gain representation on important committees.

Bring in outside experts (consultants) to bolster your position.

Source: Hatch (1997)

DISTRIBUTING POWER: THE EMPOWERMENT ENVIRONMENT

The extent to which employees have a sense of personal power and control has become recognised as central to their performance and well-being. Employee empowerment is an essential feature of the new organisation scenario, but conditions must be right for empowerment to thrive. In many organisations, empowerment has become a buzz word, and although often used, the term is often not understood. Where does empowerment begin? What must organisations be like in order for empowerment to occur? There is often agreement about the way an empowered employee should behave, but much less so on which conditions are necessary for fostering enough empowerment to change a traditionally hierarchical organisation into a more participative one. Dobbs (1993) advances four necessary conditions to encourage empowerment: participation, innovation, access to information and accountability. These factors combined produce an organisational feeling and tone that can have a dramatic, positive effect on employees.

- **Participation:** People must be actively and willingly engaged in their jobs. They must care about improving their daily work processes and work relationships. Such involvement does not simply come about, but rather it has to be fostered.

- **Innovation:** It is almost impossible for empowerment to exist in environments in which innovation is ignored or stifled. Empowerment cannot exist in an organisation that expects employees to do their jobs the way they have always done them. Employees need to be given permission to innovate. As Shepard (1967) suggests:

  > The most successful corporate innovation systems aren't systems at all. They are environments that are hospitable to interesting people with innovative ideas – environments that encourage people to explore new paths and take meaningful risks at reasonable costs ... Innovation is as much a core value as is an acceptable return on investment.

- **Access to information:** In many organisations information can be a source of power. In traditional organisations, the senior managers decide who receives what kind of information. In organisations in which employees are empowered, people at every level make decisions about what kind of information they need for performing their jobs.

- **Accountability:** Too many workplaces have traditionally stifled enterprise, initiative and entrepreneurship and have failed to create a climate where individuals perceive a sense of personal power. The result is that individuals go elsewhere to engage in activities that provide them with the stimulus to innovate and where they demonstrate far more skill than most employers encourage them to show at work. Many managers still hold the mistaken belief that to empower subordinates is to undermine or indeed lose one's own power. Hollander and Offermann (1990) suggest that an effective way of overcoming such a perception is to ensure that those managers who do empower their employees are not blamed for their people's mistakes and/or failures, nor ignored when their people succeed.

THE POSITIVE USE OF POWER

Power is often a dirty word, as in 'power corrupts'. Yet, without the power to make things happen, managers can't build organizations.

Managers need to understand the dynamics of power in four arenas and harness and direct energies in ways that are not just effective and efficient, but also deeply satisfying and empowering of self and the others who lend their energy toward goals.

Power has two primary components: a vision – a goal to achieve – and energy – the impetus or force needed to bring the vision into reality. This offers an equation: Vision multiplied by energy produces the power to accomplish goals! However, opposing energies can vitiate even a great vision supported by enormous energy.

Here, then, is a more realistic equation for power:

$$Power = Vision \; x \; Energy/Resistance$$

Applying this simple equation is not so simple. Once being powerful was a perquisite of managers. People did what their managers wanted them to do. Wages were provided in return for obedient labor.

Today, managers need new ways to generate power and influence if they are to harness and focus the energy of their people into power sufficient for excellence and continued success.

Finite and Infinite Perspectives

I see two basic views of power:

The finite perspective says that power is scarce, limited, and finite – that there is not enough to go around, that someone will win, and someone must lose. This limited view of power limits the power we might accrue. A win/lose perspective of power actually creates resistance, as those who believe they will lose if you win, will fight aggressively and passively to turn the tables.

The infinite view sees power as abundant, unlimited, and infinite. In this view, power is accrued through partnering with and learning from others – including those who might resist. The quantity and quality of available power from this perspective is potentially infinite, facilitating great energy.

Harnessing infinite power depends on mastering six principles:

- **Focus your energy** – focusing, releasing, and managing the energy of your thoughts, emotions, and behaviors to achieve your goals.
- **Think systemically** – seeing that every thing and every action exists within some system of other things and actions, and that every thing and action within a system impacts and is impacted by every other thing and action with that system.
- **Learn from differences** – using differences to accrue knowledge and skill, not to foster contention or conformity.

- **Seek sound and current data** – operating from accurate, up-to-date information rather than from opinion, interpretation, assumption, or speculation.
- **Empower others** – supporting self and others to identify and resolve their issues and discover their excellence.
- **Use support systems** – developing and using a diverse group of supporters who contribute to achieving. Support systems achieve their goals as they reach critical mass.

Four Arenas of Power

Successful managers apply each of these principles within four arenas:

1. **Personal power.** Managers must access the untapped capacity we, individually, have for personal power. Integrating our intellectual, emotional, and physical energies, the arena of personal power is the groundwork.

2. **Interpersonal influence.** We can't achieve organizational goals alone, regardless of how much personal power we have. Personal power does, however, enable us to achieve interpersonal influence. Influence is the impact we have on others simply because we are part of the same system. Such influence is too often undefined and undirected. *Interpersonal influence* connotes a specific focus of impact; that is, our ability to support others to willingly use their energy on behalf of our goals in ways that get rid of power struggles that waste energy. Instead, the focus is on improving the quality of our relationships to enhance interpersonal influence.

3. **Team synergy.** A group is formed anytime people come together to accomplish something. We may call them departments, divisions, work units, teams, task forces, or committees. Meetings are a group activity. Groups must be turned into a source of meaningful power. Team synergy, the most potent manifestation of group power, exists when the whole generates more power than the sum of its parts. Turning groups into high-performing, synergetic teams requires creating safe, conflict-competent, empowering groups that learn from differences and make good decisions.

4. **The infinite organization.** The pay-off occurs in a final arena, *The Infinite Organization*. In this arena our skills of personal power, interpersonal influence, and team synergy are applied in three areas: leadership and the executive team, structures and policies, and management practices that have created the benefits of the infinite perspective of power and its related principles. With these tools, managers can create the positive and self-sustaining culture that characterizes an infinite organization. When all three areas are fully developed, aligned, and congruent, the focus, energy, and success of *The Infinite Organization* will be evident.

Source: Broom (2003)

POLITICS AS POWER IN ACTION

Politics is about access to power and mobilising power. When reviewing how power is utilised in organisations, one inevitably must address the issue of organisational politics, or what Tyson and Jackson (1992: 94) term those 'strategies individuals and groups adopt in order to maintain their power, to prevent others from taking their power, or to enlarge their power.' Politics in organisations involves 'those activities taken within the company to acquire, develop and use power and other resources to obtain one's preferred outcomes in a situation in which there is uncertainty or dissension about choices' (Pfeffer 1981: 7). Bacharach and Lawler (1980: 1–2), in their observations on politics, note that:

> Organizations are neither the rational, harmonious entities celebrated in managerial theory, nor the arenas of apocalyptic class conflict projected by Marxists. Rather, it may be argued, a more suitable notion lies somewhere between these two – a concept of organizations as politically negotiated orders. Adopting this view, we can observe organizational actors in their daily transactions, perpetually bargaining, repeatedly forming and reforming coalitions, and constantly availing themselves of influence tactics … politics in organizations involve the tactical use of power to retain or obtain control of real or symbolic resources. In describing the processes of organizations as political acts, we are not making a moral judgement; we are simply making an observation about a process.

Politics permeates organisations because organisations are collections of people who have differing past experiences, differing current circumstances and therefore potentially differing interests (Hickson 1990). If there was no opposition within an organisation to what a manager wanted to do, then it would be largely unnecessary for them to engage in political activity. The central issue here, then, is influence, exercised according to the power source one is drawing from (reward, coercive, legitimate, referent and/or expert). The task of accommodating everyone's interests when something is being decided is largely a political one based on influence. In this respect, four general political tactics can be identified, namely inducement, coercion, persuasion and obligation. Inducement implies the ability to control the situation and the outcome is perceived as beneficial by others involved. This is a positive situation. During coercion, the situation is again controlled but the outcome is perceived in negative terms. Specific acts of coercion might include the threat of dismissal, no further promotions or the withdrawal of privileges. Using the tactics of persuasion requires the strategist to sell the benefits of acting in a certain way. This could be the promise of rewards, promotions, greater job security, more authority and responsibility. The outcome in this case should be positive. Obligation, on the other hand, is an intentional tactic where people are persuaded to behave and act in a particular way by appealing to obligation. The obligation could be something that they are said to owe the company, that they owe particular favours or have obligations towards a particular group of people. The outcome in this case is negative.

Table 14.3 Advantages and Disadvantages of Specific Political Tactics in a Change Scenario

	Advantages	Disadvantages
Inducement	• Break down resistance to change. • Employees can see some benefits of the change. • Individual managers have positive feelings about the change. • The situation is under control.	• Will incur additional costs for the organisation. • Must deliver on the inducements offered. • Change may still be resisted. • Its success depends on previous initiatives.
Coercion	• Management is in control of the situation. • Suitable in situations where quick decisions have to be made for survival. • Management are exerting management prerogative.	• The coercion will have dysfunctional consequences. • Employees will usually find ways of resisting the change. • Makes future changes very difficult because it creates negative precedent.
Persuasion	• The need for change is communicated. • There are attempts to educate the organisation on the need for change. • The change has a better chance of being implemented. • It is a way of getting undesirable changes implemented.	• Employees may not believe in the promises made. • Management credibility may be low. • Can be costly for the organisation. • Slows down the pace of strategic change.
Obligation	• Does not involve additional costs to the organisation. • Suitable tactic where there is high commitment to the organisation. • Change can be quickly introduced.	• The outcome will most likely be negative. • Employees may see the tactic for what it is. • Employees may expect rewards in return for their commitment.

Source: Garavan *et al.* (1993)

In his examination of the influence process between specialists and executives in organisations, Pettigrew (1974) details a series of political ploys frequently drawn upon as part of their political repertoire (see below).

STRATEGIES USED BY EXECUTIVES

- **Strategic rejection:** If executive is self-assured and powerful, rejects the report.
- **Mobilising political support:** Executive calls in the credits from colleagues.
- **Nitty-gritty tactic:** Minor details are questioned and mistakes in details are raised to try to discredit the whole report.

- **Emotional tactic:** Relies on appeals to emotional states, such as personal consequences of action.
- **But in the future:** Argument that data may be historically accurate but does not consider future changes.
- **Invisible man:** Avoidance, often with a secretary's support, so no discussion can take place.
- **Further investigation required:** Specialist is sent away to collect more information, either because terms of reference are changed or to follow up the more interesting issues in the report.
- **Scapegoat:** A suitable scapegoat, who is raised as a threat to any change proposed.
- **Deflection:** Discussion is deflected away from the main areas by concentrating the attention on less crucial matters.

THE MOST POLITICAL PROCESSES

Hickson (1990) argues that the making of particular strategic decisions in organisations may be a highly political affair or may involve very little political activity, depending on the exact nature of the decision.

> The overall character of the processes differ a great deal. The making of one strategic decision may be a most political affair, the next much less so, a third least political of all. This does not denote their importance. All will be strategic with costly and far-reaching consequences, yet some will be more political than others (Hickson 1990: 178).

He labels the processes that are likely to be politically charged 'sporadic processes'. Those less politically charged are termed 'constricted processes', while those that are least politically prone he describes as 'fluid processes'.

Sporadic processes are likely to be highly politically charged, as they deal with particularly weighty and controversial matters. According to Hickson, these are matters with potentially serious consequences, drawing in a multiplicity of information and views from numerous departments and external sources.

> Many of those involved have interests which come from differing objectives. In short, such a matter is diversely involving, contentious, with external influences, from which come its political nature. Typical examples would be decisions on novel new products and on take-overs (Hickson 1990: 179).

Constricted processes are likely to be less politically loaded than sporadic ones. A constricted process typically refers to a relatively normal and recurrent matter that has some familiarity about it, e.g. a business plan or a budget. Matters of this nature have been dealt with previously, and the way it will be dealt with is largely understood and accepted.

Hickson (1990: 179) notes that its consequences will not likely concern everyone and 'in particular they do not implicate external interests. If strong interests have to be reckoned with they will be from inside the organisation … Such a matter is comparatively well known, with consequences that are more limited, influenced by internal interests only.'

Fluid processes are least likely to encounter controversy, and consequently, according to Hickson, they are least politically prone. They especially focus on common but non-controversial matters, and while the consequences will likely be felt more broadly, they are not likely to be as serious as those described as constricted or sporadic. Typically, fewer interests are involved and their interests are generally highly compatible. Influence is generally evenly spread among the stakeholders. 'Though such a matter can be quite novel and have diffuse consequences, it is not excessively serious nor contentious so it is likely to be dealt with in a relatively smooth, steadily paced, formally channelled, speedy way' (Hickson 1990: 180).

ETHICS: ETYMOLOGY AND MEANING

While, as Irvin (2002) suggests, the subject of ethics tends to be laden with religious connotations, the relationship of managerial values and resulting behaviour is indisputable. The etymology of the word 'ethics' relates to the Greek word '*ethos*', meaning 'custom' or 'character'. Consequently, Solomon (1984) suggests that the fundamental concerns of ethics are with individual character and the social rules of right and wrong. However, as Turnipseed (2002: 1) observes:

> There is neither a universally accepted definition of ethics nor a standard measure that allows an individual or event to be uniformly judged as ethical or unethical. Two individuals judged by many as highly ethical may have divergent views on such issues as capital punishment, abortion, affirmative action, layoffs, plant closings, environmental issues or discrimination. Two ethical individuals may act consistent with their values and arrive at different conclusions about a given decision, as the meaning of ethical is individual specific … Ethics must be evaluated with respect to personal values, which are underlying beliefs and attitudes that are partial determinants of individual behaviour.

In an overarching review, Turnipseed identifies and characterises five different views of ethics prominent in the extant literature, namely egotism, utilitarianism, moral rights, justice and relativism.

Egotism as a belief suggests that the pursuit of one's long-term self-interests constitutes ethical behaviour. For an ethical egoist, moral rules are irrelevant. All that matters is whether an action is in the agent's self-interest. If the individual's long-term interest can be accommodated by self-sacrificingly serving the interests of an organisation, then in his or her self-interest the ethical egoist will take this action. The self-interest of the ethical egoist may be to act altruistically or to seem to do so because this serves his or her self-interests. To a strict ethical egoist, however, altruism is untenable. Many commentators have noted that ethical egoism is the underlying value of many business enterprises, both for corporations and individuals.

Utilitarianism considers actions as moral if they do the greatest good for the greatest number of people. There are many forms of utilitarianism, two of which are relevant to the focus of this chapter: act and rule utilitarianism. Act utilitarianism justifies an action as right if it maximises utility (value); in other words, it maximises benefits for the greatest number of people. Act utilitarianism is concerned with the calculation of costs and benefits. The right action is the one that maximises benefits over costs. For a long time this theory had significant influence in government and politics, but perhaps less so in a business and strategic context. Rule utilitarianism represents a reformulated form of act utilitarianism. It attempts to overcome the criticisms that are generally levelled at act utilitarianism, such as the claim that costs and benefits cannot adequately be measured in ethical terms and that maximising utility does not take into consideration the rights and justice issues as far as individuals are concerned. According to rule utilitarian, an act is right, in a specific situation, if everyone affected by the rule is better off than anyone under an alternative rule. Thus, a rule is acceptable if it results in maximising utility.

Moral rights considers behaviour ethical if people are treated impartially and fairly, respecting the fundamental rights of life, liberty and fair treatment. Based on the philosophies of Thomas Jefferson and John Locke, in a contemporary context it embodies such issues as privacy, due process, free speech and health and safety issues.

Justice provides another lens through which to explore ethics. Ethical behaviour can be viewed as a form of procedural or distributive justice. This view is grounded in the belief that ethical decisions result in impartial and fair treatment according to rules and standards of behaviour. Derived from Rawls's work (1971), he addressed the principles that he perceives underlie justice as 'fairness' from a social contract perspective. Rawls derives his theory from two questions:

1. What are the fundamental principles we would choose, supposing we had the opportunity to do so, that would govern society?
2. What are the principles of justice that can be derived from Question 1?

The two basic principles of justice as fairness and equality that Rawls derives from his analysis of the original position are:

1. Each person has an equal right to the most extensive scheme of basic liberties compatible with a similar scheme of liberties for all.
2. Social and economic inequalities are to meet two conditions: they must be to the greatest expected benefit of the least advantaged and attached to offices and positions open to all under conditions of fair opportunity.

Relativism suggests that aspects of ethics may be considered situational. For example, cultural relativism refers to the belief that ethical behaviour in foreign cultures should be guided by the rights and wrongs in the foreign setting (see the discussion at the end of this chapter on 'Business Ethics in the International Context').

DETERMINANTS OF INDIVIDUAL ETHICS

What kind of factors determine an individual's ethics? Individuals begin to form ethical standards as children during the formative period in response to their perceptions of their parents' behaviour and the behaviour that parents allow them to enact. Similarly, individuals are influenced by peers with whom they interact on a continuous basis. Clearly, if these peers have high ethical standards and reject certain behaviours, then the individual is more likely to adopt similar high standards. Obviously, important events may also shape individuals' lives and contribute to their ethical beliefs and behaviour, which may be both positive and negative. Situational factors could also determine ethical behaviour. Individuals might find themselves in unexpected situations which cause them to act against their better judgment. Furthermore, a person's values and morals contribute to ethical standards as well. For example, an individual who places financial gain and personal advancement as high priorities will adopt a personal code of ethics that promotes the pursuit of wealth. However, a good, solid character arguably does not completely prepare one to deal with the many ethical dilemmas that they will face in their working lives. Rest (1988) says that to assume that any twenty-year-old of good character can function ethically in professional situations is no more warranted than assuming that any logical twenty-year-old can function as a lawyer without any special education.

This raises the question of whether ethics can actually be taught. Many dissenters take the view that educational institutions can do little if students have not already learned ethics from their parents and families, friends, schools and significant others (Hanson 1988; Levin 1990). However, the critical point here relates to the notion of learning. If ethical codes and standards are learned, and clearly they are, then they can be unlearned and new standards can be acquired to replace them with.

BUSINESS ETHICS

Many people find it hard to take the concept of business ethics seriously, and according to Green (1994) they view it as an oxymoron because business misconduct has fostered the view that businesspeople are unconcerned with ethics and are even prepared to break the law if they can get away with it. Despite this, or perhaps in response to it, over the past twenty years or so the field of business ethics and social responsibility has achieved a recognised place in business education. While developing a real paradigm remains problematic, there is now a community of scholars who share a common desire to clarify and foster the basis of ethics in business (Collier 1998). Management ethics are those standards of behaviour that guide individual managers in their work, while social responsibility can be viewed as that set of obligations an organisation has to protect and enhance the society in which it functions. According to Buckley (2001), many organisations now see ethics as 'good business' in terms of enhanced image, reputation and a source of competitive advantage.

SHOULDN'T EMPLOYEES ALREADY KNOW THE DIFFERENCE BETWEEN RIGHT AND WRONG?

A belief is that any individual of good character should already know right from wrong and should be able to be ethical without special training. You probably think of yourself as an individual of good character. So think about the following real dilemma.

You are the VP of a medium-sized organisation that uses chemicals in its production processes. In good faith you have hired a highly competent person to ensure that your company complies with all environmental laws and safety regulations. This individual informs you that a chemical that the company now uses in some quantity is not yet on the approved Environmental Protection Agency list, although it is undergoing review and is scheduled to be placed on the approved list in about three months because it has been found to be safe. You can't produce your product without this chemical, yet you are not supposed to use the chemical until it is approved. Waiting for approval would require shutting the plant for three months, putting many people out of work and threatening the company's very survival. What should you do?

Source: Trevino and Nelson (1995)

Management researchers began to study business ethics and social responsibility during the 1960s by conducting surveys of managers' attitudes towards business ethics (Baumhart 1961). Since then, Trevino and Nelson (1995) note that interest in the area has grown substantially in the last thirty years to the point where articles and books proliferate in the academic and professional press.

Management ethics are the standards of behaviour that guide individual managers in their work. However, it is important to note that ethical or unethical actions do not occur in a vacuum. The actions of peers, managers and top management combined with the organisation's culture all contribute to the organisation's ethical context. That said, the starting point for understanding the ethical context of management is the individual's own ethical standards. Garavan *et al.* (1993) identify three areas where managerial ethics are most significant:

1. **Relationship of the firm to its employees:** The behaviour of individual managers defines the ethical standards according to which the company treats its employees. Examples of such areas include hiring and firing, wages and working conditions, employee privacy, support for religious beliefs, etc.
2. **Relationship of employees to the firm:** Issues which arise here include conflicts of interest, secrecy, honesty in keeping expense accounts, not making secret profits, accepting gifts from potential clients, etc.
3. **Relationship of the firm to others:** This would include relationships with customers, suppliers, behaviour towards competitors, dealing with stockholders, unions and the local community.

Carr (1968) argues that business has an ethics of its own, different from that which governs our ordinary personal relationships. For the sake of profits and economic success, this ethic permits conscious mis-statements, concealment of pertinent facts and exaggeration. He likens business ethics to a game of poker governed by an acceptable set of formal rules.

> No one expects poker to be played on the ethical principles preached in churches. In poker it is right and proper to bluff a friend out of the rewards of being dealt a good hand. A player feels no more than a slight twinge of sympathy, if that, when – with nothing better than a single ace in his hand – he strips a heavy loser who holds a pair of the rest of his chips. It was up to the other fellow to protect himself ... Poker's own brand of ethics is different from the ethical ideals of civilised human relationships ... No one thinks any worse of poker on that account. And no one should think any the worse of the game of business because its standards of right and wrong differ from the prevailing traditions of morality in our society (Carr 1968: 145).

This view, according to Green (1994: 9), while holding some truth, also distorts the reality of managerial ethical responsibility. 'Managers are sometimes validly thought of as game players. But game ethics must be replaced by more familiar moral standards when managers' actions seriously impact on persons not playing the business game.'

MANAGING ETHICAL BEHAVIOUR IN THE BUSINESS CONTEXT

Recent years have witnessed numerous ethical scandals with the result that many organisations have begun to place more emphasis on employees' ethical behaviour. Significant here are attempts by management to:
- set a good example and act as role models in relation to ethical behaviour;
- establish and manage an organisation's culture so that it clearly delineates what is acceptable and unacceptable behaviour;
- offer employees training and development on how to cope with ethical dilemmas;
- establish an ethics committee that reports directly to the board of directors;
- prepare guidelines that detail how employees are to treat suppliers, customers, competitors and other stakeholders; and
- develop codes of ethics, which are written statements of the values and ethical standards that guide a company's actions.

BUSINESS ETHICS AND IRISH MANAGEMENT

Introduction

Do ethical considerations influence the key business dialogues or will the next generation of up and coming top Irish management similarly slip having learnt little from the recent exposés? In effect, what do Irish managers really think about ethics, morality, and business practice?

The study

930 senior managers were surveyed – 530 UK, 100 Republic of Ireland, and 300 US. The sample only involved senior managers, the managerial roles varying from general managers to executive directors and main or subsidiary board members. Differences in sample size reflect the challenge of gaining access to senior level managers and the range and number of medium to large sized organisations in each of these countries. Questionnaires were distributed to named individuals invited to participate in the study, with the result that an over 70 per cent response rate ensued. 83 per cent of the total sample are between the ages of 36 to 55 years.

Findings

* Irish managers are significantly more convinced than UK, but less than US, managers that every company and every industry should have a code of ethics.
* Irish managers give significantly greater importance than UK or US managers to the influence which increasing public concern about ethical standards has on behaviour in business.
* UK managers agree significantly less strongly than Irish or US managers in three areas, namely that business schools should include more ethics training for students, or with the capacity of public opinion to influence a businessperson's ethical behaviour, or with every company and every industry having a code of ethics.
* US managers are significantly more in favour than UK or Irish managers of consultancy intervention in helping managers to deal with ethical issues.
* Irish managers agree significantly more strongly than UK or US managers that ethical beliefs should be a consideration in the selection of managers.

Ethical standards in Irish business today

Managers were asked whether they believed ethical standards in business have fallen, stayed the same or risen over the last ten years. 37 per cent believe they had fallen, 42 per cent believe they have stayed the same, and 11 per cent believe they have risen. For those who say standards have fallen, greed, self-centredness, increased competition, and social tendency towards a 'me first' mentality are the chief reasons put forward. Some argue that standards are the same, and that it is merely our awareness of malpractices that has been increased.

The duality of the Irish

These findings are representative of a major duality in the ethical stance of Irish management. On the one hand, the study reveals a generally high awareness of ethical issues and issues surrounding the implementation of ethics in business, but on the other, reveals what is essentially a preparedness to place as highest priority the interest of corporate stockholders. Essentially, the situation is one in which Irish managers may espouse ethical intentions until the need arises to satisfy stockholder needs. A narrow view of corporate responsibility, confined only or mainly to stockholder interests, is evidence of profoundly short-term thinking.

Considerations towards enhancing ethical behaviour

Based on the findings of the research, there are a number of practical suggestions which can be made to Irish managers to increase awareness of ethics in business, and enhance the potential for ethical behaviour in organisations.

Shareholder impact

Of prime importance is highlighting to Irish managers the inherent dangers of attributing so great a corporate responsibility solely to stockholders, the most significant of which is the likelihood of creating an organisational culture at senior level which is built around the principle of satisfying stockholder interests at any costs. Such cultures are inevitable breeding grounds of potentially unethical behaviour both among management and staff. There is evidence from the research that Irish managers do indeed recognise the need for a broader concept of organisation stakeholders and consequently of corporate responsibilities. This broader concept should be encouraged through reinforcement, education, and training at all levels.

Training and education

Inclusion of business ethics teaching within Irish business schools and university business-oriented courses is considered desirable. Ethics education and training is shown by previous research (Delaney and Sockell 1992) to have a positive effect on sensitivity to and awareness of potential influences on behaviour, ethical issues, and ethical conflicts, yet few Irish managers have received any ethics education at all.

The role of top management

Enhancing awareness of the crucial role which top management plays in the creation of a culture of ethical behaviour within organisations is equally desirable. Alongside emphasis on the role of top management competence in visioning, communication, and creation of mission and culture outside the ethical dimension in management development, the importance of competence in the ethical dimension should also be highlighted.

Source: Extracts from Alderson and Kakabadse (1994)

CODES OF ETHICS

The benefits of ethical codes highlighted in the literature focus on benefits to both the organisation and to stakeholders. Munro (1996) suggests that an obvious use of a company code of ethics is as a public relations exercise. However, Winfield (1990) reports evidence to suggest that companies tend to restrict their codes to top management and shareholders and rarely distribute them to outside interest groups, suggesting that many companies do not fully exploit the public relations potential of ethical codes. Some codes of ethics give explicit recognition to a wide range of stakeholder interests, including customers, suppliers, employees and the local community. Some commentators point out, however, that shareholders are one of the least-mentioned interest groups.

Codes of ethics have the potential to address a wide range of issues, yet there is evidence that their enforcement is somewhat haphazard. Weaver (1993) argues that compliance with codes of ethics can best be characterised as 'too general and sporadic, too legalistic and stultifying.' There is also evidence of unequal application, resulting in discrimination and injustice. Garavan (2000) draws attention to a study conducted by Arthur Anderson's Ethics and Responsibility Practices Group in the US (1999) (a report which predates the Enron debacle), which reports that a key factor in the success or failure of ethics and compliance codes and programmes in organisations is employees' perceptions of management's motivation for establishing such codes and programmes in the first place. Where employees perceived that the code was implemented as a guide to behaviour as well as seeking to establish a shared set of company values already rooted in the company culture, the code was more likely to be successful than where it was designed primarily for compliance purposes. Where employees perceived that the code was specifically developed to prevent, detect or punish violations of law or to enhance the company's image, the impact of the code was diminished.

ADVANTAGES AND LIMITATIONS OF WRITTEN CODES OF ETHICS

Advantages

1. They are a concrete indication of the organisation's commitment to high standards of ethical behaviour.
2. They clearly establish parameters within which individuals must behave.
3. They give employees a commitment that no one will be called upon to do anything in the line of duty that is morally, ethically or legally wrong.
4. It provides employees with a legitimate basis to inform top management of unethical behaviour and have it dealt with.
5. The code may help employees to resolve actual or potential ethical dilemmas.

Limitations

1. They may prescribe what people should do, but they often fail to help people understand and live with the consequences of their choices.
2. The code may be ignored by key people in the organisation, thus openly undermining its effectiveness.

3. Managers may not be prepared to make ethical choices because of the possibility of unpleasant outcomes, such as firing, rejection by colleagues or the loss of monetary gain.

4. Individual managers must be prepared to confront the consequences of their own decisions and weigh up the options available when making difficult ethical decisions. A code will not do this for them.

5. The code may not cover all possible situations that may arise.

6. The code may be unsuccessfully communicated and may not support appropriate procedures, i.e. discipline procedures and avenues to inform on unethical behaviour.

In relation to broader social responsibility, organisations relate to their environment in ways that may often involve ethical dilemmas and decisions. Garavan *et al.* (1993) argue that organisations exercise social responsibility towards three primary interests, namely organisational constituents, the natural environment and the wider society.

Organisational constituents are defined as people and other organisations that are directly affected by the organisation's behaviour and who have a stake in its performance, such as customers, creditors, suppliers, employees, owners/investors, local government, etc. To maintain a social responsibility to investors, for example, requires financial managers to follow proper accounting procedures, provide appropriate information to stakeholders about the company's financial performance and manage the organisation to profit shareholders' rights and interests. Insider trading, illegal stock manipulation and withholding financial data are examples of unethical behaviour in this area.

In relation to the natural environment, there has been an increasing awareness of its importance in recent years. Examples of issues that are emerging here include:

*   developing feasible ways to avoid contributing to acid rain and global warming;
*   developing alternative methods of handling sewage, hazardous wastes and ordinary wastage;
*   developing safety policies that cut down on accidents with potentially disastrous environmental results;
*   initiating crisis management plans to deal with disasters, such as the 1989 Exxon Valdez oil spill or the 2002 Prestige spill and sinking off Spain's Atlantic coast; and
*   using recycled materials.

Many believe that promoting the general welfare of society is a central aspect of business social responsibility. Examples of positive activity in this area include:

*   making contributions to charities, philanthropic organisations and non-profit foundations and associations;
*   supporting culturally enriching activities;
*   taking an active role in public health and education; and
*   acting to combat the political inequalities that exist in the world.

Arguments For and Against Social Responsibility

Arguments for
- Business creates problems and should therefore help to solve them.
- Corporations are citizens in our society.
- Business often has the resources necessary to solve problems.
- Business is a partner in our society, along with the government and the general population.

Arguments against
- The purpose of business is to generate profit for owners.
- Investment in social programmes gives business too much power.
- There is potential for conflicts of interest.
- Business lacks the expertise to manage social programmes.

Activity 14.1 The Human Relationships Questionnaire

Developed by Richard Christie, the test attempts to predict whether a person becomes emotionally involved with other people or simply uses them for his/her own ends. Also known as the Machiavelli Test, it is used to measure Machiavellian tendencies. A high score on the test will give you a high Machiavellian tendency.

The following questions ask you about how you behave at work, what you believe about human relationships and what value you place on them. Each question is presented as a statement and you are asked to choose one of five possible responses: strongly agree, agree, don't know, disagree or strongly disagree.

There are no right answers and no wrong answers, so please be as honest as you can. (See p. 423 for the scoring key.)

	Strongly agree	Agree	Don't know	Disagree	Strongly disagree
1. You should only tell someone the real reason for doing something if it serves a successful purpose.	☐	☐	☐	☐	☐
2. People who lead upright and respectable lives will get on in the world.	☐	☐	☐	☐	☐
3. Bravery is inherent in most people.	☐	☐	☐	☐	☐
4. You should always assume that people can be villainous and that this will appeal if given a chance.	☐	☐	☐	☐	☐

5. Telling people what they want to hear is the best way to deal with them. ☐ ☐ ☐ ☐ ☐

6. The old saying 'there's one born every minute' is not true. ☐ ☐ ☐ ☐ ☐

7. Lying to other people cannot be forgiven. ☐ ☐ ☐ ☐ ☐

8. Giving the actual reason rather than ones which may carry more weight is the way to behave when asking someone to do something for you. ☐ ☐ ☐ ☐ ☐

9. It is sensible to pander to important people. ☐ ☐ ☐ ☐ ☐

10. It is hard to be successful in an organisation without cutting corners. ☐ ☐ ☐ ☐ ☐

11. What differentiates criminals from other people is that they are foolish enough to get caught. ☐ ☐ ☐ ☐ ☐

12. Euthanasia should be a choice for those with an incurable disease. ☐ ☐ ☐ ☐ ☐

13. In the final analysis, most people are good and well meaning. ☐ ☐ ☐ ☐ ☐

14. You should only act when it is morally defensible. ☐ ☐ ☐ ☐ ☐

15. Humility coupled with honesty is a better combination than dishonesty and self-importance. ☐ ☐ ☐ ☐ ☐

16. Unless forced to work hard, most people will stretch themselves. ☐ ☐ ☐ ☐ ☐

17. Being good in all respects is quite possible. ☐ ☐ ☐ ☐ ☐

18. The death of a parent is more easily forgotten by most people than the loss of a piece of property. ☐ ☐ ☐ ☐ ☐

19. It is simply asking for trouble to trust someone else completely. ☐ ☐ ☐ ☐ ☐

20. It is best always to be honest.   ☐   ☐   ☐   ☐   ☐

Scoring key for human relationship questionnaire

Question number	Strongly agree	Agree	Don't know	Disagree	Strongly disagree
1	5	4	3	2	1
2	1	2	3	4	5
3	1	2	3	4	5
4	5	4	3	2	1
5	5	4	3	2	1
6	1	2	3	4	5
7	1	2	3	4	5
8	1	2	3	4	5
9	5	4	3	2	1
10	5	4	3	2	1
11	5	4	3	2	1
12	5	4	3	2	1
13	1	2	3	4	5
14	1	2	3	4	5
15	1	2	3	4	5
16	5	4	3	2	1
17	1	2	3	4	5
18	5	4	3	2	1
19	5	4	3	2	1
20	1	2	3	4	5

Calculate your overall score. Score =

Score	Comment
20–38	Goodness shines through you. How do you survive?
39–54	No is not an impossible word to say – you only think it is.
55–69	An honest cynic – at least relatively honest.
70–84	Congratulations – you could be an honorary member of the Borgia family.
85–100	You might even be able to teach Machiavelli something. ('Never give a sucker an even break.' – W.C. Fields)

Source: Tyson and Jackson (1992)

ONGOING DEBATES/ADVANCED CONCEPTS IN POWER, POLITICS AND ETHICS

BUSINESS ETHICS IN THE INTERNATIONAL CONTEXT

The international business arena presents a particular set of ethical issues. Commonly cited difficulties include employment issues, marketing, effects on the natural environment, the cultural impact of transnational activities, economic development issues and relationships with the home country.

Two distinct schools of thought have emerged concerning transnational responsibilities, which may be called the 'minimalist' and 'maximalist' schools (Garavan 2000). The 'minimalist' school, he notes, suggests that a transnational corporation's moral responsibilities are tied directly to its economic purposes, i.e. to make profits for its investors and products or services for the public. Minimalists deny that it is the corporation's responsibility to help the poor, encourage the arts or contribute to social causes – except in so far as doing such things is consistent with its more fundamental mission of making profits. Minimalists assert that transnational corporations have moral responsibilities, but that they can sometimes put them under the heading of 'not harming' and not directly violating others' rights.

In contrast, the maximalist school argues that corporations are unique in their level of organisation and ability to control wealth, and therefore they have the duty to reach out and help others. If housing and water supplies are substandard in the local area, then the company should work toward their improvement. Similarly, if malnutrition is a serious problem, the transnational corporation should both develop nutrition programmes and facilitate their implementation. Both minimalists and maximalists agree that transnational corporations should meet certain minimum ethical standards in conducting their business, but they disagree about whether transnationals should exceed the minimum.

Garavan (2000) notes that the most often-used means of expressing minimum standards is through the moral language of rights. All individuals, nations and corporations are said to have rights and correlative duties in connection with these rights. Many commentators argue that these duties include only refraining from depriving people of the objects of rights directly, but also, at least in some instances, helping to protect people from being deprived of their rights. For example, a transnational operating in a developing country has correlative duties regarding the right to minimal education. In turn, the transnational would violate the right to minimal education if it hired young children as full-time, ongoing labour and thus deprive them of the opportunity to learn to read and write. The violation in this case would be passive rather than active; it would happen not through the corporation actively removing the means of minimal education, but by passively failing to protect the right from deprivation. Garavan quotes DeGeorge (1993), who advances ten guidelines that he believes apply to multinationals operating in less-developed countries. According to him, such multinationals should:

- do no intentional direct harm;
- produce more good than harm for the host country;
- contribute by their activity to the host country's development;

- respect their employees' human rights;
- respect the local culture and work with it, not against it;
- pay their fair share of taxes;
- co-operate with the local government in developing and enforcing fair background institutions;
- recognise that majority control of a firm carries with it the ethical responsibility for the actions and failure of the firm;
- make sure that hazardous plants are safe and run safely; and
- when transferring hazardous technology to less-developed countries, be responsible for redesigning suitable technology so that it can be safely administered in the host country.

The consequence of this line of thinking, Garavan suggests, is that one of the most difficult contexts for transnational business ethics involves clashes between home and host country norms or laws. The problem is particularly problematic when the norm or law appears substandard from the perspective of the transnational's home country. When wage rates, pollution standards, norms prohibiting bribery and treatment of minorities appear substandard in a foreign country, should the transnational corporation take the high moral ground and adhere to the home country standards, or should it take the expedient route of embracing the host country's standards? It is argued that attempts to embrace either extreme would be morally problematic. Adopting the home country standard would sometimes disadvantage the host country. It is also argued that to continually adopt the host country's standard would be pernicious. Laws and regulations in many developing countries are frequently unsophisticated, and a lack of technological knowledge coupled with inefficient bureaucratic mechanisms may preclude effective government control of industry.

INSTITUTIONALISING THE ACT OF WHISTLEBLOWING

In 2002, Sherron Watkins (formerly of Enron) was the recipient of several accolades, including *Time Magazine*'s 'Person of the Year' award. She was honoured for her courage as a whistleblower in speaking out and exposing the accounting scandal at Enron Corporation that rocked the US financial and corporate world. Often dismissed as troublemakers, when forced to speak out, whistleblowers often experience a deep conflict between their obligations of loyalty to the organisation and their obligation to prevent harm to individuals or the public at large. Garavan (2000) suggests that whistleblowing is generally defined as a practice in which employees or ex-employees of an organisation have knowledge that their company is engaged in activities that:

- cause unnecessary harm to the consumer or others;
- are in violation of human rights;
- are considered illegal in that they breach some common law or statutory provision;
- run counter to the defined purpose of the organisation; or
- are considered to be immoral.

The whistleblower then decides to inform the public or some government agency of these activities. The disclosure is made in the reasonable belief that there is malpractice coupled with the belief that it is made in good faith, without malice and ultimately perhaps in the public interest.

Some commentators view whistleblowing as an act of disloyalty and consequently the only justification for overriding the obligation to the company is a countervailing obligation to the public. Other commentators argue that whistleblowing is simply an act of disloyalty and is never justified, to a more extreme position that employees have no obligation to the company but instead have a right to freedom of expression that allows the employee to ethically disclose whatever they wish about the company, except where an employment contract in some way prohibits this. Among the conditions under which whistleblowing is permissible are the following.

- The whistleblowing should be done for the purpose of exposing some unnecessary harm, illegal activity, violation of human rights or activity that runs counter to the organisation's expressed purpose.
- There is a duty to the part of the whistleblower to make sure that their belief that inappropriate actions are ordered or have occurred. The standard in the case of this condition is one of reasonable grounds.
- The whistleblower is mandated to act only after careful analysis of the danger.
- The literature clearly posits the notion that the whistleblower should exhaust all internal channels before informing the public.

SUMMARY OF KEY PROPOSITIONS

- Power, politics and ethics are important concepts for explaining behaviour in organisations.
- Power relates to the extent to which individuals or stakeholders are able to pursue or convince others to take a certain course of action. Politics can be viewed as power in action and consist of strategies and tactics drawn upon for the purpose of influencing individuals and groups. Management ethics are the standards of behaviour that guide individual managers in their work. Social responsibility refers to the set of obligations an organisation has to protect and enhance the society in which it functions.
- Authority is the right to manipulate or change others. Power need not be legitimate. Influence is usually conceived of as being broader in scope than power and involves the ability to alter others in general ways, such as by changing their satisfaction and performance.
- The impetus for the study of power in organisations came from two rather different directions. One stream of research focused on the existence of conflicting, competing interests and has examined power from the perspective of domination. The second major research root associated with power examined how groups acquire and wield power not granted to them under official arrangements.
- Several bases of power exist, reflecting the different bases or resources that power

holders might rely upon. The sources identified are reward, coercive, legitimate, referent and expert power.

- Employee empowerment, referring to the extent to which employees have a sense of personal power and control, has become recognised as a central feature of the new organisation scenario.
- Four general political tactics can be identified, namely inducement, coercion, persuasion and obligation.
- Processes that are likely to be highly politically charged are described as sporadic. Those less politically charged are termed constricted processes, while those that are least politically prone are labelled fluid processes.
- Organisations exercise social responsibility towards three primary interests, namely organisational constituents, the natural environment and the wider society.

DISCUSSION/SELF-ASSESSMENT QUESTIONS

1. What do you think the main sources of power within an organisation are?
2. What political tactics might you employ to bring about large-scale, speedy change in an organisation?
3. Is the use of power in an organisational context ethical?
4. Identify key factors that determine individual ethics.
5. Describe five types of unethical behaviour.
6. Think of some examples of firms that are making attempts to be socially responsible. Identify exactly what courses of action they are taking to be so.

MULTIPLE CHOICE QUESTIONS

1. The essence of power is control over others' behaviour. True or false?
2. Power differs from authority because:
   (a) While authority usually operates in vertical directions down the organisational hierarchy, power typically operates in any direction.
   (b) While authority is often accepted by subordinates, power may not be accepted by those it is exercised upon.
   (c) In the organisational context, authority is vested in specific roles or positions in the organisation, whereas power may arise from different sources.
   (d) Authority can be identified from the organisation chart, but power is less observable in this concrete way and consequently it is more difficult to identify and label.
   (e) All of the above.
   (f) None of the above.
3. Coercive power:
   (a) Derives from the individual's control over resources and is dependent upon the power wielder's ability to confer valued material rewards.
   (b) Is that which is exercised in accordance with organisational rules and with the organisation's authority.

    (c) Refers to the power to punish or withhold reward, the power to threaten and to use one's position to force others to take action.

    (d) Is contingent upon the charisma, interpersonal skill and/or personal attraction of the individual.

    (e) All of the above.

    (f) None of the above.

4. The sources of exchange power for an internal organisational stakeholder include:

    (a) Specific resource.

    (b) A technical skill.

    (c) Specific information.

    (d) All of the above.

    (e) None of the above.

5. The cultural values of a society have an impact on the influenceability of its people. True or false?

6. According to Dawson (1996), three main sources of constraint that limit attempts to exercise power in pursuit of interest are:

    (a) Regency, leniency and intent.

    (b) Technological, administrative and ideological.

    (c) Trainability, transfer and outcomes.

    (d) Physiological, emotional and somatic.

7. According to Dobbs (1993), the four necessary conditions to encourage empowerment are:

    (a) Employability, willingness, engagement and determination.

    (b) Preparation, planning, monitoring and evaluation.

    (c) Participation, innovation, access to information and accountability.

    (d) Planning, leadership, co-ordination and control.

8. According to Hickson (1990), the processes around strategic decision making that are the most political are best described as fluid processes. True or false?

9. Utilitarianism as a view of ethics suggests that:

    (a) The pursuit of one's long-term self-interests constitutes ethical behaviour.

    (b) Behaviour may be considered ethical if people are treated impartially and fairly.

    (c) Actions are moral if they do the greatest good for the greatest number of people.

    (d) Aspects of ethics may be considered situational.

    (e) All of the above.

    (f) None of the above.

10. Ethical codes and standards are learned by the individual. True or false?

11. Among the advantages of a written code of ethics is that:

    (a) It provides a concrete indication of the organisation's commitment to high standards of ethical behaviour.

    (b) It establishes parameters within which individuals must behave.

    (c) It may give employees a commitment that no one will be called upon to do anything in the line of duty that is morally, ethically or legally wrong.

(d) It may provide employees with a legitimate basis to inform top management of unethical behaviour and have it dealt with.

(e) All of the above.

(f) None of the above.

FIVE KEY READINGS

Collier, J., 'Theorizing the ethical organization', *Business Ethics Quarterly*, VIII/4 (1998), 621–54.

Fiol, C.M., O'Connor, E.J. and Aguinis, H., 'All for one and one for all? The development and transfer of power across organization levels', *Academy of Management Review*, XXVI/2 (2001), 224–42.

Hardy, C. and Clegg, S., 'Some dare call it power', in S. Clegg, C. Hardy and W. Nord (eds), *Handbook of Organization Studies*, London: Sage 1996.

Hickson, D., Hinings, C., Lee, C., Schneck, R. and Pennings, J., 'A strategic contingencies theory of intraorganisational power', *Administrative Science Quarterly*, XVI/2 (1971), 216–29.

Trevino, L. and Nelson, K., *Managing Business Ethics: Straight Talk About How To Do It Right*, New York: Wiley 1995.

REFERENCES

Alderson, S. and Kakabadse, A., 'Business ethics and Irish management: a cross cultural study', *European Journal of Management*, XII/4 (1994), 432–41.

Alen, R., Madison, D., Portor, L., Renwick, P. and Mayers, B., 'Organizational politics: tactics and characteristics of its actors', *California Management Review*, XXII (Fall 1979).

Bacharach, S. and Lawler, E., *Power and Politics in Organizations*, London: Jossey-Bass 1980.

Baumhart, R., 'How ethical are business men?', *Harvard Business Review*, XXXIX/4 (1961), 6–8.

Bernard, C., *The Function of the Executive*, Cambridge, MA: Harvard University Press 1938.

Broom, M., 'Positive use of power', *Executive Excellence*, XX/2 (2003), 11.

Buckley, R., 'Ethical issues in human resource systems', *Human Resource Management Review*, XI/1/2 (2001), 11–29.

Carr, A., 'Is business bluffing ethical?', *Harvard Business Review*, XLVI/1 (1968), 145.

Collier, J., 'Theorizing the ethical organization', *Business Ethics Quarterly*, VIII/4 (1998), 621–54.

Cyert, R. and March, T., *A Behavioral Theory of the Firm*, Englewood Cliffs, NJ: Prentice Hall 1963.

Dahl, R., 'The concept of power', *Behavioural Science*, II/1 (1957), 201–15.

Dawson, S., *Analysing Organisations*, 3rd ed., London: Macmillan 1996.

DeGeorge, R.T., *Competing with Integrity in International Business*, New York: Oxford University Press 1993.

Dixon, M., 'The world of office politics', *Financial Times*, 10 November 1982.

Dobbs, J., 'The empowerment environment', *Training and Development*, (February 1993), 55–7.

Drory, A. and Romm, T., 'Politics in organization and its perception within the organization', *Organization Studies*, IX/2 (1988), 165–79.

Finchman, R. and Rhodes, P., *The Individual, Work and Organization: Behavioural Studies for Business and Management Students*, London: Weidenfeld & Nicolson 1988.

Fiol, C.M., O'Connor, E.J. and Aguinis, H., 'All for one and one for all? The development and transfer of power across organization levels', *Academy of Management Review*, XXVI/2 (2001), 224–42.

French, J. and Raven, B., 'The bases of social power', in L. Cartwright and A. Zander (eds), *Group Dynamics: Research and Theory*, London: Tavistock 1959.

French, L. and Bell, H., *Organization Development: Behavioral Science Interventions for Organization Improvement*, Englewood Cliffs, NJ: Prentice Hall 1995.

Garavan, T., 'Business ethics and corporate social responsibility', in M. Morley and N. Heraty (eds), *Strategic Management in Ireland*, Dublin: Gill & Macmillan 2000.

Garavan, T., Fitzgerald, G. and Morley, M., *Business Analysis: Books I and II*, London: Certified Accountants Educational Trust 1993.

Green, R., *The Ethical Manager: A New Method for Business Ethics*, New York: Macmillan College Publishing 1994.

Hanson, K., 'Why we teach ethics in business school', *Stanford Business School Magazine*, (February 1988), 14–16.

Hardy, C. and Clegg, S., 'Some dare call it power', in S. Clegg, C. Hardy and W. Nord (eds), *Handbook of Organization Studies*, London: Sage 1993.

Hatch, M.J., *Organization Theory: Modern, Symbolic and Postmodern Perspectives*, Oxford: Oxford University Press 1997.

Hickson, D., 'Politics permeate', in D. Wilson and R. Rosenfeld, *Managing Organizations: Text, Readings and Cases*, London: McGraw-Hill 1990, 175–81.

Hickson, D., Hinings, C., Lee, C., Schneck, R. and Pennings, J., 'A strategic contingencies theory of intraorganisational power', *Administrative Science Quarterly*, XVI/2 (1971), 216–29.

Hollander, E. and Offermann, L., 'Power and leadership in organizations', *American Psychologist* (February 1990), 184.

Irvin, L., 'Ethics in organizations: a chaos perspective', *Journal of Organizational Change Management*, XV/4 (2002), 359–81.

Lasswell, H., *Politics: Who Gets What, When, How*, New York: McGraw-Hill 1936.

Levin, M., 'Ethics courses: useless', *New York Times*, 25 November 1990.

Luthans, F., *Organizational Behavior*, 6th ed., New York: McGraw-Hill 1992.

Munro, I., 'Codes of ethics: some uses and abuses', in P. Davies (ed.), *Current Issues in Business Ethics*, London: Routledge 1996.

Pettigrew, A., *The Politics of Organisational Decision-Making*, London: Tavistock 1973.

Pettigrew, A., 'The influence process between specialists and executives', *Personnel Review*, III/1 (1974), 24–30.

Pfeffer, J., *Power in Organisations*, London: Pitman 1981.

Porter, M., *Competitive Advantage: Creating and Sustaining Superior Performance*, New York: The Free Press 1985.

Rawls, J., *A Theory of Justice*, Cambridge, MA: Harvard University Press 1971.

Reitz, H., *Behavior in Organizations*, 3rd ed., Homewood, IL: Irwin 1987.

Rest, J., 'Can ethics be taught in professional schools? The psychological research', *Easier Said than Done* (Winter 1988), 22–6.

Shepard, H., 'Innovation resisting and innovation producing organisation', *Journal of Business*, XL (1967), 470–7.

Statt, D., *Psychology and the World of Work*, London: Macmillan 1994.

Trevino, L. and Nelson, K., *Managing Business Ethics: Straight Talk About How To Do It Right*, New York: Wiley 1995.

Turnipseed, D., 'Are good soldiers good? Exploring the link between organization citizenship behavior and personal ethics', *Journal of Business Research*, LV/1 (2002), 1–15.

Tyson, S. and Jackson, T., *The Essence of Organizational Behaviour*, Hemel Hempstead: Prentice Hall 1992.

Walumbwa, F., 'Power and politics in organizations: implications for OD professional practice', *Human Resource Development International*, II/3 (1999), 205–16.

Weber, M., *The Theory of Social and Economic Organization*, New York: The Free Press 1947.

Winfield, M., *Minding Your Own Business: Self Regulation and Whistleblowing in British Companies*, London: Social Audit 1990.

THE DYNAMICS OF EFFECTIVE STRATEGY

15

Learning Objectives

- To introduce different definitions and perspectives on the behavioural dynamics of strategy in organisations.

- To highlight how effective strategic activity is seen by some researchers as contingent on key behavioural dynamics within an organisation.

- To present the problems and contributions of the rational approach to strategy in organisations.

- To indicate the importance of language and talk at work and how important a role it can play in strategic development.

- What strategic management requires, why it is important and how it can be developed.

- How different 'strategic climates' can be identified and how different types of climates can give rise to different strategic processes in organisational settings.

INTRODUCTION

Given its current prevalence, it is hard to believe that the term 'strategy' was relatively rarely used in organisational or management contexts before the 1980s (Schendel and Cool 1988). The increasing popularity of the notion of strategy in organisations can be at least partly attributed to the management education boom of the 1980s, along with global political developments in which the aggressive pursuit of competitive advantage became an increasingly central concept (Whipp 1996). This is not to say that strategy was completely ignored before its emerging popularity within the last twenty-five years, but the assumptions with which it has been associated have changed and developed quite dramatically since then. This chapter will explore some of the central aspects of strategy in organisational settings and show how changes in definitions of strategy provide a useful backdrop for understanding key developments in the field. It will explore the requirements and dynamics of effective strategy in organisations and the advanced concepts section will focus particularly on the dynamics of dialogue and decision making. This chapter uses evidence-based concepts to help highlight what organisational and strategic management requires, why it is important and how it can be developed.

WHAT IS STRATEGY?

Strategy in organisations has traditionally been seen as a field of inquiry that is almost completely separate from the field of organisational behaviour (for example, see Watson 2002). Indeed, many texts on organisational behaviour today still do not address the area of strategy in any explicit way, even if they do refer to the related dynamics of managing change or making decisions (for example, see Gordon 2002).

Over the years, strategy has been defined in many different ways. Below we outline a range of orientations towards strategy, each highlighting different perspectives on what strategy is, and some revealing assumptions about its associated dynamics.

DEFINITIONS OF STRATEGY

'Strategy is something done out of sight of the enemy' (James' military dictionary 1810).

'Strategy is rivalry amongst peers for prizes in a defined and shared game' (Andrews 1971).

'Strategy relates to all actions that contribute to the long-term survival of an organisation' (Thompson and Strickland 1981).

'Strategy is something an organisation needs or uses in order to win, or establish its legitimacy in a world of competitive rivalry … Strategy is what makes a firm unique, a winner, a survivor' (Thomas 1993).

'Strategy is a discourse and a mechanism of power' (Knights and Morgan 1991).

'Strategy is a statement of an organisation's basic mission, purpose and goals as well as the means for accomplishing them' (Gordon 2002).

'Strategy answers two basic questions: where do you want to go and how do you want to get there?' (*The Economist* 1997).

'Strategic decision making is the fundamental dynamic capability in excellent firms' (Eisenhart 1999).

Strategy from a modernist perspective can be seen as 'top management's planned efforts to influence organisational outcomes by managing the organisation's relationship with its environment' (Hatch 1997).

Strategy from a postmodernist perspective can be defined as 'the complex processes of enacting, making sense of or socially constructing an organisation' (Hatch 1997).

DEFINITIONS OF KEY CONCEPTS

Strategic capability
An organisation's general capacity to formulate and implement strategy to ensure its long-term viability.

The competition imperative
The assumption that competition is central to organisational survival.

The rational strategy process
An approach to strategy that assumes a rational sequence of analysis, formulation and implementation. Note that the rational process rarely describes actual strategic behaviour in organisations.

Top management team strategy climates
Strategic climates in the top management team can differ according to diversity of view and willingness to address issues that merit attention. Strategic climate refers to the psychological conditions in which top management teams operate that can affect their ability to think and act strategically.

KEY DIMENSIONS OF STRATEGIC CAPABILITY

An organisation's strategic capability seems to be central to its ability to perform and survive. Strategy formulation and implementation is not an easy process. It relies on the talents of the top management team, on the commitment of all organisational members, on the co-ordination of activities and the intangible contributions of the dynamics of trust, structure, culture, climate and organisational dialogue. The top management team (TMT) should play a central role in the establishment of these dynamics: providing appropriate leadership, creating effective vision, focusing on the long-term survival and viability of its organisation and developing a strong, collective sense of purpose. Such responsibilities are demanding. There are 'mutually reinforcing barriers that block strategy implementation and organisational learning' (Beer and Eisenstat 2000: 29) that form the basis for senior management frustrations, inactivity and inappropriate defensive action (Argyris 1990).

THE COMPETITION IMPERATIVE

Much of the management literature carries the assumption that competition is central to organisational survival. Alongside the existence of strategic obstacles and frustrations, there appears to be a stronger imperative than ever before for organisations to be able to 'compete successfully with anybody, anywhere at any time' (Hitt *et al.* 1998). This imperative seems to be becoming more intense for a whole spectrum of organisational types and industries, particularly as emerging information technologies take hold of business processes from the design to the delivery of products and services. Watson (2002: 171), however, argues that while survival is the fundamental aim of all organisations, it is inappropriate to assume that achieving that aim is 'merely a matter of winning battles with competitors.' This assumption represents a simplification of organisational responsibility and activity.

Is it all about competition? Does strategic activity inevitably have to put competitive advantage at its centre? Watson argues that organisational survival can be achieved through co-operation, coalition and collaboration with other organisations – even those with which the organisation also competes. It can be asserted that to promote competition as the essence of strategic activity is to privilege the market-orientated, commercial, fast-paced, high-tech end of the market rather than the many other organisations that provide services to people, such as health, education, safety and justice. Thus, while competition is a central concept in understanding strategy and permeates many of the definitions and orientations that have been outlined above, there are other features and goals of strategy that need to be considered in different organisational contexts.

RATIONALITY, IRRATIONALITY AND STRATEGIC ACTIVITY

One of the most persistent criticisms of traditional strategic theory and research is that it assumed that strategy was capable of being pursued in a rational, objective, linear way. Early theorists generated great comfort among practitioners by providing neat, rational, sequential models that they claimed provided actionable templates for the effective management of strategy. Porter (1980) developed a model which presented three strategies that he argues can be pursued in order to secure sustainable competitive advantage within any organisational setting. The three strategies he proposes are based on rationalistic assumptions that hold that organisational strategic decision makers can analyse their environment successfully, and from this analysis select and pursue one of the three following strategies:

1. **Cost leadership:** Finding ways of producing goods and services at a lower cost than those of one's competitors.
2. **Differentiation:** Commanding a higher price for goods or services because of some factor that favourably differentiates one's product or service from others'.
3. **Focus:** Targeting a niche strategy so successfully within a given marketplace that competition is virtually eliminated.

Since they were articulated in the early 1980s Porter's propositions have been presented to countless management students. They present a tidy, comforting template for strategic progress and tally with rationalistic assumptions about how organisations can orientate themselves effectively towards their environments. While Porter focuses on the 'what' of strategy, process theorists emerging at the same time focused on the 'how' (for example, see Steiner 1979; Argenti 1980). Their assumptions hold that the strategy process can be broken down into a series of logical and effective steps.

- **Step 1 – Analysis:** By analysing the organisation's internal and external environment, by focusing on opportunities and threats in the environment, by scanning that environment, by examining networks and by watching trends, the rationalist approach to the strategy process suggests that an organisation can equip itself with all of the knowledge that it needs to make effective strategic progress.

- **Step 2 – Formulation:** The rationalist approach also suggests that once the organisation's internal and external contexts have been effectively analysed, strategy formulation can follow in logical sequence. Strategy formulation involves considering alternative courses of action based on the analysis that has preceded, establishing conditions under which alternatives will be selected and engaging in rational comparison between alternatives in order to make the optimum strategic choice.

- **Step 3 – Implementation:** Once the optimum choice has been selected, the rational model suggests that implementation is the next separate but connected step. This involves mobilising resources in order to activate the decisions, developing systems of control and monitoring and setting up structures, policies and procedures in order to ensure that required action is supported.

The rationalistic templates do tell us something about the need for managers and strategists to reduce uncertainty in their environments and to develop templates for action that make their complex tasks feel manageable. However, they fail to take account of the non-rational behavioural processes that are inherent in strategic activity in organisations. As Mintzberg (1994: 226–7) puts it:

> Nowhere in the [rational planning approach to strategy] has there been any indication whatsoever that efforts were made to understand how the strategy making process really does work in organisations. [Rational theorists] merely assumed a correspondence between strategic planning, strategic thinking and strategy making. [In fact,] the research tells us that strategy making is an immensely complex process involving the most sophisticated, subtle and at times subconscious of human cognitive and social processes.

The rational model can be criticised from a number of perspectives.

- It assumes and encourages false divisions between different parts of the strategy process (Hatch 1997).

- It does not recognise that strategy is an iterative process that will benefit from analytical inputs at any stage in the process, not at some initial discrete phase (Mintzberg 1997).

- It fails to account for the bounded rationality that characterises human decision-making processes (Lindblom 1957; March and Olsen 1976; March 1994).

- It makes recommendations that can create problems with communication, receptivity, flexibility and relevance of particular streams of strategic activity and it assumes that structure can be easily reconfigured to adopt new strategic decisions without recognising emotional, political and other processes that pursue patterns not predicted by 'rational', business-based assumptions (Weick 1987).

In summary, to assume that strategy is a rational process is to provide an account of strategy that is arguably impoverished and inaccurate. (For an excellent critique of rational approaches to strategy and strategic planning in organisations, see *The Rise and Fall of Strategic Planning* by Henry Mintzberg.) However, Hatch (1997) reminds us that the rational planning model of strategy has made some important contributions to the field. First, it tracked historical thinking about strategy and represented the first formal attempt to bring knowledge about strategy to organisations. Second, the ideal of rationality may be an important principle to consider, both for theory and practice in the field. Rationality is a 'powerful symbol of modernity' (Hatch 1997: 116) that allows us to adopt a series of coherent assumptions about the environment that may still be useful as a way of making sense of many of the complexities and uncertainties in organisational environments. In addition, the appeal of the rationalist approach to strategy is still strong, particularly in real business settings. As Whipp (1996: 263–4) points out:

> The attraction of the rational model of strategy is considerable. Indeed, it is possible to point to those professional groups within organisations who have failed in their status and their influence because of their inability to embrace the [rationalistic] discourse of strategy.

STRATEGY AS DECISION MAKING

Eisenhart (1999) defines strategy as decision making. Her research shows that these decisions need to be characterised by three essential features – decision speed, decision support and decision quality – if they are to be effective, i.e. fast, widely supported and high in strategic quality in the contexts in which they are applied. She and her colleagues have argued that it is possible to produce decisions with these features by managing behaviour within strategic decision-making groups. Brown and Eisenhart (1988) have shown that, contrary to many assumptions that there are inevitable trade-offs between decision speed, support and quality, it is possible to produce decisions that are high on all three of these essential features by ensuring that the following behavioural dynamics exist within decision-making groups: a collective sense of intuition, stimulated conflict, decision pace and momentum and defusing political behaviour.

A collective sense of intuition helps a strategic decision-making group to become better at scanning and developing a complex understanding of the environments in which they operate. Effective strategic decision-making groups engage in intense and regular communication with one another, participating in what Eisenhart refers to as 'must attend' meetings in which important metrics from different functional leaders are compared and considered. It seems that evidence still suggests that rationalistic scanning and regular collective analysis provide a crucial bedrock for effective strategic action in organisations. Eisenhart argues that developing a collective sense of intuition is something that requires regular, comparative analysis of important data, both inside and outside the organisation, as well as intense interaction among strategic decision makers.

Stimulated conflict helps decision makers to consider issues from a variety of perspectives, to confront divergent views and to produce courses of action that are based on ideas of superior quality. It is often tempting to avoid conflict and confrontation at work. Interactions about issues over which strategic actors disagree are often difficult or uncomfortable, and in the advanced concepts section of this chapter you will see how different cultures tend to avoid confronting issues that are sensitive within a group, often to the detriment of effective strategic development. Finding effective processes to stimulate conflict may represent an important route to strategic success. Vocal groups that are not averse to conflict may be more likely to create the conditions for creativity that are necessary to tackle the complexities of uncertain strategic environments.

Throughout any strategic decision-making process, attention needs to be paid to the pace and momentum of the strategy. Eisenhart (1999: 69) refers to the importance for decision makers to 'follow the natural rhythm of strategic choice', which requires allocating enough time for effective consideration and activation to take place, but not too much that energy and commitment to achieving the strategy are lost. Gersick (1995) also demonstrates that there are optimum time frames for the achievement of certain strategies, and that paying attention to them can represent an important route to strategic success.

Defusing political behaviour helps strategists to dismantle barriers that can slow down or thwart the progress of important decisions. While political behaviour is inevitable, particularly in large organisations with high differentiation between function and levels, evidence suggests that for the important strategic decisions, creating a clear, shared vision to which most people commit is highly important (for example, see Pinkley and Northcraft 1994).

When strategy is viewed as decision making, the four features of strategic decision making listed above provide broad guidelines for the effective management of the strategy process. Another theoretical perspective on strategy views it through the discourse lens, which is outlined briefly in the following section.

STRATEGY AS DISCOURSE AND NARRATIVE

Discourse can be referred to as 'a set of interconnected concepts, expressions and statements that constitutes ways of talking or writing about an aspect of the world, thus framing and influencing the ways people understand and act with regard to that world' (Watson 2002: 118). If we see strategy as discourse, we recognise, as Huff (1982) and Spender (1989) already have, that discourse produces a 'dominant logic' through language that restrains and structures the ways in which people think and act, and determines what types of strategies are selected in organisational settings as well as ways in which they are pursued.

By paying attention to the ways in which language is used in organisations, particularly among those with the responsibility for forging strategy, we can come to understand strategic priorities and principles and learn something important about the types of strategies that are most likely to be pursued. Knights and Morgan (1991) applied linguistic theory to the study of strategy. Seeing strategy as discourse allows us to consider some important principles of linguistic theory: that language shapes the ways in which we think, that language serves important functions within social settings (including organisational ones) and that being able to participate in certain types of discourses (such as strategic conversations or meetings) bestows different levels of power on people within their organisational settings.

Another way of treating strategy as discourse is through the interactive narrative orientation towards strategy. Barry and Elmes (1997: 433) say that:

> From a narrative perspective, the successful strategic story may depend less on such tools as comprehensive scanning, objective planning or meticulous control or feedback systems and more on whether it stands out from other organisational stories, is persuasive and invokes retelling. What the story revolves around, how it is put together and the way it is told, all determine whether it becomes one worth listening to, remembering and acting upon. Thus, strategic effectiveness from a narrative perspective is intimately tied to acceptance, approval and adoption.

Taking a narrative viewpoint, the power of the strategic story, who is telling it and how it is being told become central considerations and may require leaders and strategists who are emotionally intelligent (see Chapter 5) and transformational (see Chapter 12). From this viewpoint, it can be argued that in order to create successful strategies, they must be both believable and novel (Matjeka and Pomorska 1971; Bann and Bowlt 1973). From this perspective it may be argued that:

> Successful strategic narratives may need to take account of the need for inspiring novelty as well as the need for an anchor of credibility to hold the vision together. Analysing the narratives that occur in real business settings can be seen as an important way of evaluating the extent to which successful strategic stories are being told (Moore 2000: 119).

ONGOING DEBATES/ADVANCED CONCEPTS IN STRATEGY

This section focuses on two key aspects of strategic behaviour that have recently been subjected to analysis and theorising, namely diversity of views and active dialogue as important ingredients for strategic activity. More specifically, this section explores the existence of a diversity of views among top management teams and the willingness of strategists to engage in active dialogue about strategic issues. The following discussion revisits results from a comprehensive leadership survey and explores these in light of emerging literature on strategic leadership. Key findings will be examined in order to engage in a comparative analysis between national cultures. A matrix exploring four hypothesised 'strategic climates' will also be presented.

STRATEGIC LEADERSHIP

As you have seen in Chapter 12, leadership is a multifaceted concept requiring both individual and collective competencies and involving both style and substance. It demands skills in both the formulation and implementation of strategy. Its ultimate aim still tends to be seen as focusing on boosting organisational reputation and securing sustainable competitive advantage (for example, see Petrick *et al.* 1999). Evidence-based research shows that such leadership is becoming increasingly global, that it requires considerable behavioural complexity (Hart and Quinn 1993) and that there are several associated performance criteria involving equal focus on profitability and productivity, continuity and efficiency, commitment and morale and adaptability and innovation (Dennison *et al.* 1995). This need for multiple foci highlights the paradoxes and tensions associated with strategic leadership and leadership capability. The Cranfield study (1995) sheds further light on these paradoxes and provides data that allows for international comparisons in order to allow a greater understanding of the nature of leadership capability.

LEADERSHIP CAPABILITY: THE CRANFIELD STRATEGIC LEADERSHIP SURVEY

A total of 5,500 top manager respondents representing private sector organisations in eleven countries highlighted some interesting issues with respect to top management team perceptions and leadership capability. This section focuses on two dimensions that were explored in the study: perceived diversity of views between members of top management teams and perceived reluctance to talk about issues or sensitivities meriting attention.

Diversity of Views

Much of the literature on effective organisational leadership refers to the importance of a clear, shared vision among top management team members (for example, see Floyd and Woolridge 1992; Beer and Eisenstat 2000). It is difficult to be decisive and sustained in the development of an effective strategy unless decision makers share the same view of the future direction of their organisation. Yet the basis of a workable consensus should not be that of a bland or acquiescent conformity to dominant views. There is a responsibility among top managers to recognise that there are diverse perspectives and alternatives (otherwise there would be no decisions to be made) and to undertake an informed, complex, interactive dialogue that allows a united position to be adopted and then pursued. Recognising that there is a diversity of views may be the first important step in the iterative development of an effective strategy. Finding a workable integration of these views is also necessary if the top management team will be able to commit to a long-term strategy in a coherent way. Such workable integration can only be achieved through dialogue, particularly focusing on difficult issues where divergence of views exists.

Existing literature suggests that top management team diversity, or conversely, top management team homogeneity, are both double-edged swords. On the one hand, diversity of views about strategic future may provide top management teams with a range of important benefits, including a rich diversity of inputs, a range of sources of information and antidotes to organisational myopia. These benefits facilitate responsiveness to complexity and change in their organisations' environments (Bantel and Jackson 1989; Jackson 1992; Sanders and Carpenter 1998). On the other hand, top management team diversity (including diversity of views) may cause team disintegration, excessive or dysfunctional conflict and an inability to create a platform for effective strategic progress (Carpenter and Frederickson 2001). A homogenous group, sharing related or identical strategic views, can bring benefits such as group cohesiveness, team harmony and the clarity and momentum that accompanies a strong shared vision (O'Reilly *et al.* 1993). However, senior team homogeneity of view can also give rise to strategic blind spots, 'groupthink' and other rational dysfunctionalities (for example, see Janis 1970). Findings in this area remain inconclusive. What is clear is that the extent to which strategic viewpoints differ has an impact on the strategic climate of any top management team and requires exploration if strategic activity is to be more fully understood.

Dialogue between Members of the Top Management Team

The purposes of any communication within organisations may include such political goals as cultivating a favourable impression (Goffman 1959), demonstrating competence (Fielden 1982), expressing confidence (Jackall 1988), being liked (Wofford *et al.* 1997), developing a base of support (Allen *et al.* 1979), aligning oneself with more powerful others (Bacharach and Lawlor 1980) and controlling access to information (Steele 1975). Dialogue between members of the same group is often seen to serve the function of enhancing relationships and developing cohesiveness among group members (for example, see Frost *et al.* 1985). Anderson and Martin (1995) show that business conversations are driven by individual motives for pleasure, escape, inclusion, affection, duty, control and relaxation.

Argyris (1990) argues that much of the collective communication or interaction within organisations serves to reinforce people's sense of themselves and to help them avoid facing up to problems that might need urgent attention. He identifies several defensive patterns that appear to recur in the ways people interact in organisations, arguing that many organisational decision makers identify faults in the system but abrogate responsibility for correcting those faults. They accentuate negative aspects of the organisation, but in ways that protect them from criticism; they espouse values that they argue cannot be implemented due to problems with the system; and furthermore, they identify these problems as ones they did not cause and cannot be expected to solve. The rationalising behaviour of decision makers can thus do damage to their organisation's long-term viability and at the very least creates routines that undermine effective collaborative action.

Top managers need to be aware of these embedded, defensive routines. It may not be possible to avoid or eliminate this type of behaviour, but knowing that it exists provides more control and allows for a more deliberate approach to making organisationally sound decisions. Communication can also serve the function of pooling knowledge in order to address problems or achieve objectives. To do this requires recognising the hidden dynamics of organisational dialogue, examples of which have been outlined above.

Defensive routines are more likely to emerge when strategists are attempting to tackle sensitive issues, and it is these very issues that are more likely to show the way to structural or strategic problems that need to be changed.

RESULTS FROM THE CRANFIELD LEADERSHIP STUDY

The Cranfield study on leadership capability tapped into a large sample of top managers in the private sector. Among the many concepts and dimensions explored were two questions designed to uncover the extent to which top managers perceived there to be a diversity of strategic view and the extent to which issues/sensitivities merited but did not receive attention at senior management level. These questions were worded as follows:
- 'Do the members of the senior executive hold different views as to the future direction of the organisation?' (Abbreviated as 'diversity of views'.)
- 'Are there issues or sensitivities that merit attention but do not receive attention at senior management levels?' (Abbreviated as 'reluctance to talk'.)

Diversity of Views

Irish (forty-eight per cent), Spanish (forty per cent) and French (thirty-nine per cent) top managers are most likely to report higher diversity of views about the future direction of the organisation. Swedish and Japanese respondents are least likely to highlight differences of views concerning strategic direction at senior management levels. It is important to note that different cultures may respond to these questions in similar ways, but for different reasons. The similarity between Swedish and Japanese responses almost certainly masks other cultural dynamics. It may be that top managers from some cultures deny the existence of diverse views, whereas others work to surface and resolve it (for example, see Hofstede 1990).

Figure 15.1 Perceived Diversity of Strategic Views by Nationality

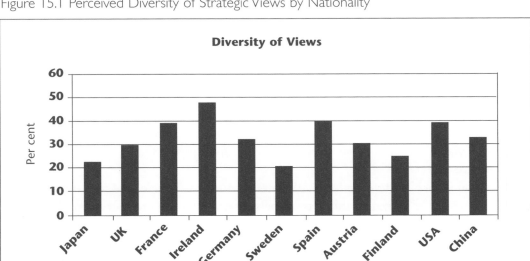

Many cultural factors make it difficult to compare national responses. Whatever the reasons, Irish top managers are most likely to report diverse views among top management team members. This may be based on some positive cultural dynamics, perhaps linked with such factors as a culturally induced tolerance for diverse views or a willingness to live with ambiguity and divergent perspectives. It may also indicate a damaging set of symptoms that could stunt progress towards the development of coherent organisational strategies. The high level of response frequency could point to a top management team climate that is genuinely more likely to experience 'splits of vision' (Kakabadse 1990) than their counterparts in other countries.

Reluctance to Talk

Effective strategic dialogue is associated with the capability to address and/or resolve issues of sensitivity at senior management levels. Figure 15.2 demonstrates the extent to which there is a perceived reluctance to engage in strategic dialogue at top management levels. The Chinese (eighty per cent), Japanese (seventy-seven per cent) and Irish (sixty-eight per cent) respondents are most likely to indicate a reluctance to address important strategic issues. In general, the perception that sensitive issues remain unaddressed is more prevalent than that of the existence of divergent strategic views.

Figure 15.2 Perceived Reluctance to Address Sensitivities/Issues that Merit Attention (by Nationality)

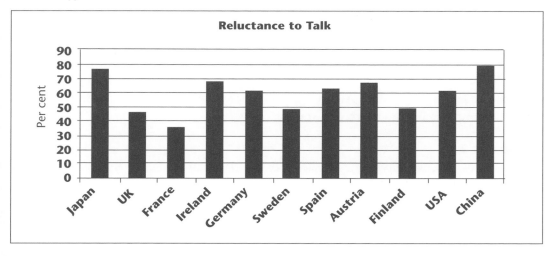

TOP MANAGEMENT TEAM STRATEGY CLIMATES

The degree to which top managers share the same views about their organisation's future and the extent to which top managers are prepared to discuss sensitive issues have been identified in this section and in previous literature as two central constructs in the development of effective strategy (for example, see Hambrich 1995; Beer and Eisenstat 2000). Indeed, it can be argued that the combination of these two factors may influence the climate for strategy in organisations and could be linked to other cultural differences.

Combining 'diversity of view' with 'reluctance to talk' yields four hypothetical quadrants, in which there may be different prevailing strategic climates, each with its own set of assets and liabilities. The proposed differences between these strategic climate quadrants are outlined below and summarised in Table 15.1.

Quadrant 1

*Low levels of perceived diversity combined with **high** levels of perceived reluctance to address sensitivities that merit attention.*

A strategic climate in which perceived diversity is low and reluctance to talk about sensitive issues is high risks being characterised by the following types of negative conditions:

- a prevailing naïveté in which strategies developed pass uncriticised and without constructive analysis or debate;
- an oblivion to possible sources of conflict or divergence of views;
- apathy or blind acceptance of the lead taken by a dominant leader;
- a suppression of any dissenting view to the point that none is expressed; and
- an unexplored impression of conformity to a single view or strategic direction.

However, in this quadrant there may also be revealed a positive strategic climate based on the following climactic assets: compliant harmony, high levels of group cohesiveness and an unspoken, implicit understanding of the 'right strategic path'. There is a possibility that top management groups falling into this quadrant may have developed a strong commitment to a single vision that no longer requires discussion or analysis. However, the long-documented and oft-quoted 'groupthink' phenomenon presented by Janis (1970) is characterised by this combination and poses a real risk under these circumstances.

In the Cranfield survey and according to a comparison of relatively high and low response rates, Japan, China, Austria and Germany fall into this quadrant, with the Japanese sample being most likely to appear in this quadrant (see Figure 15.3).

Quadrant 2

*Low levels of perceived diversity combined with **low** levels of perceived reluctance to address sensitivities that merit attention.*

This quadrant represents a strategic climate that risks being dominated by the false impression of active agreement. It is one in which much discussion and analysis is combined with the frequent expression of high levels of related viewpoints. There is a possibility that the sense of active agreement is just a false impression, reinforced by constant reminders of points of concurrence between members. It is also possible that the strategic vision is derived from homogenous, complacent dynamics. On the other hand, those groups falling into this quadrant that have achieved a genuine, robust shared vision are more likely to have achieved this as a result of hard-won agreement attained through negotiation and informed dialogue. In this case, the active, ongoing commitment to the development of a strong shared vision is likely to be a strategic asset.

Sweden, Finland and the UK fall into this quadrant, with Sweden and Finland being more likely to appear in this quadrant based on the Cranfield survey findings.

Quadrant 3

High *levels of perceived diversity combined with* **low** *levels of perceived reluctance to address sensitivities that merit attention.*

This quadrant creates a climate in which there is a risk of open hostility and aggressive disagreement between top management team members. Where strategic views are divergent and sensitive issues are subject to regular discussion there is no automatic guarantee of the identification of workable solutions. These are conditions in which dysfunctional, persistent and cyclical conflict may become the norm, and in such conditions people's acclimatisation to high levels of conflict may desensitise top managers from having to find viable ways forward.

Nevertheless, when utilised effectively these conditions can create situations in which healthy conflict is tolerated, devil's advocacy is incorporated rather than suppressed and where there is a prevailing willingness to address and engage with the differing viewpoints and convictions that exist between members.

Based on the Cranfield survey results, France is the only nationality that falls into this quadrant.

Quadrant 4

High *levels of perceived diversity combined with* **high** *levels of perceived reluctance to address sensitivities that merit attention.*

This combination gives rise to a strategic climate in which cynicism may dominate the dynamics of strategic activity. Conflict may be actively suppressed alongside a complacent acceptance of the inevitability of strategic splits of vision. As a result there may be inaction in tackling any strategic problems head on. On the other hand, this strategic climate may be more realistic and accepting of the diversity and complexities of organisational strategy. There may also be an implicit tolerance of ambiguity that may sit less comfortably in other strategic climates.

Overall, however, top management groups with divergent views and a reluctance to talk are likely to encounter real problems in tackling intransigent strategic issues and may engage in ritualised routines of strategic behaviour that do not recognise the needs of the changing environment, that do not adapt or innovate and that may be deaf to any voices highlighting the very issues that need attention.

In the Cranfield survey, Ireland, Spain and the US fall into this quadrant. Note that the Irish respondents in the sample are those most likely to appear in this quadrant (see Figure 15.3).

The similarities and differences between senior managers of diverse national cultures are interesting to examine. Figure 15.3 plots the interaction between senior managers' perceptions relating to 'reluctance to talk' and 'diversity of views' at strategic levels. The proximity of national cultures on this graph indicates the similarity/differences between national responses found in the Cranfield survey.

Table 15.1 The Assets and Liabilities of Four Different Strategic Climates

	Low levels of diversity of views among top managers	High levels of diversity of views among top managers
High levels of reluctance to talk about sensitive issues that merit attention	**Possible liabilities**	
	Naïveté. Oblivion regarding divergent views. Intolerance of devil's advocacy and genuinely critical voices. Unawareness of intransigent strategic problems. False impression of compliance.	Cynicism. Suppression of conflict. Tolerance of 'splits of vision'. Inaction in tackling intransigent strategic problems head on.
	Possible assets	
	Compliant harmony. Existence of and commitment to a single vision.	Realism. Implicit acceptance of differing points of view. Understanding of the complexities and diversity of strategic positions at the top. Tolerance of ambiguity.
Low levels of reluctance to talk about sensitive issues that merit attention	**Possible liabilities**	
	False impression of active agreement. Homogenous, complacent but frequently reaffirmed approach to strategy.	Open hostility. Dysfunctional, persistent, cyclical conflict. Conflict tolerance.
	Possible assets	
	Harmony achieved through continuous, active dialogue. Vigorous, ongoing commitment to the development of a strong shared vision.	The regular identification of strategic problems that require change. Willingness to address and engage with differing viewpoints and convictions.

Figure 15.3 Strategic Climates: Plotting National Cultures for Broad Comparison

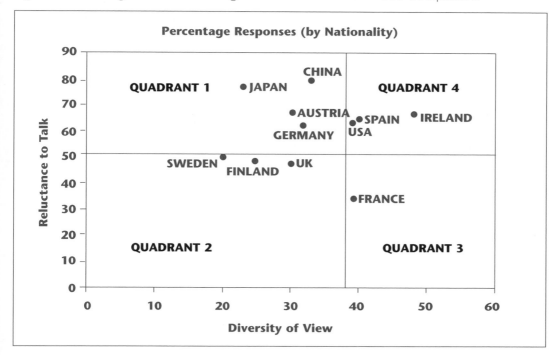

Any climactic 'typology', including the four types of strategic climate outlined above, will by definition be a simplified version of the realities it aims to describe. As Karl Weick famously proposed, 'the territory is not the map'. Strategic territory is a particularly difficult terrain to encode.

STRATEGIC PARADOXES

A major dimension of effective strategic leadership relates to a strong ability to cope with ambiguity and paradox. It is difficult to prescribe the extent to which strategic views should be shared and to which sensitive issues should be discussed. Each strategic climate is unique and complex.

Different opinions may be unavoidable in the complex, ambiguous environments faced by senior teams. Some top team climates may encourage this diversity of view, others may ignore or suppress it, while still others may attempt to confront and integrate these views in a way that facilitates progress.

The data provided in this section inevitably only tells part of the story. The fact that some groups of top managers see their team as sharing the same vision may be due to suppression, unawareness or active and successful integration of views that were formerly diverse. Whatever the reasons for the responses derived from different nationalities, all combinations highlight that strategic climates are replete with paradox and ambiguity. Agreement is something that we may naturally find solace in and seek in the face of paradox and complexity. Behavioural theory has long identified the human truth that it feels good to agree (Heider 1957). This is no less true for the members of top management teams. 'Confrontation is scary. [Furthermore,] it is a normal human tendency to shrink from confronting one's own deficiencies' (Beer and Eisenstat 2000: 36). But agreement may lead to blind spots and a lack of creativity, while different views pose difficulties for the achievement of strategic direction.

It may be the confrontation of those very differences that could give rise to strategic breakthroughs leading to the emergence of competitive ideas and courses of action. Talking about differences and addressing sensitive issues may be vital at certain stages in the development of strategy. On the other hand, such discussions may at other times simply paralyse the group or lock them into ritualistic, unproductive cycles, giving rise to little or no strategic development or performance.

What demands are made on leaders that allow for these dynamics to take place? Why do individuals find it difficult to reach a point of understanding that allows them to make strategic breakthroughs? What prevents them from facing major hurdles in the discussion of issues that are important to them and their enterprise? The results from the Cranfield study suggest that the majority of top managers from all national backgrounds had a reasonable insight into their organisations' environments and could even foresee specific implications for their organisations if certain issues were not attended to.

It seems that the possession of important strategic knowledge and understanding is not sufficient to initiate strategic action. Leaders face pressures that can prevent them from taking concerted strategic action. Those pressures may be considerably different depending on national culture, top management team demographics, strategic paradoxes and varying responses to complexity and feedback paradoxes. Leaders of organisations are continually urged to provide direction while encouraging participation, to delegate while being 'hands on', to provide decisive leadership while taking into consideration a variety of organisational perspectives and to control powerful personalities while promoting consensus.

These paradoxes are difficult to reconcile. Forming a unique view as to how to interpret such common directives is the challenge faced by every strategic leader in his or her specific context.

LEADERSHIP DEVELOPMENT

Similar challenges face a wide range of business leaders from different contexts. The Cranfield study has found that many of the same issues are relevant to international business leaders, leaders of health organisations and top civil servant government leaders. While the symptoms of problems may be different, the underlying pressures are comparable across a spectrum of business contexts. The feeling of 'not having one's act together' is commonplace among top management teams, but that feeling may arise for a range of different reasons. What distinguishes a mediocre organisation from a high-performing one is the manner in which leaders are prepared to accept responsibility for working with and resolving problems. This may require tackling different aspects of a top management team's strategic climate, depending on a range of factors, including the national cultural influences on behaviour that have been explored in this section.

Learning How to Resolve Conflicting Agendas

Recognising the reality of how key senior managers relate to each other and how they communicate mixed messages to the rest of the organisation is often a reality that needs to be accommodated. Living in a world of conflicting agendas while still having to manage the organisation is a prospect that most leaders of organisations are likely to face. Leaders may need help in surfacing conflicting agendas that allow the identification of workable strategic progress.

Knowledge of Organisational Structure and Understanding of Alternatives to Current Configurations

The careful structuring or restructuring of work groups can enhance the ways in which diverse views are integrated and strategic dialogue is facilitated. The ability to visualise the form and shape of the desired organisation is a conceptual challenge. Knowing how to configure an organisation to achieve its purpose requires knowing the alternatives to existing organisational structures along with the strengths and weaknesses associated with different organisational forms. It is important for senior managers to be keenly aware of how current organisational structures facilitate or prohibit the achievement of organisational goals.

Enhancing Vision Capability

The Cranfield surveys highlight the development of an effective vision as a key element of corporate leadership, the development of which requires the collective tackling of the following questions.

- What is the current and likely future shape and configuration of key client/community/stakeholder groups?
- What is required now and what will be required in the future to service these user groups?
- What are the needs of important suppliers/distributors and how can an understanding of these needs be used to nurture the organisation's relationship with them? How will these needs change in the future?
- How committed are various parts of the organisation to actionable innovation or to the improvement of performance in the service of key groups?
- How committed are various parts of the organisation to the enhancement of co-operation?
- What levels of expenditure are required to provide for the delivery of existing/developing/new products and services?

The answer to these questions requires access to and understanding of details concerning the management of organisational departments and units. It is through a detailed yet creative analysis of the following types of information that meaningful conclusions can be formed regarding the level of expenditure required:

- the expectations and requirements of stakeholder groups;
- the behaviour of suppliers;
- the needs and likely demands of external agencies;
- the life cycles of any service or provision; and
- the level of speed and responsiveness required by different client/community groupings.

Leaders need informed views about the organisational size and cost base associated with proposed strategic developments, a keen understanding of how departments and units are structured and how to position new and current products/services and they need to be able to understand and reconcile different views, to which a mix of emotional, intuitive and analytical human processes have given rise.

From this detailed view, leaders need to be able to extrapolate and determine appropriate ways forward. An effective leader needs to be concerned with detail and broader debate, with intimate day-to-day understanding of the functioning of the organisation and with a broader picture of future challenges and how to proceed in order to face them. The Cranfield studies showed that it is from relevant details that meaningful visions are formed. An effective vision involves the capability for broad conceptualisation while focusing in an active way on important details within the organisation.

Most importantly, the effective engagement in organisational dialogue in order to reconcile differences and craft a workable vision is central to bridging the difficult gap between the formulation and implementation of strategy. This may represent the very essence of effective leadership.

SUMMARY OF KEY PROPOSITIONS

- This chapter has outlined and explored some of the important concepts associated with the dynamics of effective strategy at work. It outlined different orientations towards defining strategy and encouraged the exploration of the implications of these different definitions for real-life strategic situations.
- It explored key dimensions of strategic capability and critically analysed some central strategic assumptions that persist among many strategists, namely the competition imperative and the rationalist approach to strategic decision making.
- It analysed strategy through different lenses, showing that when strategy is viewed as a rational process, the ideas and activities with which it is associated may be quite different than if it is defined as decision making or as discourse.
- The advanced concepts section explored some of the important dimensions associated with effective strategic leadership. Revisiting the Cranfield data of 1995, it has highlighted national cultural differences, analysed key features of strategic climate and outlined central paradoxes and challenges accompanying strategic leadership. Recommendations relating to leadership development focus on capabilities associated with the development of an effective vision, structural knowledge, analytical competence and effective dialogue.

- With reference to national similarities and differences, it is interesting to see that the Irish sample stands out somewhat, but can be placed in closest proximity to Spain and the US on two essential dimensions of strategic climate: it yields the highest proportion of top managers indicating that the top management team holds different views concerning the direction of the organisation and it is ranked third highest in terms of perceived reluctance of top management team members to talk about issues that merit attention. Possible liabilities associated with the typical Irish response patterns include top management team cynicism, suppression of conflict, splits of vision and inaction in tackling strategic problems head on. However, possible assets might include a sense of strategic realism, the tolerance of ambiguity and an implicit recognition of diverse perspectives.

- Recent events show that we have reached a point in history where the active dialogue between groups with differing perspectives may be more important than at any other time in history. Strategic leaders have a part to play in the initiation and maintenance of effective dialogue within and beyond their own organisations. The perception and recognition of diverse views is a necessary precondition for active dialogue. In Irish organisational settings, the perception of a diversity of views is something that may be less of a challenge than the active tackling of those differences (and the sensitivities to which they give rise) through active, open dialogue. For many organisational leaders, moving towards active dialogue requires a risky leap of faith, which among other things may go against deeply ingrained cultural predispositions. Nevertheless, it is a leap of faith that holds much promise, and one that is worth taking.

DISCUSSION/SELF-ASSESSMENT QUESTIONS

1. At the very beginning of this chapter a series of definitions of strategy was presented which suggested that different orientations towards strategy are possible. What do these different orientations imply about the role that strategy might play within any organisation? Identify common themes that run through all or most of these orientations. Identify key differences in these orientations that might point to fundamentally different ways of approaching the field of strategy.
2. Highlight some of the advantages of a rationalist approach to strategy in organisations. Why has the rationalist approach been seen more recently as an impoverished and inaccurate orientation towards strategy?
3. Identify Porter's three strategies for sustainable competitive advantage.
4. According to Eisenhart (1999), what three essential features do good strategic decisions have?
5. If you adopt a discourse approach to strategy, what features of strategic activity are important to pay attention to and why?
6. Using the four strategic climates outlined in the advanced concepts section of this chapter, identify a strategic group with which you are familiar, e.g. a political party, a top management team, etc., suggest which quadrant it occupies and provide evidence for your selection.

MULTIPLE CHOICE QUESTIONS

1. Porter's approach views strategy as:
    (a) A rational, analytical process.
    (b) A non-rational, communicative process.
2. Different cultures have been found to occupy different 'strategic climates'. True or false?
3. In the Cranfield study outlined in this chapter, what nationality of managers was most likely to express a diversity of strategic views?
    (a) Finnish.
    (b) Japanese.
    (c) Irish.
    (d) American.
4. In the Cranfield study outlined in this chapter, managers of which nationality were least likely to report a reluctance to address issues of sensitivity in their strategic groups?
    (a) French.
    (b) German.
    (c) Chinese.
    (d) Swedish.
5. Strategy was an organisational term relatively rarely used in organisational or management contexts before the 1980s. True or false?
6. Competition is the essence of strategic activity. True or false?
7. In reality, strategic activity is completely rational. True or false?
8. Eisenhart argues that strategic decision making needs to be characterised by three essential features. Which three features does she identify?
    (a) Speed, wide support, quality.
    (b) Complexity, ambiguity, closure.
    (c) Simplicity, elegance, agreement.
9. According to Brown and Eisenhart, decision pace and momentum is an essential feature of strategic decision making. True or false?
10. Top management team diversity is an automatic asset for enhancing strategy. True or false?

FIVE SUGGESTED KEY READINGS

Anderson, C. and Paine, F., 'Managerial perceptions of strategic behaviour', *Academy of Management Journal*, XVIII (1995), 811–23.

Beer, M. and Eisenstat, R.A., (2000) 'The silent killers of strategy implementation and learning', *Sloan Management Review* (Summer 2000), 29–40.

Floyd, S.W. and Woolridge, B., 'Managing strategic consensus: the foundation of effective implementation', *Academy of Management Executive* (November 1992), 27–39.

Knights, D. and Morgan, G., 'Strategic discourse and subjectivity: towards a critical analysis of corporate strategy in organisations', *Organisation Studies*, XII/2 (1991), 251–73.

Mintzberg, H., *The Rise and Fall of Strategic Planning*, Hemel Hempstead: Prentice Hall 1994.

REFERENCES

Allen, R.W., Madison, D.L., Poreter, L.W., Renwick, P.A. and Mayes, B.T., 'Organisational politics, tactics and characteristics of its actors', *California Management Review*, XXII/1 (1979), 77–83.

Anderson, C. and Paine, F., 'Managerial perceptions of strategic behaviour', *Academy of Management Journal*, XVIII (1995), 811–23.

Andrews, K., *The Concept of Corporate Strategy*, Homewood, IL: Irwin 1971.

Argyris, C., *Overcoming Organizational Defences: Facilitating Organizational Learning*, Boston, MA: Allyn & Bacon 1990.

Bachrach, S. and Lawlor, E., *Power and Politics in Organizations*, San Francisco: Jossey-Bass 1980.

Bantel, K. and Jackson, S., 'Top management and innovations in banking: does the composition of the top management team make a difference?', *Strategic Management Journal*, XXVIII (1989), 845–64.

Barry, D. and Elmes, M., 'Strategy retold: toward a narrative view of strategic discourse', *Academy of Management Review*, II (1997), 429–52.

Beer, M. and Eisenstat, R.A., 'The silent killers of strategy implementation and learning', *Sloan Management Review* (Summer 2000), 29–40.

Carpenter, M. and Fredrickson, J., 'Top management teams, global strategic posture, and the moderating role of uncertainty', *Academy of Management Journal*, XLIV/3 (2001), 533–45.

Fielden, J.S., 'What do you mean you don't like my style?', *Harvard Business Review*, LX/3 (1982), 128–38.

Floyd, S.W. and Woolridge, B., 'Managing strategic consensus: the foundation of effective implementation', *Academy of Management Executive* (November 1992), 27–39.

Frost, P.J., Moore, L.F., Louis, M.R., Lundberg, C.C. and Martin, J. (eds), *Organizational Culture*, Beverly Hills, CA: Sage 1985.

Goffman, E., *The Presentation of Self in Everyday Life*, New York: Doubleday 1959.

Hambrich, D., 'Fragmentation and the other problems CEOs have with their top management teams', *California Management Review*, XXXVII/3 (1995), 110–27.

Hatch, M.J., *Organisation Theory: Modern, Symbolic and Postmodern Perspective*, London: Oxford University Press.

Hitt, M.A., Ireland, R.D. and Hoskisson, R.E., *Strategic Management: Competitiveness and Globalization*, 3rd ed., Cincinnati, OH: South-Western Publishing 1998.

Hofstede, G., *Culture and Organizations: Software of the Mind*, London: McGraw-Hill 1990.

Jackall, R., *Moral Mazes: The World of Corporate Managers*, Oxford: Oxford University Press 1988.

Jackson, S., 'Consequences of group composition for the interpersonal dynamics of strategic issue processing', in P. Shrivastiva, A. Huff and J. Dutton (eds), *Advances in Strategic Management*, viii, Greenwich, CT: JAI Press 1992, 345–82.

Kakabadse, A., *The Wealth Creators*, London: Sage 1990.

Knights, D. and Morgan, G., 'Strategic discourse and subjectivity: towards a critical analysis of corporate strategy in organisations', *Organisation Studies*, XII/2 (1991), 251–73.

Lindblom, L., 'The science of muddling through', *Public Administration Review*, XIX (1959), 78–88.

March, J. and Olsen, J., *Ambiguity and Choice in Organisations*, Bergen: Universitetsforlaget 1976.

Mintzberg, H., *The Rise and Fall of Strategic Planning*, Hemel Hempstead: Prentice Hall 1994.

O'Reilly, C., Snyder, R. and Boothe, J., 'Effects of executive team demography on organizational change', in G. Huber and W. Glick (eds), *Organizational Change and Redesign*, New York: Oxford University Press 1993, 145–75.

Petrick, J.A, Scherer, R.F., Brodzinski, J.D., Quinn, J.F. and Ainina, M.F., 'Global leadership skills and reputational capital: intangible resources for sustainable competitive advantage', *Academy of Management Executive*, XIII/1 (1999), 58–69.

Pinkley, R. and Northcraft, G., 'Conflict frames of reference: implications for dispute processes and outcomes', *Academy of Management Journal*, XXXVII (1994), 193–205.

Porter, M., *Competitive Strategy*, New York: The Free Press 1980.

Sanders, W. and Carpenter, M., 'Internationalisation and firm governance: the roles of CEO compensation and board structure', *Academy of Management Journal*, XLI (1998), 158–78.

Schendel, D. and Cool, K., 'Development of the strategic management field', in J. Grant (ed.), *Strategic Management Frontiers*, Greenwich, CT: JAI Press 1988.

Spender, J., *Industry Recipes*, Oxford: Blackwell 1989.

Steele, F., *The Open Organization: The Impact of Secrecy and Disclosure on People in Organizations*, Reading, MA: Addison-Wesley 1975.

Watson, T.J., *Organising and Managing Work*, Essex: Prentice Hall 2002.

Weick, K., 'Substitutes for corporate strategy', in D.J. Teece (ed.), *The Competitive Challenge: Strategies for Industrial Innovation and Renewal*, Cambridge, MA: Ballinger 1987.

Whipp, R., 'Strategy and organizations', in S.R. Clegg, C. Hardy and W. Nord (eds), *Handbook of Organizational Studies*, London: Sage 1996.

Woofford, J.C., Gerloff, E.A. and Cummins, R.C., *Organizational Communication: The Keystone to Managerial Effectiveness*, New York: McGraw-Hill 1997.

THE DYNAMICS OF ORGANISATIONAL CHANGE AND DEVELOPMENT

16

Learning Objectives

- To describe what is meant by organisational change.

- To provide an understanding of the process of change management in organisations.

- To differentiate between various models of managing change.

- To highlight key reasons why individuals resist change.

- To introduce and outline the various techniques of organisational development.

INTRODUCTION

A considerable literature has developed in recent years on organisational change and change management, with the central message of many of the 'change gurus' being that change is the only constant in life. Similarly, McConalogue (2003) suggested that the well-known adage, 'nothing is so certain as change', has become an increasing reality for Irish organisations in the past decade. Vaill (1989) argues that organisational environments are characterised by chaotic change, while Peters (1987) suggests that general uncertainty pervades contemporary environments. Organisations, like everyday life, are not static. Hussey (1995) argues that change is one of the most critical aspects of effective management and that the turbulent business environment in which most organisations operate means that not only is change becoming more frequent, but that the nature of change may be increasingly complex and the impact of change is often more extensive. Tersine *et al.* (1997: 45) suggest that:

> Change has joined death and taxes as life certainties. Some businesses have been quick to accept and adopt changes, others are struggling to cope with it. Specialists and individualism have been replaced by teams and co-operation. People are being asked to do more with less on a regular basis from a litany of change, innovate, re-engineer, continuously improve, and then change again.

The forces for change arise both in the macroenvironment and inside the organisation. For the most part environmental changes cause problems and these forces cannot be resisted. The exception occurs when the business has sufficient power to manage the environment to its own advantage. Examples include monopoly suppliers or government protection from competition. Managers of other organisations know that they must adapt or disappear. Within the organisation, change stems from internal processes and decisions. Managers may change the company or departmental goals, innovation may establish new directions or employees and their trade unions may make new demands along the way to share the benefits of their efforts.

In this chapter the origins of change management are examined from a theoretical perspective, pertinent models of organisational change are discussed, a number of key variables that lead to resistance to change initiatives are explored and finally, we focus on organisational development as an independent technique in managing successful change.

DEFINITIONS OF KEY CONCEPTS

Radical change
Large-scale, organisation-wide transformation programmes.

Incremental change
Small-scale, localised projects to solve a particular project.

Performance gap
A mismatch between what is desired and what is being achieved.

Action research change model
Rational, systematic analysis to problem solving.

Three-step change model
Unfreezing, change, refreezing.

Planned change model
Sequential stages that must be gone through to ensure change.

Emergent change model
A process of change that unfolds.

Change agent
Person responsible for managing change.

Force field analysis
Analysis of the strength of forces for and against change.

Organisation development
A process of planned change and improvement.

Management development process
Analysing present and future management needs.

UNDERSTANDING CHANGE

In general, change can be characterised as either radical or innovative. Radical change relates to large-scale, organisation-wide transformation programmes involving the rapid and wholesale overturning of old ways and old ideas and their replacement by new and unique ones. Such change represents a conscious and decisive break with the past and thus is often referred to as revolutionary change. Incremental change, on the other hand, refers to relatively small-scale projects that are localised and designed to solve a particular problem or enhance the performance of a subsection or part of the organisation. This type of change is sometimes referred to as evolutionary since it can often be incremental, unco-ordinated and indeed piecemeal. This is not to suggest, however, that it is unimportant. In fact, more often it is the incremental changes that keep the organisation on an even keel and so are essential for organisational survival from day to day. Tersine *et al.* (1997) provide an interesting characterisation of change which details that the magnitude and the rate of change can be measured from normal to severe relative to technical/economic and human/social issues. They argue that while severe change might be absorbed on one or the other dimension, it may not be integrated in both at the same time.

Figure 16.1 Taxonomy of Change

Technical/Economic	
• New product introduction • Opening new facilities • Fluctuation in stock value • Open new market • New competitor enters market	• Introduction of revolutionaary new technology by competitor • Economic depression • Hostile takeover of company • Significant change in regulatory environment
Normal Change	**Severe Change**
• Acquisition • Hiring new personnel • Relocation of personnel • Reorganisation	• Radical downsizing • Re-engineering • Significant legal action taken against organisation • Facility closing • Entering international marketplace • Establishing virtual organisation
Human/Social	

Source: Tersine *et al.* (1997)

Managing change is not unproblematic. Both Blacker and Brown (1986) and Burnes (1996a) suggest that the introduction of initiatives such as total quality management often fail because companies lack ability in terms of planning and managing change, motivating and involving employees and designing and implementing suitable job and work structures. Wilson (1993) cautions that change of any kind is threatening, for not only is there the uncertainty of the new but also the loss of a trusted friend – 'the way we have always done things around here.' Pascale *et al.* (1997) tracked the change efforts of the Fortune 100 companies and found that although most of them had implemented costly change programmes in the previous fifteen years, only thirty per cent had produced any significant improvement in the bottom-line results. A survey by Hunt (2000) of more than 400 leading international organisations reported similar success rates of around thirty per cent, suggesting that failure to deliver on change is a global phenomenon.

PERFORMANCE GAP

The need for change can come from identifying a performance gap, which is a mismatch between what is wanted and current or forecast outcomes. It can arise either from shifts in what managers consider desirable, that is, a raising of ambition, or from failure or decline in current business. If the gap is recognised, managers will seek action to close it. According to Naylor (1999), there is a danger in thinking that the need for change is obvious. Managers would be expected to swiftly close the gap, yet many do not. Kotter (1996) attributes this to weaknesses in leadership. Changes fail because staff do not share a sense of urgency.

Burnes (1996b) argues that change management is not a distinct discipline with rigid and clearly defined boundaries. Rather, the theory and practice of change management draws upon a number of social science disciplines and traditions. In particular, three distinct perspectives are evident – the individual perspective, group dynamics and open systems.

The Individual Perspective

Advocates of the individual perspective suggest that the focus of change should centre around the individual and their behaviour. Drawing upon the behaviourist theories of the human learning school of thought, the perspective argues that strong individual incentives are required in order to ensure that individuals behave in a manner desired by the organisation. This perspective also draws upon many of the principles of effective employee motivation in order to reinforce new behavioural outcomes.

Group Dynamics

Lewin (1958) propounded the notion that since organisations represent collections of individuals who are organised as groups (formal/informal), the most effective means of achieving permanent organisational change is through the changing of group norms, roles and values.

Open Systems

The open systems perspective views organisations as organic entities that are comprised of a number of interconnected subsystems, such as cultural systems, managerial systems, technical systems and social systems. Scott (1987) suggests that any change in one of these subsystems will necessarily impact on all of the others and thus have repercussions for overall performance.

THEORIES AND MODELS OF CHANGE MANAGEMENT

Approaches to change and change management vary considerably from organisation to organisation, and indeed from country to country. Handy (1986) argues that there is a strong link between culture and managerial practices, thus in different countries managers' approaches to a change initiative will be inherently influenced by the prevailing culture of their situation. In an attempt to describe the underlying concepts of organisational change, a number of models of change management have been developed over the years. Some of the most commonly referenced models are reviewed here.

ACTION RESEARCH MODEL

The term 'action research' (or action learning) was coined in the late 1950s and is based on the premise that an effective approach to solving organisational problems must involve a rational, systematic analysis of the issues in question. Burnes (1996a) argues that it must be an approach that secures information, hypotheses and action from all parties involved, as well as evaluating the action taken towards the solution of the problem. French and Bell (1984: 98–9) describe action research in the following terms:

> Action refers to programs and interventions designed to solve a problem or improve a condition … action research is the process of systematically collecting research data about an ongoing system relative to some objective, goal or need of that system; feeding these data back into that system; taking action by altering selected variables within the system based both on the data and on hypotheses; and evaluating the results of action by collecting more data.

In essence, therefore, action research advocates a dual/collective approach to managing change. First managers, workers and a change agent get together to identify a problem and agree a plan of action to eliminate this problem. This stage requires the frank exchange of information and is open to inquiry. However, action research also recognises that successful action/change is predicated upon the correct diagnosis of the situation and so it requires that those involved in the change initiative formulate a number of alternative scenarios delineating the nature of the problem under review, coupled with action plans for each scenario. Only through a process of elimination based on critical analysis of each action plan will a final solution be agreed on, which forms the basis for the change to be implemented. While this sounds complicated, it really advocates that decision makers, through a process of consultation and participation, take cognisance of the range of possible alternatives before deciding on a particular course of action. In this way organisations learn from past decisions and individuals are more likely to be committed to the outcomes. Cummings and Huse (1989) argue that despite its long history, action research remains a highly regarded approach to managing change.

THREE-STEP CHANGE MODEL

Lewin (1958) suggests that behaviour in organisations is a combination of two particular forces: those that are intent on maintaining the status quo and those that are pushing for change. Where both sets of behaviours are about equal, then equilibrium is maintained. If the organisation wishes to reach this state of equilibrium then it must either decrease the forces maintaining the status quo or increase those forces pushing for change. Lewin suggests that change is more acceptable if the organisation can manage to decrease or modify the strength of the forces maintaining the status quo rather than imposing change.

Lewin proposes that in order to ensure that the desired change becomes a permanent feature of organisational life and that new behaviour is successfully adopted, the old behaviour has to be discarded. In developing his model of organisational change, he identified three stages in the change process.

1. **Unfreezing:** Here the organisation must first reduce those forces that are maintaining the organisation's behaviour at its present level. Typically, an organisation might introduce an information/education/communication strategy in an attempt to persuade individuals/groups to modify their behaviour.
2. **Change:** At this stage the organisation is active in developing new behaviours, values and attitudes that are consistent with its desired behavioural outcomes. This is usually achieved through structural and process changes.
3. **Refreezing:** Once the change has occurred the organisation is concerned to ensure it remains in what is now a new state of equilibrium. To this end, it focuses on developing systems, values, norms and a culture that facilitate and reinforce this changed behaviour.

The three-stage model of organisational change was, and is, perceived to be relatively broad, thus successive theorists have sought to develop and extend Lewin's work.

PLANNED CHANGE MODEL

In an effort to expand on Lewin's three-step model, a number of writers, e.g. Lippitt *et al.* (1958), Bullock and Batten (1985), Cummings and Huse (1989), have developed various models that are based on a planned set of successive steps or phases that must be followed in order to bring about organisational change. Cummings and Huse (1989) suggest that, in itself, the concept of planned change implies that organisations exist in different states at different times and so it is possible to follow a predesigned plan to move from one phase to another. Organisations therefore must appreciate not only the process of change, but also the various sequential stages that must be gone through to ensure this change.

Illustrative of this planned change thesis, Lippitt *et al.*'s model (1958) provides for the introduction of a change agent to oversee and manage a planned change programme. While a varying number of steps have been attributed to this model, it essentially involves four main phases. First, the change agent explores the current stage of play in terms of meeting various internal actors and collecting required information. He/she then develops a systematic plan of the required behaviour change, taking into account organisational processes and systems and bearing in mind possible resistance that might be encountered. The third stage involves implementing the change. The fourth and final stage is integration, whereby the change is evaluated to ensure consistency with existing systems and processes and adjustments are made as required. This final stage also represents closure. Once the change is implemented and integrated with the organisation system, the change project is closed.

Burnes (1996b) cites a number of criticisms that have been levelled at the planned change models, which are worth noting here.

- They are based on the assumption that organisations operate under stable conditions and can move from one stable state to another in a preplanned manner. However, both Garvin (1993) and Stacey (1993) argue that such assumptions are increasingly tenuous and that organisational change is a more continuous and open-ended process than a set of discrete, self-contained events.
- The planned change models emphasise incremental or small-scale change and so are not applicable in situations that require rapid radical and/or transformational change.
- They are based on the premise that common agreements can be reached and that all parties involved in the change process are interested in and support the change initiative. The planned change models largely ignore the realities of organisational conflict and politics.

EMERGENT CHANGE MODEL

The emergent approach to change management, as advocated by both Dawson (1996) and Wilson (1992), is based on the premise that the planned model of change management has limited application in a turbulent business environment that is characterised by uncertainty and complexity. Burnes (1996b) describes the emergent model as an approach to change that views it as a process that unfolds through the interplay of multiple variables (context, political processes and consultation) within the organisation. The model is perceived to be less prescriptive and more analytical than the planned change models and allows for a more comprehensive understanding of managing change in a complex environment. Dawson (1996) argues that change can best be perceived as a period of organisational transition that is characterised by disruption, confusion and unforeseen events that emerge over long time frames. Perceived this way, organisational change becomes a continuous process that requires considerable learning and adaptability on the part of organisational members. Benjamin and Mabey (1993: 181) argue that '... while the primary stimulus for change remains with those forces in the external environment, the primary motivator for how change is accomplished resides with the people inside the organisation.'

In a review of the major proponents of the emergent change model, Burnes (1996b) identifies some of the main tenets of the emergent change thesis.

- Organisational change is perceived as a continuous process of experimentation and adaptation aimed at matching an organisation's capabilities to the needs and dictates of a dynamic and uncertain environment.

- While comprised of many small and incremental changes, over time the change process can constitute major organisational transformation.
- Managers' key role in this change scenario is to create and/or foster an organisational structure and climate that encourages and sustains experimentation and risk taking and to develop a workforce that will take responsibility for change and implementing it.
- Managers are also charged with creating and sustaining a vision of what the changed organisational scenario might be so that successive change initiatives can be judged against this vision.
- Central to this change initiative are the organisational activities of information gathering, communication and learning.

A cursory examination of much of this emergent change management literature might lead one to the conclusion that this budding change model is based less on change management principles and more on the burgeoning 'learning organisation' literature – or indeed, vice versa – since both sets of literature depict an organisation that is environmentally driven to adopting a continuous process of transformation and development.

A contingency approach to change management has been proposed by, among others, Dunphy and Stace (1993), who argue that since organisations operate under different circumstances, there must be more than one approach to change management. The choice then facing managers is to adopt the change approach that best suits their particular circumstances.

To review, then, it would appear that both the planned and emergent models of organisational change advocate different approaches to change management. The planned model has greater application in an environment that is relatively stable and predictable and where change can be driven from the top down. The emergent model, on the other hand, is geared towards dynamic, complex environments that are characterised by high risk and unpredictability, so in such situations it is not possible to successfully effect change from the top. Having said this, however, it is clear that both models suggest that internal practices must be changed in order to meet the demands of the situational environment and thus assume that managers do not have any discretion in terms of the choices available to them. However, the strategic management literature (for example, see Child 1972; Montgomery and Porter 1991; Pettigrew and Whipp 1993) would suggest that managers have considerable discretion and room for manoeuvre in terms of the strategic choices they make concerning the environment within which they operate, thus not only can they influence the nature of their situational environment (choices made concerning the product/service markets they decide to compete in) but they may also determine their approach to change management (related to their preferred management style, workforce characteristics and so forth).

A Change Agent

Early in the process, the organisation may seek the assistance of a change agent – a person who will be responsible for managing the change effort. The change agent may also help management to recognise and define the problem or the need for change and may be involved in generating and evaluating potential plans of action. The change agent may be a member of the organisation or an outsider, such as a consultant. Under the change agent's direction and management, the organisation implements the change through Lewin's unfreeze, change and refreeze process.

The final step is measurement, evaluation and control. The change agent and the top management team assess the degree to which the change is having the desired effect, that is, they measure progress towards the goals of the change and make appropriate changes if necessary. The more closely the change agent is involved in the change process, the less distinct the steps become. Throughout the process the change agent brings in new ideas and viewpoints that help employees look at old problems in new ways. Through the measurement, evaluation and control phase, management determines the effectiveness of the change process by evaluating various indicators of organisational productivity and effectiveness or employee morale.

The Change Manager as Consultant

Managing change and consultancy often go together. Typically, consultants are seen as being external to the change team, people who are brought in from another part of the organisation or from specialist consultancy firms to provide assistance. There is another dimension to change management consultancy, however, and this is where the change manager is seen as a consultant on their own change project.

The term 'consultant' has come to mean many things, from the expert advisor to the process facilitator. A consultant can adopt a range of different roles. Some organisations will want the consultant to 'just fix the problem', others will want the consultant to help them define the problem, while others will want the consultant to provide ideas as to how the problem might be solved.

According to Armstrong (1994) it is necessary to make use of basic project management guidelines in drawing up specifications for consultants before they are offered a contract, which can be summarised as follows.

- Take care to ensure that there is a valid and justifiable reason for employing consultants in the first place, that the project is worth doing and that it cannot be done as well in house.
- Ensure that the objectives and deliverables for the project are specified in a way that clearly indicates the desired results. Plan the project so that terms of reference, deadlines, methods of monitoring and review and reporting arrangements are clearly laid down. Ensure that both parties fully understand their respective roles in the relationship.
- Take care that the project is managed in line with the objectives and deliverables and that the company continues to receive value-for-money services. Wherever possible it is desirable to foster a partnership approach.
- Special care is required over the implementation, involvement and communication processes during and after the project.

FORCE FIELD ANALYSIS

Force field analysis had its origin in the work of the pioneering behavioural scientist Kurt Lewin. Lewin's model is based on laws of physics that hold that an object at rest will remain so unless the forces exerted on the object (to move it) are greater than the forces working against it (to keep it at rest). He put forward the idea that change occurs when change drivers collectively overcome restraining forces. A behaviour that is positioned between two forces, one opposing change and one pushing to change, will not change if the opposing forces are equal and thus cancel each other. In almost any change situation there are forces acting for and against the change. According to this model, behavioural change will occur if the forces for change are strengthened, if the forces against change are weakened or if a combination of the two is applied. To facilitate the change, management should start by listing each set of forces and then try to tip the balance so that the forces facilitating the change outweigh those hindering it.

Figure 16.2 Force Field Analysis

Step 1: Define the problem in terms of the present situation, with its strengths and weaknesses, and the situation you would wish to achieve. Define the target situation as precisely and unambiguously as possible.	**Step 4:** Agree on actions that appear most likely to help the problem of achieving change.
Step 2: List the forces working for and against the desired changes. These can be based on people, resources, time, external factors or corporate culture.	**Step 5:** Identify the resources that will be needed to take the agreed actions and how these resources may be obtained.
Step 3: Rate each of the forces for and against change in terms of strength (high, medium or low). Give the strength ratings numerical values: five for high, three for medium and one for low, which allows totals for driving and resisting forces to be calculated.	**Step 6:** Make a practical action plan designed to achieve the target situation, which should include timing of events, specified milestones and deadlines and specific responsibilities (who does what).

Source: Adapted from Carnall (1995); Huczynski and Buchanan (2001)

MANAGING THE CHANGE PROCESS

As indicated earlier, change can occur at any level within the organisation and can represent incremental or fundamental changes to individuals' lifestyles. Baron and Greenberg (1992) suggest that reactions to change can be categorised along a continuum.

Quitting	Active resistance	Opposition	Acquiescence	Reserved acceptance	Acceptance	Active support

The most extreme reaction is to leave the job because the change is perceived to be intolerable. Active resistance involves personal defiance and encouraging others to resist the change initiative. Opposition essentially involves a lack of co-operation and trying to delay proceedings. Acquiescence occurs where individuals may be unhappy about the change but feel powerless to prevent it, so they put up with it as best they can. Reserved acceptance occurs where the main thrust of the change is accepted but where individuals may bargain over details. Acceptance is characterised by passive co-operation with the change but no overt wish to participate in it. Finally, at the other extreme there is active support, where individuals welcome change and actively engage in behaviours that increase the chances of that change becoming a permanent feature of organisational life.

In view of the myriad of likely responses to change and the breadth of scope of many change initiatives, it is recommended that a number of key stages be involved in managing the change process (see Figure 16.3).

Figure 16.3 Activities Contributing to Effective Change Management

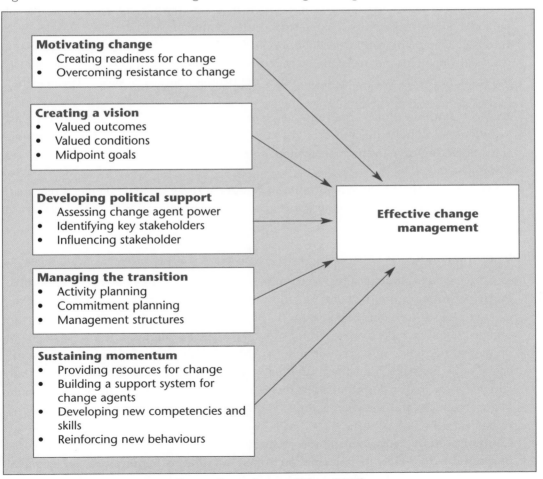

Source: Cummings and Huse (1989)

A number of the stages highlighted in Figure 16.3 are worthy of further elaboration here. The first concerns creating readiness for change by demonstrating the necessity for change in terms of the organisation's desired goals and current practice. It will also involve considerable discussion on the value of change and the positive impact such change will have on organisational members. The second step is more complex and involves overcoming likely resistance to change.

RESISTANCE TO CHANGE

It is probably fair to say that while humans are amazingly adaptable beings, individuals are often wary of change since it invariably disturbs the status quo and carries with it some degree of uncertainty. Hussey (1995) identifies a range of factors that might explain the root causes of resistance.

- **Actual threats:** Changes that are perceived as having an impact on the value of an individual's job generally tend to raise fears and uncertainties. In particular, individuals may fear loss of employment or resist change that requires them to develop new knowledge and skills – often it is less the fear of change as fear of personal failure or inability to cope that results in much resistance.
- **Imposed change:** In many cases individuals do not understand why changes are being imposed on them and resist them as a result. In other situations anything that is imposed, rather than discussed, can often 'get people's backs up' simply because they had no voice or say in the matter.
- **Lack of faith in those making the change:** This is largely dependent on past experiences and how previous changes were managed. Unsuccessful or uncomfortable transitions can leave individuals feeling 'hard done by' and thus more likely to avoid future changes.
- **The head and the heart:** While individuals appear to agree that change is required, they may be happier to retain the status quo – they like the continuity of things staying as they are.

REDUCING RESISTANCE TO CHANGE

At least three generic strategies for overcoming resistance to change have been identified.

- **Participation and involvement:** Organisational members are given ownership of the change process by being involved in its inception and development. From an organisational perspective, a strategy of participation allows for a vast array of opinions to be taken into account and it is likely that problem diagnosis will be more effective as a result. From the individual's perspective, organisational members are allowed a say in decisions that affect them and, as a result of being involved, are more likely to understand the change and the rationale for it, thereby reducing fears and resistance.
- **Communication:** Since one of the primary reasons for resisting change concerns uncertainty and lack of information, often all that is required is an effective communications exercise designed to eliminate misinformation and misinterpretation

of information. Employees can be encouraged to ask questions and share their concerns and thus gain a better understanding of the necessity for change.

- **Training and education:** This strategy is particularly useful where the change initiative involves restructuring jobs and processes. Fear of being unable to function in a new structure can cause unnecessary stress and can lead to decreased productivity even before the change is introduced. It is therefore necessary to adopt a strategic approach to managing the change process so that the required training and education programmes and systems can be put in place long before the change is introduced.

Kotter and Schlesinger (1979) outline the particular strengths of these and other methods of reducing resistance to change (Table 16.1).

Table 16.1 Methods of Reducing Resistance to Change

Approach	Situational Use	Advantages	Drawbacks
Education and communication	Where there is lack of information or inaccurate information about the change.	Once persuaded, people often will help with the implementation of the change.	Can be time consuming if many people are involved.
Participation and involvement	Where the initiators do not have all the information they need to design the change and where others have considerable power to resist.	People who participate will be committed to implementing change and any relevant information they have will be integrated into the change plan.	Can be time consuming if participants design an inappropriate change.
Facilitation and support	Where people are resisting because of adjustment problems.	No other approach works as well with adjustment problems.	Can be time consuming, expensive and still fail.
Negotiation and agreement	Where someone or some group will clearly lose out in a change and where that person/ group has considerable power to resist.	Sometimes it is a relatively easy way to avoid major resistance.	Can be too expensive for others to negotiate for compliance.
Manipulation and co-optation	Where other tactics will not work or are too expensive.	It can be a relatively quick and inexpensive solution to resistance problems.	Can lead to future problems if people feel manipulated.
Explicit and implicit coercion	Where speed is essential and the change initiators possess considerable power.	It is speedy and can overcome any kind of resistance.	Can be risky if it leaves initiators discredited.

Figure 16.3 above further highlights that the creation of a vision that can be shared by organisational members is a significant aspect of ensuring the smooth introduction of a change initiative. This will involve developing an organisation mission that employees can identify with and outlining a range of strategies to achieve this mission. Organisations are political entities and thus support from the key stakeholders plays a vital role in ensuring the transition from old to new. Finally, the evaluation of the organisation environment in terms of its culture, policies, systems and procedures is required to ensure that the change becomes a permanent feature of organisational life. It is evident that effective change management involves considerable strategic planning and communication at all levels of organisational life, but how is this achievable? In the following section we explore the various dimensions of organisation development as one particular mechanism for managing change.

THE MAIN BLOCKS TO CHANGE IN IRISH ORGANISATIONS

In a series of in-depth interviews with thirty managers in five organisations that have undergone major changes in the past five years, McConalogue (2003) found that although Irish organisations have become more enlightened in their approach to change, there are still many unanticipated blocks that persist. The main blocks to change are as follows.

1. Insufficient buy-in and ownership.
    • Lack of commitment from the top.
    • Lack of middle-management ownership.
    • Insufficient support at all levels.
2. Unrealistic timescale for change.
    • Loss of energy.
    • Lack of resources.
3. Lack of trust.
    • Failed attempts at change.
    • Lack of vision or a process.
    • Inadequate internal communications.
4. Lack of readiness for change.
    • Problems with letting go.
    • Overt and covert resistance.

Source: McConalogue (2003)

ORGANISATION DEVELOPMENT

Organisation development is the process of planned change and improvement of organisations through the application of knowledge of the behavioural sciences. First, organisation development involves attempts to plan organisation changes, which excludes spontaneous, haphazard initiatives. Second, the specific intention of organisation development is to improve organisations, which means excluding changes that merely imitate those of another organisation, are forced on the organisation by external pressures or are undertaken merely for the sake of changing. Third, the planned improvement must be based on the knowledge of the behavioural sciences, such as organisational behaviour, psychology, sociology and related fields of study, rather than on financial or technological considerations. As a broad strategy, organisation development can be defined as:

> A long-term effort, led and supported by top management, to improve an organisation's visioning, empowerment, learning, and problem-solving processes, through an ongoing collaborative management of organisation culture – with special emphasis on the culture of intact work teams and other team configurations – utilising the consultant-facilitator role and the theory and technology of applied behavioural science, including action research (French and Bell 1984: 15).

Generally, organisation development programmes focus on the prevailing culture of various groups and of the organisation as a whole. There is a conscious effort to examine beliefs, values, norms and goals to see which are useful and which need to be changed. The above definition also refers to action research, which is the process of gathering information, feeding it back and developing plans for implementing desired changes. In a typical organisation development programme, action research involves gathering information (usually through interviews and questionnaires), making that information visible (for example, reporting interview themes to a group), then facilitating employee participation in problem-solving effort.

Over the years it has been common to use the term 'organisation development' more or less synonymously with organisation change or, in fact, to combine the two terms into one label – organisation change and development. Moorhead and Griffin (2001), however, suggest that over the past thirty years, organisation development has emerged as a distinct field of study and practice.

Lundberg (1991: 9–11) differentiates organisation development with reference to the critical tasks of most modern organisations.

- **Organisations have to manage their internal affairs:** The focus here is on making continuous internal adjustments to ensure that goals are achieved and plans and standards are followed. This internal adjustment constitutes organisation change and will include those activities and processes designed and activated to overcome internal problems and bring performance in line with goals, standards and the like.
- **Organisations have to survive in their external environments:** As environments become more complex and uncertain, organisations will have to continuously realign themselves with portions of their environment. Lundberg suggests that this lies at the heart of organisation development, which focuses on those activities and processes designed to achieve a more appropriate alignment between an organisation and its relevant environment. Enhanced alignment, he suggests, will include those activities and processes that modify the basic character or culture of the organisation, redesigning an organisation's structures, strategies, systems, membership, etc. so they become more appropriate for future functioning.

- **Organisations have to anticipate and prepare for their probable future:** Essentially this third task requires that organisations be capable of dealing with the unknown and so exist in a state of readiness or be 'anticipatively aligned' with their operating environment. Lundberg proposes that dealing with anticipation can be labelled 'organisation transformation' and that transformation almost always requires both organisation change and development.

Organisation development is aimed at the development of individuals, groups and the organisation as a total system. In their seminal work, French and Bell (1984: 15) describe organisation development thus:

> Organisation development is a top management-supported long-range effort to improve an organisation's problem-solving and renewal processes, particularly through a more effective and collaborative management of organisation culture … with the assistance of a change agent or catalyst, and the use of theory and technology of applied behavioural sciences, including action research.

It can be said, therefore, that organisation development is planned and adopts a systems approach, that is, it operates at all levels within the organisation. It is designed to improve organisational functioning, both in the short and long term, by focusing on problem solving and human interaction and socialisation. It is concerned with ensuring that the organisation operates at its most effective and has the capacity to adapt to future change requirements. Warrick (1984) suggests a number of positive benefits of organisation development (see below).

TEN POSITIVE RESULTS FROM ORGANISATION DEVELOPMENT

1. Improved organisational effectiveness (increased productivity and morale, more effective goal setting, planning and organising, clearer goals and responsibilities, better utilisation of human resources and bottom-line improvements).
2. Better management from top to bottom.
3. Greater commitment and involvement from organisational members in making the organisation successful.
4. Improved teamwork within and between groups.
5. A better understanding of an organisation and its strengths and weaknesses.
6. Improvement in communications, problem solving and conflict resolution skills, resulting in increased effectiveness and less wasted time from communications breakdowns, game playing and win-lose confrontations.
7. Efforts to develop a work climate that encourages creativity and openness, provides opportunities for personal growth and development and rewards responsible and healthy behaviour.
8. A significant decrease in dysfunctional behaviour.

9. Increased personal and organisational awareness that improves the organisation's ability to adapt to a continuously changing environment and to continue to grow, learn and stay competitive.

10. The ability to attract and keep healthy and productive people.

Source: Warrick (1984)

Robbins (1991) suggests that organisation development is comprised of a number of change techniques, from organisation-wide changes in structures and systems to psychotherapeutic counselling sessions with groups and individuals undertaken in response to changes in the external environment that seek to improve organisational efficiency and employee well-being. He identifies a number of principles of organisation development that are worth highlighting here.

- **Respect for people:** Individuals are perceived as being responsible, conscientious and caring and should be treated with dignity and respect.
- **Trust and support:** The effective and healthy organisation is characterised by trust, authenticity, openness and a supportive climate.
- **Power equalisation:** Effective organisations de-emphasise hierarchical authority and control.
- **Confrontation:** Problems shouldn't be swept under the carpet, but rather should be openly confronted.
- **Participation:** The more that people who will be affected by a change are involved in the decisions surrounding that change, the more they will be committed to implementing those decisions.

Organisation development is more compatible with organic structures, yet those organisations that might best benefit from organisation development are probably those that are most likely to resist it, i.e. bureaucratic, mechanistic, highly formalised organisations.

IMPLEMENTING ORGANISATION DEVELOPMENT

The implementation of organisation development interventions can be broadly classified as structural interventions, task/technology interventions and people-focused interventions.

Structural Interventions

These are designed to make the organisation more organic and responsive to changing environmental demands. Robbins (1991) highlights three common structural interventions.

1. **Structural reorganisation:** This type of organisation development intervention is highly disruptive since it involves a systems change that impacts on all organisational members. Such change is characteristic of the move from a hierarchical structure to a more decentralised, flatter one in order to respond to change more quickly. The move

towards organisational delayering often occurs in tandem with a push for greater flexibility and the adoption of a team approach to organisation design, which requires employees to take responsibility for their work and oftentimes to learn new skills. Such change is fundamental since it primarily represents a change in what has essentially become a way of life and so its successful implementation is highly dependent on full consultation and participation.

2. **New reward systems:** The typical purpose here is to reinforce a particular type of behaviour, so organisations might seek to link individuals' pay with performance. This may be organisation wide or limited to particular sections or groups of workers, but again, this type of intervention can meet with considerable opposition, particularly in unionised environments. The purpose of this form of organisation development, as with many others, is to ensure greater operational efficiency, thus it seeks to provide a motivating environment where increased effort and greater output are rewarded.

3. **Changing culture:** It has long been argued that culture is a fluid concept that is virtually impossible to interpret, never mind manage or change. However, cultures can become obsolete and thus inhibit organisation growth and renewal in a dynamic environment. Cultural change interventions are concerned with developing values, beliefs and norms that are appropriate to an organisation's strategic direction and environmental conditions.

Task/Technology Interventions

Task/technology interventions emphasise changing the jobs that people do and/or the technological processes involved in performing them. Three particular approaches have been developed, namely job redesign, socio-technical systems approach and the quality of working life (QWL) movement.

People-Focused Interventions

This approach to organisation development focuses on changing individuals' attitudes and behaviours within the organisation through communication, decision making and problem solving. A number of specific techniques have been developed to achieve these changes.

1. **Sensitivity training:** Often termed T-group training, sensitivity training requires that small, unstructured groups of individuals are set up that meet on a regular basis without a planned agenda. This is designed to provide members with experiential learning about group dynamics, leadership and interpersonal relations. Over time, as members of the group interact with each other, they begin to learn more about themselves, each other and how others might perceive their behaviour. The objective of this form of organisation development is to heighten sensitivity to emotional reactions and thus facilitate improved decision making, communication and conflict resolution.

2. **Survey research and feedback:** In essence, this form of organisation development involves conducting an attitude survey of all organisational members to determine views on various organisational processes and systems. A survey questionnaire is

developed and administered to all employees. In some organisations, focus groups are set up comprising employees from various sectors and departments to discuss many aspects of work in that organisation. The data from the surveys is then collated and interpreted and generally presented to the management team. The results are fed back to employees through meetings that are set up to discuss the results and matters arising. This form of organisation development is becoming increasingly popular in Ireland and many organisations are commissioning third-level educational institutions to conduct such research on their behalf. The purpose of this is twofold: first, the organisation buys in expertise in the form of an experienced researcher who is adept at designing, administering and interpreting such surveys, and second, the use of an independent consultant can often reassure employees about responding in a frank manner to the questions posed.

3. **Process consultation:** Here the organisation buys in external expertise in the guise of an organisation development consultant whose role is to observe how individuals interact with each other. His/her role is to review organisational systems and processes in terms of their effect on organisational communication, individual interaction and work behaviour. In practice the aim of this type of organisation development may be to diagnose the solution to such problems as dysfunctional conflict, poor communications and ineffective norms. The idea is that over time group members can learn to deal with such problems themselves.

4. **Team building:** This form of organisation development focuses on team dynamics within the organisation. In particular it examines task allocation and the patterns of human behaviour within the work group. Based on Lewin's approach (1958), it assumes that organisational effectiveness is dependent on the effectiveness of teams; therefore, improvements in how the team operates will likely result in greater organisational efficiency. It goes beyond merely examining group processes and looks at tasks to be achieved and role allocation within the team as well.

Walton (1975) and Guest (1990) both argue that organisation development as a change mechanism is often limited and rarely diffuses throughout the organisation. Guest in particular suggests that much of the innovation is piecemeal and lacks the critical ingredient of strategic integration, and that as a result it is unlikely to have a positive impact on organisational performance. Burnes (1996b) provides a classification of change management approaches that encapsulate many of the organisation development interventions described here (see Table 16.2).

Furnham (1997) cautions that the generation, implementation and diffusion of new ideas and processes in an organisation are particularly difficult and stresses that organisations must take cognisance of their range of support structures and systems to ensure close coherence with defined goals and objectives. Given the inherent problems associated with generating behavioural changes and the perceived difficulties of maintaining meaningful change, organisations must have a carefully constructed and clearly articulated means of introducing and sustaining a change initiative.

Table 16.2 A Classification of Change Management Approaches

Focus	Approach	Techniques	Involvement
Individual	Behaviourist or Gestalt-Field	• Life- and career-planning activities. • Role analysis technique. • Coaching and counselling. • T-group (sensitivity training). • Education and training to increase skills, knowledge in the areas of technical task needs, relationship skills, decision making, problem solving, planning, goal-setting skills. • Job redesign.	High
Teams and groups	Group dynamics	• Team building. • Process consultation. • Third-party peacemaking. • Quality circles. • Survey feedback. • Role analysis. • Education in decision making, problem solving, planning, goal setting in group settings.	Medium–high
Intergroup relations	Group dynamics	• Integroup activities (process and task directed). • Organisational mirroring. • Techno-structural interventions. • Process consultation. • Third-party peacemaking at group level. • Survey feedback.	Medium–low
Total organisation	Open systems	• Techno-structural activities. • Confrontation meetings. • Strategic planning activities. • Culture change. • Survey feedback.	Low

Source: Burnes (1991: 176–7)

THE MANAGEMENT DEVELOPMENT PROCESS

As managers are major decision makers in any organisation, an effective management development process is crucial to organisational success. For all organisations, therefore, the management development process is a potentially powerful 'strategic tool'

(Osbaldeston and Barham 1992). Essentially, the management development process involves three tasks:

- the analysis of present and future management needs;
- the assessment of the existing and potential capability of managers against those needs; and
- producing and implementing policy, strategy and plans to meet those needs.

These tasks involve decisions about individuals' career routes, management succession and organisational performance. Management development design is often dominated by a highly systematic approach, leading to blocks of training and development aiming to 'teach' managers (and potential managers) their roles and tasks in an orderly, sequential fashion and help them acquire sets of functional skills. Organisational life, however, is not ordered or predictable, so the management development process should help managers to prepare for uncertainty and turbulence.

Lippitt (1983) cautions that management development must be centrally concerned with organisational values and with attitudinal change. One aspect of that concern is the attitudes of those being developed. Dogmatic attitudes in managers mean that they are unlikely to be able to function effectively in a changing world because they cannot accept that they themselves need to change. Therefore, management development that does not focus on attitudes can unwittingly simply ensure the perpetuation of old attitudes to the detriment of new learning.

Harrison (2000) suggests that work-based learning can be stimulated in many ways. Currently the most popular methods and processes include development through project work, self-development, action learning, coaching and mentoring. No single approach to development, however, is likely to be able to guarantee managerial effectiveness over time. Careful consideration must certainly be given to the kind of work-based experiential learning that can achieve improved performance and strengthen the ties between managers and the organisation.

Osbaldeston and Barham (1992) identify six characteristics that make a management development process effective, no matter what management development methods are used:

- a clear management development process mission linked to the organisation's business strategy;
- specific programme objectives that relate to the external challenges the organisation is facing;
- a focus on major internal organisational issues;
- programmes tailored to organisational and individual needs;
- the systematic assessment of management development needs, aims and outputs; and
- a professional, business-led approach to the management development process.

Therefore, the development of managers is a political process in any organisation and needs effective collaboration between the key parties if it is to succeed. If longer-term outcomes are to be achieved, the management development process must be integrated with wider employee resourcing policy and practice in order to be consistent across the process of planning, recruitment, selection, appraisal, rewards and development. This argues for the human resource function to have a central involvement in planning and managing the management development process.

ONGOING DEBATES/ADVANCED CONCEPTS IN ORGANISATIONAL CHANGE AND DEVELOPMENT

RE-ENGINEERING

For many organisations there is no time for long-range comprehensive change programmes of organisational development to take effect. Often, the changes they need are more radical than improvements to current practices could yield. The current term for fundamental change to all systems within the organisation is 're-engineering', or since the focus is on process improvements to better serve customers, 'business process re-engineering (BPR)'. Leading proponents Hammer and Champy (1993) argue that the link between products and success needs to be turned around. They define business process as a 'collection of activities that takes one or more kinds of input and creates an output that is of value to the customer.' Good products do not lead to success, but successful businesses deliver good products, therefore managers must get it right. The following features are generally associated with BPR:

- practitioners take a process view;
- the business is redesigned, starting with a 'clean sheet' to create the ideal;
- the whole system discards old habits and adopts new methods;
- BPR sees stability as abnormal and instead continually seeks improvements;
- 'stretch' targets are set, looking for major breakthroughs in factors such as performance, profit, quality and costs;
- leaders seek ways of decentralising decision making and control; and
- teamwork among multiskilled employees is favoured.

Information technology has been an important influence here. Inspired by ideas drawn from systems engineering and supported by advances in information systems capacity, re-engineering has often concentrated on the 'hard' aspects of management, while 'softer' aspects, such as attitudes, values and culture, are played down. Re-engineering, as seen by Hammer and Champy, is essentially a top-down programme that assumes neither an upward flow of involvement nor consensus decision making. They assert that people lower down the organisation lack the perspective to visualise the changes that are needed, although they do point out that it is important to pay attention to the company's human resource and organisational infrastructure and that it is important to reward behaviour that exhibits the appropriate values pertaining to customers, teamwork and ownership of problems. They also see the manager's role changing from being a boss to that of a coach, which is consistent with the experience of organisations that develop self-managed teams. Overall, however, in typical practice re-engineering tends to be a top-down, non-participative, industrial engineering attempt to improve efficiency and profitability.

Mumford and Hendricks's main criticism (1996) of re-engineering is that people are forgotten. They also find failure in other areas, such as the following.

- **The tendency to copy:** Security for managers is found in following others. This is unsuccessful if the following firm does not need the same therapy.
- **The absence of a theory:** Pioneers have admitted that rhetoric replaced theory, yet without theory there is little chance of giving guidance on management or evaluating experience. It is sometimes said that engineering works because it works.
- **The use of consultants:** Without detailed methodology, consultants were left to invent their own, often old techniques recycled to suit the new fad.

CHANGE PROJECT MANAGEMENT

All macro-level and most micro-level areas of change are amenable to managing as change projects. Grundy (1994: 95) suggests that 'change project management is the focusing of change into one or more discrete projects to reach a pre-planned result within a specified time and cost whilst managing interdependencies with other projects and activities.'

The benefits of change projects as a management process are that they:

- help managers to 'diagnose' and plan the change process more thoroughly as well as define a clear objective for change;
- provide a vehicle for control;
- can help identify the key stakeholders in the project;
- provide clear ownership for the change; and
- necessary resources are highlighted and can be mobilised in good time.

Some of the identified problems of using change project management processes include:

- the specific change is seen in isolation and unlinked to other activities or areas of change;
- the process becomes weighed down with too much control bureaucracy; and
- project management is not seen as fitting the organisational pattern and may be resisted.

The introduction of project management as a major tool for implementing change across the organisation may require changes in structure (through greater role flexibility) as well as style. In the transition period, managers may perceive the changeover to project management as generating more rather than less work in the short term. This requires careful management of expectations to ensure that managers are not rapidly switched off this technique. It also requires evaluation to show that project management is genuinely both achieving benefits and saving time.

In summary, project management provides powerful infrastructure to the change process, which enables teams to mobilise for change far more effectively and efficiently than is feasible purely within functional and hierarchical structures.

SUMMARY OF KEY PROPOSITIONS

- Organisation change is one of the most critical aspects of effective management, and the turbulent business environment in which most organisations operate means that not only is change becoming more frequent, but that the nature of change may be increasingly complex and the impact of change is often more extensive.
- Change can be either incremental and localised or fundamental and organisation wide.
- Organisations may seek a change agent's or management consultant's assistance in their efforts to manage change. The change agent or management consultant may use force field analysis in their attempts to implement change.
- Resistance to change can occur at many levels, but primarily is a result of fear of the unknown, inadequate knowledge or loss of status. Strategies for overcoming resistance include participation and involvement, training and education and communication.
- Every work organisation strives to be effective. Organisation development is concerned with the diagnosis of organisational health and performance and adaptability to change.
- Organisation development is action oriented and tailored to suit individual needs and is based on organisational behaviour.
- Organisation development intervention can be classified as structural interventions, task/technology interventions and people-focused interventions.
- Management development is closely linked with organisation development, as it involves decisions about individual organisational managers, which in turn affects organisational performance.

DISCUSSION/SELF-ASSESSMENT QUESTIONS

1. Outline the various models of change management. Which model has the greatest applicability in modern organisations?
2. Why do individuals resist change? How can organisations overcome resistance to change?
3. What are the advantages and disadvantages of having an internal change agent rather than an external change agent?
4. Which stage of the Lewin model of change do you think is most often overlooked? Why?
5. How does organisation development differ from organisation change?

MULTIPLE CHOICE QUESTIONS

1. Substantive modification of any part of an organisation is:
   (a) Organisation development.
   (b) Organising.
   (c) Organisation change.
   (d) Organisational structure.

2. During the unfreezing process, which of the following occurs?
    (a) People resist change because of self-interests.
    (b) Managers select a change technique.
    (c) Individuals are led to recognise why change is needed.
    (d) Those who adapt well to the change are rewarded.
3. The most effective technique in overcoming resistance to change is generally considered to be:
    (a) Participation.
    (b) Facilitation.
    (c) Division of labour.
    (d) Education.
4. Which of the following is *not* one of the three major areas in which organisation change takes place?
    (a) Social responsibility.
    (b) Organisational structure and design.
    (c) Technology and operations.
    (d) People.
5. Generally, the most difficult thing for management to do is to attempt to change:
    (a) Technology.
    (b) Control systems.
    (c) Performance.
    (d) Attitudes.
6. The changing of attitudes and values is called organisation:
    (a) Change.
    (b) Design.
    (c) Development.
    (d) Behaviour.
7. All but which of the following is an assumption of organisational development?
    (a) Employees have strong social needs.
    (b) Management-employee collaboration is needed.
    (c) Employees have strong growth needs.
    (d) Employees normally take an adversarial stance to the organisation.
8. Which of the following would normally exert the most powerful force for change?
    (a) Change in the balance of trade figures.
    (b) Increase in the average age of the population.
    (c) Increase in the budget deficit.
    (d) New product development by a competitor.
9. Studies of the organisation change process found that participation:
    (a) Reduced the need for communication.
    (b) Encouraged employees to adopt differing perceptions.
    (c) Increased productivity and co-operation.
    (d) Led to higher training costs.

10. Organisation change by means of change in technology/operations occurs when:
    (a) The management information system is upgraded.
    (b) Jobs are redesigned.
    (c) People are given training in new skills and abilities.
    (d) Line and staff relationships are changed.
11. Which of the following factors is an internal force for change?
    (a) Increases in the prime lending rate.
    (b) Increased union attempts to organise new companies.
    (c) A change in workers' attitude towards unannounced layoffs.
    (d) New technology makes the factory obsolete.
12. Force field analysis is a technique that:
    (a) Helps managers overcome resistance to change.
    (b) Does not recognise change.
    (c) Does not involve employee participation.
    (d) Suggests all factors for change are external.
13. The preferred method of change is to implement the change:
    (a) Quickly so that resistance does not have time to build up.
    (b) After various sequential stages of planning have been gone through.
    (c) With no employee involvement.
    (d) From a top-down management approach.
14. Changing employee attitudes and values is:
    (a) One of the easier forms of organisation change.
    (b) One of the most difficult forms of organisation change.
    (c) Technical change.
    (d) Refreezing.
15. A change agent is a person who:
    (a) Resists change.
    (b) Is responsible for change.
    (c) Does not plan change.
    (d) Does not use facilitation for change.
16. One of the major reasons people often resist change appears to be:
    (a) Employee participation.
    (b) Recognising the need for change.
    (c) Change models.
    (d) The uncertainty generated by change.
17. Action research is designed to:
    (a) Maintain the status quo.
    (b) Refreeze.
    (c) Solve a problem.
    (d) Eliminate employee involvement.
18. The primary motivator for how change is accomplished is:
    (a) The employees.

    (b) The stakeholders.

    (c) The technological environment.

    (d) The legal environment.

19. Organisation development is:

    (a) Tailored to suit individual needs.

    (b) Part of the external environment.

    (c) Resisting change.

    (d) Confrontational.

20. The emergent change model does *not* involve:

    (a) Gathering communication.

    (b) Developing employees.

    (c) A vision for change.

    (d) A stable environment.

FIVE SUGGESTED KEY READINGS

Kotter, J.P., *Leading Change*, Boston, MA: Harvard Business School 1996.

Mumford, A., *Management Development: Strategies for Action*, London: CIPD 2000.

Pearn, M. (ed.), *Individual Differences and Development in Organisations*, Chichester: John Wiley & Sons 2002.

Porras, J., Pascale, R., Collins, J. and Duck, J.D., *Harvard Business Review on Change* (August 1998).

Senge, P.M., *The Dance of Change: The Challenges to Sustaining Momentum in Learning Organizations*, New York: Doubleday 1999.

REFERENCES

Armstrong, M., *Using the Human Resource Consultant: Achieving Results, Adding Value*, London: IPM 1994.

Baron, R. and Greenberg, J., *Behavior in Organizations*, Boston: Allyn & Bacon 1992.

Benjamin, G. and Mabey, C., 'Facilitating radical change', in C. Mabey and B. Mayon-White (eds), *Managing Change*, 2nd ed., London: The Open University/Paul Chapman 1993.

Bennis, W., *Organizational Development: Its Nature, Origins and Prospects*, Reading, MA: Addison-Wesley 1969.

Blacker, F. and Brown, C., 'Alternative models to guide the design and implementation of the new information technologies into work organisation', *Journal of Occupational Psychology*, 59 (1986), 287–313.

Bullcok, R.J. and Batten, D., 'It's just a phase we're going through: a review and synthesis of OD phase analysis', *Group and Organisational Studies*, X (December 1985), 383–412.

Burke, W., *Organizational Development*, Boston, MA: Little, Brown 1982.

Burnes, B., *Managing Change*, London: Pitman 1991, 176–7.

Burnes, B., *Managing Change*, 2nd ed., London: Pitman 1996a.

Burnes, B., 'No such thing as a "one best way" to manage organisational change', *Management Decision*, XXXIV/10 (1996b), 11–18.

Carnall, C., *Managing Change in Organizations*, London: Prentice Hall 1995.

Child, J., 'Organisational structure, environment and performance: the role of strategic choice', *Sociology*, VI/1 (1972), 1–22.

Cummings, T. and Huse, E., *Organization Development and Change*, St Paul, MN: West Publishing 1989.

Dawson, P. (1996), *Organisational Change: A Processual Approach*, London: Paul Chapman 1996.

Dunphy, D. and Stace, D., 'The strategic management of corporate change', *Human Relations*, XLVI/8 (1993), 905–18.

French, W. and Bell, C., *Organizational Development*, Englewood Cliffs, NJ: Prentice Hall 1984.

Furnham, A., *The Psychology of Behaviour at Work*, London: Psychological Press 1997.

Garvin, D.A., 'Building a learning organization', *Harvard Business Review* (July/August 1993), 78–91.

Grundy, T., *Implementing Strategic Change*, London: Kogan Page 1994.

Guest, D., 'HRM and the American dream', *Journal of Management Studies* (July 1990), 388.

Hammer, M. and Champy, J., *Reengineering the Corporation: A Manifesto for Business Revolution*, London: Nicholas Brealey 1993.

Handy, C., *Understanding Organisation*, Harmondsworth: Penguin 1986.

Harrison, R., *Employee Development*, 2nd ed., London: CIPD 2000.

Huczynski, A. and Buchanan, D., *Organizational Behavior, Student Workbook*, Hemel Hempstead: Financial Times/Prentice Hall 2001.

Hunt, J., 'The change-able organisation', *Journal of the Strategic Planning Society* (September 2000).

Hussey, D.E., *How to Manage Change*, London: Kogan Page 1995.

Kotter, J.P., *Leading Change*, Boston, MA: Harvard Business School 1996.

Kotter, J.P., 'Leading change', *Fortune*, CXXXIV/3 (5 August 1996), 168–70.

Kotter, J. and Schlesinger, L., 'Choosing strategies for change', *Harvard Business Review* (March/April 1979), 106–14.

Lewin, K., 'Group decisions and social change', in G.E. Swanson, T.M. Newcomb and E.L. Hartley (eds), *Readings in Social Psychology*, New York: Holt, Rhinehart & Winston 1958.

Lippitt, G., 'Management development as the key to organisational renewal', *Journal of Management Development*, I/2 (1983), 36–9.

Lippitt, R., Watson, J. and Westley, B., *The Dynamics of Planned Change*, New York: Harcourt, Brace & World 1958.

Lundberg, C., 'Towards a conceptual understanding of organisational development', *Journal of Organisational Change Management*, IV/4 (1991), 6–15.

Luthans, F., *Organizational Behavior*, New York: McGraw-Hill 1992.

Mabey, C. and Mayon-White, B., *Managing Change*, 2nd ed., London: The Open University/Paul Chapman 1993.

March, J., 'Footnotes on organisation change', *Administrative Science Quarterly*, XXVI/4 (1981), 563–72.

McConalogue, T., *Dealing with Change: Lessons for Irish Managers*, Cork: Oak Tree Press 2003.

Montgomery, C.A. and Porter, M., *Strategy: Seeking and Securing Competitive Advantage*, (Harvard Business Review book series), Boston: Harvard Business School Publishing 1991.

Moorhead, G. and Griffin, R.W., *Organizational Behavior: Managing People and Organizations*, 6th ed., New York: Houghton Mifflin 2001.

Mullins, L., *Management and Organisation Behaviour*, London: Pitman 1991.

Mumford, A., *Management Development: Strategies for Action*, London: CIPD 2000.

Mumford, E. and Hendricks, R., 'Business process reengineering RIP', *People Management*, (2 May 1996), 22–9.

Naylor, J., *Management*, London: Financial Times/Pitman Publishing 1999.

Osbaldeston, M. and Barham, K., 'Using management development for competitive advantage', *Long Range Planning*, XXV/6 (1992), 18–24.

Pascale, R., Millemann, M. and Gioja, L., 'Changing the way we change', *Harvard Business Review* (November/December 1997).

Pearn, M. (ed.), *Individual Differences and Development in Organisations*, Chichester: John Wiley & Sons 2002.

Peters, T., *Thriving on Chaos*, New York: Knopf 1987.

Pettigrew, A. and Whipp, R., *Managing Change for Competitve Success*, London: Blackhall 1993.

Porras, J., Pascale, R., Collins, J. and Duck, J.D., *Harvard Business Review on Change* (August 1998).

Robbins, R., *Organizational Behavior: Concepts, Controversies and Applications*, Englewood Cliffs, NJ: Prentice Hall 1991.

Schein, E., 'Organizational culture', *American Psychologist* (February 1990), 117.

Scott, W.R., *Organizations: Rational, Natural and Open Systems*, Englewood Cliffs, NJ: Prentice Hall 1987.

Senge, P.M., *The Dance of Change: The Challenges to Sustaining Momentum in Learning Organizations*, New York: Doubleday 1999.

Stacey, R., *Strategic Management and Organisational Dynamics*, London: Pitman 1993.

Tersine, T., Harvey, M. and Buckley, M., 'Shifting organisational paradigms: transitional management', *European Management Journal*, XV/1 (1997), 45–57.

Vaill, P.B., *Managing as a Performing Art*, San Francisco: Jossey-Bass 1989.

Walton, R., 'The diffusion of new work structures: explaining why success didn't take', *Organisational Dynamics*, (Winter 1975), 3–22.

Warrick, D., *Modman: Managing Organisational Change and Development*, Englewood Cliffs, NJ: Science Research Associates Inc. 1984.

Wilson, D.C., *A Strategy of Change*, London: Routledge 1992.

Wilson, G., *Making Change Happen*, London: Pitman 1993.

SECTION FOUR

CONTEMPORARY DEBATES IN ORGANISATIONAL BEHAVIOUR

MANAGING DIVERSITY

Learning Objectives

- To define diversity and identify the essential elements of a diversity policy.
- To analyse dimensions of workplace diversity.
- To assess the role of the human resource manager in diversity initiatives.
- To identify the business benefits of workplace diversity.
- To explain the link between workplace diversity and good management practice.

INTRODUCTION

Diversity is nothing new – human diversity has existed throughout the world from the beginning of time. Gender differences were evident in the Garden of Eden and multilingualism emerged with the Tower of Babel. Ethnic, cultural and racial differences were found within tribes and other groups of people across the continents before recorded history. Indeed, the history of humankind is a story of multiculturalism and diversity. Over the years, all civilisations have included people who are different from one another by virtue of age, gender, race, sexual orientation, class and physical ability.

Yet denying multiculturalism and diversity is as old as diversity itself. This denial has taken the form of holy wars, colonisation of one country by another and other movements designed to homogenise people (Arredondo 1996).

The workforce in organisations today is becoming increasingly diverse, a development that affects workers' lives and poses numerous challenges for managers. In some organisations the increase is due to changing demographics among the general population of society, whereas in other situations the increasing diversity is caused by the globalisation of an organisation's products, services, suppliers, customers and employees. The issues of demographic change have been summed up by Johnston and Packer (1987) and specifically relate to the changing nature of the workforce, and in particular to:

- gender – increasing numbers of women entering the labour market;
- ethnic minorities – they will be forming an increasing part of the workforce; and
- age – the ageing of the working population.

The changing demographic situation will have an effect on organisations and on society. Much of the work on managing diversity has stemmed from trying to identify what this impact will be and how organisations can prepare themselves for it. Regardless of the cause of the diversity in organisations, the result is that management must deal with and develop ways to manage it. This chapter examines the different types and sources of diversity affecting organisations today. In exploring diversity, this chapter highlights definitions of diversity and summarises models in relation to this concept. This chapter also outlines the role of the human resource manager in managing a diverse workforce.

DEFINITIONS OF KEY CONCEPTS

Diversity
Enabling every employee to perform to his or her potential.

Discrimination
Treating people differently because of prejudice.

Equal opportunities
Legislating against discrimination.

Diversity management
Organisational approach to workforce diversity development.

Primary dimensions of diversity
Inborn factors.

Secondary dimensions of diversity
Factors that can be adapted or changed.

Valuing diversity
Highlighting the importance of individuality.

Assimilation
Minority groups are forced to learn majority group ways.

Stereotyping
Individuals from the same group are regarded as having the same characteristics.

DEFINING AND DIMENSIONALISING DIVERSITY

In many organisations the conversation continues to centre around the issue of what diversity actually is. Many definitions of managing diversity have been produced; for example, Thomas (1990) suggests that managing diversity 'means enabling every member of your workforce to perform to his or her potential. It means getting from employees, first, everything we have a right to expect, and, second, if we do it well – everything they have to give.' Kandola and Fullerton (2001) propose that:

The basic concept of managing diversity accepts that the workforce consists of a diverse population of people. The diversity consists of visible and non-visible differences which will include factors such as sex, age, background, race, disability, personality and work style. It is founded on the premise that harnessing these differences will create a productive environment in which everybody feels valued, where their talents are being fully utilised and in which organisational goals are met.

Therefore, the term 'diversity' is often broadly used to refer to many demographic variables, including but not limited to:

- race;
- religion;
- colour;
- gender;
- national origin;
- disability;
- sexual orientation;
- age;
- education;
- geographic origin; and
- skill characteristics.

The term 'diversity' has also come to designate not only a variety of demographic and cultural differences, but also

> a workforce made distinct by the presence of many religions, cultures or skin colours, both sexes (in non-stereotypical roles), differing sexual orientations, varying styles of behaviour, differing capabilities, and usually unlike backgrounds (Canadian Institute of Chartered Accountants 1996).

Diversity has to be considered as being different from discrimination, as diversity is about variety and differences while discrimination concerns treating people differently through prejudice. This means that a worker can behave unfairly towards another person or group, but it is usually because of prejudice about one or more of the components of diversity listed above.

EQUAL OPPORTUNITIES AND MANAGING DIVERSITY APPROACHES

Diversity also has to be considered as being different from equal opportunities and not as a new label for an old concept. Equal opportunities has traditionally been a concept that sought to legislate against discrimination and was often seen as the concern mainly of personnel and human resource managers. Managing diversity, however, is seen as the concern of all employees, especially managers within an organisation.

In comparing equal opportunities with managing diversity, one assumption is that the difference is purely one of appearances – that this new concept represents no more than a change in language, perhaps because of frustration at the slow speed of change to date.

Indeed, the point has been made that such language change is itself helpful, that 'new terms as well as new solutions have to be found for old problems if the issue is to be kept alive' (Shaw and Perrons 1995). However, comparisons between these two approaches have been made that relate to differences other than simply language. The goal of equal opportunities has been described in terms of social justice and of redressing past wrongs: 'to correct an imbalance, an injustice, a mistake' (Thomas 1990).

The fundamental purpose of equal opportunities policies and practices in organisations has been described in terms of the search for equality, i.e. the creation of conditions where women and men are treated the same and are not advantaged or disadvantaged because of their gender. The shift, therefore, is from a solely gender-related perspective to one which focuses on all employees. The term 'managing diversity' highlights the importance of difference and suggests a view where difference is welcomed and is perhaps even to be celebrated (Ross and Schneider 1992).

DIVERSITY MANAGEMENT

Diversity management refers to a strategic organisational approach to workforce diversity development, organisational culture change and workforce empowerment. It represents a shift away from activities and assumptions defined by affirmative action to management practices that are inclusive, reflecting the workforce diversity and its potential. Ideally, it is a pragmatic approach in which participants anticipate and plan for change, do not fear human differences or perceive them as a threat and view the workplace as a forum for individuals' growth and change in skills and performance with direct cost benefits to the organisation (Arredondo 1996).

As the diversity of people will always exist, so will the need to work with factors of change, which will be both internal and external, domestic and international and driven by need as well as the potential for emerging markets. Diversity management interacts with all other aspects of business, i.e. leadership, management practices, product development, human resources, marketing and sales, financial projections and community and global communications.

Diversity management requires a shift in thinking. Company leaders must engage in a re-education process to comprehend the scope and potential of a diversity management approach. Shifts in thinking allow for simultaneous consideration of business needs that are universal or culturally relative. Seeing each individual as a 'customer', whether an employee, client, vendor or member of the board of directors, becomes a valid consideration in business planning (Arredondo 1996).

According to Digh (1998), if an organisation wishes to concentrate on diversity it must 'articulate, clearly and simply, what it means by diversity and what approach it is going to take. That is, are the members of the organisation going to tolerate, value, celebrate, manage, harness, or leverage diversity.' Managing diversity does not mean giving preferential treatment to non-productive employees, but it does mean fully utilising the potential of all employees regardless of age, gender, colour, religion, national origin and disability. To manage diversity is to minimise or remove performance barriers that result from diversity-related problems, such as turnover, absenteeism, low productivity, work quality and group cohesiveness. It is also argued that effective recruitment and management of a diverse workforce can enhance a company's competitive advantage by adding expertise relevant to addressing increasingly diverse markets, expanding creativity in problem solving and increasing organisational flexibility, goal achievement and profitability (Cox 1991).

PRIMARY DIMENSIONS OF DIVERSITY

The primary dimensions of diversity are those factors that are either inborn or exert extraordinary influence on early socialisation. These include age, race and ethnicity, gender, physical and mental abilities and sexual orientation and make up the essence of who we are as human beings. These characteristics are enduring aspects of our human personality and they sometimes present complex problems to managers.

SECONDARY DIMENSIONS OF DIVERSITY

Secondary dimensions of diversity include factors that matter to us as individuals and to some extent define us to others, but which are less permanent than primary dimensions and can be adapted or changed. These include educational background, geographic location, income, marital status, parental status, religious beliefs and work experience.

The impact of secondary dimensions may differ at various times in our lives. Moving to another part of the world may be traumatic for a parent with children, whereas a person with no close ties or dependants may find it exciting. Family experiences may also influence a manager's degree of sympathy with the disruptions of work life that sometimes occur because of personal responsibilities.

Employees enter the workforce with unique experiences and backgrounds that affect their perspective of work rules, work expectations and personal concerns. Although employees may have essentially the same work hours, job description and pay, their reactions to the work situation may differ significantly because of differences in these primary and secondary dimensions of diversity.

THE VALUE OF DIVERSITY

Valuing diversity means putting an end to the assumption that everyone who is not a member of the dominant group must assimilate. Valuing diversity is not just the right thing to do for workers, it is the right thing to do for the organisation, both financially and economically. One of the most important benefits of diversity is the richness of ideas and perspectives that it makes available to the organisation. Rather than relying on one dominant group for new ideas and alternative solutions to increasingly complex problems, organisations that value diversity have access to more perspectives on a problem.

Overall, an organisation benefits when it truly values diversity. An employee the organisation values is more creative and productive. Valued workers in diverse organisations experience less interpersonal conflict because the employees understand each other, and when employees of different cultural groups, backgrounds and values understand each other, they have a greater sense of teamwork, stronger identification with the team and deeper commitment to the organisation and its goals. A key element is to move towards 'cultures of inclusion' (Thornberg 1994), recognising that various organisational practices often lead to certain groups feeling left out or unwelcome. Exponents of the management of diversity perspective argue that all differences must be valued, including those of white males.

ASSIMILATION

Assimilation is the process through which members of a minority group are forced to learn the majority group's ways. In organisations this entails hiring people from diverse backgrounds and then attempting to mould them to fit into the existing organisational culture. One way that organisations attempt to make people fit in is by requiring that employees speak only one language. Organisations develop systems such as performance evaluation and incentive programmes that reinforce the values of the dominant group. By universally applying the values of the majority group throughout the organisation, assimilation tends to perpetuate false stereotypes and prejudices. Employees who are different are expected to meet the standards for dominant group members.

STEREOTYPING

One of the biggest obstacles in managing diversity is stereotyping. People entering organisations bring their own assumptions and preconceptions with them and they use those ideas to form new impressions about other groups in the organisation and society. Harré and Lamb (1986) state that stereotypes are 'usually considered to be oversimplified, rigid, and generalised beliefs about groups of people in which all individuals from the same group are regarded as having the same set of leading characteristics.' Adherence to stereotypes leads to certain groups being treated differently from others.

One of the effects of stereotyping, therefore, is to deny individual uniqueness. A person is often responded to only as a member of a group instead of an individual with his or her own unique characteristics. Managing diversity means attempting to break down stereotypes and make people aware of their dangers.

IMPLEMENTING A DIVERSITY STRATEGY

Kandola and Fullerton (2001) note that eleven models for managing diversity have been identified in the literature. These models overlap to a great extent, but no two are identical. Several recent models suggest a developmental process for the implementation of diversity management programmes in organisations. A current approach developed by Wilson (1997) uses a scale he refers to as an equity continuum to place organisations in terms of their practices in dealing with issues of fairness to employees.

Wilson's continuum is based on an earlier framework developed by Schwartz (1992) from her studies of the progress of women into positions of influence in companies in the US. Schwartz found that the companies she had exposure to fell into patterns in terms of their motivation to develop opportunities for women. She identified six stages, which she labelled unaware, regulatory, morality, multiple initiatives, levelling field and true equality.

THE SCHWARTZ MODEL

Generally, Schwartz labelled companies that believed they simply had no problem as 'unaware'. In such companies, she believed there was little appreciation of any benefit they might derive from developing women, describing them as dead to the issue. In some companies there were policies and tracking systems in place to satisfy labour laws, but no initiatives to respond to women's needs. Schwartz categorised these as 'regulatory'. A third category where women's needs were beginning to be perceived as important and where a few policies related to child care and part-time jobs at the clerical level were in place she categorised as driven by 'morality'. The next pattern in the spectrum that she identified appeared in organisations that had 'multiple initiatives' to promote women. These organisations tended to focus on acceptance and valuing talent across cultural and other differences, broadening the focus beyond the promotion and development of women. Finally, there was a stage wherein she saw a few organisations trying to move toward a 'level playing field'. Schwartz also suggested a stage beyond the level playing field, which she labelled as 'true equality'. She suggests that this state is an unreachable, utopian one in the context of current thinking in organisations.

THE WILSON MODEL

Wilson (1997) built on Schwartz's model to develop a scale he refers to as an equity continuum. The continuum, similar to Schwartz's, is based on the underlying motivations for organisations' adoption of equitable employment practices. Wilson's stages, again based on Schwartz's, include zeros (No Problem Here!), ones (Legislated Fairness, or the Sheriff is on the Corner), twos (Good Corporate Citizens), threes (The Business Reasons), fours (Transition) and fives (Still Only a Goal). Wilson found that approximately fifty per cent of organisations in his Canadian study could be classified as being between stages 0 and 1, that is, between lacking awareness that human resource diversity is an issue at all and complying with labour legislation. None of the organisations in his sample were in the level 4–5 stage, the 'mythical stage' where employment systems are equitable in the perception of the employees themselves.

Some models focus entirely on the process that should be followed in successfully managing diversity, while others include a mix of both process and content, i.e. the initiatives that should be put in place. A synopsis of the models would indicate the following core process:

- audit the current situation: culture, attitudes, systems and procedures;
- identify aspects that hinder managing diversity;
- implement a strategy to eradicate the hindrances; and
- continually evaluate progress of the managing diversity strategy.

Kandola and Fullerton's (2001) model outlines eight elements as separate components that should be looked upon as the range of activities that need to permeate the entire organisation if managing diversity is to be successful. Each element has its own specific focus, but the model itself should not be seen as sequential. The eight elements are as follows.

Organisational Vision

If diversity is to become a business issue then the organisation must have a clear vision of what it intends to achieve and why this vision is important. Thomas (1990) claims that the vision an organisation needs to communicate is one of fully harnessing the needs of every employee. The vision should encapsulate the principles of managing diversity, communicating a shared vision of where the organisation is going and the expected rewards. If managing diversity is to be accepted as an organisation-wide concern then the vision and policy must be seen to actively support the business goals.

Top Management Commitment

McEnrue's (1993) model for managing diversity suggests the following three reasons for gaining commitment from top management.

- It communicates a vision that motivates employees by focusing their energy on a common goal.
- Only top management are in a position to ensure that all the initiatives concerning key management processes, i.e. recruitment, selection, induction, appraisal, promotion, are initiated, co-ordinated and monitored.
- A commitment of time and resources is required, which will often need to be sanctioned by top management. Senior management commitment needs to be visible, active and ongoing. Employees need to be aware of the commitment – it must be clearly communicated not only in writing but also in actions.

Auditing and Assessment of Needs

When setting out to manage diversity, a first step for organisations is to take a look at their culture, the systems and procedures in operation and the composition of their human resources, which requires collecting data and auditing the key management processes.

Cox and Blake (1991) state that this research stage is necessary for the following reasons:

- it identifies issues to be addressed in diversity awareness;
- it identifies areas where changes are needed and gives suggestions on how to make them; and
- it provides useful baseline data for the evaluation stage.

Another reason for conducting a managing diversity check on the organisation is that it aims to uncover sources of potential bias and ways in which the organisational culture, structure and processes can overtly and covertly discriminate against certain individuals. However, it is important to note that the auditing and assessing element of the model is an ongoing activity, not a discrete first stage. The data uncovered provides both a starting point and a baseline against which to measure progress.

Clarity of Objectives

Having identified the areas that require attention, it is necessary to establish the objectives for implementation. A coherent strategy must have clear, quantifiable objectives with set timescales. Only then can progress be measured and reviewed in a consistent fashion.

Objectives and action plans reinforce a strategic approach where ownership is organisation wide. Given that the objectives are based on the information gathered from the workforce, a strong sense of support and commitment to the objectives should result, which will be strengthened through effective communication of the objectives.

Clear Accountability

Once actions have been initiated, accountability must be established. If diversity is to be effectively implemented, the diversity policies and strategies need to be properly understood by employees. Accountability must extend across the entire organisation. Every employee should not only be aware of what is required of them, but they should also be accountable for their responsibilities in the implementation of initiatives. Cox and Blake (1991) advocate the importance of accountability and claim that managing diversity should be no different from any other business activity – there must be key people at all levels of the organisation who will support and guide the change. Traditionally these people have been human resource professionals, but they should not hold exclusive responsibility for managing diversity.

Effective Communication

To be effective, communication regarding managing diversity must ensure that all employees have a full understanding of the issues, the organisational vision and the benefits to be gained. Staff need to be continually updated on progress, and feedback on how to proceed should be solicited from them. Communication on progress to all employees also serves to enhance confidence in senior management commitment and will go a long way to reduce scepticism that diversity is just another initiative that will go nowhere.

Co-ordination of Activity

While top management commitment is essential, the implementation of the strategy needs to be co-ordinated either by individuals or groups at all levels of the organisation. It is important that a co-ordinator role be established for the efficient implementation of the strategy. Cox and Blake (1991) and Harris and Kleiner (1993) believe that 'diversity champions' are needed, especially at lower organisational levels to ensure cross-functional and hierarchical involvement. Champions should be known throughout the organisation and their role clearly communicated to emphasise that they are not responsible solely for managing diversity, but rather for managing it effectively and smoothly.

Evaluation

Evaluation should be regarded as an ongoing process, constantly reviewing progress of the managing diversity strategy towards the realisation of the vision. Continuous evaluation also ensures that information is fed back on an ongoing basis. This information can be acted upon quickly in order to realign actions or initiatives where necessary.

The information gathered during the evaluation should not be retained by management – if diversity is to be the responsibility of all employees, then they too should receive this information. Information on progress will serve as a reminder of the importance of diversity and may also elicit feedback from staff on how to proceed.

In order to ascertain that an organisation has implemented its policy, it is essential that it addresses eight key areas of its business – it is within these areas that a check can be made to ensure that diversity is in practice:

- marketing, sales and customer service;
- recruitment;
- retention of talent;
- enhanced productivity;
- management of teams;
- globalisation;
- adherence to legislation, including EU directives; and
- ethical and social factors.

In summary, Kandola and Fullerton (2001) suggest that managing diversity must pervade the entire organisation if it is to be successful. They propose a MOSAIC vision, which summarises the key characteristics of the diversity-oriented organisation. MOSAIC is an acronym for Mission and values, Objective and fair processes, Skilled workforce: aware and fair, Active flexibility, Individual focus and Culture that empowers. In highlighting these key characteristics it is clear that the focus becomes that of ensuring all individuals within an organisation can maximise their potential, regardless of any groups they may belong to.

THE ROLE OF HUMAN RESOURCE MANAGEMENT

Human resource management has been generally defined as the process of placing the right people with the right skills in the right place at the right time, with the right motivation to achieve organisational objectives (Schuler *et al*. 1987). Of special concern to human resource management is ensuring that those individuals selected for employment are moulded into the type of employees who can abide by the organisation's corporate culture (Pascale 1985). The ultimate purpose of this moulding process is to change the values of those selected to match the value system subscribed to by the organisation's corporate culture (Higgins 1991). Cross-cultural research suggests that current human resource management models neglect the potential impact that diversity might have on organisations (Laurent 1983). The research further suggests that human resource managers are of the opinion that a strong corporate culture moderates the effect of diverse values that individuals bring to the workplace. The assumption is that employees, even if they are from different ethnic, cultural or racial backgrounds, leave their socially instilled values at the doorway as they enter the workplace. If they do not, the assumption is that the prevailing corporate culture will neutralise potential influences that their values might have on the organisation's value system. Subsequently, new employees are expected to respond to situations within the organisation in ways that are consistent with the prevailing value system (Hopkins 1997).

The issues of globalisation, ethics in business and workforce diversity underpin the human resource function and the human resource manager needs to raise the subjects in the many areas associated with the employment of people. It is particularly applicable in the twenty-first century, where there has been a change of emphasis from personnel management to human resource management.

THE IMPACT OF DIVERSITY ON ORGANISATIONS

Diversity can have a significant impact on organisations, as it provides both opportunities and challenges. Many organisations are finding that diversity can be a source of competitive advantage in the marketplace. Organisations that manage diversity effectively will become known among minorities as good places to work, and in turn these organisations will generally have lower levels of turnover and absenteeism.

Organisations with diverse workforces will also be better able to understand different market segments than less diverse organisations. If an organisation is dominated by one population segment, it follows that its employees will generally adhere to norms and ways of thinking that reflect that segment. The diverse organisation, however, will be characterised by multiple perspectives and will be more likely to be more creative and generate new ideas and ways of doing things.

According to Joplin and Daus (1997), however, diversity in an organisation can also become a major source of conflict, which can arise for various reasons. One potential avenue for conflict is when an individual thinks that someone has been hired, promoted or fired because of his or her diversity status. Suppose a male manager, for example, loses a promotion to a female manager. If he believes that she was promoted because the organisation simply wanted to have more female managers rather than because she was the better candidate for the job, he will likely feel resentment towards both her and the organisation.

DeNisi and Griffin (2001) conclude that managers need to appreciate the numerous positive benefits of diversity. In addition, though, they should also recognise that it can be a serious source of conflict and must be prepared to address any and all diversity-related issues that might arise in the organisation.

ONGOING DEBATES/ADVANCED CONCEPTS IN MANAGING DIVERSITY

MANAGING DIVERSITY IN IRELAND: IMPLEMENTING THE EMPLOYMENT EQUALITY ACT 1998 AND THE EQUAL STATUS ACT 2000

The Employment Equality Act 1998 is arguably one of the most wide-ranging single pieces of legislation of its type in the world (Fullerton and Kandola 1999). The new Act replaces and repeals the 1974 and 1977 Acts. When the earlier legislation was introduced it was against a background of discrimination against women. The Anti-Discrimination (Pay) Act

1974 was brought in specifically to address the issue of women being paid at lower rates, even though they may be carrying out the same work. The Employment Equality Act of 1977 was introduced to tackle non-pay matters and to outlaw employment discrimination on the grounds of sex and/or marital status. The new Acts, however, recognise not only that other forms of discrimination exist, but also that there is much greater pressure within society generally that all forms of unfair discrimination should not be tolerated.

The Acts describe discrimination as the treatment of one person in a way that is less favourable than that in which another person is, has been or would be treated. The Acts cover employees in both the public and private sectors as well as applicants for employment and training. Discrimination is outlawed on nine distinct grounds.

1. **Gender.**
2. **Marital status:** Marital status means single, married, separated, divorced or widowed. Single people are included for the first time, which means that benefits that have typically been provided for the employee and their spouse could now be considered discriminatory.
3. **Family status:** Family status has been defined as having responsibility either as a parent or as a person *in loco parentis* for someone below eighteen years of age or as a parent or resident primary carer for someone over eighteen years with a disability who requires a high degree of support and attention.
4. **Sexual orientation:** This covers heterosexual, homosexual or bisexual orientation.
5. **Religious beliefs:** This includes religious background or outlook.
6. **Age:** This covers people between the ages of eighteen and sixty-five.
7. **Disability:** The act defines disability as:
   (a) 'the total or partial absence of a person's bodily or mental function, including the absence of a part of a person's body;
   (b) the presence in the body of organisms causing, or likely to cause, chronic disease or illness;
   (c) the malfunction, malformation or disfigurement of a part of a person's body;
   (d) a condition or malfunction which results in a person learning differently from a person without the condition or malfunction;
   (e) a condition, illness or disease which affects a person's thought processes, perception of reality, emotions or judgement or which results in disturbed behaviour' (Section 2 1 – 1998 Act).
8. **Race:** This includes race, colour, nationality, ethnic or national origins.
9. **Membership of the Traveller community**.

THE EQUALITY AUTHORITY

The Equality Authority replaces the Employment Equality Agency and is charged with a statutory duty to work towards the elimination of discrimination and the promotion of equality of opportunity in employment on the nine discriminatory grounds covered by the Act.

Codes of practice developed by the new Authority will have a legal basis for the first time, which means that they will be admissible in evidence and taken into account in determining any relevant case. The Authority will also have new powers to carry out equality reviews. Taken together, these powers mean the new Authority will be able to be more proactive in ensuring that issues of equality are taken seriously in organisations.

Hill and Stapleton v. Revenue Commissioners and Department of Finance [1998] IRLR 466.

Ms Hill and Ms Stapleton were employed as clerical assistants in the Revenue Commissioners. Ms Hill worked in a full-time capacity from 1981 to 1988, when she began job-sharing (half-time). Ms Stapleton was recruited into a job-sharing position (half-time) in 1986. The job-sharing scheme provided that each employee would move one point up the incremental pay scale with each year of service and that they were paid 50 percent of salary applicable to the point they had reached on the scale.

The full-time scheme treated each year's job share as only equivalent to six months full-time employment. Because of this, when Ms Hill and Ms Stapleton took up full-time employment, they were placed on a lower point of the full-time scale than they otherwise would have been.

They claimed that equating two years' job-sharing service to one year's full-time service constituted indirect sex discrimination on the basis that more female workers than male workers spent part of their working lives in a job-sharing capacity.

The European Court of Justice found in their favour, stating:

> Rules which treat full-time workers who previously job-shared at a disadvantage compared with other full-time workers by applying a criterion of service calculated by length of time actually worked in a post and therefore placing them on the full-time pay scale at a level lower than that which they occupied on the pay scale applicable to job-sharing must, in principle, be treated as contrary to Article 119 and the Equal Pay Directive where 98 percent of those employed under job-sharing contracts are women.

The court went on to state: 'Nor was it relevant that there was an established practice within the Civil Service of crediting only actual service …'. This highlights the need to monitor all systems in relation to their impact on certain groups. A historic criteria, valid in a particular area at a particular point in time, does not ensure its wide-ranging applicability or long-term relevance.

Source: Fullerton and Kandola (1999)

SOCIAL AND MORAL OBLIGATIONS TOWARDS DIVERSITY

If the rationale is that business organisations have a social responsibility to increase their profits (Friedman 1970) and if a diverse workforce will help organisations to be more competitive and thus more profitable, then organisations are being socially responsible as well as fulfilling a moral obligation by promoting diversity (Hopkins 1997). On the other hand, some organisations believe that they do not have a moral obligation to promote diversity. The belief is that whether the goal is equal performance (in terms of competitiveness and profitability) or superior performance, the way to achieve this goal is to stop treating diversity as a moral issue and start treating it as a business issue (Gordon 1992). It might be argued, however, that these two issues are inextricably linked. For example, social responsibility is fundamentally an ethical concept and the very term 'responsibility' has moral overtones, implying that business organisations have an obligation to someone or something. Therefore, when organisations engage in socially responsible behaviour by promoting diversity, they are not only addressing a business issue but a moral issue as well. Moreover, whether they act voluntarily or in response to societal or regulatory pressures, when organisations act in a socially responsible manner towards diversity they are essentially demonstrating their moral, if not legal, obligation to diversity (Hopkins 1997).

MULTICULTURAL, DIVERSE ORGANISATIONS

Because workforces are becoming increasingly more diverse, organisational cultures must integrate systems effectively to motivate, maintain productivity and use diversity as a resourceful, competitive advantage. Essentially, a major aim of an organisation-wide cultural diversity programme is to create a multicultural organisation. A multicultural organisation not only has a diverse cultural workforce, it also values diversity. A multicultural organisation has the following characteristics.

A Culture that Fosters and Values Cultural Differences

Creating an effective multicultural organisation involves creating an environment and climate in which all members can excel. This is done through hiring and promoting people who endorse the organisation's values, reinforcing and instilling these values in performance and evaluation systems and communicating with and educating all employees.

Using Pluralism to Acculturate Employees

Using pluralism as an acculturation process involves integrating minority culture perspectives into core organisational values and norms. This is accomplished through such programmes as valuing diversity and language training, new employee induction programmes and explicitly managing diversity in mission statements.

Instilling Structural Integration and Informal Networks

Creating integration in the organisation means blending the community with the organisation, which involves incorporating diversity into major committees and implementing affirmative action, education and targeted career-development programmes. Informal integrating networks are accomplished through company-initiated mentoring programmes and social events.

Eradicating Institutional Bias

Changing institutional bias involves auditing and changing inequities in reward, appraisal, benefits and performance systems. Such policies and procedures as hiring, training and retraining, promoting, child care arrangements, work schedules and parental leave should have no biases in their process or content. Also, performance regarding the management of diversity goals and processes should be included in the policies and procedures.

Managing Intergroup Conflict

A multicultural organisation must minimise interpersonal and intergroup conflicts related to group identity and must promote understanding of cultural differences. This goal may be addressed through conflict management and resolution training, which focus on identifying and stripping stereotypes and assumptions about out-groups, enhancing relationships, training awareness and personal empowerment (Weiss 1996).

SUMMARY OF KEY PROPOSITIONS

- This chapter explored the concept of diversity, which enables every employee to perform to his or her potential. The primary and secondary dimensions of diversity were discussed, the main difference being that primary dimensions are more permanent than secondary dimensions.
- Diversity differs from discrimination in that discrimination treats employees differently because of prejudice. Diversity also differs from equal opportunities in that equal opportunities are designed to correct an imbalance.
- The changing workforce suggests that managing diversity is a key challenge for human resource managers in particular, as organisations are moving from the traditional personnel management to the more modern concept of human resource management.
- To implement a diversity strategy, organisations need to audit their current situation, identify aspects that hinder managing diversity and subsequently implement the strategy to eradicate these hindrances. The strategy's progress should then be continually evaluated.

DISCUSSION/SELF-ASSESSMENT QUESTIONS

1. Outline the differences between the primary and secondary dimensions of diversity. Which particular dimension seems to be the most difficult for organisations to deal with?
2. Explain how managing diversity could lead to an organisation gaining competitive advantage.
3. Discuss the role of the human resource manager in implementing a diversity strategy.
4. What are the main reasons for the workforce becoming increasingly diverse?
5. What is the difference between assimilation of minority groups and valuing diversity in organisations?

MULTIPLE CHOICE QUESTIONS

1. Which of the following would *not* be included in primary dimensions of diversity?
   (a) Age.
   (b) Gender.
   (c) Income.
   (d) Race.

2. Which of the following would *not* be included in secondary dimensions of diversity?
   (a) Marital status.
   (b) Religious beliefs.
   (c) Work experience.
   (d) Ethnicity.

3. Assimilation is the process through which:
   (a) Minority groups are forced to learn the ways of the dominant group.
   (b) Minority groups are valued for their differences.
   (c) Minority views are welcomed and encouraged.
   (d) The similarity of minority views is considered important.

4. Stereotyping is:
   (a) Valuing individualism.
   (b) Generalising about individuals.
   (c) Managing diversity.
   (d) Valuing diversity.

5. Valuing diversity means:
   (a) All employees must assimilate.
   (b) Treating all employees as individuals.
   (c) Making judgments about employees.
   (d) Stereotyping employees.

6. Equal opportunity initiatives were begun in order to:
   (a) Correct an imbalance.
   (b) Assimilate employees.
   (c) Create stereotypes.
   (d) Encourage prejudices.

7. Secondary dimensions of diversity:
   (a) Can be adapted or changed.
   (b) Are inborn.
   (c) Are based on race and ethnicity.
   (d) Are gender specific.

8. Primary dimensions of diversity:
   (a) Can be adapted or changed.
   (b) Are inborn.
   (c) Are based on educational background.
   (d) Are based on work experience.

9. Diverse organisations encourage employees to:
    (a) Perform to their potential.
    (b) Reinforce beliefs about superiority and inferiority.
    (c) Make judgments about others, ignoring individuality.
    (d) Learn the ways of the majority.

10. Implementing a diversity strategy is generally done by:
    (a) The marketing manager.
    (b) The human resource manager.
    (c) The public relations manager.
    (d) The finance manager.

11. In implementing a diversity strategy, which of the following is *not* included?
    (a) Vision.
    (b) Top management commitment.
    (c) Assessment of needs.
    (d) No co-ordination of activities.

12. Discrimination is:
    (a) Prejudicial treatment of certain categories of employees.
    (b) Valuing employees' individualism.
    (c) Correcting an imbalance.
    (d) Enabling employees to perform to their potential.

13. Valuing diversity is often brought about because of:
    (a) A move from personnel management to human resource management.
    (b) A move from human resource management to personnel management.
    (c) Treating people like the majority group.
    (d) Employees with similar backgrounds.

14. Which of the following factors is *not* part of the changing workforce?
    (a) Gender.
    (b) Ethnic minorities.
    (c) Age.
    (d) Decline in international business.

15. The implementation of a diversity strategy requires commitment from:
    (a) Top management.
    (b) Customers.
    (c) Competitors.
    (d) Stereotyped employees.

16. Which of the following is *not* part of implementing a diversity strategy?
    (a) Clarity of objectives.
    (b) Co-ordination of activities.
    (c) Evaluation.
    (d) Non-communication.

17. Diversity workforce management requires:
    (a) A strategic organisational approach.

(b) Commitment from human resource management only.

(c) Affirmative action.

(d) Giving preferential treatment to some employees.

18. Evaluating a diversity strategy does *not* include:

(a) Feedback.

(b) Reassessing organisational needs.

(c) Communication.

(d) Stereotyping.

19. Managers need to recognise that employees from different backgrounds are:

(a) Totally similar.

(b) Not at all similar.

(c) Similar in some respects and different in others.

(d) Totally different.

20. The primary dimensions of diversity:

(a) Exert extraordinary influence on early socialisation.

(b) Are less permanent.

(c) Can be changed.

(d) Can be assimilated.

FIVE SUGGESTED KEY READINGS

Cox, T.H. and Blake, S., 'Managing cultural diversity: implications for organizational competitiveness', *Academy of Management Executive*, V (1991), 45–56.

Jackson, S.E., *Diversity in the Workplace: Human Resource Initiatives*, New York: The Guildford Press 1992.

Kandola, R. and Fullerton, J., *Diversity in Action: Managing the Mosaic*, London: Chartered Institute of Personnel and Development 2001.

Point, S. and Singh, V., 'Defining and dimensionalising diversity: evidence from corporate websites across Europe', *European Journal of Management*, XXI/6 (2003), 750–61.

Powell, G.N., 'One more time: do female and male managers differ?', *Academy of Management Executive* (August 1990), 68–76.

REFERENCES

Arredondo, P., *Successful Diversity Management Initiatives: A Blueprint for Planning and Implementation*, London: Sage 1996.

Cox, T.H. and Blake, S., 'Managing cultural diversity: implications for organizational competitiveness', *Academy of Management Executive*, V (1991), 45–56.

DeNisi, A.S. and Griffin, R.W., *Human Resource Management*, New York: Houghton Mifflin 2001.

Digh, P., 'Coming to terms with diversity', *HR Magazine* (November 1998), 1–5.

Friedman, M., 'The social responsibility of business is to increase its profits', *New York Times Magazine* (13 September 1970), 122–6.

Fullerton, J. and Kandola, R., *Managing Diversity in Ireland: Implementing the Employment Equality Act 1998*, Dublin: Oak Tree Press 1999.

Gordon, J., 'Rethinking diversity', *Training Magazine* (January 1992), 1–9.

Harré, R. and Lamb, R., *The Dictionary of Personality and Social Psychology*, Oxford: Blackwell 1986.

Harris, D.S. and Kleiner, B.H., 'Managing and valuing diversity in the workplace', *Equal Opportunities International*, XII/4 (1993), 6–9.

Higgins, J.M., *The Management Challenge*, New York: Macmillan 1991.

Hopkins, W.E., *Ethical Dimensions of Diversity*, London: Sage 1997.

Jackson, S.E., *Diversity in the Workplace: Human Resource Initiatives*, New York: The Guildford Press 1992.

Johnston, W.B. and Packer, A.H., *Workforce 2000: Work and Workers for the 21st Century*, Indianapolis, IN: The Hudson Institute 1987.

Joplin, J.R.W. and Daus, C.S., 'Challenges of leading a diverse workforce', *Academy of Management Executive*, (August 1997), 32–44.

Kandola, R. and Fullerton, J., *Diversity in Action: Managing the Mosaic*, London: CIPD 2001.

Laurent, A., 'The cultural diversity of Western conceptions of management', *International Studies of Management and Organization*, XIII (1983), 75–96.

McEnrue, M.P., 'Managing diversity: Los Angeles before and after the riots', *Organizational Dynamics*, XXI/3 (Winter 1993), 18–29.

Pascale, R.T., 'The paradox of culture: reconciling ourselves to socialization', *California Management Review*, XXVII (1985), 26–41.

Point, S. and Singh, V., 'Defining and dimensionalising diversity: evidence from corporate websites across Europe', *European Journal of Management*, XXI/6 (2003), 750–61.

Powell, G.N., 'One more time: do female and male managers differ?', *Academy of Management Executive* (August 1990), 68–76.

Ross, R. and Schneider, R., *From Equality to Diversity – A Business Case for Equal Opportunities*, London: Pitman Publishing 1992.

Schuler, R.S., Galiente, S.P. and Jackson, S.E., 'Matching effective human resource practices with competitive strategy', *Personne* (September 1987), 18–27.

Schwartz, F., *Breaking with Tradition: Women and Work, The New Facts of Life*, New York: Warner 1992.

Shaw, J. and Perrons, D. (eds), *Making Gender Work: Managing Equal Opportunities*, Buckingham: Open University Press 1995.

Talbot-Allan, L., 'Measuring the impact of diversity', *CMA Magazine* (June 1996).

Thomas, R.R., 'From affirmative action to affirming diversity', *Harvard Business Review* (March/April 1990), 107–17.

Thornberg, L., 'Journey towards a more inclusive culture', *HR Magazine* (February 1994), 79–96.

Weiss, J.W., *Organizational Behavior and Change: Managing Diversity, Cross-Cultural Dynamics, and Ethics*, New York: West Publishing 1996.

Wilson, T., *Diversity at Work*, Toronto: John Wiley & Sons 1997.

WOMEN IN ORGANISATIONS

Learning Objectives

- To assess the impact of the glass ceiling for women in organisations.

- To identify the overt and covert barriers that hinder women from attaining senior positions in organisations.

- To illustrate the strategies used by women in organisations for career advancement.

- To understand the benefits of mentoring and networking for women in organisations.

- To recognise the factors that contribute to different career development processes for men and women in organisations.

INTRODUCTION

Since 1994 there has been a gradual increase in the percentage of women in the workforce in almost all countries in the Western hemisphere. A study conducted by Whirlpool Foundation (1996) noted that the 'biggest change in the nature of the European labour force is the tremendous increase in women's participation within the past decade, and the permanence of that change.' Until the late 1970s, women managers were virtually invisible in most countries. As Ho (1984: 7) observes:

> Statistics show that women represent one-third of the world's workforce, do two-thirds of the world's working hours, but they earn only one-tenth of the world's income and own one-hundredth of the world's goods ... they hold less than one percent of the world's executive positions.

While it seems relatively easy for women to gain employment at the lower levels of the organisation, it is proving very difficult for them to reach upper, middle and senior management positions. To understand why women have not been more successful in moving up to higher managerial positions, it is useful to examine the mechanisms through which power is acquired, maintained and exercised in organisations. Arroba and James (1987) suggest that sources of power in organisations are frequently biased towards men, which is the result of generations of socialisation and internalisation effects that produce organisational structures, norms and cultures with inbuilt power balances towards men. As Arroba and James note, 'organisations are designed and run by men and therefore the prevailing culture tends to be alien to women.' Similarly, Still (1994) maintains that 'enough evidence now exists to prove that organisational culture is a major impediment to women's progress into senior management because of the gender bias of the culture.' She also suggests that all organisations embody a male managerial culture because when both organisations and management systems were first formed, only males were in the workforce, leading to what Kanter (1977) describes as organisational structure that has been constructed to exacerbate and exploit gender differences.

Despite the advent of women into both the workforce and management and the introduction of anti-discrimination, equal opportunity and affirmative action laws, Still (1994: 4) notes that 'there has been little fundamental change to the underlying culture.' This culture can work against women in many ways, for instance, by organising opportunity structures and career progression in ways that enable men to achieve positions of prestige and power more easily than women. Because it is a culture rather than a formal visible structure that is biasing power, it becomes more difficult to change through legislation.

Cross-cultural studies and reviews that have been undertaken in order to compare males and females in organisations in terms of managerial efficiency and performance have produced results which reveal that there are far more similarities than differences in terms of managerial efficiency and performance. Where differences do occur, they tend to be found not so much in the way each gender 'manages', but stem from factors associated with the low proportion of female managers, attitudinal differences, prejudices, discrimination and different life circumstances and stresses of female managers in comparison to male managers. Many of these differences are regarded as negative and therefore hamper women's career advancements in organisations.

DEFINITIONS OF KEY CONCEPTS

Glass ceiling
Invisible barriers preventing women from gaining senior positions.

Having it all
Having a successful career, personal relationship and children.

Work-family conflict
When work and family roles are mutually incompatible.

Mentoring
Support, information and advice given from a senior to a junior person.

Tokens
Members of minority groups in organisations.

Networking
Peer relationship support.

THE GLASS CEILING

As more women enter the workforce, their failure to reach the highest management positions has become the cause for considerable research and debate, both in their home countries and in international management. Women are better educated and hold more jobs worldwide than ever before, yet most women continue to suffer from occupational segregation in the workplace and rarely break through the so-called 'glass ceiling' separating them from senior-level management and professional positions.

In a number of countries, while women are gaining managerial experience, they still encounter a glass ceiling – a term used to describe 'a barrier so subtle that it is transparent, yet so strong that it prevents women and minorities from moving up the managerial hierarchy' (Morrison and Von Glinow 1990: 200). According to Morrison and Von Glinow, the glass ceiling is not simply a barrier based on the person's inability to handle a higher-level job, it 'applies to women as a group who are kept from advancing higher because they are women' (1990: 200). This ceiling represents a real barrier that is difficult to break but is also so subtle that it can be hard to see. In the case of the 'glass wall', lateral movement is also prevented. Jackson (2001) observes that once hired, women are initially placed in genderised fields, channelled into staff or highly technical or professional jobs that are not traditional positions that track to the top, resulting in a glass wall. Davidovich (2000) suggests the barriers that make up the glass ceiling are nothing but an insidious form of sex discrimination, in violation of law.

There are major organisational barriers that constitute the glass ceiling, including a lonely and non-supportive working environment, treating differences as weaknesses, excluding people from group activities because of their differences and failure to help individuals to prepare to balance work and personal life issues (Morrison 1997). According to Schwartz (1989), however, the metaphor of the glass ceiling is misleading, as it suggests an invisible barrier created by corporate leaders to hinder the promotion of women managers. Schwartz (1989: 68) believes that:

> A more appropriate metaphor would be the kind of a cross-sectional diagram used in geology. The barriers to women gaining senior management positions occur when potentially counterproductive layers of influence on women – maternity, tradition, socialisation – meet management strata pervaded by the largely unconscious preconceptions, stereotypes, and expectations of men. Such interfaces do not exist for men and tend to be impermeable for women.

The specific problems and pressures that have been identified as unique to female managers include burdens of coping with the role of the 'token' woman, being a test case for future women, lack of role models and feelings of isolation, strains of coping with prejudice and sex stereotyping and overt and indirect discrimination from fellow employees, employers and the organisational structure and climate (Linehan 2000). Summarising a review of stress literature, Burke and McKeen (1994) conclude that working women experience more stress than working men, and the sources of that stress are related to the expected and actual roles of women in society and to the fact that women still occupy minority status in organisations. Korac-Kakabadse and Kouzmin (1997) agree that the glass ceiling is an invisible barrier, but is a very real impediment when vying for career progression, particularly for ethnic, coloured and aboriginal women, adding that the barrier is concrete for such employees.

In relation to the glass ceiling, Powell (2000) suggests that the most basic force to be considered is the societal context. Throughout recorded history, a patriarchal social system in which the male has power and authority over the female has almost always prevailed. Women's presence in top management positions violates the norm of men's higher status and superiority to a greater extent than women's presence in lower-management positions. This norm is reinforced in more subtle ways in societies today, such as in stereotypes of what constitutes an effective leader and in the cognitive processes of decision makers.

Berthoin-Antal and Izraeli (1993), in a worldwide overview of women in management, state that 'probably the single most important hurdle for women in management in all industrialised countries is the persistent stereotype that associates management with being male' (1993: 63). Similarly, Schwartz (1989) summarises that 'to think manager equals think male' and adds that:

> Men continue to perceive women as the rearers of their children so they find it understandable, indeed appropriate, that women should renounce their careers to raise families … Not only do they see parenting as fundamentally female, they see a career as fundamentally male (1989: 67).

Female entrepreneur and founder of The Body Shop, Anita Roddick, states:

> I don't believe that the proverbial glass ceiling is going to be shattered in my lifetime. Some reports indicate that if women continue to progress in business at the current rate, it will be 500 years before they have equal managerial status in the world, then another 475 years before they hold equal political and economic status to men. Nearly 1,000 years to go isn't progress (Roddick 2000: 115).

Research has indicated that women in lower management levels are likely to encounter the glass ceiling, thus preventing their advancement into middle management. However, Simpson and Altman (2000) suggest that the glass ceiling may now be 'punctured', thereby allowing some women to progress upwards. Their research suggests that young women may find it easier to override barriers lower down in the organisation and perhaps reap the rewards in the earlier stages of their careers. At the senior levels of management, however, the glass ceiling intensifies as networks and the 'men's club' become increasingly important in facilitating further progress. Simpson and Altman conclude that career barriers up to a certain stage in the hierarchy may be broken down by some women, but above that level women may encounter more intractable barriers that are difficult to overcome.

Wirth (2001) reports that almost universally, women have failed to reach leading positions in major corporations and private sector organisations, irrespective of their abilities. She concludes that despite recent progress, the glass ceiling is still relatively intact.

Breaking Through the Glass Ceiling

According to national surveys, women's overall share of management jobs rarely exceeds twenty per cent. The higher the position, the more glaring the gender gap. In the largest and most powerful organisations the proportion of top positions going to women is generally two to three per cent.

Breaking the glass ceiling, therefore, is a significant challenge for women, especially given that the gatekeepers and power brokers in organisations tend to be white males (Smith 2000). In his analysis of how to reduce sex stereotyping and promote egalitarian male-female relationships in management, Maier (1993: 290) indicates what must occur for women to advance:

> For women, as a group, to break the glass ceiling depends on the extent to which men are prepared to work with them as equals, offering them the same types of informal as well as formal supports that men have themselves historically relied on for advancement. For this to happen, men have to assume an active role as equal team-mates and allies of women, which requires identifying compelling reasons to do so.

Research conducted by Linehan (2000) with fifty women, all of whom reached senior management positions, indicates that the glass ceiling is still in place for women in organisations in all countries. The women believe that they broke through the glass ceiling in their own careers because they are as well qualified, or in some cases more qualified, more ambitious and more mobile, than male managers. In addition to these traits, they persistently asked for their next career move, rather than waiting for it to be offered, and were better than their male counterparts at balancing a number of functions at the same time. The women suggested that they developed this ability of balancing a number of functions simultaneously from their childhood experiences and their socialisation as children. They recalled from their childhood socialisation their fathers being singularly focused on work outside the home, whereas their mothers needed to develop the ability to balance a number of different responsibilities.

An IBEC (2002) report outlines a range of practical measures which could be adopted to help with the advancement of women's careers.

- A number of recruitment and promotion measures, such as establishing procedures to make recruitment and promotion more objective and making the recruitment and promotion process more structured and transparent.
- Potential positive action measures, such as setting up a task force to identify and remove barriers, put an action plan in place and assign deadlines for meeting targets and instructing recruitment officers and agencies to make special efforts to find women candidates.
- Equal opportunity measures, including launching an executive development

programme with the objective of providing equal development opportunities for all employees, ensuring that performance assessment procedures use neutral and measurable criteria and making employment and development policies gender neutral.

- A focus on diversity management. It is suggested that determinants of a diversity programme could include strong senior management support, an assessment and modification of organisational culture, the provision of education and training and the development of the business case for promoting diversity, inclusion and equal opportunity.

- Training measures which would increase the pool of qualified women. Companies could identify potential women managers and ensure that they receive 'cross-training' (training in different areas to gain broad experience) to equip them with higher line management skills, remedy any factors that might limit women's access to training and provide equal opportunities training.

- Family-friendly and work-life balance policies, which are viewed as important for bridging the gender divide, as are career tracking and mentoring. Career tracking involves identifying women with high potential and helping them gain experience through challenging and high-profile assignments. It is suggested that mentoring could take the form of a planned long-term corporate mentoring programme for talented individuals.

Table 18.1 shows the factors that women in Europe believe are important for improving women's advancement at different management levels.

Table 18.1 Factors Women in Europe Believe Are Important for Improving Women's Advancement in Management

Factors	Junior Management	Middle Management	Senior Management
Equal opportunity programme	41%	39%	29%
Company child care	44%	36%	24%
Special courses for women managers	78%	68%	43%
Revised selection or promotion process	24%	33%	41%
Mentoring	39%	47%	46%
Quotas for female representation	13%	14%	22%
Reducing workload	10%	16%	13%

Source: Women in Management in Irish Business (IBEC)

The table indicates that women in junior and middle management positions would appear to favour special courses to support women in management, followed by company child care provision and mentoring. Women in senior management positions appear to favour mentoring, followed by special courses to support women in management and revised selection and promotion procedures. Success and commitment are two characteristics which are associated with breaking through the glass ceiling and are discussed below.

SUCCESS

Definitions of success are different for men and women. The informally accepted definition of success in an organisation tends to more closely match the one held by men. This often results in women being perceived as less ambitious. Interviews conducted by Vinnicombe and Harris (2000) with male and female managers in a major international service organisation showed that all of the women defined success in terms of achievement, personal recognition or influence, rather than 'material' career success. The content of their jobs was more important to them than their grade.

Most of the men believed that their position in the hierarchy was a measure of their career success, either through status or influence. The strongest differences between men and women were in external material criteria, such as position and pay. While not irrelevant to women, these factors were never central to their descriptions of career success. Men, however, saw these as central and indispensable markers of success related to the status they wanted.

Men described hierarchical positions as targets for which they were aiming. Women, on the other hand, talked about progression in terms of meeting sets of challenges. They did not have the same 'survival of the fittest' mentality as men. Women also thought of career success as only one part of what they wanted to achieve in their lives. Balance was often described as part of their definition of success. While some of the men wanted balance, life success for them was essentially driven by career success.

COMMITMENT

Female managers are often reported as being less committed than their male counterparts. According to Vinnicombe and Harris (2000), informal organisational culture and a predominance of men in senior management tends to favour male definitions of commitment. Their research with male and female managers in England and Sweden revealed that the managers' definitions of commitment included active behaviours, such as task delivery, 'putting yourself out', involvement and quality.

While overall men's definitions of commitment were closer to top managers' definitions, top women's meanings were also similar to those of top men. They shared the concepts of being proactive, ready for a challenge, creative and business aware. Women also defined commitment more in terms of 'good citizenship', while men tended to talk about it in ways that benefited themselves as well as the organisation. Men and women also used different strategies to convey commitment. Men are more likely to work late, while more women may have child care commitments. Men tended to push more for career development and to talk more loudly about their work and to talk of their team's work as if it were solely their own achievement.

Previous research has shown that women often need to spell out to their managers that they want challenging assignments or it will be assumed that they are not interested. In essence, women's commitment is less visible than men's.

HAVING IT ALL

Research conducted by Hewlett (2002) reveals that at mid-life, between one-third and half of all successful career women in the US do not have children. In fact, thirty-three per cent of such women (business executives, doctors, lawyers, academics, etc.) in the 41–55 age bracket are childless – and that figure rises to forty-two per cent in corporate America. These women have not chosen to remain childless – the vast majority, in fact, yearn for children. Indeed, some have gone to extraordinary lengths to bring a baby into their lives. Hewlett's research indicates that for many women, the demands of ambitious careers, the asymmetries of male-female relationships and the difficulties of bearing children late in life conspire to diminish the possibility of having children.

Women in organisations pay a greater price for long hours spent at work because the early years of career building overlap almost perfectly with the prime years of childbearing. It is very difficult for women to hold back that stage of a career and expect to catch up later. When it comes to career and fatherhood, high-achieving men do not have to deal with difficult trade-offs – seventy-five per cent of men in Hewlett's survey have children. Only thirty-nine per cent of high-achieving men are married to women who are employed full time, while nine out of ten married women in the high-achieving category have husbands who are employed full time or self-employed.

Similar findings emerge from European research conducted by Linehan (2000). Forty-seven of the fifty senior women executives interviewed believed that it is more difficult for females than for their male counterparts to 'have it all', that is, a successful career, a good personal relationship and children. These managers believed that females are forced to choose between a career and marriage because of the extra responsibilities of balancing home and work life. They further suggested that men in organisations do not have to make the same sacrifices, as it is still generally accepted by organisations and society that the male breadwinner's career will be prioritised .

Hewlett (2002) believes that the challenge to employers is to craft more meaningful work-life policies. Professional women who want both a family and a career need reduced-hour jobs and careers that can be interrupted, neither of which is readily available yet. They also need to be able to partake of such benefits without suffering long-term damage to their careers. The high-achieving career women who participated in Hewlett's survey were asked to consider a list of policy options that would help them achieve long-term balance in their lives. They endorsed the following cluster of work-life policies that would make it much easier to get off conventional career ladders and eventually get back on.

- **A time bank of parenting leave:** This would allow for three months of paid leave, which could be taken as needed, until the child turned eighteen.
- **Restructured retirement plans:** In particular, women want to see the elimination of penalties for career interruptions.

- **Career breaks:** Such a leave of absence might span three years, unpaid, but with the assurance of a job when the time came to return to work.
- **Reduced-hour careers:** High-level jobs should be created that permit reduced hours and workloads on an ongoing basis but still offer the possibility of promotion.

A challenge to women in organisations is to convince employers that they are entitled to both a career and children. According to Hewlett (2002), even in organisations whose policies support women, prevailing attitudes and unrelenting job pressures undermine them. Women's lives have expanded, but the grudging attitudes of most company cultures weigh down and constrain what individual women feel is possible.

WOMEN IN IRISH ORGANISATIONS

A report from the Irish Business and Employers Confederation (IBEC) launched in 2002 highlights the increase in the labour market participation rate of women in Ireland, from twenty-eight per cent in 1971 to just over fifty per cent in 2001. In the period between 1971 and 2001, the number of females at work in Ireland grew by 140 per cent compared with twenty-seven per cent for men. The highest female participation rate is among women in the 25–34 age group (nearly seventy-seven per cent in 2001). The participation rate for married women is 46.4 per cent compared with 25.7 per cent in 1991. The increase in the female participation rate is attributed to factors such as higher educational attainment, falling fertility rates, the removal of the 'marriage bar' in public service, equality legislation and higher earning capacity for women.

Despite women's high level of participation in the workforce, female CEOs are in a remarkably small minority in Ireland's top 1,000 companies. There are only ten women chief executives in the *Business & Finance* top 1,000 companies, and there is only one in the top ten (Corcoran 2002). Similarly, IBEC's *Women in Management in Irish Business* (2002) shows that women continue to be under-represented at senior management level in Ireland. In a survey of 6,000 managerial/professional people, it found that eight per cent of chief executives, twenty-one per cent of senior management and thirty per cent of middle managers were women. When these three categories are combined, women make up only a quarter of all managers, while making up half of the working population. However, Harrison, director of social policy at IBEC, acknowledges that these figures are somewhat skewed as the sample of 6,000 companies included a considerable number of small and medium-sized enterprises. Therefore, Harrison believes that 'among Ireland's large companies the figure is closer to 3 percent for senior managers, and very little has changed over the last few years' (in Thesing 2003: 30).

In the past, Harrison would have been quite positive on the scope and change in Ireland for female senior managers, whereas now she recognises that it is unlikely that any sort of critical mass will reach the top in the near future. Thirty years ago women made up four per cent of all company directors and managers, with a labour force participation of twenty-eight per cent. At junior management level, forty-five per cent of employees are female. Human resource management/personnel is the only function where there are more women than men at the level of head of function or senior management. Moreover, the more senior the position, the wider the gender gap is. Company profile is also an important factor. For instance, more female chief executives are likely to be found in small companies, in Irish-owned companies and in the service sector. At the next level of management, the larger the company, the less likely it is to have female heads of function or senior managers.

Table 18.2 Irish Women in Senior Positions, by Sector

Year	Sector	Position	Women (%)
1997	Civil service	Assistant secretary	10
		Principal officer	12
1998	Corporate Ireland	Managing director	3
		Senior manager	2
		Middle manager	23
1998	Higher education	Professor	5
		Senior lecturer	16
		Lecturer	37
2000	Dáil Éireann	Government minister	20
		Junior minister	12
		TDs	12
2000	Judiciary	Supreme Court	29
		High Court	7
		Circuit Court	19

Source: IBEC, *Women in Management in Irish Business* (2002)

An Irish study on women and work with 515 women aged between nineteen and forty-four, commissioned by BUPA Ireland and *Business & Finance*, found that one in three women believe that the glass ceiling still exists and half of the women said that they had experienced its negative effects. Other significant findings from the report highlight that women believe that they have to work harder than men to get promoted and that they are expected to perform too many roles in terms of work and family and as a result they are suffering from stress-related illnesses. The married women surveyed believe that having children affects their career prospects and that single women have a better chance at succeeding at job interviews.

A recent report by the National Women's Council of Ireland (2003) examines the current level of women's participation in national and local politics, on regional authorities, state boards and national development plan monitoring committees. The council argues that the current electoral system plays an important role in limiting the number of women elected to the Dáil. It recommends that the government and political parties should agree a proactive strategy to increase the percentage of women elected to the Dáil and to bring about equal representation of women and men in the Oireachtas. It

Table 18.3 Breakdown of Women to Men in Irish Politics and State Boards

	Women	Men
Cabinet	2	13
TDs in Dáil Éireann	22	144
Medical Council	6	23
National Economic and Social Council	5	26
Board of the Court Service	6	11
Central Bank	0	12
South Dublin County Council	7	19
South East Regional Authority	2	32
Irish Congress of Trade Unions Executive Council	4	25

Source: Irish Politics – Jobs for the Boys (2003)

also urges the government to make the 40:60 gender balance for nominations to state boards a statutory obligation. The report also calls on the government to introduce legislation to make fifty per cent of funding for political parties dependent on a 40:60 gender balance among local and general election candidates. The report further recommends setting quotas to require political parties to have an equal representation of women and men within party executives to support greater participation by women in national and local politics.

Recent Irish research conducted on the legal profession by academic lawyers Bacik *et al.* (2003) reveals that only nine per cent of all senior counsel are women and only one managing partner from thirteen large solicitors' firms in Dublin is a woman, despite the large increase in the number of women entering both the legal profession as solicitors and barristers. Women now make up two-thirds of entrants to university law schools and half of the students taking professional courses at Blackhall Place and the King's Inns. There is also a large discrepancy in earnings, with forty-two per cent of male lawyers earning more than €100,000 compared with only nineteen per cent of female layers. The gap is even more marked at senior levels, where sixty per cent of male lawyers aged over fifty earn more than this, in comparison with only twenty per cent of women of the same age.

The reasons for this are complex, according to Bacik, and many of them apply equally to other professions. The long-hours culture, the continued role of the old boys' networks in professional advancement and the difficulty women still experience in balancing work and home life are all contributory factors. The difficulty of combining motherhood with work has led women to postpone pregnancy, for example, until they believed their careers were established. Forty per cent of all men have partners full-time in the home in comparison to only four per cent of women. The number increases dramatically when there are children: sixty-five per cent of lawyer fathers rely on a partner for child care, compared with nine per cent of women.

One of the most alarming facts revealed in the survey is that women lawyers who have experienced discriminatory behaviour in interviews or at work did not feel they could seek redress through the raft of Irish equality legislation, as they feared that doing so would damage their careers. Despite anti-discrimination legislation, questions about husbands, children and child-minding are still asked of women in interviews for places in barristers' chambers, along with questions such as 'Are you a feminist?'.

The recent IBEC report *Women in Management in Irish Business* attempts to summarise the reasons for women's lack of progress in Irish organisations, which include the following.

- Unclear selections criteria for promotion, which allows for considerable scope for discretion by senior management. This discretion is likely to be influenced by their personal views and attitudes towards women.
- Occupation segregation, whereby the selection process can favour men or women for certain jobs.
- Exclusion from informal networks or the 'old boys' club'.
- Women's ability to combine both management and family responsibilities is often questioned by their male senior management colleagues.
- Women often cannot work the long hours required of managers because of the lack of back-up or family support structures.
- Women are said to be more job focused than career focused and are often not aware of the strategic importance of the decisions they make around their careers.
- Lack of female role models.
- Lack of affordable, good-quality, consistent child care.
- Male-dominated corporate cultures.
- Characteristics considered to be masculine, e.g. forceful, aggressive, independent, objective, competitive, are generally regarded as traits required for management, rather than so-called feminine characteristics, e.g. co-operative, flexible, subjective, intuitive, emotional, which can be viewed as ineffective management traits.
- Women's tendency to move into 'support' or 'non-strategic' functions, such as human resource management and administration at junior management level, rather than into line management functions that lead to more senior positions.
- Married women are considered unsuitable for jobs that require frequent travel.
- A reluctance to hire women to head departments that are staffed by men.

Another factor that illustrates inequality in Irish organisations is salary. Research by Barrett *et al.* (2000) shows that women are still paid less than their male counterparts for the same or similar types of work. In 1997, for example, the average hourly earnings of women were 84.5 per cent of those of men. The authors explain that the pay gap is referred to the 'discrimination index', or the extra amount a woman would have earned had her characteristics been rewarded in the same way as a man's. According to the research, some of the factors that have given rise to this pay gap include occupational segregation, lack of female role models in senior positions and personal and social expectations held by men and women. The report also highlights that male employees are more likely than female employees to benefit from a variety of non-pay elements of compensation, such as pension benefits, free or subsidised health schemes or medical insurance, free or subsidised leisure and sport facilities and housing-related benefits such as subsidised mortgages.

According to a gender pay gap study commissioned by the Department of Justice, Equality and Law Reform (2003), Irish mothers are finding it difficult to access affordable full-time child care of an acceptable quality, which is curbing their ability to join or return to the workforce. According to the Equality Authority, the greatest number of queries the body receives each year are related to gender discrimination, and as women are still bound by outside responsibilities such as child care they are discriminated against in their careers because of it.

Recent Irish research conducted by Phoenix (2002) with women in Irish organisations and Irish female politicians reveals that the main reasons for women's poor representation in senior positions in Irish organisations are cultural and structural barriers, the old boys' network, work-family conflict, lack of female role models and women themselves. Statistical evidence indicates that while it seems relatively easy for women to gain employment at the lower levels of organisations, it is still proving very difficult for them to reach upper, middle and senior management positions.

BARRIERS TO WOMEN IN ORGANISATIONS

Many of the constraints that often hinder women in attaining senior managerial positions are quite similar in most countries. For example, there are cultural, educational, legislative, attitudinal and corporate constraints in most countries. The relative importance of each constraint varies from society to society. Research by Izraeli and Adler (1994: 13) suggests that the specific image of an ideal manager varies across cultures, 'yet everywhere it privileges those characteristics that the culture associates primarily with men.' They point out from their research that this belief is widely supported by male managers and that successful management is associated with masculinity. Research conducted by Morrison (1997) with 196 managers working in organisations that had been somewhat successful in supporting the career advancement of women and minority managers and professionals revealed consensus among the managers concerning the six critical barriers to advancement. The barriers were prejudice (treating differences as weaknesses), poor career planning, a hostile working environment, lack of organisational savvy, exclusion from informal networks and difficulty in balancing career and family. In observing the current environment for executive women, Nelson and Burke (2000) conclude that there has been progress, but many obstacles remain. The main barriers to women in organisations are discussed below.

Work-Family Conflict

A significant barrier that women in organisations have to overcome is the stress and pressures resulting from work-family conflict. This is experienced when pressures from the work and family roles are mutually incompatible, such that the participation in one role makes it more difficult to participate in the other. According to Hochschild (1989), because of the uneven distribution of household work, women are said to work a 'second shift' at home in addition to their first shift at work. Hochschild believes that women continue to work this second shift because their jobs are considered to be less important than those of their husbands. Women's family ties are seen as obstacles to promotion because they stand in the way of their availability for work, and being available is seen as essential for promotion. It is women who are mainly responsible for organising the household and it is women who take time off from their professional lives to devote time to their children. In a survey of 5,000 women, the health magazine *Top Sante* found that ninety per cent of women are 'stressed out' by the twin pressures of managing work and home and that eighty per cent would happily 'bail out' of corporate life and spend the time with their children at home. The same eighty per cent believed that they are 'the most responsible' for their children.

The work functions and duties performed by managers in all industrialised countries appear to be based on total commitment measured in terms of time spent at the workplace. Career breaks for women managers for bearing and rearing children show incompatibilities with the job of management, which is presumed to be a full-time and continuous job. Career breaks are seen to indicate a lack of commitment and re-entry is also problematic. Despite women's increased involvement in the workforce, research over time and across cultures continues to document the persistence of inequality in the allocation of household work and family responsibilities, even among couples with 'modern' ideologies and in countries with commitment to gender equality at home and at work.

Women's extra domestic responsibilities can create role conflict and overload and can reduce the potential for achievement in their careers. Most women feel that promotion in their careers has been achieved at the expense of time with their children and of the quality of family life. Therefore, family responsibilities involving marriage, child care and household activities can hinder women managers' career achievements. These family responsibilities produce work-family conflicts to which women may respond by reducing their employment involvement, which in turn restricts career opportunities and advancement.

Employers often see women as being less ambitious, not worth training or promoting (because they may leave to have children), less reliable (because of domestic responsibilities) and generally less committed to work than male counterparts. According to Davidson and Cooper (1992), the typical employer attitude that women are 'poor training and promotional investments' – who leave work on marrying and/or starting a family – is particularly detrimental to those who work continually after marriage and to single women who do not marry, a profile which fits many women in organisations.

MENTORING, TOKENISM AND NETWORKING

Covert barriers such as lack of mentors, being members of minority groups in organisations and lack of networking also hinder females in organisations. Generally, a mentor provides information, training, advice, direction, achievement of social and professional integration in organisations and psychosocial support for a junior person in a relationship lasting over an extended period of time. Although mentoring relationships may be particularly important for the advancement of women in organisations, there is a smaller supply of mentors available for women than to men and women may be less likely than men to develop these relationships. According to Ragins (1989: 6), one reason why women may be less likely than men to seek mentors is that they may fail to recognise the importance of gaining a sponsor and may 'naïvely assume that competence is the only requisite for advancement in the organisation.' Vinnicombe and Colwill's research (1995) reveals that when asked to describe the characteristics of their ideal junior person to mentor, both men and women choose people who are similar to themselves. As Vinnicombe and Colwill note, 'there are few top-level executives whose mirror reflects a woman', which suggests that most male and female junior managers will be mentored by men.

Owing to the severe shortage of female mentors at the top of organisations and to the fact that males hold more central positions, a male mentor may be valuable. However, there may be particular difficulties associated with cross-gender mentoring relationships. Resentment from co-workers is one difficulty, another is that the pair must manage the closeness in the mentoring relationship along with outsiders' perceptions of the relationship. Females also experience more social distance, discomfort and over-protectiveness from male mentors than do males (Bowen 1985).

No firm statistics exist, but the number of dedicated in-house mentoring programmes across Europe is limited. Although larger companies, such as Microsoft Corporation, Deloitte Touche Tohmatsu and Deutsche Bank AG, have launched mentoring plans, they are in the minority. Wittenberg-Cox, a career coach at the Insead business school in France, cautions that mentoring programmes for women are only effective as part of larger corporate-wide gender-diversity efforts and notes that many companies still fall short in that area. Companies that identify mentoring as a part of their business strategy are most likely to create successful programmes, but many companies still do not see it as part of a broader approach to cultivating and retaining talented women executives. She also suggests that because of the scarcity of senior women in most European organisations, a better approach is to form external networks for mentoring, sharing top executives from a number of member companies (in Chipman 2002).

Closely linked with the lack of female mentors is the difficulty of belonging to a minority group. Additional strains and pressures are experienced by female managers that are not felt by dominant members of the same organisational status. Women entering managerial and executive positions are often the first of their gender to take such posts. Being the first, or one of a kind, illustrates what has been termed a 'token' status. Kanter was one of the first to suggest that if women comprise less than fifteen per cent of a total category in an organisation they can be labelled tokens, as they could be viewed as symbols of their group rather than as individuals. She observes that token women in a large organisation are highly visible and subject to greater performance pressures than their male counterparts. Other demands include serving as representatives or spokespersons for their category, feeling isolated and outside the informal network, being seen in stereotyped roles, highlighting comparisons with other tokens and fears of earning the displeasures of the majority group. According to Freeman (1990), being a token woman not only means having no female peer support, but working in an environment which provides no role models of women in senior positions. Female role models in higher managerial positions act as important influences in terms of career aspirations for other women.

Peer relationships and interpersonal networks should provide a source of organisational support for female managers, particularly in the absence of mentors and because of their additional difficulties as members of a minority group. Peer relationships are different from mentoring relationships in that they often last longer, are not hierarchical and involve two-way helping. Peer relationships have advantages, particularly since a significant number of both women and men may not have had mentors. Burke and McKeen (1994: 75) suggest that 'it seems clear, however, that managerial women are still less integrated with important organisational networks, and it is these internal networks that influence critical human resource decisions such as promotion and acceptance.'

Women have been largely excluded from 'old boys' networks', which are traditionally composed of individuals who hold power in an organisation. Scase and Goffee's research (1989) establishes that attempts by male managers to exclude females from joining old boy networks merely reinforces existing stereotypes of negative male attitudes towards female managers. Davidson and Cooper (1992: 89) also suggest that certain established, traditional male institutions have developed exclusively male customs and traditions, which perpetuate the 'old boy network and safeguard it from female intrusion.' They suggest that it is up to organisational policymakers to take active steps to break down 'male organisational cultures' that perpetuate the 'old boy ghetto' syndrome.

WHY WOMEN ARE 'BAILING OUT' OF CORPORATE LIFE

Many executive women are leaving organisations to start their own businesses. Research conducted with 800 female and male business owners in the US by Commeau-Kirschner (1998) sought to determine the reasons behind the trend, as this corporate exodus among women is occurring at a rate double the national average. Among women, glass ceiling issues, feeling unchallenged and the desire for more flexibility were the top reasons for leaving. In addition, the persistent wage gap, stereotypes about women being less committed to work because of family responsibilities and the demand that employees spend significant time in the office were key things that drove women away from organisations. Several companies have been concerned about this 'brain drain', which negatively affects the organisation's health.

Proctor & Gamble saw two disturbing trends in the 1990s. Women made up forty per cent of their new employees, yet the company's attrition rate for these women was significantly higher than that of men. In addition, women were seldom found in the brand management area at Proctor & Gamble, the 'grooming spot' for high potential managers. Proctor & Gamble formed a task force on the advancement of women that was managed with the same attention the company gives to brand businesses (Catalyst 1999). Outcomes were measured and reported annually. Key parts of the initiative included building coaching skills through mentoring programmes and additional work/life programmes, such as work on reduced schedules for extended periods of time, that were introduced through policy changes. The payoff of Proctor & Gamble's actions was substantial: women at the general manager and vice-president level have tripled and by 1997 women made up thirty-one per cent of the vice-president and senior management positions at the company. Thus, Proctor & Gamble's interventions benefited both women's careers and the organisation's well-being.

According to Nelson and Burke (2000), in addition to, and perhaps more important than, formal programmes, women want more informal flexibility at work in order to balance work and personal lives. Providing entrepreneurial challenges at work and greater compensation are other ways to prevent the exodus of women. Nelson and Burke also note that, while significant, organisational policies by themselves may not make much difference in managerial and professional women's work and life experiences. Many organisations develop policies but fail to back them up. This often results from seeing work and family issues as an either-or situation, that is, individuals who fulfil family or personal life needs do so at the expense of work commitments. A more meaningful approach is to identify work values and practices that, if changed, would facilitate both work performance and family and personal life concerns, a linking of work practices and family life. Such culture change benefits all organisational employees, not just women.

ONGOING DEBATES/ADVANCED CONCEPTS IN WOMEN IN ORGANISATIONS

MAXIMISING HUMAN RESOURCES

Current debates on more flexible managerial styles and approaches (with a view to maximising human resource utilisation), together with the interest of enterprises in attracting and retaining qualified and talented women in a competitive environment, could provide positive perspectives for increasing women's share of managerial jobs in the future.

Over the years, governments, enterprises and organisations have committed themselves to policies and programmes to advance women. While these have met with varying degrees of success, they have undoubtedly had a positive effect, especially on younger generations of men and women. Given women's increasing level of qualifications and work performance, it might have been expected that they would have moved more quickly up the career ladder in recent years. Yet this has not been the case and for many the pace of change is just too slow. Participation in decision making is proving to be one of the most resistant areas yet for gender equality.

In many instances, the development of detailed career plans within organisations has been shown to be instrumental in promoting equal opportunities in career progression. Special support through networks, coaching, mentoring and training has also been found to be effective in encouraging women and making them more visible. Not only is specific action required to ensure that women's careers are not stymied, but increasingly their opportunities will be enhanced by the creation of workplaces that are more dynamic, flexible, value diverse and are more people oriented and family friendly.

Men in positions of power must recognise that it is in the organisation's interests to eliminate the obstacles that prevent women from advancing to senior managerial positions. Kottis (1993) suggests that for an organisation to operate efficiently and succeed in a highly competitive world, it must use the best talent available, irrespective of gender. Since organisations spend large amounts of money on recruiting, training and developing their personnel, they should try to make the best use of their resources. Women in managerial positions have a much higher turnover rate than their male counterparts, mainly owing to 'lack of opportunities for advancement for women.'

One of the greatest challenges that remains is how to make the structures and dynamics within organisations more conducive and sensitive to gender equality concepts and practice. This is particularly crucial in environments where new management structures and work roles involve restructuring, downsizing, decentralisation and delayering in the bid to be more globally competitive. Without such change from within organisations, in the years to come women will continue to experience glass ceilings and glass walls as invisible barriers to positions of management.

Career Development for Women in Organisations

As highlighted above, females in organisations face more overt and covert barriers to career advancement than their male counterparts. Because of these barriers the career development process for women is different from that of men and far more complex in terms of frequent shifts between home and work. Research on adulthood in women has focused on the family cycle at the expense of the work cycle, which means that no formal theory of women's occupational behaviour exists.

Fitzgerald and Crites (1980) believe that career development for women is more complex because of the differences in socialisation and in the combination of attitudes, role expectations, behaviours and sanctions that constitute it. The socialisation of women to give primacy to nurturing roles, and secondary or negligible priority to career or achieving roles, leads to home-career conflict, lack of serious career planning and restriction of options to sex-stereotypical occupations. According to Astin (1995), the basic motivation is the same for men and women, but women make different choices because of their differing early socialisation experiences and structural opportunities. Diamond (1989) points out that a variety of attitudes and behaviours still set up barriers to women's optimal career development, particularly to their participation in non-traditional occupations. Women are often discouraged from entry into non-traditional professions, and for those who do enter, they are subjected to harassment and hostile behaviour.

Bardwick (1980) and Gilligan (1982) believe in a distinct theory of female adult development. These researchers note that women emphasise the importance of relationships and attachments and that, even for accomplished professional and career women, traditional roles and interpersonal commitments remain a core part of female identity. Bardwick argues that there is a distinctly different phase of adult life for men and women between the ages of thirty and forty. For men, she states, this is a period of enhanced investment in career, while women require much more than career and professional success.

Career theory researchers agree that a clear picture of the career-developmental process for women has not yet emerged. Diamond (1989) and Larwood and Gutek (1987), however, suggest that there is a need to develop a theory of women's career development. Larwood and Gutek state that if a comprehensive theory of women's career development were to be developed, particular attention should be given to career preparation, opportunities available in society, the influence of marriage, pregnancy and children and timing and age. Diamond (1989: 25) also suggests that more research is needed in this field, yet such research 'must not be based on the male model but must be relevant to the many unique aspects of women's experience and involve broad enough samples of women to embrace all the pertinent variables – socio-economic, demographic, educational, environmental, biological and psychological.' Diamond suggests that the research should be tested empirically and longitudinally. Only then can the process of career development for women, and its similarities to and differences from the career development process for men, be more fully understood.

SUMMARY OF KEY PROPOSITIONS

- This chapter explored the impact of the increased participation of women in the workforce and highlighted that in all industrialised countries it is still proving difficult for women to reach senior managerial positions.
- The concept of the glass ceiling was discussed in order to illustrate the hidden or covert barriers that prevent women from reaching top positions in their organisations.
- To enable women to break through the glass ceiling, organisations need to consider a number of practical measures regarding recruitment, training, promotion, equal opportunities, diversity and family-friendly and work-life balance policies.
- The difficulties for women of 'having it all', i.e. a successful career, a personal relationship and children, were explored.
- The under-representation of women in senior positions in Irish organisations was discussed, illustrating that among Ireland's largest companies approximately only three per cent of senior positions are held by women, with very little change over the past few years.
- Other significant barriers to women in organisations include work-family conflict, lack of mentoring, being members of minority groups and lack of access to male influential networks.

- Organisations need to attract and retain talented women in order for them to maximise their human resources, which in turn could provide them with a competitive advantage in an increasingly competitive environment.
- Career development for women is different from their male counterparts, yet research illustrates that there is no distinct career-developmental process for women. Various researchers have suggested that there is a need to develop a career model specifically for women in order to more fully understand the additional barriers and difficult lifestyle choices women in organisations face.

DISCUSSION/SELF-ASSESSMENT QUESTIONS

1. Do you think that the glass ceiling is a thing of the past? Why or why not?
2. Identify the main barriers for women in organisations and suggest methods for overcoming such barriers.
3. What policies could organisations put in place to redress the imbalance of women in senior positions in organisation?
4. Discuss the advantages and disadvantages of implementing a formal mentoring programme in organisations.
5. Identify the main similarities and differences in the career development of men and women in organisations.

MULTIPLE CHOICE QUESTIONS

1. The glass ceiling is:
   (a) Formal organisational policies.
   (b) Obvious barriers.
   (c) Hidden barriers.
   (d) Only in the US.
2. The glass ceiling applies to:
   (a) Men in organisations.
   (b) Women in organisations.
   (c) Human resource managers.
   (d) Chief executive officers.
3. Various research studies have illustrated that the glass ceiling is:
   (a) Relatively intact.
   (b) Non-existent.
   (c) Made up of obvious barriers.
   (d) Confined to the old boys' network.
4. A glass wall occurs when:
   (a) Lateral movement is prevented in organisations.
   (b) Women are prevented from entering organisations.
   (c) Women reach senior positions in organisations.
   (d) Men and women earn equal salaries.

5. Success and commitment are associated with:
   (a) Creating the glass ceiling.
   (b) Discrimination in organisations.
   (c) The glass wall.
   (d) Breaking through the glass ceiling.
6. Having it all suggests having a:
   (a) Successful career.
   (b) Successful home life.
   (c) Successful career, relationship and children.
   (d) Successful mentoring relationship.
7. Women in Irish organisations generally earn:
   (a) More pay than their male colleagues.
   (b) Less pay than their male colleagues.
   (c) Equal pay to their male colleagues.
   (d) Similar pay to their male colleagues.
8. The successful characteristics associated with management are usually compared to:
   (a) Women.
   (b) Men.
   (c) Supervisors.
   (d) Token women.
9. A mentoring relationship is generally formed with a:
   (a) Senior organisational member.
   (b) Peer.
   (c) Junior organisational member.
   (d) Minority group.
10. A token in an organisation means being a member of:
    (a) The old boys' network.
    (b) A mentoring relationship.
    (c) A minority group.
    (d) A female network.
11. Peer relationships:
    (a) Are hierarchical.
    (b) Involve two-way helping.
    (c) Involve mentors.
    (d) Are exclusive to males.
12. The old boys' network generally:
    (a) Includes women.
    (b) Excludes women.
    (c) Provides female role models.
    (d) Provides equal opportunities.

13. Female role models in organisations provide:
    (a) Access to the old boys' network.
    (b) Career aspirations for junior women.
    (c) Peer relationships.
    (d) Limited career development opportunities.
14. Junior female managers are usually mentored by:
    (a) Peers.
    (b) Junior male managers.
    (c) Junior female managers.
    (d) Senior male managers.
15. Career development for women in organisations is more complex because of:
    (a) Their over-representation at senior level.
    (b) Inclusion in the old boys' network.
    (c) Mentoring by senior women managers.
    (d) Childbearing and childrearing factors.
16. At senior management level in Irish organisations, women are usually:
    (a) Over-represented.
    (b) Under-represented.
    (c) Part of the old boys' network.
    (d) Earning more than their male colleagues.
17. Being a member of a minority group creates:
    (a) Additional strain and stress.
    (b) Opportunities for career advancement.
    (c) Opportunities for higher pay.
    (d) Better networking opportunities.
18. Women in organisations are perceived to be:
    (a) Less ambitious than their male colleagues.
    (b) More ambitious than their male colleagues.
    (c) More successful than their male colleagues.
    (d) More committed than their male colleagues.
19. Work-family conflict is generally experienced more by:
    (a) Men in organisations.
    (b) Women in organisations.
    (c) Senior male managers.
    (d) Members of the old boys' network.
20. Token women in senior positions in organisations are usually:
    (a) Test cases for future women managers.
    (b) Less ambitious than their male colleagues.
    (c) Less successful than their male colleagues.
    (d) Less committed than their male colleagues.

FIVE SUGGESTED KEY READINGS

Adler, N.J. and Izraeli, D.N. (eds), *Competitive Frontiers: Women Managers in a Global Economy*, Oxford: Basil Blackwell 1994.

Burke, R.J. and Burgess, Z. (eds), 'Women on corporate board of directors', *Women in Management Review*, XVII/7 (2003, special issue).

Linehan, M., *Senior Female International Managers: Why So Few?*, Aldershot: Ashgate 2000.

Powell, G.N. and Graves, L.M., *Women and Men in Management*, Thousand Oaks, CA: Sage 2002.

Vinnicombe, S. and Colwill, N.L. (eds), *The Essence of Women in Management*, London: Prentice Hall 1995.

REFERENCES

Adler, N.J. and Izraeli, D.N. (eds), *Competitive Frontiers: Women Managers in a Global Economy*, Oxford: Basil Blackwell 1994.

Arroba, T. and James, K., 'Are politics palatable to women managers?', *Women in Management Review*, III/3 (1987), 123–30.

Astin, H.S., 'The meaning of work in women's lives: a sociopsychological model of career choice and work behaviour', *The Counselling Psychologist*, XII (1985), 117–26.

Bacik, I., Drew, E. and Costello, C., *Gender Injustice: Women in Law Project*, Dublin: School of Law, Trinity College 2003.

Bardwick, J., 'The seasons of a woman's life', in D. McGuigan (ed.), *Women's Lives: New Theory, Research and Policy*, Ann Arbor, MI: University of Michigan Centre for Continuing Education of Women 1980.

Barrett, A., Callan, T., Doris, A., O'Neill, D., Russell, H., Sweetman, O. and McBride, J., *How Unequal? Men and Women in the Irish Labour Market*, Dublin: Oak Tree Press 2000.

Berthoin-Antal, A. and Izraeli, D.N., 'A global comparison of women in management: women managers in their homelands and as expatriates', in E.A. Fagenson (ed.), *Women in Management: Trends, Issues and Challenges in Managerial Diversity*, London: Sage 1993.

Bowen, D.D., 'Were men meant to mentor women?', *Training and Development Journal*, XXXIX (1985), 32–4.

Burke, R.J. and Burgess, Z. (eds), 'Women on corporate board of directors', *Women in Management Review*, XVII/7 (2003, special issue).

Burke, R.J. and McKeen, C.A., 'Career development among managerial and professional women', in M.J. Davidson and R.J. Burke (eds), *Women in Management: Current Research Issues*, London: Paul Chapman 1994.

Burke, S., 'Women: undervalued, underpaid', *The Irish Times* (17 June 1999).

Catalyst, '*Catalyst Best Practice: Putting a Stop to the Female Brain Drain*', New York: Catalyst 1999.

Chipman, A., 'Finding mentors can be tough, but it's worth it', *The Wall Street Journal Europe* (27 February 2002), A14.

Commeau-Kirschner, C., 'Keeping female execs in the house', *Management Review*, LXXXVII (1998), 7–8.

Corcoran, S., 'Women overboard', *Business & Finance*, Top 1,000 Companies in Ireland Supplement (23 May 2002), 18–20.

Davidovich, N., 'The glass ceiling – has it prevented employment to your full potential?' (available online at www.talk-law.com/glass.shtml, downloaded on 16 October 2001), 2000.

Davidson, M.J. and Cooper, C.L., *Shattering the Glass Ceiling: The Woman Manager*, London: Paul Chapman 1992.

Diamond, E.E., 'Theories of career development and the reality of women at work', in B.A. Gutek and L. Larwood (eds), *Women's Career Development*, Beverly Hills, CA: Sage 1989.

Fitzgerald, L.F. and Crites, J.O., 'Towards a career psychology of women: what do we know? What do we need to know?', *Journal of Counselling Psychology*, XXVII/1 (1980), 44–62.

Freeman, S.J.M., *Managing Lives: Corporate Women and Social Change*, Amherst, MA: University of Massachusetts Press 1990.

Gilligan, C., *In a Different Voice: Psychological Theory and Women's Development*, Cambridge, MA: Harvard University Press 1982.

Hewlett, S.A., 'Executive women and the myth of having it all', *Harvard Business Review*, LXXX (April 2002), 66–73.

Ho, S., 'Women managers in Hong Kong: traditional barriers and emerging trends', *Equal Opportunities International*, III/4 (1984), 7–29.

Hochschild, A., *The Second Shift*, New York: Viking 1989.

IBEC: *Women in Management in Irish Businesss*, Dublin 2002.

Izraeli, D.N. and Adler, N.J. (eds), *Competitive Frontiers: Women Managers in a Global Economy*, Oxford: Basil Blackwell 1994.

Jackson, J.C., 'Women middle managers' perception of the glass ceiling', *Women in Management Review*, XVI/1 (2001), 30–41.

Kanter, R.M., 'Some effects of proportions of group life: skewed sex rations and responses to token women', *American Journal of Sociology*, LXXXII (1977), 965–90.

Korac-Kakabadse, N. and Kouzmin, A., 'Maintaining the rage: from "glass and concrete ceilings" and metaphorical sex changes to psychological audits and renegotiating scripts', *Women in Management Review*, XII/5 (1997), 182–95.

Kottis, A.P., 'The glass ceiling and how to break it', *Women in Management Review*, VIII/4 (1993), 9–15.

Larwood, L. and Gutek, B., 'Working towards a theory of women's career development', in B. Gutek and L. Larwood (eds), *Women's Career Development*, Newbury Park, CA: Sage 1987.

Linehan, M., *Senior Female International Managers: Why So Few?*, Aldershot: Ashgate 2000.

Maier, M., 'The gender prism: pedagogical foundations for reducing sex stereotyping and promoting egalitarian male-female relationships in management', *Journal of Management Education*, XVII/3 (1993), 288–317.

Morrison, A.M., *The New Leaders*, San Francisco: Jossey-Bass 1997.

Morrison, A.M. and Von Glinow, M.A., 'Women and minorities in management', *American Psychologist*, XLV/2 (1990), 200–8.

National Women's Council of Ireland: *Irish Politics: Jobs for the Boys*; Dublin 2003.

Nelson, D.L. and Burke, R.I., 'Women executives: health, stress, and success', *Academy of Management Executive*, XIV/2 (2000), 107–21.

Phoenix, A.M., 'The glass ceiling: a persistent barrier for women in management in Irish business', unpublished dissertation in partial fulfilment for the Degree in Management (Marketing), Dublin: Dublin Institute of Technology 2002.

Powell, G.N., 'The glass ceiling: explaining the good and bad news', in M.J. Davidson and R.J. Burke (eds), *Women in Management: Current Research Issues*, ii, London: Sage 2000.

Powell, G.N. and Graves, L.M., *Women and Men in Management*, Thousand Oaks, CA: Sage 2002.

Ragins, B.R., 'Barriers to mentoring: the female manager's dilemma', *Human Relations*, XLII/1 (1989), 1–22.

Roddick, A., *Business as Usual*, London: Thorsons 2000.

Scase, R. and Goffee, R., *Reluctant Managers: Their Work and Lifestyles*, London: Unwin Hyman 1989.

Schwartz, F.N., 'Management women and the facts of life', *Harvard Business Review*, LXVII/1 (1989), 65–76.

Simpson, R. and Altman, Y., 'The time bounded glass ceiling and young women managers: career progress and career success – evidence from the UK', *Journal of European Industrial Training*, XXIV (2000), 2–4.

Smith, D.M., *Women at Work: Leadership for the Next Century*, Englewood Cliffs, NJ: Prentice Hall 2000.

Smith, C.R. and Still, L., 'Breaking the glass border: barriers to global careers for women managers in Australia', paper presented at 5th International Human Resource Management Conference, San Diego, CA, 24–28 June 1996.

Still, L., 'Where to from here? Women in management – the cultural dilemma', *Women in Management Review*, IX/4 (1994), 3–10.

Thesing, G., 'Women at the helm', *Business & Finance*, Top 1,000 Companies in Ireland, (2003, special issue), 24–30.

Vinnicombe, S. and Colwill, N.L., *The Essence of Women in Management*, London: Prentice Hall 1995.

Vinnicombe, S. and Harris, H., 'Women and leadership', *People Management*, VI/1 (2000), 27–32.

Whirlpool Foundation, *Women Setting New Priorities, European Study*, Bauknecht: Whirlpool Foundation 1996.

Wirth, L., *Breaking Through the Glass Ceiling: Women in Management*, New York: International Labour Organization 2001.

INTERCULTURAL ADJUSTMENT AND WORKING ABROAD

19

Learning Objectives

- To introduce key themes in the literature on working abroad.

- To present the U-curve hypothesis as a theoretical device for explaining the likely pattern of adjustment experienced by the individual on entering a novel culture.

- To outline the psychic-distance paradox.

- To review the personal factors, job factors and organisational factors that explain the pattern of intercultural transitional adjustment experienced by the individual working abroad.

INTRODUCTION

Recent years have shown a marked increase in the internationalisation of business in areas such as international strategic alliances, joint ventures, foreign subsidiaries and overseas offices. In this context of an ever-increasing evolution towards global activity in business venturing, the likelihood of one spending time working abroad has become a reality for many people. So-called 'international assignments' or 'expatriate assignments' are becoming a key part of many people's careers. Planning and managing these international assignments is now a key activity for many organisations as they can pose many challenges, both to the organisation sending the individual abroad and to the individual themselves. Culture shock, differences in work-related norms, isolation, homesickness, differences in health care, housing, schooling, cuisine, language, customs, sex roles and the cost of living are just some of the things that have contributed to making expatriate failure one of the most significant problems facing today's multinationals. Other major issues identified in the expatriate literature include inadequate selection criteria, poor predeparture training, poorly designed compensation packages, failure of the expatriate and/or their family to adjust to the new culture and poor repatriation programmes.

In this chapter we focus on key issues associated with working abroad, namely the psycho-social process of adjusting to working and living abroad, the key factors that facilitate this intercultural transitional adjustment and finally, the value of a repatriation programme dedicated to assisting the reintegration of the individual on returning from working abroad.

DEFINITIONS OF KEY CONCEPTS

Expatriate

An employee of an organisation who is sent on a temporary work assignment in a different country from their home country.

Intercultural adjustment

The psycho-social process by which the individual working in a foreign environment becomes comfortable with and achieves a degree of functional mastery of that host environment.

U-curve hypothesis

The U-shaped pattern of adjustment whereby on entering a foreign environment the individual experiences a period of elation, followed by a period of culture shock which is eventually followed by period of adjustment and eventual comfort in operating in the host environment.

Cross-cultural training

Training interventions, exercises and simulations designed to increase the trainee's level of cultural awareness in order that he/she can successfully and effectively work in the host environment and interact with host nationals and the broader environment.

Repatriation

Refers to the return and re-entry of the expatriate to the home country on completion of the work assignment abroad.

INTERCULTURAL ADJUSTMENT AND THE U-CURVE HYPOTHESIS

Expatriate intercultural adjustment has been described as the process by which 'overseas employees become comfortable with, or acculturated to, the host-country' (Parker and McEvoy 1995), 'the degree of psychological comfort experienced with various aspects of the host environment' (Black and Gregersen 1991), 'the re-establishment of routines that provide valued outcomes and feelings of control that are predictable' (Brett 1980) or 'the process by which the individual (with his unique set of abilities and needs) acts, reacts and comes to terms with his environment' (Dawis *et al.* 1964). Thus, adjustment can be said to occur when the individual adopts new behaviours which produce similar results to those behaviours that were used prior to the transfer.

Cleveland *et al.* (1960) highlight that most people who go abroad generally expect things to be different in large and predictable ways. There may be unusual scenery, a strange language and other major inconveniences that may be encountered as part of working abroad. They argue that what appears to be the trouble is something subtler and more intimately subversive, namely a feeling of inadequacy that results from not quite knowing how to act. Consequently, the process of developing a minimum threshold of 'adequacy' in responding to the demands of the host environment in all its different facets is important. This response adequacy, acquired by the expatriate through a process of adjustment, is marked by increased effectiveness in different life domains.

A number of contributors have suggested, and indeed some have successfully demonstrated, that the pattern of adjustment can often take the form of a U-curve, whereby following a period of elation after entering the host environment, the expatriate experiences a type of culture shock which, in the context of a successful assignment, is followed by a period of adjustment and subsequently a degree of competence in operating in the host environment. According to Black and Mendenhall (1991: 226), the U-shaped curve 'represents one of those rare cases in which a theoretical perspective has been applied to cross-cultural research' (see Figure 19.1).

Figure 19.1 The U-Curve in Intercultural Transitional Adjustment

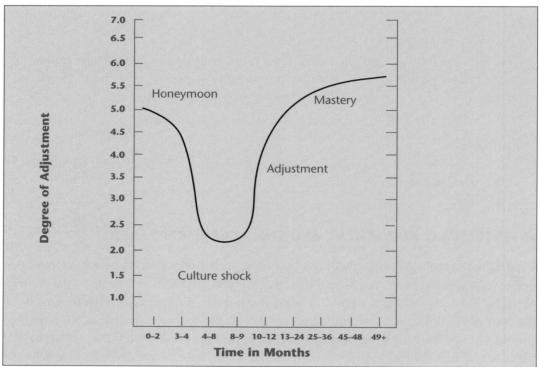

Lysgaard's work (1955) is generally cited as the research that initiated the empirical testing of the U-curve. In this original work Lysgaard compared three groups of Norwegian students who had received Fulbright scholarships to study or do research in the US. He divided the students into three groups according to the amount of time they had spent in the US, i.e. zero to six months, six to eighteen months and eighteen months or more. Using several items to examine 'professional-educational' and 'personal-social'

adjustment, Lysgaard found that 'good' adjustment was reported by the first and third group, whereas the second group was 'less well' adjusted. The research pointed to the existence of a curvilinear relationship, a phenomenon subsequently referred to as the U-curve hypothesis in intercultural adjustment.

Sappinen (1993) draws upon Oberg's treatise (1960) on the phenomenon of culture shock, viewing it as a successful addition to the U-curve theory in that it explicates the various stages of the curve. In his original work Oberg argues that adjustment to new cultural environments is characterised by four distinct phases, namely the honeymoon stage, which may last from a few days or weeks to six months depending on circumstances, then a culture shock phase, which Oberg views as a 'hostility ... which grows out of the genuine difficulty which the visitor experiences in the process of adjustment' (1993: 178); followed by a phase of recovery; and eventual adjustment and mastery. Simeon and Fujiu (2000: 595) also judge this work to be valuable in that it focuses on how the 'awareness and acceptance of what is considered appropriate behaviour in different environments can reduce uncertainty and ease the difficulty of adjustment.'

Torbiörn (1982) argues that this description and explanation of the U-curve advanced by Oberg is only a reflection of a deeper process of adaptation in cognitive terms. He suggests that the reason for the drop in satisfaction is not caused by the fact that the individual can no longer ignore their problems, is not due to the fact that they have come to grips with everyday life, is not due to the increasing demands on the individual, nor is it that they feel the need to extend their relationship with the host country culture. Torbiörn also notes that the deterioration in subjective adjustment is not primarily dependent on the loss of approval as the new arrival ceases to be a novelty and the locals' welcoming attitude declines. Rather, he proposes that the direct cause of the decline in subjective adjustment is the individual's loss of confidence in his or her own ideas. The individual's understanding and handling of reality become weakened and worn down by contact with a real world that provides him or her with no reinforcement.

Overall, while the U-curve hypothesis is often invoked in the intercultural and expatriate management literature to describe the various stages of the adjustment process, some commentators note that there is a dearth of evidence to suggest the value of the curve as a way forward in explaining the experience of all those who go on a foreign assignment. A number of authors state that on the whole there is not a huge amount of accumulated empirical evidence to suggest that all individuals experience an adjustment process that follows any one pattern. Brewster (1991) suggests that while all respondents in his survey could identify with the U-curve pattern, the process of adjustment varied significantly among respondents. Only one respondent in his survey experienced an adjustment process that conformed to the U-curve pattern. Similarly, DeCieri *et al.* (1991) also found support for the different stages of the adjustment process, but not for the actual pattern of the U-curve. Finally, arising from their review, Black and Mendenhall (1991: 232) conclude that 'based on empirical evidence, it seems unreasonable to either accept or reject the U-curve theory.'

CULTURE SCHOCK AND CULTURAL INTEGRATION

Beyond the actual pattern of adjustment, a key question is how the process takes place and precisely what it is we actually have to adjust to. Berry *et al.* (1988) have outlined four different approaches to adjustment: assimilation, integration, separatism and marginalisation. Assimilation takes place when the individual wishes to integrate with host nationals and has no desire to maintain their own culture. Integration occurs when the individual continues to have an interest in their own culture while also interacting with host nationals. The individual adopts a separatist mode of acculturation when they want to keep their cultural identity without any desire to integrate with host country nationals. Marginalisation arises when there is no desire to identify with one's own culture or to mix with host nationals. Marginalisation and separation do not lead to successful expatriate adjustment. The most common approach to successful expatriate adjustment is integration. In an attempt to integrate, expatriates may try a variety of approaches before establishing a new set of behavioural norms that will enable them to adapt to the new environment. Aptly labelled as 'sense-making' by Louis (1980), the objective is to allow the individual to develop a 'map' of his/her new environment.

Early formulations dedicated to examining and interpreting intercultural transitional adjustment centred on the unitary notion of culture shock (Oberg 1960; Gullahorn and Gullahorn 1963), a conceptualisation which received a degree of attention because it is both common and disturbing to the international assignee. Originally coined by Oberg (1960) as the 'occupational disease' of people who suddenly find themselves located in a culture very different from their own, it rather quickly established itself as the major theoretical lynchpin for understanding intercultural transitional adjustment and its associated difficulties. The general characterisation of culture shock is one of a feeling of inadequacy that results from not quite knowing how to act as a result of the removal of familiar cues, what Oberg (1960: 178) originally referred to as 'our signs and symbols of social intercourse.' Recovering from the loss of these cues and acquiring a fluency in the new social order is essential for expatriate performance and the overall success of an intercultural assignment, yet we know it to be difficult. Foster (1990) contends that few first-time, longer-term sojourners recover from culture shock in less than six months, and significantly, a single culture shock experience will not immunise one against future shocks, although future experiences may be less severe and the readjustment periods somewhat shorter.

WHAT FACTORS EXPLAIN HOW THE INDIVIDUAL ADJUSTS TO WORKING AND LIVING ABROAD?

Much has been written about the factors that facilitate or inhibit adjustment when going to work abroad. For the purposes of our discussion here, the factors can be grouped into personal factors, job factors and organisational factors.

PERSONAL FACTORS AS PREDICTORS OF ADJUSTMENT

Gender

There is relatively little empirical research on the impact of gender on adjustment, largely due to the fact that there are so few female expatriates. Adler (1995) suggests that probably the single most uncontroversial, indisputable statement one can make about women in management is that there are very few of them. To this end, it has been noted that many researchers refer to the gender of expatriates as male throughout their research. Indeed, Black's account (1988) of work role transitions among American expatriate managers in Japan is derived from an all-male sample and his 1990 treatise on the relationship between personal characteristics and the adjustment of Japanese expatriate managers is based on sixty-seven usable questionnaires returned by male expatriate managers (Black 1990: 127).

Where evidence does exist on the gender-impact question, one of the core arguments is that female expatriates in certain cultures can experience difficulties if they are to play a role that is not 'appropriate' to their perceived role. However, Adler (1995) suggests that the societal and cultural rules governing the behaviour of local women that limit their access to managerial positions and responsibility do not apply to foreign women, and therefore host nationals may in fact be more willing to accept female expatriates playing roles that may be seen as inappropriate for local females. She discovered that the most difficult hurdle in the female's international career involved getting sent abroad in the first place and not, as most had anticipated, gaining the respect of foreigners and succeeding once sent. In her study, almost all the female expatriate managers (ninety-seven per cent) reported that their international assignments were successful and the data pointed to a success rate considerably higher than that reported for North American male expatriates. Referring specifically to this managerial group, Torbiörn (1982) empirically examined the impact of gender on adjustment and found no significant connection between sex and subjective adjustment, while more recent work by Harris (1999) and Linehan (1999) suggests that women can be as successful internationally as men.

Marital Status

Associated with the debate on the 'trailing spouse', the expatriate's marital status also features in the literature as a variable of considerable importance. The failure of the spouse to adjust on a foreign assignment has been highlighted as one of the most common reasons for male expatriate failure and early return from international assignments. Aycan (1997) suggests that spousal support is an important positive influence where the spouse is well adjusted himself or herself. In this situation, Kraimer *et al.* (2001) argue that the expatriate who travels with his or her spouse enjoys a degree of 'social support' whereby the spouse can act as an information provider along with acting as a source of affirmation for the expatriate, something which is seen to be important in the context of a stressful international assignment. The support provided by the spouse can also have a spillover effect and positively impact work outcomes. Kraimer and colleagues predicted that spousal support would be positively related to the expatriate's work and general adjustment but did not find support for this, a result which they found 'surprising because the literature is replete with suggestions that spousal support is critical to expatriate adjustment' (2001: 92).

Age

Mamman's treaties (1995) on the socio-biographical antecedents of intercultural effectiveness point towards age as an important factor in subsequent adaptation to a foreign setting. He maintains that younger people are more flexible in adapting to a new environment and suggests, for example, that most expatriates will probably find that their children have adapted faster than they have. However, in some societies age has significant status connotations – the older the person, the wiser he or she becomes and the more likely to command respect, with the result that in such settings older expatriates can have advantages over younger expatriates during social interactions. Furnham and Bochner (1986) maintain that although the research is equivocal on the matter of age and adjustment, it is generally the case that older, more experienced people cope better with the problems of geographic movement. Similarly, Church (1982) speculates that more mature expatriates may adjust better to other cultures, something which Parker and McEvoy (1993) take to be theoretically plausible when one considers that job satisfaction is an important part of the work adjustment concept and that older workers are generally more satisfied with their job than their younger counterparts. Notwithstanding, empirically they did not find a significant correlation between age and work, interaction or general living adjustment, thus lending support to Torbiörn's (1982) conclusion that age does not seem to have affected the satisfaction of either men or women on overseas assignments.

Education

In his analysis of the personal adjustment required for living abroad, Torbiörn (1982) assuredly notes that people who have received higher education are more content than those with fewer formal educational attainments. This applies to both men and women, regardless of the professional orientation of the education concerned. Similarly, in terms of smoothing the expatriate experience, Mamman (1995) notes that in many societies educational qualifications are highly valued and can be a significant determinant of social and economic status. Therefore, it is predicted that expatriates perceived to have higher levels of educational attainment may command a greater level of respect and hence improve their chances of receiving favourable responses during interactions, something which smooths the adjustment process.

Personality

While there now appears to be a substantial list of personality traits that an expatriate should possess in order to satisfactorily adjust while on foreign assignment, many of which equate with the typical dimensions of extroversion, some earlier researchers did not support the concept that the expatriate's personality might significantly affect adjustment during the course of such an assignment. For example, Brein and David (1971) describe the conceptualisation of the sojourner's adjustment in terms of typical behaviour or social patterns and personality typologies, traits and constellations as 'interesting', 'entertaining' and 'somewhat anecdotal', while more recently Ward and Chang (1997: 525) suggest that 'anecdotal musings and armchair theorising have frequently highlighted the role of personality in the process of cross-cultural transitions and adjustment.'

By and large, though, Aycan (1997) notes that there here has been an upsurge of interest in personality traits as predictors of job behaviour in recent years, with the consequence that the application of personality tests to predict adjustment and performance is considered fruitful. Among the various personality traits, extroversion and openness to new experiences have been found to be significant predictors of cross-cultural adjustment. Parker and McEvoy (1993) note that extroversion and open-mindedness are both positively related to sociability and interpersonal involvement, and by extension, they anticipate they are also related to interaction adjustment abroad. Aycan (1997) suggests that individuals who have such personality traits are more likely to initiate and maintain meaningful interactions with host nationals, portray a greater interest in learning host values and approach such new experiences with respect and empathy.

Personal Competencies or Skills and the Adjustment Process

Beyond the personality investigations, the research on expatriate adaptation also indicates that success in overseas work assignments depends upon the possession and utilisation of other skills. Black (1990: 123) notes:

> The basic premise in the literature for why these personal dimensions are important assumes that individuals must understand and be willing to execute behaviours which are appropriate in the new cultural context and that certain personal dimensions either facilitate or inhibit this process.

Mendenhall and Oddou (1988) provide a typology of such skills, namely personal skills, people skills and perception skills. They argue that techniques and attributes which facilitate the expatriate's mental and emotional well-being may be thought of as 'personal skills' and could include meditation, prayer or other means of finding solitude, all of which, they argue, tend to decrease the executive's stress level. Ratiu (1983) describes the engagement of such activities as 'stability zones' – when situations become overly stressful the expatriate can retreat to these activities. Such temporary withdrawals, he suggests, produce a rhythm of engagement and withdrawal in the manager's involvement with unfamiliar environments. It is withdrawals of this nature, Mendenhall and Oddou (1986) note, that allow the expatriate to more gradually acculturate to the host culture through the utilisation of a familiar psychological support system as a means of alleviating the initial impact of culture shock.

People skills in Mendenhall and Oddou's schema include effective interaction with others, particularly foreigners, and involvement, which according to Torbiörn (1982) is well short of going native, but nonetheless potentially important as a device for building a bridge from one culture to another. Wills and Barham (1994) suggest that the effective portrayal of cultural empathy requires a holding or bracketing of one's assumptions in order to open oneself completely to the other's perspectives. While the authors appreciate that this is not an easy task, the success of the activity, they suggest, allows the participants involved to be able to move more freely in each other's subjective worlds, perceiving as they perceive, feeling as they feel and experiencing as they experience. Ultimately both parties are led to progressively greater heights of acceptance and understanding.

Two important relational skills associated with coping with stress while on foreign assignment are identified by Aycan (1997), namely cultural flexibility and conflict resolution skills. Cultural flexibility refers to the ability to orient oneself to a new cultural setting, an important aspect of which includes the ability to substitute activities in the new culture for those enjoyed in the home country. According to Torbiörn (1982), cultural flexibility might also be suggestive of the avoidance of prejudice in one's opinions and behaviours and a willingness to alter one's behavioural pattern when the situation plainly demands it.

Aycan (1997) suggests that conflict resolution skills enable one to cope with stress, especially in interpersonal conflicts. They include an understanding of others' viewpoints and an effort to relate to them, initiating a collaborative approach and increasing mutual respect. Conflict resolution is also expected to facilitate cultural learning. In their accounts of intercultural effectiveness and relations, Abe and Wiseman (1983) and Hawes and Kealey (1981) have unearthed a significant relationship between conflict resolution skills and adjustment, while Black *et al.* (1991) have found a significant correlation between both conflict resolution and cultural flexibility and all three facets of adjustment.

The Expatriate's Intercultural Communication Abilities

Mendenhall and Oddou (1985) maintain that the executive who desires or needs to communicate with others, who is willing to try to speak the foreign language (even when not necessary) and who does not worry about making linguistic mistakes is much more likely to be successful than the executive who is introverted, self-conscious or otherwise uncomfortable when interacting with foreigners. However, as Osland (1995) suggests, problems can still arise even where there is a similarity of language. She highlights that while people usually expect fewer difficulties when they move to a country where the same language is spoken, this is often a mistake, as aside from the language barrier, the culture can present enough difficulties to make adjustment a challenge. Similarly, Hall (1992) maintains that the greatest confusion in intercultural communication can be traced to a failure to correctly interpret the subtle cues that precede and surround verbal communication. In his account of the 'silent language of overseas business' he notes that while a person may understand the actual spoken message, they may be totally unaware of the non-verbal messages that are occurring at the unconscious level. Thus, as Brein and David (1971) highlight, the subtle, yet important, differences between cultures may not be understood, with the result that what may be perceived by the sojourner as 'the most laudable of intentions' may be perceived by the host country nationals as an insult.

JOB FACTORS AS PREDICTORS OF ADJUSTMENT

Role Novelty

Black (1988) proposes that role novelty involves the difference between the past role and the new one. Role novelty essentially increases the degree of unfamiliarity with the new role, which probably decreases the degree of predictability. He notes that if the new position is substantially different from the previous one, the expatriate may experience greater feelings of uncertainty and unpredictability with the result that it may be more difficult to understand which behaviours are appropriate for the new situation. Pinder and Schroeder (1987) highlight that transfers that entail moving from one functional area to another and that promote expatriates to jobs with greater responsibility than before will probably be more stressful than transfers that feature less change in geographic areas and work dimensions. Although they define job transfer as a relatively permanent job reassignment that entails the movement of an organisation's employee from one of its operating sites to another and is considered more permanent than expatriation, it appears that the theory for transfers can be applicable to expatriation. If the new job demands are sufficiently different from those they left behind, a decrease in job performance and feelings of lack of confidence are likely to be especially pronounced (Pinder and Schroeder 1987). Teagarden and Gordon (1995) also point out that if the job is novel to the expatriate during the overseas assignment, they would expect significant learning curves and this would influence the expatriate's success in the early stages of the expatriate posting.

Role Ambiguity

Handy (1985) notes that the four most frequently cited instances of role ambiguity in a work situation are uncertainty about how one's work is evaluated, uncertainty about scope for advancement, uncertainty about scope of responsibility and uncertainty about others' expectations of one's performance. He argues that if the individual (the focal person) is unclear about the role he/she performs or if their conception of the role differs from that of the others in his role set (the group of people with whom he interacts), there will be a degree of role ambiguity. Rizzo *et al.* (1970) affirm that role theory states that role ambiguity – lack of the necessary information available to a given organisational position – will result in coping behaviour by the role incumbent, which may take the form of attempts to solve the problem to avoid the sources of stress or to use defence mechanisms that distort the reality of the situation. Rizzo *et al.* (1970) note that according to role theory, ambiguity should increase the probability that a person will be dissatisfied with his/her role, experience anxiety, distort reality and thus perform less effectively. Most major role transitions have some associated role ambiguity (Black 1988). Black (1988) highlights that the greater the role ambiguity, the less the individual is able to predict the outcome of various behaviours and the less the individual is able to utilise past successful behaviours or determine new behaviours.

Role Conflict

Role conflict refers to a 'collection of roles that do not precisely fit' (Handy 1985: 63) and results from the necessity for a person to carry out one or more roles in a given situation. Role theory states that when the behaviours expected of an individual are inconsistent (one kind of role conflict), he/she will experience stress, become dissatisfied and perform less effectively than if the expectations imposed on him/her did not conflict (Rizzo *et al.* 1970). Role conflict can therefore be seen as resulting from violation of the two classical principles and causing decreased individual satisfaction and decreased organisational effectiveness. Rizzo *et al.* (1970) note that people reporting role conflict stated that their trust in those who imposed the pressure was reduced, they liked them less on a personal basis, they held them in lower esteem, they communicated less with them and that their own effectiveness was decreased. Black notes that individuals in new roles experience conflicting signals about what is expected of them, stating that 'when an individual experiences conflicting messages about expected behaviours, he or she is less able to determine which messages to ignore and which to follow and thereby execute the appropriate behaviours' (Black 1988: 281). In this way, he suggests it is hardly surprising that researchers have found that the greater the role conflict that exists, the greater the difficulty of the role transition.

Role Overload

Irrespective of occupation or status, the most obvious cause of stress at work is 'sheer overload' (Statt 1994: 94). If managers have too many demands placed upon them, they will be less able to respond adequately to them (Black 1988) and role overload will have a negative influence on work role and expatriate adjustment. Role overload has been found to be negatively associated with successful role transitions (Tung 1982). Role overload may occur due to the parent company's lack of awareness of what the overseas position actually involves, which might reduce the expatriate's ability to perform the job satisfactorily, thus making adjustment more difficult.

ORGANISATIONAL FACTORS AS PREDICTORS OF ADJUSTMENT

The Selection Process Endured

Staffing overseas positions is a very serious issue facing multinational corporations. Harvey (1996) highlights that international human resource managers and academic researchers attribute a significant portion of the expatriate failure rates to poor selection of candidates for overseas assignments and he argues that the selection of candidates with a higher probability of foreign assignment success must become a high priority for multinationals (MNCs) if they are to be successful in the long-run global marketplace. Black *et al.* (1991) point out that most US MNCs do not select the candidate from a pool of competitive or comparable candidates, while earlier Hixon (1986) noted that there was an almost ingrained practice of hiring from within, which he suggested had become one of the unwritten rules of international staffing. Hixon suggests that this mattered because poor selection, coupled with the stress of living and working overseas, may be viewed as potential contributory factors to, among other things, psychosomatic problems, alcoholism and divorce. The problem of recruiting from within the organisation is that it limits the potential selection pool – in many cases eliminating those with pertinent cross-cultural experience and skills.

Researchers have investigated the absence of using valid expatriate selection criteria. Hixon (1986) determines that poor staffing decisions occur simply because companies are forced to act quickly to remain competitive in a market sector. Shilling (1993) notes that too often, expatriates are selected in a knee-jerk reaction to the need to fill a new or unexpected vacancy in foreign soil. Hixon (1986) warns that in moving too quickly, a company may fail to consider all possible candidates and pressurise the selected candidate to accept the position or forego cross-cultural training. Harvey (1996) describes this as a 'reactionary mentality' for overseas assignments. He indicates that frequently there is little time for a company to put out a 'foreign fire', which results in an obsession with currently employed candidates who possess the technical and managerial qualifications necessary to solve the short-term problem. This lack of time for appropriate selection procedures appears to be a well-seasoned problem. Baker and Ivancevich (1971) recommend that longer and more deliberate policies must be used in selecting and evaluating candidates for overseas service.

Other explanations for the absence of valid selection criteria have been proposed by Hixon (1986) and Zeira and Banai (1984). Hixon (1986) claims that organisations rely on technical ability as a selection criterion because the crucial variables affecting an individual's or a family's adjustment are difficult to identify and measure. He also notes that the complex relationship between personality factors and the ability to adapt overseas is seldom understood. Zeira and Banai (1984) espouse that a general problem that characterises most selection studies, irrespective of the research tool used, is the failure to provide operational definitions for the selection criteria. Concepts such as adaptability, maturity, sensitivity, potential, creativity, independence and stability are specified as desirable in expatriates, but since they are not operational they cannot be measured.

This difficulty in measuring and defining desired competencies in the selection of expatriates is also recognised by Torbiörn (1982) and Teagarden and Gordon (1995). In attempting to explain why MNCs ignore certain important predictors, Teagarden and Gordon (1995) found that such predictors are ignored because they may be difficult to measure, are too controversial or private or because the candidates are simply presumed to possess the desired ability or trait. The final factor relates to certain criteria that are seen as unimportant, as they are not relevant to the job requirements (Teagarden and Gordon 1995).

Alas, Foster and Johnson (1996) emphasise that commentators on international assignments can recommend selection criteria as much as they like without MNCs necessarily paying attention to them. In their study of expatriate management policies in fifteen organisations in the UK, they found that the selection criteria recommended by many commentators are much more sophisticated than those actually employed by the companies studied. This problem is also recognised in the US by Mendenhall *et al.* (1987), who affirm that a trend seems to have developed in the 1970s and continued into the 1980s, which is that human resource divisions of US MNCs consistently overlook key criteria that are predictive of overseas success in their recruitment and screening of potential overseas workers. Mendenhall *et al.* (1987) maintain that researchers have consistently called for changes in this system based on their findings, yet the trends continue. Swaak (1997) proposes that one would assume that companies would have developed comprehensive systems to select global executives for key posts to protect their investments. However, he acknowledges that unfortunately this is not the case, as many MNCs still take a haphazard approach to filling international positions. This is underscored by Harvey (1996), who asserts that even when MNCs take a more deliberate approach to the selection of managers, they do not follow a formal, standardised process, unlike many competitors from other countries.

The Provision of Cross-Cultural Training

The basic goal of cross-cultural training (CCT) is:

> to bring about cultural awareness in the participant so that he can successfully interact with host nationals and the environment and effectively carry out his managerial responsibilities. Cultural self-awareness, cultural other awareness and acquisition of learning and conceptualising skills are seen as sub goals contributing to this overall goal (Thiagarajan 1971: 74).

Harrison (1994) affirms that a major purpose of CCT is to develop more cosmopolitan managers who can better understand cultural differences and who can apply this knowledge in cross-cultural situations. CCT's goal is to minimise 'culture shock' when on foreign deployment and to enhance the manager's cross-cultural experience.

Numerous researchers contend that training facilitates expatriate performance and effectiveness, thus facilitating adjustment. Brewster (1995) asserts that CCT has long been advocated as a means of facilitating adjustment to the expatriate environment. He maintains that effective preparation and training can shorten non-productive 'running-in' periods while the expatriate adjusts to the new environment.

On investigating the use of rigorous selection and training procedures, Tung (1982) found that in the American and Western European samples studied, there was a definite relationship between the rigour of selection and training procedures used and the expatriates' ability to successfully perform in a foreign environment. The more rigorous the selection and training procedures used, the fewer incidents of poor performance or failure to work efficiently in a foreign country. Tung (1982) affirms that this indicates the need for MNCs to adopt more meticulous procedures in the areas of expatriate selection and training.

In Black and Mendenhall's (1990) review of twenty-nine US empirical studies on CCT, they found a positive relationship between CCT and the development of appropriate perceptions relative to members of another culture, i.e. training was positively correlated with adjustment and positively related to performance. Hogan and Goodson (1990) examined a survey of forty MNCs in Japan and found that a combination of reliable selection and training strategies increases the potential for expatriate success.

Baker and Ivanecvich (1971) determine that the failure of US executives overseas is not alleviated by predeparture orientation in the host country's language, customs, culture and business practices. In their study a large number of managers indicated that proper predeparture preparation is needed to improve overseas American managers' performances. These managers believe that Americans transferring overseas must be made aware of such factors as the environmental differences between the US and the host nation, the differences among people and their customs in the host nation and the national attitudes towards American customs.

Thiagarajan (1971) highlights that managers conditioned to a specific cultural environment experience considerable difficulty in adjusting to and working in an alien cultural milieu. CCT efforts that deal with this issue are crucial for the successful completion of overseas assignments, as CCT's purpose is to make managers sensitive to the influence of culture on their own behaviour and on the behaviour of the host nationals (Thiagarajan 1971). On examining predeparture training programmes, Baker and Ivanecvich (1971) found that some managers believed that more intensive predeparture training programmes are needed to prepare managers for the 'culture shock' of transferring abroad. Harrison (1994) states that CCT's goal is to minimise culture shock when on foreign deployment and enhance the managers' cross-cultural experience, while Katz and Seifer (1996) contend that CCT serves to reduce the severity of culture shock and the time necessary to reach an acceptable level of cultural proficiency. In addition, CCT leads to more realistic expectations, greater job satisfaction and lower intentions of returning early from cross-cultural assignments (Black and Mendenhall 1990). Caudron (1991) notes that with CCT, the potential for costly failure is significantly reduced.

Cavusgil et al. (1992) affirm that it has been agreed that well-planned training and orientation programmes can ease an expatriate's and family's transition and adjustment and can improve the expatriate's on-the-job performance. Findings by Brewster and Pickard (1994) indicate that expatriates and their partners are very positive towards formal training for expatriation. According to them, expatriates and their spouses believe that training helps to adjust to living and working in the host country. Brewster (1991) highlights that expatriates themselves are significantly enthusiastic about training programmes and languages. He stresses that the support implicit in the provision of training, the opportunity to reflect in a time of turmoil and the chance to absorb valuable information should lead one to expect that any help that expatriates can be given will be gratefully received. It will be acknowledged by the expatriate not only for its own intrinsic value, but as evidence that the organisation sending him/her is aware of the potential problems and is willing to help.

Building upon this concept of support that is implicit in training, Black and Gregersen (1991) contend that a lack of predeparture cross-cultural training can reinforce low levels of commitment to the parent firm and to the location of the operation. Lack of firm-sponsored training can contribute to the view that 'the company doesn't care about me, so why should I care about it?'. Lack of training can also inhibit the expatriate from understanding the foreign culture and becoming committed to the local operation (Black and Gregersen 1991).

Despite the support that training affects the expatriate's performance, effectiveness and subsequent adjustment, there appears to be a lack of sufficient training programmes provided by organisations. Hogan and Goodson (1990) claim that many companies do not realise the potential bottom-line impact of expatriate success and fall short in their efforts to prepare expatriates for their assignments. This is underscored by Foster and Johnson (1996), who contend that the principal reason given for the problem of high expatriate failure levels and underperformance is that most companies do not provide sufficient attention to the selection, training and monitoring of staff and their families on international assignments. Adler and Ghadar (1992) pinpoint the problem to American firms, as they maintain that American firms generally have not recognised the importance of the relationship between CCT and the subsequent effectiveness of the expatriate's performance. Rahim (1983) claims that the classic international business blunders could probably have been avoided if MNCs had given adequate attention to the development of their international managers.

The scarcity of expatriate training has long been recognised by researchers. In Baker and Ivanecvich's study (1971) of 124 firms, they found that a clear majority of firms do not administer predeparture training programmes. Blue and Haynes (1977) assert that it is painfully apparent that many US companies have failed, and are continuing to fail miserably, when it comes to selecting and preparing the managers responsible for developing overseas markets. The deficiency of training programmes offered by US companies continued through the 1980s, as Torbiörn (1982) notes: 'very little appears to be provided in the way of special predeparture training by companies in the USA.'

Torbiörn (1982) also acknowledges that the picture regarding training has improved a little in recent years, and more large companies now provide some predeparture training geared more directly to adjustment and adaptation in the host country, with spouses likely to be included. However, he contends that systematic training according to appropriately designed programmes is still rare. On practical issues such as arranging transport and housing, etc., companies are generally very helpful. However, Torbiörn (1982) highlights that the picture is not as bright when it comes to preparation intended to ease the process of adaptation and adjustment in the host country.

At the same time, Tung (1982) examines training procedures adopted by US, European and Japanese MNCs. In the US sample, she detects that only thirty-two per cent of the respondents indicate that their company has formalised training programmes to prepare candidates for overseas work. In contrast, sixty-nine per cent of the respondents in the Western European sample and fifty-seven per cent of the Japanese MNCs sponsor training programmes to prepare candidates for overseas assignments. This research also reveals that a full sixty-eight per cent of the respondents did not have any type of training to prepare them for CCT encounters.

Brewster (1991) and Brewster and Pickard (1994) maintain that despite the extensive literature on the preparation of expatriates for their foreign assignments, the clearest message that appears is that very little preparation actually takes place. Despite the importance of expatriate positions, the high costs associated with expatriation and the extensive and largely non-productive 'running-in' periods, it is still the case that most organisations provide no formal training (Brewster 1991).

More recent research by Oddou (1991) reveals that this lack of training still exists in organisations. Oddou's study (1991) of over 165 expatriates discovered that sixty-five per cent of the expatriates in the survey received no training at all. He finds that, surprisingly, even the best companies do not spend a lot of time or money preparing their expatriates for the cultural transition. This is also supported by Black and Mendenhall (1990), who claim that roughly seventy per cent of all US expatriates receive no predeparture cross-cultural training.

Harrison (1994) notes that the use of CCT in the corporate setting is very limited, primarily because such training is considered unnecessary or ineffective by most top managers. Brewster (1995) highlights the fact that so many expatriates are sent abroad without specific training or preparation reflects the difficulty of organising such events in the often turbulent circumstances. Selectors are either unfamiliar with any scientific grounds for selection or they have little confidence in their validity, and the same can be said of their attitude to existing training programmes (Torbiörn 1982). Behind all of this uncertainty lies the inadequacy of present knowledge about the psychological mechanisms involved in adapting and adjusting to new cultural conditions.

Further justification offered for this lack of training is that since people assigned to overseas assignments frequently go out one or two at a time, it becomes awkward or impractical to assemble a group for training, which many companies mistakenly assume can only be done in a group (Murray and Murray 1996). Tung (1987) maintains that this reluctance to invest large sums of money in training stems from the fear that employees may leave the company. She contends that this fear is justified to a large extent because of the high mobility of the US workforce.

Compensation and Benefits

Parker and McEvoy (1993) affirm that expatriates – especially those from the US – are often well compensated for their work, both in direct pay and in benefits such as home leave, income tax equalisation, housing allowances and cash premiums for 'hardship' posts. Wederspahn (1992) emphasises that the financial stakes for organisations sending expatriates are high. Typical first-year expenses of an expatriate assignment for a family of four are three times the US executive's base salary. In Foster and Johnson's (1996) study of expatriate management policies they find that the relocation packages that many companies provide are often extremely financially generous and wide ranging. Parker and McEvoy (1993) advocate that higher compensation should enhance general living adjustment, yet at the same time they point out that it may encourage the expatriate to live much differently than the host country nationals, i.e. in isolated expatriate communities in which interaction opportunities, and hence interaction adjustment, are impeded. Yet Parker and McEvoy (1993) find that compensation has a positive relationship with work adjustment only. The hypothesised negative relationship with interaction adjustment is not found. Foster and Johnson (1996) warn that organisations may well be making the mistake which many UK companies made in the expansive 1980s of simply throwing money at the problem of mobility rather than treating it as both an important element of strategic human resource management and a key part of the career development of staff and dependants during international relocations.

Adler (1995) notes that most expatriate benefit packages have been designed to meet the needs of traditional families (employed husband, non-employed wife and children). She recommends that companies should be prepared to modify their benefit packages to meet the needs of managers who are single (female or male) or dual-career couples. Modifications that are recommended should include increased lead time in announcing assignments, executive search services for the partner in dual-career couples and payment for 'staying connected', including telephone and airfare expenses, for couples who choose some form of commuting rather than both simultaneously relocating abroad (Adler 1995).

As mentioned above, the research proposes that US expatriates generally receive high compensation, which can lead to increased general adjustment. To examine this concept in the context of this study, the following propositions are advanced.

Overall Organisational Support

Sieveking *et al.* (1981) warn that regardless of how valid the selection is and how thorough the orientation is, most employees will encounter difficulties. These difficulties may occur in job performance, maintenance of family harmony or adaptation to the host culture. Mendenhall *et al.* (1987) maintain that the stronger the support system and the more it is focused towards the needs of the spouse and family, the more likely the expatriate manager will succeed in their overseas assignment. Foster and Johnson (1996) and Pinder and Schroeder (1987) suggest that through providing support such as counselling following the move and off-the-job support services in addition to an already generous relocation package, international firms can help to ease the adjustment process by reducing uncertainty and increasing the sense of control which families have over the move (an important buffer against stress).

Katz and Seifer (1996) recognise that problems are often found with the adaptation of the expatriate and their family to the host country's cultural environment. They affirm that often support groups, led by more senior expatriates, will facilitate the adaptation of expatriates and their families to the local culture. Solomon (1994) maintains that ongoing support is as important as preparation, while Tung (1988) recommends that companies should establish and co-ordinate a support system that attends specifically to the needs and aspirations of expatriate employees. Solomon (1994) also suggests that human resource managers must create educational tools and in-country support to help employees handle difficulties.

According to Katz and Seifer (1996), many of the larger US MNCs have a division whose sole purpose is to look after expatriates' needs. However, Mendenhall and Oddou (1987) highlight that US MNCs have still fallen short of providing a comprehensive support system or network for expatriate managers. According to Tung (1987), European and Japanese MNCs provide a more comprehensive support system to allay expatriate concerns about problems of repatriation. Research indicates that the low failure rate of Japanese MNC expatriation partly comes from the firms' efforts to maintain communication and supervisory relations with the expatriates (Tung 1987). An example of one such support mechanism is that of 'parenting' or mentoring. Tung (1987) describes the mentoring process as the pairing of an expatriate to a superior in the corporate headquarters who takes on the role of sponsor. The sponsor, who is usually a member of senior management, regularly informs the expatriate about the situation at home and has the responsibility of finding a position for the expatriate upon his/her return. The mentor can also provide information and support that aids the expatriate in adjusting to the culture outside of the workplace.

Cavusgil *et al.* (1992) note that part of an expatriate's stress comes from the uncertainty of what position he/she will assume upon returning from the overseas assignment. They suggest that a mentor in the home office should be assigned to the expatriate who retains career communication and should also 'look out for' the expatriate's interests on the home front. Solomon (1994) emphasises that it is critical that individuals keep connections with people at home as well as abroad, maintaining that mentors are an excellent way for expatriates to keep in touch with headquarters while also getting support. Osland (1995) affirms that cultural mentors also contribute a great deal to reducing the uncertainty that expatriates feel. As Hiltrop and Janssens (1990) suggest, providing organisational information on the politics and day-to-day activities of the headquarters helps reduce the 'out of sight, out of mind' dilemma.

Osland (1995) found that expatriates in his study who had cultural mentors in whom they could confide and who could explain the local culture to them generally fared better than those who did not have such mentors – they are more fluent in the foreign language, perceive themselves as being better adapted to their work and general living conditions abroad, are more aware of the paradoxes of expatriate life and receive higher performance appraisal ratings from both their superiors and themselves. In addition to these quantitative measures, expatriates with cultural mentors generally describe their overseas experience in more glowing terms. According to Tung (1987), where there is no sponsor-expatriate pairing most companies have separate departments or divisions that are responsible for overseeing expatriates' material well-being and career path. Some companies have a senior manager in their overseas subsidiaries who has a 'part-time responsibility as a career manager or godfather.'

The writings reviewed in this area appear to agree that the provision of support to the expatriate while on assignment can help him or her to adjust to both the job and the general environment. Research indicates that where the new job was perceived to be more difficult, any support provided helped minimise the time to become proficient in the new position. There would appear to be a degree of consensus in the literature that having a mentor while on assignment provides the expatriate with support that can facilitate adjustment to the work and to the general environment, thus the following concepts are proposed.

ONGOING DEBATES/ADVANCED CONCEPTS IN THE LITERATURE ON WORKING ABROAD

CULTURAL AND PSYCHIC DISTANCE

In making the successful transition to working and living abroad, an important question relates to whether fewer adjustment difficulties arise in the situation where the individual is moving to a culture classified to be broadly similar and close to their own.

Thus, for example, Leiba-O'Sullivan (2001), drawing upon O'Grady's 'psychic-distance paradox' (1994) which suggests that cultural similarity can paradoxically lead to extreme levels of culture shock due to the emergence of unrealistic expectations, discovered a high level of culture shock among Canadian expatriates and their spouses in Ireland. A majority of expatriates in her qualitative investigation reported having experienced a very difficult first year abroad and several reported ongoing adjustment problems beyond their first year. Leiba-O'Sullivan notes that several reported experiencing culture shock to the extent that they did because they had not expected to experience any adjustment challenges, something which she suggests lends support to the psychic-distance paradox.

Selmer's work (1997) points to a similar conclusion. In an investigation of the difficulty of adjusting to a similar culture, he reports evidence supporting the 'paradoxical proposition' that it might prove as difficult for an expatriate to adjust to a similar culture as to a highly novel or different culture. Drawing upon data gathered from ethnic Chinese and Western expatriates working in the Peoples' Republic of China, he demonstrates that although Chinese expatriates experienced a lower degree of cultural novelty than their Western counterparts, they were generally less well adjusted than their Western counterparts.

Lastly, in a previous pilot study of expatriates and their spouses on assignment in the Mid-West region of Ireland, Moore and Punnett (1994) report that while there was a positive correlation between cultural similarity and satisfaction with the assignment, a majority in their sample still reported the need to develop strong support groups to assist in the adjustment process, even in a highly similar cultural context.

SUMMARY OF KEY PROPOSITIONS

- Expatriate intercultural adjustment has been described as the process by which 'overseas employees become comfortable with, or acculturated to, the host country' or the degree of psychological comfort experienced with various aspects of the host environment.
- The general characterisation of culture shock is one of a feeling of inadequacy that results from not quite knowing how to act as a result of the removal of familiar cues.
- A number of contributors have suggested, and indeed some have successfully demonstrated, that the pattern of adjustment experienced by an individual on entering a novel culture can often take the form of a U-curve, whereby following a period of

elation after entering the host environment, the expatriate experiences a type of culture shock which, in the context of a successful assignment, is followed by a period of adjustment and subsequently a degree of competence in operating in the host environment.

- Four different approaches to adjustment have been outlined: assimilation, integration, separatism and marginalisation.
- The factors that facilitate or inhibit adjustment when going to work abroad have been grouped into personal factors, job factors and organisational factors.
- The personal factors that have been drawn upon to explain adjustment include gender, age, marital status, personality, personal competencies and skills and intercultural communicative ability.
- The core job factors employed to assist in explaining adjustment patterns are role novelty, role ambiguity, role conflict and role overload.
- The organisational factors included the selection procedure, cross-cultural training provision, the nature of the compensation and benefits offered and overall organisational supports during the period when the individual is working in the host culture.

DISCUSSION/SELF-ASSESSMENT QUESTIONS

1. What is intercultural transitional adjustment?
2. What do you understand by the 'psychic-distance paradox'? Do you think it is useful in research on working and living abroad?
3. Outline what key interventions you think might be important in a cross-cultural training programme for individuals going (a) to a culture close to their own and (b) a highly distant and novel culture.

MULTIPLE CHOICE QUESTIONS

1. International strategic alliances, joint ventures, foreign subsidiaries and overseas offices all represent important routes to business internationalisation. True or false?
2. Culture shock is:
   (a) A kind of silent sickness that afflicts the inexperienced traveller or unaware expatriate.
   (b) Especially experienced by those who have never been away from home.
   (c) Caused by an abrupt loss of the familiar signs and symbols of social intercourse, causing a sense of isolation and diminished self-importance.
   (d) All of the above.
   (e) None of the above.
3. Intercultural adjustment can be said to occur when the individual adopts new behaviours which produce similar results to those behaviours that were used prior to the move into the new culture. True or false?

4. The researcher closely associated with originally empirically testing the U-curve theory is:
   (a) Lursey.
   (b) Guarda.
   (c) Lysgaard.
   (d) Strack.

5. According to Oberg, adjustment to new cultural environments is characterised by four distinct phases, namely:
   (a) The satisfaction phase, the surprise phase, the sense-making phase and the settling-in phase.
   (b) The honeymoon stage, the culture shock phase, the recovery phase and the adjustment and mastery phase.
   (c) The novelty phase, the engagement phase, the response phase and the mastery phase.

6. According to Berry *et al.* (1988), 'marginalisation' as an approach to intercultural adjustment occurs when:
   (a) The individual wishes to integrate with host nationals and has no desire to maintain their own culture.
   (b) The individual continues to have an interest in their own culture while also interacting with host nationals.
   (c) The individual wants to keep their cultural identity without any desire to integrate with host country nationals.
   (d) The individual displays no desire to identify with their own culture or to mix with host nationals.

7. Cultural flexibility refers to the ability to orient oneself to a new cultural setting, an important aspect of which includes the ability to substitute activities in the new culture for those enjoyed in the home country. True or false?

8. Role conflict refers to:
   (a) A collection of roles that do not precisely fit.
   (b) An uncertainty about scope of responsibility and uncertainty about others' expectations of one's performance.
   (c) The difference between the past role and the new one.
   (d) All of the above.

9. The purpose of cross-cultural training (CCT) is to:
   (a) Bring about cultural awareness in the participant so that he or she can successfully interact with host nationals and the environment and effectively carry out his or her managerial responsibilities.
   (b) Increase cultural self-awareness, cultural other awareness and acquisition of learning and conceptualising skills.
   (c) To develop more cosmopolitan managers who can better understand cultural differences and who can apply this knowledge in cross-cultural situations.

(d) To minimise culture shock when on foreign deployment and to enhance the manager's cross-cultural experience.

(e) All of the above.

(f) None of the above.

10. The psychic-distance paradox suggests that cultural similarity can paradoxically lead to extreme levels of culture shock due to the emergence of unrealistic expectations. True or false?

FIVE SUGGESTED KEY READINGS

Aycan, Z., 'Expatriate adjustment as a multifaceted phenomenon: individual and organizational level predictors', *The International Journal of Human Resource Management*, VIII/4 (1997), 434–65.

Black, J.S., 'Work role transitions: a study of American expatriate managers in Japan', *Journal of International Business Studies*, XIX/2 (1988), 277–94.

Black, J.S. and Mendenhall, M., 'The U-curve hypothesis revisited: a review and theoretical framework', *Journal of International Business Studies*, XXII/2 (1991), 225–47.

Oberg, K., 'Culture shock: adjustment to new cultural environments', *Practical Anthropologist*, 7 (1960), 177–82.

Torbiörn, I., *Living Abroad: Personal Adjustment and Personnel Policy in the Overseas Setting*, New York: John Wiley & Sons 1982.

REFERENCES

Abe, H. and Wiseman, R., 'A cross-cultural confirmation of the dimensions of intercultural effectiveness', *International Journal of Intercultural Relations*, VII/1 (1983), 53–67.

Adler, N., 'Expatriate women managers', in J. Selmar (ed.), *Expatriate Management: New Ideas for International Business*, London: Quorum Books 1995.

Aycan, Z., 'Expatriate adjustment as a multifaceted phenomenon: individual and organisational level predictors', *International Journal of Human Resource Management*, VIII/3 (1997), 434–65.

Baker, J. and Ivancevich, J., 'The assignment of American executives abroad: systematic, haphazard or chaotic?', *California Management Review*, XIII/2 (1971), 39–44.

Berry, J., Kim, R. and Boski, P., 'Psychological acculturation of immigrants', in Y. Kim and W. Gudykust (eds), *Cross Cultural Adaptation: Current Approaches*, Beverly Hills: Sage 1988.

Black, J.S., 'Work role transitions: a study of American expatriate managers in Japan', *Journal of International Business Studies*, XIX/2 (1988), 277–94.

Black, J.S., 'The relationship of personal characteristics with the adjustment of Japanese expatriate managers', *Management International Review*, XXX/2 (1990), 119–34.

Black, J.S., 'Coming home: relationship of expatriate expectations with repatriation adjustment and job performance', *Human Relations*, XLV (1992), 177–92.

Black, J.S. and Gregersen, H., 'Antecedents to cross-cultural adjustment for expatriates in Pacific Rim assignments', *Human Relations*, XLIV/5 (1991).

Black, J.S. and Gregersen, H., 'When Yankee comes home: factors related to expatriate and spouse repatriation adjustment', *Journal of International Business Studies*, XXII/4 (1991), 671–94.

Black, J.S. and Mendenhall, M., 'Cross-cultural training effectiveness: a review and a theoretical framework for future research', *Academy of Management Review*, XV/1 (1990), 113–36.

Black, J.S. and Mendenhall, M., 'The U-curve adjustment hypothesis revisited: a review and theoretical framework', *Journal of International Business Studies*, XX/2 (1991), 225–47.

Black, J.S., Mendenhall, M. and Oddou, G., 'Towards a comprehensive model of international adjustment: an integration of multiple theoretical perspectives', *Academy of Management Review*, XVI/2 (1991), 291–317.

Black, J.S. and Mendenhall, M., 'The U-curve hypothesis revisited: a review and theoretical framework', *Journal of International Business Studies*, XXII/2 (1991), 225–47.

Brein, M. and David, K., 'Intercultural communication and the adjustment of the sojourner', *Psychological Bulletin*, LXXVI/3 (1971), 215–30.

Brett, J., 'The effect of job transfer on employees and their families', in C. Cooper and R. Payne (eds), *Current Concerns in Occupational Stress*, London: Pitman Press 1980.

Brewster C., *The Management of Expatriates*, London: Kogan Page 1991.

Brewster, C., 'The paradox of expatriate adjustment', in J. Selmer (ed.), *Expatriate Management: New Ideas for International Business*, Westport, CT: Quorum Books 1995.

Brewster, C., Mayrhofer, W. and Morley, M., *New Challenges for European Human Resource Management*, London: Macmillan 2000.

Brewster, C. and Pickard, J., 'Evaluating expatriate training', *International Studies of Management and Organisation*, XXIV/3 (1994), 18–35.

Caudron, S., 'Training ensures overseas success', *Personnel Journal*, 27 (1991), 27–30.

Cavusgil, T., Yavas, U. and Bykowicz, S., 'Preparing executives for overseas assignments', *Management Decisions*, XXX/1 (1992), 54–6.

Church, T., 'Sojourner adjustment', *Psychological Bulletin*, XCI/3 (1982), 540–72.

Cleveland, H., Margone, G. and Adams, J., *The Overseas American*, New York: McGraw-Hill 1960.

Dawis, R., England, G. and Lofquist, L., 'A theory of work adjustment', *Minnesota Studies in Vocational Rehabilitation*, Bulletin 38 (January 1964).

DeCieri, D., Dowling, P. and Taylor, K., 'The psychological impact of expatriate repatriation on partners', *The International Journal of Human Resource Management*, II/3 (1991), 377–414.

Feldman, D. and Tompson, H., 'Expatriation, repatriation and domestic geographical relocation: an empirical investigation of adjustment to new job assignments', *Journal of International Business Studies*, XXIV/3 (1993), 507–30.

Finn, G. and Morley, M., 'Expatriate selection: the case of an Irish MNC', in M. Linehan, M. Morley and J. Walsh (eds), *International Human Resource Management and Expatriate Transfers: Irish Experiences*, Dublin: Blackhall Publishing 2001.

Foster, N., 'Employee job mobility and relocation', *Personnel Review*, XIX/6 (1990), 18–24.

Foster, N. and Johnson, M., 'Expatriate management policies in UK companies new to the international scene', *International Journal of Human Resource Management*, VII/1 (1996), 179–205.

Furnham, A. and Bochner, S., *Culture Shock: Psychological Reactions to Unfamiliar Environments*, New York: Methuen 1986.

Gullahorn, J. and Gullahorn, J., 'An extension of the U-curve hypothesis', *Journal of Social Issues*, XIX/3 (1963), 33–47.

Hall, E., 'The silent language in overseas business', in H. Lane and J. DiStefano (eds), *International Management Behavior*, Boston, MA: PWS-Kent Publishing Company 1992.

Hamill, J., 'Expatriate management policies in British multinationals', *Journal of General Management*, XIV/4 (1989), 18–33.

Handy, C., *Understanding Organisations*, London: Penguin Books 1985.

Harris, H., 'Women in international management: why are they not selected?', in C. Brewster and C. Harris (eds), *International Human Resource Management: Contemporary Issues in Europe*, London: Routledge 1999, 258–76.

Harrision, J., 'Developing successful expatriate managers: a framework for the structural design and strategic alignment of cross cultural training programs', *HR Planning*, XIX/2 (1994), 17–30.

Harrison, J., Chadwick, M. and Scales, M., 'The relationship between cross-cultural adjustment and the personality variables of self-efficacy and self-monitoring', *International Journal of Intercultural Relations*, XX/2 (1996), 167–88.

Harvey, M., 'The selection of managers for foreign assignments: a planning perspective', *Columbia Journal of World Business*, 31 (1996).

Hawes, F. and Kealey, D., 'An empirical study of Canadian technical assistance', *International Journal of Intercultural Relations*, V/2 (1981), 239–58.

Hiltrop, J. and Janssens, M., 'Expatriation: challenges and recommendations', *European Management Journal*, VIII/1 (1990).

Hogan, G. and Goodson, J., 'The key to expatriate success', *Training and Development Journal*, XLIV/1 (1990), 50–2.

Katz, J. and Seifer, D., 'It's a different world out there', *Human Resource Planning*, XIX/2 (1996), 32–48.

Kobrin, S., 'Expatriate reduction and strategic control in American multinational corporations', *Human Resource Management*, XXVII/1 (1988), 63–75.

Kraimer, M., Wayne, S. and Jaworski, R., 'Sources of support and expatriate performance: the mediating role of expatriate adjustment', *Personnel Psychology*, 54 (2001), 71–99.

Leiba-O'Sullivan, S., 'The psychic distance paradox revisited: multiple perspectives of Canadian expatriates' adjustment to Ireland', in M. Linehan, M. Morley and J. Walsh (eds), *International Human Resource Management and Expatriate Transfers: Irish Experiences*, Dublin: Blackhall Publishing 2001.

Linehan, M., *Senior Female International Managers*, London: Ashgate 1999.

Linehan, M., Morley, M. and Walsh, J., *International Human Resource Management and Expatriate Transfers: Irish Experiences*, Dublin: Blackhall Publishing 2001.

Loo, R., 'A structured exercise for stimulating cross-cultural sensitivity', *Career Development International*, IV/6 (1999).

Louis, M., 'Surprise and sense making: what newcomers experience in entering unfamiliar organisational settings', *Administrative Science Quarterly*, XXV/2 (1980), 226–51.

Lysgaard, S., 'Adjustment in a foreign society: Norwegian Fulbright grantees visiting the United States', *International Social Science Bulletin*, 7 (1955), 45–51.

Mamman, A., 'Socio-biographical antecedents of intercultural effectiveness: the neglected factors', *British Journal of Management*, VI/2 (1995), 97–114.

Mendenhall, M. and Oddou, G., 'The dimensions of expatriate acculturation: a review', *Academy of Management Review*, X/1 (1985), 39–47.

Mendenhall, M. and Oddou, G., 'Acculturation profiles of expatriate managers: implications for cross-cultural training programs', *Columbia Journal of World Business*, XXI/4 (1986), 73–7.

Mendenhall, M. and Oddou, G., 'The overseas assignment: a practical look', *Business Horizons*, XXXI/5 (1988), 78–84.

Mendenhall, M., Dunbar, E. and Oddou, G., 'Expatriate selection, training and career-pathing: a review and critique', *Human Resource Management*, III/3 (1987), 331–45.

Moore, S. and Punnett, B.J., 'Expatriate and spousal adjustment: a pilot study in the Mid-West region', *Journal of Irish Business and Administrative Research*, XV/1 (1994), 178–84.

Morley, M., Burke, C. and O'Regan, T., 'The Irish in Moscow: a question of adjustment', *Human Resource Management Journal*, VII/3 (1997), 53–65.

Oberg, K., 'Culture shock: adjustment to new cultural environments', *Practical Anthropologist*, 7 (1960), 177–82.

Odden, G., 'Managing your expatriates: what the successful firms do', *Human Resource Planning*, XIV/4 (1991), 301–8.

O'Grady, S., 'The psychic distance paradox', paper presented at the Academy of International Business Conference 1994.

Osland, J., *The Adventures of Working Abroad*, San Francisco: Jossey-Bass 1995.

Parker, B. and McEvoy, G., 'Initial examination of a model of intercultural adjustment', *International Journal of Intercultural Relations*, XVII/2 (1993), 355–79.

Parker, B. and McEvoy, G., 'Expatriate adjustment: causes and consequences', in J. Selmar (ed.), *Expatriate Management: New Ideas for International Business*, London: Quorum Books 1995.

Philips, N., 'Cross cultural training', *Journal of European Industrial Training*, XVII/2 (1993).

Pinder, C. and Schroeder, K., 'Time to proficiency following job transfers', *Academy of Management Journal*, XXX/2 (1987), 336–56.

Rahim, A., 'A model for developing key expatriate executives', *Personnel Journal*, LXII/4 (1983), 312–17.

Ratiu, I., 'Thinking internationally: a comparison of how executives learn', *International Studies of Management and Organisation*, XIII/1 (1983), 139–50.

Rizzo, J., House, R. and Kirtzman, S., 'Role conflict and ambiguity in complex organisations', *Administrative Science Quarterly*, 15 (1970), 150–63.

Ronen, S., 'Training the international assignee', in I. Goldstein and Associates (eds), *Training and Development in Organizations*, San Francisco: Jossey-Bass 1989.

Sappinen, J., 'Expatriate adjustment on foreign assignments', *European Business Review*, XCIII/5 (1993), 3–11.

Scullion, H. and Brewster, C., 'The management of expatriates: messages from Europe?', *Journal of World Business*, XXXVI/4 (2001), 346–65.

Selmer, J., 'The difficulty of adjusting to a similar culture: ethnic Chinese vs. Western expatriates in the PRC', Business Research Centre Papers on Cross-Cultural Management, Hong Kong: Baptist University 1997.

Shaffer, M., Harrison, D. and Gilley, K., 'Dimensions, determinants, and differences in the expatriate adjustment process', *Journal of International Business Studies*, XXX/3 (1999), 557–81.

Shilling, M., 'Avoid expatriate culture shock', *HR Magazine*, XXXVIII/7 (1993), 57–63.

Simeon, R. and Fujiu, K., 'Cross-cultural adjustment strategies of Japanese spouses in Silicon Valley', *Employee Relations*, XXII/6 (2000), 594–611.

Statt, D., *Psychology and the World of Work*, Basingstoke: Macmillan 1994.

Stenning, B. and Hammer, M., 'The cultural context of expatriate adaptation: American and Japanese managers abroad', *Academy of Management Best Paper Readings* (1989), 121–5.

Stephens, G. and Black, S., 'The impact of spouse's career orientation on managers during international transfers', *Journal of Management Studies*, XXVIII/4 (1991), 417–28.

Swaak, R., 'Expatriate failures: too many, too much cost, too little planning', *Compensation and Benefits Review*, XXVII/6 (1997), 47–55.

Teagarden, M. and Gordon, G., 'Corporate selection strategies and expatriate manager success', in J. Selmer (ed.), *Expatriate Management: New Ideas for International Business*, London: Quorum Books 1995.

Thiagarajan, K., 'Cross cultural training for overseas management', *Management International Review*, (1971), 69–85.

Torbiörn, I., *Living Abroad: Personal Adjustment and Personnel Policy in the Overseas Setting*, New York: John Wiley & Sons 1982.

Torbiörn, I., 'Staffing for international operations', *Human Resource Management Journal*, VII/3 (1997), 42–52.

Tung, R., 'Selecting and training of personnel for overseas assignments', *Columbia Journal of World Business*, XVI/1 (1981), 68–78.

Tung, R., 'Selection and training procedures of US, European and Japanese multinationals', *California Management Review*, XXV/1 (1982), 57–71.

Tung, R., 'Corporate executives and their families in China: the need for cross cultural understanding in business', *Columbia Journal of World Business*, XXI/1 (1986).

Ward, C. and Chang, W., 'Cultural fit: a new perspective on personality and sojourner adjustment', *International Journal of Intercultural Relations*, XXI/4 (1997), 525–33.

Ward, C. and Kennedy, A., 'Where's the culture in cross-cultural transition?', *Journal of Cross Cultural Psychology*, XXIV/2 (1993), 221–49.

Wederspahn, G., 'Costing failures in expatriate human resource management', *Human Resource Planning*, XV/3 (1992), 27–36.

Weissmann, D. and Furnham, A., 'The expectations and the experiences of a sojourning temporary resident abroad: a preliminary study', *Human Relations*, XL/5 (1987), 313–26.

Wills, S. and Barham, K., 'Being an international manager', *European Management Journal*, XII/1 (1994), 49–58.

Zeira, Y. and Banai, M., 'Present and desired methods of selecting expatriate managers for international assignments', *Personnel Review*, XIII/3 (1984), 29–35.

INDEX

Cellular and Molecular Neurobiology

Second Edition

C. Hammond
Institut de la Méditerraneé
INSERM Unité 29
Marseille
France

ACADEMIC PRESS

A Harcourt Science and Technology Company

San Diego   San Francisco   New York   Boston
London   Sydney   Tokyo

Copyright © 2001 by ACADEMIC PRESS

First edition © 1996

Academic Press
A Harcourt Science and Technology Company
Harcourt Place, 32 Jamestown Road, London NW1 7BY, UK
http://www.academicpress.com

Academic Press
A Harcourt Science and Technology Company
525 B Street, Suite 1900, San Diego, California 92101-4495, USA
http://www.academicpress.com

ISBN 0-12-311624-4 (Ppbk)
    0-12-311625-2 (Hdbk + CD)

Library of Congress Card Number: 00-111699
A catalogue record for this book is available from the British Library

Typeset by Wyvern 21 Ltd, Bristol
Printed and bound in Great Britain at The Bath Press, Colour Books, Glasgow

01 02 03 04 05 06 BP 9 8 7 6 5 4 3 2 1